ADVANCES IN VISUAL FORM ANALYSIS

Proceedings of the Third International Workshop on Visual Form

ADVANCES IN VISUAL FORM ANALYSIS

Capri, Italy May 28-30, 1997

Edited by

Carlo Arcelli
Istituto di Cibernetica
Consiglio Nazionale delle Ricerche
Naples, Italy

Luigi P. Cordella
Dipartimento di Informatica e Sistemistica
Università di Napoli Federico II
Naples, Italy

Gabriella Sanniti di Baja
Istituto di Cibernetica
Consiglio Nazionale delle Ricerche
Naples, Italy

World Scientific
Singapore • New Jersey • London • Hong Kong

Published by

World Scientific Publishing Co. Pte. Ltd.

P O Box 128, Farrer Road, Singapore 912805

USA office: Suite 1B, 1060 Main Street, River Edge, NJ 07661

UK office: 57 Shelton Street, Covent Garden, London WC2H 9HE

British Library Cataloguing-in-Publication Data
A catalogue record for this book is available from the British Library.

ADVANCES IN VISUAL FORM ANALYSIS
Proceedings of the Third International Workshop on Visual Form

ISBN 981-02-3258-6

This book is printed on acid-free paper.

Printed in Singapore by Uto-Print

FOREWORD

This book contains the papers presented at the 3rd International Workshop on Visual Form (IWVF3), held in Capri, Italy, 28-30 May 1997. IWVF3 was sponsored by the International Association for Pattern Recognition, and organised by the Dipartimento di Informatica e Sistemistica of the University of Naples and the Istituto di Cibernetica of the National Research Council of Italy. Two previous sessions of the workshop were held in Capri in 1991 and 1994, organised by the same institutions.

During IWVF3, problems and prospects of current interest in 2D and 3D shape analysis and recognition were discussed extensively in order to provide an updated view of research activity in the field. Both theoretical and applicative aspects of visual form processing were analysed, with special reference to shape representation, decomposition, description and recognition. The papers in this book cover important topics and constitute a collection of recent results achieved by leading research groups from several countries. Contributions were reviewed by an international board of referees listed separately. Invited talks were given by Kim L. Boyer, Jan-Olof Eklundh, Robert M. Haralick, Jan J. Koenderink, Michael Leyton, Gerard Medioni, Jean Serra, Harry Wechsler, and Steven W. Zucker. The scientific contribution and enthusiasm of all the IWVF3 participants resulted in the great success of the meeting.

IWVF3 and this book, which originates from it, would not have been possible without the financial support of the universities, research institutions and other organisations that contributed generously. The precious help given by the referees in selecting the papers to be included in the scientific program of the workshop is gratefully acknowledged. We also wish to thank all the authors who have contributed to this book and made it enjoyable for the readers.

Carlo Arcelli
Luigi P. Cordella
Gabriella Sanniti di Baja

June 1997

ACKNOWLEDGMENTS

IWVF3 has been financially supported by the following organizations:

Area di Ricerca di Napoli - CNR
Azienda Autonoma di Cura, Soggiorno e Turismo - Isola di Capri
Comitato Scienze di Ingegneria e Architettura - CNR
Comitato Scienze e Tecnologia dell'Informazione - CNR
ELSAG Bailey S.p.A.
Gruppo Nazionale di Cibernetica e Biofisica - CNR
Istituto di Cibernetica - CNR
Regione Campania
Università degli Studi di Napoli Federico II
Università degli Studi di Salerno

The help of Mr. Salvatore Piantedosi in the preparation of this book is also gratefully acknowledged.

LIST OF REVIEWERS

Keiichi Abe (Japan)
Sergey V. Ablameyko (Belarus)
Claus S. Andersen (Denmark)
Hans J. Andersen (Denmark)
Alberto Biancardi (Italy)
Joergen Bjoernstrup (Denmark)
Gunilla Borgefors (Sweden)
Alfred Bruckstein (Israel)
Elisabetta Bruzzone (Italy)
Virginio Cantoni (Italy)
Bruno Caprile (Italy)
Dmitry Chetverikov (Hungary)
Anna Maria Colla (Italy)
Bruno Crespi (Italy)
Larry Davis (USA)
Leila De Floriani (Italy)
Dov Dori (Israel)
Leo Dorst (The Netherlands)
Gregory Dudek (Canada)
Cesare Furlanello (Italy)
Tarak Gandhi (USA)
Ullas Gargi (USA)
Giovanni Garibotto (Italy)
Gösta Granlund (Sweden)
Erik Granum (Denmark)
Richard Hall (USA)
Rangachar Kasturi (USA)
Benjamin Kimia (USA)
Josef Kittler (UK)
Tat Yung Kong (USA)
Walter Kropatsch (Austria)
Chia-Hoang Lee (Taiwan)
Luca Lombardi (Italy)
Huizhu Luo (USA)
Claus B. Madsen (Denmark)
Paola Magillo (Italy)
Stefano Messelodi (Italy)
Evangelos E. Milios (Canada)
Thomas B. Moeslund (Denmark)
Annick Montanvert (France)
Giorgio Musso (Italy)
George Nagy (USA)
Gianluca Nicchiotti (Italy)
Ingela Nyström (Sweden)
Ennio Ottaviani (Italy)
Theo Pavlidis (USA)
Enrico Puppo (Italy)
Pier Carlo Ravasio (Italy)
Marina Rosso (Italy)
Hanan Samet (USA)
Franc Solina (Slovenia)
Minas E. Spetsakis (Canada)
Luuk Spreeuwers (Hungary)
Albert Vossepoel (The Netherlands)
Thorbjoern G. Vynne (Denmark)
Piero Zamperoni (Germany)

CONTENTS

GROUPING BASED HYPOTHESES VERIFICATION IN OBJECT RECOGNITION

A. AMIR, M. LINDENBAUM
Computer Science Department, Technion, Haifa 32000, ISRAEL
arnon@cs.technion.ac.il, mic@cs.technion.ac.il

Verification is the final decision stage in many object recognition processes. It is carried out by evaluating a score, usually calculated as a sum of evidence obtained from every data feature in the image, and choosing the hypotheses associated with the highest score. This additive approach often fails in the presence of occlusions, other objects and clutter.
We propose an alternative verification paradigm, which does not rely on summing the evidence from individual data features. The basic observation is that the group of data features which belong to the object according to the hypothesized object instance, should be a "good group". Therefore it should agree with local grouping information, which can be measured from the image independently of the object recognition process.
We use a probabilistic framework, and choose the hypothesis which maximizes the joint likelihood of all available grouping cues. We prove that this criterion is consistent (in the statistical sense). Experiments with synthetic and real images show that although the additive approaches is often satisfactory, the proposed grouping-based non-additive approach works better in many difficult cases.

1 Introduction

Verification is the final decision stage in many object recognition processes. It is carried out by evaluating a score as a measure of "goodness" for every hypothesis [6,7,11], and using it to decide whether to accept or to reject the hypothesis. The performance of an object recognition system highly depends on the reliability of the verification method. In this paper we focus only in the verification stage, and suggest a new scoring method, which leads to a more reliable recognition result.

Traditionally, the verification score is calculated as a sum of evidence obtained from every data feature in the image. In its simplest form it is just the number of edgels[a] in the image which lie close enough (within the error tolerance) to the boundary of the projected hypothesized object instance[8,4]. More elaborate methods rely on a probabilistic error model (usually Gaussian), and measure the evidence, associated with every data feature, by its likelihood (see e.g.[13,10]). Some recognition algorithms do not contain an explicit verification

[a] An edgel is an edge pixel plus gradient direction.

stage but yet rely on a similarly calculated score (e.g. the Hough transform). We shall refer to all methods which evaluate some consistency measure for every data feature and calculate the score as the sum of these measures as *additive score methods*. The additive score approach often fails in the presence of other objects and clutter. Typical failure mechanisms are shown in Figure 1. Such failures are very common in practical situations, and limit the reliability of recognition systems [10,14,5]. They are also predictable by theoretical considerations [6,9]. Failures happen even when it is visually clear to a human observer, which object instance is indeed present in the scene.

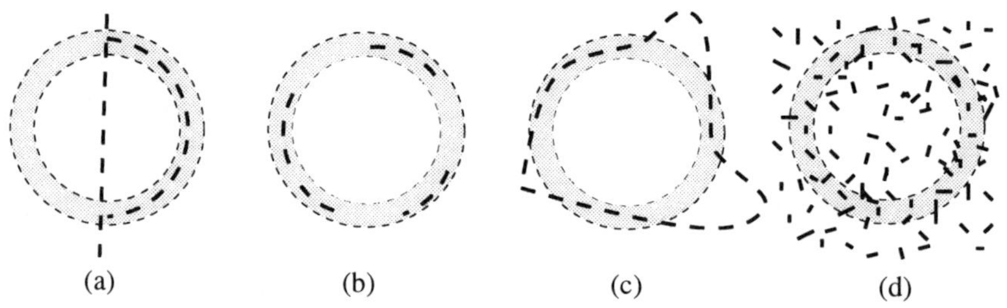

Figure 1: Four hypotheses of a circle which may be associated with the same additive score. Every small line segment denotes an edge pixel, with its direction. The first case, (a), stands for a half-occluded circle, and expected to get the highest score from all four. In (b) it is not clear why some parts of the boundary are missing, although it may looks as a correct hypothesis. The hypotheses in cases (c) (partially match with different object/s) and (d) (match with clutter, noise edges) are clearly incorrect.

In a statistical context, the additive score approach corresponds to an implicit independence assumption on the data feature's errors. This basic assumption often fails in real situations. The nature of edge detection processes, for example, implies that continuous edge segments are more likely than edgels which are scattered along the boundary. Therefore, the consistency of the former edgel subset gives a stronger evidence to the presence of the object in the scene and should be weighted higher in the verification stage [5]. Another example is the absence of some parts of the object's boundary due to occlusion, which may be identified and taken into account in the verification stage [12]. Indeed, verification method which is based on these observations perform nicely in many cases where the additive approach fails.

The basic theme of this work is that verification should measure the consistency of the hypothesis in the context of the whole image data, and should take into account especially its mutual dependencies, which may be quantified by grouping cues. We consider a probabilistic model for the grouping cues [2], and use the conditional joint likelihood of all available grouping cues, given the hypothesis, as the score. Then, by the maximum likelihood principle, the hypothesis associated with the highest score is selected. The method is controlled by one parameter, which should be selected based on the expected error mechanism. We prove that this method is consistent in the statistical sense; that is, in the presence of only one object in the scene, the correct hypothesis is expected to get the highest score. In a way, the systematic and quantitative method proposed here, generalizes and unifies some of the criteria suggested in [5,12].

2 Perceptual Grouping: Cues and Their Graph Representation

The mutual dependencies between data features are measured by perceptual grouping cues. To describe the grouping information available to the verification process we use the framework developed in our work on generic grouping algorithms and their analysis [3]. In this framework, *grouping cues* are considered to be random binary functions of data features pairs (e.g. pairs of edge points). For a pair of edgels, $e = (u, v)$, the grouping cue $c(e)$ provides a decision which may be either that the two edgels belong to the same group ($c(e) = 1$) or that they do not ($c(e) = 0$). Let $t(e)$ denote the true association between the data features u and v. That is, if both features indeed belong to the same group then $t(e) = 1$, otherwise $t(e) = 0$. Using this notation, the cues' reliability may be quantified by the probabilities that the cues provide wrong decisions,

$$\epsilon_{fa} = Prob\{c(e) = 1 \mid t(e) = 0\} \qquad \epsilon_{miss} = Prob\{c(e) = 0 \mid t(e) = 1\}. \quad (1)$$

This model is easily extendible to more general cue functions which provide a non-binary output, such as the likelihood of the feature pair to be in the same group. Cues which operate on three or more data features are also a direct extension (see [1]). In our experimentation the grouping cue is a smoothness criterion; a function which decide whether or not two edgels belong to the same smooth curve. The reliability of grouping cues, quantified by $\epsilon_{miss}, \epsilon_{fa}$, may be estimated analytically or experimentally.

We use graphs to represent the grouping information. The *underlying graph*, $G_u = (V, E_u)$, represents the set of edgel pairs to be tested by the cue. Each node represents an edgel, and each arc represents a tested pair. The *measured graph*, $G_m = (V, E_m)$, represents the cue results. It has the same nodes set as G_u, but only the subset of arcs associated with positive cue ($c(e) = 1$). Here G_u is build up by connecting each edgel to its k nearest neighbors. We would like to mention, however, that this graph representation of perceptual grouping information is not limited to smoothness based grouping and k connected graphs, and is useful for other applications and grouping domains[1].

3 The Grouping-Based Hypothesis Score

In order to define our score, we shall use the following observation; the hypothesized object instance h induces a partition of the data feature set (e.g., all edgels) into two subsets; the data features associated with the hypothesized object are put in the *object set*, O, and the rest are put in the *background set*, B. In the examples considered in this work, the object set consists of those edgels which lie close enough to the hypothesized object boundary. The grouping information supports certain hypotheses. A grouping cue, for example, may provide a positive evidence that two data features belong to the same object. Such an evidence will support hypotheses which put both data features in the object set. However, it will work against hypotheses which put only one of these data features in the object set.

Quantitatively, observe that the feature partitioning induces a further partition of the arcs (and their corresponding cues) into three disjoint subsets: the *object-object set*, OO, includes all cues corresponding with two data features in the hypothesized object set. The two other sets, the *object-background set*, OB, and the *background-background set*, BB, are similarly defined. Consider some particular cue which corresponds to some feature pair e. If this feature pair belongs to the OO set, it means that the hypothesis puts this pair of data features in the same object. In this case, the likelihood of the value "0" is $L\{c(e) = 0|e \in OO\} = \epsilon_{miss}$ and the likelihood of the value "1" is $L\{c(e) = 1|e \in OO\} = 1 - \epsilon_{miss}$. Similarly, if e belongs to the OB set, then $L\{c(e) = 1|e \in OB\} = \epsilon_{fa}$ and $L\{c(e) = 0|e \in OB\} = 1 - \epsilon_{fa}$. Calculating the likelihood of cues corresponding to feature pairs in the BB set (both features belong to the background) is not straightforward. Let us denote $L\{c(e) = 1|e \in BB\} = \epsilon_{bg}$ and $L\{c(e) = 0|e \in OB\} = 1 - \epsilon_{bg}$, where ϵ_{bg} is a parameter which should be tuned according to the expected failure mechanism[2]. For the moment, assume that the likelihood may be calculated for all cues.

To calculate the joint likelihood of all the cues, we assume that the cues are independent and identically distributed (iid) random variables. This assumption may be challenged, but note that it is different (and weaker) from the assumption (made by all additive-score verification methods) that the location of a data features is determined by a random iid process. Here we allow, and in fact, build on the dependencies between data features. We just assume that the grouping tests (cues) fail (or succeed) independently on different pairs.

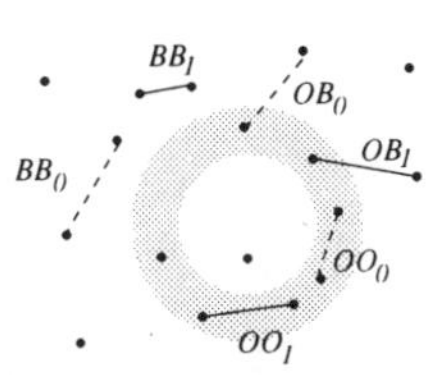

Cue-based classification	Hypothesis-based classification			total
	OO set	OB set	BB set	total
$c(e)=0$	N_0^{OO}	N_0^{OB}	N_0^{BB}	N_0
$L\{c(e)=0\}$	ϵ_{miss}	$1-\epsilon_{fa}$	$1-\epsilon_{bg}$	
$c(e)=1$	N_1^{OO}	N_1^{OB}	N_1^{BB}	N_1
$L\{c(e)=1\}$	$1-\epsilon_{miss}$	ϵ_{fa}	ϵ_{bg}	
total	N^{OO}	N^{OB}	N^{BB}	$N=\lvert E_u\rvert$

Figure 2: The set of arcs (feature-pairs), tested by the grouping cue, is divided into $2\times 3=6$ classes. Left: an example for one arc of each class. Every arc is associated with its grouping cue result, which is either "0" (dashed line) or "1"(solid line). Every hypothesis infer a further partition of E_u into three disjoint sets, denoted as OO, OB, BB (the points inside the gray torus form the object set, O). Therefore, we have 6 disjoint subsets. Right: the table specifies the notations for the number of arcs in each category, and the likelihood of every one.

Using this independence assumption, the joint likelihood of all the cues is just the product of all individual likelihoods. This joint likelihood is highly related to the consistency measure proposed in this work. To make the expressions simpler we use the logarithm of this likelihood as the actual score. Recall that every one of the cues corresponds to some arc, e, of the *underlying graph* $G_u=(V,E_u)$, this log-likelihood is

$$logL_h \stackrel{\text{def}}{=} \sum_{e\in E_u} logL\{c(e)|h\}. \quad (2)$$

Hence the consistency of the hypothesized object does not depend only on the number of consistent data features, but also on their relative locations and orientations, captured by the grouping cues. This is therefore a non-additive score. The likelihood of every cue $c(e)$ depends on its value and on the set to which e belongs. Therefore all arcs may be classified into 6 categories. The arcs in each category are associated with the same likelihood value. Figure 2 summarize the notations for the number of arcs in these categories and their likelihoods. Using these notations, eq. (2) becomes

$$\begin{aligned} logL_h &= N_0^{OO}\log(\epsilon_{miss})+N_0^{OB}\log(1-\epsilon_{fa})+N_0^{BB}\log(1-\epsilon_{bg}) \\ &+ N_1^{OO}\log(1-\epsilon_{miss})+N_1^{OB}\log(\epsilon_{fa})+N_1^{BB}\log(\epsilon_{bg}). \end{aligned} \quad (3)$$

For the special *empty hypothesis*, which associates all the data features with the background set, $B=V$, the object set is empty, $O=\emptyset$, $N_0^{OO}=N_1^{OO}=N_0^{OB}=N_1^{OB}=0$, and the log-likelihood expression shrinks to $logL_\emptyset = N_0\log(1-\epsilon_{bg})+N_1\log(\epsilon_{bg})$. The log-likelihood of the empty hypothesis, $logL_\emptyset$, does not depend on any other hypothesis h, and thus may be regarded as a constant bias level. We shall use the relative log-likelihood,

$$\begin{aligned} score(h) \stackrel{\text{def}}{=} logL_h - logL_\emptyset &= N_0^{OO} \log \frac{\epsilon_{miss}}{1-\epsilon_{bg}} + N_1^{OO} \log \frac{1-\epsilon_{miss}}{\epsilon_{bg}} \\ &+ N_0^{OB} \log \frac{1-\epsilon_{fa}}{1-\epsilon_{bg}} + N_1^{OB} \log \frac{\epsilon_{fa}}{\epsilon_{bg}} \end{aligned} \tag{4}$$

as the verification score, for evaluating any other hypothesis. This final form differs from the log-likelihood, $logL_h$ (eq. 2) only by a constant, $logL_\emptyset$. Note that this criterion is local, and depends only on feature pairs associated with the hypothesized object (only the OO set and the OB set). This score may be interpreted as the joint log likelihood ratio, comparing some hypothesis, h, against the empty hypothesis. In this comparison, the feature pairs corresponding to the BB set, get the same likelihood for both hypotheses, and do not effect the score. This form is also computationally more practical, because it avoids the need to count N_0^{BB} and N_1^{BB}. It relies only on the much smaller sets of arcs, OO and OB, connected to the nodes of the hypothesized object. Therefore, the grouping cues associated with the other feature pairs, does not have to be evaluated at all. This dramatically decreases the computational cost, especially if only a small number of hypotheses are considered. In our implementation, where the degree of each node in the graph is bounded, the number of evaluated grouping cues for each hypothesis is therefore linearly bounded relative to the hypothesis size, $|O|$.

It may be shown that the score defined in eq. 4 is a consistent estimator. in a statistical sense. That is, the correct hypothesis is expected to get the highest score. This property holds if there is one object in the scene. The parameter ϵ_{bg} provides a tradeoff between the two failure mechanisms, described in Fig 5(c)(d), and controls the relative weights of the different types of arcs in eq. 4. We elaborate on this issue in the full version [2].

4 Experimentation and Discussion

The new score was tested and compared with an additive score, on synthetic and on real images. The first two examples demonstrate the discrimination power of the proposed method for two different failure mechanisms associated with the additive score. In the first example (Figure 3) additive verification fails due to the presence of a similar object in the scene (first failure mechanism, Fig. 1(c)). The hypothesized object is a circle. It turns out that the additive score associated with placing the object on the hexagon in the image, is higher than the score associated with placing it on the half occluded circle. Therefore, the use of the additive score leads to localization error. The grouping based method, on the other hand, rightfully prefers the circle. The grouping score of the hexagon is lower because of the negative contribution of the N_1^{OB} term to the score (eq. 4). Note that in this case, even more elaborate additive score methods, which use, for example, the gradient direction information, are expected to fail.

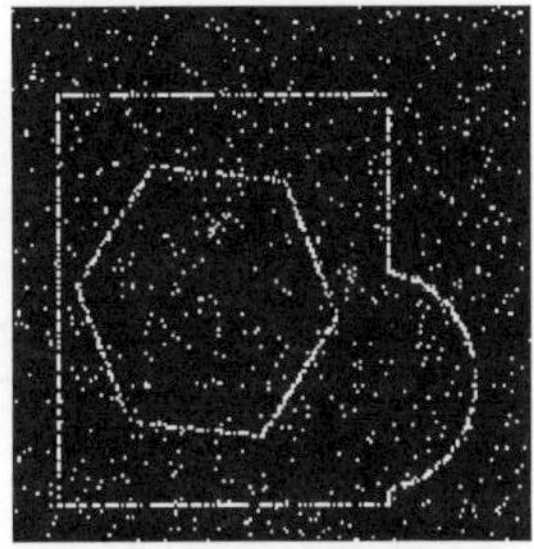

a. Edgels image.

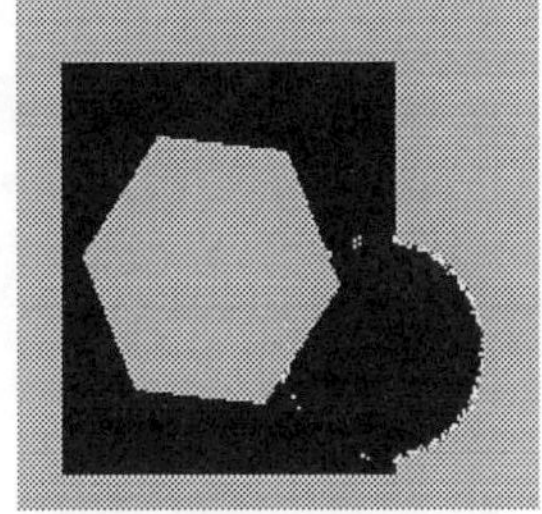

b. The correct hypothesis

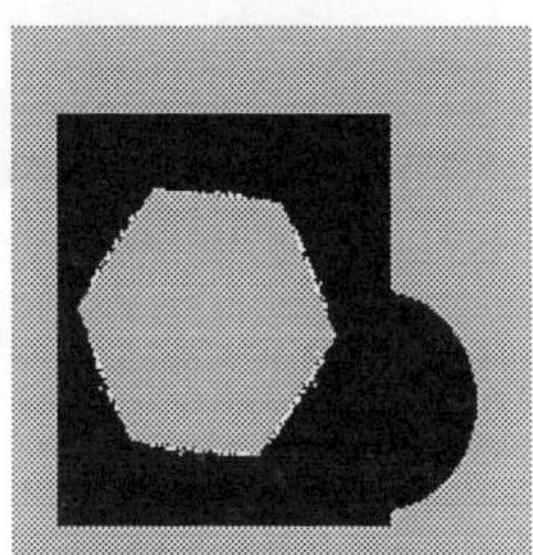

c. A wrong hypothesis

Figure 3: Example for the first failure mechanism (see Fig. 1(c)). The additive scores of the correct hypothesis (b) and of the wrong hypothesis (c) are 3.58 and 3.95, respectively. The grouping based scores of (b) and (c) are 405 and 251, respectively.

In the second example (Figure 4), the synthetic edge image (a) includes a very small, partially occluded, 2D "pigeon" shape (like in (f)), together with other objects and high clutter. Image (b), a magnification of the center of the original noise-free image, shows the object (black region), and the correct hypothesis. Five of the wrong hypotheses, numbered $1-5$, got an additive score, higher than the correct one (the 6th hypothesis), as shown in (d). The grouping-based score for the same 45 hypotheses is given (in the same order) in (e). The correct hypothesis (no. 6), got the highest score, which is clearly much higher than all others. In this context the erroneous hypotheses are created by a random accumulation of clutter, as illustrated in (f), which may be discriminated from the correct hypothesis mainly by the negative contribution of the N_0^{OO} term to the score (eq. 4).

The Third example (Figure 5) demonstrates the utility of the method to $3D$ realistic objects in a very cluttered image. The object is an apple, its boundary modeled by a simple hand-drawn $2D$ spline. 45 hypotheses were verified by an additive score (g) and by the grouping based score (h). The additive scores of 31 wrong hypotheses, numbered $1-31$, are higher than the score of the correct one (the 32nd hypothesis). With the grouping-based score, the correct hypothesis got the highest score, which is clearly much higher than all others. In this real situation, the erroneous hypotheses are created by a

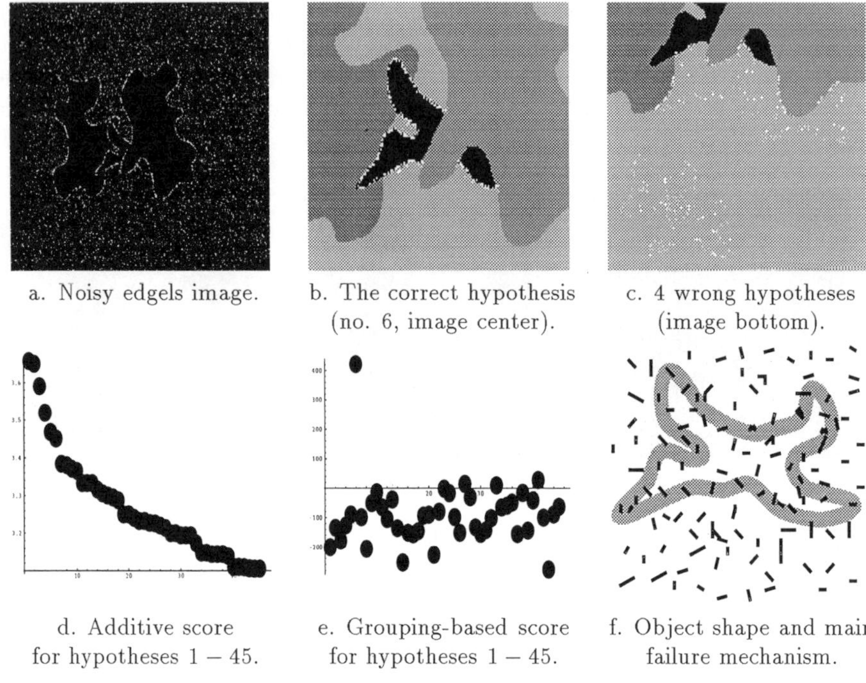

a. Noisy edgels image. b. The correct hypothesis (no. 6, image center). c. 4 wrong hypotheses (image bottom).

d. Additive score for hypotheses $1 - 45$. e. Grouping-based score for hypotheses $1 - 45$. f. Object shape and main failure mechanism.

Figure 4: Example 2: a very small, partially-occluded, 2D "pigeon" shape (like the one in (g)), in the presence of other objects and high clutter (see text).

random accumulation of clutter in some regions of the edge image, which is a mixture of the above two failure mechanisms.

5 Conclusions

We propose a new hypothesis verification method, which is based on perceptual grouping information. The experimentation show that this method is better than additive score in difficult scenes. For easier scenes, both the additive score and the grouping based score perform well.

The proposed non-additive verification process seems to be more reliable than additive verification because it does not take into account only the consistency of data features along the hypothesized boundary, but also its "inconsistency" with its larger neighborhood, outside the hypothesis. In perceptual grouping terms, we prefer hypotheses that are "good groups".

The paper raises again the old question: what is an evidence for some

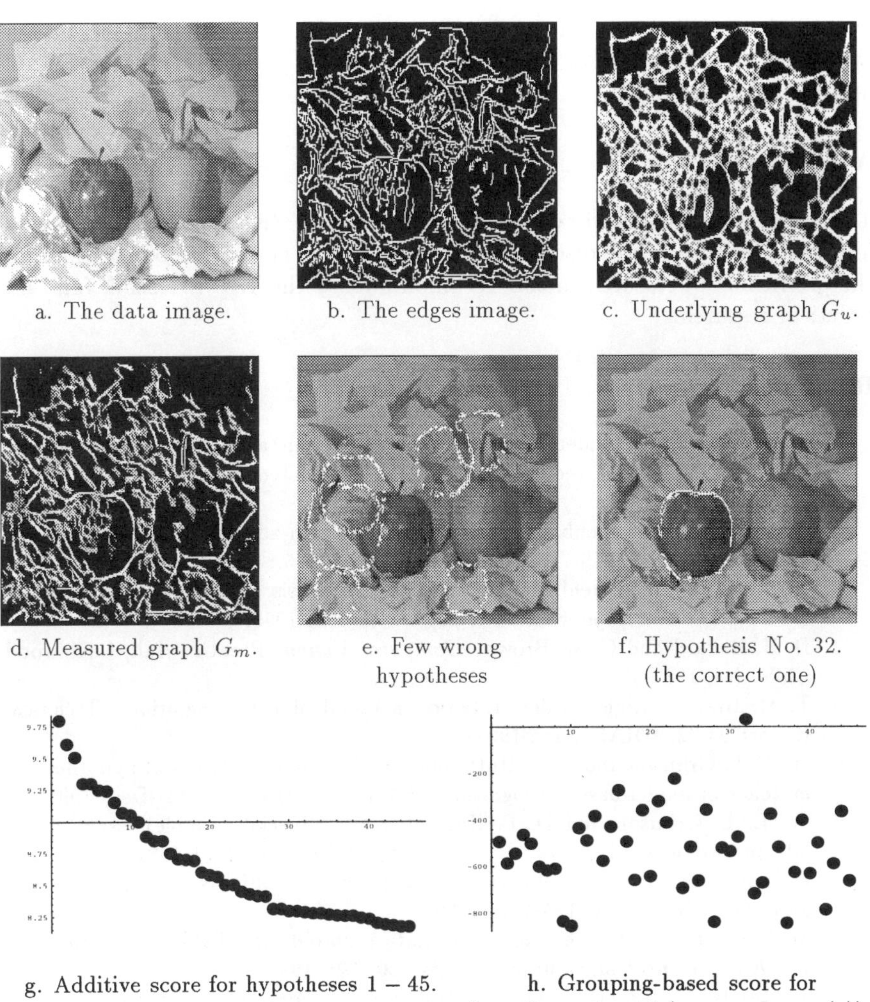

a. The data image. b. The edges image. c. Underlying graph G_u.

d. Measured graph G_m. e. Few wrong hypotheses f. Hypothesis No. 32. (the correct one)

g. Additive score for hypotheses 1 – 45. **h. Grouping-based score for hypotheses 1 – 45 (same order as (g)).**

Figure 5: Example 3: Finding an apple in a real image (see text). Note that the grouping information, represented by the set of tested grouping cues (G_u)(c), and their results (G_m) (d), emphasizes the smooth edges.

hypothesis? We believe that in the context of object recognition the answer we proposed is better than the additive approach. It is clear, however, that much is left to be done.

Acknowledgments

The motivation to this work was raised by Andrew Zisserman, and we thank him for these interesting discussions. This work was supported by the fund for the promotion of research in the Technion and by the J.D. Erteschik fund for practical research.

References

1. A. Amir and M. Lindenbaum. The construction and analysis of a generic grouping algorithm. Technical Report CIS-9418, Technion, Israel, Nov. 1994. accepted to T-PAMI.
2. A. Amir and M. Lindenbaum. Grouping-based non-additive verification. Technical Report CIS-9518, Technion, Israel, Oct. 1995.
3. A. Amir and M. Lindenbaum. Quantitative analysis of grouping processes. In *ECCV-96, Cambridge*, volume 1, pages 371–384, 1996.
4. D. H. Ballard and C. M. Brown. *Computer Vision*. Prentice Hall, Englewood Cliffs, NJ, 1982.
5. T. M. Breuel. Higher-order statistics in visual object recognition. Technical Report 93-02, IDIAP, June 1993.
6. W. E. L. Grimson and D. P. Huttenlocher. On the verification of hypothesized matches in model-based recognition. *PAMI*, 13(12):1201–1213, Dec. 1991.
7. W. E. L. Grimson and D. P. Huttenlocher. Special (double) issue on the interpretation of 3d scenes. *PAMI-13(10) and PAMI-14(2)*, 1991.
8. D. Huttenlocher and S. Ullman. Recognizing solid objects by alignment with an image. *IJCV*, 5(2):195–212, 1990.
9. M. Lindenbaum. On the amount of data required for reliable recognition. In *ICPR-94, Jerusalem*, volume 1, pages 726–729, 1994.
10. J. Mundy, C. Huang, J. Liu, W. Hoffman, D. Forsyth, C. Rothwell, A. Zisserman, S. Utcke, , and O. Bournez. Object recognition system based on geometric invariants. In *IUW-94*, pages 1393–1402, 1994.
11. J. L. Mundy and A. Zisserman. *Geometric Invariance in Computer Vision*. The MIT press, 1992.
12. C. Rothwell. Reasoning about occlusions during hypothesis verification. In *ECCV-96, Cambridge*, volume 1, pages 599–609, 1996.
13. K. B. Sarachik and W. Grimson. Gaussian error models for object recognition. In *CVPR*, pages 400–406, 1993.
14. A. Zisserman. *personal communication*.

MODELING APPEARANCE CHANGE IN IMAGE SEQUENCES

M.J. BLACK
Xerox Palo Alto Research Center
3333 Coyote Hill Rd., Palo Alto, CA 94304

Y. YACOOB
Computer Vision Laboratory, University of Maryland
College Park, MD 20742

D.J. FLEET
Department of Computing and Information Science, Queen's University
Kingston, Canada K7L 3N6

As non-rigid and non-cohesive objects move or change state, their projected appearance on the image changes. These "appearance changes" due to deforming, articulating or eruptive/emergent events can be accounted for by two classes of image-based events. The first accounts for the deformations and articulations of the object in the image plane; we describe such *form* changes using optical flow. The second class accounts for intensity changes not captured by image motion. These result from occlusion, disocclusion, and changes to material properties, and we refer to these as *iconic change*. The evolving appearance of non-rigid and non-cohesive objects is modeled using a "mixture" of image deformation and iconic change. We propose a method for learning parameterized models of image deformation and iconic structure, and an algorithm that exploits these to recover appearance changes in image sequences.

1 Introduction and Motivation

Changes in the image appearance of a rigid object can be characterized by the 3D shape of the object, its surface reflectance properties, the scene illumination, and the relative motion between the object and the camera. For non-rigid objects or complex scenes with many objects occluding one another the situation is less clear. Consider for example a complex deformable object such as a human face as shown in Figure 1. Unlike simple rigid objects, image sequences of faces exhibit a variety of appearance changes. These include smooth changes of image structure, referred to here as "image deformation." They also include intensity variations caused by occlusion, disocclusion, reflectance changes, and changes in material properties. We refer to these as "iconic change."

In this paper we begin to develop a theory to describe the changes that non-rigid and non-cohesive objects can undergo in an image sequence. We will define, first intuitively and then mathematically, what we mean by changes

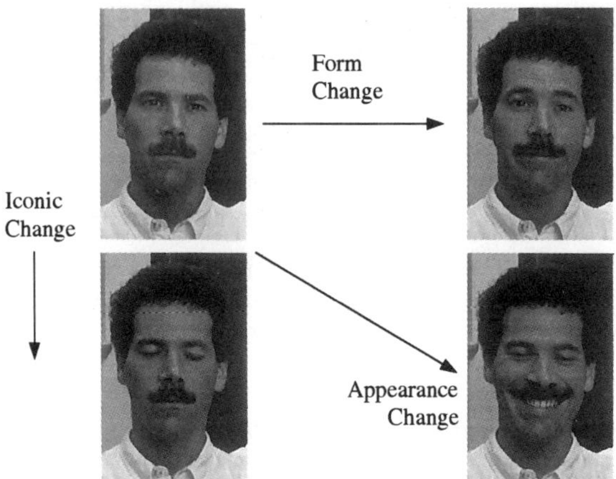

Figure 1: Appearance changes involve image deformation and iconic change.

in image form and iconic structure. We propose a method for automatically constructing simple parameterized models of image deformation and iconic structure that can be used to model the appearance changes of complex objects over time and we demonstrate this formulation in the domain of human mouths.

To develop an understanding of what we mean by deformation and iconic change, consider the human face in Figure 1. The figure illustrates two types of "intensity change." Some of the changes can be modeled by a smooth deformation (warping) from one frame to another. The curving and deformation of the mouth, or the translation and deformation of the eyebrows can be modeled in this way.[1] These *form* changes can be described by the *motion* of pixel intensities between frames, and can be measured with optical flow techniques.

There are other changes that images of faces undergo that are not well modeled by smooth deformations (optical flow). We call these "iconic change".[a] The blinking of the eye in Figure 1 is one example of a change between the images that is not well modeled by the warping of one image into the other. Still other dynamic image variations involve both image deformation *and* iconic change. For example, when a person smiles there is often a significant deformation of the lips, as well as the appearance of the teeth, tongue, and mouth cavity. Such changes in image appearance are common with complex

[a] While many words describe changes in form (eg. metamorphosis) we were unable to find a general term which describes the notion of an appearance change that does not involve a change in shape. These types of changes are common in nature, and we coin the term "iconic change" to describe them.

deformable objects, and with motion textures such as articulated human motion, or the motion of plants, flags, water, etc. Our goal in what follows is to formalize more precisely what we mean by appearance change and to show how to factor appearance change into image deformation and iconic change.

Of course, one might attempt to understand and model changes in image appearance by inferring 3D shape, surface reflectance, and the multitude of complex occlusion relationships in the scene. However, for many objects this seems untenable since, as Gibson [2] noted, scenes contain surfaces which "often flow or undergo stretching, squeezing, bending, and breaking in ways of enormous mechanical complexity."

In this paper we advocate "image-based" modeling of non-rigid and non-cohesive objects rather than a 3D or physically-based approach. In this approach, an object such as a human mouth undergoes deformations *in the image plane* (2D image motion), and changes in iconic structure. One motivation for developing the theory of image-based appearance change stems from our interest in recognizing non-rigid and articulated motion, such as human facial expressions. Previous work in this area focused on image motion of face regions such as the mouth.[1] But focusing on the image motion alone ignores much of the available information in image sequences of people talking. The systematic appearance/disappearance of the teeth and tongue during speech and facial expression appears to provide important cues to human observers. For machine recognition we would like to be able to model these intensity variations.

2 Modeling Appearance Change

As an object moves or deforms we often assume that only the geometry of its projection onto the imaging plane changes. This is usually formalized as the *brightness constancy assumption*

$$I(\mathbf{x}, t) \;=\; I(\mathbf{x} - \mathbf{u}(\mathbf{x}),\, t+1), \tag{1}$$

that is, that the appearance of the object at pixel $\mathbf{x} = (x, y)$ at time t is the same as that at time $t+1$ offset by the image motion, $\mathbf{u}(\mathbf{x}) = (u(\mathbf{x}), v(\mathbf{x}))$. We refer to this motion as "image deformation" (a change in image form).

It is well known that the brightness constancy assumption is violated in many situations involving changes in diffuse reflectance, specularities, shadows, occlusion, etc. Most methods for estimating optical flow treat these violations as a source of error and attempt to reduce their significance. For representing and recovering the changes in appearance of non-rigid objects we do not want to ignore them. Rather, we wish to explicitly model their structure.

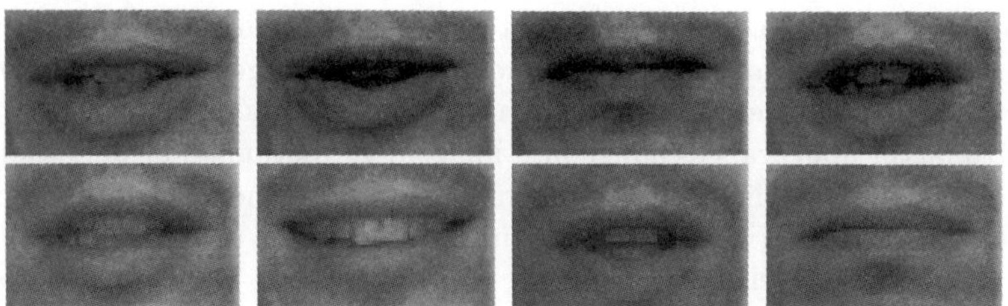

Figure 2: Example frames taken from the 600 image training sequence.

Our approach is to learn parameterized models of the deformation and iconic structure of an object such as a mouth. Image motion is first computed from a training image sequence using a robust optical flow method [3] and then principle component analysis (PCA) is used to compute a low-dimensional model of the deformation.[4] PCA is also used to construct a low-dimensional model of the individual frames of the training sequence to allow us to account for iconic change. Finally, we generalize the brightness constancy assumption to account for both types of appearance change. We then show how to estimate the parameters of the models directly from an image sequence.

Throughout this paper we use the motion of a human mouth for illustration. Figure 2 shows sample frames from a training sequence of 600 images in which a single subject spoke several words and smiled.

2.1 Modeling Image Deformation (Optical Flow)

We first compute image motion for the training sequence using the brightness constancy assumption and a robust optical flow algorithm.[3] The robust method is essential as it allows violations of the brightness constancy assumption that occur due to the appearance/disappearance of the teeth, tongue, and mouth cavity. The training set from which we construct a model of image deformation is a set of p optical flow fields. For images with $s = n \times m$ pixels, each flow field contains $2s$ quantities (i.e., the horizontal and vertical flow components at each pixel). For each flow field we place the $2s$ values into a column vector of length $2s$ by scanning the horizontal components of the flow, $u(x, y)$, and then vertical components, $v(x, y)$, in standard lexicographic order. The resulting p vectors become the columns of a $2s \times p$ matrix F.

PCA is then used to compute a low-dimensional model for the spatial structure of the flow fields.[4] Toward this end, let the Singular Value Decomposition (SVD) of F be written as

$$F = M\Sigma_m V_m^T \tag{2}$$

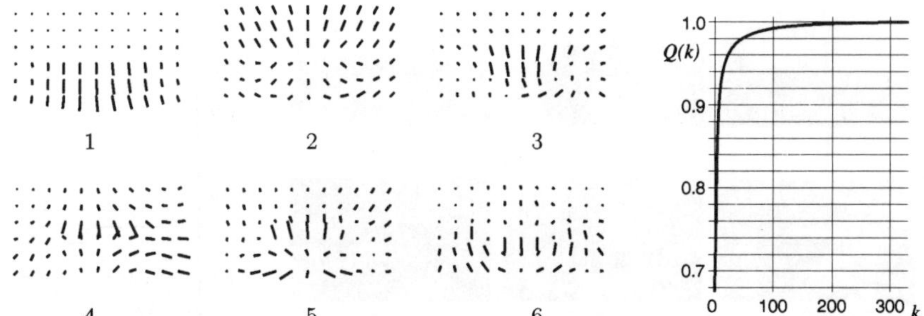

Figure 3: First six basis flow fields, $M_1(\mathbf{x})$ ... $M_6(\mathbf{x})$, and the fraction of variance $Q(k)$ in the first k eigen-directions.

where $M = [M_1, \ldots, M_p]$ is a $2s \times p$ matrix, the columns, M_i, of which form an orthogonal basis for the columns of F, Σ_m is a $p \times p$ diagonal matrix containing the singular values, $\lambda_1, \lambda_2, \ldots, \lambda_p$ sorted in decreasing order, and V_m^T is a $p \times p$ orthogonal matrix that encodes the coefficients used in expanding each column of F as a weighted sum of the principle component directions M_i.

Because there is redundant information in the training flow fields, the rank of F will be lower than p. We can therefore approximate flow fields like those in the training set as

$$\mathbf{u}(\mathbf{x};\, \vec{\mu}) \;=\; \sum_{i=1}^{k} \mu_i\, M_i(\mathbf{x}), \tag{3}$$

where $k < p$, $M_i(\mathbf{x})$ denotes the ith column of M expressed as a 2D vector field, and $\vec{\mu} = (\mu_1, ..., \mu_k)$ are the model parameters. These learned models are like the affine models commonly used in optical flow methods, but are tailored to the domain of interest here. Finally, the quality of the approximation given by the first k columns of M is characterized by the fraction of the variance of the training set that is accounted for by the selected components, i.e.,

$$Q(k) \;=\; (\sum_{i=1}^{k} \lambda_i^2) \,/\, (\sum_{i=1}^{p} \lambda_i^2). \tag{4}$$

The motion of the mouth is highly constrained, the training set contains redundant information, and the singular values drop off quickly. The first six basis flow fields, $M_i(\mathbf{x})$, shown in Figure 3, account for 89% of the variance in the training data. For the experiments below, we use ten basis flow fields which account for 93% of the variance. Hallinan referred to basis flows such as our $M_i(\mathbf{x})$ as *EigenWarps*.[5] They can also be thought of as *motion templates* [6] that can be combined to produce motion fields.

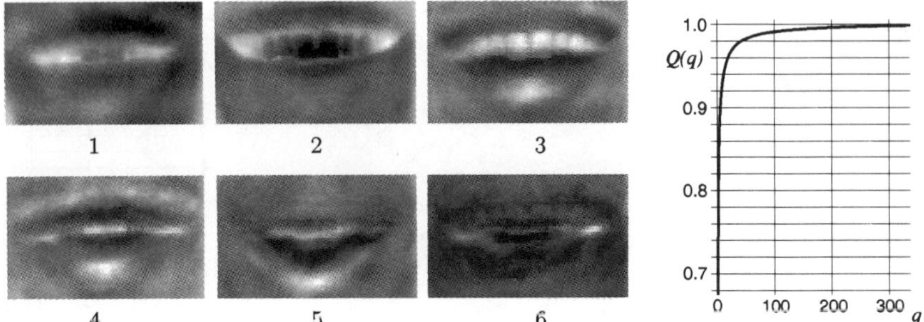

Figure 4: First six basis appearance images, $A_1(\mathbf{x})$ ... $A_6(\mathbf{x})$, and the fraction of variance $Q(q)$ in the first q eigen-directions.

2.2 Modeling Iconic Change

In order to account for iconic change in image sequences we first construct a low-dimensional model for the spatial image structure in the training set using PCA. For each $n \times m$ training image we scan the pixels in lexicographic order into a 1D column vector which becomes a column in a $nm \times p$ matrix B. As above, we compute the SVD of B to obtain

$$B = A\Sigma_a V_a^T . \tag{5}$$

Here, the columns, A_i, of A, are the principle component directions for the training set, Σ_a is a diagonal matrix containing the singular values in decreasing order, and the $p \times p$ orthogonal matrix V_a^T encodes the coefficients used in expanding columns of B in terms of the principle component directions.

We can express the ith column of A as a 2D basis image $A_i(\mathbf{x})$ and we can approximate some new $n \times m$ image I using q basis images as

$$I_A(\mathbf{x}; \vec{\alpha}) = \sum_{i=1}^{q} \alpha_i A_i(\mathbf{x}) , \tag{6}$$

where the α_i are scalar parameters of the model. The fraction of the variance in the mouth training set that is captured in the first q columns of A is shown in Figure 4. As in the case of deformation, we use ten basis images which account for 93% of the variance; six of these are shown in Figure 4.

2.3 Modeling Appearance Change: Mixture of Deformation and Iconic Change

Mixture models[7] have been used previously in motion analysis for recovering multiple motions within an image region.[8,9,10] Here we use the idea to account for mixtures of deformation and iconic change. Specifically, we model the image at time t as a motion term plus an iconic change term:

$$I(\mathbf{x},\, t) \;=\; w_0(\mathbf{x})I(\mathbf{x}-\mathbf{u}(\mathbf{x};\vec{\mu}), t+1) \;+\; w_1(\mathbf{x})I_A(\mathbf{x};\vec{\alpha})\,. \tag{7}$$

where w_i are "weights" between zero and one that indicate the extent to which a pixel is modeled by either deformation or iconic change. The weights are constrained to sum to one at each pixel location. Equation (7) can be generalized to model generic scene events including shadows, illumination variations and specularities.[11]

Note that $I(\mathbf{x}, t)$ will likely be similar to one of the training images, and could be explained by the iconic model, I_A, without deformation. To ensure that we recover information about motion in the scene, we include a *prior* that favors the deformation explanation.

To recover the parameters $(\vec{\mu}, \vec{\alpha})$ and weights (w_i), we formulate an objective function to be minimized

$$\sum_{\mathbf{x}} \rho\left(\left[w_0(\mathbf{x})I(\mathbf{x}-\mathbf{u}(\mathbf{x};\vec{\mu}), t+1) + w_1(\mathbf{x})I_A(\mathbf{x};\vec{\alpha}) - I(\mathbf{x},t) + \beta w_1(\mathbf{x})\right], \sigma\right). \tag{8}$$

This objective function includes the appearance constraint in (7) and a penalty term, βw_1, that enforces a preference for an explanation of the appearance change as a deformation. The function, ρ, is a robust error norm [3] given by $\rho(r,\sigma) = r^2/(\sigma^2+r^2)$, where σ is a scale factor. This function is used to reduce the influence of "outliers" which are appearance changes that are not well modeled by either of the learned deformation or iconic models.

The parameters $\vec{\mu}$, $\vec{\alpha}$, w_0 and w_1, are estimated using a variant of the EM algorithm.[7] The solution iterates between solving for the weights given estimates of the model parameters (the Expectation step) and solving for the model parameters with the weights held fixed (the Minimization step). Details of our EM algorithm using the robust norm are given elsewhere.[4,11]

3 Experimental Results

We present some experiments with human mouths to illustrate this model of appearance change. We collected a test sequence containing 150 frames of the same person from the training set both smiling and speaking (30 frames/sec, NTSC). We estimated the parameters for deformation $\vec{\mu}$, iconic change $\vec{\alpha}$, and the mixture weights w_i between each consecutive pair of frames by minimizing Equation (8).[11] The optimization scheme performs coordinate descent at each level in a coarse-to-fine strategy. A continuation method that lowers the value of σ during the optimization is employed to avoid local minimia.

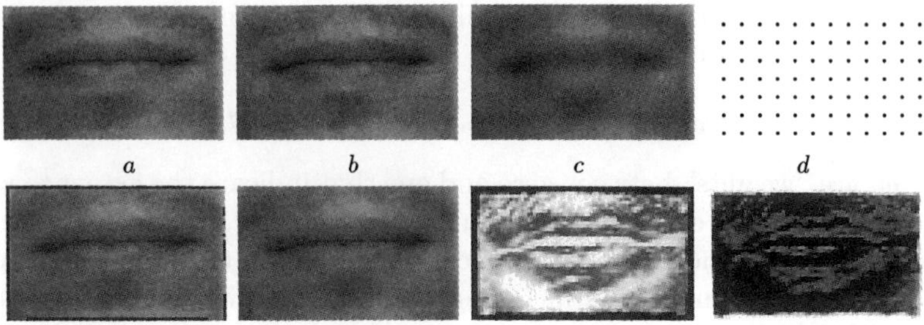

Figure 5: *(a,b)* first and second frames; *(c,d)* iconic model and recovered flow field; *(e,f)* image stabilized using motion alone, and with a mixture of motion and iconic models; *(g,h)* mixture weights for motion and appearance (white = 1, black = 0).

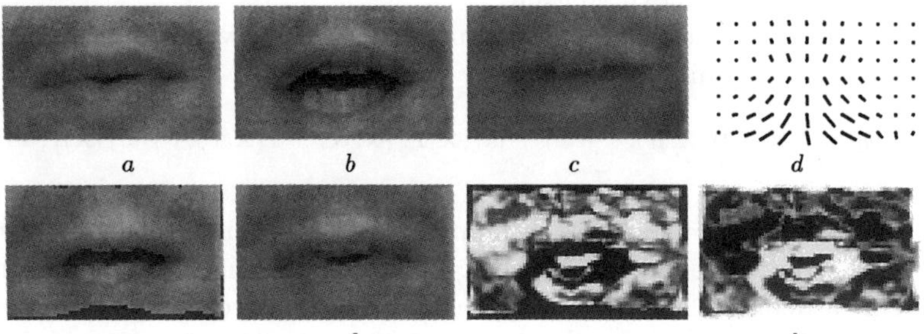

Figure 6: *(a,b)* first and second frames; *(c,d)* iconic model and recovered flow field; *(e,f)* image stabilized using motion alone, and with a mixture of motion and iconic models; *(g,h)* mixture weights for motion and appearance (white = 1, black = 0).

First consider the example in Figure 5 which contains no image motion. Figure 5*c* shows that the iconic model does a good job of reconstructing the image at time t (it is blurred owing to the small number of basis images used). Figure 5*d* shows the recovered flow which is near zero. The mixture weights w_0 and w_1 are shown in Figures 5*g,h*. The motion weights $w_0(\mathbf{x})$ are nearly one throughout, but the the explanation is shared between both models in some places. Finally, Figures 5*e,f* show the image "stabilized" using the recovered flow model alone, (i.e., $I(\mathbf{x} - \mathbf{u}(\mathbf{x}; \vec{\mu}), t+1)$), and then using both deformation and iconic models. (i.e., $w_0(\mathbf{x})I(\mathbf{x} - \mathbf{u}(\mathbf{x}; \vec{\mu}), t+1) + w_1(\mathbf{x})A(\mathbf{x}; \vec{\alpha})$).

Figure 6 shows another example from the test sequence. The change between the frames is large and cannot be modeled well by motion alone. The recovered iconic model of the first frame is shown Figure 6*c* and the recovered flow field in Figure 6*d* clearly shows the opening of the mouth. As above, the stabilized image using just deformation is in Figure 6*e*. The motion does a good job of stabilizing the upper lip for example, but brightness constancy is violated by the teeth and mouth cavity. This can be seen by examining the weights, w_0, for the motion term in Figure 6*g*. Note how the stablized image (Figure 6*f*) that uses both models resembles the original image in Figure 6*a*.

4 Discussion

Our motivation in exploring image deformation and iconic change is to address a general theory of appearance change in image sequences. Optical flow characterizes changes that obey brightness constancy. While it captures the appearance changes of many objects, it is only one class of appearance change. Occlusion/disocclusion is another class in which one surface *progressively* covers or reveals another. While optical flow and occlusion/disocclusion have been studied in detail, other types of appearance variations have not. The color of objects can change due to chemical processes (eg., oxidation), a change in state (eg., evaporation, dissolving), or a radical change in structure (eg., exploding, tearing, rupturing, boiling). With mouths, many of the appearance changes between frames are not deformations that conserve brightness.

One could ask: "Why model image deformation"? While all image changes might be modeled by iconic change this does not reflect the natural properties of objects (their "structural texture" [2]) and how they change. Motion is a natural category of appearance change that is important to model and recover. Therefore we impose a preference in our model that accounts for changes in appearance with motion when possible and with iconic change when motion fails. This preference for image deformation over iconic change is well motivated by the physics of natural objects.

One could also ask: "Why model iconic change"? While optical flow methods exist that can ignore many appearance changes that do not obey brightness constancy, it is important to account for, and therefore model, these image changes. Iconic change may be important for recognition. For example, we postulate that the systematic appearance/disappearance of teeth should be a useful cue for aiding speech and expression recognition. In addition, we believe that the temporal change of some objects may not be well modeled as image deformation. Bushes and trees blowing in the wind provide important examples exhibiting spatiotemporal texture. The appearance of leaves changes as their orientation with respect to the light direction changes and as they are occluded/disoccluded by other leaves. The result appears as "flicker". Although a detailed 3D model of branches and leaves could be used to account for the spatiotemporal intensity variation, this is impractical at all but a very fine spatial scale. A more natural approach is to account for the coarse motion of the branches and leaves, and model the "flickering" of the leaves as iconic change.

Appearance change in images is rarely due to image deformation or iconic change alone. Appearance changes result from a complex combination of events and processes. Here, we have proposed a simple model of appearance change as a mixture of deformation and iconic change. Future work will focus on a richer classification of appearance changes.[11]

Acknowledgments: We thank L. Davis and A. Jepson for their comments. DJF also thanks NSERC Canada and Xerox PARC for financial support.

5 References

1. M. J. Black and Y. Yacoob. "Tracking and recognizing rigid and non-rigid facial motions using local parametric models of image motions." *Proc. ICCV*, pp. 374–381, Boston, June 1995.
2. J. J. Gibson. *The Ecological Approach to Visual Perception.* Houghton Mifflin, Boston, MA, 1979.
3. M.J. Black and P. Anandan. "Robust estimation of multiple motions: Parametric and piecewise-smooth flow fields." *CVGIP:IU*, 63:75–104, Jan 1996.
4. M. J. Black, Y. Yacoob, A. Jepson, and D. Fleet. "Learning parameterized models of image motion." *Proc. CVPR*, Puerto Rico, June 1997.
5. P. Hallinan. *A deformable model for the recognition of human faces under arbitrary illumination.* PhD, Harvard Univ., Cambridge, MA, Aug 1995.
6. G. D. Hager and P. N. Belhumeur. "Real-time tracking of image regions with changes in geometry and illumination." *Proc. CVPR*, pp. 403–410, San Francisco, June 1999.
7. G.J. McLachlan and K.E. Basford. *Mixture Models: Inference and Applications to Clustering.* Marcel Dekker Inc., N.Y., 1988.
8. A. Jepson and M. J. Black. "Mixture models for optical flow computation." *Proc. CVPR*, pp. 760–761, New York, June 1993.
9. Y. Weiss and E. H. Adelson. "A unified mixture framework for motion segmentation: Incorporating spatial coherence and estimating the number of models." *Proc. CVPR*, pp. 321–326, San Francisco, June 1996.
10. S. Ayer and H. Sawhney. "Layered representation of motion video using robust maximum-likelihood estimation of mixture models and MDL encoding." *Proc. ICCV*, pp. 777–784, Boston, 1995.
11. M. J. Black, Y. Yacoob, and D. J. Fleet. "Mixture models for appearance change in image sequences." *Submitted: ICCV*. Bombay, Jan 1998.

ACCURATE RECOVERY OF DENSE DEPTH MAP FROM VIDEO SEQUENCES

M Bober, N Georgis and J Kittler
Centre for Vision, Speech and Signal Processing,
School of Electronic Engineering, Information Technology and Mathematics
University of Surrey, Guildford GU2 5XH, United Kingdom
email: {M.Bober,N.Georgis,J.Kittler}@ee.surrey.ac.uk

The problem of scene structure recovery from image motion is considered in the context of motion compensated video coding. In order to compensate for full 3D motion of the camera, the scene depth map together with camera egomotion need to be estimated from the image sequence. An important prerequisite of the shape and motion recovery is the establishment of correspondences between the points in two successive frames of a video sequence. In the paper we abandon the traditional feature based approach and develop a correspondence analysis technique based on robust matching of local image intensities under affine transformation. We show that the technique not only establishes true correspondences, but the resulting field of corresponding points is dense, and their displacement is obtained with a subpixel accuracy and free of bias. We demonstrate that these dense high quality matches yield accurate estimates of the imaging geometry which are several orders of magnitude better than estimates obtained with feature based methods. This accuracy is reflected in a superior quality of estimates of the scene structure. The experiments are performed with images of a scene with known geometry, obtained using a calibrated camera. The obtained depth estimates are dense, with error of the order of 1% which contrasts with the sparse depth map and greater than 10% errors offered by a typical feature based approach.

1 Introduction

Scene structure recovery from X (stereo, motion, shading) has been one of the main preoccupations of vision research for decades. The interest stems from the range of vision applications the shape from X technology would enable which includes vision based navigation, 3D scene modelling, and 3D scene interpretation. Our particular interest in structure recovery is in the context of video coding. One of the most effective ways of removing information redundancy from moving image sequences is to predict image motion from one frame to another. Information compression is then achieved by transmitting the motion parameters together with any errors between the actual frame and its motion compensated prediction coded to remove any spatial redundancies.

Conventionally, 2D apparent motion in the image plane is estimated to motion compensate the next frame in a video sequence. However, this approach can be shown to work well only when the camera motion is limited to zoom, panning, tilting or rotation. When the camera motion includes also translation, motion compensation based on the apparent image motion fails to predict the next frame correctly because the apparent motion is a function of the distance of the scene from the camera. Motivated by this observation we have embarked on a research programme the aim of which is to compensate for the apparent image motion even when it is created by a translating camera. This approach involves the computation of the camera egomotion from the image sequence and estimation of the depth map. Once these two prerequisites are available, one can project pixels from one frame to another, which is the basis of motion compensation coding. The process should result in small prediction errors which can then be spatially coded in a conventional manner to achieve very low bit rates for video representation and transmission.

This paper is concerned with the problem of scene structure recovery from image motion. Traditionally the process of shape from motion estimation involves the extraction of image features such as corners and/or edges. The correspondence is then established between pairs of feature points in two consecutive frames which relate to the same physical point or structural primitive in the scene. Once these correspondences are determined, one can then estimate the fundamental matrix constraining the transformation of the pixels from one frame to another. From the fundamental matrix one can determine the essential matrix using the camera intrinsic parameters which can be obtained either via a camera calibration process [1] or alternatively from the video sequence using the Kruppa equations [2]. The essential matrix can then be decomposed into camera translation and rotation and this information, together with the pairs of corresponding points is sufficient to recover the scene depth.

Our initial experiments with the above scheme have identified very serious drawbacks associated with the feature based approach to structure from motion recovery. First of all, by definition, features are relatively sparse and do not facilitate the recovery of a dense map which is needed for coding purposes. More over, the depth and pixel projection estimates from one frame to another have been found to be prone to very serious errors which would render the more sophisticated approach to motion compensation useless. It was found that these latter problems were caused by the error sensitivity of the fundamental matrix. The errors and bias in the relative position estimates of the corresponding feature were sufficient to destabilise the process of fundamental matrix computation even when robust statistical techniques were used to guard against outliers. The problem is accentuated specifically for video data where the camera motion from frame to frame is likely to be very small.

In this paper we abandon the classical feature based approach to correspondence analysis for a novel image intensity based method to address both of the above problems. We show that the robust Hough method of local image intensity matching proposed in the paper, which assumes a locally affine transformation between two frames, establishes pixel correspondences to subpixel accuracy and free of bias. As the correspondence analysis is image intensity based, a dense field of correspondences can be established. We demonstrate that these dense high quality matches yield accurate estimates of the imaging geometry which are several orders of magnitude better than estimates obtained with feature based methods. This accuracy is reflected in a superior quality of estimates of the scene structure. We argue that these improvements make the investigated approach to image coding viable.

The paper is organised as follows. In Section 2 we present the proposed correspondence analysis method. The structure from motion recovery method is over-viewed in Section 3. Section 4 presents and discusses experiments in depth map estimation using the proposed approach and a traditional feature based scheme. Finally, Section 5 summarises the main contributions of the paper and their implications.

2 Correspondence Analysis

We base the correspondence analysis on textured regions in the image rather than point features. By texture we mean any type of intensity variation in a local region, including greylevel profiles around features such as corners and edges.

Let us define the transformed pixel difference as $\epsilon(\vec{a}, p) = I_0(p) - I_1(p')$, where $I_0(p)$ and $I_1(p')$ are the grey-level intensities at pixel location p and p' in the reference I_0 and consecutive frame I_1 respectively. Displacements of pixels within the region, and consequently their positions p and p' are constrained by the mapping $T_{\vec{a}}$: $p' = T_{\vec{a}}(p)$ where $T_{\vec{a}}(p)$ is a geometric transformation with parameter vector $\vec{a}$. For each pixel p (except for uncovered or occluded regions) one can find a displacement vector $\vec{d_p} = (d_x, d_y)$ such that $p' = p + \vec{d_p}$. Displacement $\vec{d_p}$ is defined for translational, quasi-affine and affine models as follows:

$$\vec{d_p} = (a_1, a_2) \tag{1}$$

$$\vec{d_p} = (a_1 x - a_2 y + a_3, a_2 x + a_1 y + a_4) \tag{2}$$

$$\vec{d_p} = (a_1 x + a_2 y + a_3, a_4 x + a_5 y + a_6) \tag{3}$$

In the cases of the four parameter transformation model (eq. 2) and the affine transformation model (eq. 3) displacement is a function of the position of pixel in the image.

In the Robust Hough Transform the support h from any pixel p for a parameter vector $\vec{a}$ is defined by a kernel function $\rho(\cdot)$:

$$h(\vec{a}, p) = \rho(\epsilon(\vec{a}, p)) \quad (4)$$

$$H(\Re, \vec{a}) = \sum_{p \in \Re} \rho(\epsilon(p, \vec{a})) \quad (5)$$

Eq. (5) expresses the total amount of support $H(\Re, \vec{a})$ received by the transformation parameter vector $\vec{a}$ from the region $\Re$. The estimate of the block transformation(s) is recovered from the position of the maximum of function H defined in the multidimensional transformation parameter space. Since it is convenient to define the problem as minimisation, we redefine the support function (for example by multiplying by factor -1) so that strong support corresponds to small values of H.

The Hough Space may have up to six dimensions (for the affine transformation model) and therefore the exhaustive search for a minimum has to be ruled out as being too computationally costly. However the support function (Hough space) H is well-behaved in the vicinity of the minimum and, consequently, one of the gradient based methods may be applied. We use the steepest descent search on a multiresolution discrete grid (in Hough space)[3,4].

A well–behaved confidence measure should reflect the quality of the local transformation estimate. Firstly, it should reject grossly erroneous estimates which could strongly bias the final estimate. Secondly, if we assume that the random errors have unimodal distribution, the confidence measure should reflect the spread of such distribution. Finally, we would like to have a warning about the transformation model failure. To achieve the above objectives, the final confidence measure is based on several factors.

The first confidence factor C_t reflects how much grey-level texture the region exhibits. It is computed before the estimation process, based on a region of interest in the reference frame. This confidence factor is based on the assumption that the accuracy of the estimate depends on how sharp and high the peak of the support function is. In practice, for n-dimensional transformation model, the confidence measure C_x is an $n \times n$ dimensional matrix with the elements c_{ij} defined as: $c_{ij} = \frac{\partial H}{\partial a_i} \frac{\partial H}{\partial a_j}$. C_t is the smaller eigenvalue of the matrix C_x. The second confidence factor C_e is used to reject gross errors. The total support for the region of interest H_{ROI}^{min} is compared to the average support for all regions in the image $\hat{H}^{min}$. Note, that for a region with no texture, there would be a high level of support (low minimum values of H) for all transformation parameters.

Finally, we examine the proportion of outliers in the region, to detect cases where the region overlaps the transformation boundary (there could be some moving objects in the scene) or depth discontinuity. Information about outliers is provided by the RHT module.

We have selected the four parameter transformation model, with the Tukey biweight kernel [4]. It seems that the four parameters transformation model offers a good trade-off between complexity and performance. We noticed that using more complex transformation models (affine) does not improve the accuracy of the final estimate and makes it more susceptible to noise. This is hardly surprising – we give the algorithm two extra degrees of freedom, that are not really needed, given the size of the region of support used.

Two resolutions in the image space and four resolutions in the Hough space are used. For the experimentation, rectangular regions of 15×15 pixels in size were used as region of support.

3 Recovery of 3D Structure

Once pairs of corresponding points are determined we can adopt standard techniques to recover the 3D structure of the imaged scene. Exploiting the epipolar geometry constraint a pair of corresponding points in two consecutive frames $\mathbf{q}$ and $\mathbf{q}'$, expressed in the homogeneous coordinate system, must satisfy $\mathbf{q}'^{\mathbf{T}} F \mathbf{q} = 0$, where F is the 3 x 3 fundamental matrix. By taking a number of corresponding pairs we can solve for F by minimizing $\sum_i \mathbf{q}_\mathbf{i}'^{\mathbf{T}} F \mathbf{q}_\mathbf{i}$. We have shown [5] that for our technique the accuracy of the corresponding pairs is such that a simple linear algorithm gives a satisfactory solution for the fundamental matrix, without the need to resort to any normalisation of the input data or to nonlinear techniques.

Using the intrinsic parameters of the camera we were able to compute the essential matrix. By decomposing the essential matrix the camera rotation matrix $\mathbf{R}$ and translation vector $\mathbf{t}$ were determined. The depth map was then computed [7].

4 Experiments

The proposed algorithm (RHT) has been tested on a set of 11 images of a static scene with accurate information about object locations in 3D. The calibration parameters were also available and could serve as the ground truth. These images are available to the vision community via ftp[a] and were taken with a scientific camera in an indoor setting, at the Calibrated Imaging Laboratory at CMU. All calibrated images were taken by moving the camera from place to

[a] ftp.cs.cmu.edu

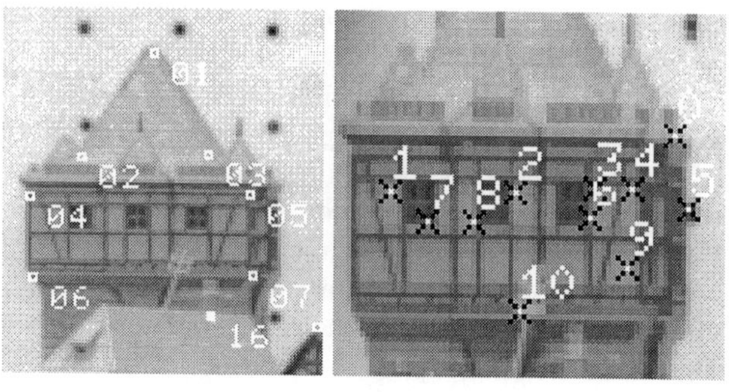

(a) Ground Truth (b) Features given by REF

Figure 1: The CMU house sequence

place using an automated jig platform. Object position and lighting remained constant during the camera motion, and there was no (significant) camera rotation.

Comparison of our results with the results obtained by a *typical* feature-based approach (REF) is also presented. We use the implementation of the Zhang technique [8], which uses correlation and relaxation to obtain matches. The binaries can be obtained from the INRIA ftp server[b]. The selection of this technique as a benchmark was based on the fact that it represents a classical approach to the low-level feature extraction. It should be noted that, at this stage, we have only used the feature extraction/matching front end of the complete system.

4.1 3D reconstruction accuracy on house image

In the first experiment two images from the *House* sequence (figure 2.a) were used. The RHT technique was used to obtain correspondences for 10 points for which the ground truth image coordinates on both images as well as their position in the world coordinate system (in mm) is known. In table 1 it shown that very accurate reconstruction (7.5 mm average depth variation at a distance of about 1.5 meters away from the object) can be obtained from just 2 images resulting from simply translating the camera by 20mm. For the purpose of comparison we used the REF technique to reconstruct features obtained in a region enclosed by the ground truth points 4, 5, 6 and 7 (figure 1a). The 11 features obtained by REF were then reconstructed and the results are shown

[b] `ftp://krakatoa.inria.fr/pub/`

Table 1: Reconstruction of 10 points for which the ground truth (GT) is known for the House sequence using the RHT technique.

Left (pixels)		Method	Right (pixels)		World (mm)		
x	y		x	y	x	y	z
46.50	92.62	GT	71.31	92.67	385.2	432.0	320.5
		RHT	71.61	92.89	387.5	433.2	295.6
63.73	123.39	GT	88.55	123.31	399.9	457.7	304.1
		RHT	88.70	123.49	400.9	458.2	291.5
76.66	135.52	GT	101.53	135.39	411.1	468.0	290.9
		RHT	101.46	135.35	410.7	467.8	296.5
77.40	159.15	GT	102.25	158.97	411.4	487.2	290.4
		RHT	102.05	158.94	410.1	486.9	307.0
131.69	233.27	GT	159.57	232.90	468.9	545.0	42.6
		RHT	159.55	232.94	468.9	545.0	43.3
60.44	171.68	GT	87.31	171.47	410.3	499.1	144.2
		RHT	87.34	171.45	410.6	499.1	141.4
91.63	174.64	GT	119.44	174.40	439.4	502.3	63.3
		RHT	119.39	174.52	439.2	502.3	66.3
222.61	158.32	GT	247.18	158.04	529.9	488.0	267.1
		RHT	247.12	158.03	529.8	487.9	272.0
255.89	141.30	GT	280.37	141.00	557.1	474.3	274.8
		RHT	280.40	140.98	557.1	474.3	272.3
272.49	96.75	GT	296.58	96.44	570.9	436.7	312.9
		RHT	296.54	96.47	570.9	436.6	316.0
235.25	72.65	GT	259.22	72.40	540.1	415.9	325.6
		RHT	259.17	72.39	540.0	415.7	329.8

in table 2. From the ground truth information available it is expected that the depths obtained should be between 290 mm and 295 mm (in the world coordinate system). However, great variations in the depth (more than 100 mm) were obtained by the feature based approach. It should be noted that errors of 0.1 pixel in the correspondences obtained can result in significant errors in the reconstructed points (see table 2).

Using frames 1 and 2 of the house image we also obtained a reconstruction of frame 9 (the original image is shown in figure 2.a and the reconstructed image in figure 2.b). Figure 2.c illustrates the grey–level difference between the original and the reconstructed image. The RHT confidence levels are shown in figure 2.d where dark regions are regions of low confidence for the corresponding pairs obtained. The computed dense depth map is shown in figure 2.e where

Table 2: Reconstruction of 10 points for the House sequence using the feature based technique. From the ground truth data it is expected that all z coordinates of the reconstructed points should lie between 290 and 295 mm

Left (pixels)		Right (pixels)		World (mm)		
x	y	x	y	x	y	z
84.98	132.67	108.71	132.83	410.6	463.3	385.4
15.88	141.06	41.96	141.07	368.7	473.7	235.2
46.81	141.17	71.69	141.34	385.7	472.2	308.7
66.06	140.89	90.94	140.91	402.1	472.3	296.1
74.33	140.57	99.21	140.55	409.2	472.1	291.1
88.17	143.40	112.03	142.78	414.2	472.8	369.4
64.64	145.16	89.67	144.93	402.0	475.9	284.0
25.49	146.05	51.39	145.54	375.4	477.3	240.3
36.92	145.79	62.67	145.81	383.8	477.3	244.8
74.16	152.63	99.01	152.55	408.7	481.9	292.7
47.89	159.05	74.86	159.30	401.1	489.6	145.3

the darker the grey level, the closer the scene to the camera. Note that some geometrical features are distorted, e.g. the tip of the steeple. Such distortion arises due to an inherent motion ambiguity in regions with a uniform greylevel background. Fortunately, for such regions the error in the depth map will not cause any errors in the motion compensated prediction of the next frame as can be seen from figure 2.b.

Finally, figure 2.f shows the features that would be used by a typical feature based technique to obtain the depth map. Its sparsity would render it useless for motion based frame compensation.

5 Conclusions

The problem of scene structure recovery from image motion was considered in the context of motion compensated video coding. In order to compensate for full 3D motion of the camera, the scene depth map together with camera egomotion need to be estimated from the image sequence. An important prerequisite of the shape and motion recovery is the establishment of correspondences between the points in two successive frames of a video sequence. In the paper we abandoned the traditional feature based approach and developed a correspondence analysis technique based on robust matching of local image intensities under affine transformation. We showed that the technique not only establishes true correspondences, but the resulting field of corresponding

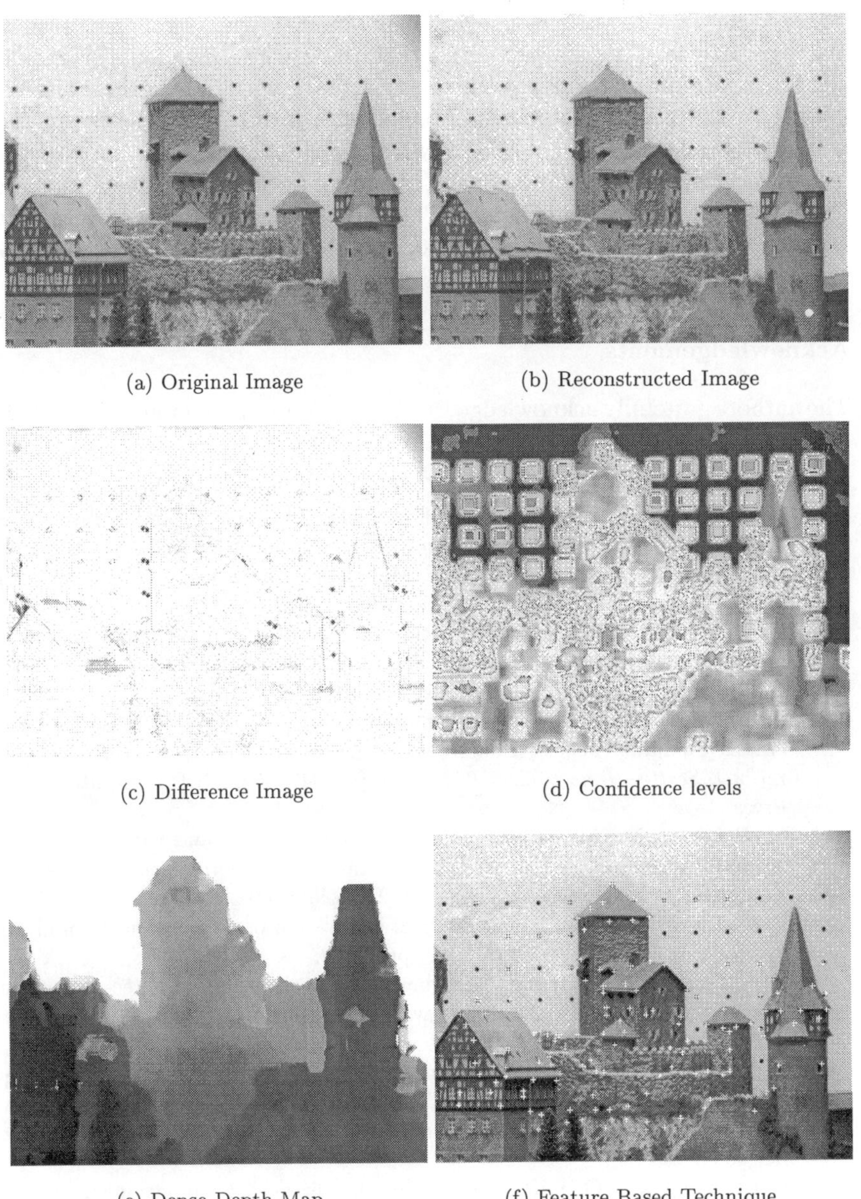

(a) Original Image

(b) Reconstructed Image

(c) Difference Image

(d) Confidence levels

(e) Dense Depth Map

(f) Feature Based Technique

Figure 2: Reconstruction of image frame 9 from frames 1 and 2 using RHT

points is dense, and their displacement is obtained with a subpixel accuracy and free of bias. We demonstrated that these dense high quality matches yield accurate estimates of the imaging geometry which are several orders of magnitude better than estimates obtained with feature based methods. This accuracy is reflected in a superior quality of estimates of the scene structure. The experiments were performed with images of a scene with known geometry, obtained using a calibrated camera. The obtained depth estimates were dense, with error of the order of 1% which contrasts with the sparse depth map and greater than 10% errors offered by a typical feature based approach.

Acknowledgements

The authors gratefully acknowledge EPSRC for support under grant GR/J52563 and Esprit for support under Project "RETINA".

1. R. Y. Tsai, "A versatile Camera Calibration technique for high-accuracy 3D machine vision metrology using off-the-shelf TV cameras and lenses", *IEEE Journal of Robotics and Automation*, vol RA-3, no. 4, pp 323-344, Aug 1987.
2. O.D. Faugeras, Q. T. Luong, and S. Maybank, "Camera self-calibration : Theory and experiment", in *2nd ECCV*, Genoa, 1992.
3. M. Bober and J. Kittler, "Estimation of general multimodal motion: an approach based on robust statistics and Hough transform", *Image and Vision Computing*, vol. 12, no. 12, pp. 661–668, 1994.
4. M. Bober and J. Kittler, "Robust motion analysis", in *Proceedings, CVPR '94 (IEEE Computer Society Conference on Computer Vision and Pattern Recognition), Seattle, June 20-24, 1994.* 1994, pp. 947–952, IEEE Computer Society Press.
5. M. Bober an N. Georgis and J. Kittler, "On accurate and robust estimation of fundamental matrix", in *British Machine Vision Conference*, R Fisher, Ed., Edinburgh, UK, September 1996, vol. 2, pp. 595–604, BMVA Press.
6. Q.-T. Luong and O.D. Faugeras, "Self-calibration of a camera using multiples images", in *Proc. 11th ICPR*, 1992, pp. 9–12.
7. R.Y. Tsai and T.S. Huang, "Uniqueness and estimation of three-dimensional motion parameters of rigid objects with curved surfaces", *IEEE Trans. Pattern Analysis and Machine Intelligence*, vol. 6, pp. 13–27, 1984.
8. Z. Zhang, R. Deriche, O. Faugeras, and Q.-T. Luong, "A robust technique for matching two uncalibrated images through the recovery of the unknown epipolar geometry", *Artificial Intelligence Journal*, vol. 78, pp. 87–119, October 1995.
9. Q.T. Luong and O.D. Faugeras, "On the direct determination of epipoles: A case study in algebraic methods for geometric problems", in *International Conference on Pattern Recognition, ICPR-A*, 1993, pp. 243–247.

MULTI-SCALE SKELETONS VIA PERMANENCE RANKING

GUNILLA BORGEFORS
Centre for Image Analysis, Swedish University of Agricultural Sciences
Uppsala, Sweden, E-mail: gunilla@cb.uu.se

GIULIANA RAMELLA, GABRIELLA SANNITI DI BAJA
Istituto di Cibernetica, Italian National Research Council
Arco Felice, Naples, Italy, Email: [gr, gsdb]@imagm.na.cnr.it

Multiresolution shape representations are highly desirable, as they provide a flexible tool that fits the user's needs better than single resolution systems. In this paper, the skeletons of a 2D pattern recorded onto a binary AND-pyramid are extracted at all resolution levels. The so obtained skeletons are then transformed into multiresolution skeletons by ranking skeleton subsets, based on their permanence in the skeleton at the various scales. The potential of multiresolution representation is exploited in this way, since the skeleton is available at various scales and, at each scale, skeleton components are furthermore ranked according to their permanence along the pyramid levels.

1 Introduction

Multiresolution representations[1-3] of discrete patterns in 2D binary images are often convenient for pattern recognition applications, as they reduce the complexity of the matching phase. Typically, the pattern to be recognised is represented by a graph, as are all the different, available prototypes. The number of graph nodes depends on the pattern resolution. Some special features of the pattern at hand are preserved at different resolution levels, at least within a given range, while other features only appear at higher resolution levels. Graph comparison can first be performed using all prototypes but only at lower resolution levels, where a smaller number of nodes are involved, to sort out the most promising matchings. Detailed comparison can then be performed with a reduced number of prototypes at higher resolution levels, where a larger number of nodes have to be taken into account.

Multiresolution representations can be obtained by first converting the pattern to some representation, recognised as a more flexible tool for shape analysis, and then identifying and ranking the components of the adopted representation, to transform it into a multiresolution structure. For example, the skeleton of the pattern could be adopted as a convenient representation scheme and skeleton subsets could then be suitably ranked to create a multiresolution skeleton[4]. Alternatively, the binary image can be recorded on a resolution pyramid, which transforms a single-scale data set into a multi-scale data set, and then a multi-scale representation can be obtained by extracting the selected representation scheme at all pyramid levels. If the adopted representation is again the skeleton, this process would lead to a number of differently structured skeletons[5], each of which represents the pattern at a different scale.

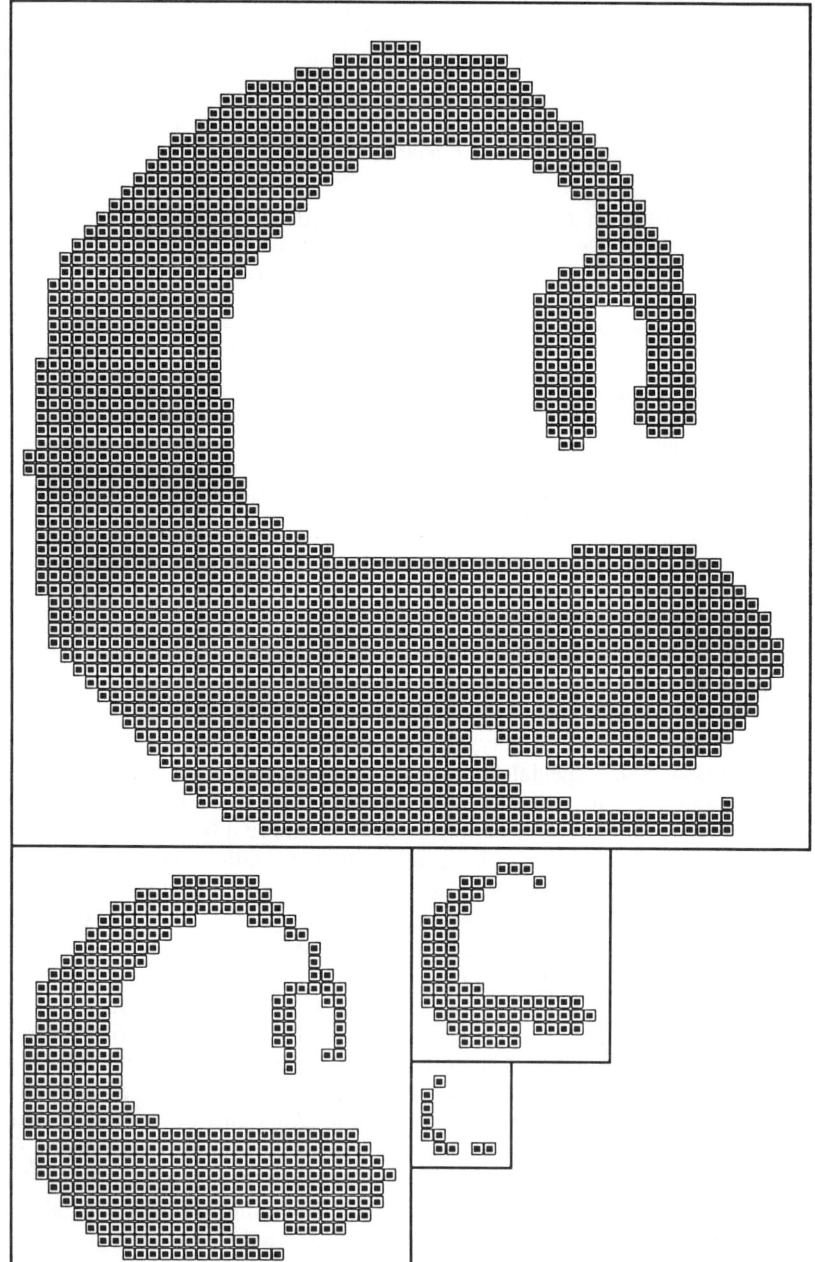

Figure 1. The four significant levels of the AND-pyramid of a test $2^6 \times 2^6$ image.

The 2×2 AND-pyramid is the most straightforward example of a multi-scale binary image. The highest, original, resolution level in the pyramid is a bitmap representation, where pixels are either black (pattern) or white (background). The next, lower, resolution level is built by partitioning the bitmap in 2×2 blocks of pixels, the *children*, and associating a single pixel, the *parent*, to each block. The colour of the new pixel (black or white) is determined by the logical AND operation. The process is repeated for the previously computed lower resolution representation, and then further iterated to build all the resolution levels regarded as significant in the problem domain. For an original image of size $2^n \times 2^n$, n+1 resolution levels are possible, the lowest resolution level consisting of a single pixel. Generally, the last levels are not meaningful for shape representation and will not be used in the following.

The skeleton is a stick-like representation of a 2D pattern which encodes topological and geometrical properties of the pattern, such as connectedness, symmetry, and elongation.

In this paper, we use both the approaches mentioned previously and create a multiresolution representation of a 2D pattern, at all resolution levels of a binary pyramid. The skeleton of the pattern is extracted at all levels of the pyramid, where the pattern is initially recorded. The so obtained skeletons are then transformed into multiresolution skeletons by identifying and ranking skeleton subsets, based on their permanence in the skeleton at the various scales. The resulting skeleton representation will thus show two different types of hierarchy which will both contribute to facilitate recognition. The first type of hierarchy is intrinsic from the fact that the pyramid includes various resolution levels, so that a number of skeletons at different scales are indeed available. This type of hierarchy allows one to initially match roughly using only skeletons at lower scales, where only the most significant parts of the pattern are represented. Only the prototypes for which matching at lower scales is successful will then be examined again at higher scales, to achieve an exact match. The second type of hierarchy is established at each level of the pyramid by identifying and ranking skeleton subsets according to their permanence in the skeleton when the scale changes. This hierarchy facilitates matching at any single resolution level. In fact, it allows for consideration initially only the most significant subsets of the single-scale skeleton, thus reducing the number of prototypes for which a more detailed comparison is necessary, that involves also less significant components of the single-scale skeleton.

2 Skeleton Extraction

Let B and W be the sets of black and white pixels of a binary picture P with size $2^n \times 2^n$. For simplicity, we suppose that the pattern B consists of a single 8-connected component. No assumption is made on the number of 4-connected components of W, but we assume that all pixels on the border of P are white.

The picture P is stored in the highest resolution level (also called the first level) of an AND-pyramid. The successive lower resolution level is built from the preceding level in the following way: every pixel of level k, k>1, is black or white,

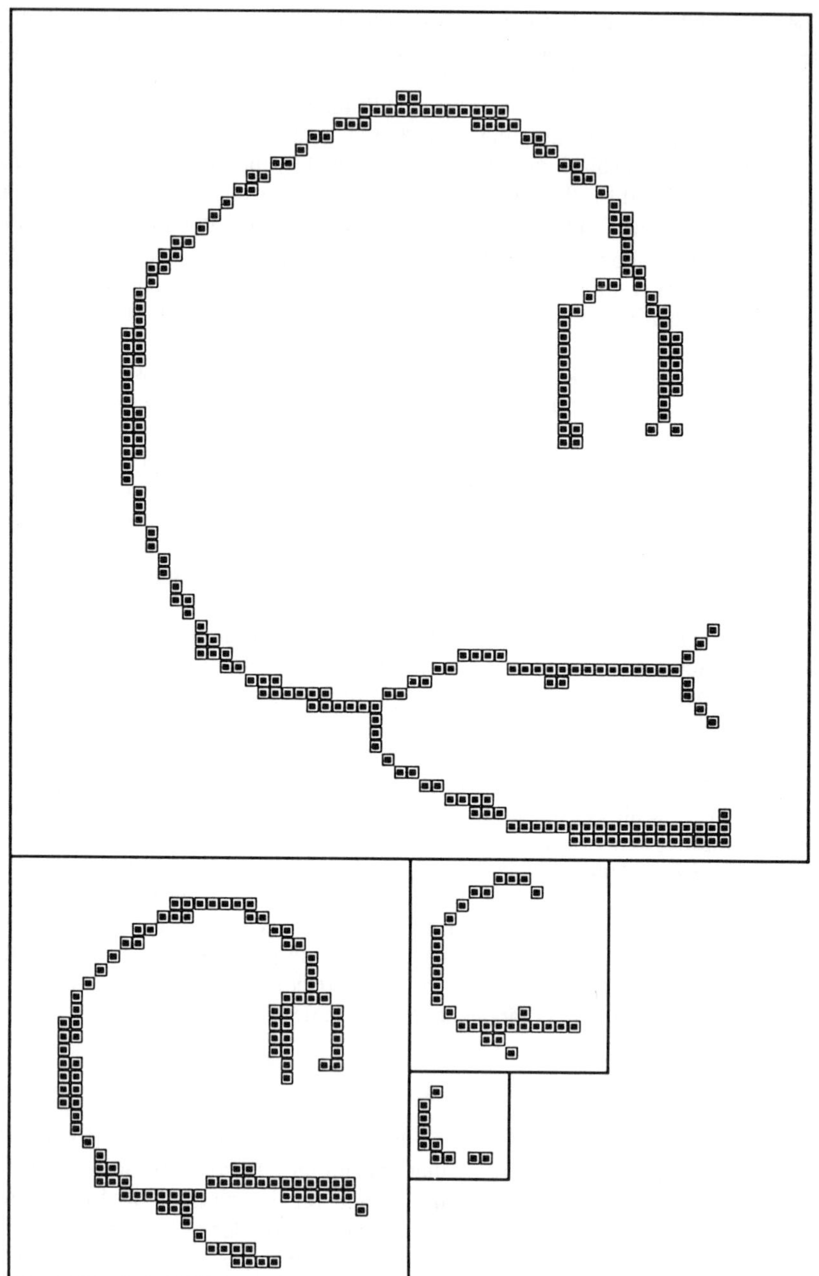

Figure 2. Sets of skeletal pixels found at all levels of the AND-pyramid.

depending on whether all its four children at level k-1 are black. Resolution levels sized 4×4, 2×2 and 1×1 pixel are not meaningful for shape description or skeletonization purposes. Therefore, we will consider the 8×8 pixel image as the last pyramid level, giving n-2 levels in the pyramid. As an example, see Figure 1 where the n-2 significant levels of the AND-pyramid of a test pattern are shown. The first level of the pyramid has size $2^6 \times 2^6$. We note that when the resolution decreases the pattern becomes narrower and narrower so that some of the initial regions either completely vanish or become disconnected[6]. Thicker regions appear at all resolution levels and constitute the most significant pattern components.

Skeletonization is accomplished simultaneously at all resolution levels in two phases. The first phase uses an iterative process that, at each iteration, identifies and removes (i.e., changes to white) in a parallel fashion all the pixels on the pattern contour that are not skeletal pixels. At each iteration black pixels having at least a horizontal/vertical white neighbour constitute the current contour, all the other black pixels are internal pixels; a contour pixel p is a skeletal pixel if at least one of the following conditions holds:

1. No pair of horizontally or vertically aligned neighbours of p exists, such that one neighbour is white and the other is a black internal pixel;
2. A 2×2 block of pixels, including p, exists, such that the diagonal neighbour of p is a contour pixel and the other two neighbours are white.

The first phase of skeletonization terminates when all black pixels are skeletal pixels. The number of iterations depends on the maximal pattern thickness at the highest resolution level. The resulting sets of skeletal pixels are at most two-pixel wide. The sets of skeletal pixels found at all levels of the AND-pyramid of the test pattern are shown in Figure 2.

The second phase of the process, also referred to as final thinning, reduces the sets of skeletal pixels to unit wide skeletons. Skeletal pixels are sequentially inspected at all resolution levels. Pixels whose 3×3 neighbourhood matches any of the configurations shown in Figure 3, where letters "b" and "w" denote black and white pixels and dots denote don't care pixels, are changed to white. One inspection of all pyramid levels is generally sufficient to obtain the desired results.

w	·	·
·	b	b
·	b	·

·	·	w
b	b	·
·	b	·

·	b	·
b	b	·
·	·	w

·	b	·
·	b	b
w	·	·

Figure 3. Removal operations used during final thinning. Letters "b" and "w" denote black and white pixels, respectively. Dots are don't care pixels.

3 Skeleton Hierarchy

The main idea behind building the skeleton hierarchy is the observation that skeleton components present at lower resolution levels are definitely also present at higher levels.

The connected components of the skeleton are identified at the lowest resolution level (8×8 level). (Any connected component labelling algorithm could be adopted for this purpose[7].) Each component is expected to be the *parent* of a *child* component at the next level (16×16), *grandparent* of a *grandchild* at level 32×32, and so on, until the highest resolution level is reached and all the descendants have been found. Skeletal pixels at level 16×16, that do not belong to any already identified child component, are in turn grouped into connected components. These components are labelled by the connected component labelling process and are then interpreted as parent components originating at level 16×16. Their children and grandchildren can be found in the higher levels. Similarly, new parent components and their descendants can be found at all levels.

Using the parent-child relationships among components at different scales, skeleton components at each single pyramid level could be assigned a *permanence number*, by counting the number of levels we should pass through to find the most remote corresponding ancestor component. All skeleton components found at (the lowest resolution) level 8×8 directly originate at that level and should accordingly be assigned permanence 1; components at level 16×16 should be ascribed permanence 2 or 1 depending on whether they are generated from components at level 8×8 or originate directly at level 16×16; generally, components at level $2^n \times 2^n$ should be assigned permanence n-2, n-1,..., 2, 1, depending on whether their most remote ancestor component are found at level $2^3 \times 2^3$, $2^4 \times 2^4$,..., $2^{n-1} \times 2^{n-1}$, or they originate directly at level $2^n \times 2^n$.

At any individual pyramid level, components with the same permanence number can be distinguished from each other if the label assigned to their parent component by the connected component labelling process is also transmitted from parents to children. Permanence number and connected component label can be suitably combined into a unique label. In our case, the label ascribed to any skeletal pixel p is obtained by multiplying the relevant permanence number by 100 and by adding the number assigned to the connected component including p. Of course this labelling is possible only provided that less than 100 skeleton components exist on every single pyramid level.

In general, skeletal pixels in a child component, are expected to be children of some skeletal pixel in the corresponding parent component. Thus, they could be identified (and assigned the relative combined label) by means of a *projection* process from lower resolution levels onto higher resolution levels: every skeletal pixel p in a (parent) skeleton component projects over a 2×2 set of children at the immediately higher resolution level, and assigns the skeletal pixels present therein to the corresponding child skeleton component. Any child component should have the same connected component label as its parent component, while its permanence number should be equal to the permanence number of the parent component plus one. Thus, the combined label of any child component will be equal to the combined label of its parent component plus 100.

The projection process can be followed with reference to the example shown in Figure 4. The pixels in the parent skeleton component are shown as grey pixels (Figure 4a) and their 2×2 sets of children are enclosed by thick frames (Figure 4b);

among the children, only the (grey) skeletal pixels are interpreted as belonging to the child component.

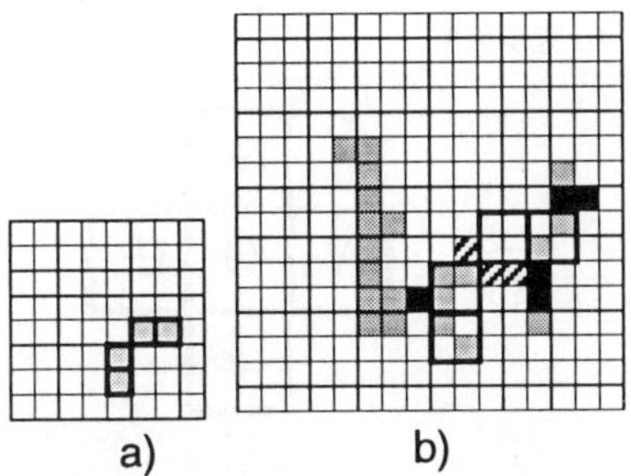

Figure 4. Pixels (grey squares) in a parent skeleton component, a), and their corresponding skeletal children (grey squares in the 2×2 sets enclosed by thick frames), b). Dashed squares and black square respectively denote pixels identified by the expansion process and the propagation process.

Unfortunately, due to the discrete scheme used to build the binary pyramid and to the process for extracting the unit wide skeleton from the two-pixel wide set of skeletal pixels, a child component might be slightly shifted compared to its expected position. To limit the bias in the position of a child component that can be introduced by the final thinning, we apply the projection process to the two-pixel wide set of the skeletal pixels and postpone the reduction to unit width till after the establishment of the parent-child correspondences. This notwithstanding, the children of the pixels in a parent skeleton component could all be white, so that the parent-child correspondence would not be established, or a child component might appear as non connected. See Figure 4b.

To cope with the more intrinsic shifting caused by the discrete scheme used to build the pyramid, one should interpret as belonging to the current child component not only the pixels defined by the projection process, but also a suitable number of neighbouring skeletal pixels. To identify these extra pixels, we use two processes, respectively termed *expansion* and *propagation*.

Let Q be the 2×2 *quadruplet* of children of a given skeletal pixel q, and N_Q, S_Q, W_Q, E_Q be the four neighbouring 2×2 quadruplets. See Figure 5. During the projection process, an expansion onto N_Q, S_Q, W_Q and E_Q is performed whenever Q is empty, i.e. includes only white pixels. The expansion process interprets as belonging to the current child component the skeletal pixels of the neighbouring quadruplets, provided that these pixels have not already been marked as belonging to other child components.

The pixels identified by the expansion process are shown as dashed squares in Figure 4.

The propagation process is accomplished after all pixels of the parent components have been projected (and possibly expanded) on the next higher resolution level. For every pixel p in a child component, the propagation ascribes to the same component also the neighbours of p, provided that they belong to the skeleton and have not yet been labelled. The pixels identified by the propagation are shown as black squares in Figure 4.

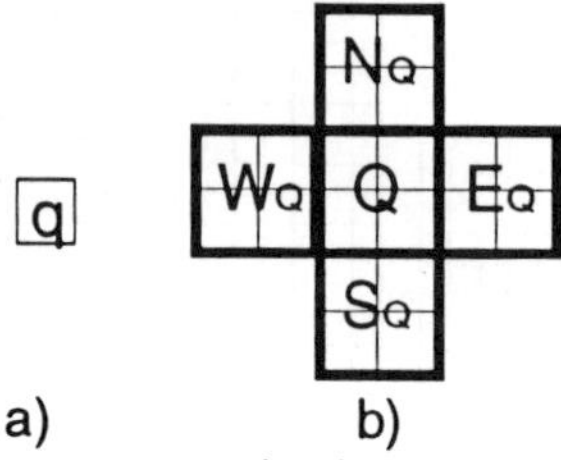

Figure 5. A skeletal pixel q at level $2^k \times 2^k$,a); the quadruplet Q corresponding to q and the neighbouring quadruplets at level $2^{k+1} \times 2^{k+1}$, b).

Pixels assigned to a component by the propagation process are distinguished (and differently treated) from those assigned by the projection and expansion processes, to prevent an excessive spreading of child components over the skeleton during the successive projection onto higher resolution levels. In our case, distinction is done by assigning negative sign to the labels of the pixels due to propagation. (In Figure 6a, dashed and black squares respectively denote pixels ascribed to the same component by the projection and expansion processes and by the propagation process.)

Pixels ascribed to every component at level $2^k \times 2^k$ by the projection and expansion from $2^{k-1} \times 2^{k-1}$ (dashed squares in Figure 6a) are projected and expanded first on the next level $2^{k+1} \times 2^{k+1}$ (dashed squares in Figure 6b). Then, the remaining pixels in the component at level $2^k \times 2^k$ (black squares in Figure 6a) undergo the projection on level $2^{k+1} \times 2^{k+1}$. For these pixels a slightly different process is accomplished: let q be any of these pixels and Q the corresponding quadruplet on the next level. Among the pixels of Q belonging to the skeleton and not yet ascribed to any other component, only those having at least one neighbour already labelled as belonging to the current component are interpreted as belonging to the current child component. For the quadruplets corresponding to the black squares of Figure 6a, these pixels are the squares starred in Figure 6b. Note that not all skeletal pixels of the quadruplets are necessarily ascribed to the child component. Moreover, no expansion is accomplished when the quadruplets are empty. Finally, the propagation on the neighbouring pixels takes place at level $2^{k+1} \times 2^{k+1}$ (black squares in Figure 6b).

After all components at level $2^k \times 2^k$ have been projected (and expanded) onto level $2^{k+1} \times 2^{k+1}$, and for each projected child component propagation has also been accomplished, a final processing is done on level $2^{k+1} \times 2^{k+1}$ before the components directly originating at level $2^{k+1} \times 2^{k+1}$ are identified by connected component labelling. Pixels due to propagation (i.e., pixels with negative label) are examined.

The label of any such a pixel p is changed into positive if all skeletal pixels in the neighbourhood of p belong to the component including p (i.e., the label of p and that of its skeletal neighbours are equal in absolute value).

The effect of expansion and propagation for connectedness preservation is evident in Figure 6b. Without these processes, the child component originating from a connected parent component would not be connected.

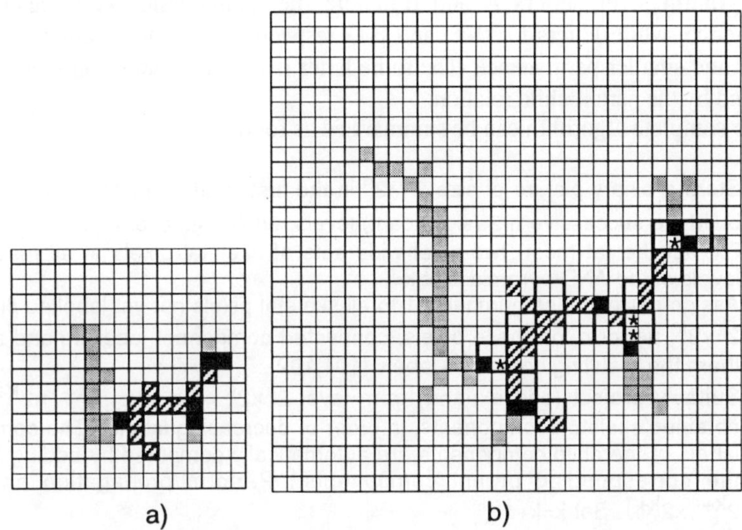

Figure 6. Dashed and black squares denote pixels identified by the projection and expansion processes and by the propagation process, respectively. In the child component, b), starred squares are pixels identified by suitably projecting the pixels denoted by black squares in the parent component.

Skeleton components at any pyramid level are processed in order of decreasing permanence number. Components with the highest permanence number are processed first to identify the corresponding child components. Components with smaller and smaller permanence number assign to their child components only the children that have not yet been included in other child components with larger permanence number. The criteria used to establish the parent-child correspondence favours skeleton components that are more stable, that is present at many pyramid levels.

After all skeleton components have been identified and labelled, final thinning is performed on all pyramid levels. Removal operations shown in Figure 3 are used, but an iterative thinning process is preferred, to favour preservation of pixels belonging to the more significant skeleton components. At each iteration, removal is active only on pixels having a given permanence number, starting from the lowest permanence number. The number of iterations required is equal to the maximum permanence in the hierarchy, i.e., is equal to the number (n-2) of pyramid levels. The increase in computation cost of this iterative final thinning is repaid by a higher significance and stability of the resulting skeleton hierarchy.

A post-processing is then performed to improve skeleton aesthetics by straightening zig-zags, that can be created during final thinning[8].

The resulting skeleton hierarchy for the test pattern can be seen in Figures 7. At each pyramid level, letters A and B denote the components with the highest permanence, while letters C, D-E, and F-G respectively denote components with smaller and smaller permanence. The same letter is used to denote components that are found by the parent-child relation.

The complete algorithm can be summarised as follows:

1. Store a binary picture of size $2^n \times 2^n$ in the first level of an AND-pyramid and build the successive n-2 (significant) levels, ending at level $2^3 \times 2^3$.
2. Extract the (at most) two-pixel wide sets of skeletal pixels at all resolution levels of the AND-pyramid. Set k=3
3. Assign permanence number = 1 to all skeletal pixels not yet labelled on level $2^k \times 2^k$; perform, on these pixels, connected component labelling and assign them the resulting combined labels (101,102,...).
4. Suitably project (and expand) from level $2^k \times 2^k$ onto level $2^{k+1} \times 2^{k+1}$ the obtained skeleton components, in order of decreasing labels. (The combined labels of the child components are automatically computed by adding 100 to the corresponding parent components.) Perform propagation on level $2^{k+1} \times 2^{k+1}$. Set k=k+1.
5. If k<n, go to 3.
6. Apply the iterated final thinning to all resolution levels, according to increasing permanence value.
7. Reduce the zig-zags possibly affecting the skeletons.
8. Display the skeleton hierarchy and stop.

4 Conclusion

A method to hierarchically rank components of the skeletons computed at all resolution levels of an AND-pyramid has been suggested. The skeleton representation obtained in this way includes two different types of hierarchy which could both contribute to facilitate object recognition. The first type of hierarchy is intrinsic in the fact that the pyramid includes different resolution levels. It allows one to match initially only the parts of the pattern having large size. The prototypes for which matching is favourable, are then compared with the pattern to be identified at the next higher resolution level. The second type of hierarchy facilitates matching at a given resolution level, since the components of the corresponding skeleton can be ranked according to some relevance criteria (their permanence in the skeleton along the resolution levels, in our case).

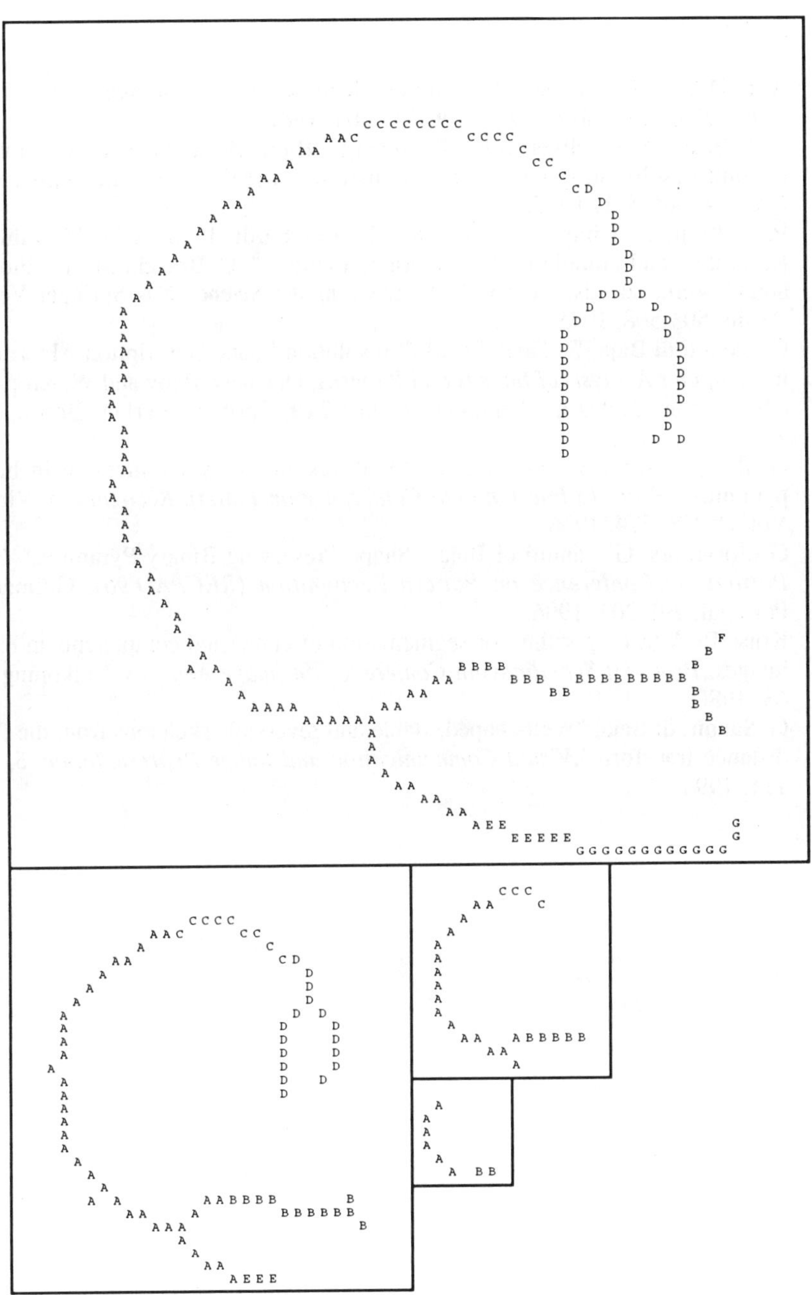

Figure 7. Skeleton hierarchy.

5 References

1 A.R. Dill, M.D. Levine, P.B. Noble, "Multiple resolution skeletons," *IEEE Trans. Patt. Anal. Mach. Intell.* **9**, 495-504, 1987.

2 S.M. Pizer, W.R. Oliver, S.H. Bloomberg, "Hierarchical shape description via the multiresolution symmetric axis transform," *IEEE Trans. Patt. Anal. Mach. Intell.* **9**, 505-511, 1987.

3 P. Bottoni, L. Cinque, S. Levialdi, L. Lombardi, P. Mussio, "Combining Resolution and granularity for pattern recognition", C. Braccini, L. De Floriani and G. Vernazza eds., Lecture Notes in Computer Science **974**, Springer-Verlag, Berlin, 503-508, 1995.

4 G. Sanniti di Baja, E. Thiel, "A Multiresolution Shape Description Algorithm," in *Computer Analysis of Images and Patterns,* D. Chetverikov and W. Kropatsch eds., Lecture Notes in Computer Science **719**, Springer-Verlag, Berlin, 208-215, 1993.

5 G. Borgefors, G. Sanniti di Baja, "Multiresolution skeletonization in binary pyramids", *Proc. 13 International Conference on Pattern Recognition,* Vienna, Vol. D, 570-574, 1996

6 G. Borgefors, G. Sanniti di Baja, "Shape Preserving Binary Pyramids," *Proc. Portoguese Conference on Pattern Recognition (RECPAD'96),* Guimarães, Portugal, 197-203, 1996.

7 Kruse B, A fast algorithm for segmentation of connected components in binary images, *Proc. 1st Scandinavian Conference on Image Analysis,* Linköping, 57-63, 1980.

8 G. Sanniti di Baja, "Well-shaped, stable and reversible skeletons from the (3,4)-distance transform",*Visual Communication and Image Representation,* **5**, 107-115, 1994.

CHARACTERISING SHAPE AND SHAPE TRANSFORMATION BY REWRITING SYSTEMS

P.BOTTONI, L.CINQUE, S.LEVIALDI, B.NEBBIA
Dipartimento di Scienze dell'Informazione, Università di Roma,
Via Salaria 113, 00198 Roma, Italy
E-mail: {bottoni,cinque,levialdi}@dsi.uniroma1.it
http://www.dsi.uniroma1.it/{bottoni,cinque,levialdi}.html

P.MUSSIO
Dipartimento di Elettronica per l'Automazione, Università di Brescia,
Via Branze 38, 25123 Brescia, Italy
E-mail: mussio@bsing.ing.unibs.it

This paper presents a methodology to specify the action of image processing operators in terms of the transformations induced on structures in an image. Transformations are specified via conditional attributed rewriting rules operating on attributed strings describing the shape of the structures. The methodology is based on an analysis of the characteristics of an operator with respect to the adopted segmentation technique and is illustrated through an example of Gaussian filter characterisation. Applications are foreseen in automatic generation of image processing and interpretation strategies, considering the operator's capability of preserving shape.

1 Introduction

A problem in defining automatic systems for image processing (IP) and interpretation is that of characterising IP operators (IPO), so that it becomes possible to establish which operators are more suitable in a given process. IPO characterisation is usually based on properties of transformations induced on images, typically relative to numerical features of the image signal, e.g. noise or texture [1]. A different perspective is here taken: generalising the approach in [2], IPO are characterised by specifying the transformations they induce on structures in images, defined in terms of their shape. Structures are described as strings of attributed symbols identifying pixels in which the contour changes its direction [3]; shapes are characterised by grouping these attributed symbols into shape descriptions [4]. In this line transformations operated on an image by IPO are characterised by defining the transformations of the descriptions of the structures present in the input and output images. The diagram of Fig.1 summarises this view.

Given an image I, an operator Tr maps I into I'. The analysis algorithm *anl* [3] derives a description D of image I and a description D' of the image I'. The problem is to identify the description transformation *?* such that the diagram commutes (i.e. identical results are obtained by combining Tr and *anl* or *anl* and *?*). In this way, we can characterise the operator Tr.

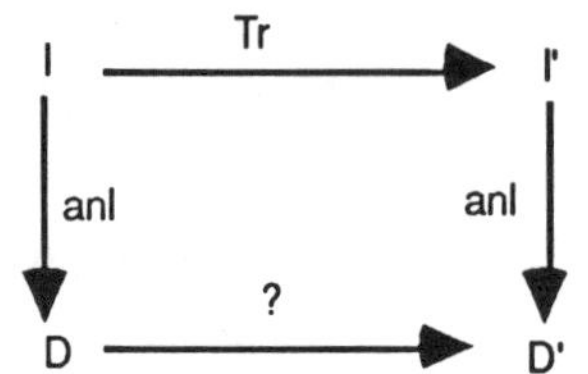

Fig.1 The diagram of image / description transformations

In this paper we show that the transformation of the descriptions - i.e. strings of attributed symbols - can be characterised by means of CAILs (*Conditional Attributed L-System with Interaction*) [4] and we present an analytical methodology to extract CAIL rules defining the transformations from the numerical specification of the given operators. To illustrate the feasibility of the methodology, we discuss an experiment to study the action of the Gaussian filter [5] on symmetrical geometrical structures. A long tradition of computational and empirical studies has led to qualitative and quantitative definitions of the action of specific IPO. For instance, characteristics of edge detectors have been studied in relation to the kinds of borders they can extract [6]; smoothing algorithms have been studied in relation to their effect on edges [7]; the action of non-linear filters has been characterised in qualitative terms [8], but formal notions also exist, such as that of root signal, which defines the class of signals which remain invariant after a number of iterations of filter application [9]. Several parameters are usually employed to perform such characterisations. Here we describe the action of IPO on the structural features of the contour of an object present in an image. A preliminary work in this sense is contained in [10]. Rewriting systems have been applied to define the action of IPO on pixels, in terms of particular types of finite state automata [11] of cellular automata [12], or of L-systems [13,14,15] also with reference to mathematical morphology operations [16]. The novelty of our approach lies in the use of rewriting systems to describe the action of IPO in terms of structural transformations. To this end, we also introduce some notations for the description of symmetrical structures, used for the experimental part. The outline of the paper is as follows. The method for structure description is introduced in Section 2. In Section 3 the method for characterisation of shape transformations is illustrated via a specific example, and Section 4 draws conclusions.

2. Describing shape

A structural description of an image enumerates the structures recognised in it. Each structure is described by a name, identifying its type and denoted by a *symbol*, and a vector of *properties*, the values assumed by a set of variables, called *attributes*. Structures of different types can be characterised by different sets of attributes. Structures can be decomposed into simpler ones. A family exists of elementary structures, called *primitive* structures, which are not further decomposable.

Following [3], we adopt as primitive structures those pixels in which the contour changes its direction locally. Such pixels are called *multiple elements* and are associated with the symbol *ME*, with attributes: *code*, summarising the pixel's 8-neighbourhood, ordered as in Fig.2, and *coordinates*; *code* is computed by the formula: (1), where u_i is *1* if the pixel p_i is white, *0* if it is black.

p_1	p_2	p_3
p_0	**p**	p_4
p_7	p_6	p_5

Fig.2 The ordering of 8 neighbourhoods.

$$c(p) = \sum_{i=0}^{7} u_i \cdot 2^i \qquad (1)$$

In [3] it is shown that such a description is sufficient to reconstruct the original image and an algorithm is described which obtains such a description from a black and white image. For example, when describing the structure of Fig.3, textured pixels marked with A, B and C are the multiple elements, black pixels represent the inside of the triangle. A is associated with the code *31*, B with the code *6* and C with code *12* and the triangle *Tr* is described by the string of three attributed symbols: $Tr{:}\langle\langle ME,6,4,1\rangle \circ \langle ME,31,1,4\rangle \circ \langle Me,12,4,7\rangle\rangle$.

The set of types of structures of interest in real cases is finite, so that the set *V* of their names is assumed as an alphabet. Each single structure is described by an attributed symbol, formed by the symbol in *V* identifying its type and by the vector of its properties. The description of an image is thus formalised via strings of attributed symbols.

The description of a structure based on primitive structures is formalised by *Conditional Attributed L-System with Interaction* (CAIL) [4]. CAILs extend the grammars traditionally used in syntactic pattern recognition [17] in two main ways. First, they allow the use of one single alphabet, not partitioned in terminal and non-terminal ones. Hence, each symbol denotes a structure, rather than a possible derivation of it. Second, they allow the use of parallel direct generation. These two aspects are typical of Lindenmayer systems [18].

Def. 1 A CAIL is defined by a rewriting system $RW=(V,P,\Rightarrow)$ and a semantic domain $D=(\Omega, \Phi, \Gamma)$, where: *V* is a finite set of symbols called the alphabet. *P* is a finite set of productions of the form $\langle\langle \omega_1, \delta, \omega_2\rangle, \varepsilon\rangle$, meaning that for δ to be rewritten as ε, it must be embedded in the context represented by

$\omega_1, \omega_2 \in V^*$; $\delta \in V+$ is called the rewriting part of the antecedent, $\varepsilon \in V^*$ is called the consequent. $\Omega = \{D_1,\ldots,D_k\}$ is a finite set of domains. Φ is a set of functions. Γ is a set of predicates, also comprising the constant predicates *true* and *false*.

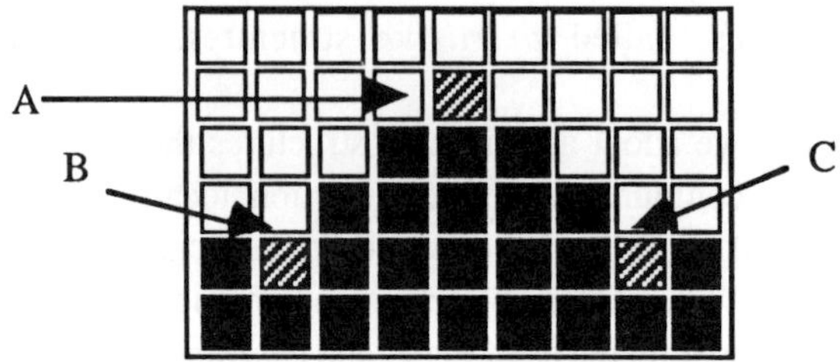

Fig.3. An upward triangle associated with the sequence of codes (6,31,12).

The rewriting system and the semantic domain are related as follows:

$\forall x \in V, \exists A(x)$, set of attributes, $\forall \alpha \in A(x), \exists D_i \in \Omega$, which specifies the possible values that the attribute α can assume when associated with the symbol x. $\forall p \in P, \exists \gamma \in \Gamma, \gamma: D_{i_1} \times \ldots \times D_{i_s} \rightarrow \{true, false\}$. γ is the *condition* to be satisfied for p to apply. $\forall p \in P, \exists r_p$, a finite set of semantic rules of the form $\varepsilon_j.\alpha_i = f_i(\omega_{1_1}.\alpha_{i_1},\ldots,\omega_{2_m}.\alpha_{i_n})$, where $f_i \in \Phi$. Semantic rules compute attributes of the consequent as a function of those of the antecedent.

The rewriting relation $\Rightarrow$ specifies that rules in P are applied in parallel to directly generate a string Z from a string W (in symbols $W \Rightarrow Z$). A rule is applied if an instance of its antecedent (left and right context and rewriting part) is found in W and the attributes of the instance satisfy the condition. Semantic rules in the set r_p are computed when a rule p is applied.

Here, attributed symbols describe multiple elements as well as geometrical structures, and rewriting rules provide a specification of a structure, as well as a specification of its transformation. The symbols describing adjacent structures appear consecutively in the description of a structure contour, considered as a cyclic string. A *side* is a segment connecting two adjacent multiple elements. The *length* of a side is $length(p_1,p_2) = (|x_1-x_2|, |y_1-y_2|)$ where x_i, y_i are the coordinates of the extremal points of the side.

A *symmetrical image* is an image such that an axis exists dividing the image into two isomorphic parts. A *symmetrical structure* (SS) is a structure such that the minimal subimage containing it (up to rotations) is symmetrical. A *run* is a sequence of adjacent black pixels, orthogonal to a symmetry axis. Here an axis is a line in the real plane and not in the digital space. The axis extends across the middle pixel if the run has odd length, between the two middle pixels if the run has even length. In the following examples, we consider types of SS -with either horizontal or vertical symmetry axis - protruding from the contour of components. For these types an intuitive geometrical notion exists, derived from classical geometry. We provide a formal definition of them in terms of strings of attributed symbols. In particular a type of structure is defined by a CAIL.

2.1 Description of isosceles triangle

An *i-triangle*, as the one shown in Fig.3, is the digital version of a rectangular isosceles i-triangle. Hence, there is a finite number of possible sequences of multiple elements which can delimit an i-triangle. The *base* of an i-triangle is the length of the run from the first to the third multiple element, including these two. The *height* of an i-triangle is the length of the run from the second multiple element to the nearest pixel in the base. An *i-triangle*, denoted by the symbol *tri*, is defined by the rule in Fig.4. The elements in *TRI* define the clockwise sequences of codes for the extremal points of an i-triangle. The associated semantic rule r_p allows the computation of the base and height of the i-triangle as follows.

r_p: $tri.base = |ME_1.x - ME_3.x| + 1$, $tri.height = |ME_2.y - ME_1.y| + 1$

<<,$ME_1 \circ ME_2 \circ ME_3$,> , *tri*>
γ: $(length(ME_1,ME_2) = length(ME_2,ME_3)$ && $((ME_1.code, ME_2.code, ME_3.code) \in TRI)$
where
$TRI=\{(6,31,12), (3,199,129), (192,241,96), (48,124,24), (12,31,6), (129,199,3), (96,241,192), (24,124,48)\}$

Fig.4 The rule for defining an i-triangle

These semantic rules are used for upwards and downwards triangles. The case for leftwards and rightwards triangles derives in the obvious way. Constraints exist on *base* and *height* of an i-triangle and on their relations. In particular, the lowest values for *height* and *base* are 2 and 3 respectively. Due to structure symmetry, for each pixel added to *height*, the *base* increases by two pixels. Hence, for an i-triangle with *base* = b and *height* = h, $b = b(h) = 2h-1$. Similarly, we can define *square* and *trapeze* as digital versions of a square and a trapeze, through suitable rewriting rules.

2.2 Description of symmetrical structures.

Structure symmetry is used to define a notation helping in the definition of structure transformation. Indeed, each SS is formed by a sequence of parallel runs. With each run a number is associated representing its length (number of pixels).

Hence a SS can be described by coding the sequence of lengths of its runs. The following theorems provide the rationale for this representation. Proofs are omitted for brevity.

Theorem: For each type *T* of SS there is a language *L(T)* of strings of natural numbers, coding the sequences of lengths, each string uniquely describing a structure of type *T* up to localisation.

The proof is based on the following lemma.

Lemma A SS is composed only of runs of the same parity.

As an example, the i-triangle of Fig.3 (odd parity), is described as $tri(4) = 1^\circ 3^\circ 5^\circ 7$, where *1* denotes the vertex of the i-triangle, considered as a run of length one; *3* and *5* are the lengths of the following runs and *7* is the length (number of pixels) of the base. The symbol '°' denotes concatenation. We call such a sequence a *length-sequence.*

Based on these definitions, the sequence associated with an i-triangle is inductively defined as follows: $tri(1)=1$, $tri(h)=tri(h-1)^\circ(b(h-1)+2)=tri(h-1)^\circ(2h-1)$. For squares we have: $sqr(l) = l^l$.

Another useful notation associates a SS with the sequence of variations in the length of the runs.

Theorem: For each type *T* of SS there is a language *L*(*T*) of strings of natural numbers, coding variations in length of the runs, each string uniquely describing a structure of type *T* up to position and length of the top run.

For example: $tri(4) = 1^\circ 3^\circ 5^\circ 7 \equiv 2;2;2 = 2^3$, $sqr(3)=3^\circ 3^\circ 3=3^3 \equiv 0;0 = 0^2$.

In general, an i-triangle of height *h*, as well as a trapeze of height *h*, is associated with the string: $tri(h)=trpz(h)= 2;2;....;2=2^{h-1}$, where ';' is now used to denote concatenation. In a similar way, a square is associated with the string: $sqr(l)= 0;0;....;0=0^{l-1}$. Note that symbols in the strings associated with SSs are even numbers. We call such a sequence a *variation-sequence.*

3. Characterising shape transformations

In this Section we illustrate the methodology for analytical extraction of rewriting rules, using as example the transformations induced by a Gaussian filter, in the case that the segmentation operator is thresholding. We use a Gaussian filter with kernel of size 5, and we consider the same size for the neighbourhood of pixels. The convolution kernel is symmetrical, generated from the vector $1/20\times[1,5,8,5,1]$, through the law: $w(i,j)=w(i) \times w(j)$. Due to the symmetry characteristics of both the filter and the considered structures, it is possible to identify some lowest values for the size of the structures, in order for the transformation to be characterised by a regular, formalisable behaviour.

In a binary image, a centre pixel in a neighbourhood is one of the following:

1. internal pixel: all the pixels in the neighbourhood are black.
2. pixel close to the background: the central pixel is black and the neighbourhood contains both black and white pixels.
3. pixel close to the foreground: the central pixel is white and the neighbourhood contains both black and white pixels.
4. background pixel: all the pixels in the neighbourhood are white.

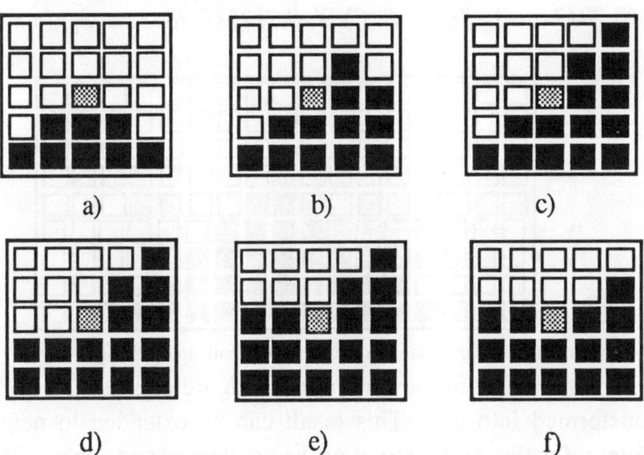

Fig.5 Some configurations of a neighbourhood on the contour of an i-triangle.

We refer to grey level images with values in a set $\{0,...,255\}$, where 0 corresponds to white and 255 to black. The segmentation algorithm is a simple thresholding, producing a new image p_i from an original image i, applying the threshold th, as mapping pixels to the value 255 if they exceed th, to 0 otherwise

In the following we discuss results for $th=200$. Hence, a pixel of coordinates (n,m) is transformed into a pixel with grey value 255 if and only if:

$$\left(\sum_{i,j\in\{-2,+2\}} w(i,j)\cdot[g(n+i,m+j)=255] \right) \geq \frac{200}{255} = 0.7843 \tag{1}$$

where $[g(n+i,m+j) = 255]$ denotes the elements with value 255.

The value of the sum is indicated with W. To define the effect of the filtering on the segmented image, neighbourhood configurations are exhaustively analysed to identify those allowing the central pixel to be transformed into 255. As an example, Fig.5 describes some possible neighbourhood on the contour of an i-triangle.

3.1 Transformation of an i-triangle

In this paragraph the method described above is used for the case of the i-triangle. In Fig.6, A indicates the pixel starting from which all pixels maintain the same value, while descending toward the base. In Fig.7 B indicates the pixel until which the value is maintained. For all the neighbourhoods in Fig.5, the central pixel is transformed into 0. Indeed, they give rise to the following values:
(a) $W=0,435<0,7843 \Rightarrow G_{bin}(n,m)=0$; (b) $W=0,63<0,7843 \Rightarrow G_{bin}(n,m)=0$; (c) $W=0,645<0,7843 \Rightarrow G_{bin}(n,m)=0$; (d) $W=0,6575<0,7843 \Rightarrow G_{bin}(n,m)=0$; (e) $W=0,7775<0,7843 \Rightarrow G_{bin}(n,m)=0$; (f) $W=0,7125<0,7843 \Rightarrow G_{bin}(n,m)=0$.

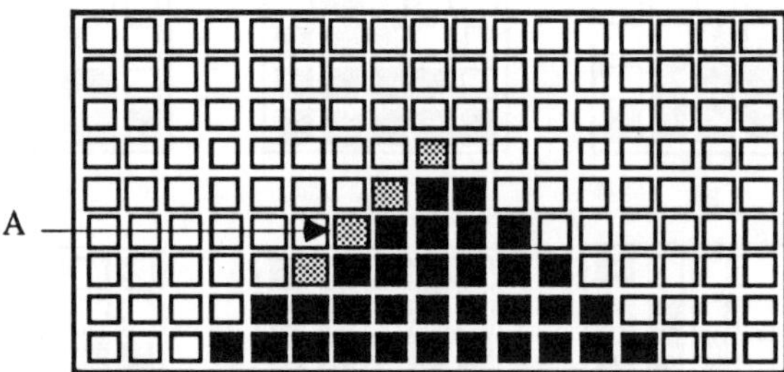

Fig.6. The initial configurations on the contour of an i-triangle

All the other pixels in the i-triangle which are close to the background are instead transformed into *255*. This result can be extended to neighbourhoods resulting from reflection and rotation of the neighbourhoods above. We have now considered all the combinations of interest for the analysis of the Gaussian transformation. There exists a minimal height, viz. *4*, above which a general law can be identified. Below this height, the methodology is however able to describe the behaviour of the transformation for the single cases.

Theorem (i-triangle). The variation-sequence for an i-triangle of *height* $h \geq 4$ is transformed by a Gaussian filter in a variation-sequence, by the law: $2^{h-1} \rightarrow 2^{h-2}$.

Note that the overall transformation of the structure erases the vertex of the i-triangle, while preserving the base length. Hence, an i-triangle is transformed into a trapeze and the structural transformation induced by the Gaussian filter is summarised by the following rule, where the function g is defined by the theorem.

$<<segm_1, tri, segm_2>, trpz>$
γ: $(tri.heigh \geq 4)$ && $(segm_1.length \geq 3)$ && $(segm_2.length \geq 3)$
r_p: $trpz.height = tri.height-1$, $trpz.base = tri.base$, $trpz.varseq = g(tri.varseq)$

As an example, for the case of Fig.8 we have: $G[(tri(5))]=2^3$ Analogous rules and theorems hold for trapezes and squares.

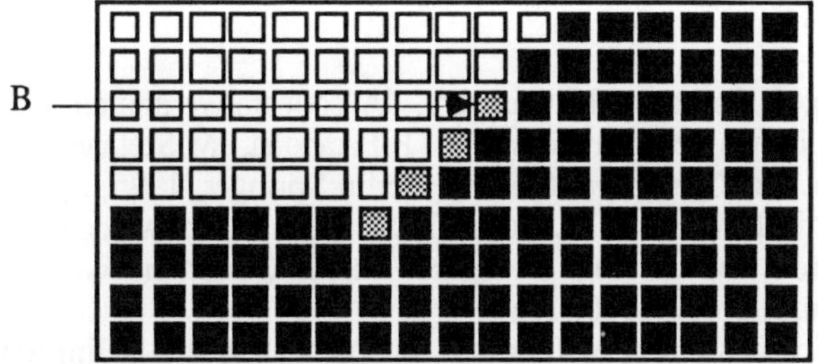

Fig.7. The final configurations on the contour of an i-triangle

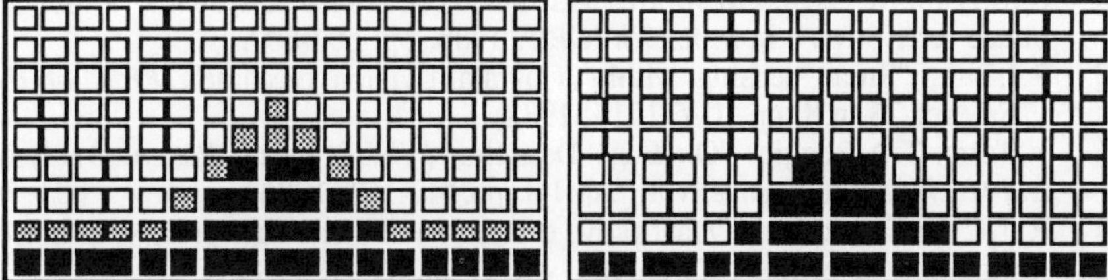

Fig.8. Gaussian transformation of an i-triangle.

4. Conclusions

We have illustrated a methodology for the definition of rewriting rules expressing the transformations induced by IPO on structural descriptions of images. The methodology is based on an analysis of the characteristics of the operator with respect to the adopted segmentation technique.

This methodology can be applied in the automatic generation of IP and interpretation strategies, in case one wants to consider also the operator's capability of preserving structural features of the image. In particular, it can be used to distinguish which types of structures constitute structural invariants for a transformation, and to characterise families of structures with respect to the transformation under which they remain invariant. The conditions for its application are that SS have to be composed of adjacent pixels along the object contour, and that the structure size be sufficient to avoid high-frequency effects.

Future developments in this line are the definition of a language for the description of the operators and of a metalevel interpreter able to select suitable operators based on such descriptions. Automatic learning tools are being experimented to characterise the effect of transformations on structures defined in terms of domain-semantics and not only of geometrical characteristics.

5. References

[1] C.Spinu, C.Garbay, J.M.Chassery, "A cooperative and adaptive approach to medical image segmentation", in P.Barahona, M.Stefanelli, J.Wyatt eds., *Artificial Intelligence in Medicine*, Berlin:Springer, 1995, pp.379-390

[2] P.Bottoni, P.Mussio, M.Protti, R.Schettini, "Knowledge-based contextual recognition and sieving of digital images", *Pattern Recognition Letters*, vol.10, n.2, pp.101-110, 1989

[3] P.Mussio, D.Merelli, M.Padula, "An approach to the Definition, Description and Extraction of structures in Binary Digital Images", *Computer Vision Graphics & Image Processing*, vol. 31, pp. 19-49, 1985.

[4] P.Mussio, M.Padula, M.Protti, "Attributed conditional L-systems: a tool for image description", in *Proc. 9th ICPR*, 1988, pp. 607-609.

[5] P.J.Burt, "Smart sensing within a pyramid vision machine", *Proc. of the IEEE*, vol.76, n.8, pp.1006-1015, 1988.

[6] V.Torre, T.A.Poggio, "On Edge Detection", *IEEE Trans. Pattern Analysis and Machine Intelligence*, vol.PAMI-8, pp.147-163, 1986

[7] R.T.Chin, C.-L.Yeh, "Quantitative evaluation of some edge-preserving noise-smoothing techniques", *CVG&IP.*, vol.23, pp.67-91, 1983

[8] R.M.Hodgson, D.G.Bailey, M.J.Naylor, A.L.M.Ng, S.J.McNeill, "Properties, implementations and applications of rank filters", *Image and Vision Computing*, vol.3, n.1, pp.3-14, 1985

[9] N.C.Gallagher Jr, G.L.Wise, "A theoretical analysis of the properties of median filters", *IEEE Tr. ASSP*, vol.ASSP-29, pp.1136-1141, 1981

[10] V.Cantoni, L.Cinque, C.Guerra, S.Levialdi, L.Lombardi, "Tree pattern matching for 2D multiresolution objects", in *Proc. CAMP*, 1993, pp.43-46

[11] K.Culik II, P.Rajcani, "Iterative weighted finite transductions", *Acta Informatica*, vol.32, pp.681-703, 1995

[12] E.R.Dougherty, C.R.Giardina, *Mathematical Methods for Artificial Intelligence and Autonomous Systems*, Englewood Cliffs: Prentice-Hall, 1988

[13] A. Favre, H. Keller, "Parallel Syntactic Thinning by Recoding of Binary Pictures", *CVG&IP*, vol.23, pp.99-112, 1983

[14] A. Rosenfeld and R. Siromoney, "Pictorial Languages", *Languages of Design*, vol.1, pp.229-245, 1993.

[15] Di Lernia, N.Bianchi, G.Marveggio, A.Morabito, P.Mussio, G.Rubbia, Rinaldi, "Topographic modeling of #1 G-banded chromosome", *Jour. of Biological Systems*, vol. 3, n.1, pp.27-39, 1995.

[16] J. Serra, Image analysis and mathematical morphology, London: Academic Press, 1982.

[17] K.S.Fu, *Syntactic Pattern Recognition and Applications*, Englewood Cliffs: Prentice-Hall, 1982.

[18] G.T.Herman, H.Rozenberg, *Developmental Systems and Languages*, Amsterdam: North-Holland, 1975.

OBJECT RECOGNITION USING LARGE STRUCTURAL MODELBASES

K. L. BOYER & K. SENGUPTA

Signal Analysis and Machine Perception Laboratory, Department of Electrical Engineering, The Ohio State University, Columbus, OH 43210, USA

We present an architecture for fast object recognition from large modelbases in computer vision. Scene objects and models are stored as graph theoretic abstractions because object parts and their spatial relations, including models for the uncertainty in these quantities, can be effectively embedded in a graph. To avoid a brute force linear search over the modelbase during recognition we first partition the library into submodelbases of grossly similar objects using spectral features derived from matrices based on simple indicators of shape. Each resulting partition is next organized hierarchically using an information theoretic structural dissimilarity measure. During recognition one or two partitions likely to contain the correct object model are first identified using spectral features derived from the object hypothesis (in the scene) together with a perturbation model developed to account for noise and sensor distortion, self-occlusion, and scene clutter. Once a small number of plausible partitions are selected, one matching process is invoked between the scene object and the partition representative. To do this, we introduce a new technique for structural matching derived as an extension to the geometric hashing concept and which uses the hierarchical organization of the partition. Next, we perform a tree search of the partition to identify the correct model. This search is inexpensive because of the particular way the corresponding tree is constructed. We conclude by summarizing the results of extensive experimental results on a CAD modelbase of more than 100 objects and numerous range images.

1 Introduction

Model based recognition techniques can be broadly classified as graph theoretic and non graph theoretic. In graph theoretic systems, an object is described as an assembly of several parts, each represented as a node in a graph. The arcs in this graph encode the relationships among the parts. In other methods, local features are used to describe the object. Increasing the size of the model library increases the capability of a model based system, but adversely affects the recognition time.

Despite the historically superior performance of non graph theoretic methods for large libraries, we have pursued the graph theoretic approach because graph theoretic methods allow us to inject additional intelligence into spatial reasoning and CAD objects can easily be described in graphical form. To make graph theoretic methods feasible for large library sizes, we structure the modelbase such that recognition time increases sublinearly with its size. In prior

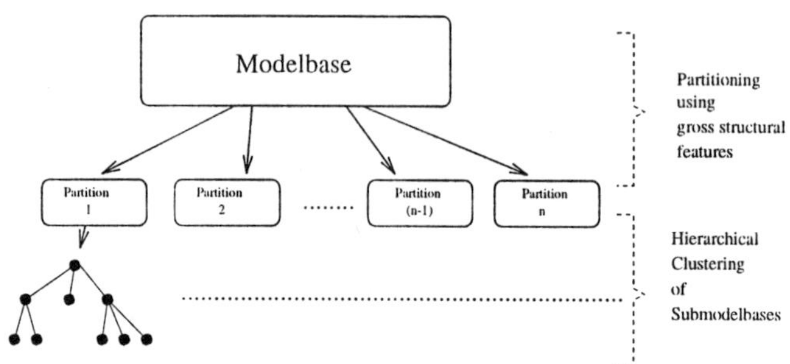

Figure 1: An illustration of the two tiered organization strategy for a large modelbase.

work, Sossa and Horaud [1] index a library of graph based models using the coefficients of the second immanantal polynomial derived from the Laplacian matrix that describes the graph. However, the graphs are not attributed and the system is restricted to polyhedra. Shapiro and Haralick [2] organize models in a tree according to an intermodel distance metric. Extending these concepts to more sophisticated models is the thrust of this paper; we show how a graph theoretic modelbase architecture can be constructed to yield the speed of indexing approaches, while retaining the graph theoretic advantages.

2 An Architecture for Structural Modelbase Organization

We propose a two tiered organization strategy, illustrated in Fig. 1. First, we segregate the modelbase into structurally homogeneous *partitions* by grouping models with similar overall structural features. Next, the models in each partition are hierarchically organized, using the theory developed in [3].

We represent *object models* in the library by random parametric structural descriptions (RPSD) and scene *observations* using parametric structural descriptions (PSD). The PSD is a pair $\mathbf{G} = (\mathbf{P}, \mathbf{R})$ with $\mathbf{P}$ a set of primitives (*e.g.*, surfaces) and $\mathbf{R}$ a set of named parametric relations over $\mathbf{P}$ (*e.g.*, adjacency). A primitive is characterized by attributes (*e.g.*, area), while a relation is characterized by parameters (*e.g.*, relative orientation).

A random parametric structural description is a pair, $\mathcal{G} = (\mathcal{P}, \mathcal{R})$, in which $\mathcal{P}$ is a set of *random primitives* and $\mathcal{R}$ is a set of named *random parametric relations*. The RPSD captures the randomness in an object's appearance. For

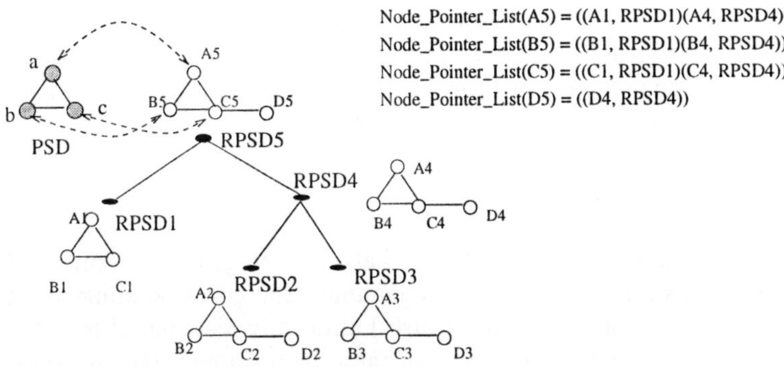

Figure 2: Mapping functions between PSD and RPSD primitives can be determined from the node pointer lists.

example, we have a random variable for the area attribute of a surface primitive to capture the effect of viewpoint variation or noise. Similarly, for a random relationship tuple, the parameter value is random.

In [3] we define an information theoretic RPSD-RPSD dissimilarity measure to organize the modelbase hierarchically. The RPSDs of specific object models are placed at the leaves and intermediate node RPSDs are formed by merging the RPSDs below by recursive clustering. This continues to a single, root RPSD representing the full range of models in the tree. This merging operation computes the best interprimitive mapping between the RPSDs (slowest increase in entropy) and produces a *node pointer list* for each primitive in the merged structure. Using this map of the tree's construction, the search is fast.

During recognition, the only potentially expensive matching process is between the scene PSD and the root RPSD. Section 5 presents an embedded surface-based geometric hashing approach that yields an extremely fast matcher. Using this match result, the organized hierarchy, and the node pointer lists, the remaining work simplifies to a logarithmic number (in the size of the modelbase) of linear (in the number of primitives) tests through subsequent levels of the tree. According to theory, the speedup by this method over linear search through the model set approximates $N : 1$, for N models. However, this was quite difficult to obtain using the hierarchy alone because the root RPSD can be large. Therefore, the PSD to root RPSD match can be far more expensive than the match between the PSD and any single model RPSD. The hierarchical clustering of RPSDs which are not too dissimilar yield well-structured trees with smaller root RPSDs and, correspondingly, better performance. These observations motivated the developments below.

This work has been developed in the context of range images, but the essential concepts should adapt well to other domains. We begin by segmenting the input range image into surfaces, using Flynn and Jain's BONSAI system [4], followed by simple perceptual organization [5].

3 Partitioning the Modelbase

For partitioning, we require features that capture gross structural information over all possible viewpoints. We compute the corresponding set of gross structural features for 128 points (nearly) uniformly distributed over the viewsphere. *It is the distribution of each of these features over the viewsphere that characterizes the object's overall shape.*

3.1 The Features

We define a set of three matrices whose eigenvalues describe the model from a given viewpoint:

- **Area Matrix**: Entry (i, i) is the visible area of surface i. Entry (i, j) is 1 for surfaces i, j adjacent in the given view, 0 otherwise. Used only in partitioning; unreliable for recognition.
- **Nullity Matrix**: Entry (i, i) is 1 if any part of the ith surface is visible from this viewpoint, 0 otherwise. Entry (i, j) is as in the Area Matrix.
- **Angle Matrix**: Diagonal entries are 0. Entry (i, j) is the angle between surfaces i, j, if both are visible and share an edge. If either surface is spherical, this entry is 0. If one is planar and the other cylindrical, we choose the acute angle between the cylinder's axis and the planar surface normal. For two cylinders, we use the acute angle between the two axes.

We use (the distributions of) eigenvalues as our features because they offer a rich, yet concise description of the overall appearance, they are permutation invariant and so require no expensive matching of shape primitives, and because eigenvalues vary smoothly with the data. The eigenvalues for each matrix are stored in descending order by algebraic value, quantized uniformly over $L = 50$ levels from their maximum to minimum value over the modelbase.

The size of the property matrix and, consequently, the number of features extracted for a particular view of an object depend on the number of visible surfaces. Since the primitive count varies with both model and viewpoint, we consider m eigenvalues for every matrix, where m is the largest primitive (surface) count over the entire modelbase. For an object with $n < m$ visible surfaces, we insert zero eigenvalues into the set. We calculate the eigenvalues of each property matrix, for each of 128 viewpoints and compute the histogram for each, assuming equiprobable poses. Scaling the histogram appropriately yields the estimated probability mass function of this eigenvalue, for this property matrix, for this model.

3.2 The Gross Dissimilarity Measure

Let the probability mass function of the ith eigenvalue (for one matrix) of model M_1 be $\{P_i^{M_1}(k) \mid k = 1.\cdots, L\}$. To compare two models M_1 and M_2, we adapt the mass function similarity measure in [6]:

$$C_{diss}(M_1, M_2) \quad = \quad 1 - \frac{1}{m} \sum_{i=1}^{m} \sum_{k=1}^{L} \frac{P_i^{M_1}(k)}{\mid P_i^{M_1} \mid} \frac{P_i^{M_2}(k)}{\mid P_i^{M_2} \mid} \tag{1}$$

where $\mid P_i^{M_1} \mid = \sqrt{\sum_{k=1}^{L} P_i^{M_1}(k)^2}$. The overall dissimilarity between two models is the average over all three properties.

Once the dissimilarities between all model pairs are computed, the modelbase is segregated such that all pairs in a common partition are within a dissimilarity value of t, using the clustering algorithm in [7]. The threshold t corresponds to a significant minimum in the histogram of pairwise dissimilarities. The mass functions of the $3m$ eigenvalues for each partition are computed by averaging the individual model mass functions, assuming the models are equiprobable.

3.3 Entropy

For a partition C, let the probability mass function (for one matrix) for the ith eigenvalue be $\{P_i^C(k) \mid k = 1, \cdots, L\}$. Its entropy is

$$H_i^C = -\sum_{k=1}^{L} P_i^C(k) \log_2 \left(P_i^C(k)\right); \; 0 \leq i \leq m \tag{2}$$

The entropy of an eigenvalue measures its average information content. Eigenvalues with high entropies are therefore the most useful.

4 Identifying the Correct Partition

We begin with surface segmentation and simple perceptual organization as mentioned above to define a set of surface clusters. Each cluster represents an object hypothesis, and the initial task is to find a small set of partitions likely to contain the hypothesis. The surface segmentation and clustering will not be perfect and some surfaces will be occluded, so the eigenvalues of the property matrices corresponding to the surface cluster are perturbed from those of the corresponding model or partition. We have modeled this perturbation in terms of surface count error probabilities, and we use this model to correct the eigenvalue mass functions for recognition.

4.1 Modeling Eigenvalue Perturbation

We limit the study to eigenvalue perturbations caused by missing or extra surfaces and relations. For Nullity Matrices, this suffices because the entries are just ones and zeros. For the Angle Matrix, off-diagonal entries are also perturbed by errors in the surface parameters. However, this effect is insignificant compared to that of missing or extra surfaces, and we neglect it.

Let X'_N be an $n \times n$ Nullity Matrix corresponding to some surface cluster, and X_N be the $k \times k$ Nullity Matrix for the hypothesized model under ideal conditions. In other words, X_N is synthetically generated from the object model when its pose is exactly the same as that of the hypothesized object in the image. Suppose $n > k$. Since eigenvalues are permutation invariant, without loss of generality we assume that the ith surface in the model matches the ith surface in the scene ($i = 1, \ldots, k$). If a particular surface is missing from the cluster, the corresponding row and column entries in X'_N are all 0.

Let $\lambda(X_N)$ and $\lambda(X'_N)$ be the eigenvalues of X_N and X'_N, respectively, both sorted in descending order. Also, let $\lambda_i(X_N)$ be the ith eigenvalue of X_N. To find the mathematical relationship between these two sets of eigenvalues, we use what we call the *eigenvalue perturbation theorem*[8]. It states that if we can construct a matrix $Q \in \Re^{n\times k}$ which has the property $Q^T Q = I_k$, and if

$$X'_N Q - Q X_N = E_N$$

then there exist $\mu_1, \mu_2, \ldots, \mu_k \in \lambda(X'_N)$ such that

$$|\mu_i - \lambda_i(X_N)| \leq \sqrt{2}||E_N||_2; \quad i = 1, \ldots, k \tag{3}$$

where $||E_N||_2$ is the 2-norm of E_N.

Here, because the ith scene surface is assumed to match the ith model surface, the construction of matrix $Q = [q_{ij}]$ ($i = 1, \ldots, n$ and $j = 1, \ldots, k$) is quite simple;

$$\begin{aligned} q_{ij} &= 1;\ \text{if } i = j. \\ &= 0;\ \text{otherwise.} \end{aligned}$$

Also, E_N is an $n \times k$ matrix, where $E_N = \left[e_{N_{ij}}\right]$ ($i = 1, \ldots, n$ and $j = 1, \ldots, k$). From linear algebra, we know that

$$||E_N||_2 \leq ||E_N||_F = \sqrt{\sum_{i=1}^{n} \sum_{j=1}^{k} e_{N_{ij}}^2}$$

where $||E_N||_F$ is the Frobenius norm. Thus Eqn. 3 can be rewritten as:

$$|\mu_i - \lambda_i(X_N)| \leq \sqrt{2 \sum_{i=1}^{n} \sum_{j=1}^{k} e_{N_{ij}}^2}; \quad i = 1, \ldots, k \tag{4}$$

In general, we don't know the Q matrix but it captures, with ones in the appropriate positions, the mapping of the k model surfaces onto the n cluster surfaces. Thus, k of its n rows will contain a single one; the rest contain all zeros. Moreover, each of its k columns will contain a single one.

We declare a *Count Error* when $e_{N_{ij}}^2 = 1$. Therefore, the *Total Count Error* ($\mathbf{n_C}$) can be expressed as:

$$\mathbf{n_C} = \sum_{i=1}^{n} \sum_{j=1}^{k} e_{N_{ij}}^2 \geq \left(||E_N||_2\right)^2 \tag{5}$$

If we define $(\lambda_i(X_N) - \mu_i)$ as λ_{i,e_N}, then Eqn. 4 can be rewritten as:

$$|\lambda_{i,e_N}| \leq \sqrt{2\mathbf{n_C}} \tag{6}$$

We assume $\mathbf{n_C}$ is exponentially distributed:

$$\Pr\left[\mathbf{n_C} = n_c\right] = \left(1 - e^{-\alpha}\right) e^{-\alpha n_c}, \text{ for } n_c \geq 0 \tag{7}$$

Using the bound in Eqn. 6 we assume λ_{i,e_N} is uniformly distributed over $\left[-\sqrt{2n_c}, \sqrt{2n_c}\right]$. Thus, its probability density function, conditioned on n_c is:

$$f_{\lambda_{i,e_N}|\mathbf{n_C}}\left(x|n_c\right) = \frac{u\left(x + \sqrt{2n_c}\right) u\left(-x + \sqrt{2n_c}\right)}{2\sqrt{2n_c}}$$

where x is a real number and $u(x)$ is the unit step. When $\mathbf{n_C} = 0$, $f_{\lambda_{i,e_N}|\mathbf{n_C}}(x|0) = \delta(x)$. Finally, the total probability density is

$$\begin{aligned} f_{\lambda_{i,e_N}}(x) &= \sum_{n=0}^{\infty} f_{\lambda_{i,e_N}|\mathbf{n_C}}\left(x|n_c\right) \Pr\left[\mathbf{n_C} = n_c\right] \\ &= \left(1 - e^{-\alpha}\right) \left(\delta(x) + \sum_{n_c=1}^{\infty} e^{-\alpha n_c} \frac{u\left(x + \sqrt{2n_c}\right) u\left(-x + \sqrt{2n_c}\right)}{2\sqrt{2n_c}}\right) \end{aligned} \tag{8}$$

This density function models the perturbation of a Nullity matrix eigenvalue $\lambda_i(X_N)$ about its true value. We discretize this function as $P_{i,\lambda_{e_N}}$. For $n < k$, a similar analysis yields the same mass function.

Recall that $\lambda_i(X_N)$ is used to create the ith eigenvalue mass function P_i^C (for a partition C). The observed eigenvalue is the sum of this random variable with that representing the perturbation. Thus, the density function of the observed eigenvalue is $P'^C_i = P_i^C * P_{\lambda_{i,e_N}}$, the *convolution* of P_i^C and $P_{\lambda_{i,e_N}}$, and is computed prior to recognition.

The analysis for the angle matrix eigenvalues is similar, but a bit more complicated because surface types (planar, cylindrical, or spherical) must be accounted for [9].

4.2 Partition to Surface Cluster Dissimilarity

We first consider the dissimilarity calculation based on one property. For a partition C, the probability mass function corresponding to the ith (perturbed) eigenvalue is P'^C_i $(i = 1, 2, \ldots, m)$. Let the n quantized eigenvalues computed from the surface cluster (with n surfaces) be $\{\overline{\lambda_i}\}_{i=1}^n$. We define the dissimilarity between the jth eigenvalue of the surface cluster and $\overline{\lambda_i}$ as:

$$diss\,(i,j) = -\log\left(P'^C_i\left(\overline{\lambda_j}\right)\right);\ 1 \le i \le m \text{ and } 1 \le j \le n \tag{9}$$

where $P'^C_i\left(\overline{\lambda_j}\right)$ is the value of the mass function at $\overline{\lambda_j}$. The measure of Eqn. 1 is monotonic with this information theoretic measure (proof in [9]), allowing us to use the first for partitioning and the second for identification.

Next, we need a 1:1 mapping function $\mathcal{M}$ from the n scene eigenvalues to the m possible eigenvalues of partition C. Since both sets are sorted, $\mathcal{M}(i) > \mathcal{M}(j)$, if $i > j$. The dissimilarity between the surface cluster SC and the partition C is defined as:

$$\delta_I\,(C, SC) = \arg\min_{\mathcal{M}} \sum_{i=1}^{n} diss\,(i, \mathcal{M}(i)) \tag{10}$$

We do not evaluate Eqn. 10 exhaustively; we approximate the result by dynamic programming.

The entropies of the eigenvalue distributions tell us how much information they convey on average and, therefore, how useful they are. So we scale the δ_I function in Eqn. 10 by a factor κ to favor functions using the partition's "better" eigenvalues:

$$\kappa = \frac{\sum_{i=1}^{m} H_i^C - \sum_{i=1}^{n} H_{\mathcal{M}(i)}^C}{\sum_{i=1}^{n} H_{\mathcal{M}(i)}^C} \tag{11}$$

We average the results from both properties to arrive at the final surface cluster to partition dissimilarity. The decay parameter α in Eqn. 7 is unknown. So, for each partition, we average the overall dissimilarity for $\alpha = 1, 2, \ldots, 5$. The partition having the lowest average dissimilarity, and all others within 20% of this minimum, are then searched for the best model.

5 Hierarchically Embedded Geometric Hashing

Our remaining obstacle to fast recognition is the cost of the root match for a given partition. That is, once the partition is selected, as above and in [9], but before we search it, as in [3], we must (quickly) determine the mapping of observed PSD primitives onto RPSD primitives. We use a novel surface-based geometric hashing *embedded within the partition hierarchy* for this. We first construct separate hash arrays for each model. The hash array corresponding to an intermediate node RPSD is formed by merging those of its children, continuing to a single, root hash array used to find the root match. The lower hash arrays are used only to build the root array; they are not used online.

5.1 Hash Arrays for Model RPSDs

For now assume the primitives are planar surfaces. Three surfaces form a *basis set*; additional ones act as *voting surfaces.* We invoke quaternary, named, ordered relations to describe the geometry of a fourth primitive with respect to a basis primitive triple. For the three different surface types we consider (planar, cylindrical, and spherical), there are 81 of these possible. A constituent 4-tuple is (p^1, p^2, p^3, p^4), where each p^i is a surface primitive with normal $\mathbf{n}_1$, (p^1, p^2, p^3) is the basis, and p^4 is the voting primitive. The parameter vector $(\beta_1, \beta_2, \beta_3, \ldots, \beta_8)$ describes the geometry of the tuple:

$$\beta_1 = \text{Relation Identifier} \qquad \beta_2 = (\mathbf{n}^1 \times \mathbf{n}^2) \cdot \mathbf{n}^4 \qquad \beta_3 = (\mathbf{n}^2 \times \mathbf{n}^3) \cdot \mathbf{n}^4$$
$$\beta_4 = (\mathbf{n}^3 \times \mathbf{n}^1) \cdot \mathbf{n}^4 \qquad \beta_5 = \mathbf{n}_1 \cdot \mathbf{n}_2 \qquad \beta_6 = \mathbf{n}_2 \cdot \mathbf{n}_3$$
$$\beta_7 = \mathbf{n}_3 \cdot \mathbf{n}_1 \qquad \beta_8 = (\mathbf{n}_1 \times \mathbf{n}_2) \cdot \mathbf{n}_3 \tag{12}$$

Note that β_2, β_3 and β_4 capture the geometry of the voting primitive p^4 with respect to the basis (p^1, p^2, p^3), while β_5, β_6, β_7 and β_8 capture the geometry of the basis itself. The parameter vector indexes the hash array, pointing to the model, the basis triple, and the voting primitive. Hypothesizing the model to scene basis triple match helps us later to complete the mapping between the unmatched scene and model surfaces.

For the same basis, parallel voting surfaces index the same location. Therefore, we also store the maximum and minimum distances of the voting surface (planar or cylindrical) from the first surface in the triple to resolve such ambiguities. We define consistent methods of dealing with all other basis-voter combinations in [10], but omit the (tedious) details here.

5.2 Merging Hash Arrays

To build the hash array for the root RPSD, we merge the hash arrays of all the model RPSDs *as we create* the hierarchy. We obtain the entries in a particular location of the array of merged model M by merging the entries in the corresponding locations of the hash arrays of (say) M_1 and M_2, as determined by the interprimitive mapping function between the two corresponding RPSDs. The primitive identities in each of these entries are modified to their corresponding primitive identities in M. It is possible that there will be two separate entries for the same triple after merging. These are replaced by just one entry such that each voting primitive appears just once in the merged list. The distance range associated with each voting primitive is set to encompass the range for its children in M_1 and M_2.

5.3 Using the Hash Arrays

We use hashing to identify not only the best partition, but also the interprimitive mapping from the observation to the partition's root RPSD. Hashing consists of *voting*, in which we identify the promising root RPSD triple to scene PSD triple matches, followed by *verification*, wherein the qualifying triple matches from the voting stage are evaluated and the best one chosen. Fig. 3 diagrams the process.

Voting

Given a scene triple, for each of the remaining surfaces in the scene we index into the root hash array using the same method followed to create the arrays. A basis triple (and its corresponding model) present in this location receives a vote if the voting scene surface satisfies the locational constraints for at least one of the voting model surfaces associated with this basis triple.

After all scene primitives not included in the scene basis triple have voted, we tally the votes for each model triple. Any model triple receiving more than, say, v_t votes is a possible match for the scene triple. The selection of the vote threshold can be critical. If it is too low we will choose many incorrect model basis triples, a problem that worsens with noise. Although these erroneous triples can be eliminated in verification, reducing v_t means more to verify and longer recognition time. If v_t is too high, the correct basis triple may not be

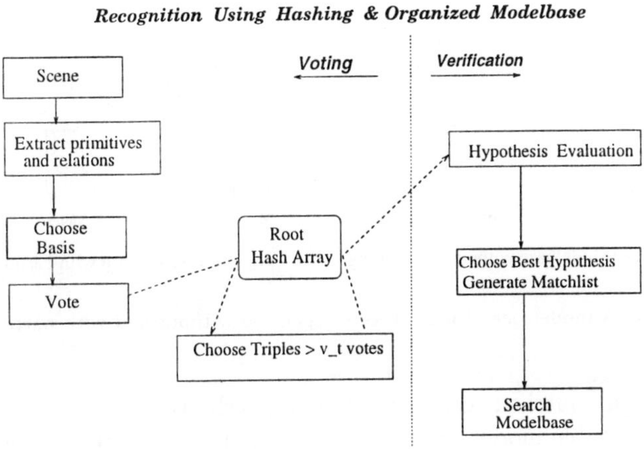

Figure 3: The flow diagram of the hashing process.

selected at all. Hashing embedded in an organized hierarchy leads to sparser (merged) hash arrays than standard (recognition based on hashing alone), and the choice of v_t is far less critical as a result. Indeed, we can afford to explore every model triple receiving at least one vote.

Although the analysis is too lengthy for this space, we have studied the effect of bounded sensor error on the hashing indices. Using these results, we allow each surface triple to access a range of bins in the array. We have also analyzed the effect of this strategy on the probability of false positives as a function of the sensor error and scene clutter. The merged hash array is only slightly more prone to false positives than standard hashing in high noise. In low to moderate noise, and for all degrees of clutter, the two are virtually indistinguishable with respect to error rate.

Verification

Given a root RPSD triple to scene triple match hypothesis, we use the hash array to complete the interprimitive mapping efficiently. For a given unmatched scene primitive, the locations to be accessed in the hash array are determined by its parameter vector with respect to the scene basis triple as above. The hypothesized model basis triple should be present at this location. Otherwise, this unmatched scene surface maps to null. At this location in the hash array, each of the voting root RPSD surface primitives associated with the hypothesized root RPSD basis triple is a potential match for the scene surface.

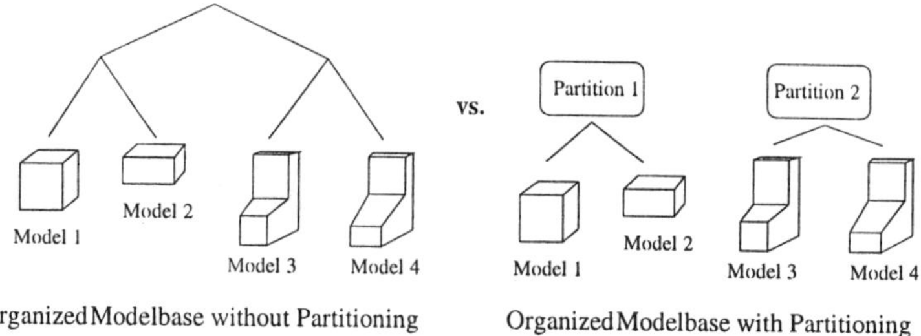

Figure 4: A modelbase of four objects organized without and with partitioning.

For each unmatched scene primitive not included in the scene basis triple, a list of all possible model surfaces is determined as described above. All one-to-one mapping functions still possible are then evaluated using the PSD to root RPSD dissimilarity measure defined in [3]. That mapping function having the lowest dissimilarity value (cost) is chosen. Among all the triple match hypotheses, that with the minimum cost is retained. Thus, verification also completes the mapping between observed surfaces and root model surfaces.

6 Experimental Results

6.1 Speedup from Partitioning

We demonstrate the dramatic speedup available using the modelbase of just four polyhedral objects in Fig. 4. Without partitioning, the recognition time for Model 1 is 5.61 cpu-seconds. With partitioning, this drops to 3.16 cpu-seconds, 0.59 seconds for partition selection, and 2.57 seconds for the tree search. For Model 3, the recognition time without partitioning is 11.18 cpu-seconds. With partitioning, it is 10.27 cpu-seconds, 0.96 seconds for partition selection and 9.31 seconds for the tree search[a]. These results do not use the embedded hashing technique.

Even on such a small example partitioning has a remarkable impact. It is readily apparent that partitioning is extremely powerful when scaling to truly large, heterogeneous modelbases.

6.2 Partitioning a 125-Object CAD Modelbase

In this modelbase, 115 objects are polyhedral; the remainder include cylindrical and spherical surfaces. These two sets were partitioned separately. A typical

[a] HP9000/715 machine, timing by Unix utility.

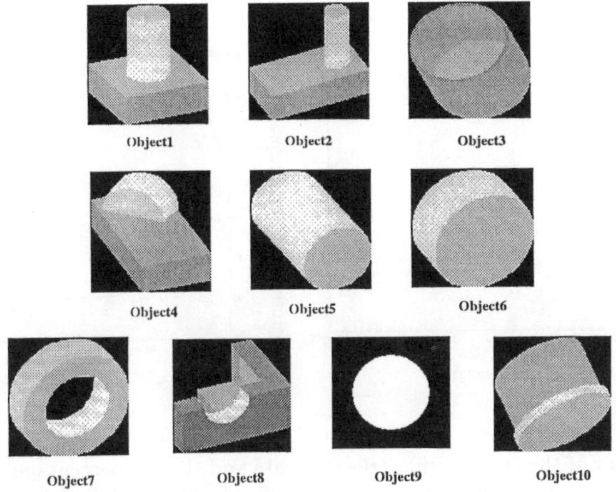

Figure 5: A typical view of each of the 10 nonpolyhedral objects.

view of each of the nonpolyhedral objects appears in Fig. 5. We grouped these using the threshold $t = 0.24$, which corresponds to one of the deepest minima in the histogram of pairwise dissimilarities. The three partitions are {Object1, Object2, Object4, Object8}, {Object5, Object6, Object9}, and {Object7, Object3, Object10}. All models in the first partition include boxes. In the other two, planar surfaces are not dominant. The set of 115 polyhedral objects generated 7 partitions.

Corresponding to each property matrix, we computed m (= 27) representative eigenvalue probability mass functions for each partition. We tested each of the 128 views for every object. For the nonpolyhedral objects, the overall correct selection rate is 93.05%. For Object3 the correct partition selection rate is low (62.5%) because from several viewpoints it looks much like Object5 or Object6. For those viewpoints, only the second partition was selected, as a human observer would tend to do. For the polyhedral objects, the overall correct partition selection rate is 89.40%. Recall that all partitions within the acceptance range (20%) of the minimum dissimilarity value are chosen for search. In Fig. 6 we present the effect of varying this parameter from 10% to 100%; 100% means we search partitions of dissimilarity up to twice that of the best.

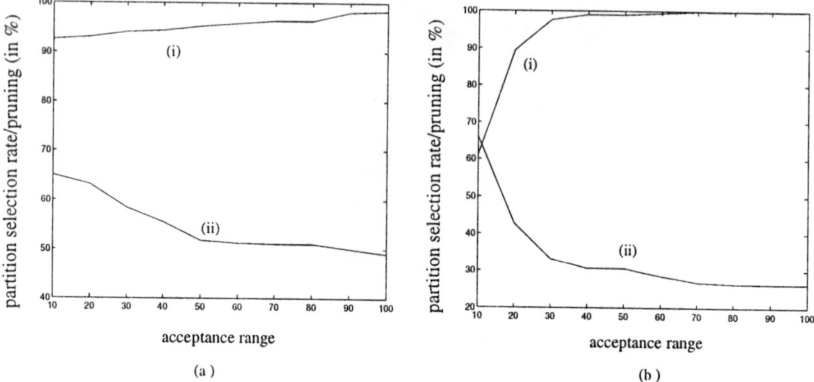

Figure 6: The plot of the (i) partition selection rate and the (ii) percentage of the modelbase pruned as we vary the acceptance range from 10% to 100%. Plots (a) and (b) are for the nonpolyhedral and polyhedral (sub)modelbases, respectively.

6.3 Partition Selection Using Real Range Images

To test our perturbation model, we performed partition recognition experiments without surface clustering to force count errors. We ran these (at first) on range images of single objects against a plain tabletop-wall background, giving two extra surfaces and some extra adjacency relationships. Typically, a 59% pruning of the modelbase occurred. *When the perturbation function was invoked, no partition selection errors occurred in these cases. Without the perturbation function, the correct partition was never selected.*

Fig. 7 presents a typical cluttered range image and the correct object models corresponding to each surface cluster produced. Partition selection was repeated for each of the six object hypotheses (clusters). Note that there are a few missing and extra surfaces from the object hypothesized in SC1, yet the modelbase is pruned by 80%. For SC2 and SC6, the pruning rate is 41% and 63%, respectively. For clusters SC3, SC4, and SC5, the correct partition was not chosen. SC3 suffers from heavy oversegmentation, and SC4 and SC5 actually belong to the same object, pointing to errors in both segmentation and grouping in these fairly extreme situations. Partitions storing smaller objects were chosen for these clusters.

Overall, for the set of range images we considered and using the 20% acceptance range, when the perturbation function was considered, the correct partition was selected for 15 out of 18 hypothesized scene objects. When the perturbation function was not considered, the correct partition was selected

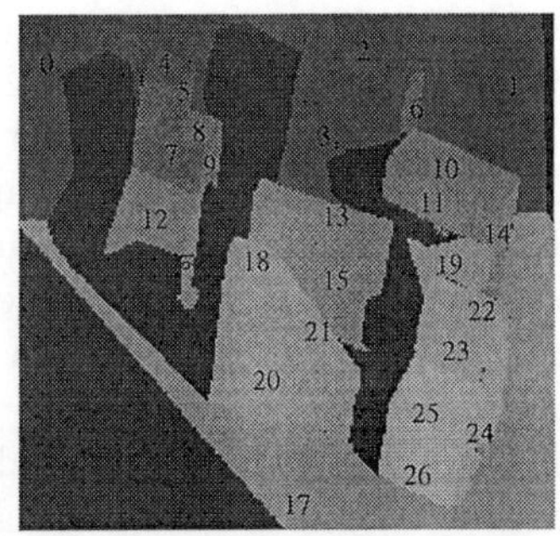

SURFACE CLUSTERS

SC1 = {4, 5, 7, 8, 9, 12, 16}
SC2 = {22, 23, 24, 25, 26}
SC3 ={2, 3, 6}
SC4 = {13, 15}
SC5 = {18,21,20}
SC6={10,11, 14,19}

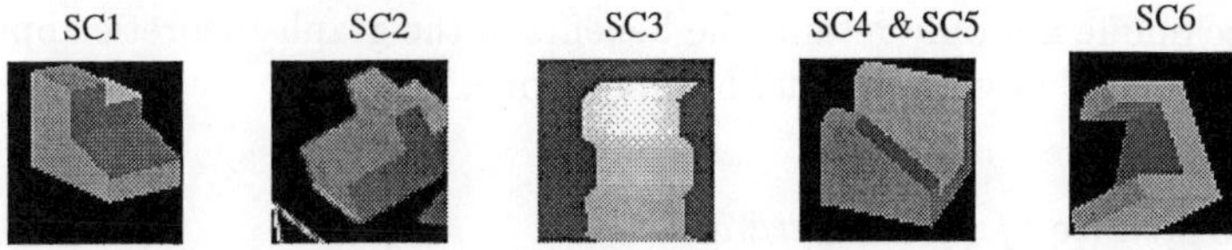

Figure 7: The cluttered, segmented range image. We list the surface clusters extracted from the image. The bottom row shows the CAD models for each of the clusters.

only 5 out of 18 times. *This dramatically underscores the neccessity of modeling the effect of perturbation on the probability density functions of the eigenvalues.*

6.4 Embedded Geometric Hashing on a 35-Object Modelbase

We first implemented the hashing strategy on an organized modelbase of 35 models. Starting from the hash arrays of individual models, we created hash array HA1 corresponding to the root RPSD of the organized modelbase. For comparison, we also created a second hash array HA2 such that the entries are the (Model, Triple) pair for every model in the library. This is basically the nonmerged version of the root RPSD hash array, or "normal" geometric hashing for the same set of models.

The number of different surface triples in HA1 is just 834, compared to 7416 in HA2, for a reduction of nearly 90%. This set of models has a preponderance of surfaces meeting at right angles, so some locations in HA2 are heavily overpopulated even though we discard basis triples having a zero triple product. This problem is mitigated in HA1 because of the merging of similar triples at each location in the hash array. *The merged hash array is both more sparsely and more uniformly occupied than the "regular" array.* Both of these attributes are highly desirable for speed and accuracy.

In our tests on this modelbase, embedded hashing enjoyed a typical advantage over standard hashing of 8:1 in verification load. Voting typically reduced the verification load by 20% in either array. Of course, the exact improvement in any given situation depends on the range and number of shapes in the modelbase. The speedup in finding the root RPSD match ranged from more than 2:1 to nearly 150:1 with respect to our standard structural matcher, itself reasonably fast. Actual root match times, including everything, ran from just over one second to just under 50 seconds.

We should note that HA2 (conventional geometric hashing) identifies a particular model, while HA1 (hybrid scheme) only identifies a modelbase partition (or a small set of partitions). However, the time taken for tree search in our system is virtually negligible alongside these other values. Thus, the hybrid technique not only retains the benefits of the graph-theoretic approach, it is also faster than conventional hashing alone.

6.5 A Modelbase of 115 Polyhedral Objects

Next we conducted recognition experiments using a modelbase of 115 polyhedral objects, divided into seven partitions and organized hierarchically, as above. Since our models have as many as 27 surfaces, for memory considerations we created array entries only for those basis triples whose normals have a nonzero scalar triple product, and having at least two adjacent surface pairs. Any model triple receiving at least one vote qualified for verification.

We first conducted experiments on several range images containing a single object. Voting times ranged from 3.47 to 17.91 seconds, and the time to complete the evaluation and tree search ranged from 2.91 to 14.47 seconds. The correct model RPSD was selected in all cases but one. Owing to serious segmentation errors in this case, the match from the PSD to the root RPSD of the selected partition was incorrect, so the correct model was not selected by the tree search. Obviously, no recognition method can be expected to work in the presence of seriously flawed low and intermediate level results.

For the cluttered scene shown earlier, six surface clusters were identified: $SC1, SC2, \ldots,$ and $SC6$ (ignoring the background surfaces 0, 1, and 17). The partitions selected for each surface cluster were searched. Since geometric hashing as we do it requires the hypothesized object to have at least four surfaces (three basis surfaces plus one to vote), we could not perform recognition for SC3, SC4, and SC5. For the surface clusters SC1, SC2, and SC6, the basis triples chosen were (4 7 12), (24 25 26) and (10 11 14), respectively. The time taken for voting was 28.92, 53.56, and 31.32 cpu seconds, respectively. Note that for SC2, this number is a little higher because it has to vote into four hash arrays corresponding to its four "favorable" partitions, compared to two each for SC1 and SC6. The time taken for hypothesis evaluation and tree search was 8.33, 274.30, and 4.29 seconds, respectively. The basis triple for SC2 has surfaces meeting at right angles, and therefore a crowded portion of the hash array was accessed, which led to a higher verification load (in each of its four "favorable" partition's arrays). The correct object model was identified for SC1 and SC2, but not for SC6. The object corresponding to SC6 is too heavily occluded to be recognizable.

7 Final Comments

Although presented in the experimental context of range images of CAD models, many of the ideas in this work can be applied or extended to other sensing modalities and object types. In particular, the overall architecture of partitioning and hierarchically organizing structural models according to appropriate dissimilarity measures offers wide promise.

We should point out that in a fully developed, working system, one would not be bound by the initial partition selection result. For instance, suppose the surface grouping algorithm presented a false collection of surfaces to the matcher that yielded a particular partition. While it is possible that the eigenvalue features derived from this set of surfaces mimics those of the partition, it is far less likely that any individual model in the partition will prove a good match once all of the specific object information in the RPSD is considered. So object recognition would correctly fail at that point.

8 References

1. H. Sossa and R. Horaud, "Model indexing: The graph-hashing approach," in *Proceedings of The IEEE Computer Society Conference on Computer Vision and Pattern Recognition*, pp. 811–815, 1992.
2. L. G. Shapiro and R. M. Haralick, "Organization of relational models for scene analysis," *IEEE Transactions on Pattern Analysis and Machine Intelligence*, vol. PAMI-4, pp. 595–602, Nov. 1982.
3. K. Sengupta and K. L. Boyer, "Organizing large structural modelbases," *IEEE Transactions on Pattern Analysis and Machine Intelligence*, vol. 17, pp. 321–332, Apr. 1995.
4. P. J. Flynn and A. K. Jain, "BONSAI: 3D object recognition using constrained search," in *International Conference on Computer Vision*, pp. 263–267, 1990.

5. R. B. Fisher, *From Surfaces to Objects: Computer Vision and Three Dimensional Scene Analysis.* New York: John Wiley and Sons, 1989.
6. S. Sarkar and K. L. Boyer, "Integration, inference, and management of spatial information using Bayesian networks: Perceptual organization," *IEEE Transactions on Pattern Analysis and Machine Intelligence*, vol. 15, pp. 256–274, Mar. 1993. Special Issue on Probabilistic Reasoning.
7. A. K. Jain and R. Dubes, *Algorithms for clustering data.* Information and System Sciences Series, Englewood Cliffs, NJ: Prentice Hall Advanced Reference Series, 1988.
8. G. H. Golub and C. F. V. Loan, *Matrix Computations.* The Johns Hopkins University Press, 1989.
9. K. Sengupta and K. L. Boyer, "Modelbase partitioning using property matrix spectra," Tech. Rep. SAMPL-96-01, SAMP-Lab, Dept. of EE, OSU, January 1996. Accepted to *Computer Vision and Image Understanding.*
10. K. Sengupta, *Object Recognition Using Large Modelbases.* PhD thesis, The Ohio State University, 1996.

ON LEARNING TO RECOGNISE 3-D SHAPE DEFECTS

TERRY CAELLI, EROL OSMAN AND GEOFF WEST
Deparment of Computer Science, Curtin University of Technology,
Perth, Western Australia. 6019
(tmc, erol, geoff)@cs.curtin.edu.au

In this paper we consider the problem of comparing 3D sensed data with models for tolerancing and where the correspondence between models and data needs to be solved in robust and efficient ways. We explore the use of machine learning as an efficient method for solving correspondence, pose estimation as well as automatically generating tolerancing conditions from training data. In particular, we show how a new relational learning technique, termed CRG (Conditional Rule Generation) is well-suited to solve such problems. As an additional but necessary issue, we also consider the use of view-independent covariance methods for the extraction of surface features which are used for determining shape signatures and which correspond to curvature-like surface attributes. Such features are utilized in the relational learning model.

1 Introduction

In general terms the process of inspecting an object for *localized* faults or deformations from known models involves aligning objects to models and making some kind of comparison between corresponding parts (see Requicha[1]). Most approaches to this generally assume that the correspondence aspect of the problem is solved or is assumed to be adequately solved using least squares matching of complete models or their features (see, for example Cootes et al.[2]). The aim of this project was to develop an approach to (3D) surface tolerancing which is capable of (1), extracting surface features which can be physically interpreted with respect to different surface geometries; (2) automatically determining the correspondences between model and data features in an efficient but robust way; and (3), learning tolerence conditions as feature (part) attribute bounds.

Figure 1 illustrates the type of tolerancing model being explored. Key components of this approach involve training the system with known valid, or "correct" models and inducing part and relational attribute bounds which

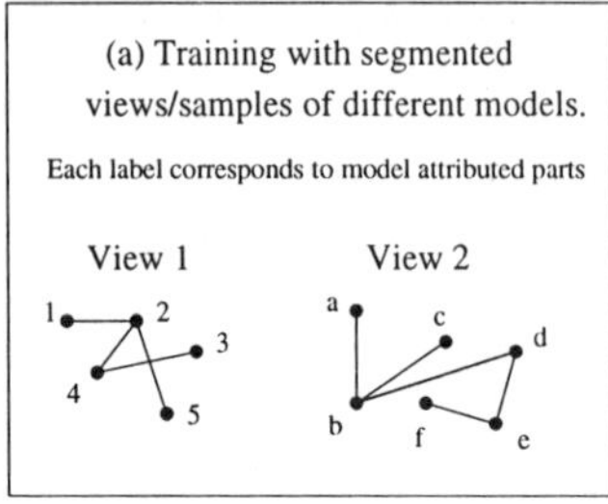

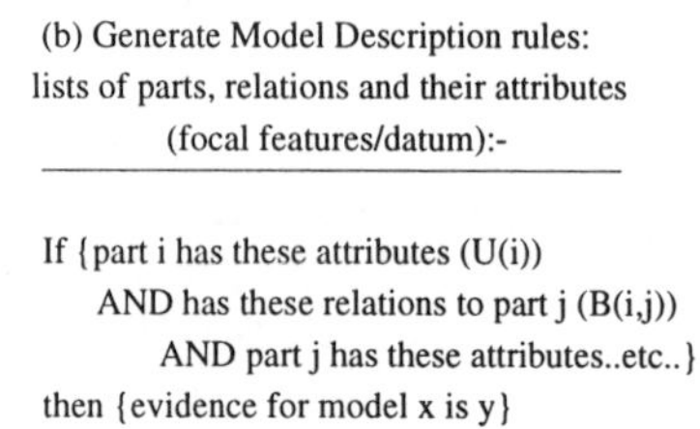

(b) Generate Model Description rules: lists of parts, relations and their attributes (focal features/datum):-
If {part i has these attributes (U(i))
AND has these relations to part j (B(i,j))
AND part j has these attributes..etc..}
then {evidence for model x is y}

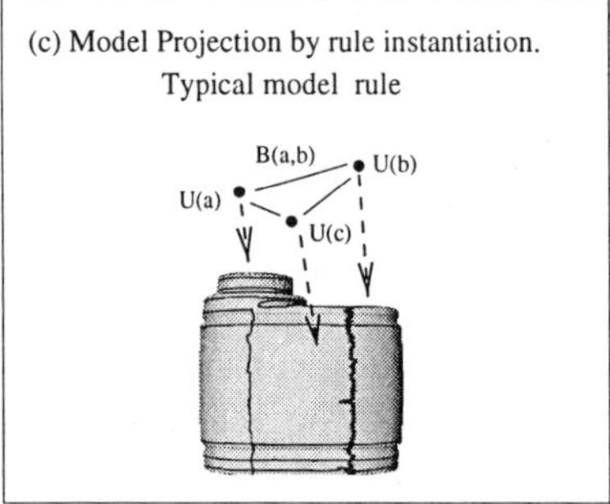

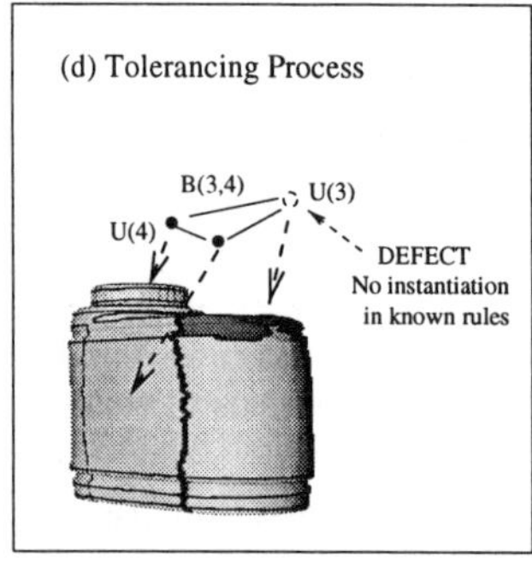

Figure 1: Shows basic outline of the tolerancing system where correspondences between models and data are derived from instantiating relational rules which uniquely define model, example and pose information (U: unary or part attributes; B: binary or relational attributes)

encapulate the training data using least generalisation - that is, restricting attribute bounds not beyond what is presented during training. Detection of faults, then, involves projecting models onto new data via rule instantiation and determining faults from parts which cannot be instantiated in the relational structures learnt during training.

In this approach model samples are defined by labelled and attributed parts and relations - represented by the graphs shown in Figure 1a. Machine Learning (ML) is then used to summarise such positive (acceptable) samples in terms of rules which determine bounds on part and relational attributes which cover all the training data in the form of lists of conjunctions of parts, relations, and their attribute bounds which uniquely define one model (see Figure 2b). Finally, during matching features are extracted from new data which will or will not instantiate rules. New data/objects are rejected if they contain parts/relations which have attributes which do not fall within rule bounds.

Uses of ML to generate object descriptions have typically been restricted to standard Horn clause form (Jain and Hoffman[3]) from decision trees (Quinlan[4]) or neural networks and of the form:

IF (part and/or relations have these attributes)
THEN (evidence for model X is Y)

Although these methods allow for generalisations from training data and, in some cases, recognition from fragments, they are typically not rich enough to encode the full relational nature of models and directly determine the projections of models/samples onto observed data - correspondence. This latter requirement necessitates rule generation techniques which can result in rules of the form:

IF (part a has these attributes
AND is related to part b with those attributes
AND part b has those attributes..etc..)
THEN (it is model X with projections $(X_i -> a; X_j -> b..)$

Defect detection versions of such rules could assume the following form:

IF (part a has these attributes
AND is related to part b with those attributes
AND part b has these attributes..etc..)
THEN (it is model X with projections $(X_I -> a; X_j -> b..etc..)$
AND IF (part c does is not instantiated THEN it is a defect)

These types of rules encapulate two important aspects of tolerancing. One, recognition is initiated by the presence of model fragments, and their relations, which fall within acceptable attribute bounds by model projection using rule instantiation. Two, given such reference features (datum), defects can be detected.

However, such an approach is dependent upon adequate part extraction, data segmentation and the attributes selected. This is particularly problematic for manufactured objects and for range-based sensing where the feature extraction process needs to be sensitive enough to register deformations and discontinuities while, at the same time, encode smooth regions. Problems with the use of (computational) Differential Geometry for characterising range surfaces lie essentially with determining the best form of differentiation to use which can both retain corners and other discontinuities while also encoding smooth surfaces and not be too affected by the typically view-dependent nature of the sensors. In the following section we describe a new view-independent covariance-based feature extraction method to attain such goals. It extracts surface features in terms of the intrinsic eigenstructures extracted from estimates of the surface shape, per se, and not its projections onto a view-dependent plane.

2 View-independent surface feature extraction

View-independent surface eigenstructures are computed by the following procedure. We first define the "surface weighted neighbourhood" (SWN) of a given surface position by a gaussian weighting function of adjacent surface points - using a shortest path on the Deloney triangulation of the points in 3-D. We then determine, at each surface point, the (x, y, z) covariance matrix of the SWN and its eigenstructure. From this, the expected surface normal is determined as the eignevector orthogonal to the other two which form the best-fitting "tangent" plane at the surface point. We then compute the SWN of these "surface normal" eigenvectors to result in second-order covariance eigenvalues which are similar to surface principal curvature(Berkmann and Caelli[5]). For a locally flat (planar) surface, all the normal vectors will map after projection onto the tangent plane into a single point. Accordingly, both eigenvalues will be zero. If the surface is locally developable (parabolic), the projected normal vectors will map onto a line. Therefore one eigenvalue will be non-zero. Finally in the case of a generally curved surface, both eigenvalues will be non-zero. Since the model surface is not view-dependent "jumps" (an other view-dependent surface features) can be simply defined via the degrees to which surface points are isolated from others. For this reason, jump points are labeled by using a threshold on their distance from their nearest neighbours: every point with at least one neighbour further apart than the given threshold is labeled as a jump point.

In this research we have used a CyberScan scanner for obtaining range data. It produces a full 360 degree cylindrical view of objects. With such range sensors and surface descriptors, it is then possible to classify each surface point into one of these different view-independent surface shape types.

Finally, regions were formed by connecting all neighbouring points which have the same label computed by the procedures described above. Regions which were below a certain minimal size and completely surrounded by another region were merged with that region - determining the spatial scale. Otherwise all the points of such a region were labelled invalid - a necessity due to the chararistic of such scanners to produce isolated spurious range values.

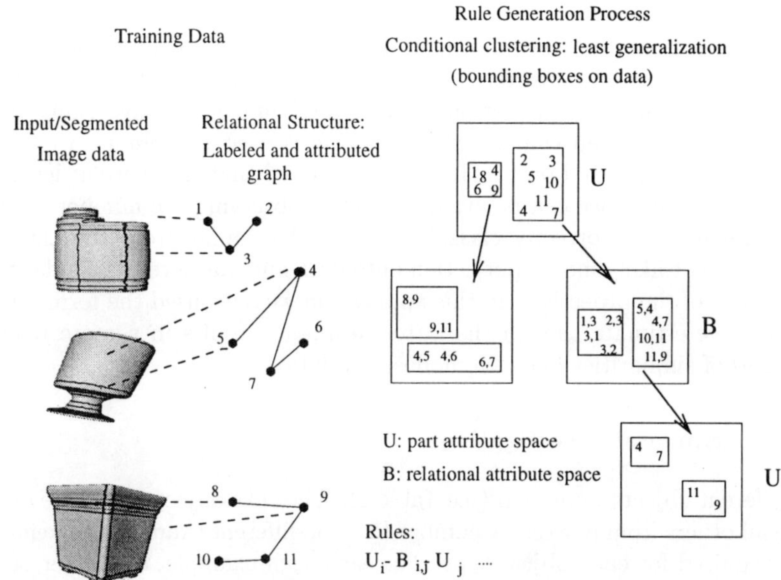

Figure 2: Shows Relational Structure Model for Tolerancing Rule Generation:CRG

3 Relational Learning and Matching

To generate rules we have used Conditional Rule Generation (CRG), a technique for learning structural relations that generates trees of hierarchically organised rules(Bischof and Caelli[6]). The rules are defined as clusters in conditional feature (attribute) spaces which correspond to either unary or binary features of the training data. The clusters in a given attribute space are generated by splitting attributes (partitioning feature spaces) in such a way that each selected attribute splitting operation creates new regions (defining rule bounds) which contribute better evidence for fewer classes. In our approach, such rules (lists of labelled and attributed parts and relations) are generated conditionally through controlled decision tree expansion and a cluster refinement procedure - as shown in Figure 2. For tolerancing it is necessary to use *least generalization*: fitting bounding boxes to just enclose the known data as the essential idea behind this work is that defects constitute examples where the observed attribute values fall beyond what they have been observed to be for a given valid part or relation.

Recognition and Pose Estimation. For matching, CRG rules are activated in a parallel, iterative deepening method. Starting from each scene part, all possible sequences of parts, termed *chains*, are generated and classified using the CRG rules. In this application we have used an evidence averaging model where the set $\mathcal{C}_p$ of all chains that start at p is used to obtain an evidence vector for each observed part p. It should be noted that there are at least two ways that performance can be evaluated. One, observing the number of parts which are initially correctly classified. Two, determine, from the classified parts the most likely model porjection onto data and measure the similarity or correctness of the proection. In this application we have used the former more conservative estimate though the latter technique results in a more realistic measures of similarities between modes and data.

4 Experimental Investigations

Six different objects were used (see Table 1). The cake object was made of wax while all others from plastic. A number (5-7) of different example range images were acquired for each object type. For each such example, a number of features were extracted by varying the feature extraction thresholds around those set by "expert" judgement to result in identifiable parts (see Table 2). Features from the examples without defects were used to train the CRG system and the resultant rules were used to determine whether new objects had defects or not. In this case, the defects were generated by heat treating the object and typical examples are shown in Table 1. As shown, we were only interested in local deformations which are difficult to analyse using more traditional tolerancing and pattern recognition schemes.

Unary(part or region) attributes consisted of the principal components (ensemble (x, y, z) covariance eigenvalues computed over the complete region), means and variances of the two second-order covariance eigenvalues. The binary attributes between two regions included the difference between the average of the eigenvalues and their variance; the distance between part centroids and their area ratios. Each object was characterised by the number of segmented regions, number and range of defects, number of valid regions which were recognised correctly (hits) and the number of defect regions were recognised correctly (correct rejections). Results are shown in Table 2.

5 Discussion

In this paper we have primarily explored how to use a relational learning paradigm to develop a surface tolerancing model with particular interest in

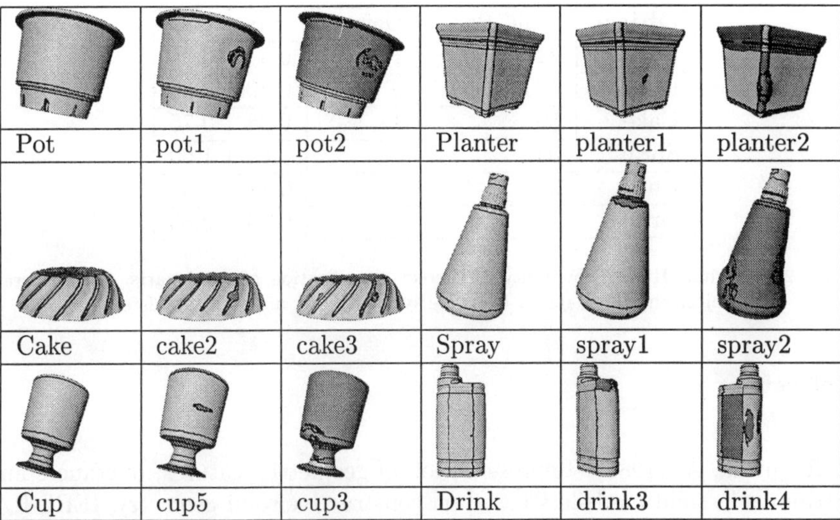

Table 1: Example models and defects

the detection and registration of different types of surface defects. Though not essential we have used Cyberscan cylindrical range maps which yield quite accurate and 360 deg. range data for objects. Our results demonstrate the feasibility of this approach and raises, we believe, a novel computational view of the complete tolerancing process - one which is derived from a common-sense approach to comparing models to data: automatically aligning the data to known critical features and then comparing model parts and relations via comparing attribute bounds which are known (learnt) to evidence different models, views or samples - with data parts.

Object	Valid Parts	Defects	Hits	CR
Pot	21	7	0.5	0.71
Planter	103	9	0.89	0.86
Cake	59	12	0.98	0.75
Spray	54	5	0.64	1.00
Cup	93	10	0.71	0.80
Drink	106	7	0.89	0.86

Table 2: Results. Hits: Probability of correct classification of valid parts. CR (Correct Rejection): Probability of correctly identifying a defect as a defect

References

1. Requicha, A. (1986). Representation of geometric features, tolerances and attributes in solid modellers based on constructive solid geometry, IEEE-RA, 2, 3, 56-165.

2. Cootes, T. , Taylor, C., Cooper, D. and Graham, J.(1992) Training models of shape from sets of examples , *BMVC-92*, 8-18.

3. Jain, A. and Hoffman, D. (1988) Evidence-based recognition of objects, *IEEE Transactions on Pattern Analysis and Machine Intelligence*,

4. Quinlan, J.R.(1993) *C4.5 Programs for Machine Learning*, San Mateo: Morgan Kaufman.

5. Berkmann, J. and Caelli, T.(1994) Computation of Surface Geometry and Segmentation using Covariance Techniques. *IEEE: Transactions on Pattern Analysis and Machine Intelligence*16, 11, 1114-1116.

6. Bischof, W. and Caelli, T. (1994) Learning structural descriptions of patterns: A new technique for conditional clustering and rule generation, *Pattern Recognition*, vol. 27, pp. 689-698.

FORMAFLUENS: A TOOL FOR DESCRIBING EVOLVING FORMS

F. CAPOBIANCO and V. CANTONI
Dipartimento di Informatica e Sistemistica
Pavia University
Via Ferrata 1, 27100 Pavia, Italy
e-mail: {capo | cantoni}@ipvvis.unipv.it
http://iride.unipv.it

In this paper we will present a new language for describing forms evolving in time: FORMAFLUENS. Following an approach for the construction of shapes oriented towards the description of the evolution, we will introduce a grammar. The derived language is composed of a set of production rules based on natural criteria which control the shape changes in time. On the basis of the language, we will propose an environment for the development and the programming of the evolution. After creating an initial form on the screen, the user can interactively modify the shape acting on some critical points (the curvature extrema) or writing code lines directly: in both cases the rules applied are memorized automatically, thus creating a program. Thereafter the program can be executed thus creating an animation of the evolution.

1 Introduction

Forms synthesis is a principal aspect of Computer Graphics; therefore many tools have been developed which allow the user to draw a curve and to modify it interactively. Often the user can modify the shape by dragging and dropping a point on the curve or on the control polygon: this is a "free" approach to the problem which lacks of a theory guiding the evaluation of the shape.

An alternative approach to form construction, oriented towards describing the evolution, introduces a grammar and a language for describing the shape changes in time: rules based on natural criteria bound the evolution of the shape.

The FORMAFLUENS project, which began in 1994, was stimulated by the need of study and expansion on this theory, together with the desire of experimenting its application. As a result, the development of an interactive environment for studying and describing evolving forms has been pursued.

On the basis of the new approach, the user needs to modify a shape following natural criteria: we can assume that the contour of a shape has been created by different processes acting on it, both internal and external. Note that these processes are applied only on the critical points of the shape (curvature extrema): form evolution is based on the modification of these processes. Thanks to the interaction mechanisms of the FORMAFLUENS graphic interface, the simulation of the natural evolution of a shape becomes easy and immediate, allowing for the development of many interesting applications.

2 The FORMAFLUENS language

FORMAFLUENS was inspired by the studies of Michael Leyton [1] about the psychological relation between shapes and time. FORMAFLUENS extends the grammar proposed by Leyton and quantifies the description of the evolution, introducing a metric. The evolution from purely qualitative becomes quantitative, in space and in time. The shape is defined on the screen by some control points (curvature extrema) and evolves following specific production rules: the contour of the forms is modified by applying the rules.

FORMAFLUENS introduces a description language, based on the new grammar: it is thus possible to program the evolution of the shape. The program can be memorized and executed: the execution results as an animation of the shape evolution on the screen.

2.1 Preliminary statements

The theory is based on the assumption that all the shapes are "natural": only forms with a smooth contour and no self-intersection are considered.

Figure 2.1 shows a shape with its curvature function, described by a parameter moving around the contour clock-wise. As shown in the figure, we assign a name to the curvature extrema; every extremum has a semantic interpretation as follows (Semantic Interpretation Role, [1]):

- Positive maximum M+ : protrusion
- Positive minimum m+ : squashing
- Negative maximum m- : indentation
- Negative minimum M- : internal resistance

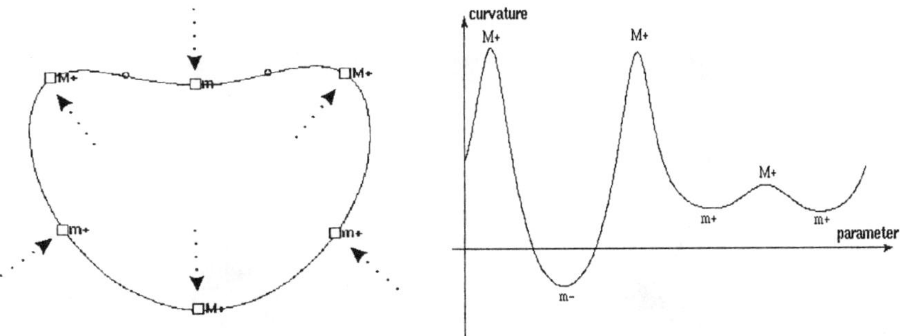

Fig. 2.1. **a)** Extrema and symmetry axes of a shape; **b)** the curvature function of the shape

Note in figure 2.1a the symmetry axes (drawn with a dotted line) terminating at the extrema: thanks to the Symmetry-Curvature Duality Theorem and the Interaction Principle is possible to state [1]:

Each curvature extremum implies a process whose trace is the unique symmetry axis associated with, and terminating at, that extremum.

Until now, we have explained the evolution processes that have occurred in the past: as we have seen, these processes operated only on the extrema. Symmetry axes can be seen as the memory of the evolution. Extending this consideration, we could state that extrema are the critical point of the shape on which the evolution process will tend to operate even in the future.

2.2. The FORMAFLUENS grammar

Let us propose a first quantification of the theory: we assign a name and a "physical" position on the screen to every extrema of a shape, thus univocally determining a form in the 2D domain. As shown in figure 2.2, every extremum has a name and a pair of values (x,y). It is now possible to distinguish the curve from the definition of its string:

"(A M+ 491 108) (B m+ 473 234) (C M+ 351 324)
(D m+ 208 253) (E M+ 175 108) (F m- 326 109)"

The past history of the evolution is completely reassumed in this string.

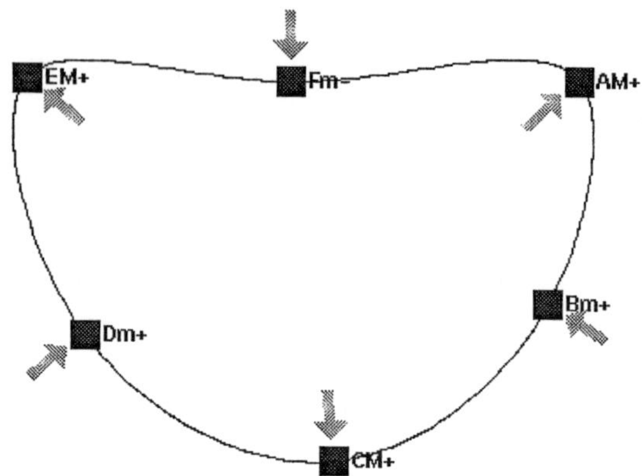

Fig. 2.2. A shape in FORMAFLUENS: curvature extrema with a name and a position in the 2D domain.

It is now possible to define the production rules of the FORMAFLUENS grammar: these rules control the evolution of the shape in *space* and *time*.

The elementary rule syntax will be:

name_production name_extremum type_extremum (direction, speed, time-length)

As already shown, productions are applied on the curvature extrema, which are characterized by a name and a type; a production can be seen as the result of a process action on the extremum.

The process acts in a direction on the screen with a certain speed; it lasts for a certain length of time. The distance can be calculated by multiplying speed and time-length; by adding the direction, we can determinate the new position of the extremum on the screen.

The grammar is composed by three different primitives: continuation, variation and bifurcation.

Continuation

A continuation on an extremum exists when the process which acted on the extremum continues without changing the nature of the critical points. In fig. 2.3 we can see a continuation on a the extremum A M+: the extremum changes its position from (xs,ys) to (xf,yf). This happens because of a process in the direction shown by the θ angle (defined in degree and growing clockwise), with a speed *s* and time-length *t*.

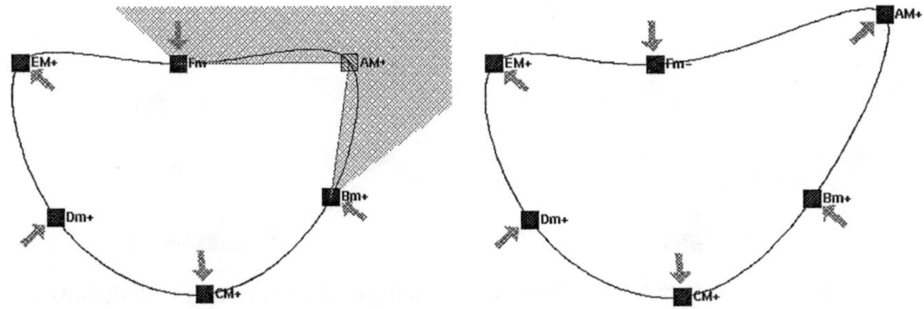

Fig. 2.3. A continuation on A M+: **a)** beginning of the production with definition of the allowable zone; **b)** conclusion of the production with the extremum in the new position.

It is possible to apply the continuation on every type of extremum: as an example let us consider the continuation on the extremum A M+ shown in figure 2.3:

$$continuation\ A\ M{+}\ (\theta,s,t) : A\ M{+}\ (xs,ys) \rightarrow A\ M{+}\ (xf,yf)$$

The user should only provide the name of the extremum and the parameters (θ,s,t) or the final position (xf,yf).

Note that with a continuation the extremum preserves its type, which is a distinctive feature of the production: the protrusion remains a protrusion. Furthermore, note the *allowable zone* for the continuation in figure 2.3a; this is a basic limit when applying a production. If the extremum exits from the allowable zone, a nearby extremum will change its type: this is not allowed by the continuation rule and cannot be admitted.

Variation

Variation is the second type of production: it is a continuation with a modification (variation) of the type of the extremum. It is possible to apply a variation on only two types of extremum, m+ and M-:

$$variation\ B\ m{+}\ (\theta,s,t) : B\ m{+}\ (xs,ys) \rightarrow B\ m{-}\ (xf,yf)$$

A variation on the extremum B m+ is shown in figure 2.4: the squashing m+ becomes an indentation m-.

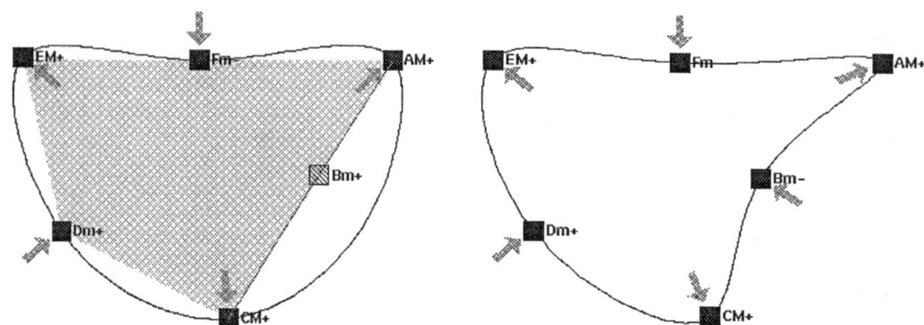

Fig. 2.4. A variation on B m+: **a)** beginning of the production with definition of the allowable zone; **b)** conclusion of the production with the new extremum m- in the new position.

Bifurcation

The last type of production is bifurcation. Imagine a new process acting in the opposite direction of the process which generated the A M+ extremum in figure 2.5: there will be a bifurcation of the existing process. Therefore two new extrema will be generated: bifurcation is the only production which increases the number of the extrema.

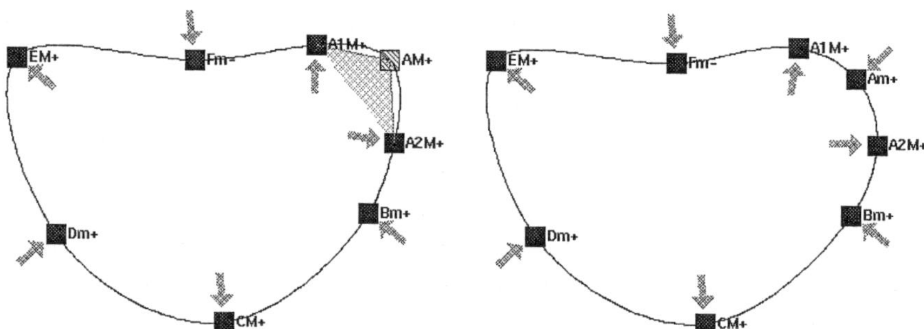

Fig. 2.5. A bifurcation on A M+: **a)** beginning of the production with definition of the allowable zone; **b)** conclusion of the production with the two new extrema.

It is possible to apply a bifurcation to every type of extremum: as an example, let us consider the bifurcation on the extremum A M+, shown in figure 2.5:

bifurcation A M+(θ,s,t) : A M+ (xs,ys) → A1 M+ (xf1,yf1) A m+ (xf2,yf2) A M+ (xf3,yf3)

A new process opposes the protrusion A M+ bifurcating its process.

Two new extrema, A1 and A2, are generated.

The grammar provides four types of bifurcation:

M+ → M+ m+ M+
m+ → m+ M+ m+
M- → M- m- M-
m- → m- M- m-

3 The interactive environment

FORMAFLUENS is a language for describing evolving forms, but is also a development environment, both visual and interactive: the user can synthesize a shape visually and apply the production described in the previous paragraph on its extrema.

3.1 The Insertion Mode

In Insertion Mode the user can create the initial form, by inserting the points of its control polygon on the screen; thereafter he/she can move these points, modifying the contour of the shape. Technically, we use NURBS (Non Uniform Rational B-Spline) [2] for describing this form: therefore the user moves the points of the control polygon of the NURBS, changing the description of the shape [3].

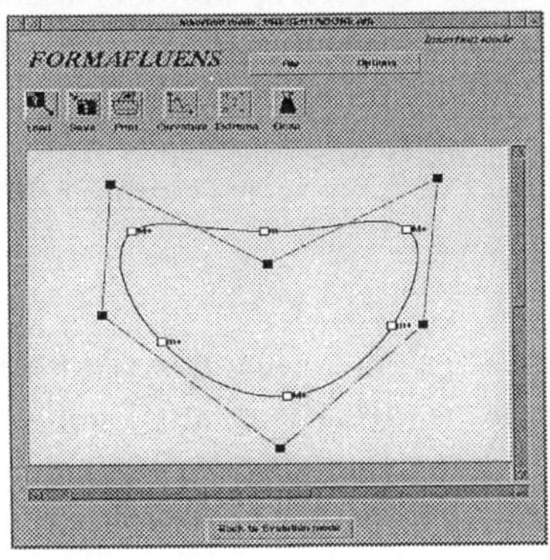

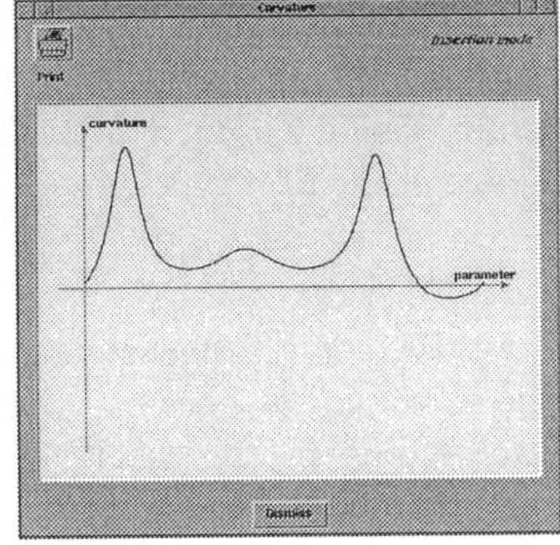

Fig. 3.1. The curvature function and the extrema on the shape in Insertion Mode.

Thanks to the analytical description of the NURBS, we are able to calculate the curvature function, which is visualized in a separate window. The curvature extrema (local maxima and minima) can be calculated automatically as well and visualized on the contour of the shape, as shown in figure 3.1.

3.2 The Evolution Mode

After creating the shape in Insertion Mode, the user can import it into Evolution Mode; thereafter he/she can modify the form applying the production of the FORMAFLUENS grammar. Two ways are proposed for shape manipulation: one interactive and one by direct coding. Technically, the shape in Evolution Mode is a Spline in tension [4], with the curvature extrema defining the control points and a fixed tension parameter.

3.2.1 Interactive evolution

In Evolution Mode, the user can click on a curvature extremum and choose a production rule. Thereafter, he/she can drag and drop the extremum in the new position (in the allowable zone). The program automatically calculates direction, speed and time-length: the last parameter can be inserted by hand, thus allowing more flexibility in the evolution [5][6].

A line code is generated automatically: therefore, the user *visually programs the evolution*. Myers divides visual languages in two main categories [7]: languages for Visual Programming and languages for Program Visualization. FORMAFLUENS in Interactive Evolution is a language of the first type.

3.2.2 Evolution by direct coding

In addition to interactive evolution, there is a second way of acting on the extrema: the user can write code lines directly ay any moment. A tool for aiding in the insertion of code has been developed: the user selects the name of the extremum and the production. Thereafter, using the three widgets shown in figure 3.2, he selects the direction, the speed and the time-length of the production. The extremum is automatically moved to the position determined by the parameters; when the user presses the 'End Production' button, the new line of code is inserted into the area below the widget.

All the program lines inserted (both visually and with direct coding) until now are shown in this area.

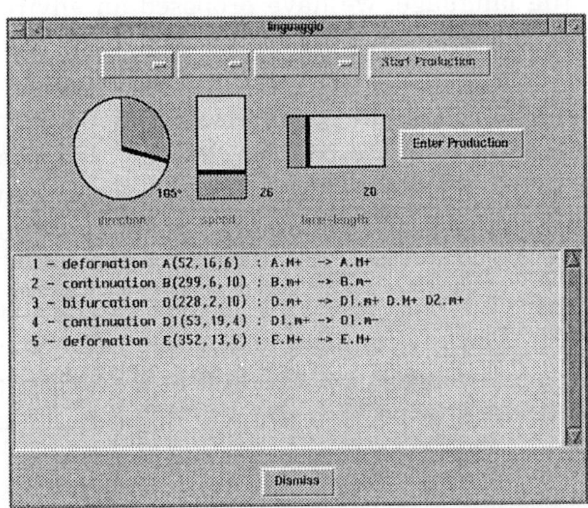

Fig. 3.2. The window for the direct coding of the program.

Looking at the classification of visual languages by Myers, as we have done previously, FORMAFLUENS can be inserted in the languages for Program Visualization as well, thanks to this second way of interaction.

3.2.3 The animation of the evolution

At the end of the code insertion, the user can execute the resulting program: an animation of the evolution, from the first form to the last one is presented on the screen. The frames between two shapes (separated by a production) are calculated with an interpolation: imagine the extremum moving along the direction which connects its position before and after the production [8]. The user can control the animation by using a tool similar to a VCR control.

4 Conclusions

We have presented a new language for describing forms evolving in time: FORMAFLUENS. We have introduced a grammar and a language by following an approach to construction of shape oriented to the description of the evolution. A set of production rules based on natural criteria control the shape changes in time.

Based on the language, we have proposed an environment for the development and the programming of the evolution. After creating an initial form, the user can interactively modify the shape acting on the extrema: the rules applied are memorized, thus creating a program (Visual Programming). It is also possible to write code lines directly: the system visualizes the results on the shape (Program Visualization). In both cases the user can execute the program, animating the evolution.

FORMAFLUENS can be used for creating animation of shapes in a natural way: the evolution is based on production rules created using a cognitive approach. The environment allows the testing and set-up of the theory, assuring an "evolution" of the FORMAFLUENS project. As an example, we are developing an algorithm for determining all the possible evolutions from one shape to a second one. Moreover, we are adding macros to the language for parallel execution of production (code lines). Finally, we intend to extend our theory to the third dimension.

5 References

[1] Michael Leyton, *Simmetry, Causality, Mind*, , MIT Press, 1992.

[2] Gerald Farin, *Curves and Surfaces for Computer Aided Geometric Design*, Academic Press, 1988.

[3] Leslie Piegl, "On NURBS: A Survey", *IEEE Computer Graphics and Applications*, pp.55-71, Jan. 1991.

[4] D.Schweikert, "An interpolation curve using spline in tension", *Journal of Math. and Phys.*, N.45, pp.312-317, 1966.

[5] E.T.Y. Lee, "Choosing the Nodes in Parametric Curve Interpolation", *Computer Aided Design*, Vol.21, N.6, , pp.589-602, Jul./Aug. 1988

[6] A.Cline, "Curve fitting in one and two dimensions using spline under tension", Comm.ACM, N.17, pp.218-223, 1974.

[7] Brad A. Myers, "Visual Programming, Programming by Example, and Program Visualization: A Taxonomy", in *CHI '86 Proceedings*, pp.59-66, 1986.

[8] G.Wolberg, *Digital Image Warping*, IEEE Computer Society Press, 1990.

GAZE TRACING BY EYE PUPIL REMAPPING USING COMPUTER VISION

C. COLOMBO
*Dipartimento di Elettronica per l'Automazione,
Via Branze 38, I-25123 Brescia, Italy*

A. DEL BIMBO
*Dipartimento di Sistemi e Informatica,
Via Santa Marta 3, I-50139 Firenze, Italy*

Gaze shifts encode relevant information on human attention and intention. In this paper, we address the problem of using computer vision to infer the location currently observed by a user placed in front of a computer screen. The proposed solution both provides a convenient way of monitoring ocular activity and suggests a method for mimicking the basic functionalities of a computer mouse using an inexpensive camera and eye-gaze information.

1 Introduction

During its normal activity, the physical apparatus of the human visual system is restless in the effort of exploiting at best the high resolution characteristics of the fovea centralis: visual inspection and world object recognition are accompanied by continuous shifts of gaze fixation.[1] Gaze shifts reflect the mental conditions of a subject, and encode relevant information on human attention and intention.[2]

Besides the simple machine monitoring of ocular activity used in psychophysics and in the medical diagnosis of eye pathologies,[3] *gaze tracing* — i.e. inferring the world locations currently observed — has important applications, ranging from market analysis and usability engineering (measuring the satisfaction of possible purchasers and users of new products) to the design of advanced human-computer interfaces.[4]

Most of the gaze tracing devices are head mounted eyetrackers with some embedded infrared systems, provided with a transmitter and a receiver, which evaluates the current pupil position;[5] similar principles are exploited in the "what you look at is what you get" strategy to infer where the user is looking using infrared light equipment;[6] other systems use either special light-emitting contact lenses or electrodes placed around the eye, which measure the contraction of the ocular muscles.[7] Much work still remains to be done with such devices, which are often very accurate but also quite expensive, intrusive and not comfortable to use.

Recently, the growth of computing power, the decrease of hardware costs and the development of specific algorithms and techniques have encouraged the use of computer vision as a non intrusive technology for advanced human-machine interaction. Experiments have been carried out using computer vision for localizing and tracking user body parts such as head, arms, hands, lips and eyes.[8,9] Some attempts have also been made to assign a semantics to the spatial configurations and temporal evolution of the tracked parameters, with the purpose of performing a visual analysis and graphical re-synthesis of human action.[10,11]

In this paper, we present a computer vision approach to gaze tracing, where the world surface of interest is the screen of a computer with its 2D graphic content. Both eyes are continuously tracked in images, eye pupil shifts are intercepted, and *remapped* onto the screen plane so as to infer the screen location currently pointed by the user. This provides an effective, contactless and non intrusive way of monitoring gaze and ocular activity. By turning eye-gaze information into an input command and providing the user with a direct visual feedback of his action, the approach can be conveniently used to define a non conventional human-machine interaction device based on *ocular pointing* and mimicking the basic functionalities of a computer mouse.

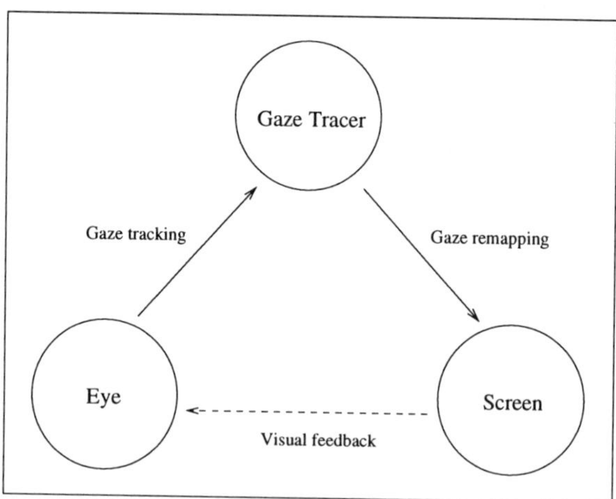

Figure 1: Gaze tracing.

2 Vision Based Gaze Tracing

Interaction. Fig. 1 illustrates the basic operations in our vision based gaze tracing approach. While the user interacts with the on-screen graphics, his gaze shifts are intercepted, tracked and finally interpreted (remapped) as screen locations by a gaze tracing module. The inferred screen location can be visualized by the graphics, thus providing the user with a visual feedback of his own activity: such a condition is useful when gaze is used as an input command for human-computer interaction, e.g. to open a window, or to draw in the screen.

As the user is placed in front of a computer screen, we assume that his gaze activity corresponds mainly to saccadic scan-paths[1] accompanied by small oscillations of the head in a plane parallel to the screen.[a] The observed screen point changes, then, according to both the orientation of the user's visual axis and the head's position.

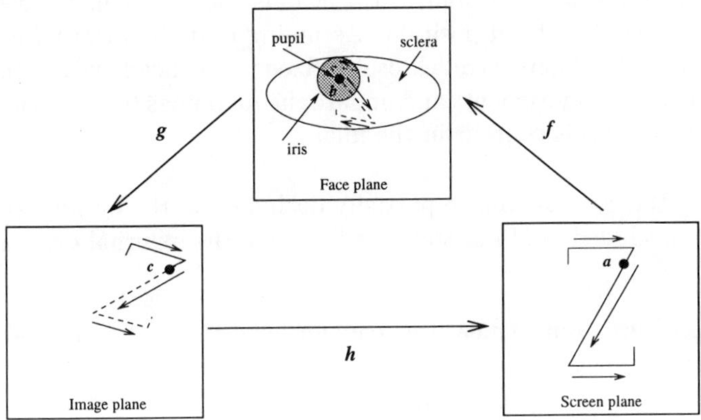

Figure 2: Geometry of gaze tracing.

Some important geometric aspects of gaze tracing are summarized in Fig. 2, showing the content of image, screen and face planes as the user inspects sequentially the outline of a Z-shaped pattern displayed in the screen.

1. Modeling the user's face (save the nose) as a plane has the effect of regarding eyeball rotations, corresponding one-one to gaze shifts, as translations in this plane.

[a] To optimize interaction, the user naturally tends to keep the face parallel to the screen.

2. From a purely geometric viewpoint, the face plane can be regarded as the image plane of *a camera with only one photo-sensitive element*, which is allocated to the pixel corresponding to the current pupil position (point $\boldsymbol{b}$ in the figure).

3. We assume an affine camera approximation [12] for both the screen-to-eye and eye-to-camera projections $\boldsymbol{f}$ s.t. $\boldsymbol{b} = \boldsymbol{f}(\boldsymbol{a})$ and $\boldsymbol{g}$ s.t. $\boldsymbol{c} = \boldsymbol{g}(\boldsymbol{b})$. As a result, the map $\boldsymbol{h}$ which backprojects camera points $\boldsymbol{c}$ onto screen points $\boldsymbol{a}$ is also linear, and defined as the linear map composition

$$\boldsymbol{h} = (\boldsymbol{g} \circ \boldsymbol{f})^{-1}, \quad \boldsymbol{a} = \boldsymbol{h}(\boldsymbol{c}). \tag{1}$$

4. The maps $\boldsymbol{f}$, $\boldsymbol{g}$ and $\boldsymbol{h}$ produce an affine-deformed version of the original pattern, which can undergo scaling, rotation and translation. The maps are time-dependent, as long as the head is allowed to move freely, as they must depend on head position. Assuming that the *external eye contour* (shown in the figure as an ellipse) is fixed to the head, we can in principle monitor head movements and update the mappings by observing the time evolution of this contour in the image.

5. While the eye iris can be partially occluded by the eyelids, the pupil is never occluded, and must always lie inside the external eye contour.

Gaze Tracking. Image measurements for head tracking and pupil detection are obtained by coupling an elastic template with the raw image data provided by the camera. The template models the external eye contour with elliptic arcs and the iris with an ellipse, whose center locates the pupil. At startup, the template is automatically initialized in the image by brightness gradient histogramming, and the approximate location of the eyes is found. At run-time, a visual tracker is started (Fig. 3, *left*), which after a few iterations attains and maintains lock onto the current eye visual appearance (Fig. 3, *right*). The segments perpendicular to the external eye contour shown in Fig. 3 represent the search paths used by the tracker predictor to find the next contour instance. The search range adaptively varies in size on the basis of a measure of the current reliability of edge point estimation. A two-step eye tracking approach is used: the next instance of the external eye contour is first found, thus providing a bound for the subsequent iris/pupil search. Besides the search bound, the current external eye location provides the time-varying information needed to measure and update the affine mapping $\boldsymbol{h}$.

Gaze Remapping. To complete the remapping process, image pupil positions are converted into the corresponding screen locations using an approximation of the affine backprojection map $\boldsymbol{h}$ — carrying metric information on eye-camera-screen interaction — and Eq. 1. This rewrites as:

$$\boldsymbol{a} = \boldsymbol{h}(\boldsymbol{g}(\boldsymbol{0})) + \mathrm{H}\,[\boldsymbol{c} - \boldsymbol{g}(\boldsymbol{0})]\,, \tag{2}$$

where

$$\boldsymbol{h}(\boldsymbol{g}(\boldsymbol{0})) = -\mathrm{F}^{-1}\,\boldsymbol{f}(\boldsymbol{0})\,, \quad \mathrm{H} = \mathrm{F}^{-1}\,\mathrm{G}^{-1}\,, \tag{3}$$

F and G being 2×2 matrices s.t. $\boldsymbol{f}(\boldsymbol{a}) = \boldsymbol{f}(\boldsymbol{0}) + \mathrm{F}\,\boldsymbol{a}$ and $\boldsymbol{g}(\boldsymbol{b}) = \boldsymbol{g}(\boldsymbol{0}) + \mathrm{G}\,\boldsymbol{b}$.[b]

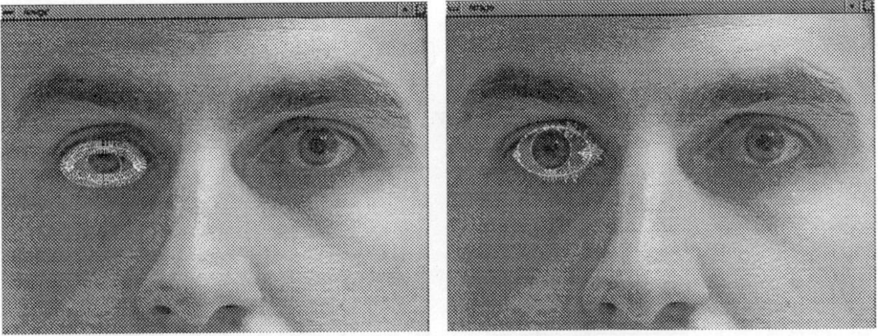

Figure 3: The visual tracker. *Left*: Automatic eye localization and template initialization. *Right*: After locking onto the eye appearance.

Before being used, the affine image-to-screen map $\boldsymbol{h} \Leftrightarrow \{\boldsymbol{h}(\boldsymbol{g}(\boldsymbol{0})), \mathrm{H}\}$ is initially estimated at system startup by means of a two-step *2D-2D calibration* procedure. First, a set of $m \geq 6$ image observations of pupil positions is collected and recorded (to reduce errors during this phase, each new observation is obtained as an average of subsequent image measurements), obtained by tracking the pupil while letting the user execute a sequence of gaze fixations on a number of given screen locations. Then the affine model is estimated, using data and observations, as the least squares solution of an overdetermined system obtained from Eq. 2.

Hence, head motions are not allowed in principle during calibration, as they determine a calibration error which depends on the extent of user displacements. However, the calibration procedure above can be easily extended to explicitly allow head displacements. Let us assume for simplicity that the

[b]By convention, each point is expressed in the native coordinates of the plane it belongs to.

two head translations parallel to the screen are dominant w.r.t. the other two degrees of freedom characterizing frontoparallel interaction (translation perpendicular to the screen, rotation in a plane parallel to the screen plane). Let us also assume that the image and screen planes are approximately parallel, and that the amount of head translation is small enough to allow the user not to rotate the eyeball in order to fixate a same point in the screen. During calibration, head translations can be compensated by normalizing the image plane observations relative to a reference $\boldsymbol{g}(\mathbf{0})$, say $\boldsymbol{g}_1(\mathbf{0})$, corresponding to the first observation. Vectors $\boldsymbol{g}_i(\mathbf{0})$ can be easily estimated in the image as the centroids of the external eye contours at discrete observation times $i = 2 \ldots m$. Compensation is accomplished by properly shifting pupil observations $\boldsymbol{c}_i$ by the amount of image translation of the head:

$$\boldsymbol{c}_i^c = \boldsymbol{c}_i + (\boldsymbol{g}_1(\mathbf{0}) - \boldsymbol{g}_i(\mathbf{0})) \,, \tag{4}$$

thus obtaining the compensated observation points $\boldsymbol{c}_i^c$.

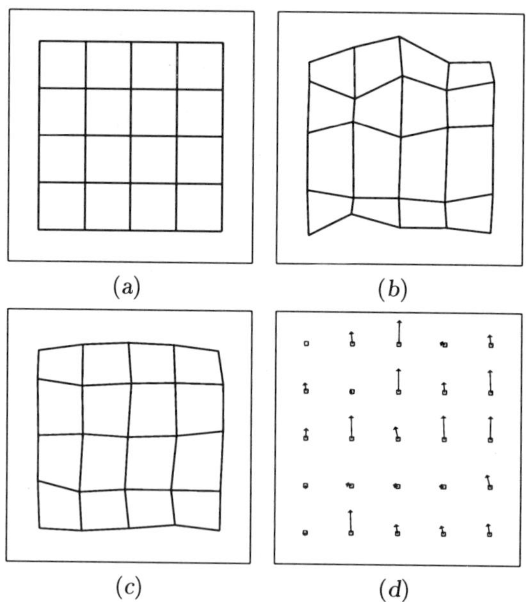

Figure 4: Calibration results. (a): theoretical calibration grid; (b): uncompensated grid; (c): compensated grid; (d): compensation vectors.

Fig. 4 shows the results of a calibration session using $m = 25$.[c] The screen points to be fixated by the user during calibration are arranged in the 5×5 grid shown in Fig. 4 (a). This is also the theoretical grid, since if calibration was perfect, the grid should be exactly reconstructed using image observations and the computed map $\boldsymbol{h}$. Figs. 4 (b,c) show respectively the reconstructed grid without and with compensation. It is evident from the figures that head motion compensation — the correction terms are shown in the needle diagram of Fig. 4 (d) — has a strongly beneficial effect on calibration performance: indeed, a non perfect compensation of head displacements is the major source of error in the remapping process. Another source of calibration errors is related to inaccuracies in the phase of pupil localization: in this respect, zooming with the camera on the user's eye region so as to track better both user eyes and pupils improves system performance.

The calibrated map is also updated at run-time by head motion compensation based on current visual data. To this aim, observe that Eq. 2 can be written at a generic time instant as:

$$\boldsymbol{a}_t = \boldsymbol{h}_t(\boldsymbol{g}_t(\mathbf{0})) + \mathrm{H}\left[\boldsymbol{c}_t - \boldsymbol{g}_t(\mathbf{0})\right], \tag{5}$$

where H is a constant independent of head translation, and the translation term at time t can be expressed as a function of the current (t) and reference ($t = 1$) centroid positions and of the translation $\boldsymbol{h}_1(\boldsymbol{g}_1(\mathbf{0}))$ obtained at calibration:

$$\boldsymbol{h}_t(\boldsymbol{g}_t(\mathbf{0})) = \boldsymbol{h}_1(\boldsymbol{g}_1(\mathbf{0})) + k_t^{-1}\left[\boldsymbol{g}_t(\mathbf{0}) - \boldsymbol{g}_1(\mathbf{0})\right]. \tag{6}$$

Head compensation at remapping time is accomplished by properly updating the translation in Eq. 5 according to Eq. 6. The scaling factor k_t in Eq. 6 equals the ratio of camera focal length and eye centroid depth. It can be measured as the ratio of the external eye width in the image (depending on t as the face moves towards or away from the screen) and in the face plane (a constant).

3 Experimental results

The gaze tracing system has been developed in C, and runs on a Silicon Graphics Indy platform, featuring a MIPS R4000/R4010 processor with a 100 MHz clock. The video acquisition software gets raw image data through a VINO frame grabber board from a B/W camera provided with zoom facilities. With such a setup, gaze tracing runs at video rate (25 Hz). We report on experiments involving the two main operating modes of the system as related to

[c] A higher number of calibration points proves to yield a better accuracy, but also to get the user bored of performing calibration.

the presence or absence of visual feedback (see Sec. 2): *scan-path analysis* and *mouse mimicking.*

Scan-path Analysis. In the scan-path analysis mode, system operation is "transparent" to the user: eye-gaze information is neither traduced into command input, nor a visual feedback of any sort is provided to the user: the remapping precision results obtained in this mode are therefore absolute, in that they are not under the user's control.

In the experiment, the user is asked to point in sequence to the centers of nine screen windows. The windows are identical, equally spaced, and arranged in a grid similar to the 5 × 5 calibration grid used for calibration. Fig. 5 shows the remapped screen points superimposed to the test grid. The figure shows that most of the remapped points are distributed in clusters around the grid points — the outliers correspond to time instants in which the user was performing a shift of fixation.

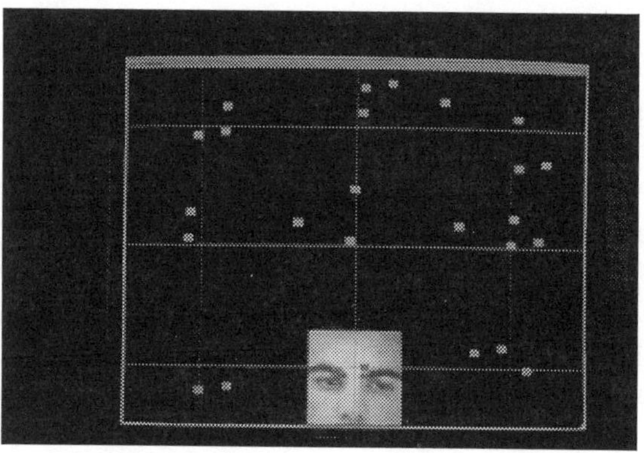

Figure 5: Scan-path analysis experiment.

Quantitative results for this test confirm the importance of doing head motion compensation also at run-time. The average remapping error, i.e. the average of the magnitude mismatch between the "true" points and the remapped ones is about 2 cm in the compensated case and more than the double (4.4 cm) for uncompensated interaction. Magnitude errors provide a resolution limit for the gaze tracing technique.

Mouse Mimicking. In the mouse mimicking mode, an icon indicating the current screen point being observed by the user is displayed in the screen. Thanks to the presence of such a visual feedback, eye-to-screen map calibration is not necessary, and a predefined matrix H of the simple form

$$\mathrm{H} = k\,\mathrm{I} \tag{7}$$

can be used, where I is the 2×2 identity matrix and k is a constant, basically related to the ocular mouse inertia.[d] The image translation term of the mapping, $\boldsymbol{h}(\boldsymbol{g}(\mathbf{0}))$, is easily derived, instead, directly from image data, assuming that at startup the user is fixating the center of the screen. At startup, the user simply "wears" the ocular pointer much in the way he finds the screen icon representing the current mouse position in a predefined location of the screen running a commercial software application. From then on, he is able to displace the icon in the screen at his will according to the given (plausible, yet arbitrary) mapping law, and control, by direct visual inspection, the results of his action.

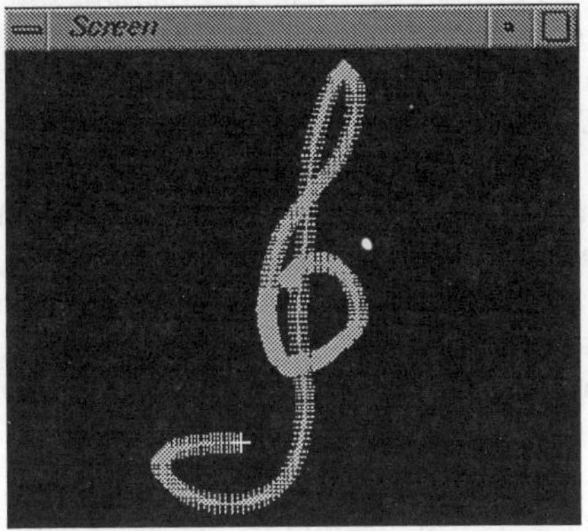

Figure 6: Mouse mimicking experiment.

The pattern of Fig. 6, representing a musical key, was sketched by a non trained user with the ocular mouse. In other tests, we are experimenting with the combined use of eye motion and persistency for producing "eye-written" text on the computer display with word separation. The use of eye pupil as a 2D mouse suggests several advanced interaction applications, such as text and graphics editing based on eye pointing and complemented by advanced pattern recognition facilities like OCR.

[d] Users prefer a pointer with some inertia. This is introduced in the system by low-pass filtering the remapped points before graphic display.

References

1. D. Noton and L. Stark. Eye movements and visual perception. *Scientific American*, 224(6):34–43, 1971.
2. A. Huxley. *The Art of Seeing.* Chatto & Windus, 1943.
3. D. Cleveland and N. Cleveland. Eyegaze eyetracking system. In *Proc. 11th Imagina International Forum on New Images IMAGINA'92*, pages 17–23, 1992.
4. R.J.K. Jacob. What you look at is what you get. *IEEE Computer*, 26(7):65–66, 1993.
5. R. Razdan and A. Kielar. Eye tracking for man/machine interfaces. *Sensors*, pages 39–42, 1988.
6. T.E. Hutchinson, K. Preston White jr. and W.N. Martin, K.C. Reichert, and L.A. Frey. Human-computer interaction using eye-gaze input. *IEEE Transactions on Systems, Man and Cybernetics*, 19(6):1527–1534, 1989.
7. J. Gips, P. Olivieri, and J. Tecce. Direct control of the computer through electrodes placed around the eyes. In *Proc. 5th International Conference on Human-Computer Interaction HCI'93*, pages 630–635, 1993.
8. R. Brunelli and T. Poggio. Face recognition: Features versus templates. *IEEE Transactions on Pattern Analysis and Machine Intelligence*, 15(10):1042–1052, 1993.
9. J.M. Rehg and T. Kanade. Visual tracking of high DOF articulated structures: an application to human hand tracking. In *Proc. 3rd European Conference on Computer Vision ECCV'94*, pages 35–46, 1994.
10. A. Azarbayejani, T. Starner, B. Horowitz, and A. Pentland. Visually controlled graphics. *IEEE Transactions on Pattern Analysis and Machine Intelligence*, 15(6):602–605, 1993.
11. C. Colombo, A. Del Bimbo, and S. De Magistris. Interfacing through visual pointers. In R. Cipolla and A. Pentland, editors, *Computer Vision in Human-Computer Interaction.* Cambridge University Press, 1997 (to appear).
12. J.L. Mundy and A. Zisserman. Projective geometry for machine vision. In J.L. Mundy and A. Zisserman, editors, *Geometric Invariance in Computer Vision.* MIT Press, 1992.

HIERARCHICAL DESCRIPTION AND RECOGNITION OF LINEAR SHAPES

L.P. CORDELLA, P. FOGGIA, C. SANSONE, M. VENTO
Dipartimento di Informatica e Sistemistica
Universita' di Napoli "Federico II"
Via Claudio 21, I-80125 Napoli, Italy
E-mail: {cordel,foggia,carlosan,vento}@nadis.dis.unina.it

The most common approach to shape recognition is based on the definition of a set of classes of interest and of a description method which, applied to the samples of a given population, provides a classifier with the information allowing to assign each sample to one of the defined classes. This goal can be achieved in a single pass or in two or more steps: in a first step, the set of samples is divided into subsets (pool-classes) according to a first level shape description. At each successive step the process is iterated, using description and classification techniques chosen according to the results obtained at the previous step, progressively increasing the selective power of the rules used to attribute a sample to one of the classes of interest. Preliminary results obtained by applying the latter approach to the description and recognition of linear shapes, namely handprinted characters, are discussed.

1 Introduction

Classifying objects according to their shape requires that objects are described in terms of suitable shape features and then grouped into classes, through a supervised or unsupervised classification process. The members of each class should share some uniformity predicates which allow to say that their shapes are similar. At the same time the predicates used to attribute an object to a class should not allow to attribute to the same class objects that, for the purposes of the recognition problem at hand, should be considered dissimilar.

This calls for descriptions detailed enough to allow to discriminate among different shapes, but at the same time so general as to allow not to distinguish among shapes that should be considered similar. The actual difficulty of many practical recognition problems mainly comes from the high variability among the shapes that should be attributed to the same class, which suggests to adopt quite general description schemes, to the detriment of the possibility to discriminate between shapes to be considered different.

Using structural features allows to obtain very expressive shape descriptions, e.g., in terms of attributed relational graphs, nevertheless even in this case it is necessary to find a trade off between generalization power and discrimination power of the adopted descriptions.

Scope of this paper is to present some preliminary results of a hierarchical approach to structural shape description and classification. The family of forms considered is that of ribbon-like shapes, making up documents of any type, from printed and handwritten texts to drawings and maps.[1,2] In particular, handprinted characters were considered: after a preprocessing which transforms the gray level image representation of a character into a set of interconnected circular arcs, a size and rotation invariant first level description of such set is derived.

Both the preprocessing and the first level description techniques devised are aimed at stressing the most general shape features of characters, attempting to smooth insignificant shape variations. This leads to obtain character representations, and then possible descriptions of such representations, which are abstract enough to hold for large sets of real characters. Simple features were used: in spite of their intrinsically structural nature, deliberately, only some of the information about the structure of the representations has been taken into account in the first level description. A first level of classification groups characters sharing similar descriptions into pool-classes which may include one or more different character classes. The discrimination among the classes within a pool-class can be achieved at a successive classification stage using information about more specific features possibly obtained from earlier representation stages.

Two different techniques have been tested to group the descriptions into clusters, both using a decision tree. In the former case, the clustering was completely unsupervised and some simple rules were used to select the feature to be searched for at each new node of the tree. In the latter case, some shape prototypes were defined on the basis of both human experience and observation of the results obtained with a training set of handprinted characters; the tree was then used to assign the descriptions of test characters to the shape pool-classes. In both cases, descriptions didn't need to be identical in order to be assigned to the same cluster, but some degree of similarity was allowed. It has been verified that each of the obtained groups of shapes include a reasonably limited number of different character classes which appear easily separable at successive classification steps by looking for simple differentiating cues.

This preliminary tests only aimed to check the description power of the features derived from the representations achieved with our preprocessing technique and the possible advantages to proceed with a hierarchical approach towards classification. Tests with description made in terms of attributed relational graphs, fully exploiting structural information, and with classification through inexact graph matching methods are in progress.

2 Preprocessing and description phases

Structural description methods[3] are typically based on the decomposition of an initial representation of the objects of interest into simple parts, so that a shape can then be described in terms of these parts, their attributes and of more or less complex relations among them. Both the preprocessing and the decomposition process give place to an image which is a more convenient representation of the initial one, since noise and not significant information have been eliminated and some particular features of the considered objects (characters in our case) have been outlined. Such representation is still susceptible of different descriptions, according to the scope and to the wideness of the class to which a given description has to be attributed.

Descriptions useful to discriminate among a small number of different objects can be much less detailed than descriptions necessary to exactly reconstruct each particular object. Instead, a too detailed description would be detrimental for recognition purposes since it could highlight the differences among objects that one would like to attribute to a same class.

Characters can be considered as ribbon-like shapes whose thickness is not significant, but in a few special cases. Thus, an appealing preprocessing technique for obtaining a synthetic representation of them is thinning. However, to be effective for recognition purposes, the obtained thin lines should preserve the shape of the original ribbons. Unfortunately, this is one of the main problems for almost all the presently available thinning algorithms. In fact, they introduce shape distortions particularly at the join and crossing of strokes. We use an original technique[4] that allows to substitute to the ribbon a polygonal line centered within it and faithfully reflecting its shape.

The polygonal line is then decomposed into pieces with the constraint that each piece can be simply described and at the same time represents a perceptively significant feature of the character. The shape of unconstrained handprinted characters, produced by a large number of writers, shows an extreme variability. Strokes having the same perceptive significance can have quite different shape and size, some strokes may be missed or added with respect to the hypothetical ideal representative of each class, and relative position of strokes may be partially altered. Nevertheless it has to be assumed that such variations are not so dramatic as to destroy the essential features making characters recognizable by a human observer. In order to cope with character variability and to single out the features most characteristic and invariant for members of a shape class, the polygonal line representing a character is decomposed into circular arcs by a fitting algorithm.[5] The circular arc has been chosen since it provides the simplest, but still good approximation of the typical strokes used to form characters. The fitting algorithm leads to represent a character as the union of arc pieces in a transformed plane (l,α), where l is the curvilinear abscissa along the polygonal and α is the angle between each segment of the polygonal and a starting segment. A circular arc in the (x,y) plane is transformed into a straight segment in the (l,α) plane. Moreover the representations in this transformed plane (see fig. 1) are rotation, translation and size invariant, making a recognition system based on them especially suitable for dealing with character strings embedded in technical drawings and geographic maps.

In order to produce descriptions appropriate for the aims of the first classification stage, after this first decomposition of the polygonal into circular arcs, a further step of approximation is performed by joining together, to form a single arc, adjacent arcs that meet suitable criteria. This step, like the previous ones, is aimed at reducing the shape variability among the samples of the same class taking care not to destroy information necessary to properly recognize the sample at successive classification stages. In other words, at the first step, the generalization power of the descriptions is privileged, favouring the confusion among similar forms and discriminating only those significantly different. Obviously, an high degree of approximation allows to group together shapes only approximately similar, however, it is not convenient to proceed with a higher tolerance since the first decomposition step, because the control of the approximation across the critical points would not be adequate. Starting from a preliminary decomposition, merging criteria tailored for the considered class of shapes can be defined. On the other hand, information about the results of the first decomposition step, so as of the preliminary steps of the process, is stored for its possible use in the successive classification stage for discriminating between characters belonging to the same pool-class.

The over-approximation is carried out by examining each pair of adjacent arcs; if a set of conditions (see below) are satisfied, the two arcs are replaced by a new one whose parameters are chosen by minimizing the mean square error in the (l,α) plane. This process is performed iteratively, in the sense that if the arc produced by merge satisfies in its turn the merge conditions, the procedure is applied again, until no more arcs can be merged. Figure 1 illustrates some steps of the decomposition process. The merge conditions ensure that merge is not attempted when the combined shape of two arcs cannot be described in a meaningful way by a single arc, so that merging would cause losing significant information about that part of the sample. The conditions, which must hold simultaneously, for merging a pair of arcs are:

- the function representing the arcs in (l,α) must be monotonic (fig. 2.a, 2.b)
- the two arcs must be connected only by their extremes (fig. 2.c)
- the angle formed by the tangents of the arcs at the contact point must be greater than a given threshold (fig. 2.d)

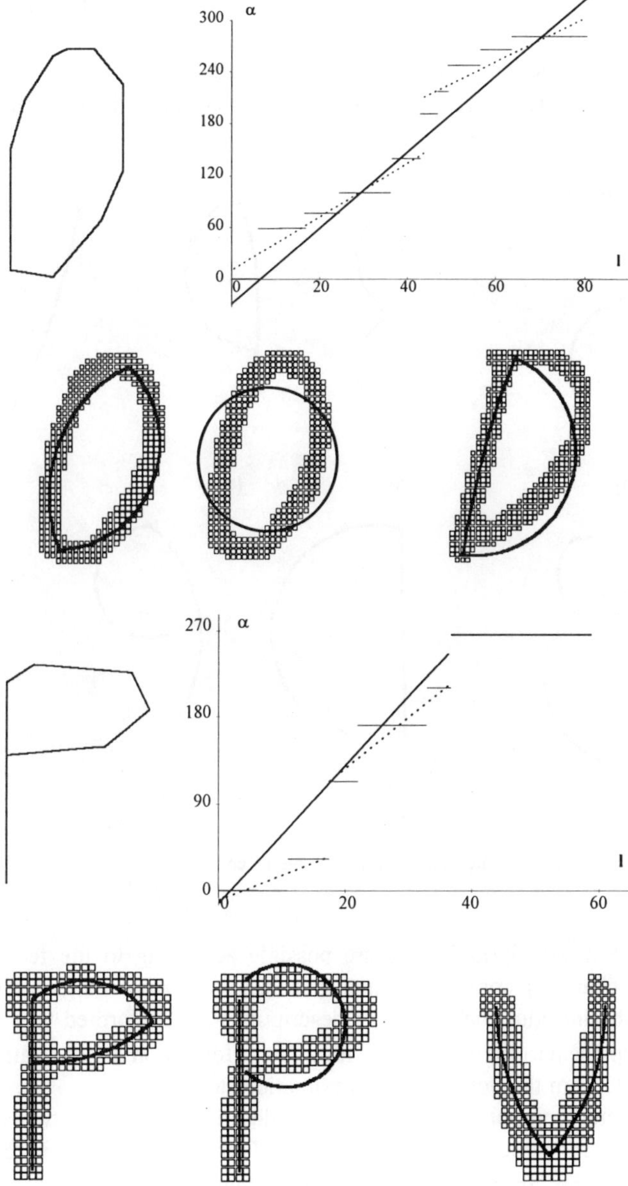

Figure 1: Two shapes and some results of the preprocessing: shape preserving skeleton, representation in the (l,α) plane, first and second step of decomposition into arcs. Two different shapes are also shown for which the over-approximation doesn't take place.

- the union of the two arcs must have no more than two contact points with any other arc (fig. 2.e)
- the arcs must not be long straight segments (fig. 2.f)
- the union of the two arcs must not span over an angle larger than a threshold depending on the relative size of the arcs (fig. 2.g)

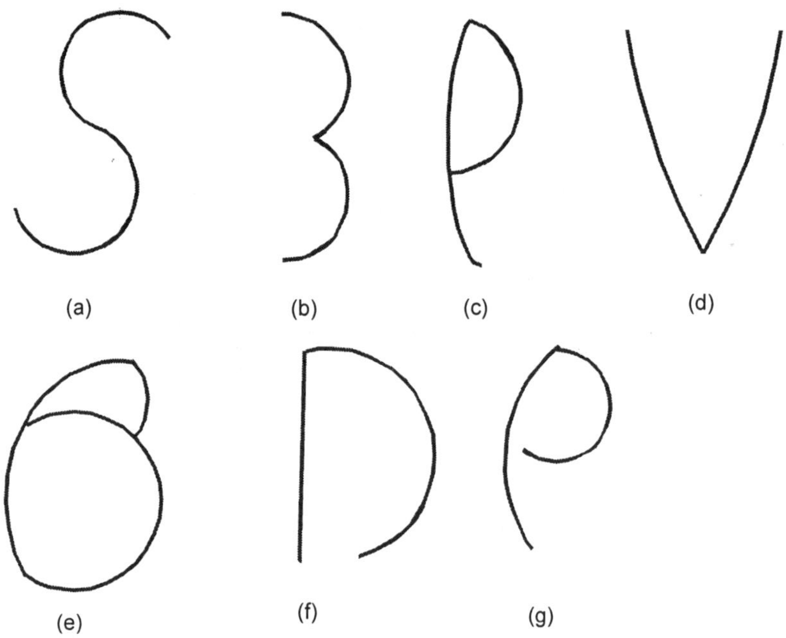

Figure 2: Examples of pairs of arcs not satisfying the merge conditions

Different description levels are possible according to the features used to characterize character components and their relations. According to the guidelines outlined in the introduction, character descriptions are performed with reference to their (l,α) representation, integrated with a few information about relations between arcs, available from the polygonal approximation step.

Character components, i.e. arcs, are described by using two features: the relative size and the angle spanned by the arc. This information is directly available in the (l,α) plane. In this transformed representation the size Δl of an arc is normalized to the size of the character, while the angle spanned by the arc is given by the difference of the α-coordinates of the extremes of the segment.

Table 1: The features used for shape description with their attributes and values. The angle values are assigned only to junctions of the V-like type.

ARCS		JUNCTIONS	
Attributes	**Values**	**Attributes**	**Values**
Size	large medium small	**Type**	T-like V-like X-like
Angular Span	straight bent loop	**Angle**	acute medium obtuse

The relations between arcs are described in terms of number and type of the contact points between them. Three types of contact are described and, in one case, the angle between arcs at the contact point is also measured. All the attribute values of both arcs and their relations are roughly quantized as shown in Table I. Anyway, as already said, the information available at any given step of the process is preserved in a suitable data structure, so as it can be recovered and used if necessary at successive steps.

This description scheme differs from others[6] since it attempts to define groups of shapes among which to discriminate, at successive classification steps, using more specific features, those belonging to the classes of interest.

3 Clustering and experimental results

In principle, there are two possible approaches to the definition of the pool-class prototype descriptions. According to the former, a certain number of prototype descriptions is assumed by the designer on the basis of the knowledge about character shapes. The latter approach leads to automatically define the pool-classes and their associated descriptions on the basis of some clustering algorithm. Both the approaches were tested on 26,000 characters (1,000 per class) from the ETL-1 data base.[7]

According to the latter approach, the pool-classes were defined by means of a symbolic clustering algorithm. The chosen method, a modification of Quinlan's ID3 learning algorithm,[8] builds a decision tree whose leaves represent the clusters in which the data set has been divided, while at non-leaf nodes the presence or absence of a given feature is tested. The path from the root to each leaf can be read as a logical expression that defines the corresponding pool-class description. The feature associated to each node was the one maximizing a goal function related to the information theoretic entropy. At each step of the algorithm, the features are examined separately, i.e. combinations of features are not taken into account. This fact implies that usually the resulting tree is not the optimal one, in the sense that it does not correspond to a global maximum of the goal function. However, the advantage of this method is that its computational cost is quite reduced, while the search of the optimal tree would have an exponential computational complexity. The obtained results obviously depend on the goal function adopted. Tests with several different functions always outlined the same problem: due to the large shape variability in the training set, a large number of pool-classes was produced, and many character classes were spread over several pool-classes. This problem was only partially overcome by merging in a second pass some of the pool-classes, using a criterion based on the similarity of the actual class distribution inside each pool-class. A possible interpretation of this results is that, since the algorithm doesn't use any a priori knowledge about the shape classes present in the data set, it may produce descriptions in terms of features that are unstable and not necessarily meaningful in the sense specified in Chianese *et al.*[6]

The former approach mentioned does not present this drawback, by definition. It was implemented by defining about 20 pool-class prototype descriptions on the basis of the visual examination of the results of the representation phase on a training set of 100 character samples per class. A decision tree classifier was then used to match the descriptions of test samples with the prototypes.

In spite of the simplicity of the prototype descriptions, admitting only a limited variability of the features attribute values, the percentage of characters not attributed to any of the pool-classes was 2.3% over a test set of 23,400 characters (900 per class). The average number of character classes present in a pool-class was about 5, so as the average number of pool-classes per character class (see Fig.3). Examples of typical shapes falling in some of the pool-classes are shown in Fig. 4. An evaluation of the recognition rate potentially achievable using a first classification stage like the proposed one has been performed in the following way. On the basis of the results obtained with the training set, to each pool-class the class labels of the characters assigned to it were associated. A label was not assigned if the percentage of characters of the corresponding class falling in a pool-class was less than 3%. Then, the characters of the test set were submitted to the classifier and consequently assigned to the pool-classes. Finally, it was checked if the identity of each character coincided with one of the labels of the pool-class it was assigned to. The percentage of unexpected characters assigned to a pool-class, representing the classification error of the first stage, was 4.7 %.

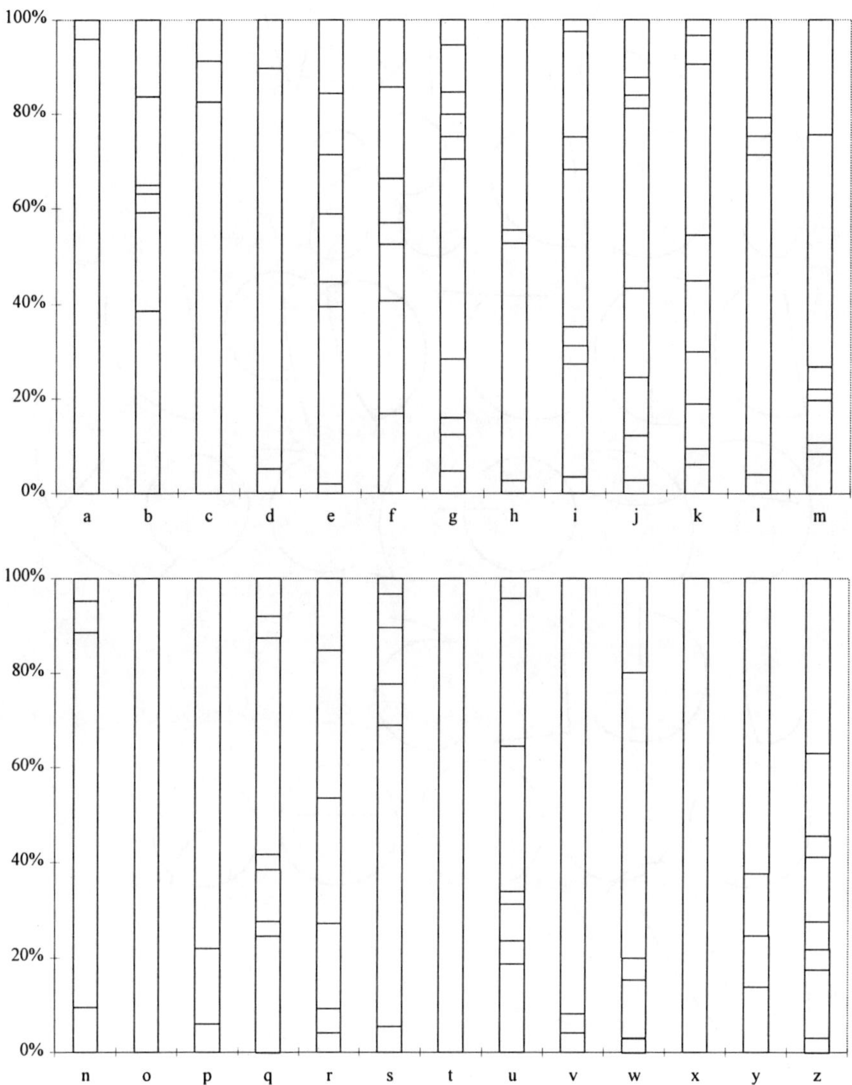

Figure 3: A bar diagram illustrating the distribution of character samples over the shape pool-classes.

Figure 4: Characteristic shapes falling within some shape pool-classes.

4 Conclusions

Some preliminary results of a hierarchical approach to structural shape description and classification have been presented. The family of forms considered is that of ribbon-like shapes, making up documents of any type. Handprinted characters were considered: after a preprocessing which transforms the gray level image representation of a character into a set of interconnected circular arcs, the character was described in terms of simple shape features and then assigned to a shape pool-class by a first classification stage. The performed tests aimed to check the description power of the features derived from the representations achieved with our preprocessing technique and the possible advantages to proceed with a hierarchical approach towards classification.

Taking into account that both the description scheme and the classification technique used in this preliminary experiment were particularly simple, the obtained results seem very promising. Future developments include the use of descriptions in terms of attributed relational graphs, exploiting structural information about the character representation with arcs. Such descriptions will enable to adopt an inexact graph matcher as first classification stage. It is expected that this new approach may lead to a reduction of the number of character classes per pool-class without increasing the number of pool-classes.

5 References

1. T. Pavlidis, S. Mori, eds., Special issue on Optical Character Recognition, *Proc. IEEE*, **80**, 1059-1194, 1992
2. J.F. Arias, R.Kasturi, Recognition of graphical objects for intelligent interpretation of line drawings, in *Aspects of Visual form Processing*, World Scientific Publ., Singapore, 11-29, 1994.
3. T. Pavlidis, *Structural Pattern Recognition*, Springer-Verlag, 1977
4. G. Boccignone, A. Chianese, L.P. Cordella, A. Marcelli, Using skeletons for OCR, in *Progress in Image Analysis and Processing*, World Scientific Publ., 1990.
5. A. Chianese, L.P. Cordella, M. De Santo, M. Vento, Decomposition of Ribbon-like Shapes, *Proc. 6th Scandinavian Conference on Image Analysis*, Oulu, Finland, 416-423, 1989.
6. A. Chianese, L.P. Cordella, M. De Santo, M. Vento, Classifying character shapes, in *Visual Form: Analysis and Recognition*, Plenum Press, 155-164, 1992.
7. ETL Database distributed by Electrotechnical Laboratory - Japanese Technical Committee for OCR, during the 2nd ICDAR, 1993.
8. J.R. Quinlan, Induction of decision trees, *Machine Learning*, **1**, 81-106, 1986.

MULTIRESOLUTION LOGO RECOGNITION

M. CORVI
Research & Development Department
Elsag Bailey, un'azienda di Finmeccanica S.p.A.
Via Puccini 2, 16154 Genova, ITALY
E-mail: marco.corvi@elsag.it

E. OTTAVIANI
Research & Development Department
Elsag Bailey, un'azienda di Finmeccanica S.p.A.
Via Puccini 2, 16154 Genova, ITALY
E-mail: ennio.ottaviani@elsag.it

A wavelet-based multiscale algorithm for the localisation and identification of logos on document images is presented. The algorithm relies only on the graphical appearance of the logo. The identification is measured by the correlation coefficient between the logo and its occurrence within the document and the localisation is achieved by a three-step procedure involving the images at different scales of resolution. The algorithm is robust against rotations and dilations of the pattern, and interference with other graphical elements.

1 Introduction

Everyday documents like mail, advertisements, official forms, etc., usually have a logo that helps the reader to identify the source of the document. The logo is generally a very conspicuous pattern easily indetifiable within the document, and is often located in key points, such as the upper-left or the upper-right region of the page. A potential application field for the Logo Recognition Algorithm is the automated document handling, e.g., mail sorting (by class), bank check reading and invoices handling. The recognition of the logo provides an input for a high level analysis of the document structure (the layout) in the context of the new approaches to document image analysis[6-8].

The logo pattern itself is an iconic feature that can therefore be used as a strong and reliable feature in a document-image database application, useful both for image indexing and for image retrieval. The use of the logo in database indexing has received little attention in spite of its potentialities[2-5].

Doermann, Rivlin and Weiss[3,4] address the logo based query by extracting the logo characteristic components: lines, circles, and text. These are organised in geometrically invariant features and are used for the recognition of the logo. In this work we assume that a logo is a graphical pattern with clear and simple geometrical features. The geometrical features can be lines, arcs, shaded areas, regular shapes, simple textures. Like Doermann et al.[3,4] Logo Recognition Algorithm strongly relies on the presence of such features. However, unlike the work of Doermann et al., in our approach the individual features are not extracted explicitly from the image. The logo is treated as a whole entity, and its recognition is based on the pattern matching of the picture itself rather than of features extracted from the picture. This global approach has the advantage of the independence of the recognition from the identification of the individual features, at the same time maintaining the computational burden to an acceptable level.

The algorithm consists of an analysis of the images, followed by the localisation and identification of the logo pattern. The logo template image and the document test image are decomposed with a multiscale analysis based on a discrete wavelet transform (DWT) a' la Mallat[9] with biorthogonal spline wavelet of Cohen et al.[10], obtaining two sequences of residue-detail image pairs at different scales. The recognition of the pattern consists of two interdependent functions: the localisation and the identification. The localisation carries out a local registration of the logo image within the test image[11].

The identification is measured by a function which evaluates the similarity between the logo image and the area of the document image where the logo has been localised. A reliable identification is important in indexing and retrieval applications for discriminating among several logos, and a good localisation is crucial for it. On the other hand the precise and accurate localisation is important for the definition of a reference co-ordinate system that can be utilised in automatic document handling applications. An estimate of the identification of the logo is necessary for the process of localisation. The localisation is described by the parameters of the mathematical transformation that maps the logo image inside the document image. This transformation is assumed to be composed of a translation, a rotation and a dilation.

The recognition of the pattern achieves the localisation of the given logo in three steps, at the same time carrying out the identification. First a rough localisation of the logo is obtained based on the coarsest scale residue images; next this localisation is improved by considering the detail images at an intermediate scale; lastly the localisation is refined in order to achieve a strong and robust identification.

This paper is organised as follows: the next section describes the algorithm; the third section discusses the implementation and the results of numerical tests; the final section is devoted to the conclusions and further comments.

2 The Logo Recognition Algorithm

The Logo Recognition Algorithm tackles a particular image registration problem consisting of the localisation of a small template image, the logo, in a larger test image. A registration algorithm[12] is characterised by four elements:

- the features used for the pattern matching;
- the class of transformations T allowed in the registration;
- the similarity function C measuring the quality of the matching;
- the search strategy used to find the best transformation.

We suppose that the template image (pattern) I has size 2^N and the test image I' has size 2^M, where $M>N$. The class of transformations that relate the template image and its occurrence within the test image is made of the affine transformations obtained by composing a rotation R (by an angle t), a dilation D and a translation (by a vector a)

$$T(x) = a + D\,R(x) \tag{1}$$

where x is a 2-dimensional vector representing a point in the template image, $R(x)$ is the vector

$$R(x) = (\cos(t)\,x_1 + \sin(t)\,x_2, -\sin(t)\,x_1 + \cos(t)\,x_2) \tag{2}$$

and D multiplies both vector components by the dilation factor d.

These transformations form a 4-parameter subgroup of the group of affine transformations. This subgroup is sufficient for the applications to digitised documents in which the logo pattern is often rotated or dilated but is not distorted.

We further assume that there are no radiometric changes between the template image and its occurrence in the test image. However slight differences between the two images are allowed, as the logo might be drawn in the test image with a style different from that in the template image, and the digitising conditions maybe different. Therefore we assume that the two images *I(x)* and *I'(T(x))* are similar, for x in the domain of the image I. The logo recognition algorithm aims to find the transformation T that maximises the similarity function of the pattern matching. For this function we use the cross-correlation,

$$C(I, I'; T) = \frac{\sum \left[I(x) - u_0 \right] \left[I'(T(x)) - u_T \right]}{S_0 \cdot S_T} \tag{3}$$

where u_0 and S_0 are the mean and the standard deviation of the template image I, and u_T and S_T are the mean and the standard deviation of the test image I', restricted to the range of T (i.e. to the region where the logo had been localised).

The features used in the Logo Recognition Algorithm are obtained from a multiresolution analysis of the two images. Both the template image and the test image are transformed with a discrete wavelet transformation (DWT) a' la Mallat[9]. This is a reiterated transformation, each iteration of which produces four images obtained by low-pass and high-pass filtering (in the X and Y directions) the generic input image denoted J, and decimating the filter outcomes:

$$\begin{aligned} J_{HH} &= H_X\, H_Y\, J \\ J_{HG} &= H_X\, G_Y\, J \\ J_{GH} &= G_X\, H_Y\, J \\ J_{GG} &= G_X\, G_Y\, J \end{aligned} \tag{4}$$

where H and G are the low-pass and high-pass filters, respectively. The subscripts denote the direction along which the filter is applied. The filter coefficients are deduced from the theory of biorthogonal wavelets applied to the cardinal splines functions.

If the generic image J has size 2^P the 4 transformed images have size 2^{P-1}. The transformed image J_{HH} is the residue image at scale level $K=N-(P-1)$, where N is the $\log_2$ size of the original image. It will be denoted J_K, and it is the input for the next iteration step. The other three images are the detail images at this scale. In particular J_0 will denote the original image, and is the input for the first iteration. The DWT of the template image and the test images is repeated up to the scale L.

The search strategy is the most important component of the algorithm. It consists of three phases and attempts to find the best registration[11] of the template image inside the test image. The first phase achieves a rough estimate of the translation vector a by maximising the function $C(I_L, I'_L;a)$, with respect to a. Here I_L and I'_L are the residue images at the coarsest scale L.

This phase is crucial for the successful logo recognition, and relies heavily on the logo being a conspicuous pattern in the document. The translation parameter a is estimated by maximising, at scale L, the correlation between the logo image and an equal-size image positioned at a in the test image. This exhaustive procedure is fast since it is carried out on images of small size, and the set of possible values of a is limited.

In the second phase of the search strategy the algorithm improves the translation parameter a while estimating the rotation angle t and the dilation factor d. It is assumed that the logos contain simple geometric features such as lines, arcs, and geometrical shapes. Therefore, the algorithm tries to correlate a sort of "edge images" of the template image and of the portion of the test image where the logo has been roughly localised in the first phase. As "edge images" we use the gradient images of the residues at the scale L_1. For each edge image E the centre of mass c is obtained,

$$c = \frac{\sum x \cdot E(x)}{\sum E(x)} \quad . \tag{5}$$

Next the radial density r, relative to c, is computed,

$$r = \left(\frac{\sum |x-c|^{-2} E(x)}{\sum E(x)} \right)^{1/2} \tag{6}$$

where x denotes the image point with co-ordinates. Then the radial distribution of edges is obtained,

$$\theta(t) = \sum_K |x-c|^2 \; E(x) \tag{7}$$

where the sum runs over the points $x = (c_1 + \cos(t)\,k,\ c_2 + \sin(t)\,k)$, k being a positive integer, and t is the angle variable.

By maximising the cross-correlation of the two radial edge distributions $e(t)$ and $e'(t)$ for the template image and the test image, respectively, we obtain the rotation angle t that relates the logos in the two images. The two functions are evaluated in *256* points and the correlation is calculated with a FFT[12] (fast Fourier transform). From the ratio of the two radial densities the dilation factor is estimated,

$$d = r \,/\, r' \tag{8}$$

where r is the radial density of the template edge image, and r' is that of the test edge image. Finally the translation parameters are adjusted to the new estimates:

$$a_{new} = a_{old} + c' - d\, R_t(c) \tag{9}$$

where c is the centre of mass of the logo edge image, and c' is that of the test image.

The last phase of the search strategy is devoted to the fine tuning of the localisation transformation T. The transformation parameters are improved by maximising the cross correlation between residue images from the scale L_2 down to the scale L_3. At each scale the parameters are adjusted with the Newton interpolation method[12]. For each parameter p of the transformation group, three correlations are evaluated at values p-Δp, p, and $p+\Delta p$. The maximum of the correlation and the corresponding value of the parameter are computed by quadratic interpolation. This procedure is repeated until for each parameter the maximum lies within a distance $\Delta p/2$ from p. The variation Δp must be chosen large enough to avoid too many repetition of the procedure, but cannot be too large otherwise the regularity of the correlation function is missed. We found that $\Delta a=1$ pixel (for each component), $\Delta d=0.05$ (a dilation of 5%), and $\Delta t=0.05$ rads (corresponding to about *3* degrees) are reasonable values.

3 Numerical Implementation and Results

The Logo Recognition Algorithm has been implemented in C on a Digital Alpha workstation *200* at *100 MHz*. The logo template images have size *128x128*. This size is large enough to contain most of the logos extracted from digital images of documents scanned at *160 dpi*. The test images have size *512x512*.

The DWT[9] was carried out up to the scale $L=4$. The first phase used the residue images at this scale. The second used detail images at scale $L_1=2$. The third used residue images at scales from $L_2=3$ down to $L_3=1$ included. The execution gives the following CPU times:

DWT	0.22 sec
1-st phase	0.02 sec
2-nd phase	0.04 sec
3-rd phase	0.36 sec

Tab.1 CPU times

The two most computing intensive parts of the algorithm are the image analysis by the DWT, and the final search phase. Overall the Logo Recognition Algorithm takes about *0.6* seconds to verify the presence of the given logo in a document image.

The numerical test was carried out on a set of US mail pieces, and aimed to retrieve a stamp with the "dove" (Fig.1). The test set consisted of *35* images of letters (see Fig.2 for an example). The "dove" stamp appeared in six images, all of which with another stamp as well. The other images contained different stamps.

Fig.1 The "dove"

The frame in Fig.2 represents the region where the logo has been localised. The results of the Logo Recognition Algorithm on the six images with the dove stamp are reported in the table 2 below. For a comparison, the highest values of the similarity for the images without the "dove" stamp are $C_1=0.31$, $C_2=0.52$, and $C_3=0.54$. It is evident that the algorithm can clearly discriminate the presence of the stamp from the absence. These results too show that the values of the similarity after the first and second phase are not sufficient for such a discrimination, and that the third phase is necessary for a robust pattern identification.

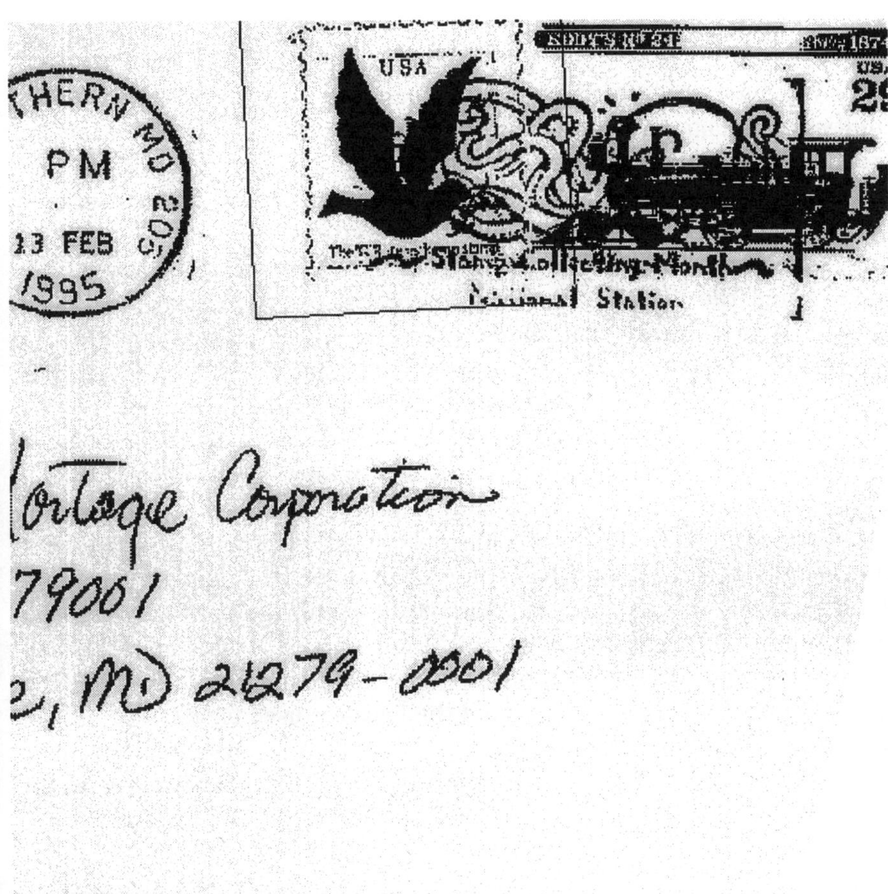

Fig.2 A part of a typical US mail

Image	C_1	C_2	C_3
dove694	0.55	0.62	0.87
dove699	0.48	0.46	0.76
dove781	0.43	0.73	0.78
dove784	0.51	0.70	0.86
dove785	0.51	0.63	0.82
dove886	0.40	0.47	0.74

Tab.2 Results of the algorithm

4 Conclusions

We have presented a logo recognition algorithm based on a multiscale image decomposition obtained through a discrete wavelet transform. The algorithm is very robust against arbitrary rotations and dilations of the pattern. It is also successful when the pattern is perturbed by some interference with other patterns.

The dependence on the wavelet filter choice is not very strong. We have tested the algorithm with different choices of biorthogonal filter derived from splines[10]. The biorthogonal spline filters are particularly interesting for numerical implementations since they have a finite number of coefficients, that are furthermore multiples of dyadic fractions. For applications to document images, low order splines appeared more appropriate, but the results did not significantly favour a particular spline. It is a three-phases procedure based on the DWT-transformed images. The first phase of the localisation is essential for the success of the recognition. The crucial point is to apply a low-pass filter to the images in order to obtain "thumbnail" copies of them for the first phase, and to use low and high passed versions richer in information for the other phases. The most important part of the algorithm is the search strategy and the features used for it.

In specific applications it is possible that this first localisation is enhanced by restricting the search focus using a-priori knowledge about the position of the logo. The second phase attempts to estimate the rotation angle and the dilation factor using the distribution of the linear elements of the images. This phase requires the logo to be composed by simple geometrical linear features, and can be hampered when the logo strongly interferes with other graphical patterns. The third phase aims to maximise the similarity function between the logo and the region of the document image where it has been localised. Many functions resulted successful, but the normalised cross correlation seems to be the best.

A future development of the algorithm might take into account also the other choices for the translation parameter a, resulting from the first phase of the localisation. The algorithm would analyse all the relevant choices locally and select the best only after the second phase. As the first two phases of the localisation do not cost much CPU, the time performances should not be impaired, while making the algorithm even more robust.

5 References

[1] http://documents.cfar.umd.edu/resources/database/UMDlogo.html UMD Logo Database

[2] F. Kanehara, S. Satoh, and T. Hamada, "A flexible image retrieval using explicit visual instructions", *Int. Conf. Docum. Analysis and Recogn.*, Montreal 1995, p. 175.

[3] D. Doermann, E. Rivlin et al., "Logo recognition", University of Maryland Report, CAR-TR-688, CS-TR-3145, Oct.1993.

[4] D. Doermann, E. Rivlin, and I. Weiss, "Applying algebraic and differential invariants for logo recognition", *Machine Vision and Applic*. Vol.9 (1996), p.73.

[5] M. Corvi, "Wavelet based logo recognition", *SIMAI Int.Conf.* 1996.

[6] A. Dengel, and A.L. Spitz "" *Proc. Document Analysis Systems*, Kaiserslautern, Germany, 1994.

[7] O'Gorman, and R. Kasturi (eds.) "Document Image Analysis", IEEE Comp. Soc. Press 1995.

[8] R. Casey, D. Ferguson, K. Mohiuddin, and E. Walach, "Intelligent Form Processing System", in Document Image Analysis, IEEE Comp. Soc. Press, p. 356.

[9] S.G. Mallat, "A theory for multiresolution signal decomposition: the wavelet representation", *IEEE Trans. PAMI*, 11 (1989) 674.

[10] A. Cohen, I. Daubechies, et al., "Biorthogonal bases of compactly supported wavelets", *Comm. Pure Appl. Math*. 45 (1992) 485.

[11] M. Corvi, G. Nicchiotti, "Multiresolution image registration", *Int. Conf. Image Process.*, Washington DC,1995.

[12] L.G. Brown, "A survey of image registration techniques", *ACM Comp. Surveys*, 24 (1992) 325.

SYMMETRY DETECTION USING A MAGNETO-STATIC ANALOGY

ANDREW D.J. CROSS, EDWIN R. HANCOCK
Department of Computer Science,
University of York,
York, Y01 5DD, UK.

This paper describes a vectorial representation that can be used to assess the symmetry of objects in 2D images. The method exploits a magneto-static analogy. Commencing from the gradient-field extracted from filtered grey-scale images we construct a vector-potential. Our magneto-static analogy is that tangential gradient vectors represent the elements of a current distribution on the image plane. By embedding the image plane in an augmented 3-dimensional space, we compute the vector potential by performing volume integration over the current distribution. The associated magnetic field is computed by taking the curl of the vector-potential. We extract edge and symmetry lines through a topographic analysis of the vector-field at various heights above the image plane. Symmetry axes are lines of where the curl of the vector-potential vanishes; at edges the divergence of the vector-potential vanishes.

1 Introduction

Symmetry is an important way of assessing the shape of both 2D and 3D objects. Several alternative ways locating axes and points of symmetry have been been suggested in the literature. Broadly speaking these can be divided into those that aim to analyse the properties of presegmented shapes [2,4,10,13] and those that aim to characterise shape as a continuous attribute [11,15]. Examples of the segmental analysis of symmetry include Friedberg's moment-based method [5], the use of spline-based representations by Cham and Cipolla [4], Ponce's idea of exploiting ribbons [10], and, the skeletal analysis of binary shapes by Wright *et al* [13]. The basic practical limitation of such methods is the availability of reliable segmental entities prior to symmetry analysis. It is for this reason that the early analysis of continuous symmetry proves an attractive alternative. For instance the Zabrodsky *et al* have to characterised the folding symmetries of 2D shapes using point-sets [15]. Reisfeld *et al* generate a continuous symmetry measure from the orientation distribution for edgels and textons [11].

We make two observations concerning the existing work on continuous symmetry characterisation. Firstly, the input image representation is a sparse pre-segmentation, e.g. points of curvature, edgels or textons. Secondly, existing work shares the common feature of using only a scalar representation to assess symmetry structure. Our standpoint in this paper is that a vectorial representation of the unsegmented image data offers a more elegant way of assessing the axial symmetries of planar shapes. This is a natural way in which to proceed since the edge tangent vectors associated with the boundaries of regular 2D shapes exhibit chiral symmetry about the vertical axis. At points of symmetry there is a cancellation of diametrically placed vectors. To exploit this property, we appeal to the mathematical concept of vector-potential from magneto-statics to generate the magnetic field associated with symmetrical currents loops.

Although several authors have exploited field analogies in the analysis of shape, these are less ambitious than the work reported here since they are electrostatic in origin [1,14]. For instance, Wu and Levine have used charge distributions to segment volumetric objects into shape primitives [14]. The work of Abdel-Hamid *et al* [1] aims to find symmetry axes by seeding a charge distribution along a binary boundary contour and computing the lines of equipotential in the resulting electric field. Our work differs from this related work in two important respects. Firstly, we do not require a pre-segmented surface or boundary from which to seed the generating distribution. Instead, we seed our field from the raw image gradient. Secondly, our analogy is magneto-static and the resulting field is generated from a vector potential rather than a scalar potential. The resulting magnetic field has a much richer differential structure which allows us the extract both source-lines (edges) and symmetry lines. Moreover, the chirality of the magnetic field means that it has a mathematical structure that is better suited to the assessment of axial symmetry than the electric field.

Our basic idea is to regard edge tangent-vectors as a raw current distribution residing in the image plane. These vectors are computed by taking the cross-product of the image gradient with the normal to the image plane. In order to compute the magnetic field we augment the 2D image space with an auxiliary vertical dimension. For each point in the resulting volume we compute the vector-potential by integrating over the current distribution residing on the embedded image plane. Following the definition of magnetic potential, the current distribution is weighted by the inverse distance between the relevant sampling point in the augmented image volume and the points on the original image plane. The magnetic field is the curl of the resulting vector-potential.

The outline of this paper is as follows. In section 2 we detail the magneto-static analogy and describe how it is exploited to compute a vector potential from the raw image gradient. Section 3 describes our analysis of the resulting vector-field. Section 4 presents a very brief description of the practical issues concerned with implementing the algorithm described in this paper. In Section 5 we present some experimental evaluation. Finally, Section 6 provides some conclusions.

2 Vector Field

Our starting point is to compute the Canny edge map [3]. We commence by convolving the raw image I with a Gaussian kernel of width σ. The kernel takes the following form

$$G_\sigma(x,y) = \frac{1}{2\pi\sigma^2}\exp\left[-\frac{x^2+y^2}{2\sigma^2}\right] \tag{1}$$

With the filtered image to hand, the Canny edge map is recovered by computing the gradient

$$\vec{E} = \nabla G_\sigma * I \tag{2}$$

In order to compute a vector field representation of the edge-map, we will need to introduce an auxiliary z dimension to the original $x - y$ co-ordinate system of the plane image. In this augmented co-ordinate system, the components of the edge-map are confined to the image plane. In other words, the edge-vector at the point $(x, y, 0)$ on the input image plane is given by

$$\vec{E}(x,y,0) = \begin{pmatrix} \frac{\partial G_\sigma * I(x,y)}{\partial x} \\ \frac{\partial G_\sigma * I(x,y)}{\partial y} \\ 0 \end{pmatrix} \tag{3}$$

For an ideal step-edge, the resulting image gradient will be directed along the boundary normal. In order to pursue our magneto-static analogy we would like to interpret the raw edge responses as elementary currents which flow around the boundaries and give rise to a vector potential. In particular we would like to explore configurations in which closed boundary edges give rise to current loops. In other words, we would like to organise the elementary currents so that they are tangential to the boundaries of physical objects. Accordingly, we re-direct the edge-vectors to that they are tangential to the original planar shape by computing the cross-product with the normal to the image plane $\hat{z} = (0,0,1)^T$. The elementary current-vector at the point $(x, y, 0)$ on the input image plane is defined to be

$$\vec{j}(x,y,0) = \hat{z} \wedge \nabla G_\sigma * I(x,y) \tag{4}$$

To be more explicit the components of this elementary current are given by the vector

$$\vec{j}(x,y,0) = \begin{pmatrix} -\frac{\partial G_\sigma * I(x,y)}{\partial y} \\ \frac{\partial G_\sigma * I(x,y)}{\partial x} \\ 0 \end{pmatrix} \tag{5}$$

The key idea underlying our image representation is to characterise edges and symmetry lines using a vector potential. Edges correspond to locations where the elementary current re-enforce one-another. In other words, the boundaries are identified as local maxima of the vector potential. Symmetry points are those at which there is cancellation between diametrically opposed elementary currents. Axes of symmetry are lines of local minimum in the vector potential. At the level of fine detail, intensity ridges or ravines (lines) give rise to local symmetry axes. According to magneto-statics, the vector-potential associated with a field of elementary currents is found by integrating over volume and weighting the contributing currents according to inverse distance. In other words, the vector potential at the point $\vec{r} = (x, y, z)^T$ in the augmented space in which the original image plane is embedded is

$$\vec{A}(x,y,z) = \mu \int_{V'} \frac{\vec{j}(x',y',z')}{|\vec{r} - \vec{r'}|} dV' \tag{6}$$

where $\vec{r'} = (x', y', z')^T$ and μ is the permeability constant which we set equal to unity.. Since the contributing currents are distributed only on the image plane, the volume integral reduces to one over the area of the image plane.

3 Magnetic Field Lines

Our basic idea in exploring the symmetry structure of grey-scale images is to regard the Canny edge map as a current-field which generates a magneto-static vector potential. In order to develop the appropriate differential operators for feature characterisation from the vector-potential we appeal to the geometry of the associated magnetic field. According to magneto-statics the magnetic field is the curl of the vector potential. It is important to stress that because it is less computationally tractable than the vector-potential, the magnetic field is never used directly in our image representation. We appeal to the magnetic field only as an auxiliary representation which yields a geometric picture which helps us to understand the differential structure of the vector-potential.

According to our representation of image structure, symmetry lines can be anticipated to follow the local minima of the vector-potential. In other words,

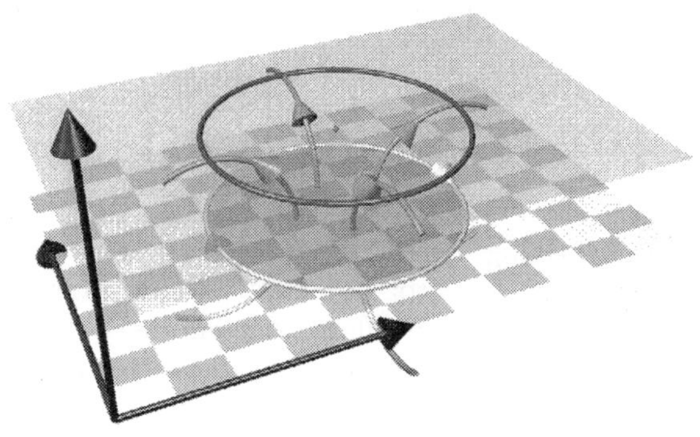

Figure 1: The geometry of the magnetic field at edge locations: The edge contour at a height z above the image plane links locations at which the field lines generated by the current loop are tangential to the sampling plane.

they connect image points where there is strong cancellation between symmetrically placed edge tangent vectors. By contrast, edge contours follow the local maxima of the vector potential. According to our representation, the edge lines connect points where there is strong directional re-enforcement between edge tangent-vectors. As we shall demonstrate later in this section, symmetry lines can be interpreted as locations where the magnetic field is perpendicular to the sampling image plane. Edges are locations where field lines are tangential to the relevant sampling plane. When viewed from perspective of the differential structure of the vector potential, symmetry lines are locations where the component of the curl in the image plane vanishes, i.e. $\hat{z} \wedge \nabla \vec{\wedge} A(x, y, z) = 0$; edges are locations where the transverse component of the divergence vanishes, i.e. $\nabla.(\hat{z} \wedge \vec{A}(x, y, z)) = 0$.

3.1 The magnetic field

Although, we do not use it directly in our image representations, the natural extension of the development of the vector potential is to compute the associated magnetic field. Again, according to magneto-statics this quantity is obtained by computing the curl of the vector potential

$$\vec{B}(x,y,z) = \nabla \wedge \vec{A}(x,y,z) \tag{7}$$

Unfortunately, searching for scale-space edges or symmetry lines by directly exploring the differential geometry of the magnetic field is not a feasible computational proposition. Instead, we confine our attention to searching efficiently for local extrema of the vector potential on individual planes of fixed height z above the input image. As mentioned in the preamble to this section, we represent the structure present in the original image gradient field by identifying lines of both maximum and minimum vector potential. In practice, we characterise these lines by seeking ridges and ravines in the topographic representation of the vector potential. We realise this process by fitting a second-order polynomial prism surface to the magnitudes of the vector-potential in a local image window. The prism surface is oriented along the direction the vector potential. The maxima and minima are marked by testing for convexity or concavity of the fitted surface. This fitting procedure is similar to that adopted by Spacek in his gradient-based edge detector [12].

3.2 Edge-lines

Before we proceed to experiment with our new symmetry detector, we will provide some analysis of the properties the underlying image representation. The simplest case is to consider the properties of edge-lines. The localisation process is effected by identifying points for which transverse derivative of the vector potential is zero. In other words we compute the derivatives of the vector-potential in the direction which is perpendicular to $\vec{A}(x,y,z)$ and which lies in the $x-y$ plane. The condition for edge lines is

$$\nabla.(\hat{z} \wedge \vec{A}(x,y,z)) = 0 \tag{8}$$

Using standard identities from vector-calculus, the required derivatives are related to the curl of the vector-potential in the following manner

$$\nabla.(\hat{z} \wedge \vec{A}(x,y,z)) = \vec{A}(x,y,z).\nabla \wedge \hat{z} - \hat{z}.(\nabla \wedge \vec{A}(x,y,z)) \tag{9}$$

Since $\hat{z}$ is a constant vector, i.e. $\nabla \wedge \hat{z} = 0$, it follows that

$$\nabla.(\hat{z} \wedge \vec{A}(x,y,z)) = -\hat{z}.(\nabla \wedge \vec{A}(x,y,z)) \tag{10}$$

Edge lines simply connect points for where the z-component of the magnetic field vanishes, i.e.

$$\hat{z}.\vec{B}(x,y,x) = 0 \tag{11}$$

In other words, the magnetic field lines become tangential to the sampling plane at the location of edge-points as illustrated in Figure 1. Viewed from this perspective the set of edges traces can be regarded as the points of tangential contact between the sampling plane and the 3D magnetic field lines.

3.3 Symmetry lines

This geometric analysis of the magnetic field can be extended to symmetry lines. Symmetry points occur where there is local cancellation of the vector potential due to a balanced current flow around an object boundary. At such points the magnetic field lines are orthogonal to the sampling plane. To understand the implication of this statement in terms of differential operators, we note that the condition for orthogonality of the magnetic field lines is

$$\hat{z} \wedge \vec{B}(x,y,z,) = 0 \tag{12}$$

Using the definition of the magnetic field in terms of the vector potential and exploiting the identities of vector-calculus

$$\hat{z}\wedge\nabla\wedge\vec{A}(x,y,z) = \nabla(\hat{z}.\vec{A}(x,y,z))+\nabla\wedge(\hat{z}\wedge\vec{A}(x,y,z))-(\hat{z}.\nabla)\vec{A}(x,y,z) \tag{13}$$

Since $\vec{A}(x,y,z)$ is confined to the image plane $\hat{z}.\vec{A}(x,y,z) = 0$ and hence $\nabla(\hat{z}.\vec{A}(x,y,z)) = 0$. In other words, the vector $\hat{z} \wedge \nabla \wedge \vec{A}(x,y,z)$ is null along lines for which the vertical derivative of current-density is zero. This condition is met at lines about which the current is symmetrically distributed. We have therefore demonstrated that the symmetry lines are orthogonal to the sampling planes.

4 Implementation

There are two distinct steps concerned with the implementation of our feature detection algorithm. The first is concerned with computing the field intensity on the sampling plane at a given height above the image. The second process is to extract the set of ridges and valleys from this field profile. In this section we will give an overview of how to implement these two stages.

4.1 Field Computation

Our goal is to compute the vector potential at a given height above the image plane. This vector potential is sourced by a set of discrete current elements located on the image plane. The key to the efficiently evaluation of this field is to appreciate that the field computations due to these current elements can be forumulated as a pair of convolution processes in the x and y direction. Since any number of sequential convolution processes can be expressed as a single multiplication in Fourier space, we can express the Gaussian differentiation and field convolution processes as a single step.

4.2 Ridge Detector

Given the field at a certain height above the image plane, we wish to determine whether there is a ridge or valley at a given point in the image. The details of this process are outside the scope of this paper, suffice to say that we use an analytic measure that is based on a polynomial approximations of the the local field intensities. These are used to scan around the edges of a pixel in order to determine the fraction the neighborhood that is in a "ridge" configeration and the fraction that are in a "valley" configeration. These fractions are used as a means of evidence for the relevant topographical features.

In practice, on an 133MHz Silicon Graphics Indy, these two processes can be implemented in about a second for a 256x256 image. The complexitiy of the overall detector is $(n.ln(n))^2$. In the real world, this process could be performed in real time using specialised Fourier Transform hardware.

5 Experiments

In this section we provide some experimental evaluation of our new image representation on natural imagery. The images under study have all been captured with a low-quality Indy-Cam.

We will now illustrate the various steps in establishing our image representation. Figure 2a shows the initial grey-scale image. Figures 2b shows the magnitude of the vector potential. Here bright regions correspond to low values while the dark areas are high values. Figure 3c shows the orientation of the vector-potential. Finally, Figure 2d shows the extracted edge and symmetry lines. Note how the two sets of lines cross at points of high curvature. There are several features worth noting in this sequence. Firstly, the minima of the vector potential are strong at both points and axes of symmetry. Secondly, the axis-structure of the symmetry map is very clean and has a very clear skeletal form. Finally, the edge and symmetry lines cross at the high curvature points on the original figure.

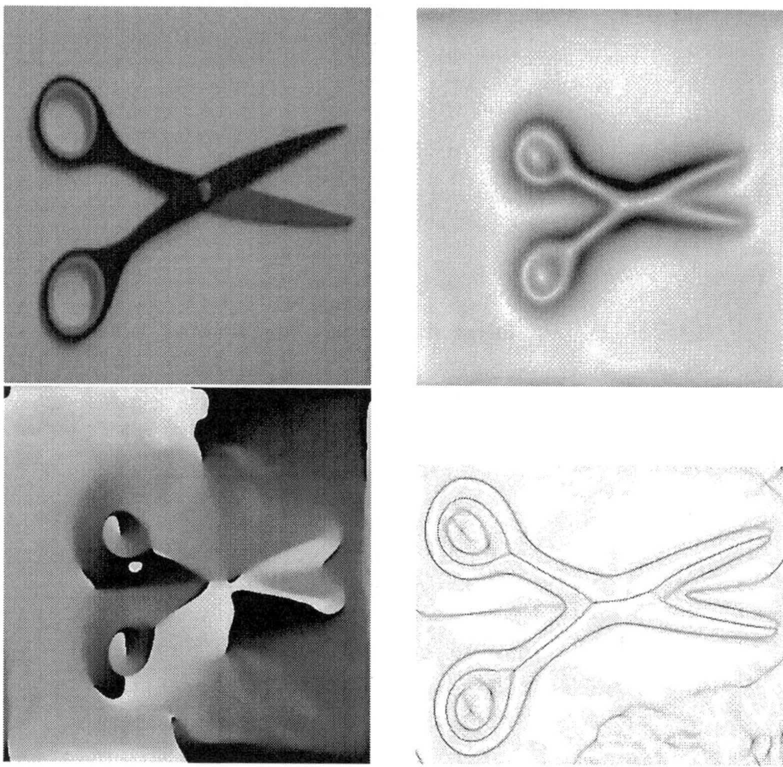

Figure 2: a) Original image, b) Field Strength, c) Field Angle, d) Edge and symmetry lines.

6 Conclusions

The main contribution of this paper is to present a new image representation based on the concept of vector potential. This potential is generated by adopting a magneto-static analogy in which the image gradient is regarded as a current distribution. We demonstrate that edges correspond to lines of zero transverse divergence in this field, i.e they are characterised by the condition $\nabla.(\hat{z} \wedge \vec{A}) = 0$. Symmetry points are characterised by the condition that the component of the curl of the vector field in the image plane vanishes, i.e. $\hat{z} \wedge (\nabla \wedge A) = 0$. In order to compute the vector potential we must embed the image plane in a 3D volume. The auxiliary dimension in this volume plays the role sampling scale in a scale-space representation of the edge and symmetry lines.

1. G. H. Abdel-Hamid and Y-H Yang, "Multi-resolution Skeletonization: A Electrostatic Field-Based Approach", *Proceedings International Conference on Image Processing*, Vol.1, pp.949–953, 1994.
2. M. Brady and H. Asada, "Smoothed local symmetries and their implementation", *Int. J. Robotics Res.*, **3**, pp.36-61, 1994.
3. Canny, J.F. "A computational approach to edge detection", *IEEE PAMI*, **8**, pp.679-698, 1985.
4. T-J Cham and R. Cipolla, "Skewed symmetry detection through local skewed symmetries", *Image and Vision Computing*, 13, pp. 439–450, 1995.
5. S.A.Friedberg, . "Finding axes of skewed symmetry", *Computer Vision, Graphics and Image Processing*, **36**, pp. 138-155, 1986.
6. L. Florack, B. TerHaarRomeny, B. Viergever and J. Koenderink, "The Gaussian scale-space paradigm and the multi-scale local jet", *International Journal of Computer Vision*, **18**, pp. 61–75, 1996.
7. R.M. Haralick, L.T Watson and T.J. Laffrey, "The topographic primal sketch", *International Journal of Robotics Research*, **2**, pp. 50-72, 1983.
8. R.M.J. Koenderink and A.J. Van Doorn, "Generic neighborhood operators", *IEEE PAMI*, **14**, pp. 597-605, 1992
9. T. Lindeberg, "Edge detection and ridge detection with automatic scale selection", *IEEE Computer Society Computer Vision and Pattern Recognition Conference*, pp. 465–470, 1996.
10. J. Ponce, . "On characterising ribbons and finding skewed symmetries", *Computer Vision, Graphics and Image Processing*, **52**, pp. 328-340, 1990.
11. D. Reisfeld, H. Wolfson and Y. Yeshurun, "Generalized symmetry: A context free attentional operator", *Progress in Image Analysis and processing III, Edited by S. Impedovo*, World Scientific, pp. 565–590, 1994.
12. L.A. Spacek, "Edge detection and motion detection", *Image and Vision Computing*, **4**, pp. 43–56, 1986.
13. M.W. Wright, R. Cipolla and P.J. Giblin, "Skeletonization using an extended Euclidean distance transform", *Image and Vision Computing*, **13**, pp. 367–376, 1995.
14. K. Wu and M.D. Levine, "3D part segmentation: A new physics-based approach", *IEEE International Symposium on Computer Vision*, pp. 311–316, 1995.
15. H. Zabrodsky, S. Peleg and D. Avnir, "Symmetry as a continuous feature", *IEEE PAMI*, **17**, pp. 1154–1166, 1995.

ELICITING VISUAL PRIMITIVES FOR DETECTING ELONGATED SHAPES

R. CUCCHIARA, M.PICCARDI
Department of Engineering
University of Ferrara
Via Saragat 1, 44100 Ferrara, ITALY
E-mail: {RCucchiara, MPiccardi}@ing.unife.it

This paper analyzes the problem of eliciting visual primitives aiming at detecting 2D objects characterized by a primarily elongated shape; such a shape is easy to perceive by human eyes but less easy to univocally define with a mathematical model. In this context, in addition to the use of standard well-known local features, an original primitive is proposed. This primitive is able to synthesize the information associated with local features and enhance detection as a more effective ensemble of proprieties of the considered model. The paper discusses the approach, shows the new primitive relying on a correlation of Hough-based features, evaluates its performance in case of noisy images and finally presents a possible application.

1 Introduction

Shape description in terms of visual primitives and their relations is commonly adopted for basic visual tasks, such as object recognition, identification, and location. In the classic data-driven approach, visual features are assembled into a possible-object description; in this bottom-up scenario, the goal is to match the object description with some models in a knowledge base. Nonetheless, visual primitives are used also in a top-down model-based approach, which starts from knowledge on the set of perceptual proprieties to look for and then searches their correspondence with sensory data [1]. Both approaches require careful selection of the feature set, particularly when shapes can not be described with well measured geometric proprieties. The selection of the set of peculiar features, or more preferably of a single primitive feature that encapsulates the saliency of a detected shape, is often more critical than its actual implementation. In this context some suggestions can be accepted by perceptual theories such as Gestalt theory which states that the visual behavior of humans leans to perceive the "global" aspect of a shape more than infer it from an analysis of details and local aspects [2].

Instead, traditional computational approaches lean to select a set of common and general-purpose local primitives, and then apply a more or less complex symbolic reasoning on them, by encoding at this high level the a-priori knowledge on the model.

In accordance with Gestalt perception and novel purposive approaches to artificial vision, our approach starts from the availability of a basic set of 2D local features and aims at finding and synthesizing a new "more global" visual primitive. The scope is to generate a suitable combination of well-known features (such as linearity of edges, high local gradient, geometrical edge relations) in order to find a primitive encoding the salient characteristics of a class of specific shapes, elongated and not well geometrically defined. This primitive enhances the information content associated with single local features and proves specifically robust in presence of noise and non-ideality of the model.

2 Combining local features for a novel visual primitive

The specific application framework we have investigated comes from a very general industrial application of automated visual inspection, i.e. the detection of defects on metallic surfaces. Defects appear as long, thin, and coarsely straight 2D shapes, generally brighter than the background; other 2D bright objects with different shapes can be due to noise, or to non-ideality of the surfaces [3]. Examples are shown in Fig. 6.

Since the main characteristic of the considered shape is its approximate rectilinearity, the use of the Hough Transform (HT) for lines is straightforward [6]. Meaningful points in the parametric space obtained by the HT identify sets of points in the source space which are "collinear" and thus gather information on linearity and length of segmented objects.

If the object contour is affected by noise so strong to degrade the segmentation process while, at the same time, the knowledge of intensity variation should be preserved, the Gradient Weighted Hough Transform (GWHT) is effectively adopted [7]. It avoids the need for initial segmentation through edge detection, since all image points vote in the parametric space in proportion to their gradient magnitude; moreover, working in the space between 0 and 2π (instead the standard 0-π range) avoid loosing information on the gradient orientation.

Therefore an immediate model of the target shape can be defined by means of local visual features, i.e. the two main straight edges, their length and rectilinearity, and their spatial relations. In the GWHT space, the main edges are represented by two peaks P1 and P2 which must be located in two different semi-spaces (0-π) and (π,2π) since they correspond to a direction change in the luminosity variation (i.e. the luminosity gradient). In the Hough space a P peak can be identified by the tuple (h,α,ρ): h is the Hough value, representing the segment length together with the average gradient; α is the angle of the normal to the segment with the x axis; ρ is the algebraic distance of the segment from the origin. The task of shape detection which exploits these basic geometrical features could be described by a relatively simple decision tree as the one indicated in Fig. 1 [4,5].

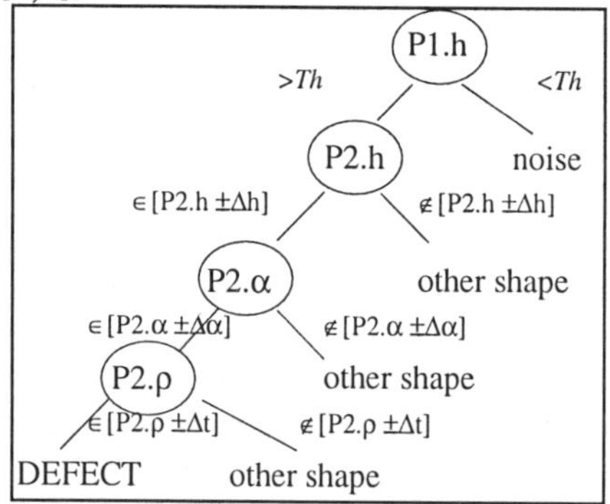

Fig. 1: Decision tree for elongated shape detection.

Tree search is guided by thresholds, which must be carefully tuned: in Fig. 1, Th is the threshold on peak intensity, which accounts for the minimum acceptable edge length (and associated gradient); Δh is the tolerance on the required similarity between edges. Δα describes the tolerance in angular displacement between edges and Δt their distances, i.e. the accepted thickness of the object. A critical step is P1 and P2 selection. In case of defect detection in images where at most a defect (or similar shape) should be present - and this is the most common case in the defined application framework-, P1 and P2 can be selected as the highest peaks in the semi-space of the Hough space characterized by having $\alpha<\pi$ and $\alpha>\pi$, respectively. The problem is more complex in case of more shapes in the same image, or noisy and confused images with a large set of local peaks, since in these cases all possible couples of local peaks should be verified with an often unacceptable increase in computational time.

Finally, while the definition of Δα and Δt is related with the “flexibility” of model definition in accepting shapes closer or less to an ideal bar shape, Th and k depend on the specific luminance condition and are strongly affected by noise.

In conclusion, if the decision process requires a large amount of difficult-to-quantify a-priori knowledge, the selection of a new visual primitive with the same, or possibly more, information content, should simplify the whole visual task.

In the specific case a new simple primitive, called CH, i.e. Correlated Hough, has been devised which the aim at explicitly exploiting correlation between semantically-connected peaks of a possible defect. In particular, calling h a point in the Hough space defined by the pair (ρ,α) with $\rho\in[-R,R]$ and $\alpha\in[0,2\pi]$, being R the limit given by discretization and quantization constraints, we can define two semi-spaces:

$H1=\{h1, : h1(\rho,\alpha)=h(\rho,\alpha), \rho\in[-R,R], \alpha\in[0,\pi[\}$ and

$H2=\{h2, : h2(\rho,\alpha)=h(-\rho,\alpha+\pi), \rho\in[-R,R], \alpha\in[0,\pi[\}$

Moreover we define for each pair (ρ,α) with $\rho\in[-R,R]$, $\alpha\in[0,\pi[$

$$h2'(\rho,\alpha)=\int_{\rho-\Delta\rho/2}^{\rho+\Delta\rho/2}\int_{\alpha-\Delta\alpha/2}^{\alpha+\Delta\alpha/2} h2(r,a)\,dr\,da \qquad (1)$$

$$h2''(\rho,\alpha)=\int_{0}^{\Delta t} h2'(\rho-t,\alpha)\,dt \qquad (2)$$

$$ch(\rho,\alpha)= h1(\rho,\alpha) * h2''(\rho,\alpha) \qquad (3)$$

The CH space is able to represent the salient shape features in a whole: the value of P_{CH} (the CH peak) is associated with the amplitude of the pair of peaks which represent two possible "wavefronts" of the luminosity gradient. Moreover, its location corresponds to one possible main edge of the shape, while it keeps information on the other edge with an adequate low-pass filter. The filter enables for preventing errors due to non-ideality of the model, while at the same time smoothes the effects of noise. Finally the transformation of Eq.(2) takes into account also different thickness, since integrates (thus making a sort of average) along an interval Δt.

This complex primitive integrates the contribution of both P1 and P2 of Fig. 1 and improves the information associated with: therefore, the final decision-making process may evaluate only this primitive without considering separately the other ones together with their relations. This new primitive has been tested on synthetic images, in order to characterize it in term of noise robustness and expressive power, also by slightly varying the model. Moreover, it has been applied to real images as will be described in the last section.

3 Detection capability in presence of noise and non ideality

In this section we assess the robustness of CH in images affected by noise and images containing objects of non-ideal bar shape. Tests are carried out by comparing the result of CH with respect to the approach of detecting two main peaks in the GWHT space and check their relations against the decision tree.

Id00

Id10db

Id-5db

Fig. 2: Test images.

In the test set of synthetic images, Id00 represents the ideal model of bar shape. Gaussian noise with mean value equal to zero has been added to Id00 with different signal-to-noise ratios per pixel, according to the formula [9]:

$$S/N = A^2/\sigma^2 \text{ or } (S/N)db = 20 \log (A/\sigma) \quad (4)$$

where A is the difference between the object luminosity and that of background (set at 16 in the tests) and σ is the variance of the Gaussian distribution.

	∞ db		20 db		10 db		0 db		-5 db	
	h	(ρ,α°)	h	(ρ,α)	h	(ρ,α)	h	(ρ,α)	h	(ρ,α)
P1	14.2	76,32	5.5	76,32	3.4	76,30	2.3	74,30	3.2	78,38
P2	15.2	84,32	7.1	84,32	2.4	82,28	2.6	84,32	2.9	36,80
P_{CH}	883	76,32	374	76,32	145	76,28	132	74,30	133	78,38

Table 1: Peaks in the transform spaces for Id00 with different S/N ratio.

Therefore we added increasing noise starting from a (S/N)db of ∞db (i.e. only signal), down to 20db, 10db (moderately noisy real images), 0 db (very noisy images) and -5db (predominating noise). Fig. 2 shows the ∞db, 10db, and -5db images.

Table 1 shows the comparison of approaches based on the standard GWHT and our primitive CH. In tables, wrong results are highlighted. The column of ∞db shows the ideal case: two peaks P1 and P2 have the same h value (with small differences due to discretization[a]), the same angular coordinate (α=32°) and mutual distance (measuring bar thickness) of |P1.ρ-P2.ρ| = 8 (the unit of length is estimated assuming square pixels). The decreasing h value for P1 and P2 in the other columns shows, obviously, that Gaussian noise causes delocalization of peaks and thus diminishes the number of "collinear" points. At the same time it smoothes the gradient, too, with the same effect on peaks. In the last case (-5 db), a wrong peak is detected instead of P2. Nevertheless CH is able to localize the right shape in each case, even with little displacement in angle and distance. The robustness and sharpness of peaks in noisy images are shown in Fig. 3, which depicts a profile of the transformed spaces projected along the ρ direction for the two images.

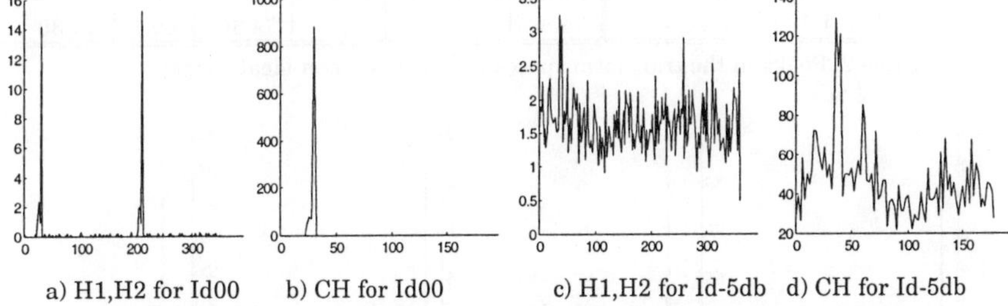

a) H1,H2 for Id00 b) CH for Id00 c) H1,H2 for Id-5db d) CH for Id-5db

Fig 3: Hough and Correlated Hough spaces for Id00 (no noise) and Id-5db .

Robustness to non-ideality of the shape has been evaluated against a test set of synthetic images with slightly irregular, divergent and curved edges (images are labelled with Ir, Di, and Cu, respectively). Fig. 4 shows three images from the test set.

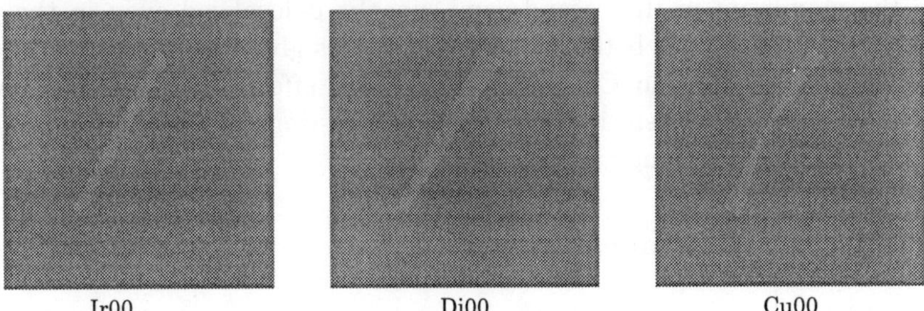

Ir00 Di00 Cu00

Fig. 4: Images with non-ideal bar-shaped objects.

Table 2 shows that in the case of a noisy contour (Ir, ∞ db), the

---

[a] Hough values are computed according to the basic GWHT algorithm in floating-point arithmetic; the gradient is computed with use of Prewitt masks. Grey-levels from 0 to 255 are previously normalized between 0 and 1.

peak's value P2.h is very low compared with the one in the ideal image (Id, ∞ db). This can lead to missing detection with the standard approach. The image with curved edge (Cu, ∞ db) manifests vote spreading and results in a Hough peak highly delocalized in the angular coordinate, that can not be associated with the peak in the other semi-space.

		Id		Ir		Di		Cu	
		h	(ρ,α)	h	(ρ,α)	h	(ρ,α)	h	(ρ,α)
∞	P1	14.2	76,32	13.6	76,32	14.2	76,32	8.7	76,32
db	P2	15.2	84,32	1.3	82,26	9.1	86,36	2.6	70,18
	P_{CH}	883.2	76,32	207.2	76,32	684.7	76,32	79.3	76,32
0	P1	2.3	74,30	2.3	74,30	2.3	74,30	2.3	74,30
db	P2	2.6	84,32	2.9	84,32	2.3	86,30	1.9	102,34
	P_{CH}	132.8	74,30	74.8	74,30	82.7	74,30	69.1	74,30

Table 2: Peaks in the transform spaces for ideal and non-ideal shapes.

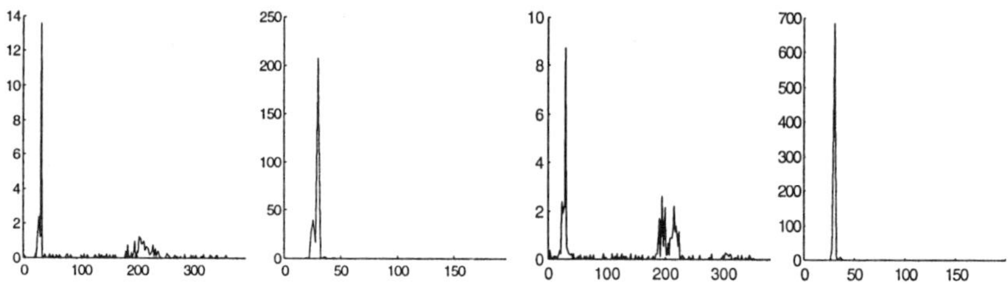

a) H1,H2 for Ir00 b) CH for Ir00 c) H1,H2 for Cu00 d) CH for Cu00

Fig 5: Hough and Correlated Hough spaces for non-ideal shapes.

Due to the combined effect of noise and curvature, in the case of 0 db the maximum in the second semi-space is delocalized even in the ρ coordinate; instead, in both cases the CH values give correct results. Fig. 5 shows Ir, ∞ db, and Cu, ∞ db, where the effects of curvature and contour noise are evident in the absence of a distinguishable, well-formed peak in the second Hough semi-space.

4 An example of application

The new operator selects a complex primitive which keeps up information on the existence in the image of a shape bright, straight enough (with an angular Δα tolerance), with a double change in luminosity variation in a very limited spatial neighborhood, i.e. something thin (with a Δt tolerance).

This primitive, thanks to its integral nature, has been shown to be very robust to noise, specially when noise results strong enough to confuse the single local features. CH has been adopted in an industrial application of defect detection. The aim is to detect the presence of an elongated shape, also in presence of noise, which is easy identifiable by human inspector but is not always detectable with the previously described classic approach.

As example of the application, three images are shown in Fig.6: Fig. 6a indicates a highly contrasted and elongated defect, Fig. 6b shows instead a shorter and blurred defect with a slight, but non negligible curvature. Finally Fig.6c is a very noisy image with a straight vertical defect in its central part.

Table 3 reports the values of the main peaks found: in the case of the first image, due to the evidence of the shape, also the classic approach based on maximal peaks in the Hough space is able to detect the defect.

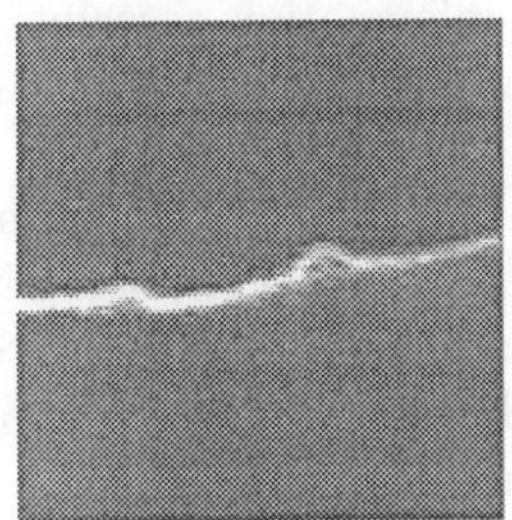
Fig. 6a

Fig. 6b

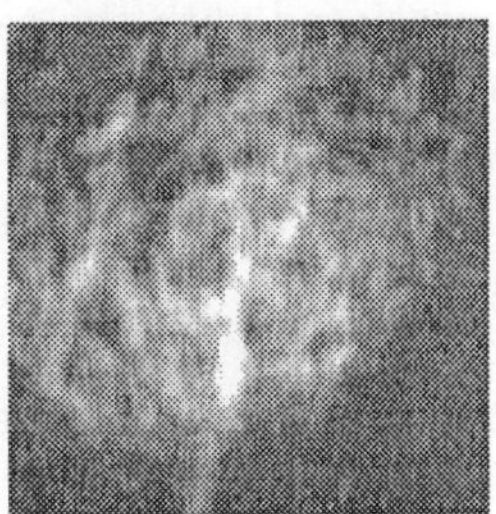
Fig. 6c

Fig. 6: Example of defects on a metallic surface.

	Fig. 6a		Fig. 6b		Fig. 6c	
	h	(r,a)	h	(r,a)	h	(r,a)
P1	8.8	76,86	2.41	86,88	3.9	34,16
P2	11.2	86,80	2.97	114,74	2.8	92,20
P_{CH}	1249.1	76,84	80.32	86,88	164.4	68,8

Table 3: Peaks for real images.

In the second example (Fig. 6b) the highest peak in the second semi-space (P2) does not correspond to the real defect but to its shadow. In this case while CH primitive directly detects the shape, the same task could be performed by the decision tree only by comparing a large set of local maxima, with high cost in term of computational time. Finally the last example (Fig. 6c) shows how, in some limit cases strongly affected by noise, the maxima found both in H1 and H2 do not correspond to real defects. They are due to blurs and spots but do not exhibit any correlation with respect to the model. Instead the effective defect is detectable at an angle of 8° and with a distance of 68 equivalent pixels, as indicated by the correspondent CH value.

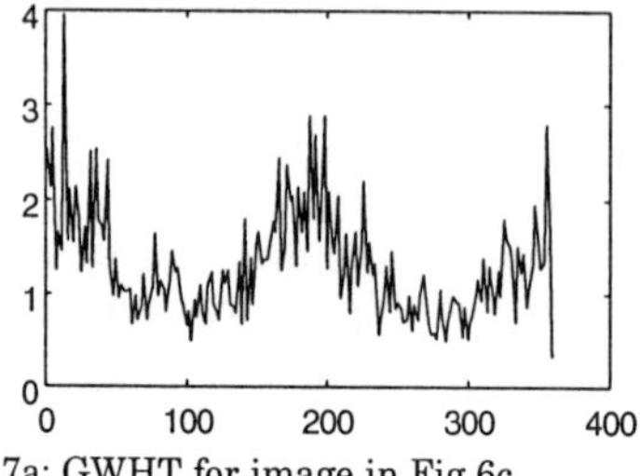

Fig.7a: GWHT for image in Fig.6c.

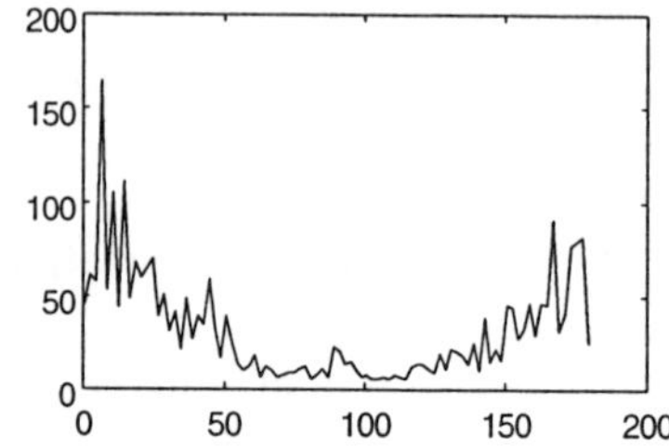

Fig .7b: CH for image in Fig.6c.

The expressive power of Correlated HT with respect to the GWHT can be intuitively argued also by comparing the graphs of Fig. 7. In real cases of non well-geometrically defined shapes, the Hough transform produces many local peaks: they can result difficult to be semantically associated with the target shape. Conversely, the information associated with CH is closer to the evaluated model and is more unbiased by local variations.

As a final consideration, the computation of correlation is not particularly critical in terms of computational time since is O(N), being N the number of points in the Hough Space. For this reason, together with the robustness of the method, we have used CH as the discriminant feature in a prototype for real-time, automated visual inspection.

This work has been also validated by an analysis performed with decision trees generated by automatic learning tools that have been used to select the most discriminant primitive among H1, H2 and CH on a statistically-significant data base of images [10].

5 Conclusion

The selection of more complex visual primitives, generated by adequate combination of local primitives is a common idea, proposed in many hierarchical visual approaches. For instance Bolle et al. in [9] define a visual system paradigm based on successive parametric transformations which, starting from local features, generate primitive features and feature assemblies, in order to validate hypotheses on the model. In our case a simple post-processing of local features allows for the selection of a suitable primitive which is able to detect the considered class of shapes even in presence of noise and blurred images.

6 Acknowledgements

The authors wish to thank Berco s.p.a for the availability of images and for grants to the research.

7 References

[1] R. Bajcsy, "Active Perception", *Proc. of IEEE*, vol. 76-8, pp. 996-1005 1988.

[2] G. Kanizsa, *Grammatica del vedere: saggi su percezione e Gestalt*, Bologna, Il Mulino, 1990.

[3] R. Cucchiara, F. Filicori, and R. Andreetta, "Detecting micro cracks in ferromagnetic material with automatic visual inspection", in *Proc. of QCAV 95*, 1995. pp. 19-24.

[4] R.T. Chin, C.R. Dyer, "Model Based Recognition in Robot Vision", *ACM Comp. Surveys*, vol. 18 n.1 pp. 67-108, 1986.

[5] P. J. Flynn, A. K. Jain, "BONSAI: 3d object recognition using constrained search", in *Proc. of IEEE Third Conference of Computer Vision*, pp. 263-267. 1990.

[6] J. Illingworth and J. Kittler, "A survey of the Hough transform", CVGIP, n. 43, pp. 221-238, 1988.

[7] T.M. Van Veen and F. C.A. Groen "Discretization errors in the Hough Transform", *Pattern Recognition*, vol. 14, pp 137-145, 1981.

[8] M. Bolle, A. Califano, R. Kjeldsen "A complete and extendable approach to visual recognition", *IEEE Trans. Pattern Anal. Machine Intell.*, vol. PAMI-14, n.5, 1992.

[9] D.J. Hunt, L.W. Nolte, A.R. Reibman "Hough transform and signal detection theory performance for images with additive noise", *CVGIP*, vol. 52, pp. 386-401, 1990.

[10] M. Bariani, R. Cucchiara, P. Mello, M. Piccardi "Data mining for automated visual inspection" in *Proc. of PADD97*, 1997, pp.51-64.

MULTIRESOLUTION REPRESENTATION AND RECONSTRUCTION OF TRIANGULATED SURFACES

LEILA DE FLORIANI, PAOLA MAGILLO
Dipartimento di Informatica e Scienze dell'Informazione – Università di Genova
Via Dodecaneso, 35 – 16146 Genova, ITALY

ENRICO PUPPO
Istituto per la Matematica Applicata – Consiglio Nazionale delle Ricerche
Via de Marini, 6 (Torre di Francia) – 16149 Genova, ITALY

A fairly general model, called a *multiresolution triangulation* (MT), for representing surfaces at different levels of detail is proposed. An MT supports efficient extraction of a representation of minimum size for a given level of detail, which may be variable over the surface. We illustrate general construction and extraction techniques, as well as applications of the MT in a variety of situations: from the approximation of CAD surfaces to the reconstruction of surfaces from scattered data. An extended version of this paper can be found in [9].

1 Introduction

Triangle meshes are a powerful tool for modelling the shape of complex objects and scenes in three-dimensional space. Due to the simplicity of their basic elements and of their connecting structure, triangle meshes are easily manipulated by analysis and visualization programs.

In several applications, surfaces are described by very dense triangle meshes. Detailed triangle meshes are obtained by scanning physical objects [13,21,1,6], or by extracting isosurfaces from high resolution datasets in volume visualization [17,21]; huge meshes are needed to describe large terrain areas [19]; displaying CAD surfaces usually involves their conversion into dense triangle meshes [16]; very large meshes may be produced in representing complex scenes in the context of virtual reality [14]. Also digital images, especially range images, can be regarded as surfaces, and their reconstruction through triangle meshes can help their processing and understanding [18,20].

Storage, manipulation, and rendering of huge meshes may easily require memory and processing resources beyond the power of state-of-the-art computers, especially in a real-time, interactive environment. Therefore, adapting the resolution of a mesh to the needs of each application is a basic issue. For example, using a lower level of detail for small, distant, or background objects may drastically improve performance in data analysis and visualization.

The aim of a multiresolution model is to provide a compact representation of a triangle mesh at several levels of detail (LODs), and to support the efficient extraction of a mesh at variable resolution upon request. In most cases, a multiresolution model may be built off-line and stored. On the other hand, meshes at a variable resolution must be extracted on-line in real time.

Here, we propose a model, called a *multiresolution triangulation*, that extends our previous proposal of a multiresolution model for scalar fields [19,7]. The model encodes a set of mesh fragments and a partial order defined on such fragments. Based on such partial order, sub-meshes can be combined together in different ways to obtain descriptions of a surface at different resolutions. In particular, the model allows the extraction of variable resolution representations, and thus it supports local control on the level of detail.

We illustrate applications of the multiresolution triangulation in two important cases: when a piecewise linear representation must be produced starting from an analytic description of a surface [16,14], and when a surface must be reconstructed from a set of sample points belonging to it [13,21,1,6].

2 Reconstruction Problems

Two major application problems motivate the use of multiresolution triangle meshes: the definition of polyhedral approximations for analytic CAD surfaces [16,8], and the reconstruction of surfaces from sampled data [1,14,4].

Problem 1

Given the boundary surface $\mathcal{S}$ of a solid object, described by a set of patches sewn together with a certain degree of continuity, produce a multiresolution representation of $\mathcal{S}$.

This kind of conversion is typically required for rendering on graphic devices, and for solving problems with finite element methods. Generating meshes at variable resolution is crucial for real-time visualization and animation of large CAD models, such as those used in virtual reality.

Problem 2

Given a set of points in Euclidean space that belong to a surface $\mathcal{S}$, produce a multiresolution representation of $\mathcal{S}$.

When a set of scattered points is the only information available, the primary issue is the definition of a topology for the input data. Special cases occur when some topological information is available:

Problem 2(a)

$\mathcal{S}$ describes a two-dimensional scalar field, *i.e., is the graph of a function $\phi : \Omega \longrightarrow \mathbb{R}$, where Ω is a compact subset of $\mathbb{R}^2$.*

In this case, the topology of the data points is induced by the neighborhood relationships among their projections on the xy-plane. Examples are the reconstruction of *terrain* models from elevation measurements in geographic information systems [19], and the segmentation of *digital images* [20,18].

Problem 2(b)
A triangle mesh T *connecting the data points is given.*
This occurs, for instance, for data extracted through laser range scanners[13,21,1,6], or for isosurfaces obtained from volume datasets [17,21].
Problem 2(c)
The data points belong to contours *obtained by intersecting a solid object with a sequence of cutting planes.*
Here, topological information is represented by the polylines connecting the points of each contour and by the sequential order of contours. This problem is important in medical applications such as CT, NMR, and PET [3].

3 The Multiresolution Triangulation

A *triangulated surface* (or *triangle mesh*) is a piecewise linear surface with triangular faces. A *triangulated approximation* of a given surface $\mathcal{S}$ is a triangle mesh T, which preserves the topological type of $\mathcal{S}$ and is geometrically "close" to $\mathcal{S}$ with respect to some *distance* measure, which depends on the specific application.

A *Multiresolution Triangulation* (MT) is made of a collection of *components* arranged in a partial order. Each component represents two triangle meshes, giving two different descriptions of a portion of the surface, at a lower and a higher resolution, respectively. The partial order of components is described by a *Directed Acyclic Graph* (DAG) having such components as nodes. There exists an arc from component N_a to component N_b if and only if one or more triangles of the mesh at higher resolution in N_a also belong to the mesh at lower resolution in N_b. The DAG is rooted at a *source* component, representing only one triangle mesh, which describes the whole surface at lowest resolution available in the model. A further *drain* component is in the DAG, which also represents only one triangle mesh approximating the whole surface at the highest available resolution.

More formally, a *multiresolution triangulation* (MT) for a surface $\mathcal{S}$ is a directed acyclic graph $\mathcal{M} = (\mathcal{N}, \mathcal{A})$, where:

1. there is a unique source node $N_0 \in \mathcal{N}$, with no incoming arcs, and a unique drain node $N_d \in \mathcal{N}$, with no outcoming arcs; both N_0 and N_d are a triangle mesh representing the whole surface;
2. each other node $N_i \in \mathcal{N}$ is a pair of triangle meshes $< T_i, T_i' >$ and describing a portion of $\mathcal{S}$: the boundaries of T_i and T_i' are coincident;
3. any two nodes $N_i =< T_i, T_i' >$, $N_j =< T_j, T_j' >$ such that $T_i' \cap T_j$ contains at least one triangle are connected by an arc $(N_i, N_j) \in \mathcal{A}$;
4. if T_0 is the source triangle mesh, then $\mathcal{A}$ contains an arc (N_0, N_i) for every node $N_i =< T_i, T_i' >$, such that $T_0 \cap T_j$ contains at least one triangle;

5. if T_d is the drain triangle mesh, then $\mathcal{A}$ contains an arc (N_i, N_d) for every node $N_i =< T_i, T_i' >$, such that $T_j' \cap T_d$ contains at least one triangle.

Figure 1 shows an MT for a scalar field. Here, a triangle mesh approximating the surface corresponds to a triangulation of the surface domain, and thus an MT is a DAG of plane triangulations.

We observe that each triangle in the model appears in exactly two triangle meshes, connected by an arc. The data structure [19] used to encode an MT represents the DAG, but for efficiency it stores triangles in arcs rather than in nodes: every arc (N_i, N_j) is labelled with the set of triangles common to N_i and N_j. The space required is linear in the number of triangles of the MT.

A cut of the DAG is a set of arcs that separate the source from the drain. The set of triangles labeling any possible cut in the DAG provides a triangle mesh representing the whole surface. Intuitively, different cuts of the DAG lead to approximations of $\mathcal{S}$ at different LODs: the mesh corresponding to a cut closer to the drain node has a higher resolution.

Formal properties of multiresolution triangulations are treated in [19,7].

An MT $\mathcal{M}$ supports the extraction of a triangulated surface, made of triangles of $\mathcal{M}$, which represents the original surface $\mathcal{S}$ within any user-defined LOD. The required LOD can be expressed as a function $\tau : \mathbb{R}^3 \rightarrow \mathbb{R}$, which defines the maximum error tolerance for the surface representation at each point of 3D space. Each triangle t in a component is characterized by an approximation error. The error value associated with t depends on the *distance* between t and the patch of $\mathcal{S}$ approximated by t. Let t be a triangle of $\mathcal{M}$; function τ either accepts or discards t depending on whether the error associated with t is smaller or greater than the minimum value of τ over t.

Given a function τ, the *simplest* triangulated representation of $\mathcal{S}$, made of triangles of $\mathcal{M}$, and such that every triangle satisfies the given error requirements must be found. The problem is equivalent to finding the nearest cut to the root of $\mathcal{M}$ such that all triangles in the associated triangle mesh have an acceptable resolution.

An algorithm for extracting a mesh at variable resolution has been proposed in [19] for two-dimensional scalar fields, and directly applies to MTs representing any kind of surfaces. Such an algorithm basically performs a traversal of the DAG of $\mathcal{M}$ in breadth-first order to locate the appropriate cut.

The result of an extraction of a triangle mesh at variable resolution representing the boundary of a solid object is shown in Figure 2; here, resolution increases in the neighborhood of a predefined point.

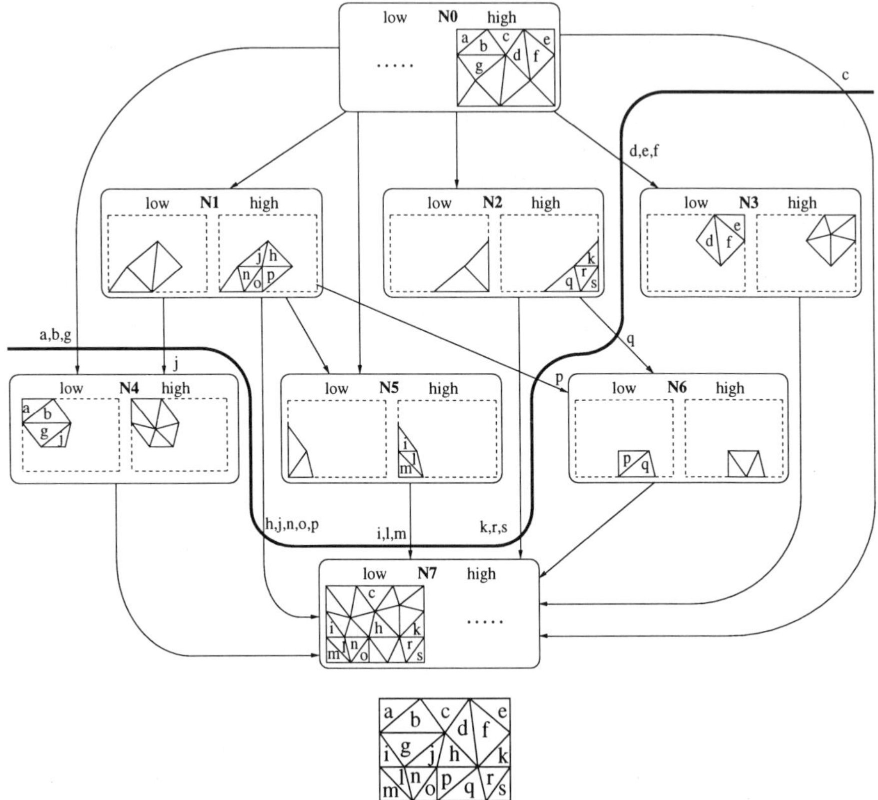

Figure 1: A multiresolution triangulation for a scalar field, a cut, and the corresponding triangulation. The labels of the triangles associated with each arc of the cut are shown.

4 Construction of a Multiresolution Triangulation

The construction of an MT relies on *incremental methods* for building triangulated surface approximations. Two basic incremental strategies exist:

- *refinement* methods, which start from a coarse approximation of the given surface and progressively refine it;
- *simplification* methods, which start from a representation at maximum resolution and progressively coarsen it.

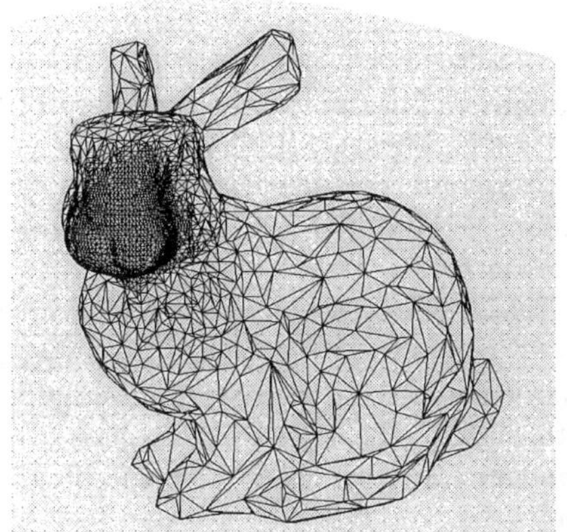

Figure 2: Representation of the boundary surface of an object at variable resolution. The approximation error is a function of the distance from a point located near bunny's nose. The variable resolution mesh uses 3,656 triangles out of 69,451 of the mesh at full resolution.

An MT is built by collecting components that correspond to local updates of a triangulated surface performed during the incremental process (each update defines a component whose triangle meshes are formed by the set of removed triangles, and by the set of of newly created triangles, respectively), and by arranging them into a DAG. The construction of an MT has the same asymptotical time complexity of the incremental method adopted.

Basic ingredients of an incremental construction method are:

1. a method for obtaining an initial triangle mesh;
2. a LOD test that decides whether a mesh must be refined/simplified further or not;
3. a criterion for selecting the point to be inserted/deleted at each step;
4. a criterion for updating the mesh because of the insertion/deletion of a point.

In the following Subsections, we discuss how such issues are faced in the context of the various problems defined in Section 2.

4.1 Building an MT for Scalar Fields

A triangle mesh T approximating a scalar field $\mathcal{S}$ given a set of sample points $\mathcal{D}$ can be obtained from a triangulation Σ having vertices at a subset of xy-projections of the points in $\mathcal{D}$. An approximating surface is defined locally on each triangle of Σ. In the case of terrains, a linear interpolant of the elevations measured at the three triangle vertices may be used; in the case of digital images, a constant or a polynomial fit to data spanned by the triangle can be adopted [18].

An initial triangulation for refinement methods can be obtained simply by considering a triangulation of the polygonal boundary of the domain of $\mathcal{S}$; an initial triangulation for simplification methods is built on all data points. The LOD test depends on an *approximation error* that is defined for each triangle $t \in \Sigma$ by the maximum vertical distance from T of those points of $\mathcal{D}$ whose vertical projection lies in t.

Most heuristics select points for insertion/deletion in a greedy way: in refinement methods, the point causing the maximum error over the whole triangulation is usually inserted at each step; in simplification methods, the point that is likely to cause the least error increase is usually selected.

A set of point and/or line features may be specified, which correspond to characteristics of the surface described by a scalar field. Point features may be included in an MT by just requiring that the initial triangulation from which a refinement method starts contains them, or that a simplification method does not remove them. Line features can be included in a multiresolution triangulation by using a *constrained triangulation* (both in refinement and in simplification). Note that the complexity of a line feature must adapt to the current level of detail. For this purpose, the construction process of the MT is split into two steps: first, a multiresolution model for the constraints is built; then, a multiresolution triangulation is built, which conforms to the multiresolution representation of the constraints.

4.2 Building an MT from Trianglulated Free-Form Surfaces

For free-form surfaces, an inital mesh at the highest available resolution is provided as input. In this case the bottom-up construction paradigm is most suitable.

The literature on mesh simplification is quite wide, and each method has its own simplification rules and error measure. For our purpose, only incremental algorithms are of interest:

- *mesh decimation* methods, which are based on the iterative elimination of vertices and on the retriangulation of the resulting holes [21,6,4,1];
- *mesh optimization methods*, which perform a sequence of elementary modifications that try to minimize an energy function defined over the mesh [14];
- *triangle collapse*, which iteratively shrinks the triangle having minimum principal curvature at its vertices to a single vertex [11].

4.3 Building an MT from Scattered Data or Cross Sections

The primary issue for building an MT of an unknown surface, given a set of scattered points, or a sequence of contours, is defining an initial topology for the data points (i.e., a triangle mesh connecting them). Such initial topology will be a triangulated surface passing through all the data points. Then, an MT can be built by using simplification methods, as described in Section 4.2.

A number of techniques have been proposed for reconstructing a triangle mesh from an unorganized set of points in space. The *sculpturing method*[2] and the *α-shape approach*[1] start from a Delaunay tetrahedralization of the convex hull and move internal data to the boundary by eliminating tetrahedra. Hoppe et al. [13] propose a different method to reconstruct a triangulated surface that does not necessarily pass through the given points, but reflects the shape of the original object.

The problem of finding a triangulated surface passing through a given sequence of cross sections is usually addressed by constructing a sequence of partial meshes, each of them connecting two contours lying on adjacent planes, and then glueing them[15,10,3].

4.4 Building an MT from CAD data

Surface patches used in CAD models are typically described as *parametric surfaces*. Triangulated approximations of a parametric surface are usually obtained by defining a triangulation of a polygonal approximation of its domain in parameter space.

When several parametric surfaces compose the boundary of a solid object, a major issue is ensuring matching between the approximations of any pair of adjacent faces. This is achieved through a two-step method[8]. First, a multiresolution model for the boundaries of each face is defined, which describes their progressively finer approximation by chains of straight-line segments. Then, a multiresolution triangulation is built separately for the interior of each face, which conforms to the multiresolution representation of its boundary. Finally, the local MTs of adjacent faces are glued together at boundary edges.

5 Concluding Remarks

We have proposed a multiresolution model of a triangle mesh, called a *multiresolution triangulation* (MT), which is based a collection of partially ordered elementary components. An MT supports the extraction in optimal time of any triangle mesh formed by triangles belonging to its components, and approximating a surface at variable resolution. We have shown applications of the MT in different contexts, and we have shown that an MT can be built from several data sources, i.e., scattared data, contours, CAD data.

Some other techniques for multiresolution surface representation based on mesh simplification methods have been recently proposed in the literature. The approaches of Hoppe[14] and of Klein and Straßer[16] are based on encoding the reverse history of a mesh simplification process, and they are aimed to minimizing information stored. The difficulty of extracting triangles meshes at variable resolution, different from the ones appeared during the simplification process, reduces the flexibility of these models: algorithms must either perform complicated computations[16], or accept a loss of precision in some areas of the object[14]. The model proposed by Ciampalini et al.[4] is based on an interval tree of triangles, and supports fast extraction of a representation only at uniform resolution. Compared with such approaches, our model requires more memory, but it is far more powerful computationally, since it can extract a mesh at variable resolution in optimal time for any given LOD.

The multiresolution triangulation has been extended to d-dimensions in[7], where this model has been shown to encompass multiresolution data structures proposed in the literature in the past. Three-dimensional refinement techniques[5] can be successfully applied to obtain an MT in 3D to support multiresolution visualization of volume data.

Further developments of the work consist in the definition of an implicit data structure for compact encoding of an MT, which avoids explicitly storing the triangles, and the development of a library of data structures and algorithms for multiresolution manipulation of surfaces in arbitrary dimensions.

Finally, we plan to investigate further the application of MTs to the multiresolution analysis of digital images, by combining this model with the adaptive approach to segmentation described in[18], and with pyramidal techniques for image analysis.

References

1. C.L. Bajaj, F. Bernardini, J. Chen, D.R. Schikore, Automatic reconstruction of 3D CAD models, *Theory and Practice of Geometric Modeling*, W. Straßer, R. Klein, R. Rau (Eds), Springer-Verlag (1996).
2. J.D. Boissonnat, Geometric structures for three-dimensional shape representation, *ACM Transactions on Graphics*, 3(4), 266–286 (1984).
3. J. D. Boissonnat, Shape Reconstruction from Planar Cross-Sections, *Computer Vision, Graphics and Image Processing*, 44, 1–29 (1988).
4. A. Ciampalini, P. Cignoni, C. Montani, R. Scopigno, Multiresolution decimation based on global error, *The Visual Computer* (to appear).
5. P. Cignoni, L. De Floriani, C. Montani, E. Puppo, R. Scopigno, Multiresolution Modeling and Visualization of Volume Data Based on Simplicial Complexes, *Proc. ACM Symp. on Volume Visualization*, 19–26 (1994).
6. J. Cohen, A. Varshney, D. Manocha, G. Turk, H. Weber, P. Agarwal, F. Brooks, W. Wright, Simplification envelopes, *Proc. SIGGRAPH 96*, 119–128 (1996).
7. L. De Floriani, P. Magillo, E. Puppo, A formal approach to multiresolution modeling, *Theory and Practice of Geometric Modeling*, W. Straßer,

R. Klein, R. Rau (Eds), Springer-Verlag (1996).
8. L. De Floriani, P. Magillo, E. Puppo, Representing parametric surfaces at variable resolution, *Tech. Rep.* DISI-TR-96-21, DISI, Univ. of Genova, Italy (1996).
`http://www.disi.unige.it/ftp/person/MagilloP/PS/disi96-21.ps`
9. L. De Floriani, P. Magillo, E. Puppo, Multiresolution representation and reconstruction of triangulated surfaces, *Tech. Rep.* DISI-TR-96-26, DISI, Univ. of Genova, Italy (1996).
`http://www.disi.unige.it/ftp/person/MagilloP/PS/disi96-26.ps`
10. H. Fuchs, S.P. Usenton, Z. Zedem, Optimal surface reconstruction from planar contours, *Communications of the ACM*, 20(10), 693–702 (1977).
11. B. Hamman, A data reduction scheme for triangulated surfaces, *Computer Aided Geometric Design*, 11, 197–214 (1994).
12. P. Hinker, C. Hansen, Geometric optimization, *Proc. IEEE Visualization*, 189–195 (1993).
13. H. Hoppe, T. DeRose, T. Duchamp, J. McDonald, W. Stuelzle, Surface reconstruction from unorganized points, *Proc. SIGGRAPH 92*, 71–78 (1992).
14. H. Hoppe, Progressive meshes, *Proc. SIGGRAPH 96*, 99–108 (1996).
15. E. Keppel, Approximating complex surfaces by triangulation of contour lines, *IBM Journal of Research and Development*, 19(1), 2–11 (1975).
16. R. Klein, W. Straßer, Generation of multiresolution models from CAD data for real time rendering, *Theory and Practice of Geometric Modeling*, W. Straßer, R. Klein, R. Rau (Editors), Springer-Verlag (1996).
17. W. E. Lorensen, H.E. Cline, Marching cubes: a high resolution 3D surface construction algorithm, *Proceedings SIGGRAPH 87*, 163–169 (1987).
18. E. Puppo, Segmentation/reconstruction of range images based on piecewise-linear approximation, *LNCS*, 974, 367–379 (1995).
19. E. Puppo, Variable resolution terrain surfaces, *Proc. 8th Canadian Conference on Computational Geometry*, 202–210 (1996).
20. F. Schmitt, X. Chen, Fast segmentation of range images into planar regions, *Proc. Computer Vision and Pattern Recognition*, 710–711 (1991).
21. W.J. Schroeder, J.A. Zarge, W. Lorensen, Decimation of triangle mesh, *Proc. SIGGRAPH 92*, 65–70 (1992).

ZERO-CROSSING EDGE BEHAVIOR IN SCALE SPACE AND ITS APPLICATION TO CONTOUR FIGURE APPROXIMATIONS

Koichiro DEGUCHI
Faculty of Engineering, University of Tokyo
Bunkyo-ku, Tokyo 113 Japan

In this paper, we propose a method to determine local inherent scales which characterize the contour edge of binary figure. In the method, we trace zero-crossing edge of the output of Laplacian-of-Gaussian (LoG) filters in scale space. Fine structures in a image are blurred out and more smoothed edge will be obtained by increasing the scale, so that the zero-crossing edge moves and we have deformations of extracted contour. Based on the change of velocity of the edge point movements in this process with respect to the scale value, we determine characteristic scale values for the edge point by point. First, we analyze how the zero-crossing edge moves depending on the scale and curvature radius of the original contour at the edge point. Then, we present an algorithm to determine characteristic scales for contour points, and propose a contour approximation using the extracted characteristic scales. Our experimental results show also the possibility of the proposed method for edge extraction of gray level images.

1 Introduction

One of the most devised techniques for scale space analysis of contour figure edge is to extract zero-crossings of the output of a Laplacian-of-Gaussian (LoG) filtering. In the technique, an input binary image is blurred by a Gaussian filter

$$\frac{1}{2\pi\sigma^2}\exp(-\frac{x^2+y^2}{2\sigma^2}) , \tag{1}$$

then output points of gradient extremum or equivalently zero-crossings of successive Laplacian filtering are extracted. The σ in (1) is commonly called a *scale*. With large value of σ, global contour features are obtained and false small notches caused by noise are avoided. But too large scale results in large deformation of extracted contour edge. A suitable value of σ to detect a proper edge depends on the shape of the original contour itself to be detected.

A pioneer research of a compromise between noise and the deformation was reported by Canny[1], in which edge maps were obtained with several σ values and merged to generate more reliable edge contour. But he only considered straight line edge contours. Lu et al.[2] reported more complicated behaviors of output zero-crossing edge contour with changes of the scale.

An example of such a complex edge behavior is shown in **Fig.1**. The zero-crossing contours are deformed from their original edge in various ways according to the scale values. These are caused by the fact that, mainly, the deformation with the scale change depends on the local curvature radius of the edge contour to be extracted. Therefore, the amount deformation differs point by point even for the same scale value. Such an edge deformation has been considered in-preferable, because the low level feature extraction should be stable and robust to small change of parameters and image noise.

In this paper, however, we claim that such a complex behavior is a kind of reflection of original contour shape, so that it should have powerful meaning in shape description[34]. We focus on the relation between the local curvature radius of the original contour and the deformation with respect to the scale. Based on this relation, observing how the local deformation occurs for the scale value, we evaluate the local curvature radius of the contour. We introduce the *velocity* of the movement of extracted edge point with respect to the scale changes. Then, we show that it changes drastically just when a local notch shape is smoothed out by the filter. The scale value at this moment is considered to characterize the size of the local feature and used to characterize contour feature at this point.

2 Edge Movements in the Scale Space

2.1 The Edge Movement by the Scale Change

The target original image is of binary figure.

The image is blurred with a Gaussian filter having a scale σ. Then the zero-crossings of the output of the Laplacian filter of the blurred image are extracted as an edge map of the original image. Practically this process is

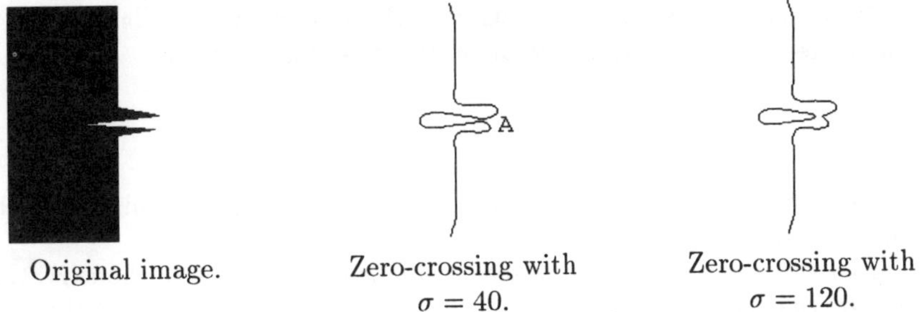

Original image. Zero-crossing with $\sigma = 40$. Zero-crossing with $\sigma = 120$.

Figure 1: An example of edge extraction by zero-crossings with various scales. The resulted edge figures are shown to have complex behaviors with respect to the scale values. Especially, around the point indicated "A" in the figure, the shown deformation cannot be expected in advance.

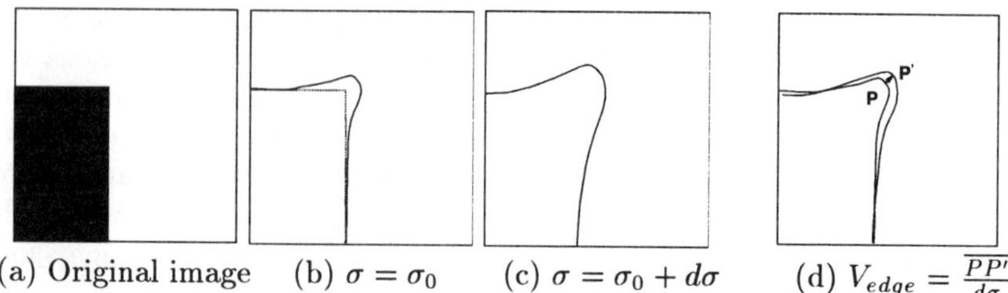

(a) Original image (b) $\sigma = \sigma_0$ (c) $\sigma = \sigma_0 + d\sigma$ (d) $V_{edge} = \frac{\overline{PP'}}{d\sigma}$

Figure 2: (a) An original binary figure, (b)zero-crossing contour of output of LoG with a scale σ_0, (c) zero-crossing contour with image blurred with a scale σ_0 then binarized, (d) zero-crossing $\sigma = \sigma_0 + d\sigma$, and (d) velocity of edge movement with increasing the scale σ.

realized by applying the simplest 3×3 so-called *LoG* (Laplacian of Gaussian) filter iteratively according to the value of σ.

Let us consider the case where, as shown in **Fig.2**, a binary image is blurred by LoG filter and extracted zero-crossing contour. Increasing the scale σ, we obtain different deformations. In this case, if the point P on the contour with scales σ corresponds to the point P' on the contour with $\sigma + d\sigma$, that is, the point P moves to P' while the scale value changes, the *velocity* of the movement with respect to the change of the scale is given as

$$V_{edge} \equiv \frac{\overline{PP'}}{d\sigma}. \tag{2}$$

This velocity becomes larger as the curvature of the edge at P becomes larger. In [3],zero-crossing edge movement was analyzed for binary circular disk blurred by LoG filters, whose scales are comparable to the radius of the disk. Following this analysis, the zero-crossing edge of output of LoG filter has always larger curvature radius. When the original curvature radius of a contour point is R, and it is filtered by a LoG with the scale σ which is comparable to R, the increment of curvature radius by this filtering is given as

$$\Delta(\sigma, R) \approx k\frac{\sigma^4}{R^3} \tag{3}$$

where k is a constant determined by the gray level edge magnitude of the original image.

From this relation, when the scale value σ is equivalent to the curvature radius R, that is $\sigma \approx R$, we have the "*velocity*" of the movement of the edge point as

$$V_{edge} = \frac{d\Delta(\sigma, R)}{d\sigma} \approx 4 \cdot k\frac{\sigma^3}{R^3} \tag{4}$$

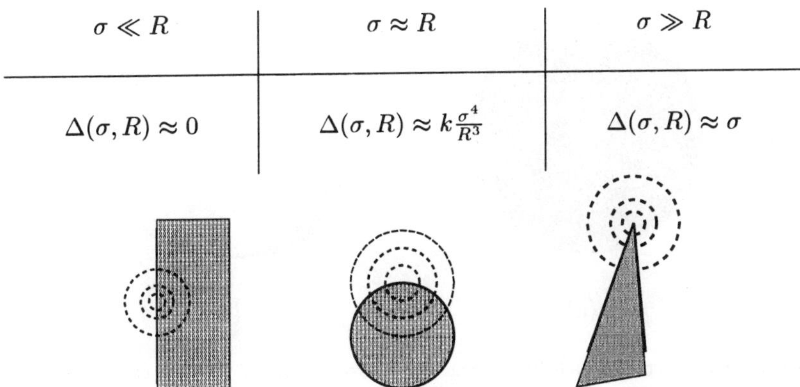

Figure 3: Summary of the edge deformations for the values of the contour curvature radius R.

On the other hand, when $\sigma \gg R$, it can be observed that $\Delta(\sigma, R) \approx \sigma$ This is acceptable when we suppose the extreme case of $R \approx 0$. For this case, the output of LoG filter with σ becomes so-called its point spread function which is the filter form itself. This implies that the output zero-crossing edge is a circle with the radius σ, and the velocity of the edge movement is given as

$$V_{edge} = \frac{d\Delta(\sigma, R)}{d\sigma} \approx 1 \quad \text{(const.)} \tag{5}$$

For the case of $\sigma \ll R$, it is clear that $\Delta(\sigma, R) \approx 0$ and the output edge is almost stable and

$$V_{edge} = \frac{d\Delta(\sigma, R)}{d\sigma} \approx 0 \quad . \tag{6}$$

Figure 3 shows the summary of these cases.

In the following section, we propose to utilize this relation. Especially, we discuss that above mentioned behavior at $\sigma \approx R$ has possibility to extract local inherent scales of an original contour figure.

2.2 Scale Selection by Edge Velocity

Figure 4(a) shows a figure which has a large structure of a global circular shape and simultaneously a small structure of a local protuberance on its edge. Blurring this image next by next by increasing the scale, the small structure will gradually be smoothed out and finally disappear. Figure 4(b) shows the

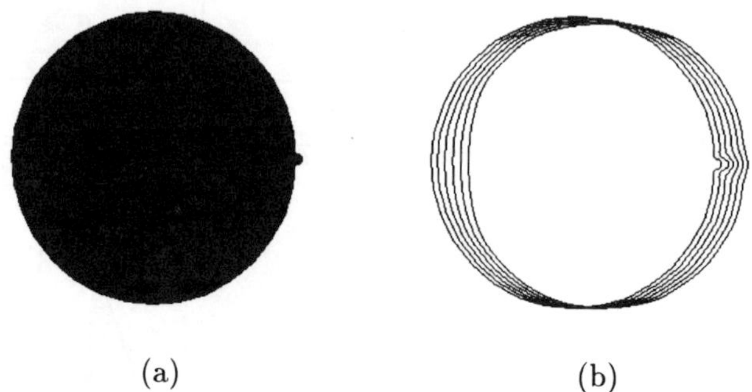

(a) (b)

Figure 4: (a) A figure which has a large structure of a global circular shape and simultaneously a small structure of a local protuberance on its edge. (b) The extracted edges with several σ's (overlaid from left to right in ascending order of σ values with small shifts).

resulted edges with several σ's (plots are overlaid from left to right in ascending order of σ values with small shifts).

We denote the curvature radius of the original edge at the small structure by R_1, and that of the large structure by R_2. For this figure, $R_1 \ll R_2$. From above discussions, for the value of σ within the range where the small structure remains and is not smoothed out, the edge velocity is given as

$$V_{edge} \approx 4 \cdot k \frac{\sigma^3}{R_1^3} \tag{7}$$

Once the small structure is smoothed out with a larger σ, it will be

$$V_{edge} \approx 4 \cdot k \frac{\sigma^3}{R_2^3} \tag{8}$$

Therefore, the ratio of velocities before and after the small structure is smoothed out has an order of $\left(\frac{R_1}{R_2}\right)^3$.

This means that the velocity of the edge point movement on the small structure will decrease drastically just when the small structure is smoothed out and disappear, because the ratio $\frac{R_1}{R_2} = 0.01$ and the velocity itself will decrease into the multiple of 10^{-6}. This also means the possibility to detect the scale σ with which a local structure is smoothed out and included into next higher structure of the hierarchical description.

However, to employ directly the above mentioned principle for the determination of characteristic scales for points on digital image, we must introduce

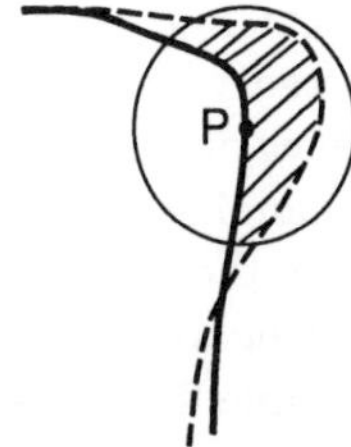

Figure 5: Area based measure F_{edge} to evaluate the edge movements for digital images.

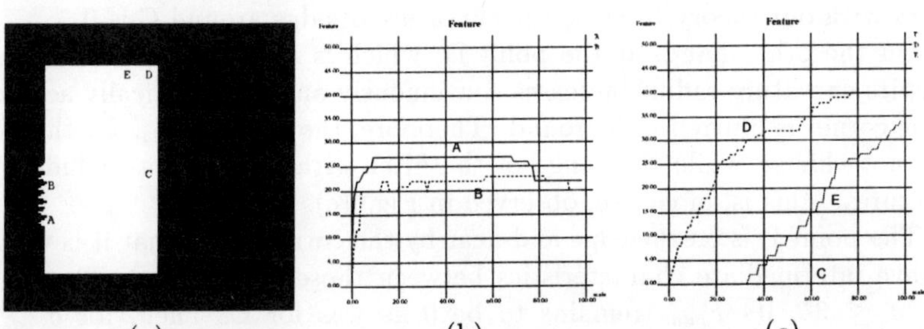

(a) (b) (c)

Figure 6: (a) An example image having both small structures and large ones. (b) Plots of F_{edge}'s at points A and B on (a) with respect to the change of σ. (c) Plots of F_{edge}'s at points C, D, and E on (a).

an alternate value to estimate the velocity. This is because, it is hard to trace point correspondences in the deformation. One of the feasible value is, as shown in **Fig.5**, an area based measure F_{edge}. Let us set a circle with radius δ and center P which is an edge point of original figure. The measure F_{edge} is defined as the *area* of the region within this circle and swept out by the moving edge while σ changes to a certain value of σ_0. The radius δ is given so as the moving edge will not run outside the circle for every σ_0.

For an edge with curvature radius R, this measure of F_{edge} is given as

$$F_{edge} \approx O(R^{-2}) \tag{9}$$

Therefore, this F_{edge} also change its rate drastically for the change of σ, as is the same case for V_{edge}, just when a small structure is smoothed out.

3 Experiments for Local Scale Detection

In this section we describe some experimental results of the behavior of F_{edge} on digital images.

First experiment shows that local edges will be well characterized by observing the velocity of edge movements. **Figure 6**(a) is an image having some sizes of structures. On this image F_{edge}'s at each points from A to E were traced while its edges are extracted with various scales. The results are plotted with respect to the scale values on Fig.6(b) and (c).

At the points A and B the changing rates of F_{edge} reduce abruptly around $\sigma = 5$ to 10. This value of σ can be thought of the characteristic scale at which the small structure around those points was smoothed out and disappeared. So that, the characteristic scale value for this small structure is about 5 to 10.

In Fig.6(c) the F_{edge} for the point C which is in the middle of right hand long straight edge is plotted as always 0 (overlapped on the scale axis). This agrees with our theory because the curvature of edge around C is 0.

On the other hand, at the point D, which is at a corner of the original edge, its curvature radius increases continuously and monotonically according as the corner is blurred to be round. Therefore, the rate of F_{edge} for this point does not change while the range of the filter with σ does not include other structures. This is, of course, observed in Fig.6(c).

The point E is on the edge and near by the corner D, so that it is thought to have intermediate characteristics between those of C and D. That is, for $0 \leq \sigma \leq 35$, its F_{edge} remains to be 0 as was for C. Then, for $\sigma > 35$, it increases monotonically as was the case for D. This means that with the smaller scale than 35 the point E is observed as a point on a straight edge, and it is observed as a corner point with larger scale than 35. This interpretation agrees with our intuitive observations.

4 Contour Approximation with Local scales

We have shown, in previous section, that characteristic scales for local edge structures can be extracted based on the behaviors of F_{edge} values for the change of σ. Here we present a method of contour approximation based on the extracted characteristic scales.

The steps of this approximation are in the followings:

1) For a given image, applying LoG filters with the increasing scale σ next by next from 0, extract edges as zero-crossings. At the same time, trace the edge movements in the scale space, and obtain F_{edge} values for all edge points.

2) For every point q on the original edge (which is an edge with $\sigma = 0$), determine the characteristic scale σ_q following the next procedures: Let w and a be input parameters. Increasing the value of σ from 0, compare the increments v_1 and v_2 of F_{edge} within $[\sigma - w, \sigma]$ and $[\sigma, \sigma + w]$, respectively. If $|v_1| \geq a \cdot |v_2|$, then register this σ as the characteristic scale σ_q for this point. A point may have several characteristic scales. If no value of σ assigned for a point, it has no structural characteristics. For such a point assign $\sigma_q = 0$.

3) Take moving averages of the characteristic scale σ_q along with nearby edge points using some weights w_p and window δ as $\hat{\sigma}_q = \sum_{p \in \delta} w_p \sigma_p$ to avoid noise effects.

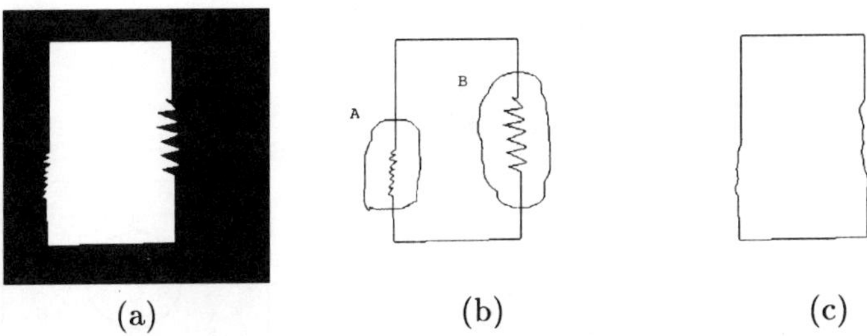

Figure 7: (a) Another example of figure image having a large structure of rectangle and two small structures on left and right side edges. (b)The distribution of obtained characteristic scales from (a). (c) The obtained approximation contour based on the characteristic scale distribution for (a).

4) Using the obtained respective characteristic scale value for every points, take the Laplacian of Gaussian filters again on the original figure, and extract the zero-crossing of the output as the approximating figure.

Figure 7(a) is an example of original image having two small structures on left and right side edges of a large structure of rectangle. Figure 7(b) shows the distribution of obtained characteristic scales. Within the region A the scales were between 17 and 25, those in the region B were between 50 and 73, and otherwise 0.

Based on these characteristic scales, the edge contour shown in Fig.7(c) was obtained, in which small structures are smoothed out but corners of large structure remain sharply as they were.

5 Edge Extraction for Textural Region and Gray Level Image

We have shown the determination of characteristic scales for point by point on edge of a given image. Here, we show some experimental results of edge extractions which demonstrate the advantages of our method to the uniform scale value filtering[6].

Figure 8(a) is a figure of circle area having texture distribution in it. For a comparison, first, we show the results of edge extraction by LoG filters with uniform scale values in Fig.8(b)–(d). As the scale value increases, point pattern edges were disappearing, but false circular edge was appearing at the same time. We could not determine proper uniform scale value to characterize global feature of this image.

Figure 8(e) is the edge extraction using F_{edge} for local scale value determination. LoG filters with locally variable scales were applied and the output zero-crossings were extracted. Its global circular shape was well extracted.

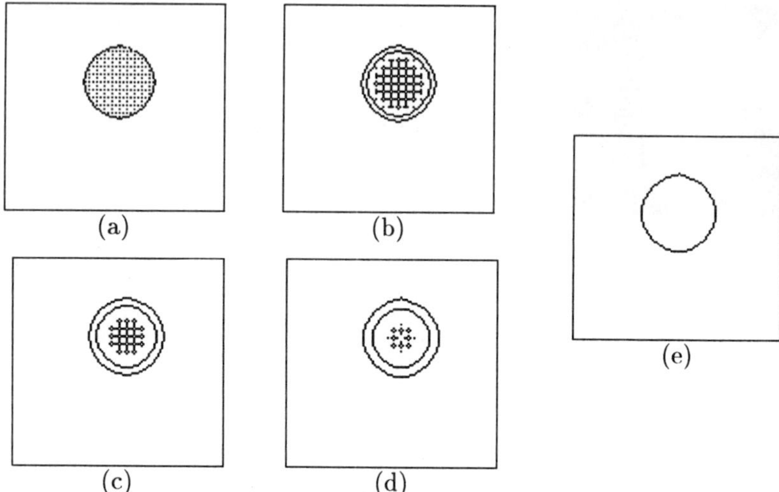

Figure 8: (a) Original image (98 × 98 pixels). The circular radius is 38, and the results of edge extraction by uniform LoG filters with scales of (b) $\sigma = 3$, (c) $\sigma = 5$, and (d) $\sigma = 7$. (e) The results of edge extraction by proposed method with local variable scales determined by using F_{edge}.

We also applied proposed method to a gray level image. The original image and its edge extraction results using some uniform scale values are shown in **Fig.9**(a)–(c) for the comparisons. Figure 9(d) is the results with local scales determined using F_{edge}. This shows also good edge extraction is achieved to characterize the image features.

6 Conclusions

In this paper, we proposed a method to determine local inherent scales which characterize the contour edge of figure. In the method, we tracked edge movements in scale space. Based on the change of velocity of the edge movements with respect to the scale value, we determined characteristic scale values for the edge points. It has been also shown that, in the resulted edge figure, global structures remain with their details while small unnecessary structures were well smoothed out. The results promises this proposed method works well for edge extraction from noisy images. The theoretical analysis of edge behavior in gray level images is still left, because for complex gray level changes produce really complex changes of F_{edge} values with respect to the scale change. But, our experimental result also promises the proposed method should have good performances for gray level images.

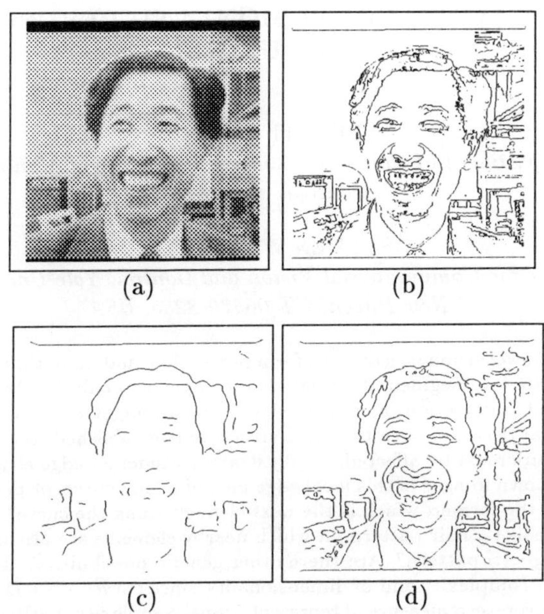

Figure 9: Edge extraction using uniform LoG filter for a gray level image, (a) Original image (512×512), (b) $\sigma = 2.0$, and (c) $\sigma = 23.0$, and (d) edge extraction with variable local scales determined by using F_{edge}.

References

[1] J.Canny. A Computational Approach to Edge Detection. *IEEE Transactions on Pattern Analysis and Machine Intelligence*, Vol.8, No.6, pp.679-698, November, 1986.

[2] Y.Lu, R.C.Jain. Reasoning about Edges in Scale Space. *IEEE Transactions on Pattern Analysis and Machine Intelligence*, Vol. 14, No. 4, pp.450-468, April, 1990.

[3] K.Deguchi, S.Aoki. Regularized Polygonal Approximation for Analysis and Interpretation of Planar Contour Figures. *Proc. 10th ICPR*, pp.865-869, June, 1990.

[4] K.Deguchi, H.Hontani. Contour Shape Approximation Based on Scale Space Analysis with A Stable Gaussian Blurring. *Proc. Asian Conf. on Computer Vision*, pp.294-298, Nov., 1993.

[5] L.J.van Vliet. Gray-Scale Measurements in Multi-Dimensional Digitized Images. *Delft University Press* ,1993.

[6] F.Mokhtarian,A.Mackworth. Scale-Based Description and Recognition of Planer Curves and Two-Dimensional Shapes. *IEEE Transactions on Pattern Analysis and Machine Intelligence*,Vol 8,No.1 ,pp.34-43, July, 1986.

COMPLEXITY, CONFUSION, AND PERCEPTUAL GROUPING

BENOIT DUBUC
Department of Computer Science, University of Montreal
Montreal, CANADA

STEVEN W. ZUCKER
Center for Computational Vision and Control, Yale University
New Haven, CT 06520-8285, USA

Intermediate-level vision is central to form perception, and we outline an approach to intermediate-level segmentation based on complexity analysis. We focus on the problem of edge detection, and how edge elements might be grouped together. This is typical because, once the local structure is established, the transition to global structure must be affected. To illustrate, consider an edge element inferred from an unknown image. Is this local edge part of a long curve, or perhaps part of a texture? If the former, which is the next element along the curve? If the latter, is the texture like a hair pattern, in which nearby elements are oriented similarly, or like a spaghetti pattern? Are there other generic possibilities? The questions raise issues of complexity and of dimensionality, since curves are 1-D and textures are 2-D. We propose a measure of representational complexity that seeks to answer these questions. A consequence of our analysis is the requirement for intermediate representations based on tangent maps, which suggests why orientation must be fundamental to the organization of visual cortex.

1 Introduction

Although edges provide the foundation upon which much of visual processing is built, it is curious that the definition of an edge remains unsettled. The usual one, which has roots back to Ernst Mach in the mid-19th century, is that edges are bright-to-dark transitions (or vice-versa), and that these transitions can be detected from measurements provided by (discrete approximations to) linear differential operators. Mach, for example, preferred the Laplacian operator, and Marr has revived modern interest in it. However, this view has turned out to be problematic, and much frustration in visual shape analysis derives from the unsatisfactory nature of early edge processing. In brief, the edges returned by standard tools do not correspond in any systematic way to boundaries of objects, and it is these boundaries–not bright-to-dark transitions–that are needed for visual shape analysis. Our goal in this paper is to propose a geometric foundation for early vision in an attempt to get right to the matter of what comprises a boundary. Our proposal is based on concepts from differential geometry and geometric measure theory. In the process of achieving this

trate on the geometric problems associated with interpreting the role an edge might be playing in an image. The geometric approach in the end leads us to conclude that one should think not in terms of edges, which are image-defined constructs, but rather in terms of tangents, which are differential-geometric constructs. It is this abstraction that reveals the connection back to boundaries.

2 Boundaries and their Detection

What, precisely, is a boundary? Mach's intuition was founded in photometry, and is based on the observation that since the reflectance of an object is typically different from the background, the object will project to an image region with different intensity from those regions to which the background projects. This intuition breaks down, however, when the object has internal structure.

To take advantage of this internal structure, consider a smooth surface such as a ball. The surface of the ball has a 2-dimensional tangent plane everywhere, and this tangent plane projects smoothly into the image except along the locus of positions at which the viewing vector just grazes the ball; at these positions the tangent plane becomes singular, and collapses to a single (one-dimensional) tangent. That it to say, the tangent plane folds away from the line of sight. An integral curve through these tangents defines the boundary of the ball. Thus, each tangent defines a proper edge element.

To see that edge elements can arise from other configurations, consider a bulge of cloth. Edges can now arise from within the cloth, with the tangent plane disappearing along the top of the bulge and then re-appearing on the other side. The tangent plane transition across a bulge (from cloth-to-cloth) is thus different from that across the ball, because it never re-appears. Moreover, this type of fold can end within the body of the cloth, as in the wrinkes around one's shirt sleeve or the muscles in one's shoulder.

2.1 Whitney's Classification Theorem

Whitney has classified the generic maps from smooth surfaces into smooth surfaces, and has shown that these two situations are the only ones that can occur generically. Generically means that the configuration does not change with small changes in viewpoint. He referred to them as the fold and the cusp (the position where the cloth fold disappears). Furthermore, by considering a view of a mountain range it is easy to observe that generic boundaries are not globally smooth; rather, they are punctuated by discontinuities. Thus we have three observations regarding boundaries:

1. *local edge elements arise in different contexts* such as exterior boundaries or interior folds. Textures, of course, provide further examples of complex contexts for edge elements.

2. *discontinuities should be expected in bounding contours* from occlusion relationships.

2.2 Normal Intensity Configurations and Logical/Linear Operators

We begin with the first observation to provide formal and computational support for the idea that local edge elements can be interpreted as tangents to contours. The first advantage is that, with the tangent direction established, one can examine the intensity profiles in the tangent and the normal directions separately. Note that most other edge operators average these together, although not necessarily uniformly. Thus we observe immediately that,

- *Normal direction:* The fold condition in Whitney's Theorem takes on a different intensity profile for a bounding edge (which involves a dark-to-light transition) from an interior fold (which involves a light-to-dark-to-light transition) or vice versa. This latter profile is often called a line, and must be separated from the former. Standard linear operators blur both together.

- *Tangential direction:* The differential interpretation demands that continuity conditions exist (that is, that the limit of one point approaching another must exist). This corresponded to continuity contrains on the intensity pattern.

A necessary condition for a tangent to exist is that one or the other of the above intensity and continuity conditions must be satisfied. We have developed a class of non-linear local operators, called logical/linear operators, that use Boolean conditions to test whether the above structural criteria are met. "Edge operators" are separated from "line operators", and lines can arise either in light-dark-light conditions (typical of a crack or a crease) or dark-light-dark conditions (typical of a highlight). Note that both of these latter conditions refer to surface markings, rather than to surface boundaries.

The tangent interpretation also leads to a solution for representing orientation discontinuities, but requires a more modern view of a discontinuity. While it is classically the case that no unique tangent exists at an irregular point on a curve, it is also the case that multiple tangents can be defined to exist there. Informally, taking a limit into the point of discontinuity from one side yields one tangent; a limit from the other side yields another. The two tangents span a 2-dimensional space, the Zariski tangent space to the curve; it is precisely this difference in dimensionality between the tangent spaces at regular and singular points that we exploit. The logical/linear operators are arranged into columns, so that multiple values of tangent orientation are possible at each point. Those points at which multiple tangents are established are the discontinuities.

Code for a system that implements the three logical/linear operators [1] in columns, one for edges, one for bright lines, and one for dark lines, is available from via anonymous ftp;

ftp://ftp.cim.mcgill.ca/pub/people/leei/loglin.tar.gz

Researchers are invited to experiment with this system. Results are shown in Fig. 1.

2.3 Edge Maps, Tangent Maps, and Grouping

The result of our logical/linear edge operator [1] at a given scale is shown in Fig. 1f on the image of the statue ("Paolina", see Fig. 1e) raises the following observations. For the shoulder region (Fig. 1c), the underlying object is simple and a curve representation seems appropriate to group the edge elements. If we examine instead regions subtending part of the hair structure (Fig. 1d), then choosing a curve representation and walking along a hair would lead very quickly to confusion, since it will be difficult to know on which part of the curve one is. A texture representation in this case seems more appropriate. The remainder of the paper will deal with these issues.

Although we have been speaking of the the logical/linear operators as if they signal tangents, actually they only return a distribution of positions at which the above intensity signatures are obtained. This is a very different notion than that of tangent. As we show in the next Section, however, there is a geometric-measure-theoretic definition of tangent that brings them back together again.

3 Continuous rectifiable curves and curve-like sets

This section is an attempt to answer the question: "what is a curve?" in the context of curve detection. The most common definition of a curve is the one of Jordan, namely that a curve Γ is the range of a continuous map α from an interval I to Euclidean space (typically $\mathbf{R}^2$ or $\mathbf{R}^3$). Two other basic notions usually follow in any study of elementary differential geometry: the one of *length*, denoted $L(\Gamma)$, and the one of best linear local approximation, namely the *tangent* to Γ at $x = \alpha(t)$, denoted $T(x)$. Within these are embedded the

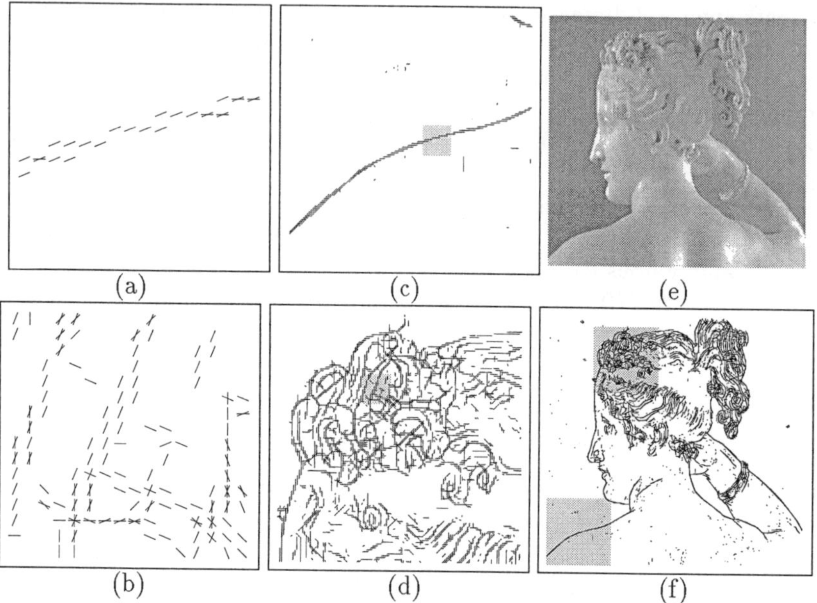

Figure 1: The subtlety of "walking through" a tangent map: (a & c) curves, (b & d) texture. Moving from right to left, the gray shaded areas are expanded to show the need for different representations to support the grouping of local edge elements. Integrating the responses of local edge detectors in the hair region is problematic. By what principles should the tangents be grouped?

notions of local representation (the tangent) and global measure (the length), which are tied together through the map α. Unfortunately, however, the map α is not given for general vision problems, but must be inferred. More abstract notions of a curve are thus required. This is why a generalization of the previous ideas through measure theory is necessary.

3.1 Geometric Measure Theory

One way to compute the length, area or volume of an object is to use the Hausdorff s-dimensional measure $\mathcal{H}^s$, where in the case of a smooth rectifiable curve, $s = 1$, in the case of a surface, $s = 2$. Consider the problem of defining the length of a set E in the plane. Hausdorff's idea was to cover the set with small circles and to take the sum of the diameters. If the balls are restricted to be smaller than some given value $\delta > 0$, and if the 'most economical' covering is chosen, we get an approximation of the length of the set at resolution δ.

Allowing arbitrary covers, instead of covers by balls, gives us an outer measure, and for $\delta > 0$ we write

$$\mathcal{H}_\delta(E) = \inf \sum_i |U_i|$$

where $|U|$ is the *diameter* of U, (i.e., $|U| = \sup\{|x-y| : x, y \in U\}$) and $\{U_i\}$ is any sequence of sets of diameter less than δ covering E. The infimum here is taken over all (countable) δ-cover $\{U_i\}$ of E and we can easily show that $\mathcal{H}_\delta(E)$ increases as δ decreases, therefore:

Definition 1 (Hausdorff measure [2]) *The* one dimensional Hausdorff measure *of E is given by*

$$\mathcal{H}(E) = \lim_{\delta \to 0} \mathcal{H}_\delta(E) = \sup_{\delta > 0} \mathcal{H}_\delta(E)$$

One important result is that if Γ is a curve, then the Hausdorff measure $\mathcal{H}(\Gamma)$ and the Jordan length $L(\Gamma)$ coincide [2]. But most importantly, we have

Definition 2 (Curve-like set [2]) *A set E with $0 < \mathcal{H}(E) < \infty$, will be called a* curve-like set.

Local structure of curve-like sets

Before discussing the existence of tangents for curve-like sets, we will present an alternate definition of a tangent that doesn't rely on a parameterization of the set. This definition is due to Besicovitch:

Definition 3 (Tangent: Besicovitch [3]) *A curve-like set E has a* tangent *$T_B(x)$ at x in the direction $\pm\theta$ if*

1. x "is on" the set E,

2. for every angle $\phi > 0$,

$$\lim_{r \to 0} \frac{\mathcal{H}(E \cap (B_r(x) \backslash S_r(x, \theta, \phi) \backslash S_r(x, -\theta, \phi)))}{r} = 0$$

where $B_r(x)$ is the ball of radius r centered at x and $S_r(x, \theta, \phi)$ is the sector of radius r at angle θ with opening ϕ.

Suppose $x \in E$, then this definition means that at x the set E is locally concentrated around the line $T_B(x)$ with orientation θ passing through x. The first condition in this definition can be formally expressed in terms of the density of the set E at x [2]. The second condition ensures that the concentration is around the tangent line only. Fig. 2b illustrates the definition, namely that

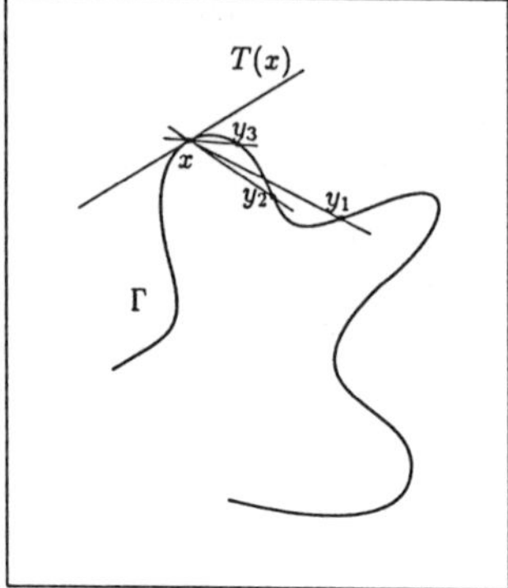

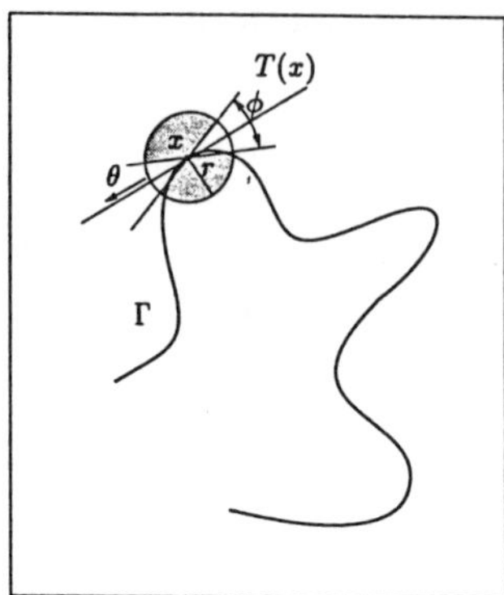

Figure 2: This figure illustrates in (a) the intuitive definition of a tangent T to a curve Γ at a point $x = \gamma(t)$. Take a sequence $\{y_1, y_2, \cdots\}$ of points on the curve converging to x. Draw the lines passing through y_i and x. The "limit line" gives us the tangent $T(x)$ to the curve at x. In (b) we illustrate the parametrization-free definition of the tangent, looking at a cone that shrinks around the point x (presented later in the text).

the second condition consists in looking at the rate of growth of what is found outside the local angular sector centered at x. If this rate of growth is much faster than r, the curve is ensured (from the first condition) to be concentrated around the line with orientation θ at x.

How does this definition of tangent relate to the usual definition of a tangent to a parameterized curve? In his seminal work, Besicovitch [3] showed that his new parameterization free definition was indeed equivalent to the usual definition. From now on we will therefore write $T(x)$ for the Besicovitch tangent.

The standard Besicovitch definition doesn't allow however for multiple tangents at a point, a key requirement in the type of sets we are studying when doing curve detection [4]. As we saw earlier, in real world situations objects occlude each other leading to discontinuities in bounding contours and to T-junctions. At these points "multiple tangents" must be represented. The following is an extension of the Besicovitch tangent to allow the representation of multiple tangents at a point:

Definition 4 (Multiple tangents) *A curve-like set E has a* tangent set $\Theta(x)$ *at x if x "is on" the set E and for every angle $\phi > 0$,*

$$\lim_{r \to 0} \frac{\mathcal{H}(E \cap (B_r(x) \backslash (\bigcup_{\theta \in \Theta(x)} [S_r(x,\theta,\phi) \cup S_r(x,-\theta,\phi)])))}{r} = 0 \tag{1}$$

but also, for each $\theta \in \Theta(x)$, $\exists\ r_0$ and ϕ_0 such that $\forall 0 < \phi < \phi_0$ and $0 < r < r_0$,

$$\mathcal{H}(E \cap (B_r(x) \cap S_r(x,\theta,\phi) \cap S_r(x,-\theta,\phi))) > 0 \tag{2}$$

As in the definition of the Besicovitch tangent, the "on the set" condition can be formally expressed in terms of densities[5]. The condition given by Eq. 1 prevents things to be too crumpled around the point, while the third (Eq. 2) ensures that indeed there is something going on in the directions contained in the tangent set.

Existence of multiple tangents It is easy to build a set with multiple tangents. The graph of the absolute value function $G_f = \{(y, f(y)) : f(y) = |y|\}$ for instance has a multiple tangent at $x = (0,0)$. In this case $\Theta(x) = \{\pi/4, 3\pi/4\}$. In both cases we have for all $r > 0$ and $0 < \phi < \pi/8$

$$\mathcal{H}(E \cap (B_r(x) \cap S_r(x,\theta,\phi) \cap S_r(x,-\theta,\phi))) = r > 0,$$

By bundling the non-empty tangent sets, we obtain our key intermediate representation, the *tangent map*:

Definition 5 (Tangent map) *Given a curve-like set E, we define the* tangent map τ *to be*

$$\tau = \bigcup_{x \in E} (x, \Theta(x)),$$

where $\Theta(x)$ is the set of tangents (in the Besicovitch sense) at x.

When the set E is rectifiable, it can be proved that multiple tangents cannot occur 'too often'.

4 From edge detection to discrete curve-like sets

One of the most interesting features of the theory of curve-like sets was the definition of the (parameterization-free) Besicovitch tangent. Notice that we are now ready to establish the connection back to the opening sections of this paper, where logical/linear operators where shown to provide a dense collection of positions at which tangents should be signaled. The main feature of the Besicovitch tangent was the dense collection of points within an elongated cone. This is exactly like what was done in edge detection except that this time one is looking at a density of pixels supporting a particular contrast distribution. There is however another major difference: the concept of finite scale. In the continuous domain, we classified objects into finite and infinite length. Those with finite length were called curve-like sets. In edge detection, the distinction will be more subtle. Since the operators will be band limited, the inferred objects will be finite but it is in some sense the "degree of finiteness" that matters and will lead a partitioning scheme for discrete curve-like sets.

4.1 From edge detection to discrete curve-like sets

When inferring curve-like objects from images, one is confronted with issues such as discretization, quantization and choice of scale. We will assume here that the scale σ at which the tangents are detected is fixed. The result of the inference will be:

Definition 6 (Discrete tangent map) *Given the responses of the linear/ logical edge/line detectors over a grey level image I, then filtered through relaxation labelling, the* discrete tangent map $\hat{\tau}$ *will be:*

$$\hat{\tau} = \{((x_i, y_i), \hat{\theta}) | \hat{\theta} \in \hat{\Theta}(x_i, y_i)\}$$

$i = 1, 2, \cdots$, *where* $\hat{\theta}$ *is a quantized orientation at the discrete image coordinate* (x_i, y_i).

Any entry in the map in fact corresponds to an equivalence class of curves passing through the cell (x_i, y_i) with orientation $\hat{\theta}$.

This approximate position and orientation at scale σ will have to be considered when assessing the complexity and integrating data. In particular, one big issue is the problem of transversality versus quantization. If at a particular position there exists more than one tangent, can it be decided whether these correspond to a quantization artifact or to the fact that two lines are actually crossing at that position? It is possible to answer this question using the following complexity measures.

5 Mapping complexity

Section 3 introduced continuous curve-like sets and their local structure. The last section made the link between edge detection and the theory in the continuous domain using the local structure of discrete curve-like sets, the discrete tangent map. In this section we will refine this classification and provide a means of deciding which representation should be used for the integration process.

5.1 From dilations to complexity

To assess the complexity of the tangent map, we will use a variant of an approach due to Minkowski. Originally it consisted in covering the object with balls of radius ϵ and computing the measure of the dilated object. The rate of growth of this measure can be linked to the complexity of the set. Our approach differs in the way that the dilation is achieved, in particular it will not be done isotropically. After reviewing the standard technique, we present our variation.

Isotropic dilations

Minkowski dilations are routinely used in mathematical morphology [6] and for the estimation of fractal dimension [2]. The approach consists in creating a new set which is the Minkowski sum with a dilating (structuring) element. The dilation is done isotropically over the set. More formally, given a subset $X = \mathbf{R}^2$, we have

Definition 7 (Minkowski sum, dilation [6]) *The* Minkowski sum *is defined in the power set of* X *by putting*

$$A \oplus B = \{a + b, a \in A, b \in B\}.$$

The translate *of* B *by* z *being* $B_z = B \oplus \{z\}$, *the set* $\{z : A \cap B_z \neq \emptyset\}$ *of the points* z *such that* A *hits the translate* B_z *is called the* dilation[a] *of* A *by* B *and is denoted* $A \oplus \breve{B}$.

An example of the isotropic dilation of a line segment with a ball is shown on Fig. 3a. In fractal analysis, the case of a dilation with a ball is often called the *Minkowski sausage*. Dilation with other shapes (squares, segments, etc.) are called *generalized Minkowski sausages*.

Oriented dilations

One of the key differences between our approach and the standard fractal analysis techniques is the fact that the dilations will not be done isotropically but will adapt to the local structure of the set. We call them *oriented dilations* and we will show that they are necessary for separating sets of different complexity. Again, taking the example of the line segment, Fig. 3b,c illustrate the concepts of both normal and tangential dilations:

[a] [6] actually calls this 'dilatation', but the term 'dilation' is more spread out in mathematical morphology.

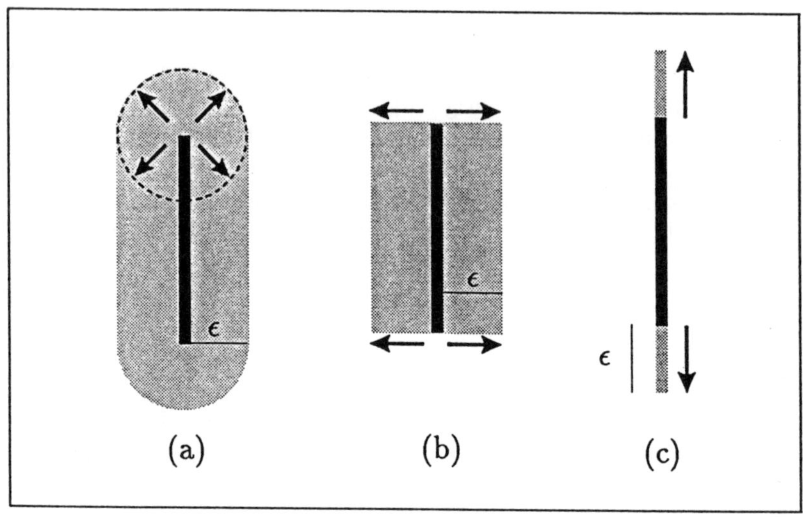

Figure 3: Isotropic and oriented dilations. (a) isotropic dilation with a ball of radius ϵ. (b) normal dilation (c) tangential dilation. Oriented dilations are possible because of the intermediate representation provided by the Besicovitch tangent sets.

Definition 8 (Normal and tangential dilations) *Let E be a curve-like set and τ its tangent map. The* normal dilation $E_N(\epsilon)$ *of E at a scale ϵ is the dilation of the set E with the segment $(-\epsilon, \epsilon)$ in the direction normal to the tangents $\theta \in \Theta(x)$ at x (Fig. 3b). The* tangential dilation $E_T(\epsilon)$ *is obtained by dilating the segment $(-\epsilon, \epsilon)$ in the direction of the tangent (Fig. 3c).*

Key observation 1 *The departure from the standard Minkowski dilation approach by using oriented dilations will be essential for our analysis since it will segregate the classification* curve *vs.* texture *(using normal dilations) from the one of* dust *vs.* curve *(using tangential dilations).*

Normal and tangential complexity

The local information contained in the tangent map τ can be used to calculate what we will call the *normal complexity* $C_N(\epsilon)$ and the *tangential complexity* $C_T(\epsilon)$ of a curve-like set at a given scale ϵ. The main idea is to be able to look at the rate of growth of the measure of the dilated sets. In the case of normal complexity, it will be $|E_N(\epsilon)|_2$ at scale ϵ. If the area of $E_N(\epsilon)$, denoted $|\cdot|_2$, is of order α, we say that the *normal complexity* $C_N(\epsilon)$ for E is $2 - \alpha$:

Definition 9 (Normal complexity) *Let E be a curve-like set. If $E_N(\epsilon)$ is the normal dilation of E at scale ϵ, and if $|\cdot|_2$ denotes its area, then the* normal complexity log-log plot *is defined as follows*

$$\left(\log\left(\frac{1}{\epsilon}\right), \log\left(\frac{1}{\epsilon^2}|E_N(\epsilon)|_2\right)\right) \tag{3}$$

moreover the normal complexity $C_N(\epsilon)$ *at scale ϵ will be the left derivative of the normal complexity log-log plot.*

¿From the structure of curve-like sets, one can show that the normal complexity is indeed well-defined.

Much in the same way as we did for the normal complexity, we will build a measure of complexity from tangential dilations and call it *tangential complexity*. The tangential complexity will be sensitive to end of lines, corners, points of high curvature and will allow to segregate between dust and curves and/or select the scale for integration.

Definition 10 (Tangential complexity) *Let E be a curve-like set. If $E_T(\epsilon)$ is the tangential dilation of E at scale ϵ, and if $|E_T(\epsilon)|_{p,1}$ denotes its perimeter, then the* tangential complexity log-log plot *is defined as follows*

$$\left(\log\left(\frac{1}{\epsilon}\right), \log\left(\frac{1}{\epsilon}|E_T(\epsilon)|_{(p,1)}\right)\right) \tag{4}$$

moreover the tangential complexity $C_T(\epsilon)$ *at scale ϵ will be the left derivative of the tangential complexity log-log plot.*

An important remark needs to be placed at this point and for this we will use a simple example. Let E be a single line or a set of lines with the same orientation. Then dilate the set tangentially and then look at the rate of growth of measure of the dilated set. For instance, a line of length l, becomes a line of length $l + 2\epsilon$ when dilated tangentially, therefore we have

$$|E_T(\epsilon)|_{(p,1)} = 2(l + 2\epsilon)$$

Notice here that the 'measure' chosen is the *length* (not the area as was the case in the normal complexity). Therefore, we expect the rate of growth, α to be between 0 and 1. We defined $C_T(\epsilon)$, the tangential complexity, to be $1 - \alpha$. In our example, when l is large with respect to ϵ, the rate of growth is small and α is "close" to zero, therefore it has a "curve" structure. Otherwise, if l is small with respect to ϵ, then α is closer to 1 and the object would be better described as having a "dust-like" structure. Although it is easy to show that on simple examples the definition is well behaved, for general curve-like sets, the validity of the tangential complexity still remains a conjecture. In the light of our results, it will become evident however that such a measure of complexity can be most valuable to the integration process.

5.2 Complexity indexes and complexity map

The complexity measures presented in the last sections had the characteristics of being local in scale. This was a major departure from the standard 'fractal analysis' approach in which the rate of growth is studied around zero. The other key difference is to make the complexity measure local in space by computing it over a given compact region $\Omega(x)$ centered at x. The normal complexity at x can be obtained by first restricting the dilation to the region $\Omega(x)$:

$$E_N(x,\epsilon) = E_N(\epsilon) \cap \Omega(x). \tag{5}$$

The case of the tangential dilation is a little more complex but basically consists into not dilating any further than the region $\Omega(x)$, therefore leading to $E_T(x,\epsilon)$

Definition 11 (Normal and tangential complexity indexes) *The* norma and tangential complexity indexes *at x over a region $\Omega(x)$ are denoted $C_N(x,\epsilon)$ and $C_T(x,\epsilon)$ and are obtained by looking at the rate of growth of their local oriented dilations. More formally they are obtained as the left derivatives of their corresponding log-log plots*

$$\left(\log\left(\frac{1}{\epsilon}\right), \log\left(\frac{1}{\epsilon^2}|E_N(x,\epsilon)|_2\right)\right) \tag{6}$$

for $C_N(x,\epsilon)$, and

$$\left(\log\left(\frac{1}{\epsilon}\right), \log\left(\frac{1}{\epsilon}|E_T(x,\epsilon)|_{(p,1)}\right)\right) \tag{7}$$

for $C_T(x,\epsilon)$.

In a similar fashion as we did in the case of the tangent map, we can bundle all the complexity indexes and build our main tool, the *complexity map*:

Definition 12 (Complexity map) *Given a curve-like set E, we define the* complexity map *C to be*

$$C = \bigcup_{x \in E} (x, C_N(x,\epsilon), C_T(x,\epsilon)).$$

Discrete complexity map

The discrete complexity map will be obtained by computing locally normal and tangential complexity at each image position subtending a non-empty tangent. The algorithm we used consisted into projecting the unit tangents from the discrete tangent map and then dilating the resulting intermediate image. Computing the area of the dilated set and estimating the rate of growth from log-log data give us two numbers, the normal and tangential complexity indexes, to be bundled into the complexity map.

5.3 Choosing the appropriate representation

How can we build from a geometric measure point of view a classification scheme for the types of objects (texture, oriented textures, curves, etc.) that can occur in curve detection? How can the complexity map be used as an index of representation? The partition of the space of discrete curve-like sets, can be done as follows, recognizing four different categories of objects:

1. a *dust-like* curve-like set: tangent map is sparse, the object almost nowhere extends along its length in the local neighborhood;
2. a *curve* curve-like set: places where a curve representation is completely adequate. The object extends along its length and the density is low almost everywhere along it in a local neighborhood;
3. *turbulent* curve-like set: characterized by objects that do not extend along their length but are dense in their normal direction;
4. a *texture flow* curve-like set: where the object extends along its length but the density in the normal direction is high.

The space of valid tangential/normal complexity pairs is a subset of $\mathbf{R}^2$, namely $[0.0, 1.0] \times [1.0, 2.0]$. This is because the tangential complexity is a number between 0.0 and 1.0 and the normal complexity a number between 1.0 and 2.0. Segmenting this space allows us to partition the space of possible patterns into equivalence classes. The following segmentation gives us the following nomenclature:

- low normal complexity - low tangential complexity : *dust*
- low normal complexity - high tangential complexity: *curve*
- high normal complexity - low tangential complexity: *turbulence*

- high normal complexity - high tangential complexity: *flow*

See Figure 4.

The four patterns listed in the introduction arise as the extrema in normal and tangential complexity space.

5.4 Applying oriented dilations

One way of understanding the implications of oriented dilations is to look at the results when applied to the Paolina tangent map. In this particular example, the dilation will be done at two scales ϵ_1 and ϵ_2. The result will display the dilated sets with two different grays: the lighter one for the smallest scale and the union of the darker and the lighter set corresponds to the dilation at the largest scale. Moreover, in all cases the projection of the tangent map has been overlaid on the resulting dilated sets. In Fig. 5 we showed the result of tangential and normal dilations on the hair and shoulder regions for the tangent map of the Paolina image. The chosen scales were $\epsilon_1 = 0.1$ and $\epsilon_2 = 0.05$ for this example. From these images we get a better feel at the underlying idea for the complexity. For the shoulder region (Fig. 5a,b), the normal dilated set seems to grow linearly while the tangential dilations don't grow at all after some point. On the hair area (Fig. 5c,d), it's the normally dilated regions that stop growing at an early stage, while it is more difficult to describe at a quick glance what is happening to the rate of growth of the tangential dilated sets.

If we apply these techniques to the Paolina tangent map, the resulting segmentation is shown in Fig. 6. Notice how the bounding contours of the head are given by the curve-like set and the turbulence set. It is these contours that will support boundary-based processing.

6 Conclusions

We have overviewed two different aspects of early vision, the first stage of edge detection and a second stage of segmentation. Processing in both stages was based on an abstraction to the level of differential geometry, with the particular abstraction that edge elements should be thought of as tangents. This abstraction was supported by the Besicovitch construction from geometric measure theory, and led to complexity measures applicable to the map of tangents.

The key advantage at both levels was the local coordinate system provided by the tangents. Edge detection was facilitated by different processing of intensities in the tangential and the normal directions, which was related to the contrast signature along and across Whitney folds. Tangent map segmentation

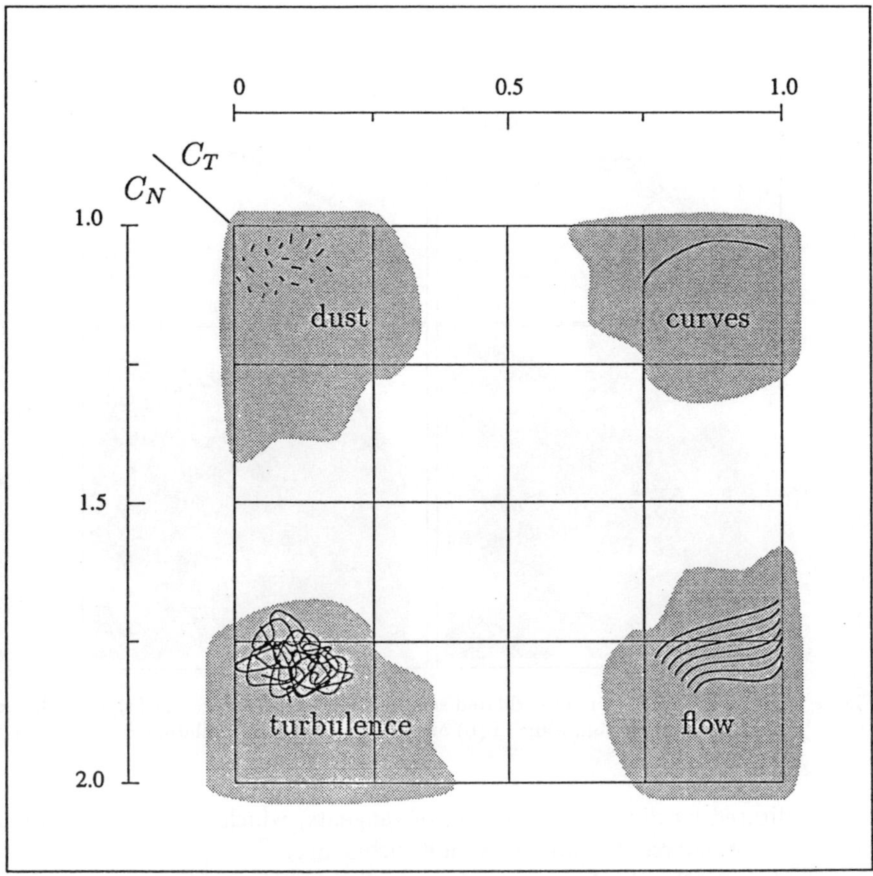

Figure 4: THE COMPLEXITY SPACE. The tiled square represents the space of complexity indexes pairs that can be encountered. The normal complexity varies between 1.0 and 2.0 while the tangential complexity is between 0.0 and 1.0. Each of the corners of the complexity space corresponds to a different type of curve-like substructure. Partitioning the complexity space will result in an image segmentation scheme bound to the structure of the objects in the visual scene.

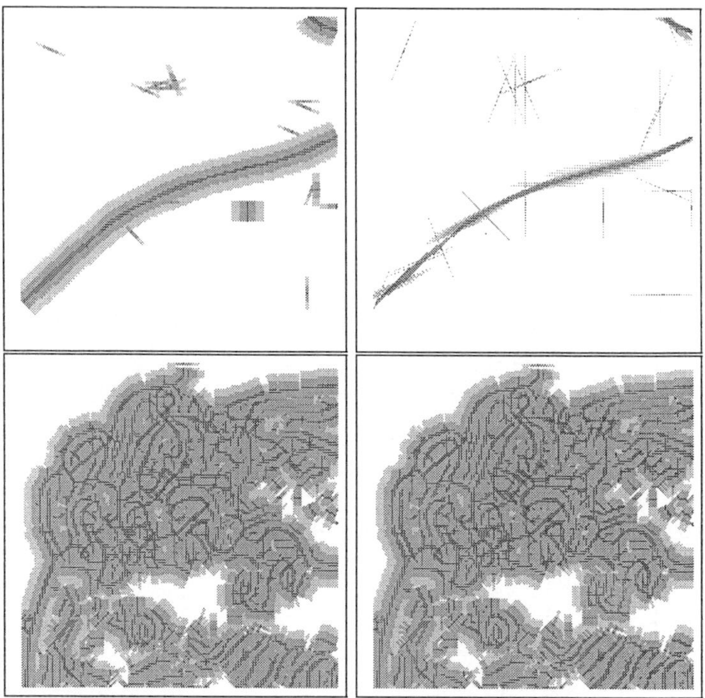

Figure 5: Close-ups on the oriented dilated sets for the Paolina image. In (a) and (c), the normal dilation, while in (b) and (d), the tangential dilation.

was facilitated by different processing of tangents, which led to a separation between dust, curves, texture flows, and turbulence.

More generally, this intermediate level of abstraction provides the foundation on which shape analysis can be performed.

References

1. Lee A. Iverson and Steven W. Zucker. Logical/linear operators for image curves. *IEEE PAMI*, 1995.
2. J. K. Falconer. *Fractal Geometry: Mathematical Foundations and Applications*. Wiley, 1990.
3. A. S. Besicovitch. On the fundamental geometrical properties of linearly measurable plane sets of points. *Mathematische Annalen*, 98:422–464, 1928.

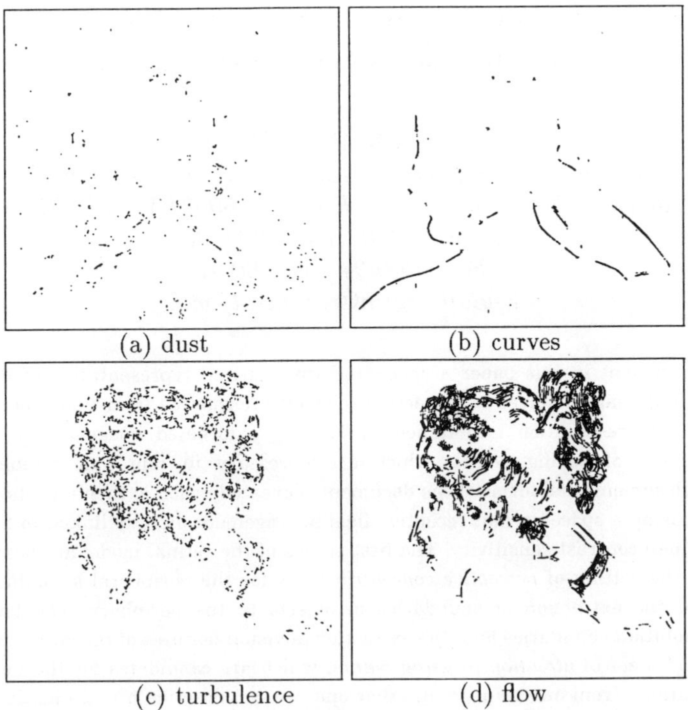

Figure 6: Segmented image of the Paolina image using the complexity map and our classification rule. The integration under a 'curve' representation should only take place within the "curves" substructure.

4. S. W. Zucker, A. Dobbins, and L. Iverson. Two stages of curve detection suggest two styles of visual computation. *Neural Computation*, 1:68–81, 1989.
5. Benoit Dubuc and Steven W. Zucker. Indexing visual representations through the complexity map. In *Fifth International Conference on Computer Vision*, 1995.
6. G. Matheron. *Random Sets and Integral Geometry.* Wiley, 1975.

LOW-RESOLUTION BOUNDARIES FOR GUIDING EYE-MOVEMENT ON A DOCUMENT

V. EGLIN, H. EMPTOZ
Laboratoire de Reconnaissance de Formes et Vision
INSA de Lyon, 20, avenue Albert Einstein 69621 VILLEURBANNE
Phone : (33) 04 72 43 80 96
Fax : (33) 04 72 43 80 97
E-mail : eglin@rfv.insa-lyon.fr

We present in this paper a space and time-variant representation of the retinal image involved in extracting relevant information from a document. This representation is obtained by forming a foveated image around a number of gazing points, which are necessary to represent complex multidimensional forms of the document. Foveated vision is then modelling by using a space-variant receptive field arrangement directly linked to the human contrast sensitivity. The first stages of the retinal model are based on the setting of *perceptive concentric rings* for the peripheral smoothing and the extraction of boundaries of objects in the periphery. The low-resolution boundaries and the extraction of visual features of the document yield a set of *attention focusing points*, which are candidates for the next fixation. From one point to an other one, we can describe a real kinetic of internal moving of attention towards the most likely peripheral target.

1 Introduction

The primal steps of vision merely take in single features of a scene. We can obtain their location in focusing our attention in some points, called *attention focusing points* [5]. Then, an attentional mechanism is necessary to represent complex multidimensional forms with a succession of gazing points. This mechanism is the impetus for the visual scan-path structuring [4]. First, the observer's eye moving is based on the organization of the *attention visual field.* This organization is directly linked to the relative independence between the attention and the fovea axis, what justify a peripheral search of information.

Our work consists, on the one hand, in expressing what the observer really *sees* on the document. That's why, we draw up a coherent representation of the retinal image of the observer. It leads us to define a set of parameters for the selection of relevant information. We will then be able to locate the different areas of the document according to different points of view (from successive gazing points), and finally, we can build the corresponding scan-path with intend to satisfy the observer's interest.

We present here what we consider as relevant information on a document and how the location of gazing points can be predicted for selecting this information.

2 The primal steps of visual perception

The control of ocular saccades has led us to define some general rules for the visual data capturing. Especially, it has been experimentally proved that *gazing points* tend to gather around *salient angles, angular points, curved lines, contrasted lines,* like beginnings or ends of lines, thick features, edges of forms...; all in all, elements which present important local discontinuities and which have in their neighbourhood a particular local relief [1]. Generally, we detect very quickly all deviations from the standard value of things. Some sudden changes in an image determine a concentration of information, like colour contrast, salient angles and boundaries.

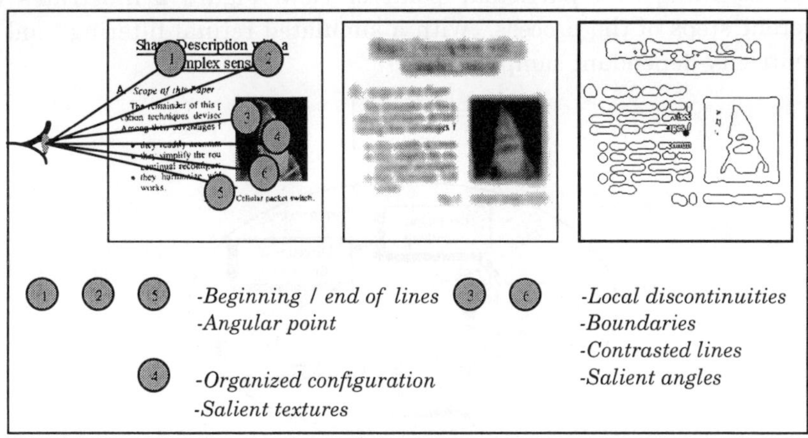

Fig.1 The primal steps of visual perception from a single fixation point. Representation of the main visual features for data capturing

As for Bonnet [2], we essentially perceive organized configurations. In fact, the eyes tend to isolate complex and concentrated areas, having a high entropy value, as if they were trying to simplify the whole visual field, so as to understand it better [9]. Those results are essential for drawing up a simplified exploratory strategy on a complex image, like a document. The observer's eyes, once fixed on the attractive points, assess the nature of the neighbouring information, more or less precisely, depending on its distance to the fovea. What is more, some findings in cognitive sciences have shown that relevant objects are extracted by independent cortical units by a pop-out effect [7]. Those units deals with the colour (as a textural information), with orientation (with the location of edges and corners), and with size (as a sampling representation of the retinal image).

Those findings have proved that frontiers of elements, their eventual global or local discontinuities, and a single or an unexpected object in the surrounding environment of the current gazing point, have all a prominent role in pattern perception. We have been inspired by this modular organization of the first stages of visual analysis, and have then decided to cut our process in as many units as necessary to recover texture, orientation and size-based information. Each unit enables us to draw up a temporary and time-dependant representation of the visual field, according to a particular point of view. Figure 2 illustrates the different steps of the process, with a simulated retinal filtering, and an eccentricity-dependant sampling.

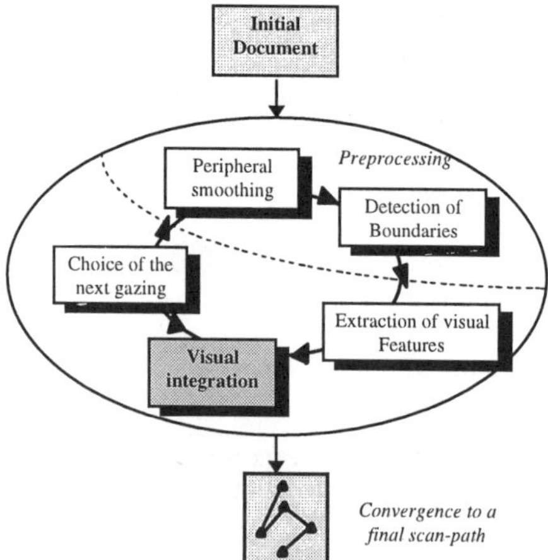

Fig.2 Representation of the hierarchical visual process (only the Pre-processing part is presented here)

3 Space variant sampling strategy

3.1 Retinal image and circular symmetry

To simulate the biological aspect of the retina, we propose a space-variant receptive field arrangement directly linked to the human contrast sensitivity. The first stage of our retinal model is based on the setting of *perceptive concentric rings*. We call *perceptive rings*, concentric circles centred on the fovea. The fovea (also called current fixation point) is noticed P_f. The radius of each ring R_i increases as an exponential function of eccentricity. This sampling strategy mimics the distribution of photoreceptors in the human retina, see Figure 3.

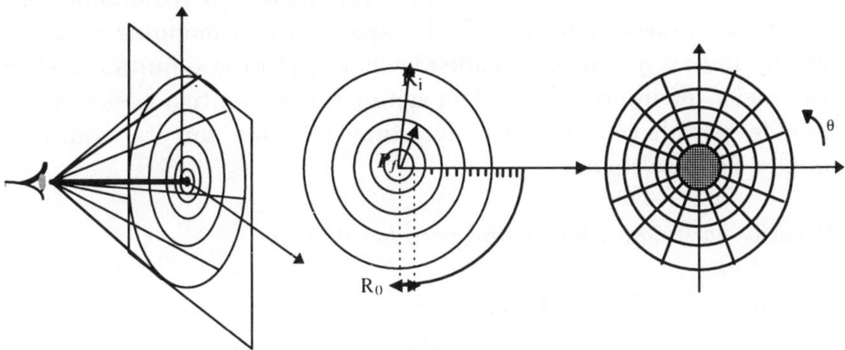

Fig.3 Successive perceptive rings centred on the fovea
Representation of the circular grid

So as to simplify the retinal representation, we have also defined the receptive field (RF) as the domain included between two successive concentric rings and two radius, making an acute angle θ, see Figure 3. Yamamoto [8] has privileged, a geometrical progression, which involves an exponential increase in rings. So as to mimic the distribution of photoreceptors in the human retina, he proposes a topological mapping of the images known as *log-polar mapping*. The log-polar mapping transforms a polar data space by taking the logarithm of each point's co-ordinates.

This mapping has a number of useful properties and will be used in our application for the edge and corner description, (see section *3.3*). First, it is conformal, that is to say that all local geometrical properties are preserved, which in turn implies that all local image processing operations such as filtering remain unaffected. What is more, the mapping is space-invariant : if a region of the document is currently being fixated by the observer, its global shape remains unchanged depending on his previous point-of-view. Finally, a large area of a peripheral region is compensated for by the corresponding drop in resolution over the periphery, thereby preserving the overall amount of visual information at the fovea.

On the other hand, the biologically motivated log-polar transform has the advantage to reduce considerably the computations [8]. Especially in document analysis, where data are voluminous and redundant, this representation proved to be useful. This space-variant mapping arises as a necessity in any system which must be able to process simultaneously a central region of interest (fovea) in detail for recognition tasks and a wide-angle peripheral view for detecting relevant targets and new candidates for gaze change.

3.2 Iterative gaussian filtering and peripheral vision

An important rule in human perception, is that visual information is always resumed in the periphery of the current fixation point. Especially text lines are perceived as homogeneous coarse blocks. Our visual system tends to extend shapes of objects (at right angles) in the orthogonal direction of real edge ends-of-lines. Coarse blocks seem all large and homogeneous, especially as they are far from the fovea. This remark is at the basis of our approach of document filtering. In a biological context, the visual filters are linearly increasing with increasing eccentricity. The large filters can be used to detect coarse edges and the small ones to detect sharply focused fine detail in the document. We are trying here to simulate all their effects, see Figure 4.

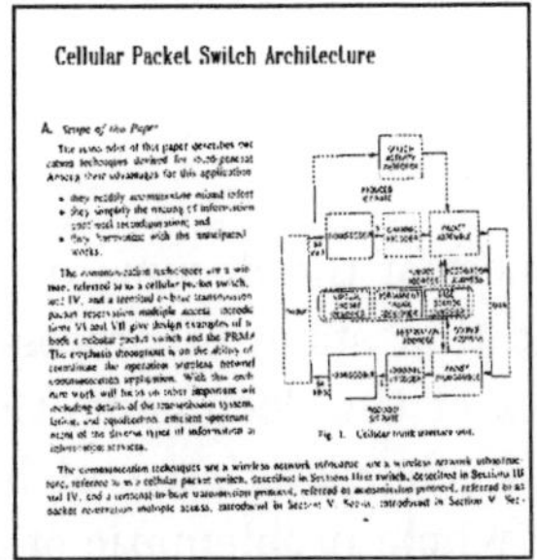

Cellular Packet Switch Architecture

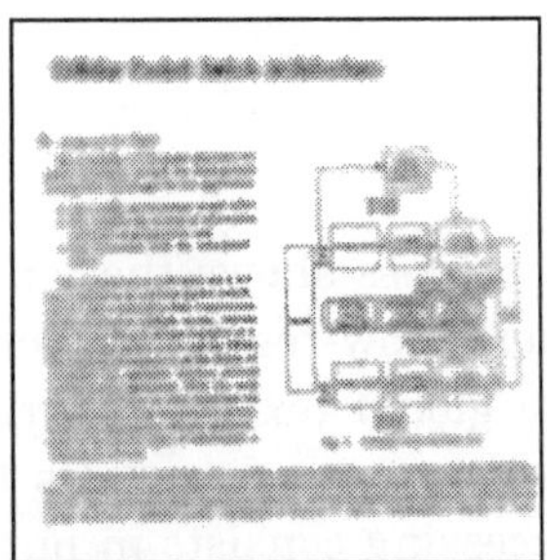

Fig.4 Iterative gaussian filtering for the simulation of foveated and peripheral vision.

The reduction of peripheral data can be obtained by smoothing high spatial frequencies in the periphery. A simple way consists in suppressing those frequencies with a low-pass filter, which shows clearly global characteristics of forms and main orientation of objects. That is why, we have chosen to implement an iterative gaussian eccentricity-dependant 3*3 sized filtering. The resulting image can be written as the *sum* of successively filtered parts of the image. The whole process consists in applying (n+1) times the smoothing spatial function g_σ with a space-constant σ on the domain $[R_n, R_{n+1}]$, n times on the domain $[R_{n-1}, R_n]$, and finally once on the domain $[R_0, R_1]$. That amounts to filter the initial image with a succession of gaussian convolution products $(g_\sigma)^k$, k $\in\{1,..n+1\}$. We note (x_i, y_i), the Cartesian co-ordinates included in the domain $[R_i, R_{i+1}]$, $i \in \{0,..n\}$. The final expression of the irregular spatially smoothed image $\hat{I}_F(x,y)$ is the following (1):

$$\hat{I}_F(x,y) = \left(g_\sigma\right)^{n+1} * I_0(x_n, y_n) + (g_\sigma)^n * I_0(x_{n-1}, y_{n-1}) + \ldots + \left(g_\sigma\right)^i * I_0(x_{i-1}, y_{i-1}) + \ldots + (g_\sigma) * I_0(x_0, y_0)$$

$$\text{that is } \hat{I}_F(x,y) = \sum_{i=0}^{n} g_\sigma^{i+1} * I_0(x_i, y_i) \qquad (1)$$

The binomial theorem allows us to write in the polar domain :

$$\hat{I}_F(r,\theta) = \sum_{i=0}^{n} g_{\sqrt{i+1}\sigma} * I_0(r_i,\theta), \theta \in [0, 2\pi]. \qquad (2)$$

This process shows the textural aspect of the document, especially for peripheral low-resolution regions. At this stage of process, we can extract the global textural characteristics of the document. Concerning the text, this approach reveals the coarse characteristics of lines. This way of processing consists in putting the whole problematic of document discrimination into the context of texture segmentation.

3.3 Low-resolution boundaries

So far, blurring images were used to extract coarse characteristics of document. But as for Marr [6], blurring images is the first step in detecting intensity changes. So, the edge detection is based here on partitioning the original image into a set of domains, which are the units of the logarithm spiral grid. Once filtered (as seen before), each domain is processed so as to detect all relevant intensity changes.

So as to predict the succession of gazing points, we have been inspired by Marr's perception modelling and we have realized a corner and edge detector, directly based on the previous space-variant filtering, that is, on difference of successive low-pass transforms, called DOLP by Crowley [3]. Those differences are computing for each portion included in the domains $[R_i, R_{i+1}]$ of the filtered image (i.e : for each units of the spiral grid), see Figure 5.

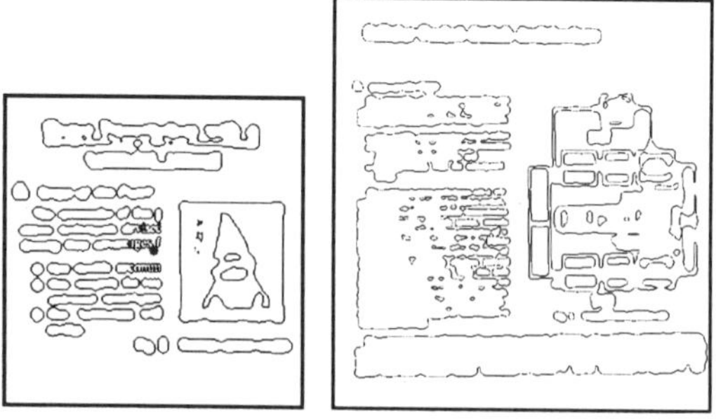

Fig.5 Difference of low-pass transforms for edge and corner extraction.

We call $b_{n+1,n}(x,y)$, the difference computed in the last peripheral domain between the two last successive gaussian convolutions, that is,

$$b_{n+1,n}(x,y) = \left[(g_\sigma)^n - (g_\sigma)^{n+1}\right](x_n, y_n). \qquad (3)$$

A simplified writing of the formula is the following : $b_{n+1,n}(x,y) = [g_n - g_{n+1}](x, y)$, and more generally, we have : $b_{i+1,i}(x,y)=[g_i - g_{i+1}](x,y)$, the difference computed between the two last successive convolution in a domain $[R_i, R_{i+1}]$. Of course, the fovea remains unchanged, because no process has been applied on it. Finally, the resulting image $\Delta\hat{I}_F(x,y)$ is the following :

$$\Delta\hat{I}_F(x,y) = \left(\sum_{i=0}^{n} b_{i+1,i}\right) * I_o(x,y) \qquad (4)$$

Practically, the space-variant filtering and the frontier extraction are computed simultaneously, so as to avoid the discontinuities between each rings. Indeed, the definition of the previous functions $b_{i+1,i}$ does not take into account the frontier values. So, the global process consists in computing the first difference $b_{1,0}$ on the whole image and then keeping the portion included in the domain $[R_0, R_1]$. The second difference is then computed for all points, which are outside the R_2 radius-sized circle. We keep then, the portion included in the domain $[R_1, R_2]$, and repeat the process until the whole document is covered.

$\Delta\hat{I}_F(x,y)$ represents all locally salient elements, like edges, corners, and frontiers of regions. Especially, this image will be used to detect coarse edges on the periphery and sharply focused fine detail around the fovea. Thanks to this representation, we are able to describe the document's components with more or less precision depending on whether they are near the fovea or not.

3.4 Polygonal approximation of blocs

We extract then a discrete contour of objects by connecting all intersection points between the outline of the object and the log-polar grid. Near the fovea, we have a precise description of the object with a large number of intersection points ; in the periphery, the low-resolution image has only produced coarse edges, what yields a coarse description of components for the extraction of visual features. Anyway, the contours are defined by the location of the intersection points. In the figure 6, we have illustrated the polygonal approximation of two portions of document from as a single centred fixation point (the original documents are illustrated in Figure 1 and Figure 4).

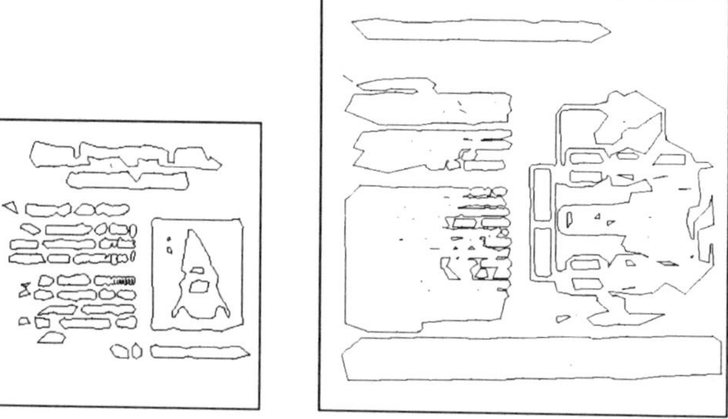

Fig.6 Polygonal approximations of blocs for the extraction of visual features
Here we have used 64 concentric rings and 64 angular sectors

4 Discussion and conclusion

With the previous processing, we have an unified representation of the visual information. This information corresponds to a particular point of view of the scene, where the central vision is privileged. So as to obtain an unified representation of the whole document, we have to multiply the points of view. To do that, we have to move our attention to the next most emergent locations, and then we have to characterize their surrounding environment in order to select the next fixation point. Finally we gather the successive representations of the document in a same map. This integration is the final representation of the complete scan-path [5], which underlines all *eye-catching points* of the document.

We propose here a representation of the retinal image in accordance with biological realities and we give the way to extract visual data relative to human perception of scene. For each shift of attention from one to another fixation point on the document, we build a temporary representation of the document. The sequences of space-variant filtering and non-uniform subsampling operations emphasize salient textural qualities of the document, such as lines or blocks of text and lay stress on primary features, such as edges and corners.

The definition of the primary visual features is another great part of the work, which has not been presented here. Those features allow us to define *attention focusing points* for the simulation of the global scan-path. This simulation is made on a test document and it will be soon compared to experimental oculometric measurement on an observer. The control of the observer's ocular saccades will yield a complete representation of the real kinetic of ocular shifting on a document, and will validate our strategies.

5 References

[1] E.H. Adelson, J.R. Bergen, Early Vision, *Computational models of visual processing, Michael S.Landy, J.A.Movskon*,1991.

[2] C. Bonnet, B. Dresp, Psychophysique de l'extraction des contours en vision humaine, *RFIA*, vol.3, pp.102-109, nov., 1991.

[3] J.L.Crowley, R.M.Stern, Fast Computation of the Difference of Low-Pass Transform, *IEEE PAMI, N°6*, pp.212-222, 1984.

[4] V. Eglin, H. Emptoz, Organisation et analyse de l'activité perceptive, *rapport de recherche RR96-08*, 88p. 1996.

[5] S.S. Hacisalihazade, L.W. Stark, J.S. Allen, Visual Perception and Sequence of Eye Movements Fixations, *IEEE SMC,* vol.22, N°3*,* pp.474-480, 1992.

[6] D. Marr, Vision.. *New-York : W.H. Freeman and Co,* p.397, 1982.

[7] A. Treisman, L'attention, les traits et la perception des objets, *Folio Gallimard,* pp.154-191, 1992.

[8] H.Yamamoto, An active Foveated Vision System, *Computer Vision and Image Understanding*, vol.63, N°1, pp.50-65, 1996.

[9] Y. Yeshurun, E.L. Schwartz, Shape Description with a Space-Variant Sensor :Algorithms for Scan-Path, Fusion, and Covergence Over Multiple Scans, *IEEE PAMI*, vol.11, N°11, pp.1217-1222, 1989.

RECONSTRUCTION OPERATORS FOR IMAGE SEGMENTATION

J.C. EVERAT, G. BERTRAND, M. COUPRIE
Laboratoire PSI, ESIEE, 93162 Noisy-le-Grand Cedex, FRANCE

The work presented in this paper is related to the segmentation of a grayscale image into regions. The image can be seen as a relief where the objects we want to extract correspond to "significant basins". Our method is made of two fundamental steps. As a raw image contains a lot of basins (significant or not), the first step of the segmentation consists in simplifying the image. The topology of the initial image is selectively modified in order to get a *regularized image*. The aim of this transformation is to have a one to one correspondence between the minima of the regularized image and the significant basins of the original image.
The aim of the second step is to recover the shape of the significant basins of the original image. In this paper, we present some *reconstruction operators* which perform this second step. These operators take as input the original image and the regularized image, and reconstruct (from the minima of the regularized image) a binary set. This set is the result of the segmentation.

1 Introduction

The work presented in this paper is related to the segmentation of a grayscale image into regions. We consider a grayscale image as a relief. The objects we want to extract correspond, in this relief, to the "dark areas" or "significant basins"[1,2]. One can think, at first, that there is a one to one correspondence between "dark areas " and *minima*; a (regional) minimum of an image is a connected set of points of uniform altitude with only strictly higher neighbors. But, in a raw image, a "dark area" which seems to be homogeneous to the human eye, contains in fact numerous minima. So, if we extract the minima of an image, we obtain an over-segmented result. This is illustrated by the example of Fig. 1; a possible segmentation of the original signal A could correspond to the black sets of the band (3). We can see that the minima (a), (b) and (c) of A correspond to the same significant basin and that the minima (d) and (e) are not significant. In order to suppress this over-segmentation, we need a method for building a simplified image B such that there exists a one to one correspondence between the significant basins of the original signal A and the minima of B. We call B a *regularized* signal (see the signal B of Fig. 1 for one possible regularization of A).

Several approaches can be used for extracting such a regularized signal B. We have already presented an automatic method [3,4] based upon topology and we will recall it in this paper (section 3). In the framework of mathematical morphology, some methods have been also proposed[5,6,7]. One of these methods consists in extracting the significant minima by thresholding the *dynamics*[8], which is a measure of the "depth" of a minimum; then building an intermediate signal C equal to A for the points of the significant minima and equal to the greatest value of A for the other points (see signal C of Fig .1). The regularized signal B is the result the *reconstruction by erosion*[2] of C over A.

Let us consider the minima of a regularized signal (see band (2) of Fig. 1). The shape of these minima does not correspond to the expected result (see band (3) of Fig. 1). So, it is necessary to use a *reconstruction operator* which allows to recover, from the minima of the regularized image, the shape of the significant basins of the original image. In this paper, we present three reconstruction operators for this purpose and we show their effects in two real segmentation problems.

It should be noted that the *watershed transformation*[9] may also be used for recovering the shape of the significant basins. A comparison with this method is beyond the scope of this paper.

2 Basic notions

2.1 Basic topological definitions

We assume that the basic notions for binary images in the square grid are well known[10]. In particular the notions of *simple point* and *homotopy* : let $X \subset \mathbf{Z}^2$ be a subset of a given binary image, then the point $x \in X$ is *simple* (for X) if there is a one to one correspondence between the connected components of X and those of $X \setminus \{x\}$, and also between the connected components of $\overline{X}$ and those of $\overline{X} \cup \{x\}$. A set Y is *homotopic* to the set X if Y may be obtained from X by deleting or adding simple points. In order to have a correspondence between the topology of X and the one of $\overline{X}$, we have to consider two different kinds of adjacency for X and $\overline{X}$: if we use the n-adjacency for X, we must use the $\overline{n}$-adjacency for $\overline{X}$, with $(n, \overline{n}) = (8, 4)$ or $(4, 8)$.

We present now some basic topological notions for a grayscale image[3,11]. A 2D grayscale image may be seen as a mapping F from $\mathbf{Z}^2$ to $\mathbf{Z}$. Let $x \in \mathbf{Z}^2$, $F(x)$ represents the gray level value of the point x. We denote $\mathcal{F}$ the set composed of all mappings from $\mathbf{Z}^2$ to $\mathbf{Z}$. Let $F \in \mathcal{F}$, we denote $F_k = \{x \in \mathbf{Z}^2, F(x) \geq k\}$ with $k \in \mathbf{Z}$; F_k is called a *section* of F. Note that a section F_k is a binary set, i.e. $F_k \subset \mathbf{Z}^2$.
We say that $F \in \mathcal{F}$ and $G \in \mathcal{F}$ are homotopic if $\forall k \in \mathbf{Z}, F_k$ and G_k are homotopic (in the binary sense). Thus, the homotopy of grayscale images may be directly derived from the homotopy of binary sets.

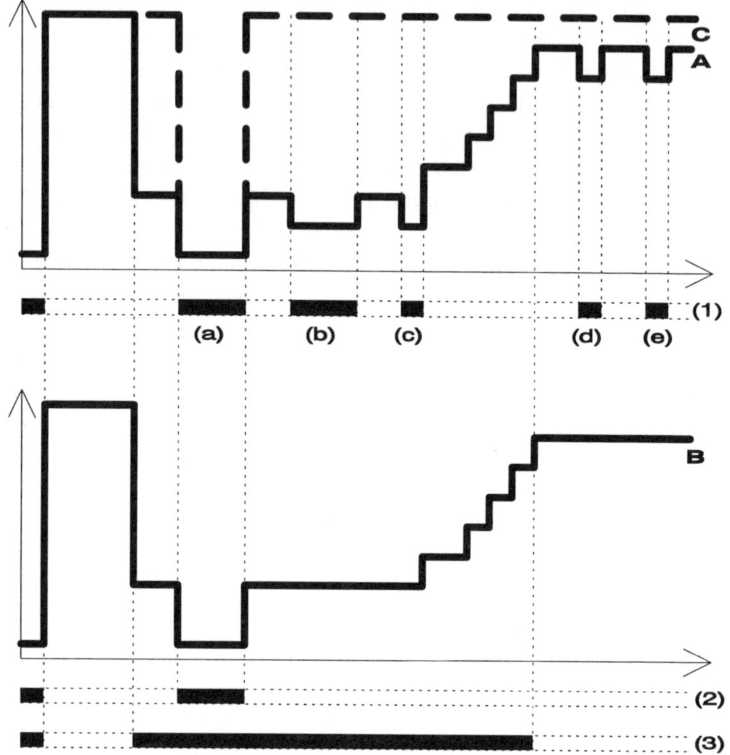

A: the original signal, B: a regularized signal for A, C: intermediate signal; (1): the minima of A, (2): the minima of B, (3): an expected segmentation result.

Figure 1: The segmentation problem.

A point $x \in \mathbf{Z}^2$ is a *peak* (for F) if x is an isolated point in F_k, with $k = F(x)$. A point $x \in \mathbf{Z}^2$ is *destructible* (for F) if x is simple for F_k, with $k = F(x)$. Note that the value of such a point can be decreased by one while preserving the topology of F. This property can be used to simplify an original image and obtain the "leveling kernel" or the "homotopic kernel".

Let $F \in \mathcal{F}$, a *leveling* (resp. *homotopic*) *kernel* of F is obtained by iteratively selecting a destructible or peak point x (resp. a destructible point x) and lowering its value. This procedure is repeated until stability. The signal D in Fig. 2 is an homotopic kernel of signal B.

Both the leveling and the homotopic kernels have the effect of spreading the minima. The homotopic kernel keeps unchanged the topology of all sections of the image, and also the topology of the minima and the topology of the maxima. The leveling kernel iteratively lowers the simply connected maxima (maxima without "holes", i.e. maxima which do not surround any minimum) while keeping the topology of the minima. We will see that the reconstruction operators presented in this paper are applied on "thin" regularized images. The *leveling* and the *homotopic* kernel transforms achieve such a thinning.

2.2 Relations

Let E be a set. Let $\mathcal{R}$ be a (binary) relation on E. Let $u \in E$. We denote $\mathcal{R}(u) = \{v \in E$ such that $u\mathcal{R}v$ is true $\}$ We denote $\mathcal{R}^\infty$ the relation defined by : $v \in \mathcal{R}^\infty(u) \Leftrightarrow$ there is a sequence $u = u_0, u_1, \cdots, u_k = v$ such that $u_i \in \mathcal{R}(u_{i-1})$. We say that v is *a kernel of* u *for* $\mathcal{R}$ if $v \in \mathcal{R}^\infty(u)$ and $\mathcal{R}(v) = \emptyset$.

The notions of relation and kernel will allow us to describe the reconstruction operators in the section 4. These operators transform an initial set X. A step of such an operator consists in adding a selected point x to the set X. The resulting set is $Y = X \cup \{x\}$. A reconstruction operator reiterates this step until stability. We describe more formally one step of such a "growing" operator by introducing a relation $\mathcal{R}$ which links X and Y. The final result of this reconstruction operator is a kernel of X for $\mathcal{R}$.

Definition : We denote $\mathcal{X}$ the set composed of all subsets of $\mathbf{Z}^2$.
A relation $\mathcal{R}$ on $\mathcal{X}$ is called a *growing relation* if we have : $\forall X, Y \in \mathcal{X}$, if $Y \in \mathcal{R}(X)$, then $\exists x \in \overline{X}$ such that $Y = X \cup \{x\}$. The *growing set* of $X \in \mathcal{X}$ is the set $GS(X) = \{x \in \overline{X}$ such that $X \cup \{x\} \in \mathcal{R}(X)\}$.

Let $F \in \mathcal{F}$ and $\mathcal{R}$ be a growing relation; we define the following relation $\mathcal{R}^F$ which is a relation on $\mathcal{X}$: $\forall X, Y \in \mathcal{X}$, $Y \in \mathcal{R}^F(X) \Leftrightarrow$
1) $Y \in \mathcal{R}(X)$; we denote x the point such that $\{x\} = Y \setminus X$; and
2) $F(x) = MAX\{F(y), y \in GS(X)\}$.
The relation $\mathcal{R}^F$ is called the *hierarchical relation associated to* $\mathcal{R}$ *(and relative to* F*)*.

For a given image, each growing relation has a corresponding hierarchical relation. This property will allow us, in the section 4, to derive from the definition of a reconstruction operator, a hierarchical reconstruction operator which better takes into account the relief of the image.

3 Regularization

As mentionned in the introduction, several methods based upon mathematical morphology or discrete topology may be used to get a regularized image. In

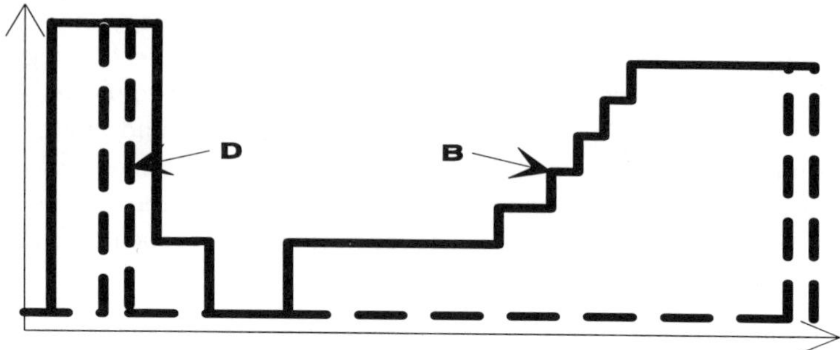

B: the regularized signal of Fig.1, D: an homotopic kernel of B.

Figure 2: Illustration of homotopic kernel.

this section, we recall the principle of a topological approach which allows to automatically regularize the leveling (or homotopic) kernel an image without any threshold or size criteria [3,4].

This approach consists in the use of two regularization operators. They respectively delete two kinds of non-significant regions of a leveling kernel :
The first one deletes the inconsistant crest lines which separate minima of similar depth.
The second one deletes the minima of small depth, with respect to the depth of the minima in the neighborhood. The characterization of these minima of small depth is possible because, in a leveling kernel, the minima are coming into contact through upper points (points which do not belong to a minimum).

Let $F \in \mathcal{F}$ be a leveling kernel. Let M be a minimum; we recall that : $\Psi(M) = MAX\{F(x), \forall x$ adjacent to $M\}$ and we denote $F(M)$ the value of the minimum M. Let x be an upper point adjacent to M.
We say that x is an *irregular upper point* if $|F(x) - F(M)| < |\Psi(M) - F(x)|$. In this case, $F(M)$ is called a *regularized value of* x.
We say that M is an *irregular minimum* if there exists a minimum M' separated from M by a point x such that $|F(x) - F(M)| < |F(M) - F(M')|$. In this case, $F(x)$ is called a *regularized value of* M.

The first regularization operator repeats the two following steps until stability : 1) Replace the values of irregular points by their regularized values; 2) Compute a leveling kernel of the result of the step 1).
The second regularization operator repeats the two following steps until stability : 1') Replace the values of irregular minima by their regularized values; 2') Compute a leveling kernel of the result of the step 1').

For obtaining a regularized leveling kernel of an image F, we apply succe-

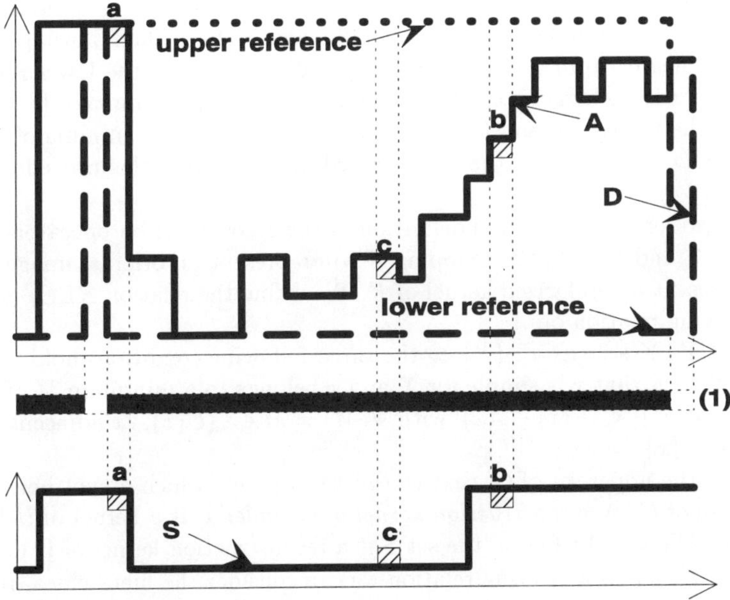

A: the original signal of Fig.1, D: the homotopic kernel of A, S: final segmentation; (1): minima of D.

Figure 3: Illustration of the reconstruction.

sively the two regularization operators to a leveling kernel of F .

We can see Fig. 4(b) and Fig. 5(b) the results of such a transformation.

4 Reconstruction operators

Let us consider a regularized kernel of an image; the minima of such a kernel is a binary set which corresponds to the expected segmentation result, up to a topological transformation. Nevertheless, the minima do not correspond, in shape, to the desired segmentation result. In this section, we present three *reconstruction* operators which modify the shape of the minima in order to recover as much as possible the shape of the significant basins of the original image.

The Fig. 3 illustrates the principle of the reconstruction; the signal A of Fig. 1 is represented as well as a regularized homotopic kernel of A, denoted D. To each minimum M of D is associated the value $\Psi(M)$ which is the maximal value of the points adjacent to M. For each point x of a minimum M, $\Psi(M)$

may be seen as an "upper reference" for x; we will use D(x) as a "lower reference" for x. We iteratively select a point x and perform the following action : if A(x) is nearer from the upper reference of x than from the lower reference of x, then x is no longer considered to be a point of the minima of D. It is the case for the points (a) and (b); the point (c) is kept in the minima of D. The set S depicted in Fig. 3 is the set obtained after iterating this procedure until stability.

We present now a formal definition of the reconstruction operators.
Let $F \in \mathcal{F}$ and $G \in \mathcal{F}$; the mapping F will represent an original image and G will represent a regularized kernel of F. We define the relation $REC_{F,G}$ which is a growing relation on $\mathcal{X}$;
$\forall X, Y \in \mathcal{X} : Y \in REC_{F,G}(X) \Leftrightarrow$ the three following conditions hold :
•$\exists x \in \overline{X}$ such that x is simple for X and x belongs to a minimum M of G,
•$|F(x) - \Psi(M)| < |F(x) - G(x)|$ with $\Psi(M) = MAX\{G(x), \forall x$ adjacent to $M\}$,
•$Y = X \cup \{x\}$.
Let U be the upper set of G, that is, the set of points which do not belong to a minimum of G. A *reconstruction kernel of G under F* is a kernel of U for the relation $REC_{F,G}$. In Fig. 3, the set S is a reconstruction kernel of D under A.

As $REC_{F,G}$ is a growing relation we can consider the hierarchical relation $REC^H_{F,G}$ and the corresponding *hierarchical reconstruction kernel.*

We can also define a *non-homotopic reconstruction kernel* which is a kernel for a modified relation $REC_{F,G}$: we do not require that the point x be simple for X.

We will see in the section 5 the advantages of the hierarchical and of the non-homotopic reconstructions with two real segmentation problems.

5 Experimental results

We present, in this section, the action of our reconstruction operators in two real segmentation problems. The Fig. 4(a) is an MRI picture of a human head; the segmentation must bring to the fore, the folds of the brain. The Fig. 5(a) is a picture of electrophoresis gel; here, the segmentation must extract the dark spots. In order to obtain the final segmentation, we have executed the reconstruction operators on the binary sets presented on Fig. 4(c) and Fig. 5(c); they are the upper sets of the regularized leveling kernels (Fig. 4(b) and Fig. 5(b)) of the original images.

We can see in Fig. 4(d) and Fig. 5(d) the segmentation obtained with the homotopic reconstruction; some badly placed black lines which alter the quality of the result can be observed. They are due to the fact that a large minimum of a regularized leveling kernel can contain, in the initial image, sev-

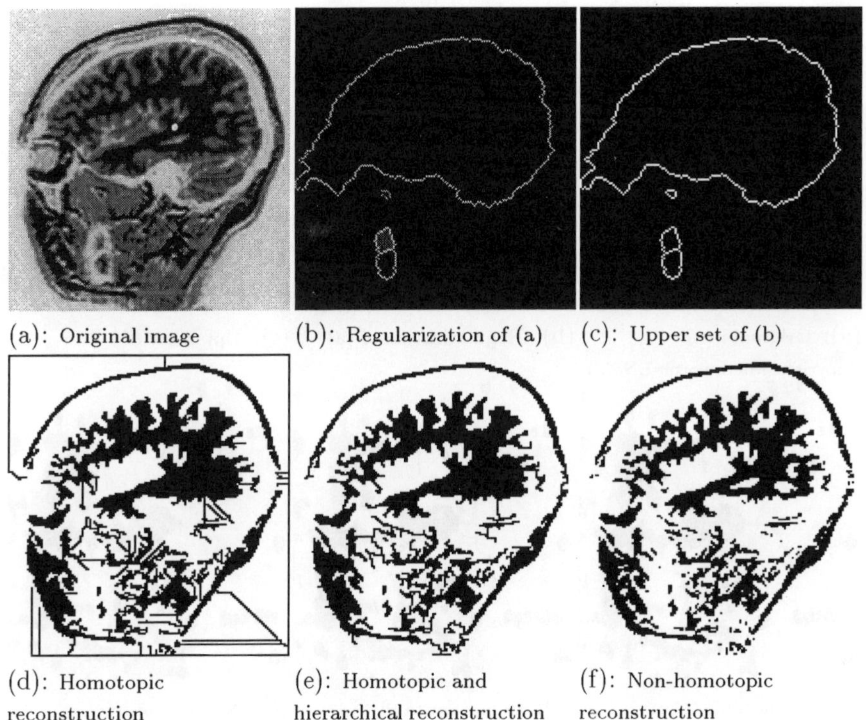

(a): Original image (b): Regularization of (a) (c): Upper set of (b)

(d): Homotopic reconstruction (e): Homotopic and hierarchical reconstruction (f): Non-homotopic reconstruction

Figure 4: A reconstruction illustration.

eral non-reconstructible areas, often with only one pixel size, and surrounded by reconstructible points. With an homotopic reconstruction operator, a path is preserved between these non-reconstructible areas. The location of this path depends only on the scanning order of the points and can take place everywhere in the picture. A solution to this problem, is to consider the hierarchical reconstruction operator. Since the points are processed according to the decreasing order of their gray level, the path between two non-reconstructible areas will be made of points of lowest possible altitude. The resulting binary image, even if it is homotopic to the one obtained by the non-hierarchical reconstruction operator, is more appropriate, because the reconstructed black set corresponds to the lowest possible pixels of the original image (see Fig. 4(e) and Fig. 5(e)).

We can also notice that with the homotopic reconstruction, hierarchical or not, some reconstructible "islands" surrounded by non-reconstructible points may never be reached. The non-homotopic reconstruction allows to recover

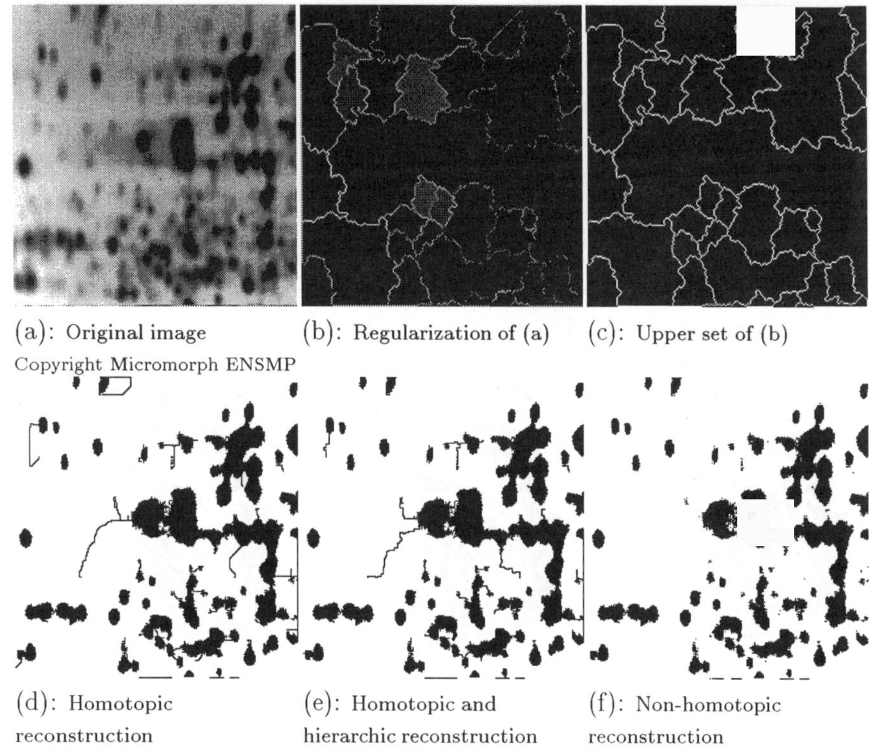

(a): Original image
Copyright Micromorph ENSMP

(b): Regularization of (a)

(c): Upper set of (b)

(d): Homotopic reconstruction

(e): Homotopic and hierarchic reconstruction

(f): Non-homotopic reconstruction

Figure 5: A reconstruction illustration.

these islands; as we can see on Fig. 4(f) and Fig. 5(f), some light and disconnected areas are recovered.

6 Conclusion

We have presented in this paper three reconstruction operators. Starting from a regularized leveling kernel of an original image, they allow to automatically recover the shape of the significant basins of this original image.

The homotopic and non-hierarchical reconstruction operator cannot be seen as an acceptable operator because it can produce some badly placed lines. The homotopic and hierarchical reconstruction operator is the better solution if the topology of the regularized leveling kernel is correct. In the adverse case, one will choose the non-homotopic reconstruction operator.

References

1. S. Beucher. *Morphologie mathématique et segmentation.* PhD thesis, École des Mines, Fontainebleau, France, 1990.
2. M. Grimaud. *La géodésie numérique en morphologie mathématique. Application à la détection automatique de microcalcifications en mammographie numérique.* PhD thesis, École des Mines, Fontainebleau, France, 1991.
3. G. Bertrand J.-C. Everat and M. Couprie. A topological approach to image segmentation. In *Proceedings of Vision Geometry* V, *Volume 2826,* pages 65–76. SPIE, 1996.
4. J.-C. Everat and G. Bertrand. New topological operators for segmentation. In *Proceedings of ICIP'96, Volume* III/III, pages 45–48. IEEE Signal Processing Society, 1996.
5. F. Meyer and S. Beucher. Morphological segmentation. *Journal of visual Communication and Image Representation,* 1(1):21–46, September 1990.
6. S. Beucher and F. Meyer. The morphological approach to segmentation : the watershed transformation. In E. R. Dougherty, editor, *Mathematical morphology in image processing,* pages 433–481. Marcel Dekker, Inc., 1992.
7. L. Vincent. Morphological grayscale reconstruction in image analysis : applications and efficient algorithms. *IEEE Transactions on Image Processing,* 2(2):176–201, April 1993.
8. M. Grimaud. A new measure of contrast : the dynamics. In *Proceedings of Image Algebra and Morphological Image Processing* III, *Volume 1769,* pages 292–305. SPIE, 1992.
9. F. Meyer. Un algorithme optimal de ligne de partage des eaux. In *Actes du* 8e *congrès de reconnaissance des formes et d'intelligence artificielle,* pages 847–859. AFCET, Novembre 1992.
10. T.Y. Kong and A. Rosenfeld. Digital topology : introduction and survey. *Computer Vision Graphics and Image Processing,* 48:357–393, 1989.
11. G. Bertrand J.-C. Everat and M. Couprie. Image segmentation through operators based upon topology. *Journal of Electronic Imaging,* to appear.

FROM VIEWER DEPENDENT TO VIEWER INDEPENDENT REPRESENTATIONS OF OBJECTS

M. FERRARO
Dipartimento di Fisica Sperimentale, via Giuria 1,
10125 Torino, Italy

T. COSTA
Dipartimento di Psicologia, via Po 14,
10125 Torino, Italy

In this note are determined necessary and sufficient conditions under which it is possible to integrate representations of an object, obtained from antipodal views, to form a representation viewer independent. In particular it is proved that, in case of orthographic projection, such integration is possible if and only if the two antipodal views share the same occluding boundary; from that it follows that their projections on the antipodal planes must have the same shape. Further, it is demonstrated a sufficient condition, concerning the properties of the surfaces, which ensures the existence of at least a pair of antipodal views from which a viewer independent representation can be determined. Finally it is shown that more than two views are needed in case of perspective projection.

1 Introduction

The ultimate goal of a biological or artificial vision system is to represent the state of the external world. Indeed, vision can be characterized as the process of deriving the identities and spatial dispositions of objects in the surrounding environment from the information contained implicitly in the images. Objects must be given a representation independent from the point of view, so that recognition can be accomplished from any view; the aim of this note is to analyze the conditions under which it is possible to integrate different views of an object in a viewer independent representation.

2 Preliminaries

Let S be the surface of an object in an arbitrary coordinate system (x, y, z). We are not interested here in abstract sufaces, but, rather, in surfaces of physical objects that are closed and bounded, and hence compact [1]. It will also be assumed that the surfaces are arcwise connected. A surface S is said to be arcwise connected if given two points $p, q \in S$ there exists a continuous curve joining p to q [1].

Surfaces can be represented in a way independent from the point of view by means of parametric or implicit representations. A parametric representation of S is a map $\vec{r}$ from an open and connected parameter domain (u, v) to $\mathbf{R}^3$,

$$\vec{r}: (u, v) \rightarrow \{x(u, v), y(u, v), z(u, v)\}. \tag{1}$$

In the implicit representation S is the zero-set of a function $F: \mathbf{R}^3 \rightarrow \mathbf{R}$; $F^{-1}(0) = S$, that is points belonging to S satisfy the equation $F(x, y, z) = 0$[1]. In the following F will be supposed to be at least of class C^1 (that is differentiable and with continuous derivatives) and, for sake of simplicity, S will be said to be C^1. This means that S has neither cusps nor sharp edges. This assumption is not satisfied by most physical surfaces, but, if fine or microscopic details are disregarded, surfaces of physical objects are at least piecewise smooth, and usually non-regular points form a set of measure zero, i.e. a set of zero area[2], thus our hyphothesis is not too restrictive.

Let γ be a curve parametrized by a parameter $t \in I$, where I is an interval in $\mathbf{R}$, and let g be the function $g = F \circ \gamma$. The curve γ and the surface $S = F^{-1}(0)$ are said to have k-fold contact at a point $p(t_0)$ if $g(t_0) = F(\gamma(t_0)) = 0$ and $g'(t_0) = \cdots = g^{k-1}(t_0) = 0$, $g^k(t_0) \neq 0$, where g^j is the j-th derivative of g with respect to t[3].

Consider a coordinate system (x, y, z) and two planes P_1, P_2, defined by $z = 0$ and $z = d$ respectively, and let the origin, the orientation of the z-axis and d be such that $F(x, y, z) = 0$ holds if and only if $0 < z < d$; this condition is not restrictive because S is bounded. Define a new coordinate system (x', y', z'), whose origin is in the plane $z = d$ and such that $x' = x$, $y' = y$, $z' = d - z$. In this new system there exists a function F' such that points of the S must satisfy the equation $F'(x', y', z') = F(x, y, d - z) = 0$.

Consider the case of orthographic projections. A line l joining a point $a = (x_0, y_0) \in P_1$ (resp. $a' = (x'_0, y'_0) \in P_2$) to a point $p \in S$ and parallel to the z-axis is said to be a line of sight. The planes P_1, P_2 will be called views. If S is a closed surface, a line of sight and S have 1-fold contacts at an even number of points; this implies that if a line of sight intersects a closed surface, and it is not tangent to it, there exist at least two points of intersection. Orthographic projections Pr_i, $i = 1, 2$ are maps from S to P_i. If one considers only projections of points visible from P_1 or P_2 the domains of Pr_1 and Pr_2 are restricted as follows: for every pair $(x_0, y_0) \in P_1$,

$$Pr_1^{-1}(x_0, y_0) = (x_0, y_0, z_0 = \min\{z | F(x_0, y_0, z) = 0\}), \tag{2}$$

and analogously for every $(x'_0, y'_0) \in P_2$,

$$Pr_2^{-1}(x'_0, y'_0) = (x'_0, y'_0, z'_0 = \min\{z' | F'(x'_0, y'_0, z') = 0\}). \tag{3}$$

This condition guarantees that a point $p \in S$ is mapped by Pr_i in P_i only if it is not occluded by some other point of S on the same line of sight; then $\forall p \in S, \quad Pr_i(p) = a \Rightarrow Pr_i^{-1}(a) = p$, i.e. Pr_1, Pr_2 are injections, one-to-one maps. Let M_1 (resp. M_2) be the domain of Pr_1 (resp. Pr_2), then M_1 and M_2 are the parts of surfaces visible, under orthographic projections, from P_1 and P_2 respectively; they have representations in the Monge form $M_1 = [x, y, z = f_1(x, y)]$, $M_2 = [x', y', z' = f_2'(x', y')]$, where the functions f_i, the depth maps, are defined by

$$f_1(x,y) = \min\{z|F(x,y,z) = 0\}, \quad f_2'(x',y') = \min\{z'|F(x',y',z') = 0\}. \quad (4)$$

Let $\vec{N}(p) = (N_x(p), N_y(p), N_z(p))$ denote the unit normal vector to S at $p \in S$, in the coordinate system (x, y, z). Assuming that the normal vectors point outward from the surface, if a point $p \in S$ is visible from P_1 then $N_z(p) \leq 0$, whereas if a point $q \in S$ is visible from P_2, $N_{z'}(q) \leq 0$, where $N_{z'}$ is the component of $\vec{N}$ along the axis z', in the coordinate system (x', y', z'). Note that in this case $N_z(q) \geq 0$.

Visible points $p \in S$ at which the lines of sight from a view P_i , $i = 1, 2$, are tangent to S form the occluding boundaries O_i^b of S for the view P_i. Occluding boundaries are sets of curves in S and if $p \in O_i^b$ then $N_z = 0$ at $p \in S$ and there exists an interval $[a, b]$ in the z-axis such that N_z takes negative values in $[a, z_0[$ and positive ones in $]z_0, b]$ [4]. In the following it will be supposed that visible points at which a line of sight is tangent to the surface form a countable set $\{p_j\}$, that is either $\{p_j\}$ is finite or it may be put in one-to-one correspondence with the positive integers. To avoid any ambiguity it will be assumed as element of O_i^b the point $p_k \in \{p_j\}$ such that its distance $d(p_k, P_i)$ from P_i satisfies $d(p_k, P_i) = \min_{p_j}\{d(p_j, P_i)\}$.

For each M_i the image of the orthographic projection Pr_i, $i = 1, 2$ is a closed region $A_i \subset P_i$. The boundary ∂A_i of each region A_i is the image of the projection of points belonging to O_i^b, the occluding boundary for the view P_i; the converse is not true, in that there may exist points $p_i \in O_i^b$ whose projection is in the interior of A_i.

3 From viewer dependent to viewer independent representations

Suppose that are given two Monge patches M_i, corresponding to two antipodal views P_1, P_2 of surface S which is $\mathcal{C}^1$, closed, bounded and arcwise connected; under which conditions is it possible to obtain a viewer independent implicit representation of S from the depth maps f_1, f_2? It is clear that it can happen only if $M_1 \cup M_2 = S$, that is if all points $p \in S$ are visible either from P_1 or from P_2. This condition is also sufficient. Preliminarily note that, by the properties of the orthographic projection, for every pair $(x, y) \in A_1$ there exists just one pair $(x', y') \in A_2$ such that $x = x', y = y'$, that is $A_1 = A_2$ modulus a translation along the z-axis. Then $f_2'(x', y') = d - f_2(x, y)$, where $f_2(x, y) = \max\{z | F(x, y, z) = 0\}$. In the coordinate system (x, y, z) the Monge patch M_1 has then representation $M_1 = [x, y, f_1(x, y)]$ and M_2 has representation $M_2 = [x, y, d - f_2(x, y)]$. Consider a point $a_1 = (x_0, y_0) \in A_1$, a point $a_2 = (x_0', y_0') \in A_2$ and let l_1, l_2 be the lines of sight from a_1, a_2 respectively. It is clear that l_1 l_2 belong to the straight line joining a_1 to a_2. For any $(x_0, y_0) \in A_1$ the there exist a point $p_1 = (x_0, y_0, z_1) \in S$ (visible from P_1) and a point $p_2 = (x_0, y_0, z_2) \in S$ (visible from P_2) that are the intersections of S with l_1, l_2. Note that these are the only intersections; if it was not the case there would be a point $p_3 \in S$ that would be visible neither from P_1 nor from P_2, contrary to the hypothesis that $S = M_1 \cup M_2$. Then the values $z_1 = f_1(x_0, y_0)$, $z_2 = d - f_2(x_0, y_0)$ are the solutions of the equation $F(x, y, z) = 0$, and they are the only solutions, because otherwise there would be a point p_3 belonging to the line joining a_1 to a_2, and it would occluded by p_1 and p_2.

Since S is a closed surface the solutions are almost everywhere distinct. Then S can be represented implicitly by

$$F(x, y, z) = z^2 - [f_1(x, y) + d - f_2(x, y)]\, z + f_1(x, y)\, [d - f_2(x, y)] = 0. \quad (5)$$

If $z_1 = z_2$ the point $p = (x, y, z_1)$ belongs to the occluding boundary, which is the same for P_1 and P_2; indeed it is easy to check that at p the line of sight is tangent to S. Thus we have

Proposition 1. *Let S be a surface and suppose that S is C^1, closed, bounded and arcwise connected. Let f_1, f_2 be the depth maps obtained by considering two antipodal views P_1, P_2 and let M_1, M_2 be the corresponding Monge patches. Then S can be given a viewer independent representation from f_1, f_2 if and only if $S = M_1 \cup M_2$. The viewer independent representation of S in implicit form is given by Eq 5.*

The implicit representation defined by Eq 5 is not unique, indeed S can be given any representation of the form $G = H \circ F = 0$, where H is a function such that $H(w) = 0$ if and only if $w = 0$; however a representation of this type is, obviously, redundant and S can be thought of as essentially represented by Eq 5.

In general it is not easy to verify if the condition $S = M_1 \cup M_2$ holds; thus some criterion must be found, based on the properties of the images of S on the planes P_1, P_2, to determine if it is possible to give the surface under observation a viewer independent representation. The first step is to show that $S = M_1 \cup M_2$ holds if and only if the views from P_1 and P_2 have the same occluding boundary.

Lemma 1. *Let S be a surface and suppose S to be C^1, closed, bounded and arcwise connected. Let M_1, M_2 be the parts of S visible from the antipodal views P_1, P_2. Then $S = M_1 \cup M_2$ if and only if $O_1^b = O_2^b$.*

Proof. If $S = M_1 \cup M_2$ then there exists a representation given by Eq 5; the occluding boundaries are set of points such that $z_1 = z_2$, where z_1, z_2 are the roots of $F(x, y, z) = 0$ for every $(x, y) \in A_1$, and this shows that $O_1^b = O_2^b$. To show that the condition is sufficent note first that a point $s = (x_0, y_0, z_0)$ is visible from P_1, (respectively P_2) if and only if $z_0 = \min\{z|F(x_0, y_0, z) = 0\}$, (respectively $z_0 = \max\{z|F(x_0, y_0, z) = 0\}$). Let $O = O_1^b \cap O_2^b$, then at $p \in O$, $\min\{z|F(x, y, z) = 0\} = \max\{z|F(x, y, z) = 0\}$. By hypothesis $O = O_1^b = O_2^b$; suppose that there exists a part $S^* \subset S$ that is occluded by $U \subset M_1$ and by M_2. Then $S = M_1 \cup M_2 \cup S^*$ and, since S is closed, for every point $c = (x, y) \in C = Pr_1(U)$ there exists a set B of points $b = (x, y, z^*) \in S^*$, such that $\min\{z|F(x, y, z) = 0\} < z^* < \max\{z|F(x, y, z) = 0\}$. Lines of sight from the boundary ∂C of C are tangent to visible points on S, i.e. the occlusion of S^* by U gives rise to a curve $\gamma \subset O_1^b$. By hypothesis S is arcwise connected, then for $q \in \gamma$ it must be $\min\{z|F(x, y, z) = 0\} \neq \max\{z|F(x, y, z) = 0\}$, and this shows that there exists a subset of O_1^b that does not belongs to O, that is O_1^b strictly includes O, a contradiction.

The next lemma relates the condition $O_1^b = O_2^b$ to properties of the projections of the occluding boundaries on the antipodal planes. Preliminarly suppose that the line of sight from a point $a_i = (x_0, y_0)$ in ∂A_i, $i = 1, 2$ can be tangent to just one point p belonging to an occluding boundary, that is we exclude the accidental alignement of occluding boundaries due, for instance, to a particular orientation of S with respect to the planes P_i. This condition is similar to the generic viewpoint assumption [5].

Lemma 2. *Two antipodal views P_1, P_2 of S have the same occluding boundary if and only if $Pr_1\left(O_1^b\right) = Pr_2\left(O_2^b\right)$ modulus a translation along the z-axis.*

Proof. It is clear that the images of projections of points $p \in O_1^b \cap O_2^b$ form the boundaries of the regions A_i, whereas the images of points belonging to just one of the occluding boundaries are in the interior of the respective regions A_1, A_2. Then the condition is necessary since, if P_1, P_2 have the same occluding boundary, $Pr_i\left(O_i^b\right) = \partial A_i$ and for every pair $(x, y) \in \partial A_1$ there exists just one pair $(x', y') \in \partial A_2$, with $x = x', y = y'$, i.e. $\partial A_1 = \partial A_2$ modulus a translation along the z-axis. To prove that it is also sufficient note that, if $Pr_1\left(O_1^b\right)$ and $Pr_2\left(O_2^b\right)$ differ only for a translation along the z-axis, for every $a_1 \in Pr_1\left(O_1^b\right)$ there is one point $a_2 \in Pr_2\left(O_1^b\right)$ such that the line l_a from a_1 to a_2 is tangent to the surface and, by the generic viewpoint assumption, l_a is tangent to S to just one point p such that $Pr_i(p) = a_i$. Then $O_1^b = O_2^b$.

From Lemmas 1 and 2, it follows

Proposition 2. *Let S be a surface and suppose that S is C^1, connected, closed, bounded and arcwise connected. Let P_1 P_2 be a pair of antipodal views. S can be given a viewer independent representation if and only if $Pr_1\left(O_1^b\right) = Pr_2\left(O_2^b\right)$ modulus a translation along the direction of sight.*

Consider now the "dual" problem, that is to determine which conditions a surface must satisfy for the existence of at least a pair of antipodal planes such that Propositon 2 holds. This can be done by using the Gauss map to analyze the distribution of the normal vectors to the surface. Let S^2 be the unit sphere. The Gauss map $\mathcal{N} : S \to S^2$ associates a point $p \in S$ to a point $s \in S^2$ such that $\vec{N}(p) = \vec{n}(s)$, where $\vec{n}$ is the normal to S^2 at s [1].

Proposition 3. *Let S be a surface and suppose S to be C^1, closed, bounded and arcwise connected. Let γ be a simple, closed curve on S. Consider the Gauss map $\mathcal{N} : S \to S^2$, and suppose that there exists a meridian m on the Gauss sphere such that $\mathcal{N}(\gamma) = m$ and $\mathcal{N}^{-1}(m) = \gamma \cup B$, where B is a countable set of points and $\gamma \cap B = \emptyset$. Then there exists a pair of antipodal views P_1 and P_2 such that the corresponding depth maps f_1, f_2 are sufficient to determine an implicit rappresentation of S.*

Proof. It is enough to prove that there exist antipodal views P_1, P_2 for which γ is the common occluding boundary, the assertion then follows from Proposition 1 and Lemma 1. The meridian m is a geodesic and hence the normal to m and the normal to the sphere coincide, since the curvature of m is just the normal curvature of the sphere. This implies that the normal vectors $\vec{n}$ to the sphere at points $s \in m$ belong to the same plane and then there exists a coordinate system $\mathcal{R}$ such that $n_z = 0$ for all $s \in m$, where n_z is the component of $\vec{n}$ in the z direction. By hypothesis $\mathcal{N}^{-1}(m) = \gamma \cup B$, then, in $\mathcal{R}$, $N_z = 0$ for all $p \in \gamma \cup B$. Points $b \in B$ cannot belong to an occluding boundary since they do not form a curve (B is supposed to be countable) and S has no cusps; on the other hand $N_z(\gamma) = 0$ and, by hypothesis, γ is the only curve in S for which this conditions holds in the coordinate system $\mathcal{R}$. Define two antipodal views orthogonal to the z-axis in $\mathcal{R}$; the lines of sight from P_1,

P_2 are parallel to the z-axis in $\mathcal{R}$ and γ is the only curve along which the lines of sight are tangent to the surface, hence $\gamma = O_1^b = O_2^b$.

Corollary 1. *Let S be a surface of revolution. Then any pair of antipodal planes parallel to the axis of revolution share the same occluding boundary.*
Proof. Obvious.

If the hypothesis of the Proposition 3 hold there exists a rotation of the coordinate system x, y, z into a new coordinate system ξ_1, ξ_2, ξ_3, in which S can be written as in Eq 5. For sake of notational compactness set $x_1 = x, x_2 = y, x_3 = z$. The new variables ξ_i can be written as $\xi_i = \sum a_{ij}(\theta, \phi, \psi)\xi_j$ where θ, ϕ, ψ are the Euler angles, the coefficents a_{ij} are elements of the matrix $A(\theta, \phi, \psi) = R_1(\theta)R_2(\phi)R_3(\psi)$ and R_i, $i = 1, 2, 3$ are rotations around the x_i-axes respectively The implicit representation of S in the new system is

$$F\left(\sum a_{1j}^*\xi_j, \sum a_{2j}^*\xi_j, \sum a_{3j}^*\xi_j\right) = F'(\xi_1, \xi_2, \xi_3) = 0, \qquad (6)$$

where a_{ij}^* are element of A^{-1}, the inverse of A. Let M_1', M_2' be the Monge patches corresponding to two antipodal views P_1', P_2' orthogonal, say, to the ξ_3-axis; then $S = M_1' \cup M_2'$ if and only if it can be given an implicit representation of the form

$$F'(\xi_1, \xi_2, \xi_3) =$$
$$H\left\{\xi_3 - [g_1(\xi_1, \xi_2) + d' - g_2(\xi_1, \xi_2)]\xi_3 + g_1(\xi_1, \xi_2)[d' - g_2(\xi_1, \xi_2)]\right\} = 0, \qquad (7)$$

where H is a function such that $H(w) = 0$ if and only if $w = 0$ and g_i are the depth maps from the new antipodal planes P_i'. Again the origin of the new coordinate system, the orientation of the ξ_3-axis and d' can be chosen such that $F'(\xi_1, \xi_2, \xi_3) = 0$ if and only if $0 < \xi_3 < d'$.

In general then, a surface S admits pairs of antipodal planes with common occluding boundary only for certain orientations of P_1, P_2. However, there exists a class of surfaces, the ovaloids, for which this property holds independently from the orientation of P_1, P_2.

Corollary 2. *Let S be an ovaloid, a surface with Gaussian curvature $K > 0$. Any pair antipodal planes share the same occluding boundary.*

Proof. It follows immediatly from the theorem of Hadamard on the characterization of ovaloids [1], since $K > 0$ implies that $\mathcal{N} : S \to S^2$ is a diffeomorphism, a map with a differentiable inverse.

Consider the case in which P_1 and P_2 are not in an antipodal position. It is obvious that in this case they cannot share the same occluding boundary, since it implies that there exists a closed curve $\gamma \in S$ such that for every $q \in \gamma$, $N_z = N_{z'} = 0$, and this can happen only if the axes z and z' are collinear, that is if P_1, P_2 are antipodal.

4 Perspective projection

In case of perspective projection, consider the projection of the surface on the hemisphere E whose center is in the focal point and whose radius r_0 is the focal lenght [6]. Without loss of generality we can set $r_0 = 1$. Let (ϕ, θ, ρ) be a system of spherical coordinates with origin O in the center of E and let $\vec{u}_r(\phi, \theta)$ be an unit vector directed along increasing ρ.

The surface S can be given a new implicit representation by replacing cartesian coordinates (x, y, z) with spherical coordinates (ϕ, θ, ρ): points $p \in S$ satisfy the equation

$$F[x(\phi,\theta,\rho), y(\phi,\theta,\rho), z(\phi,\theta,\rho)] = \Psi(\phi,\theta,\rho) = 0, \tag{8}$$

that is $S = \Psi^{-1}(0)$.

Perspective projections Πr are maps from a point $p = (\phi, \theta, \rho) \in S$ to a point $e = (\phi, \theta) \in E$, that a line of sight from $e(\phi, \theta)$ is parallel to $\vec{u}_r(\phi, \theta)$. Then it is clear that the perspective projection from S to E is just the orthogonal projection in spherical coordinates. Let E_1, E_2 be two hemispheres tangent the the planes P_1 and P_2 defined as before, and such that the line joining the center O_1 of E_1 to the center O_2 of E_2 belongs to the z-axis.

In order to ensure that a point $p \in S$ is mapped by Πr_i, $i = 1, 2$ in E_i only if is not occluded by some other point, the domains of Πr_1 and Πr_2 can be restricted in a way analogous to Eqs 2, 3: for every pair $(\phi_0, \theta_0) \in E_1$,

$$\Pi r_1^{-1}(\phi_0, \theta_0) = (\phi_0, \theta_0, \rho_0 = \min\{\rho | \Psi(\phi, \theta_0, \rho) = 0\}), \tag{9}$$

and analogously for every $(\phi'_0, \theta'_0) \in E_2$,

$$\Pi r_2^{-1}(\phi'_0, \theta'_0) = (\phi'_0, \theta'_0, \rho'_0 = \min\{\rho' | \Psi(\phi'_0, \theta'_0, \rho') = 0\}). \tag{10}$$

Visible parts of S can be given the Monge form in spherical coordinates: $M = [\theta, \phi, \rho(\theta, \phi)]$.

Let l_1 (resp. l_2) be the line of sight from E_1 (resp. E_2) to $p \in S$; it is clear that l_1, l_2 do not belong to the same straight line unless p belongs to the line joining O_1 to O_2. Then if l_1 is tangent to S at p, l_2 cannot be tangent to S at p unless,

1. p belongs to the line joining O_1 to O_2,

2. S has a cusp or a sharp edge at p, contrary to the hypothesis that F, and hence Ψ, is at least of class $\mathcal{C}^1$.

Thus occluding boundaries for E_1, E_2 can have in common at most one point, and this implies that there is a part of S which is visible neither from E_1 nor from E_2.

5 Conclusions

In this paper we have investigated which conditions are necessary and sufficient, in principle, to obtain a viewer independent representation of an object from a pair of antipodal views. It is clear that, given a pair of views P_1, P_2, the antipodal position is the one that provides the maximum possible information about S, in other words antipodal views allow to obtain viewer independent representation from the minimum number of views. Then, if the object's surface under consideration is such that conditions of Proposition 3 hold, two antipodal views suffice.

If conditions of Proposition 3 are not met more than two views are needed, in this case the resulting function F is, in general, a polynomial of degree higher than 2 and is determination is clearly more complex.

Finally it has be shown that in case of perspective projections more than two view are needed to fully recostruct the surface S.

References

1. M.P. do Carmo, 1976 *Differential Geometry of Curves and Surfaces*, Englewood Cliffs, NJ:Prentice-Hall Inc. 1976.
2. K.J. Falconer, *The Geometry of Fractal sets*, Cambridge, UK: Cambridge University Press, 1985
3. J.W. Bruce and P.J. Giblin, *Curves and Singularities*,Cambridge, UK: Cambridge University Press, 1984
4. B.K.P. Horn, *Robot Vision*, Cambridge, Mass:The MIT Press, 1986.
5. W.T. Freeman, "The Generic Viewpoint Assumption in a Bayesian Framework", *Perception as Bayesian Inference*, D. Knill and W. Richards eds., pp. 365-389. Cambridge: Cambridge University Press, 1996.
6. J. Gårding, "Shape from texture for smooth curved surfaces", *Journal of Mathematical Imaging and Vision*, vol. 2, pp. 327–350, 1992.

SURFACE DESCRIPTION BY NEURAL TREES

G.L. FORESTI AND G.G. PIERONI

Department of Mathematics and Computer Science
University of Udine
Via Delle Scienze, 208, Rizzi, 33100 Udine, Italy
E-mail: foresti@dimi.uniud.it, pieroni@dimi.uniud.it

In this paper, a neural tree (NT) architecture to perform surface recognition tasks according to the classification of the differential geometry is presented. The nodes of the NT are generalized perceptrons without hidden layers and with activation function characterized by a sigmoidal behaviour. A splitting strategy is applied to divide the training set (TS) when it is not linearly separable: such a strategy is able to assure in many cases the convergence of the tree building process. Experiments on 3D range images containing multiple surfaces are presented.

1 Introduction

A neural tree (NT) is a hybrid concept whose creation was motivated by the combination of the advantages of neural networks (NN) and decision trees (DT) [1-3]. DTs are based on information theory, while NNs rely on specific training algorithms. Both DTs and NNs subdivide, during the learning phase, the decision space into regions delimited by hyperplanes: DTs produce a set of hyperplanes orthogonal to the space axis, while NNs produce more general hyperplanes [3].

Perceptrons have solved a wide set of classification problems and are able to work in a parallel way. However, they still have difficulty when input data are not linearly separable. NNs with hidden layers, such as a multi-layer perceptron (MLP), feedfordward (FF) or back-propagation (BP), are able to handle this problem, but the exact number of hidden neurons and the connectivity between layers must be specified before the training phase. Moreover, there is not practical guarantee that correct weights will be found for a given number of neurons and a particular training set. In many cases, the number of hidden neurons is chosen by trial. A second limitation of NNs is that hyperplanes which divide the input data into regions are usually selected by an exhaustive search through arbitrarily generated splits [3].

DTs represent another popular approach to pattern recognition [4]. A DT is a recursive structure composed by two kind of nodes: (a) internal nodes having child nodes, each of which is also a DT, and (b) terminal nodes (leaf nodes) having no child nodes. The root node divides the feature space into subsets (splitting), assigning each subset to each child node. The splitting process is continued until each leaf node correspond to one class. The main problem of DTs is that it requires an exhaustive search through arbitrarily generated splits to find the best one [4].

NTs provides a solution for both the main limitations of DTs and NNs. In this paper, we introduce a NT architecture for 3D object recognition from range data. Since every object can be reduced to a collection of surfaces, the specific problem is focused on identifying different surfaces in the same scene. In particular, six classes of surfaces as a simplified subset of the height classes proposed by the differential geometry (Fig. 1) are considered. The NT, whose nodes are perceptrons without hidden layers, is grown during the learning phase and it not requires neither any a-priori information about the number of nodes nor an exhaustive search as used in training algorithms for DTs.

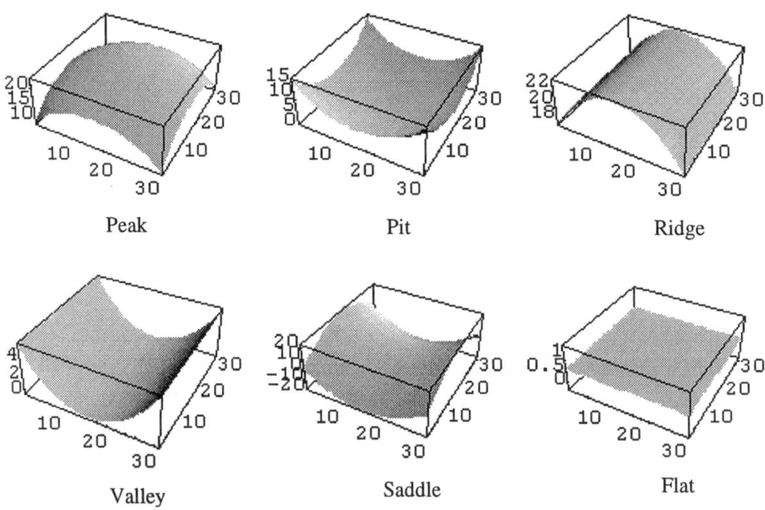

Fig. 1. Different types of surfaces used as training set

2 Neural trees and surface recognition

2.1 *Neural Trees*

The first NT, called perceptron tree, was presented in 1988 by Utgoff [1]. The architecture of this NT is composed by a DT whose internal nodes are represented by attribute tests and leaf nodes by perceptrons. An attribute test is a single node of a DT which tests a given attribute against a threshold value. The learning algorithm starts by training a perceptron at the root node. If the input patterns are not linearly separable, then the perceptron node is replaced by a decision node with an attribute test and two children nodes, one for grouping the input patterns having attribute above the threshold and the other for grouping the remaining patterns. This process is iterated until all training patterns are classified. The main disadvantage being the losing of all the training work done by the perceptron when it is replaced by a decision node. The main advantage is that the structure of the tree is determined dynamically and the resulting NT is smaller than the correspondent DT. Sirat and Nadal extended this approach to multi-class problems [2]. The training process is similar to that presented by Utgoff [1]: the root node of the tree, a perceptron node without hidden layers, is trained with all the training patterns. Then, it is used to divide the training patterns into N groups, where N is the number of output classes. An exhaustive search is done to find the best division. Each group is used as input for a new perceptron (child node) at the next level of the tree. This process is iterated recursively until all the subtrees have been terminated by leaf nodes. The main drawback consists in the necessity of an a-priori determination of the maximum size of the tree: if the tree exceeded that size, it cannot be generated. Recently, Sankar and Mammone [5] introduced a new approach. The tree is allowed to grow without size limits and a pruning phase is introduced at the end of the training phase to create a more generalized tree.

2.2 Surface recognition from range images

In the last years, segmentation of range images have been topic of intense research in the area of 3D scene analysis and robot vision. Significant work in the field has been done by Besl and Jain [6]. They used the sign of the Gaussian and Median curvatures in order to segment their images. Pieroni and Tripathy [7] attempted to apply the techniques of differential geometry to surfaces which have been triangularized. The method first triangularizes the XY plane and then projects these triangles onto the surface to yield a polyhedral representation of the surface. The segmentation and recognition of the surface will be carried out by using that polyhedral representation. Recently, Hoover et. al. proposed an experimental comparison of a large set of range image segmentation algorithms [8].

3 Neural tree architecture

In this section, a NT architecture for the solution of multi-class problems is proposed. The considered NT is a tree whose nodes are generalized perceptrons without hidden layers and with activation function characterized by a sigmoidal behaviour [9]. Let be n_h a generic node of the tree, H the total number of nodes, $l \in [0, L-1]$ a generic level and L the depth of the tree (Fig. 2). Each node takes (N+1) input (the first N input represent selected samples of a surface, x_1, .., x_N, and the last input x_{N+1} is a fixed value, i.e., $x_{N+1}=1$, with weight θ_i) and generates K outputs, called activation values. Let be $\mathbf{x}^p = \left(x_1^p, x_2^p, \ldots, x_N^p, x_{N+1}^p = 1\right)$ a generic vector of input patterns.

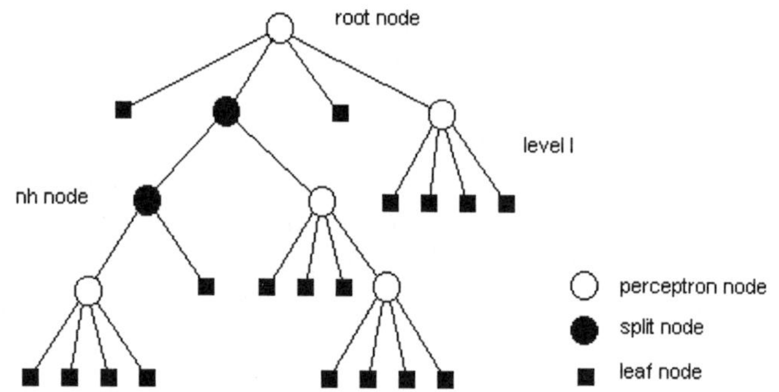

Fig. 2 - Structure of a NT with depth L=4

The root node is on level l=0. A node n_h on level l may have links at maximum to k≤K nodes on level l+1 which are the children of n_h.

3.1 *Learning phase*

Given a convenient training set, TS=[x^1,..,x^p,..,x^P], the NT has been trained according to the following algorithm.

(1) Start training a single perceptron (root node) at level l=0.

(2) If the TS is correctly classified, the NT reduces to a single leaf node. Go to (5).

(3a) The TS is split into k≤K groups, being K the number of classes to be discriminated (a pattern is assigned to the group depending the highest output value). Note that one or more groups could be empty (k<K). A new level l+1 of k perceptron nodes (children nodes) is created and each group is assigned to the corresponding child node for the

training process. The weight matrix **W** of the parent node is passed to each children node to speed up the training process [3].

(3b) If the TS is not linearly separable (the perceptron is not making significant classification improvements), then a splitting rule is applied to subdivide the TS into at least two groups (k=2).

(4) For each new perceptron, apply the perceptron training rule. If the current TS is linearly separable, set the current node to a leaf and start training the next perceptron; else go to (3a).

(5) The algorithm ends when all current nodes are leaves.

Perceptron training rule. The root node is composed by a perceptron without hidden layers and with matrix of weights **W** inizialized in a random way. It is trained with the patterns of the training set (TS) for a specified number of iterations (e.g., 500). In order to avoid the dependency of the NT generation by the rank of the patterns in the TS (e.g., first patterns without noise and then patterns with increasing noise or viceversa, etc.), the elements of the matrix **W** are computed and adjusted after presenting all of the patterns of the TS, i.e., the deltas for each weight are accumulated as the patterns are presented.

A a set of classification conditions have been defined to determine when a perceptron had correctly classified an input pattern:

(a) The input pattern must have the highest output activation value.

(b) The activation value in such a way extracted, must be above a given threshold th_1 (e.g., 0.9).

(c) The activation value as above must be at least th_2 (e.g., 0.2) higher than any other current output value.

All these three conditions must be true simultaneously for the input pattern to be considered classified.

Splitting rule. If the current perceptron is not able to classify the TS, the TS has to be divided into at least two different groups and each group must be passed to a separate child node for processing. As this process is recursive, the child nodes became more specialized while climbing the tree. In the proposed approach, we have extended the criterion introduced by Sakar and Mammone [3,5] to multi-class problems. If the TS at a given node n_h of the NT cannot reach a correct classification, the TS should be split. Two cases occur: (a) the perceptron makes a significant improvement in the classification task, (b) the perceptron repeat the same classification of the parent node. In the first case, a pattern is assigned to the group based on which of its outputs had the highest value. In the second case, a splitting node is added to the NT architecture. The patterns of the TS are grouped into different subsets according to the classes they should belong according to their final activation value, and the centroid of each class is computed. Then, the hyperplane which divides the centroids of the two classes containing more patterns is used to divide the TS into two subsets TS_1 and TS_2. Finally, such subsets are assigned to two children nodes for processing.

3.2 Classification phase

Once the NT has been successfully trained, it can be used to classify unseen patterns (test set). The classification algorithm rule follows:
(a) Present a pattern to the root of the tree.
(b) Move toward the tree in a top-down way following the path suggested by the classification given by each considered node.
(c) When a leaf node is reached, label the pattern with the classification of the current node.

The highest activation value reported from the leaf node was the classification for the pattern.

4 Surface sample collection

It is of some interest to see how surface morphology is transformed into a training set of patterns. This is a rather important step as an inconsistent presentation of patterns to the NN will inhibit the convergence of the algorithm toward a useful solution. The operation consists of creating an artificial set of specimens:

Peak $$\sqrt{R^2-((j-(\frac{n}{2}))^2+(i-(\frac{n}{2}))^2)},\{i,1,n-1\},\{j,1,n-1\}$$

Pit $$R-\sqrt{R^2-((j-(\frac{n}{2}))^2+(i-(\frac{n}{2}))^2)},\{i,1,n-1\},\{j,1,n-1\}$$

Ridge $$\sqrt{R^2-(i-(\frac{n}{2}))^2},\{i,1,n-1\},\{j,1,n-1\}$$

Valley $$R-\sqrt{R^2-(i-(\frac{n}{2}))^2},\{i,1,n-1\},\{j,1,n-1\}$$

Saddle $$\frac{(j-(\frac{n}{2}))^2}{(\frac{n}{2})^2R}-\frac{(i-(\frac{n}{2}))^2}{(\frac{n}{2})^2R},\{i,1,n-1\},\{j,1,n-1\}$$

where (n-1)*x*(n-1) is the dimension of each specimen matrix from where the training patterns will be extracted. R is the radius of curvature.

The extraction of patterns has been accomplished by picking up a limited number of pixel samples. Assuming a pixel $P_{i,j}$ belonging to the range data map M(h,k), the following matrix elements are used in order to build up a training or test pattern:

$$E[[(3+v,3+q]] = M[[i+v*step, j+q*step]] \quad (1)$$

where {v=-2,-1,0,1,2}, {q=-2,-1,0,1,2} and {step=1,2,3,..}. i,j being the indexes of the central point in case of training specimens, and any pixel in case of a test range data map. A matrix E(5x5) formed by the elevation values $Z_{i,j}$ and centered in the pixel $P_{3,3}$ will be constructed. Once that an E matrix has been completed, the 8 vectors below will be calculated:

$$v_1=\{z_{i,j-2step}, z_{i,j-step}, z_{i,j}, z_{i,j+step}, z_{i,j+2step}\}$$

$$v_2=\{z_{i-step,j-2step}, \frac{z_{i,j-step}+z_{i-step,j-step}}{2}, z_{i,j}, \frac{z_{i,j+step}+z_{i+step,j+step}}{2}, z_{i+step,j+2step}\}$$

$$v_3=\{z_{i-2step,j-2step}, z_{i-step,j-step}, z_{i,j}, z_{i+step,j+step}, z_{i+2step,j+2step}\}$$

$$v_4=\{z_{i-2step,j-step}, \frac{z_{i-step,j-step}+z_{i-step,j}}{2}, z_{i,j}, \frac{z_{i+step,j}+z_{i+step,j+step}}{2}, z_{i+2step,j+step}\}$$

$$v_5=\{z_{i-2step,j}, z_{i-step,j}, z_{i,j}, z_{i+step,j}, z_{i+2step,j}\}$$

$$v_6=\{z_{i-2step,j+step}, \frac{z_{i-step,j}+z_{i-step,j+step}}{2}, z_{i,j}, \frac{z_{i+step,j}+z_{i+step,j-step}}{2}, z_{i+2step,j-step}\}$$

$$v_7=\{z_{i-2step,j+2step}, z_{i-step,j+step}, z_{i,j}, z_{i+step,j-step}, z_{i+2step,j-2step}\}$$

$$v_8=\{z_{i-step,j+2step}, \frac{z_{i-step,j-step}+z_{i,j+step}}{2}, z_{i,j}, \frac{z_{i,j-step}+z_{i+step,j-step}}{2}, z_{i+step,j-2step}\}$$

according to the scheme in Fig. 3 which will be indicated as “numerical sensor” in the sequel. The second and fourth elements of each vector will not be used in this approach.

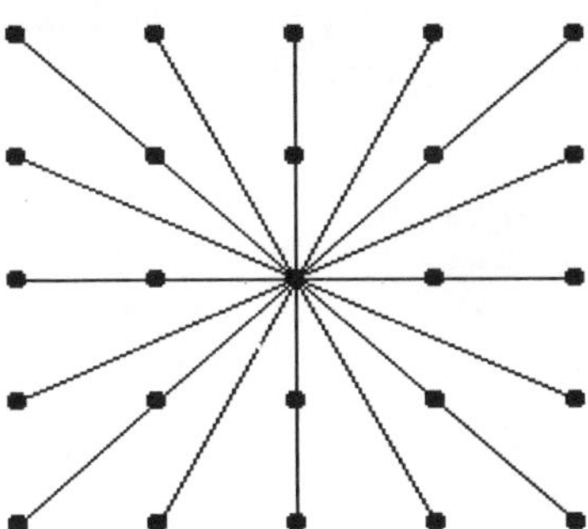

Fig 3 : Representation of the sensor arms. V_1 is the horizontal arm at the center of the scheme in the direction from left to right.

The variable “step” provides the distance between two horizontally or vertically successive nodes of the numerical sensor grid. By increasing the value of step, a larger grid is used to extract the values forming a training pattern. The digital curvature of each arm of the numerical sensor is then computed according to the following formulas :

$$dc_i = [v_i[[1]] + v_i[[5]] - 2\,v_i[[3]]] * \frac{1}{f} \tag{2}$$

where f is a function assuming the values :

$i=1$	$f=(2step)^2$	$i=5$	$f=(2step)^2$
$i=2$	$f=(2step)^2+step^2$	$i=6$	$f=(2step)^2+step^2$
$i=3$	$f=(2step)^2+(2step)^2$	$i=7$	$f=(2step)^2+(2step)^2$
$i=4$	$f=(2step)^2+step^2$	$i=8$	$f=(2step)^2+step^2$

In order to extract similar patterns when a surface has been rotated about the z axis, the numerical sensor is allowed to perform rotations of angles corresponding to the direction of each sensor arm. The adjustment of the sensor with respect to the surface rotation is obtained by calculating the minimum curvature among the sensor arms, then rotating the sensor in order to bring the minimum curvature arm to the first (horizontal) position and the other arms accordingly.

5 Experimental results

Experiments have been conducted on two different synthetic 3D range images formed by 128x128 pixels, with each pixel having a height (z value) between -1.0 and 1.0 inclusively. . Figures 4a and 4b show a continuos surface composed by peaks, saddles, and valleys, and the related 3D reconstruction, respectively.

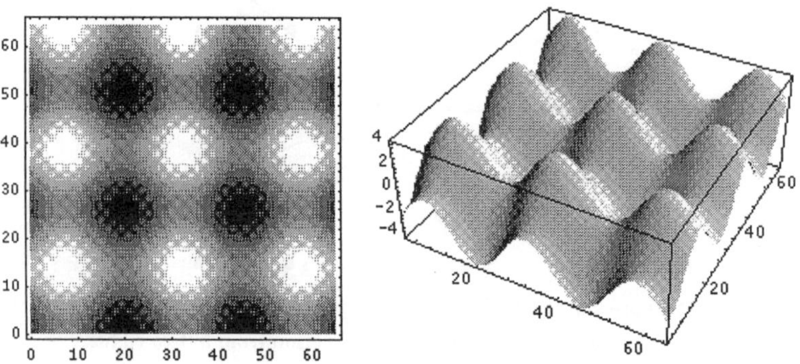

Fig. 4 (a) 128x128 range image representing three different types of surfaces (i.e., peak, pit, saddle) and (b) its 3D representation

Fig. 4c shows the classification results obtained with a NT composed by H=4 nodes with depth L=2: all surfaces are correctly classified. Figure 5a represents five different types of surfaces posed on a flat region. Evident discontinuities among different surfaces are present. Fig. 5b shows the related 3D reconstruction. Samples of synthetic depth maps with different noise levels (from 0 to 10 %) are provided to the NT as TS. A NT composed by H=15 nodes with depth L=5 has been obtained

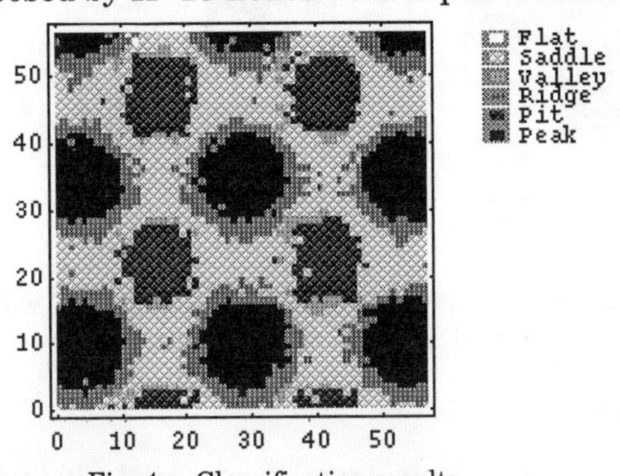

Fig. 4c - Classification results

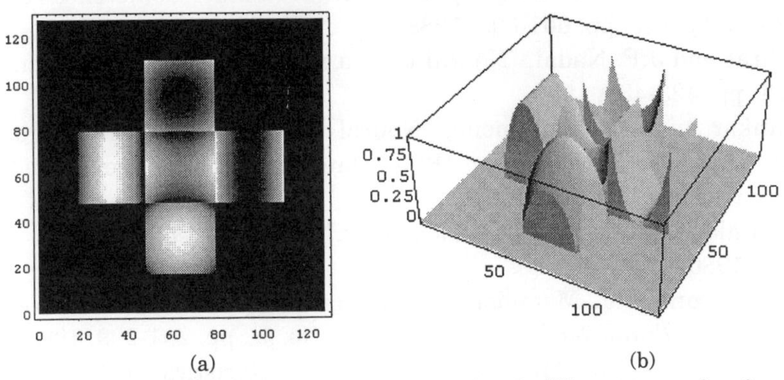

(a) (b)

Fig. 5 (a) 128x128 range image representing six different types of surfaces (i.e., peak, pit, ridge, valley, saddle, flat) and (b) its 3D representation

Fig. 6a shows the classification results. All surfaces are correctly classified. Moreover, the NT seem to be sufficiently accurate in detecting the surface boundaries. Finally, Fig. 6b shows the classification results on a noisy image obtained by corrupting the original image (Fig. 5a) with 4% noise level. The standard deviation value of this noise on the flat surface is 0.01. The NT is able to correctly classify all the surfaces, even if shows some misclassifications in the neighbourhood of the surface boundaries. Learning and classification times are about 0.5 sec and 1 sec respectively on a SUN Sparc 10 workstation.

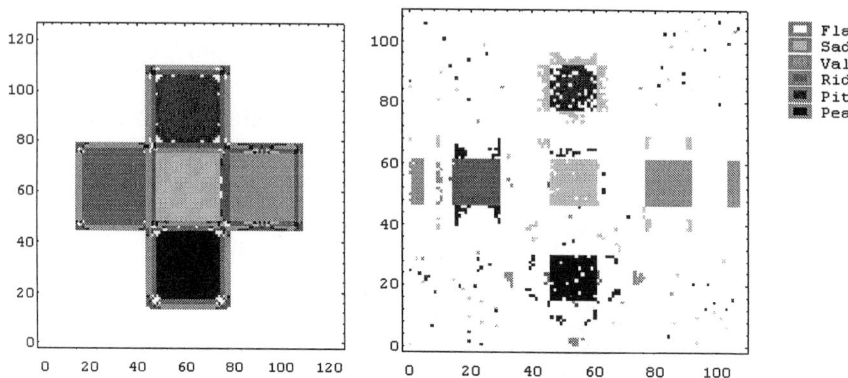

Fig. 6 - Classification results (a) in absence of noise and (b) with 4% noise level added to the original image in Fig. 4a.

6 References

[1] P.E. Utgoff, "Perceptron tree: a case study in hybrid concept representation," in *Proceeding of the VII National Conference on Artificial Intelligence,* pp. 601-605, 1988.

[2] J.A. Sirat and J.P. Nadal, "Neural tree: a new tool for classification," Network 1, pp. 423-438, 1990.

[3] A. Sankar and R.J. Mammone, "Neural tree networks," in *Neural Networks: Theory and Application* (R. J. Mammone and Y. Zeevi, Eds), Academic Press, pp. 281-302, 1991.

[4] J.R. Quinlan, "Induction of decision trees," *Machine Learning*, Vol. 1, pp. 81-106, 1986.

[5] A. Sankar and R.J. Mammone, "Growing and pruning neural tree networks," *IEEE Trans. on Computers,* Vol. 42, No. 3, , pp. 291-299, 1993.

[6] P.J.Besl and R.C. Jain, "Invariant surface characteristics for 3D object recognition in range images", *Computer Vision, Graphics and Image Processing*, Vol. 33, No.1, pp. 33-80, 1986.

[7] G.Pieroni and S.Tripathy, "A multi-resolution approach to segmenting surfaces" in *Issue on Machine Vision*, Springer Verlag, 1989.

[8] A. Hoover, et al., "An experimental comparison of range image segmentation algorithms", *IEEE Trans. on Pattern Analysis and Machine Intelligence*, Vol. 18, No.7, pp. 673-688, 1996.

[9] S. Iverson, O. Johnson, and G.G. Pieroni, "An experiment of surface recognition by neural tree," in *Proc. of IEEE Conf. on Computer Architectures for Machine Perception*, Como, Italy, pp. 443-449, 1995.

THE NON-LINEAR RECEPTIVE FIELD AS A MECHANISM FOR THE EXTRACTION OF AXES FROM OUTLINE DRAWINGS

STEVEN L. FUNK, ITSUO KUMAZAWA
Department of Computer Science
Tokyo Institute of Technology
Ookayama 2-12-1, Meguro-ku, Tokyo 152, Japan

JOHN M. KENNEDY
Department of Psychology
University of Toronto, Scarborough College
1265, Military Trail, Scarborough, Ontario, M1C 1A4, Canada

It has been demonstrated that the processing of outline drawings requires the extraction of a boundary between the object (figure), and its background (ground). However, it is insufficient to say that the boundary, is represented by the line itself[1]. The border could be represented by the center of the line, one of the contours, or some point in between the contours . The feature that we choose to represent the boundary, may vary depending on certain conditions in the image. The Non-Linear Receptive Field (NLRF) appears to provide a mechanism which accurately replicates human boundary extraction performance. The NLRF is a simple, biologically plausible, neural network architecture which is capable of complex computational tasks. An NLRF model is demonstrated, and its qualitative performance compared to results obtained from human subjects.

1 Introduction

The processing of outline images is more complex then it first appears. The most common, and universally understood outline drawings, use lines to depict the boundaries of objects. An object may contain a single boundary (as in a circle), or many boundaries (as in a square). However, the lines themselves do not represent these borders. Each line has many parts, each of which is equally capable of portraying the boundary. So, the successful processing of an outline image requires the proper extraction of features which will facilitate the extraction and selection of the appropriate margins. Three important features are the center of a line and both of its contours.

The NLRF model presented here, represents a neural network architecture which is capable of accurately emulating some aspects of human performance with outlines. This represents an important step in the simulation of human vision.

2 Outline Drawings

There are two possible reasons for using lines in outline drawings. It can either represent a change on a surface (hereafter referred to as chiaroscuro)[2] , or it can represent a boundary of a surface (including and occlusion edge or corner).

Included in the processing of chiaroscuro features is the processing of shape-from-shadow. It has been demonstrated that shape-from-shadow becomes more difficult to process if the darkness of the shadow falls on the wrong side (as in a negative image)[3]. However, if the contours between light and shadow are replaced with a single line, making the image an outline drawing, the performance drops off by a large degree[4].

In addition to shape-from-shadow contours, chiaroscuro features include boundaries between colors on a surface (e.g. equiluminance contours). In a study of the Songe (a tribe in Papua New Guinea, with no pictures in the traditional culture), Kennedy and Ross[5] found significant problems with the processing of chiaroscuro as outline. In one case the patterns shown in figure 1, were frequently mistaken for patterns made of surface contours and occlusions. Of 24 subjects tested, fully 24 correctly identified the drawing as a bird. However, only 2 correctly identified the color markings as “designs”, or the like. It was more common for the subjects to express confusion over the markings on the feathers, and remark that the bird might have been cut. So it seems that the perception of lines as representations of occlusion edges is inherent in human vision, not due to a learned convention. The identification of lines as depictions of color boundaries is less effective, learned, and not universal in human vision.

Figure 1. The outline picture used to test the Songe of Papua New Guinea. The lines which represent differences in color were not properly recognized. Some thought that the parrot had been cut by some kind of knife. From Kennedy and Ross (1975).

When examining outline pictures, it is easy to obtain an impression of local depth. However, the outlines do not give an impression of depicted colors, or brightness differences (see figure 2).

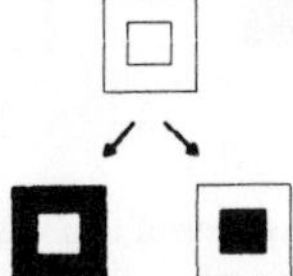

Figure 2. An outline drawing and "filled-in" variations. Note that the figure consisting only of outlines is readily seen as depicting depth. A small square in front of a large square, or a small aperture in a large square. But, the drawing does not create an impression of depicted brightness differences, such as a small white square on a black large square or the reverse, as illustrated in the lower figures.

The major use of lines in outline drawings is to depict surface edges at occlusions or corners. Depicted occlusions allow figure-ground depth impressions . The use of lines for surface edges is found in cave art throughout the world[6]. This provides strong evidence that this use is universal in human vision and not a learned convention.

3 Axis Theory

The explanation of spatial perception when using outline pictures involves an analysis of processes stimulated by lines. It is not enough to say that the line itself represents the boundary of an object, because the line has many parts. Let us call the feature of the line that acts as a depiction, the lines axis. Consider figure 3, containing 4 sets of 2 squares. In all four cases, one square appears to be in front of the other. In the first set of squares, the center of the line is often the location of the line's axis. However, in the second set, the front square is filled in. In this case the outside contour of the front square is used as the axis, while the axis of the background square remains as before. In the third set, the background square is filled in. This means that the outside contour of the background square is used as the axis. But, the inside contour of the front square is now used as the axis. Filling in the background square has forced a shift in the location of the axis of the front square. Finally in the last set of squares, the background, behind both of the squares is filled in. In this case the inside contour is used as the axis for both squares.

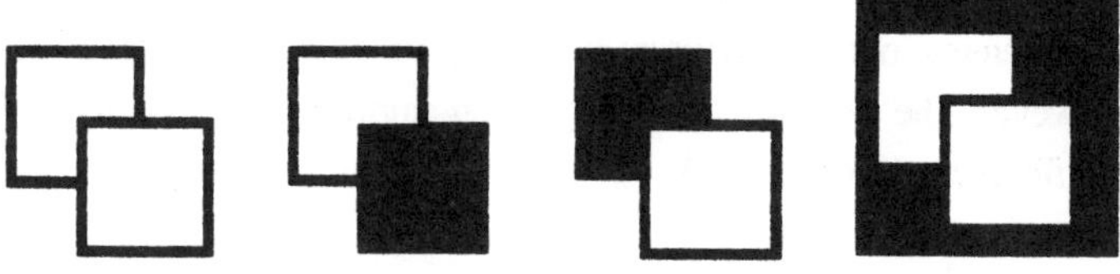

Figure 3. Four sets of squares. Each set consists of two squares, one in front of the other. Each set exhibits the same stimuli under different conditions.

So, the axis is neither the line itself, nor is it a fixed part of the line. The axis is a representation which is derived from the line and the environment in which the line exists.

Any model which seeks to describe the process of axis extraction must accurately simulate the results described here. The extraction process must be flexible, capable of extracting all possible axes, and capable of demonstrating the performance that has been documented here.

4 Other Models of Axis Extraction

There are several potential models of axis extraction. Three of these, the XOR-model, a 1-D NLRF model, and a striped receptive field model, were discussed by Kennedy and Funk[7]. None of these models were found to be entirely sufficient to represent the process of axis extraction. However, recently the NLRF model has been expanded from a system analyzing one-dimensional input to a model analyzing two-dimensional input[8]. In addition to this, there are several cellular neural networks, which demonstrate a capability which is similar to that of the NLRF model[9]. However, these tend to use a template representation of the feature to be extracted. This limits the ability of the system to extract the proper information. Anything less then the ideal input will result in a rapid degradation of the networks performance. Furthermore, the templates are limited to a single feature each. So, one network might be able to extract the convex corner from an L junction, while another could extract the corner from a V junction (an L junction rotated 45 degrees counter clockwise). But, no one template could extract a convex corner from a junction of any angle. So, while the cellular neural network architecture may provide some promising performance in the earliest stages of axis extraction, its uses seem to be limited. The proper extraction of convex corners, concave corners, and various kinds of junctions requires more then the cellular neural network can provide.

5 The Non-Linear Receptive Field Model

The model consists of many Non-Linear Receptive Fields which are uniformly distributed, and overlap with each other to a large degree. The Non-Linear Receptive field consists of 2 layers of units. All of the connections for a given receptive field are limited to a local area (in this case 5 units diameter), as in figure 4.

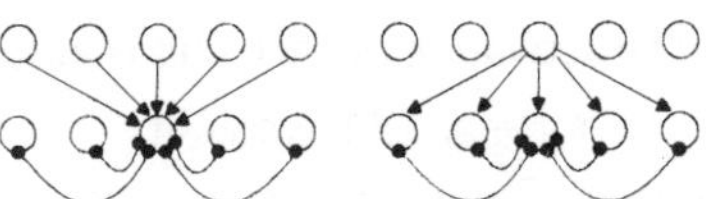

Figure 4. An NLRF in cross-section. On the left is the pattern of connectivity as viewed from the center unit of the output layer. On the right is the same pattern of connectivity as viewed from the center unit of the input layer. These connections are present for every unit, as all units are centers for clusters of five units.

A set of afferent connections connect the input layer to the output layer. In addition there is a set of lateral connections within the output layer (figure 5).

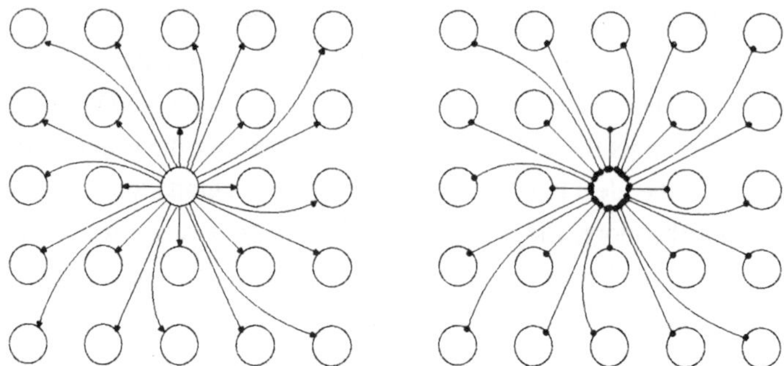

Figure 5. An NLRF as viewed from above. The figure on the left indicates the connectivity of the afferent connections, minus the connection from the center unit straight down, to the center unit in the output layer. The center unit is in the input layer , while all other units are in the output layer. The figure on the right represents the lateral connectivity. All units are in the output layer. The unit in the center of the figure on the left is directly above the unit in the center of the figure on the right.

The computation is performed when a pattern (i.e. an image) is presented to the input layer. The activation is passed from the input layer through the afferent connections to the output layer. In the output layer, the lateral connections produce competition which allows a small number of units to become dominant. This dominance occurs only under very specific conditions, allowing the network to extract specific features. The interaction of receptive field function and input pattern, combined with the uniform distribution of homogeneous receptive fields, means that the feature extraction will be performed regardless of where on the input surface the pattern is presented.

Every unit in the network is of the same type. Each uses a real activation value, with a range from 0 to 1. The activation of each unit is accumulated according to:

$$a_{i(t)} = a_{i(t-1)} + \Sigma w_{ij} a_{j(t-1)} - d \qquad (1)$$

Where: $a_{i(t)}$, is the activation of unit i, at time t, $a_{i(t-1)}$, is the activation of unit i, at time t-1, $a_{j(t-1)}$, is the activation of unit j, at time t-1, d, is the decay rate, and w_{ij}, is the weight of the connection between i and j.

The result of this equation is an activation function which is linear within a range from 0.0 to 1.0.

The pattern of connectivity is relatively simple. Every input unit distributes activation to 25 units in the output layer. Every output layer send inhibition to 24 units in the output layer, as it does not inhibit itself. The Connection weights are arranged to perform two computations, each of the two requiring a distinct set of weights. The two sets of connection weights used in this experiment are as follows:

Table 1. The connection weights used in the model. The maximum activation was 1.0, and the minimum at 0.0. The connections are symmetrical around the center of the receptive field.

Center Extraction Weights (Decay 0.225)				
	Units	Distal	Proximal	Center
Connections				
Afferent		0.0225	0.0225	0.0225
Lateral		-0.04	-0.02	0
Contour Extraction (Decay 0.02)				
	Units	Distal	Proximal	Center
Connections				
Afferent		-0.04	-0.06	1
Lateral		-0.02	-0.04	0

6 Results of the NLRF Model

When the images from figure 3 are presented to the NLRF model, two features are extracted from each image (see figure 6).

While the NLRF model is capable of extracting 4 features, only 2 of these are directly related to the process of axis extraction (assuming that both contours are considered to be 1 feature). The contours, and center of the line are extracted. However, when the centers are extracted the model may break down in an interesting way. When the line is within a certain range of thickness, the center of the line is faithfully extracted. But, when the line exceeds a certain level of thickness, the interior becomes filled with regularly distributed regions of activation and inactivation. This might be viewed a simple kind of object recognition. When the line is too thick to represent a boundary between the object and its background, it needs to be considered an object in its own right.

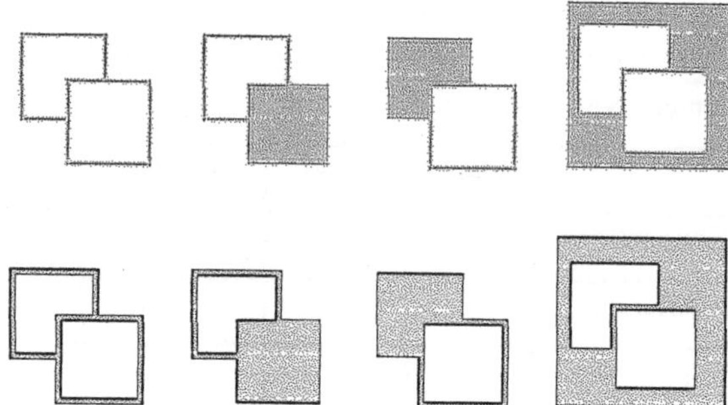

Figure 6. The results of processing the image from Figure 4. The image on the top is the result from the center extraction network, while the image on the bottom is the result from the contour extraction network (Both shown against the network input).

7 Discussion

The results obtained from the network analyzing Figure 3 have significant similarities and differences with human impressions arising from the same figure. The basic similarity is that both vision and the NLRF model emphasize contours, in some circumstances, and centers of lines in others. When the line is thin the NLRF network successfully extracts the line's center. So too does human vision, notably in viewing the top figure, composed entirely of lines. When the surrounds are filled in, and there are fewer contours, the model and human vision both treat all the contours as relevant.

However, when the square region is filled-in human vision tends to see the square as a foreground object, and separates the square from the L-shaped region. The NLRF system does not separate the filled-in square from a background.

The NLRF model is an axis-finding system. It uses contours to find axes, and can locate axes along contours or between contours. Once it has found axes, it has no way of marking some axes as foreground, and other axes as background. That is the job of an interpretive machinery, for which the axes are input.

The center axis finding combination of weights operates to find the centers of thin lines. A thin line is one that fits within the 5 unit radius of the NLRF. What happens when the line is too thick? At times lines will be 6 or more units wide. The model then fails to find a center. This failure is paralleled in human vision, since only thin lines operate as outlines showing single profiles of objects, and wide lines readily appear to show two parallel profiles. If the NLRF model receives input from a thick line, it distributes evenly-spaced nodes of activation and inactivation throughout the line's thickness. The model does not merely emphasize contours or the middle. One might describe the result as treating the line as a significant region within two contours, a primitive method of distinguishing objects from surrounding regions. This is a first step in making a figure-ground distinction.

The results of the NLRF model offer possible extensions of axis theory. Axis theory was developed to describe and account for outline depiction. But lines that are too thick to stimulate central axes generate axes at their contours and in addition a central region distinctively marked with nodes of activation and inactivation. An interpretive layer following axis-extraction could be tuned to these distinctive distributions, treating them as objects in their own right, bodies extended in two dimensions. Axes are extended along their length, and are one-dimensional. Bodies are distributed across a region in an image, projecting in two dimensions.

By way of example, Figure 8 provides both thin lines and thick lines. The thin lines can act as outlines, while the thick lines may be beyond the width optimal for outlines.

Figure 8. Concentric squares: Some use thin lines, and some thick lines. When thin, the lines may appear to mark the edge of a surface. However, thick lines can also appear to offer contours that depict occluding edges of surfaces.

If so, the thin lines can act to depict borders of edges of surfaces. But the thick lines will act as regions, not one-dimensional edges. The contours of the thick lines are capable of being emphasized, becoming triggers for axes, and thereby depictions of surface edges. If both of the contours of thick lines trigger axis extraction, then the thick line can appear as a foreground object, such as a bar or ribbon. In this case, the center-finding apparatus can fail to find a center, but it nevertheless has a role to play, it covers the region between the contours with a distribution of activity that suggests a surface stretching between its edges.

8 Conclusion

The axis theory represents a good description of the processing of outline (and some other) drawings. The NLRF mechanism provides a good model of the axis extraction process. However, the drawn objects consist of more than the axes. For example, these axes may work together to produce junctions, and they may also be involved in the production of subjective contours. So, the current NLRF model must be expanded to perform junction extraction, and in some way account for the various subjective contour phenomena.

9 References

[1] J. M. Kennedy, *Drawing and the Blind,* New Haven; Yale, 1983.
[2] K. H. Veltman, "Literature on Perspective", *Marburger Jahrbuch fur Kunstwissenschaft*, vol. 21, pp. 185-208, 1986.
[3] P. Cavanagh and Y. G. Leclerc, "Shape from shadows", *Journal of Experimental Psychology: Human Perception and Performance*, vol. 15, pp. 3-27, 1989.
[4] J. M. Kennedy, "Outline and shape from shading: the little lines that can't", *Proc. Psychonomics Society Conference*, 1988a.
[5] J. M. Kennedy and A. S. Ross, "Outline picture perception by the Songe of Papua", *Perception*, vol. 4, pp. 391-406, 1975.
[6] J. M. Kennedy and J. Silvers, "The surrogate functions of lines in visual perception: Evidence from antipodal rock and cave artwork sources", *Perception*, vol. 3, pp. 313-322, 1974.
[7] J. M. Kennedy and S. L. Funk, "Outline Perception: Three theories of axis", *Proc. International Conference on Visual Coding*, 1995.
[8] S. L. Funk et al., "The role of non-linear receptive fields in shift invariant feature extraction", *Proc. Meeting on Image Recognition and Understanding 1996*, 1996.
[9] T. Roska and J Vandewalle, *Cellular Neural Networks*,West Sussex, Wiley, 1993.

SHAPE ANALYSIS BY MEANS OF THE 'BOUNDARY INTEGRAL – RESONANT MODE EXPANSION' METHOD

P. GAMBA
Dipartimento di Elettronica, Università di Pavia, Via Ferrata, 1, I-27100 Pavia, Italy

L. LOMBARDI
Dipartimento di Informatica e Sistemistica, Università di Pavia, Via Ferrata, 1, I-27100 Pavia, Italy

In this paper the application of the Boundary Integral - Resonant Mode Expansion (BI-RME) method to the shape analysis problem is proposed. We explore the advantages for shape analysis and recognition of a BI-RME based modal matching algorithm, where each shape is represented by means of a set of eigenfunctions, solutions of the Helmotz equation with Dirichlet boundary condition. These solutions correspond to the vibration modes of an elastic sheet of arbitrary shape and fixed boundary and show some advantages over the previous approaches. It is demonstrated that the BI-RME algorithm is particularly suitable to characterize shapes with multiply connected boundary and requires small cpu-times.

1 Introduction

One of the key problems in machine vision is shape recognition, necessary for example in tracking deformable objects in image sequences. Shape recognition is also important to make correspondence among similar structures, or to compute differences between similar elements of an image. In fact, in the last years, a great deal of interest has been shown in the subject of *queries-by-sample* algorithms for image databases:[1] together with color and texture-driven searches, also shape-similarity queries are widely pursued in this field.[2]

To this aim, many image processing techniques have been proposed, that can be reduced to four classes:[3]

1. *image modelization*: model images of an object are stored and preprocessed[4];

2. *object-centered coordinate structures*: feature points of different objects are matched up by their positions with respect to an object-centered coordinate system;[5]

3. *deformable models*: similar to the first class, except for the introduction of deformations as parameterizable options of the models;[6]

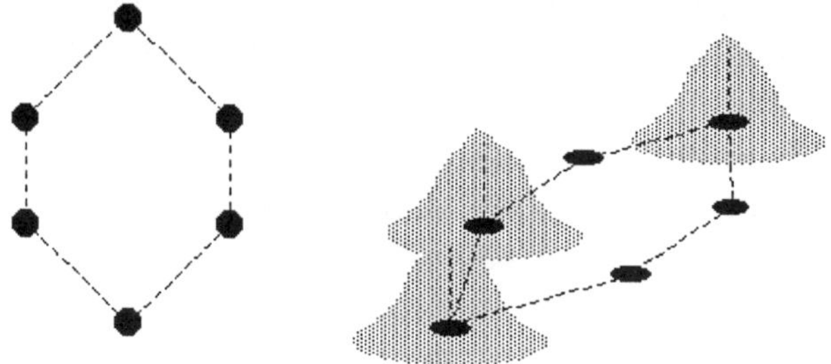

Figure 1: The representation of a shape by means of some points of its boundary, where fictitious mass elements are centered (only a few of them are shown in the figure.

4. *eigen-representations*, where suitable basis functions are used to describe the space of the functions representing the shapes.[7]

Among the last class, modal matching is a powerful tool[10] for shape analysis and recognition, but the original theory lacks in dealing with multiply connected boundaries. In this paper we want to present the application of a similar integro-differential approach, the so called Boundary Integral - Resonant Mode Expansion (BI-RME) method, that features a more efficient computation in a different eigenspace. Instead of computing the eigenvalues of a generalized linear problem built considering each object as a collection of mass points bounded by elastic relations, our approach starts by considering the shape boundaries as the fixed edge of an elastic planar surface, and the set of eigenvalues used for shape recognition are those computed by finding its resonant frequencies. This is still a modal analysis technique with a different representation basis; moreover, it allows to study shapes with simply and multiply connected boundaries, thus enlarging with respect to the original method the range of the analysis.

2 Shape analysis by modal matching

Usually, the shapes to be analyzed are obtained from raw data by low-level image processing operations, like segmentation by region growing or edge detection and grouping. Shape information is therefore easily available, but suffers from noise in the original data and from errors in the classification/edge extraction routines. A suitable shape description must be therefore able to discard local perturbations of the original object silhouette. Unfortunately, it is well assessed that some of the proposed solutions for shape recognition are affected by problems due, for instance, to sampling errors. The *modal match-*

ing approach has been introduced to overcome these difficulties (as well as parameterization and nonuniqueness errors): it allows to characterize a shape by means of some generalized deformation modes, computed and stored as a suitable basis for fast and efficient correspondence and recognition algorithms. Lower modes represent lower detailed copies of the object: retaining only a part of the computed deformation modes we are provided of a suitable noise-effective basis for the analysis.

2.1 Modal Analysis via Finite Element Method

The original modal matching technique [10] is based on the representation of an object by means of N points, generally (but not only) from its boundary. Each point is considered as a concentrated mass element (or *node*), bounded to its neighbors by elastic relations (see fig. 1). The ensemble of all the points follows the so called *"dynamic equilibrium equation"*:

$$\mathbf{M}\frac{\partial^2 \vec{U}}{\partial t^2} + \mathbf{D}\frac{\partial \vec{U}}{\partial t} + \mathbf{K}\vec{U} = \vec{R} \quad \text{in } \mathbb{R}^2 \tag{1}$$

where $\vec{U}$ denotes the vector of displacements at each node, $\vec{R}$ is the load function, $\mathbf{M}, \mathbf{K}$ and $\mathbf{D}$ are the mass, stiffness and damping matrices defined by means of a material matrix $\mathbf{C}$, the mass density ρ, and the interpolation matrix $\mathbf{H}$, that relates the basis functions to $\vec{U}$.

A matrix equation can be computed from (1) by using Gaussian basis functions $g_i(\mathbf{x}) = \exp\left(-\|\mathbf{x} - \mathbf{x}_i\|^2 / 2\sigma^2\right)$, each one centered on a node, and a FEM (Finite Element Method) procedure. By means of standard eigenvalue theory, the displacement $\vec{U}$ due to $\vec{R}$ can be expressed in terms of the solutions of the eigenvalue matrix equation:

$$\mathbf{K\Phi} = \mathbf{\Gamma}^2\mathbf{M\Phi} \tag{2}$$

where $\mathbf{\Gamma}$ is a diagonal matrix, $\mathbf{K}$ and $\mathbf{M}$ are:[10]

$$\mathbf{K} = \pi \begin{bmatrix} \gamma_1 \mathbf{A} S_{aa} \mathbf{A} & \gamma_2 \mathbf{A} S_{ab} \mathbf{A} \\ \gamma_2 \mathbf{A} S_{ab} \mathbf{A} & \gamma_1 \mathbf{A} S_{bb} \mathbf{A} \end{bmatrix} \qquad \mathbf{M} = \gamma_3 \begin{bmatrix} \mathbf{A} G \mathbf{A} & 0 \\ 0 & \mathbf{A} G \mathbf{A} \end{bmatrix} \tag{3}$$

where $\gamma_{1,2,3}, S_{aa}, S_{bb}$ and S_{ab} are useful constants and matrices and here we recall, to the aim of the successive discussion, only that $G_{ij} = \sqrt{\mathbf{G}_{ij}} = \sqrt{g_i(\mathbf{x}_j)}$, and $\mathbf{A} = \mathbf{G}^{-1}$. It is immediate to observe that $\mathbf{A}$ can easily become ill-conditioned depending on the value of the variance of the Gaussian basis functions$sigma^2$. To overcome as far as possible the problem related to the inversion of $\mathbf{G}$, a slightly different version of (2) has been proposed.[11]

However, we notice that there is no reason to start from (1): after all, it is only one of the possible choices. Therefore, we may consider a different model, and search for the eigensolutions of an other equation defined over the domain D with the Dirichlet condition over the shape boundary ∂D, namely:

$$\nabla^2\psi_i + \omega_i^2\psi_i = 0 \quad \text{in } D \qquad \psi_i = 0 \quad \text{over } \partial D \tag{4}$$

By comparison with the one-dimensional problem of a string fixed at the extremes, solving (4) in a 2-D domain means to find the resonant vibration modes of an elastic sheet fixed on its boundary.

The solution of (4) can be obtained as well by a FEM implementation: we start from a subdivision of D in simpler subdomains D_i, on which suitable basis functions $\{u_i\}$ are defined. Expanding the unknown function ψ_i and its derivatives by means of $\{u_i\}$ and using a Galerkin procedure leads to an eigenvalue matrix problem similar to (2) that gives a frequency set $\Omega = (\omega_1, \omega_2, \ldots, \omega_N)^t$ and an eigenfunction set $\Psi = (\psi_1, \psi_2, \ldots, \psi_N)^t$ as the results. Nevertheless, there is an underlying disadvantage in the FEM approach: the elementary subdomains D_i have the same dimension as the domain (i.e. for a 2-D shape, 2-D subdomains are necessary): this may be computationally onerous for large domains, or very dense discretizations.

2.2 The BI-RME approach to the problem

A different approach has been proposed by Conciauro *et al.* [12] for the solution of (4): the BI-RME (Boundary Integral - Resonant Mode Expansion) approach. It starts by representing a planar surface of arbitrary shape as an originally rectangular or circular shape S_0 modified by suitable boundary elements, which we refer to as a whole as Γ. The problem (4) is now extended to:

$$\nabla^2\psi_i + \omega_i^2\psi_i = 0 \quad \text{in } S_0 - \Gamma \quad \psi_i = 0 \quad \text{over } \partial S_0 \text{ and } \Gamma \tag{5}$$

and only the solutions of (5) that are zero in $S_0 - D$ are also solutions of (4).

We observe that ψ_i has discontinuous normal derivative over Γ, and that a formulation equivalent to (5) is:

$$\begin{aligned}
\nabla^2 u_i &= 0 \quad \text{in } S_0 - \Gamma & (6)\\
\nabla^2 v_i + \omega_i^2\,[u_i + v_i] &= 0 \quad \text{in } S_0 & (7)\\
-u_i &= v_i \quad \text{over } \Gamma \text{ and } \partial S_0 & (8)\\
u_i + v_i &= \psi_i \quad \text{in } S_0 & (9)
\end{aligned}$$

where now only u_i has discontinuous normal derivative over Γ, the discontinuity being represented by $F(s')$, s' being a coordinate following Γ. We now express

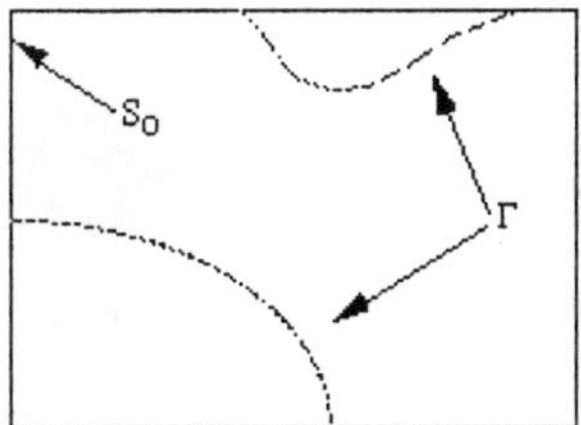

Figure 2: A simple example of definition of S_0 and Γ.

u_i by means of:

$$u_i(\vec{r}) = \int_\Gamma G(\vec{r}, s') \cdot F(s')\, ds' \tag{10}$$

$$\nabla^2 G(\vec{r}, \vec{r}\,') = -\,\delta(\vec{r} - \vec{r}\,') \quad \text{in } S_0 \tag{11}$$

$$G(\vec{r}, \vec{r}\,') = 0 \qquad \vec{r} \in \partial S_0 \tag{12}$$

By finding u_i over Γ (equal to $-v_i$, thanks to (8)), we find an integral relation (represented by the operator L) between the two functions and rewrite (7) as:

$$\nabla^2 v_i + \omega_i^2 \left[L(v_i) + v_i\right] = 0 \quad in\ S_0 \tag{13}$$

which is a linear integro-differential equation defined on a simple domain (a rectangular or circular shape).

However, the eigensolutions of $\nabla^2 x + \omega_i^2 x = 0$ for the latter cases are well-known, and available in closed form. Expanding v_i by means of these eigensolutions, and exploiting a Galerkin procedure, the method [12] computes from (13) matrix equation of the form $\mathbf{\Omega}^2\mathbf{a} = \mathbf{A}'\mathbf{a}$, where $\mathbf{A}'$ is a real-valued matrix with dimension comparable with n, the number of points of the boundary, and $\mathbf{\Omega}$ is the diagonal matrix of the eigenvalues. The solution of this last equation is straightforward, and gives the set $\{\omega_i\}$, representing the resonant frequencies of the deformation modes of (4) (fig. 3). Once $\{v_i\}$ has been computed, using the relations among all the defined functions, we obtain $\{u_i\}$ and$\{\psi_i\}$.

3 BI-RME matching and shape analysis

As a first comment, before analyzing how these deformation modes can be used for shape analysis and comparison, we must stress that all these numerical methods compute only an approximation of the modes (and of the corresponding resonant frequencies), according to the number and characteristics

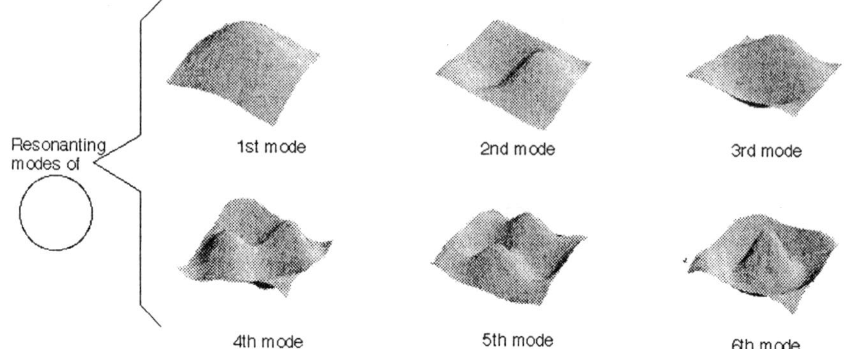

Figure 3: A simple shape and its first six resonating modes computed by means of the BI-RME approach

of the basis functions employed. In particular, defining for each frequency ω a wavelength $\lambda = 2\pi/\omega$, only the modes with λ equal or greater than the basis functions domain's mean dimension are suitably approximated. Therefore, for each shape, only lower frequency modes are extracted from the results and proposed, since these ones only are adequately characterized.

3.1 Shape comparison

Once the modal representation of a shape has been found, we need a procedure to perform a comparison between two shapes. The correspondence problem has been extensively treated in literature,[6] by means of the use of an affinity matrix $\mathbf{Z}\ /\ z_{ij} = \left\| v_i^{(1)} - v_j^{(2)} \right\|$, where $v_i^{(1)}$ is the vector of the modal deformations of the i-th point of the shape number 1.

By looking to the minimum entry for each row or column of this matrix we match the corresponding points of the compared shapes. However, some improvements to the algorithm are suggested in Sclaroff and Pentland:[10] only lower-order modes are considered as features to be matched (to discard errors due to high-order noise and numerical approximations, as outlined above), and similarity is required in both column and row-direction. The results are extremely reliable as long as there is an actual similarity between the shapes we are comparing, otherwise the correspondences are totally meaningless.[11] This is the reason why we introduced a preliminary correspondence index $c_{ab} = \frac{1}{M} \sum_{i=1}^{M} \left\| \omega_i^{(a)} - \omega_i^{(b)} \right\|$, the Euclidean distance in the frequency space, to quickly associate similar shapes and discard very different ones. In c_{ab} the

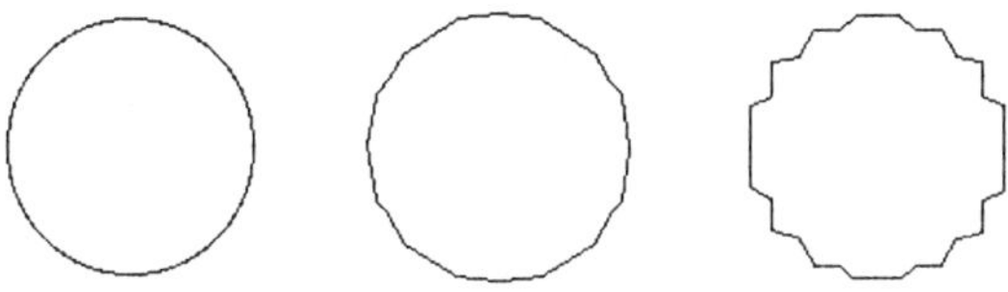

Figure 4: A circle with two 'noisy' copies of it.

indexes $(a), (b)$ refer to the two compared shapes, whose eigenvalues are found in the $\Omega^{(a)}$ and$\Omega^{(b)}$ sets. The value of c using the first 10 modes of the shapes in fig. 4 (numbered from left to right) are $c_{12} = 0.085$, $c_{13} = 0.424$, $c_{23} = 0.310$.

It must be noted that this index is related to the famous question posed by M. Kac:[13] "Can one hear the shape of a drum ?", whose answer is "No!".[14] Therefore, this index is not *in principle* a unique representation of the similarity between two objects; nevertheless, it is a powerful mean to quickly discard a lot of shapes when performing long searches.

3.2 Advantages and problems of BI-RME matching

Here we provide a comparison between the FEM and BI-RME approaches.

First of all, we observe that FEM modal matching provides a powerful orthogonal frequency-ordered description of a shape. The eigenmodes form an useful object-centered coordinate system for describing feature locations. Therefore, arbitrarily shaped objects can be easily analyzed, and correspondence between similar shapes is quick and easy. Moreover, it gives deformation parameters that are surely more globally defined than, for example, a representation of the boundary by means of a polynomial vertex approximation, because we achieve a very good shape representation by a smaller number of coefficients. However, it could be more difficult to evaluate a local variation of the contour, since it could be spanned over a number of eigenvalues: each mode takes into account the complete shape and this may be useless when small changes in shape are present. Nevertheless, since the eigenrepresentation is a kind of multiresolution analysis, its performance is always better than methods like shape Fourier descriptors. In this sense, the capability of the FEM modal matching approach to change σ^2 can be used to obtain a less or more *local* analysis of the shape: if σ^2 is small, only neighboring points are aware one of the others, and the deformation modes of the shape are more locally defined.

As for the BI-RME formulation, it leads to matrices smaller than the cor-

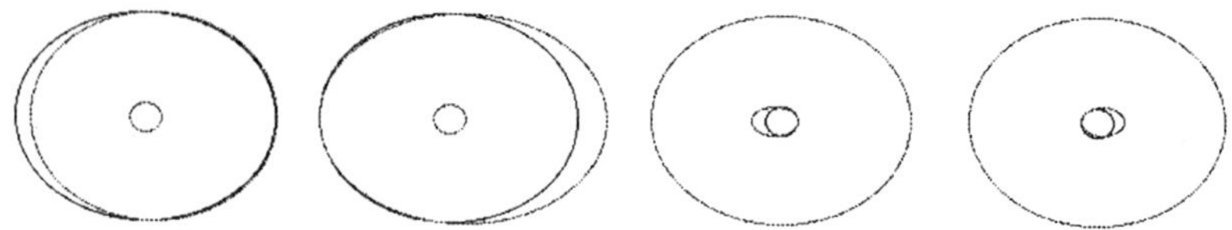

Figure 5: Two concentric circles and some of their deformation modes computed by means of the original modal matching technique.

responding FEM one. Moreover, the BI-RME approach allows to obtain the deformation introduced by the i-th mode ψ_i in any point of the whole object with simple further computations, while for the same problem the FEM solution would be limited to the boundary. As a further advantage, the BI-RME modal matching is able to deal with doubly and/or multiply connected boundaries, thus widening the field of shapes that it is possible to analyze and compare. For instance, to investigate weather-radar data to extract information on a rainfall area, we must pay attention to the complete rain system and to the interactions between the structures at the different scales of interest. Therefore, we need a tool able to analyze not only simple shapes, but also doubly and multiply connected ones. To this aim, the BI-RME implementation of the modal matching algorithm deserves a superior performance.

Finally, modal matching [10] is dependent from the sampling of the points along the shape boundary, with the constraint that it must be as regular as possible; otherwise, ill-conditioned matrices are possible. This may cause problems in analyzing shapes extracted from raw data where sampling is not exactly taken into account. The BI-RME approach to modal analysis, instead, is completely robust to each possible sampling of the same shape, i.e. it does not require that all the subdomains D_i of the basis functions must be equal or similar, but allows them to be even very different.

4 Shapes with multiply connected boundary

The shape representation of an object may require, in some circumstances, to study a boundary ∂D multiply connected. Although it doesn't happen very often, the analysis of this type of shapes is probably one of the key features of, for instance, future *query-by-sketch* algorithms for image databases. In fact, it would be extremely useful to retrieve data containing complex structures or to build a visual translation of high level queries (like "search for the photo of a man with two medals"). Moreover, the manipulation of the huge amount of remote sensing data nowadays available by means of simple databases or complex Geographical Information Systems, makes often necessary to handle such

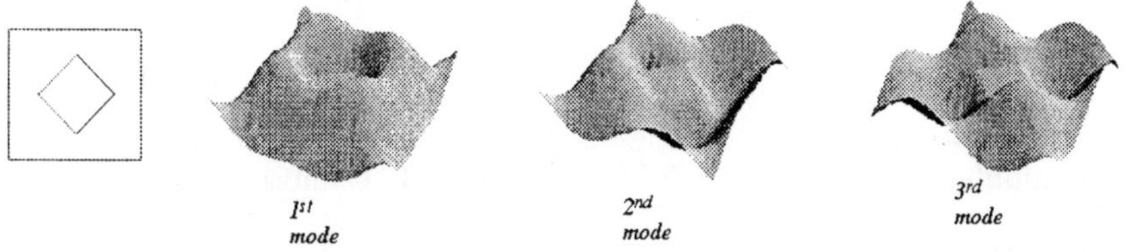

Figure 6: Two rotated squares, one inside the other, and some of their deformation modes computed by means of the BI-RME approach.

a type of shapes. Above it has been outlined the situation of rain patterns, at different scales, extracted from weather-radar data, but also structured environments information extraction and pollutant tracking are problems equally involving the analysis of multiply connected shapes. Unfortunately, many of the usual methods for shape analysis, even when able to deal with the situation, do not give an effective answer to this need. This is true for the original modal matching technique: in fig. 5 some of the deformation modes of two concentric circles obtained with this technique are reported: as it can be easily seen, those modes are not related to the whole structure, but are instead only the sum of the deformation modes of the outer and inner circles, taken separately. In fig. 6 the eigenmodes of a very similar structure (two rotated squares, one inside the other), computed by means of the BI-RME approach, are presented in a 3D fashion in order to show their physical meaning. These modes take into account both the outer and inner squares; therefore, changes in their relative positions affect both the eigenvalues $\{\omega_i\}$ and the corresponding eigenfunctions, while the same changes in the case of fig. 6 just give insignificant variations to the modes, since the two circles are analyzed as uncorrelated.

Acknowledgments

The whole Microwave Group of the University of Pavia is gratefully acknowledged for introducing P. Gamba to the original BI-RME theory. Special thanks to Prof. G. Conciauro, who first developed the BI-RME method. This work was partially supported by contract MURST 40% "Multimedia Workstation".

References

1. R. Jain and A. Pentland, Final Report,*NSF-ARPA Workshop on Visual Information Management Systems.*, Cambridge, Mass., June 1995.

2. A. Pentland, R.W. Picard, and S. Scarloff, "Photobook: Tools for content-based manipulation of image databases," *Proc. SPIE Conf. on Stor. and Retr. of Image and Video Databases II*, Vol. SPIE-2185 (1994).
3. S. Sclaroff, "Modal matching: a method for describing, comparing and manipulating digital signals" *PhD Thesis*, MIT, Cambridge, Mass., Feb. 1995.
4. T. Sedeberg and E. Greenwood,"A physically-based approach to 2-D shape blending," *Computer Graphics*, vol. 27, no. 2, pp. 25-34, July 1992.
5. B. Horn,"Closed-form solution of absolute orientation using unit quaternion," *J. of the Opt. Soc. of America A*, no. 4, pp. 629-642, 1987.
6. L. Shapiro and J. Brady, "Feature-based correspondence: an eigenvector approach," *Image and Vision Computing*, vol. 10, no. 5, pp. 283-288, June 1992.
7. G. Scott and H. Longuet-Higgins,"An algorithm for associating the features of two images," *Proc. Royal Soc. of London*, vol. B, no. 244, pp. 21-26, 1991.
8. A. Pentland and S. Sclaroff, "Closed-form solutions for physically-based shape modeling and recognition," *IEEE Trans. Pattern Analysis and Machine Intelligence*, vol. PAMI-13, no. 7, pp. 715-729, July 1991.
9. M. Kirby and L. Sirovich, "Application of the Karhunen-Loeve procedure for the characterization of human faces," *IEEE Trans. Pattern Analysis and Machine Intelligence*, vol. PAMI-12, no. 1, pp. 103-108, Jan. 1990.
10. S. Sclaroff and A. Pentland, "Modal matching for correspondence and recognition," *IEEE Trans. Pattern Analysis and Machine Intelligence*, vol. PAMI-17, no. 6, pp. 545-561, June 1995.
11. F. Dell'Acqua, P. Gamba and A. Mecocci, "Modal matching similarity search for shapes defined by a small number of points," Proc. of the *IAPR First Intern. Workshop on Image Databases and MultiMedia Search*, Amsterdam, The Netherlands, 22-23 Aug. 1996.
12. G. Conciauro, P. Arcioni, M. Bressan and L. Perregrini, "Wideband modeling of arbitrarily shaped H-plane waveguide components by the 'Boundary Integral - Resonant Mode Expension method'" *IEEE Trans. Microwave Theory and Techn.*, vol. MTT-44, no. 7, pp.1057-1066, July 1996.
13. M. Kac, "Can one hear the shape of a drum?", *Amer. Math. Monthly*, 73 (1966).
14. C. Gordon, D. Webb, and S. Wolpert, "Isospectral plane domains and surfaces via Riemannian orbifolds", *Invent. Math.*, vol. 110, pp. 1-22, 1992.

ACTIVE CONTROL OF FEATURE POINTS FOR INCREMENTAL FACTORIZATION

A. HELD, R. OKA
Real World Computing Partnership
1-6-1 Takezono, Tsukuba-shi, 305 Japan[a]

Factorization as a stable approach to the structure from motion problem has received much attention lately. However, so far, factorization has mainly been used for modeling tasks. In this paper, we investigate the possibilities of factorization applied to visual navigation tasks for a mobile robot. It is shown how it is possible to divide the tasks into smaller parts, leading to the so-called incremental factorization approach. Particular attention is payed to the problem of actively controlling the tracked feature points. This problem is reformulated as a back-projection of the recovered model on the image plane, allowing for identification of the most common problems that can occur in feature tracking.

1 Introduction

Recovering three-dimensional structure from a stream of input images, usually termed structure from motion (SFM), is a fundamental problem in computer vision. As a rather interesting approach to the structure from motion problem, Tomasi and Kanade[1] proposed to use a so-called *Factorization* method. In factorization, a number of feature points are tracked over some frames, and the coordinates of those points are compiled into one matrix. It can then be shown that this matrix, under some simplifying assumptions, is the product of the shape matrix and the motion matrix.

Lately, factorization has been expanded and used in a variety of applications, proving its versatility and generality. The problem of occlusions in the feature points and thus incomplete matrices, had been addressed already by Tomasi[2] in his thesis. The problem of more appropriate camera models, as opposed to orthographic projection, has attracted a number of researchers over the last few years. Such extensions were given by Poelman and Kanade[3] for the paraperspective case, and by Quan[4] for the affine case. Applications towards perspective factorization were treated by Yu et al.[5] and Sturm and Triggs[6]. Whereas the former use a Taylor series expansion for linearizing the problem, the latter opt to estimate projective scale factors from fundamental matrices.

An extension for the sequential update of the shape matrix was given by Morita and Kanade[7]. In their work, instead of the measurement matrix, the scatter matrix is used, transforming the singular value problem into a principal component problem where the first three modes stand for the spatial extent of the shape. Based on this sequential approach, Held[8] proposed to look only at one small part of the measurement

[a]The first author is now with ISE AG, Technoparkstr. 1, 8005 Zurich, Switzerland

matrix at a time. This approach is neither depending on the frame number nor on the total number of feature points, and it is therefore suited for navigation tasks or other tasks where reliable estimates must be available before the image stream is finished.

How to deal with the problem of multiple motions has been addressed by Costeira and Kanade[9], by computing a shape interaction matrix, allowing for the segmentation of the features into rigid motions. A similar approach was taken by Kung et al.[10], who proposed to find objects by an algebra based subspace clustering method.

Other, somewhat different approaches using factorization, are the one by Taylor et al.[11] in two dimensions, and Quan and Kanade's work[12] on a four step algorithm for line based factorization.

In this article, we revisit incremental factorization as proposed by Held[8]. It appears, incremental factorization is a useful tool for the navigation of a mobile robot, as shape updates become available at each frame, allowing for swift reaction from the controlling program. However, one problem, not only with incremental factorization but with factorization in general, is how to control the tracked feature points. One solution is the treatment of occlusions, as outlined by Tomasi[2]. However, the actual problem is how to decide when a feature point is being occluded. In addition, it would be of advantage to know of a dangerous situation well in advance, as feature points close to being occluded are rather difficult to track. This problem is even amplified in incremental factorization, where we have to rely on being able to exchange occluded feature points for new ones. The basic problem, therefore, is, how to recognize occlusions and how to deal with them.

The outline of the paper is as follows. In the next section, we will first attempt a brief review of recent factorization approaches. Following, we will show the problems we face while tracking features and outline a back projection scheme for the detection of occlusions. Finally, we will show some experiments using synthetic data, to show the performance of the proposed scheme.

2 Factorization

The original factorization, as proposed by Tomasi and Kanade, is based on a singular value decomposition, in order to obtain the shape and motion information from the measurement matrix. As the measurement matrix of this approach is of size frame number times number of feature points, shape estimates are only available after *all* frames have been processed. In order to obtain a frame-wise shape estimate, Morita and Kanade[7] proposed to work with the scatter matrix of the measurement matrix, essentially removing the frame number from the calculation. However, as the size of the measurement matrix is now given by the number of feature points, we still have to have an estimate on how many feature points will be tracked during the whole process, a helplessly difficult task in the case of a fairly complicated environment. Held[8] proposed a so-called incremental factorization approach, in which, at any time, only one small part of the whole measurement matrix is used for calculation. Incremental factorization essentially corresponds to repeated sequential factorization on different parts of the scatter matrix. The results of those partial shape estimates can then be combined by means of a recursively updateable affine transformation.

Assume we are given a world point s_p at frame f. This point will be observed at location (u_{fp}, v_{fp}) in the image plane. The measurement matrix W is then given as the matrix whose first F rows correspond to the consecutive horizontal coordinates of the P feature points and whose second F rows correspond to the vertical coordinates. W can be expressed in terms of the shape matrix S and the motion matrix R, namely

$$W = RS + T\,[1 \cdots 1], \tag{1}$$

where T is a translation vector. If we place our world origin in the center of mass of the object, the translation vector T can easily be calculated as the row average of W. Subtracting the translation T from W gives us the registered measurement matrix $\tilde{W}$.

$$\tilde{W} = W - T\,[1 \cdots 1] = \left[\begin{array}{c} \tilde{U} \\ \hdashline \tilde{V} \end{array}\right] = RS. \tag{2}$$

Tomasi and Kanade showed that it is possible to recover both, the shape and motion information from $\tilde{W}$ via Singular Value Decomposition. Namely,

$$\tilde{W} = O_1\,\Sigma\,O_2^T. \tag{3}$$

Both, O_1 and O_2 are unitary and Σ is a diagonal matrix containing the singular values of $\tilde{W}$ in decreasing order. The best possible rank three approximation to the ideal registered measurement matrix $\tilde{W}$, namely $\hat{W}$ can now be calculated as

$$\hat{W} = O_1'\,\Sigma'\,O_2' = \hat{R}\hat{S}, \tag{4}$$

where the motion matrix $\hat{R}$ and the shape matrix $\hat{S}$ can be obtained as

$$\begin{aligned} \hat{R} &= O_1'\,[\Sigma']^{1/2} \\ \hat{S} &= [\Sigma']^{1/2}\,O_2'. \end{aligned} \tag{5}$$

Instead of $\hat{W}$ we can work with the scatter matrix $Z_f = \hat{W}^T\hat{W} = Z_{f-1} + x_f\,x_f^T + y_f\,y_f^T$; hence, we are avoiding the dependence on the frame number. Shape and motion matrix, in that case, are given as

$$Z_f = \hat{W}^T\,\hat{W} = (O_1'\,\Sigma'\,O_2')^T\;\;O_1'\,\Sigma'\,O_2' = O_2'\,\Sigma'^2\,O_2'^T. \tag{6}$$

This means, by calculating the first three eigenvectors of Z_f at each frame f, we obtain the shape matrix S_f. These eigenvectors can be computed iteratively by means of the QR algorithm[13].

The shape matrix $\hat{S}$ and the motion matrix $\hat{R}$ are both linear transformations of the true shape matrix S and the motion matrix R. In other words, there exists a matrix Q such that

$$\begin{aligned} R &= \hat{R}\, Q \\ S &= Q^{-1}\, \hat{S}. \end{aligned} \tag{7}$$

Morita and Kanade[7] showed, that this matrix Q as well can be calculated sequentially. We will skip the details here.

The major problem of the sequential factorization method is that it only distributes the calculation over all the frames; still it cannot really be used while acquiring the image stream. This is so, because the dimension of the measurement matrix or its scatter matrix respectively, is now given by the number of feature points being tracked over the whole image stream. As the treatment of occlusions (see[2] for instance) has not been extended to the sequential case, the only possibility is to wait until the end of the image stream to see how many feature points could be tracked.

To overcome this problem and to explore the applicability of factorization to visual navigation tasks, Held[8] proposed an approach called incremental factorization. In incremental factorization, the sequential approach of Morita and Kanade is applied just to those feature points that are visible at that time. As it has been shown that convergence of the sequential factorization approach is rather fast (see [8]), that is, usually within 30 to 40 frames, it is not necessary to track all feature points over all frames. This means, after some time, we can discard a number of *dangerous points* and replace them with new ones. The question of what constitutes a dangerous point will be treated in the next section. In what follows, we will briefly outline incremental factorization, together with some improvements over[8].

The crucial idea in incremental factorization is to divide the image stream into sequences, see Fig. 1. We assume that the feature points do not change in one sequence.

Assume that we have been tracking a certain number of feature points over a number of frames. If now, at a certain time t_1, we reset the measurement matrix Z, replace one or several of the feature points with some new and different points, and restart factorization again, then we can expect to arrive at a converged state again within a certain number of iterations. What we have now, are two different shape matrices, which, however, share a certain number of their three-dimensional points (see Fig. 1). As those points physically are the same, they can be related to each other by means of an affine transformation, consisting of a translation and a linear map. The translation is needed to relate the two world origins, which are the centers of

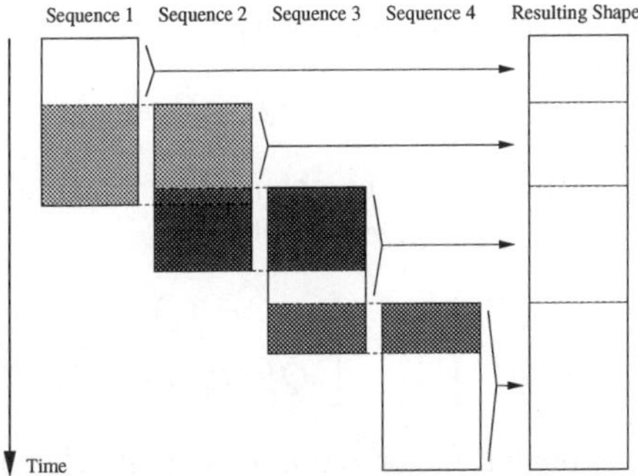

Figure 1: Incremental acquisition of shape matrix

mass of the shape matrices. Once this transformation has been obtained, we can relate the points that have been lost during the previous sequence to the present sequence. Repeating this for each sequence of the image stream allows us to gradually change our window over the environment, while still keeping track of those feature points that cannot be seen anymore.

The transformation matrix between two sequences can be calculated as follows. Assume that the two shape matrices S_1 and S_2 are given as

$$S_n = \left[\begin{array}{c} S'_n \\ \hdashline S''_n \end{array} \right], \qquad S_{n-1} = \left[\begin{array}{c} S'_{n-1} \\ \hdashline S''_{n-1} \end{array} \right]. \tag{8}$$

Without loss of generality, we can assume that the upper parts of S_n and S_{n-1}, namely, S'_n and S'_{n-1}, correspond to the same feature points, whereas the lower parts, i.e., S''_n and S''_{n-1} denote the feature points that were lost and those that are tracked newly, respectively. Using homogeneous coordinates, we have

$$S'_{n-1} = \left[\begin{array}{c:c} S'_n & 1 \end{array} \right] Q_n \tag{9}$$

where $S'_1 \in \mathbb{R}^{p \times 3}$, $S'_2 \in \mathbb{R}^{p \times 3}$, and $Q \in \mathbb{R}^{4 \times 3}$. Q could now be calculated by a normal least squares approach using the inverse of S'_n. However, due to influences of noise or unsatisfactory convergence, the calculation of the inverse is rather ill conditioned and can lead to numerical instabilities. It is therefore better to use an SVD approach for calculating the affine transform between two sequences[14], namely,

$$Q_n = \hat{V}\, \hat{\Sigma}^{-1}\, \hat{c}_1 \tag{10}$$

where

$$\hat{c}_1 = U^T\, S'_{n-1} \text{ and } \left[\begin{array}{c:c} S'_n & 1 \end{array} \right] = U\, \Sigma\, V^T \tag{11}$$

The full shape matrix at frame n is then given by

$$\ddot{S}_n = \left[\; [\; S'_n \; \vdots \; 1 \;] \; \ddot{Q}_n \; \vdots \; \ddot{S}_{n-1} \; \right]. \tag{12}$$

This means, the full shape matrix can be obtained incrementally or piece by piece. The relation between $\ddot{Q}_n$ and Q_n is given as follows.

$$\ddot{Q}_n = \begin{bmatrix} \ddot{Q}_n^R \\ \hdashline \ddot{Q}_n^T \end{bmatrix} = \begin{bmatrix} \bar{Q}_n^R \ddot{Q}_{n-1}^R \\ \hdashline \bar{Q}_n^T \ddot{Q}_{n-1}^R + \ddot{Q}_{n-1}^T \end{bmatrix} \tag{13}$$

The main feature of incremental factorization is that all calculations are of a relatively small order and do not increase with increasing frame numbers. It is therefore especially applicable for real time or near real time implementations.

3 Controlling feature points

One point of major importance in factorization, and even more so in incremental factorization is how to control the tracking of feature points. In the previous section we were mentioning that *dangerous* feature points should be discarded at a sequence transition. The question we will address in this section is what makes a feature point dangerous, that is, difficult to track.

Basically, there are three problems that can arise in the tracking of feature points: Feature points move outside visible area; Feature points are lost due to occlusion; Tracking fails due to illumination changes.

We deal with each of these points in turn. Starting with the last point, the problem of illumination changes, it has been shown that a rather simple and effective means of dealing with this problem is to apply some histogram equalization process to the image. However, although this might help in some cases, it is far from being a general tool. A more thorough treatment of this topic would involve the consideration of the reliability of the tracking result at each frame. Assuming that illumination will not change abruptly over time, discarding a feature point as soon as its reliability falls below a certain threshold should ensure that they should not be lost due to illumination changes.

The other two points require some knowledge of the camera movement in respect to the scene. The relative movement of the camera is given from Eqs. 1 and 8, namely the translation vector T and the motion matrix R. As can be seen in Morita's work[7] the motion matrix R can be obtained at each frame as the present orientation of the image plane or camera. To find out which points are in danger of being lost, we have to look ahead, by estimating what will happen within the next few frames. Based on the translation vectors of the last few frames, we are able to estimate the translational part of the motion over the next few frames as well, by assuming the motion will not change abruptly. To find points that are about to move off the visible area, it is sufficient to define an active region on the image plane. The actual extent of this active region can be deduced from the propagated translation vectors. Whenever a feature point is moving out of the active region, it is in danger of disappearing completely and should be exchanged.

For the detection of occlusions, we first have to find the actual motion of the camera, or the scene, between two frames. Given, the camera orientation at frame n is given by $R_n \in \mathbb{R}^{3\times 3}$. Clearly, as translation has been removed already, R_{n-1} and R_n are related by a pure rotation. This corresponds to finding an unitary matrix W such that the Euclidean norm of $R_n - W\, R_{n-1}$ is minimized. Again, the rotation matrix W can be calculated by means of a singular value decomposition[13]. Namely, given

$$R_n\, R_{n-1}^T = U\,\Sigma\, V^T, \tag{14}$$

then the rotation matrix W is given by

$$W = U\, V^T \tag{15}$$

It is now relatively simple to find the three rotation angles that form the matrix W.

In a next step, we have to get a surface representation of the present shape matrix, thus allowing for a pre-rotation and the detection of occlusions. Given a partial shape matrix S'_n, we apply an algorithm to find a graph that connects all the points in S'_n, such that no edges cross each other. Bearing in mind that there can not be any occlusion yet, we can neglect the depth of the points and concentrate on finding a planar graph that connects all the vertices of S'_n. In general, any triangulation of the set of vertices in the plane would do to obtain a valid surface representation. In practice, however, the Delauney triangulation[15] is the preferred tool. In general, Delauney triangulation can be carried out in $O(n \log n)$, hence, the computational burden is not excessive.

Given a reasonable triangulation of the points, we can now sort the edges such that triples form triangles or triangular surface patches; this gives us a surface representation of the shape matrix, as shown in Fig. 2 for a part of a cylinder. The task of finding the surface representation has to be done only once for each sequence, later it is sufficient to adjust the vertex positions to mirror the changes in S'_n. In addition, the whole process of finding triangular patches does not have to be repeated completely at sequence transitions either, as some parts of the shape matrices will remain intact.

Given a surface representation, we can either pre-rotate it by a multiple of the last inter frame rotation W_n or by an average of some of the last rotations $W_{n-k} \ldots W_n$. Applying a standard method for the elimination of hidden points citefol:82 to the rotated surface representation allows to identify those vertices that will disappear, given the estimated future motion. Hence, those points of the shape matrix S'_n are

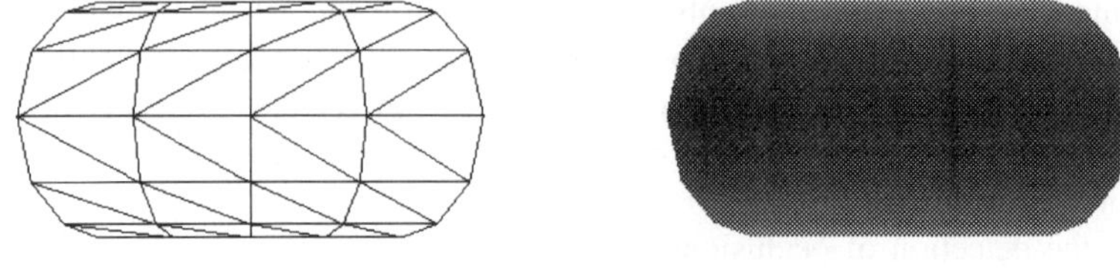

Figure 2: Surface model using triangular patches (left) and shading (right)

in danger of being occluded and should be replaced by some new, suitably chosen feature points.

4 Experiments

To show the performance of incremental factorization we selected a simple artificial model of points arranged in lines on a rotating cylinder. The input to the factorization process is given in Fig. 3.

Figure 3: Input to factorization: front view (left) and side view (right)

During factorization approximately 35 feature points are being tracked, of which, at sequence transitions, approximately 5 are being replaced. The selection of the candidate points for replacement is done according to the occlusion procedure, outlined in the previous section, leading to sequence transitions at about every 30 frames. Several stages in the acquisition of the full shape matrix are shown in Fig. 4. Although the above results are rather simple and preliminary, they show that occlusions can be treated satisfactorily by means of incremental factorization, without taking resort in elaborate schemes during the factorization stage.

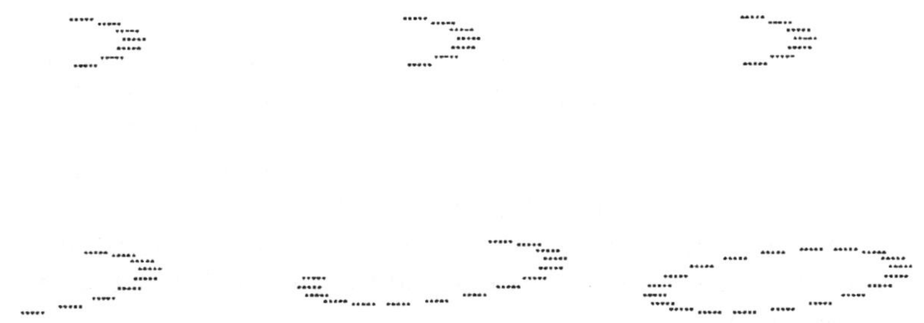

Figure 4: Partial shape matrix (top) and full shape matrix (bottom) after 110, 300, and 490 frames, respectively: perspective view

5 Conclusions

An important problem in factorization and incremental factorization as outlined in this paper, is the active control of tracked feature points. It is important that we have some control over how feature points will behave over a number of future frames, in order to distinguish between points that can be traced reliably, and points that should be discarded and replaced by new feature points. Although our experiments are relying on artificially generated feature points, the results shown in the previous section outline that the approach of propagating the motion matrix in order to estimate the future motion of the camera is applicable to the detection of occlusions and feature points moving off the visible area.

The major problem that remains to be solved for a practical application of factorization is a reliable extraction and tracking of feature points, a point that has been largely neglected in most of the work on factorization and, alas, in this paper as well. Results of factorization, as various simulation showed, heavily rely on an accurate tracking of the feature points; even more so in the case of incremental factorization where errors in the shape matrices tend to accumulate.

Acknowledgments

The authors would like to thank Dr. J. Shimada, from the Real World Computing Partnership, for providing the necessary environment for this work.

References

1. C. Tomasi and T. Kanade. Shape and motion from image streams under orthography: a factorization method. *Int. Journal of Computer Vision*, 9(2):137–154, 1992.
2. C. Tomasi. *Shape and Motion from Image Streams: A Factorization Method.* PhD thesis, Carnegie Mellon University, 1991.
3. C.J. Poelman and T. Kanade. A paraperspective factorization method for shape and motion recovery. Technical Report CMU-CS-93-219, Carnegie Mellon University, 1993.
4. L. Quan. Self-calibration of an affine camera from multiple views. *Int. Journal of Computer Vision*, 19(1):93–105, 1996.
5. H. Yu, Q. Chen, G. Xu, and M. Yachida. 3d shape and motion by svd under higher-order approximation of perspective projection. In *Proc. Int. Conf. on Pattern Recogn., ICPR'96*, pages 456–460, Vienna, 1996.
6. P. Sturm and B. Triggs. A factorization based algorithm for multi-image projectice structure and motion. In *Proc. European Conf. Comp. Vision, ECCV'96*, pages 709–720, Cambridge, 1996.
7. T. Morita and T. Kanade. A sequential factorization method for recovering shape and motion from image streams. In *Proc. 1994 ARPA Image Understanding Workshop*, pages 1177–1188, Monterey, USA, 1994.
8. A. Held. Piecewise shape reconstruction by incremental factorization. In *Proc. 7th British Machine Vision Conference*, pages 333–342, 1996. Edinburgh.
9. J. Costeira and T. Kanade. A multi-body factorization method for motion analysis. Technical Report CMU-CS-TR-94-220, Carnegie Mellon University, 1994.
10. S.Y. Kung, J.S. Taur, and M.Y. Chiu. An svd approach to multi-camera-multi-target 3d motion-shape analysis. In *Proc. Int. Conf. Image Processing, ICIP'94*, pages 573–577, Austin, 1994.
11. C.J. Taylor, D.J. Kriegman, and P. Anandan. Structure and motion in two dimensions from multiple images: A least squares approach. In *IEEE Workshop on Visual Motion*, pages 242–248, 1991.
12. L. Quan and T. Kanade. A factorization method for affine structure from line correspondence. In *Proc. Int. Conf. on Comp. Vision and Patt. Recogn., CVPR'96*, California, 1996.
13. R.A. Horn and C.R. Johnson. *Matrix Analysis.* Cambridge University Press, Cambridge, 1985.
14. C.L. Lawson and R.J. Hanson. *Solving Least Squares Problems.* SIAM, Philadelphia, 1995.
15. L.P. Chew. Constrained delauney triangulations. *Algorithmica*, 4:97–108, 1989.

AN ANTHROPOMETRIC SHAPE MODEL FOR ESTIMATING HEAD ORIENTATION

T. HORPRASERT, Y. YACOOB and L. S. DAVIS
Computer Vision Laboratory
University of Maryland
College Park, MD 20742

An approach for estimating 3D head orientation in a monocular image sequence is presented. The approach employs recently developed image-based parameterized tracking for face and face features to locate the area in which an estimation of point feature locations is performed. This involves tracking of five points (four at the eye corners and the fifth is the tip of the nose). We describe an approach that relies on the coarse structure of the face to compute orientation relative to the camera plane. Our approach employs symmetry of the eyes and anthropometric statistics to estimate the head yaw, roll and pitch.

Keywords: Face orientation, feature tracking, anthropometry.

1 Introduction

Watching people move is a favorite human pastime, and the shapes of people and their parts play important roles in the lives of both human and computer programs. Human shape is dynamic, due to the many degrees of articulative freedom of the human body, and the deformations of the body and its parts induced by muscular action. Human shape variability is also highly limited by both genetic and environmental constraints, and is characterized by a high degree of (approximate) symmetry and (approximate) invariants of body length scales and ratios. The field of anthropometry [6,14] is concerned with tabulation and modeling of the distributions of these scales and ratios, and can serve as a useful source of shape constraints for analyzing videos of people when prior information is not available about the specific individuals being viewed.

In this paper we are concerned with the problem of watching an arbitrary individual's head in a video sequence (as might be seen by a camera attached to a personal computer) and following the person's head movements in 3-D to

The support of the Defense Advanced Research Projects Agency (DARPA Order No. C635) under Contract N00014-95-1-0521 is gratefully acknowledged.

help determine, for example, where on the screen a person might be looking, whether the person is attending to the information being presented on the screen, whether the person is speaking to the machine, etc. More specifically, our goal is to recover and track the three degrees of rotational freedom of a human head, without prior knowledge of the exact shape of the head and face being observed. The approach we develop is a two stage approach in which the person being watched is first classified according to gender, race and age. This classification can be used to index into tabulated anthropometric distributions of face length scales (in our case eye fissure and nose length) to constrain as tightly as possible a head orientation recovery algorithm that integrates face symmetries with these length scale distributions. This instantaneous orientation estimation algorithm is combined with a robust motion analysis algorithm (which both aids with the tracking of facial features and provides additional constraints to an orientation tracker) to estimate the sequence of head orientations observed. In this paper we focus on both the static orientation estimation algorithm and the feature tracking method employed by the system (which employs recently developed image-based parameterized tracking[1] for face and face features to locate the area in which an estimation of the eye corner and nose tip positions is performed). We also provide an error analysis of the orientation estimation procedure, considering errors due to both image analysis and anthropometric modeling. The latter estimates expected errors in head orientation recovery using variances of subpopulations identified. This could, for example, allow adaptive control of the screen resolution with which information is presented to a user as a function of expected orientation accuracy.

There are two principal approaches in the literature to recovering head orientation: *model-* and *appearance-* based. Model-based approaches typically recover an individual's 3-D head shape using stereo or shading, and then use the 3-D model to estimate the head's orientation. On the other hand, appearance-based approaches such as view interpolation (see[5]) or eigenface approaches (see [11]) are used in conjunction with a training stage (e.g., person sits in front of a computer and is asked to look at several points on a screen by turning his head) that constructs the association between appearance and head orientation. Appearance models are expected to be less accurate than model-based approaches since they involve computing a global, lower-dimensional representation of the data (thus tuning the representation to "mean views").

Previous model-based and appearance-based algorithms include [13,7]. In Tsukamoto et al. [13], the orientation is modeled as a linear combination of disparities between facial regions and several face models. Gee and Cipolla[7] estimate head orientation based on knowledge of the individual face geometry and assuming a *weak perspective* imaging model. Their method also depends on the distance between the eyes and mouth which often changes during facial expressions. In work related to ours, DeCarlo and Metaxas[3] used anthropometry to constrain a deformable model during head tracking.

We define head orientation to be the three rotation angles in an orthogonal coordinate system located at the camera imaging plane. In this system, the roll angle is zero when the eyes are horizontal, the yaw angle is zero when the face is in frontal view and the pitch is zero when the bridge of the nose is parallel to the image plane of the camera. The pitch angle definition is somewhat arbitrary, since inclinations of the nasal bridge differ between individuals. Our objective is to develop a vision system that can recover the orientation of a head in 3-D without prior knowledge of the exact head surface shape of the people being viewed.

2 A Perspective Model for Head Orientation Recovery

The computational model for head orientation recovery is based on face symmetry and anthropometric modeling of structure. Our approach recovers orientation from the *distances* among five points: four eye corners and the nose tip. We show how these distances allow us to recover the absolute rotation angles about the Z and Y axes. However, these distances are insufficient for recovering the rotation around the X axis. Thus, a statistical analysis for face structure based on anthropometry is employed to estimate the angle of rotation about the X-axis.

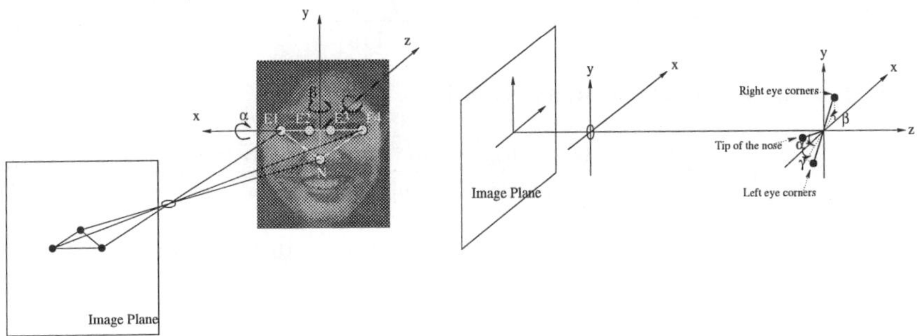

Figure 1: Geometric configuration of head orientation and coordinate system.

We employ a coordinate system fixed to the camera with the origin point being at its focal point (see Figure 1). The image plane coincides with the XY-plane and the viewing direction coincides with the Z-axis. α, β, γ (pitch, yaw and roll, respectively) denote the three rotation angles of the head about the X,Y,and Z-axis, respectively.

Our model for head estimation assumes that the four eye-corners are co-linear in 3D; this assumption can be relaxed to account for a slight horizontal tilt in the eyes of Asian subjects (see Farkas [6] for statistics on the deviation of the eye corners from co-linearity).

Let upper case letters denote coordinates and distances in 3D and lower case letters denote their respective 2D projections. Let E_1, E_2, E_3 and E_4 denote the four eye corners and e_1, e_2, e_3 and e_4 denote their projection in the image plane (((u_i, v_i) are the coordinates of the points).

A complete treatment of the estimation of these angles is given in [9]. The roll angle is trivial to compute from the eye corners. The head yaw is recovered based on the assumptions that the eyes are of equal width and E_1, E_2, E_3 and E_4 are collinear. Then, from the symmetry of the eye widths, we compute the yaw angle as a function of measured distances in the image and the focal length of the camera. Only relative distances among the four corners of the eyes are required. The method has no dependence on face structure, the distance of the face from the camera or feature translation in the image. The computation of the pitch angle assumes that the width of the eyes E and the length of the nasal bridge N are represented by a distribution function drawn from anthropometric data. The estimation of yaw is given by

$$\beta = \arctan \frac{f}{(S-1)u_1} \tag{1}$$

where f is the focal length, u_1 is given by

$$u_1 = \frac{[\Delta v \Delta u M(u_1 - v_1)] - [M^2(u_2 - v_2)(u_1 - v_1)^2]}{\Delta v(M(u_1 - v_1) - \Delta u)} \tag{2}$$

All the terms involve only distances between points in the image (see [9]). S is obtained by solving the equation

$$\frac{\Delta u}{\Delta v} = \frac{u_2 - u_1}{v_1 - v_2} = -\frac{(S-1)(S-(1+(2/Q)))}{(S+1)(S+(1+(2/Q)))} \tag{3}$$

where only distances in the image are used (Q and M involve only distances in the image). The estimation of pitch is given by

$$\alpha = \arcsin\left(\frac{f}{p_0(p_1^2 + f^2)}[p_1^2 \pm \sqrt{p_0^2 p_1^2 - f^2 p_1^2 + f^2 p_0^2}\ ]\right) \tag{4}$$

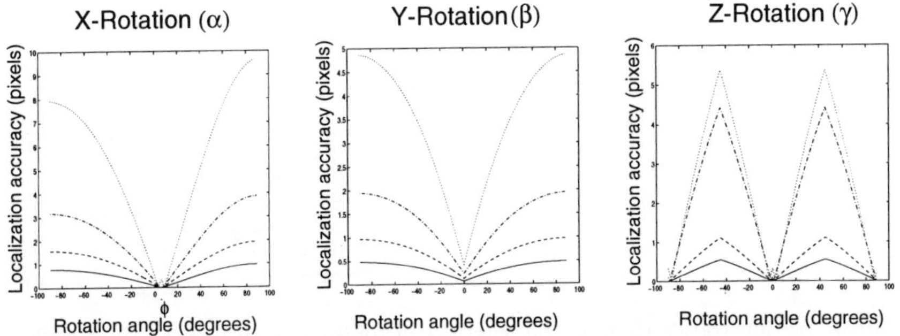

Figure 2: The localization accuracy of the rotation about each axis, while maintaining 0.5(solid line), 1(dash line), 2(dash+point line), and 5(dot line) degrees error.

where p_0 is the nasal bridge projection at 0 degrees, and p_1 is the measured projection of the nasal bridge (p_0 is estimated using anthropometry).

3 Error Analysis Simulation

In this section the effects of both image error (localization of eye corners) and model errors (due to expected variations in length from the anthropometric models) on orientation recovery are presented. In this analysis, we assume that the structure is that of an average adult American male. Thus, the expected length of the nasal bridge is 50mm, and the expected length of eye fissure is 31.3mm. The distance between model and camera is 500mm, and the focal length is 16mm. We also assume a pixel size of 16 μm (typical of what we might encounter with a PC-mounted camera).

Figure 2 illustrates the localization accuracy of image measurements required to obtain a given accuracy (0.5 to 5.0 degrees) in recovering orientation as a function of absolute orientation. As can be observed, very high localization accuracy is needed for yaw and roll of about 0 degrees. We call these angles *degenerate angles.* While the degenerate angles for yaw and roll are independent of any length scales, the degenerate angle for pitch depends on the angle $\phi = \arcsin(N/Z)$ where N is the length of the nasal bridge and Z is the distance between the face and the camera. In this particular analysis, $\phi \sim$ 5.74 degree ($arcsin\frac{50}{500}$). Generally, this angle is the angle for which the line of sight to the nose tip is tangent to the circle of radius N centered on the face (see Figure 3).

In addition to depending on the localization accuracy of the image processing, the recovery of pitch also depends on the deviation of the observed

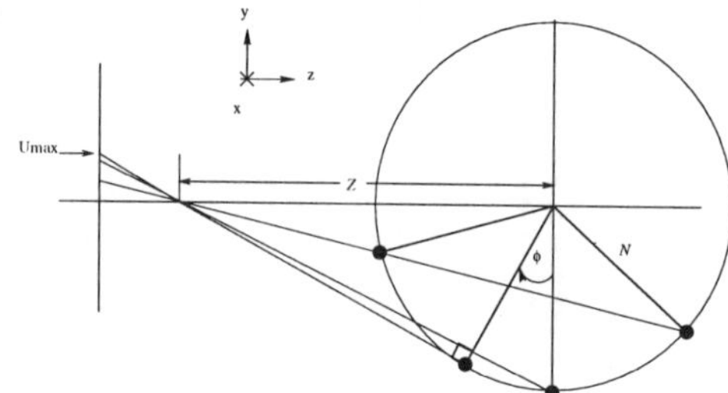

Figure 3: An illustration showing characteristic of rotating about X-axis. By considering rotations from -90 to 90 degrees, the projective point on image plane will reach the highest point when the angle of rotation is ϕ degree. This tangent angle is influenced by the distance between the original point of rotation and the lens, and the radius of the rotation.

face from the assumed face anthropometry as illustrated in Figure 4. The plots show errors in pitch recovery from applying our computational model to various face structures. The top graph display nasal bridge error for $\mu_N \pm \sigma_N$ and $\mu_N \pm 2\sigma_N$ ($\mu_N = 50mm$ and $\sigma_N = 3.6mm$). The bottom graph displays eye width error for $\mu_E \pm \sigma_E$ and $\mu_E \pm 2\sigma_E$ ($\mu_E = 31.3mm$ and $\sigma_E = 1.2mm$). Notice that the errors are small away from the degenerate angle. The horizontal axis represents the actual pitch while the vertical axis is the estimated pitch employing an average face structure.

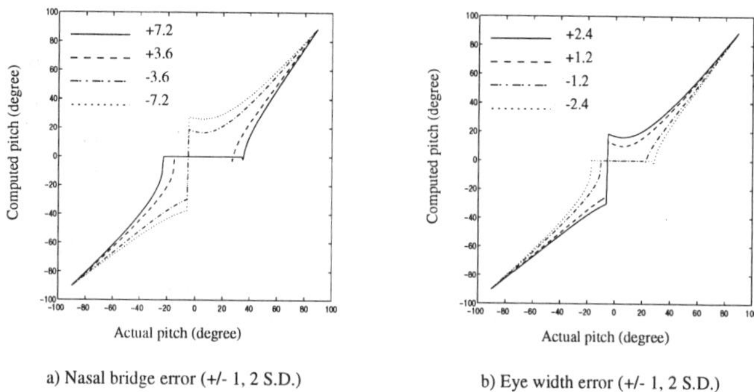

Figure 4: An illustration showing errors of our computation models to various face structures.

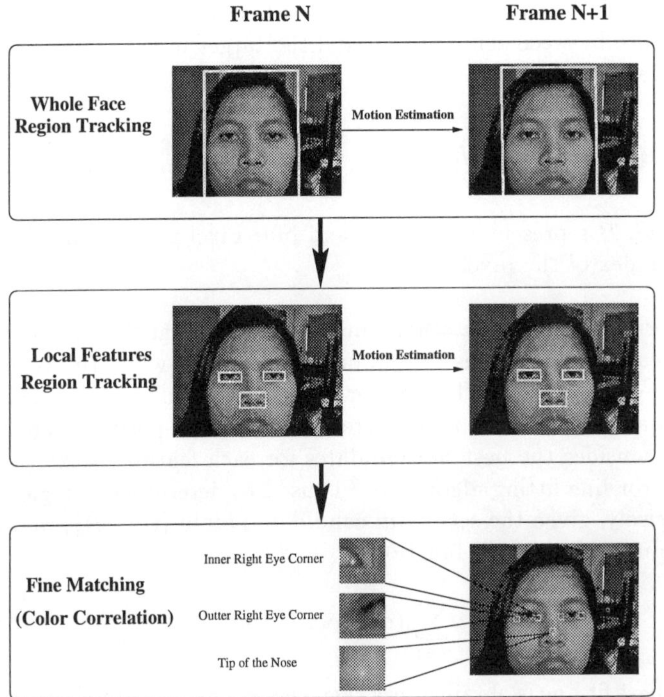

Figure 5: Diagram shows the hierarchical framework for facial features tracking.

4 Facial Features Tracking

We employ a hierarchical method for tracking the facial features used by the head orientation recovery model. We assume the initial locations of these points are given. This initialization problem has been addressed in the literature, see, e.g., [10] [8] and [12]. Given these points in the first frame, we track each point independently by employing recently developed image-based parameterized tracking [1]. This performs both *global* region tracking of the whole face and *local* region tracking of the individual facial features. We then refine our position estimates by employing color correlation. Figure 5 shows the hierarchical framework for facial feature tracking.

From face and feature tracking, the locations of feature points in the next frame are estimated. The positional refinement step involves creating a template, from the current frame, of each feature point and then performing a color correlation over a search region around the estimated location in the next frame. In the correlation, a mis-match score, M, which is a measure of the difference between template, T, and the target image, I, is determined. M is defined as follows:

$$M = \sum_{i,j} MAX(|R_{T_{i,j}} - R_{I_{i,j}}|, |G_{T_{i,j}} - G_{I_{i,j}}|, |B_{T_{i,j}} - B_{I_{i,j}}|) \tag{5}$$

where R, G, B represent red, green, and blue pixel values respectively, and i, j are the index of the pixel.

Our orientation computational model assumes that the corners of the eyes are collinear. We take this constraint into account while the corners of the eyes are being tracked. While performing correlation over the search region, the mis-match scores and their corresponding pixel positions are tabulated. Then, we consider the best m candidates for each feature. Next, a minimum-squared-error line fitting algorithm [4] is used to determine a single "eye" line. More precisely, given the set of $4m$ candidate points $\{(x_i, y_i)\}$, we find c_0 and c_1 that minimize the error function

$$\sum_{i=1}^{n}[(c_0 + c_1 x_i) - y_i]^2$$

Once the best fit line is obtained, we then choose the one, among the candidates for each eye corner, that minimizes

$$\frac{|d|}{|d_{max}|} + \frac{M}{M_{max}} \tag{6}$$

where $|d|$ is the vertical distance between the point to the line; and where $|d_{max}|$ and M_{max} are the maximum value of $|d|$ and M respectively.

Representative results of our tracking method are shown in Figure 6, and the orientation recovery results are shown in Figure 7.

5 Summary

We have presented an approach for computation of head orientation by employing face symmetry and statistical analysis of face structure from anthropometry. The rotations of the head about the Z and Y-axes can be computed directly from the relative distances among corners of the eyes and the camera focal length. The estimation of the orientation of the head about the X-axis employed anthropometric analysis of face structure. A preliminary experiment on real images has demonstrated the performance of our approach.

Figure 6: Illustration of the result from applying the hierarchical tracking method on a sequence of 24 frames, with 10 frames/sec frame rate, of a face rotating in Yaw direction. Only every other frame, starting at the first frame, is shown.

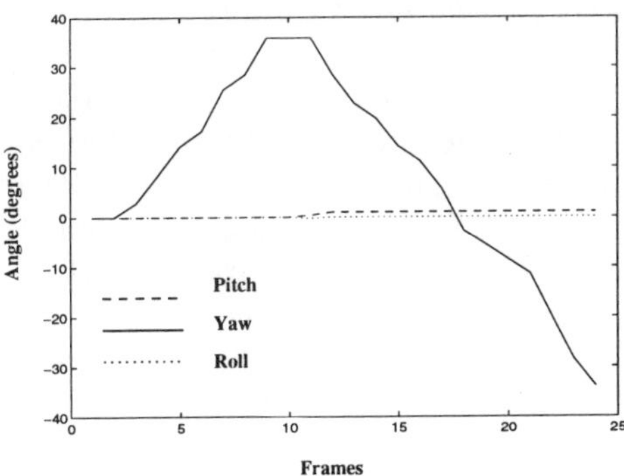

Figure 7: The plot shows the sequences of rotation angles recovered through the image sequence shown in Figure .

References

1. M. J. Black and Y. Yacoob, "Tracking and recognizing facial expressions in image sequences, using local parameterized models of image motion", *ICCV,* 1995, 374-381.
2. R. Chellappa, C.L. Wilson and S.A. Sirohey, "Human and machine recognition of faces: A survey" *Proc. of IEEE,* Vol 83, 1995, pp.705–740.
3. D. DeCarlo and D. Metaxas, "The integration of optical flow and deformable models with applications to human face shape and motion estimation," *IEEE CVPR*, 1996, 231-238.
4. R. O. Duda and P. E. Hart, "Pattern Classification and Scene Analysis", John Wiley & Sons, 1973.
5. T. Ezzat and T. Poggio, "Facial Analysis and Synthesis Using Image-Based Models," *International Conference on Face and Gesture.* 1996, 116-121.
6. L.G. Farkas, *Anthropometry of the Head and Face,* 2nd edition, Raven Press, 1994.
7. A. Gee and R.Cipolla, "Estimating Gaze from a Single View of a Face," *ICPR 94*, 758-760, 1994.
8. R. Herpers and et al., "Edge and Keypoint Detection in Facial Regions", *Proc. of Int. Conf. on Automatic Face and Gesture Recognition*, 1996, 212-217.
9. T. Horprasert, Y. Yacoob and L.S Davis "Computing 3D head orinetation from a monocular image sequence" *Proc. of Int. Conf. on Automatic Face and Gesture Recognition*, 1996, 242-247.
10. K. M. Lam and H. Yan, "Locating and Extracting the Eye in Human Face Images", *Pattern Recognition*, Vol.29, No.5, pp.771-779, 1996.
11. A. Pentland, B. Moghaddam and T. Starner, "View-based and modular eigenspaces for face recognition," *IEEE CVPR*, 1994, 84-91.
12. M.J.T. Reinders, R.W.C. Koch, and J.J. Gerbrands, "Locating Facial Features in Image Sequences using Neural Networks", *Proc. of Int. Conf. on Automatic Face and Gesture Recognition*, pp. 230-235, October 1996.
13. A. Tsukamoto, C. Lee and S. Tsuji, "Detection and pose estimation of human face with synthesized image models," *ICPR 94*, 754-757, 1994.
14. J. Young, *Head and Face Anthropometry of Adult U.S. Citizens*, Government Report DOT/FAA/AM-93/10, July 1993.

EFFICIENT COMPUTATION OF TOPOLOGICAL FUNCTIONS ON THE FACE-CENTERED CUBIC GRID

CHIH-YUAN HU, RICHARD W. HALL
Electrical Engineering Department, University of Pittsburgh, Pittsburgh, PA 15261, USA

Topological functions (e.g. identifying simple points) must be computed for topology preserving reduction processes like thinning. In 3D images there is a special need for efficient computation of such topological functions as they are typically applied over large 3D image in many passes. Time-efficient and storage efficient solutions are known for 26-6 rectangular images where faster techniques tend to have higher storage complexity. In these solutions the time complexity and storage complexity are related to the number of neighbors of the point under test. The Face-Centered Cubic grid (FCC) offers a smaller number of neighbors for such points and there may be some potential for improved time-storage performance for the computation of topological functions in such images. In this paper we explore this question by developing computations for key topological functions in FCC-based images and comparing the time-storage tradeoffs for these functions with other FCC-based approaches and with the related computations in 26-6 images.

1 Introduction

In the design of topology preserving reduction algorithms like thinning we typically use the computation of topological functions as a key part of the reduction operator. For example, in sequential processes we are often interested in knowing if a point can be removed from the foreground of a binary image without disturbing the topology of the image. Such removable points are termed *simple* points. Efficient computations for such points in 2D images are well known and easily derived – especially since the number of neighboring points in the support of the computation is rather small (e.g. eight points in 8-4 2D images) so that lookup tables can be used to directly store and compute the function. In 3D images the computation for simple points (and related functions) is complicated by the relatively large number of points in the support (e.g. 26 points in rectangular 26-6 images [8]) which makes the direct use of lookup tables unwieldy. It is particularly desirable to find good time efficiencies for these functions since they typically appear as key parts of topology preserving operators which are applied over large 3D images in many passes. In 26-6 images (defined in rectangular grids) there are a variety of methods for computing topological functions which produce a range of time and storage tradeoffs [1,2,5,9,12,13,14]. The best time efficiency has been obtained at the cost of fairly high storage complexity [5]. The complexity of computing these topological functions appears to be related to the number of points in the function support which is directly related to the number of points adjacent to the point under test. Thus, other 3D image definitions which have smaller neighborhoods of adjacent points might offer better computational properties. One such alternative definition is the face-centered cubic (FCC) grid [3] which has two natural neighborhood sizes of 12 and 18 neighbors. In this paper we explore how we can compute important topological functions in this grid and we compare time-storage tradeoffs for older and our new FCC-based functions with functions for 26-6 rectangular images.

2 Notation and the FCC Grid

We consider 3D binary images in this paper. The elements in the image (termed *points* or *voxels*) take values from the set $\{0, 1\}$. Voxels with value 1 are termed 1's and the set of such 1's is referred to as the *foreground* of the image. The set of 0's is termed the *background*. The image space is assumed to be unbounded with a finite number of 1's contained in a finite region. Thus we always assume there is a frame of 0's surrounding the 1's of the image. The traditional 3D image is assumed to be composed of cubic volume elements (voxels) which partition $\Re^3$. This leads to the well known 26-6 image[8] where foreground voxels are 26-connected and background voxels are 6-connected. We can derive the face-centered cubic (FCC) grid by considering the 3D sphere packing problem.[3] We imagine that we are placing 2D layers of spheres (say perfectly round oranges at the fruitstand stacked in a pyramid of horizontally oriented layers) upon each other such that we appear to waste no unnecessary space. In Figure 1 we show a cross-section of one layer of spheres (say an intermediate layer in our fruitstand metaphor) at the sphere centers, denoted a. Layers below and above this layer may place the sphere centers at either positions labeled b or c. We can then fill $\Re^3$ with closely packed spheres by alternately choosing positions for successive layers. Adjacent layers are only constrained to not place sphere centers at the same position, so there are an unbounded number of ways we could fill a 3D space this way by choosing different sequences from the set $\{a, b, c\}$. In this work we use the regular sequence $b, a, c, b, a, c, \ldots$ If we wish to imagine that our 3D space is fully partitioned, then we can imagine that the spheres are expanded by finding the Voronoi diagram with respect to sphere centers. From either of these metaphors we may derive two natural adjacency relations as illustrated in Figure 2. Imagine that voxel v belongs to the a layer of Figure 1 — the center such voxel in the figure. Then the *12-neighborhood* of a voxel v includes v and the 6 voxels closest to v in the a layer ($v_4 - v_9$ in Figure 2) and the 3 closest voxels with centers b in the layer

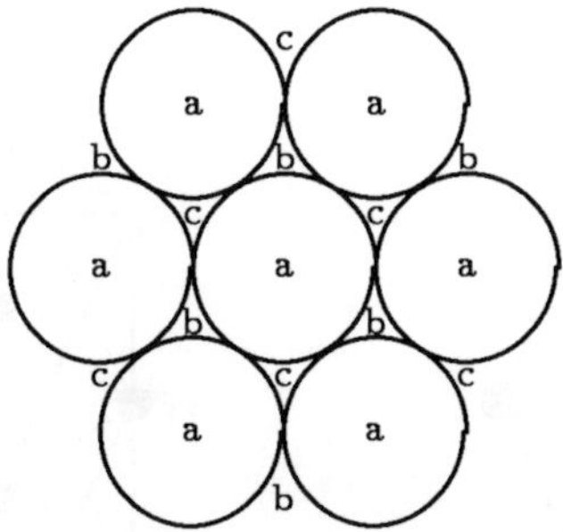

Figure 1: Defining a face-centered cubic grid via sphere packing.

below (v_{10} – v_{12} in Figure 2) and the 3 closest voxels with centers c in the layer above. (v_1 – v_3 in Figure 2) The *18-neighborhood* of v is composed of the 12-neighborhood of v with additionally the next 3 closest voxels at centers b in the layer below (v_{16} – v_{18} in Figure 2) and the next 3 closest voxels at centers c in the layer above. (v_{13} – v_{15} in Figure 2) We say v is *12-adjacent* (*18-adjacent*) to each distinct voxel in its 12-neighborhood (18-neighborhood). We use the following more compact notation to describe neighborhoods. $N_k(v)$ is defined as the set containing a point v and its k-adjacent neighbors, i.e. the k-neighborhood of v; and $N_k^*(v) \equiv N_k(v) \setminus \{v\}$, for $k = 12$ or 18. We define the *12-neighbors* of v as $N_{12}^*(v)$ and the *18\12–neighbors* of v as the six voxels in $N_{18}(v)$ which are not in $N_{12}(v)$.

We use the terms *k-path, k-connected, k-connected component* in the sense defined by Kong and Rosenfeld, [8] but with $k = 12$ or 18 based on the 12- and 18-adjacecies defined above. We use the abbreviated term *k-component* to denote a k-connected component. We define $N\xi_k(v)$ to be the number of ξ's (either 1's or 0's) in $N_k^*(v)$. We define $NC\xi_k^m(v)$ to be the number of m-components of ξ's in $N_k^*(v)$ which are m-adjacent to v. For simplicity, we use the notation $NC\xi_m(v) \equiv NC\xi_m^m(v)$ when $m = k$. When m-connectivity is used for the foreground and n-connectivity is used for the background we refer to such images as (m,n) images. A foreground point is called a *simple point* if its removal from the foreground will not affect the topology of the original image. The *genus* or *Euler characteristic* of a set of points $\mathcal{X}$ is a useful topological measure. [8] $\Delta\mathcal{G}_k^{(m,n)}(v)$ is the difference of genus for $\mathcal{X}=N_k(v)$ when v is changed. When $\Delta\mathcal{G}^{(m,n)}(v) = 0$ we say the genus or Euler characteristic is preserved and this is one possible condition for topology preservation. The

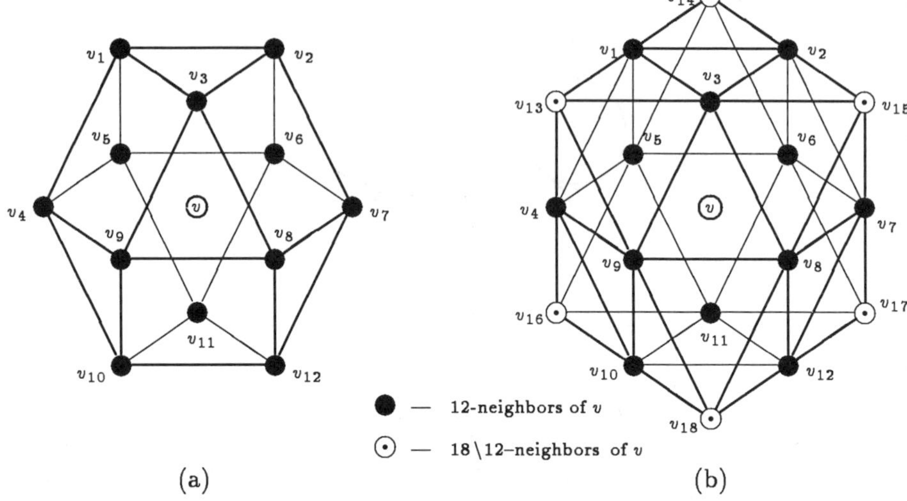

Figure 2: Neighborhoods of voxel v in the FCC grid: (a) 12-neighborhood; (b) 18-neighborhood. Lines indicate the 12-adjacencies among the neighbors of v. In (b) the 18-adjacencies among these neighbors must be inferred.

support of a function applied at a point p is the minimal set of points defined with respect to p required to evaluate the function. These are typically certain neighborhoods of p for the functions considered here.

3 Topological Functions

For rectangular (26,6) images Kong and Rosenfeld [8], Toriwaki et al. [13], and Malandain and Bertrand [2] have shown that a foreground voxel is simple iff both of the following conditions hold:

(1) $NC1_{26}(v) = 1$; and

(2) $NC0^6_{18}(v) = 1$ (or equivalently $\Delta\mathcal{G}_{26}^{(26,6)}(v) = 0$).

Kong [7] has also given new characterizations for $(18,6)$ connectivity. We can see that only local support is needed to compute 3D simple points as in the 2D cases on rectangular grid. However, the 3D realizations are not as simple as for the 2D cases, since 26 neighbors must be tested for both $(26,6)$ and $(18,6)$ images. Such realizations are particularly critical in terms of time performance for sequential implementation due to typically large 3D images. Therefore, we need time-efficient computations for 3D simple points.

Lobregt et al.[9] reported a method to compute $\Delta\mathcal{G}_{26}^{(26,6)}(v)$ by using eight 2×2×2 unit cubes in the local neighborhood of a voxel. The methodology requires relatively small lookup table storage. A similar table for $(18,6)$ connectivity has been given by Ma[10]. Unfortunately, the computation of $\Delta\mathcal{G}_{m}^{(m,n)}(v)$ alone can not determine simple points, e.g. additional analysis of foreground components in the m-neighborhood of the pixel under test would be sufficient. Binary tree searches[6] have been used, but they are computationally intensive and more time-efficient approaches have been developed. Bertrand[1] has shown how to evaluate a simple point in a (26,6) image by evaluating a small set of template matches on the neighborhood of the point under test. The use of lookup tables coupled with a variety of decompositions has been considered by several investigators[14,5,12,13]. The methods suggested in [12] and the methods described and evaluated in [5] appear to be the fastest lookup table approaches, but these methods require a good bit of storage. Reducing neighborhood size can reduce the support size for topological functions so alternative image definitions with smaller neighborhoods may be desirable to reduce computation time or storage in 3D image processing. Little attention has been given to the computational side of this issue since the early work of Toriwaki et al.[13] and Hafford and Preston.[4]

Now we define key topological functions on the FCC grid. If we wish to use a (12,12) image we find that the support of a computation for simpleness at point v is larger than $N_{12}^*(v)$. Consider the example in Figure 3 where all voxels are 0's except $v = v_3 = v_4 = r = 1$. Observe that $NC1_{12}(v)$=2 so that removal of v from the foreground leaves v_3 and v_4 unconnected in $N_{12}^*(v)$. But, if voxel $r = 1$ (r is a 12-neighbor of both v_3 and v_4) then v_3 and v_4 remain 12-connected in the foreground after removal of v. Further, no new hole or cavity is created so that v is simple in this case. Whereas if $r = 0$ topology is not preserved by removal of v from the foreground and v is not simple in this case. So r must belong to the support of the function which computes simpleness in a (12,12) image. It can be shown that the 18-neighborhood of the point under test is a necessary and sufficient support for computing simpleness in a (12,12) image. Thus, there may be no computational advantage of the (12,12) image definition as compared to the (18,12) case; and in this note we will focus on the (18,12) image definition. It can be shown in this case that a point, v, is simple iff both of the following conditions hold:

(1) $NC1_{18}(v) = 1$ and

(2) $NC0_{12}(v) = 1$.

The functions which compute $NC1_{18}(v) = 1$ and $NC0_{12}(v) = 1$ can be useful separately so we will consider the realization of three boolean functions, taking values $\{0, 1\}$, where v is the voxel under test:

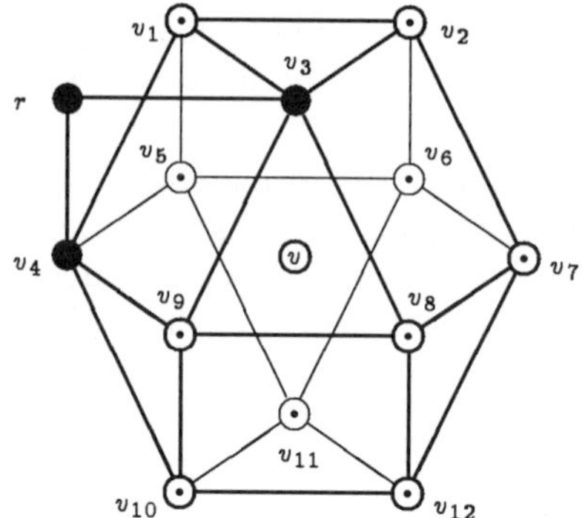

Figure 3: Illustration that the required support for a simple point computation in a (12, 12) image includes points outside the 12-neighborhood. (Note that r is v_{13} in the 18-neighborhood of v.)

(1) $\mathbf{Simple(18,12)}(v) = 1$ iff v is simple in an (18,12) image;
(2) $\mathbf{NC1_{18}}(v) = 1$ iff $NC1_{18}(v) = 1$;
(3) $\mathbf{NC0_{12}}(v) = 1$ iff $NC0_{12}(v) = 1$.

Boldface distinguishes the boolean functions from the conditions defining them. These functions are translation invariant so v is omitted where not needed.

4 Efficient Computations for FCC-based Topological Functions

Toriwaki et al.[13] gave a boolean function for computation of $\Delta\mathcal{G}_{18}^{(18,12)}(v)$. They also provided a decision tree for effectively determining $\mathbf{Simple(18,12)}$, which is based on the analyses of Euler characteristic, enumeration of $N1_{12}(v)$, and possible isolated small components of 1's. McAndrew et al. [11] have pursued a general study of FCC-based and related multidimensional image definitions. We have applied two table-based methodologies to the computation of the three FCC-based functions for (18,12) images and we sketch our methods next.

The first methodology is partially an extension of the suggestions of Saha and Chaudhuri [12] for (26,6) images to the (18,12) case and is most directly an extension of our previous merging of their suggestions with our table-based realization methods. [5] It is evident that a function lookup table with size of 2^{12} bits is sufficient to determine $\mathbf{NC0_{12}}(v)$. For $\mathbf{NC1_{18}}(v)$ our approach is conceptually similar to the $N1_6(v) = 0$ case of the methodology reported by Saha and Chaudhuri[12]. Suppose that there are all 0's among the 12-neighbors of v, then $NC1_{18}(v)$ will be equal to the number of 1's among the $18\setminus12$–

neighbors of v. Otherwise, we compute $NC1_{12}^{18}(v) = 1$, which is $NC1_{18}(v) = 1$ but assuming all $18 \setminus 12$–neighbors of v are 0's. Then $\mathbf{NC1_{18}}(v) = 1$ only if $NC1_{12}^{18}(v) = 1$ and there are no isolated $18 \setminus 12$–neighbors of v, e.g. $v_{18} = 1$ and $v_8 = v_9 = v_{10} = v_{12} = 0$. Therefore, a function lookup table which contains the resulting function for $NC1_{12}^{18}(v) = 1$, $\mathbf{NC0_{12}}(v)$, and information about possible formation of isolated $18 \setminus 12$–neighbors will be sufficient to identify all three topological functions.

First, we create a function lookup table, named $I_W[\bullet]$, composed of 8-bit bytes with one entry for each distinct pattern of 12-neighbors of arbitrary voxel, v. (i.e. $I_W[\bullet]$ is of size 4096×8 bits) The bits of each byte are defined as follows :

bit 7 (msb)	0, if $NC1_{12}^{18}(v) = 1$; 1, otherwise.
bit 6	1, if $NC0_{12}(v) = 1$; 0, otherwise.
bit 5	1, if $v_8 = v_9 = v_{10} = v_{12} = 0$; 0, otherwise.
bit 4	1, if $v_6 = v_7 = v_{11} = v_{12} = 0$; 0, otherwise.
bit 3	1, if $v_4 = v_5 = v_{10} = v_{11} = 0$; 0, otherwise.
bit 2	1, if $v_2 = v_3 = v_7 = v_8 = 0$; 0, otherwise.
bit 1	1, if $v_1 = v_2 = v_5 = v_6 = 0$; 0, otherwise.
bit 0 (lsb)	1, if $v_1 = v_3 = v_4 = v_9 = 0$; 0, otherwise.

Then the following procedure gives the three desired functions which take boolean values $\{0, 1\}$.

Method 1: Computing the 3 Topological Functions at Voxel v

Step 1: Form the 12-bit unsigned integer, *index*, using the 12 binary values of 12-neighbors of v in some designated order;

Step 2: Perform the following procedure

if (*index* = 0) **then**

$\mathbf{NC1_{18}}(v) = 1$, iff $(v_{13} + v_{14} + v_{15} + v_{16} + v_{17} + v_{18}) = 1$;

$\mathbf{NC0_{12}}(v) = 1$.

else

Form a byte, I_{18}, whose bits 0~5 are the values $v_{13}, v_{14}, v_{15}, v_{16}, v_{17}, v_{18}$, respectively, and bit 6 = 0, bit 7 =1;

$\mathbf{NC1_{18}}(v) = 1$, iff $I_W[index]$ AND I_{18})=0;

$\mathbf{NC0_{12}}(v) = 1$, iff bit 6 of $I_W[index]$ is 1.

endif

Simple(18, 12)$(v) = 1$, iff $\mathbf{NC1_{18}}(v) = \mathbf{NC0_{12}}(v) = 1$.

In our second methodology we use a mix of the ideas from [5] where the fastest 26-6 realizations are found. First, we form an index on the set of voxels in v's horizontal plane, i.e. $\{v_4, v_5, v_6, v_7, v_8, v_9\}$ as defined in Figure 2. With this index we jump through a table of 64 pointers to code which handles each of the special cases which coincides with the given index. Based on symmetries in $N_{12}(v)$ we have to do analyses on 13 special cases. For the realization of each of the 13 classes we use one of three basic approaches and we give examples of each next. For some cases the functions are derivable directly with little or no additional checking. E.g., when $v_4 = v_5 = v_6 = v_8 = v_9 = 1$ and $v_7 = 0$ $\mathbf{NC1_{18}}(v)$ is 1 regardless of values taken by other voxels in $N_{18}(v)$. Also, $\mathbf{Simple(18,12)}(v) = 1$ iff $\mathbf{NC0_{12}}(v) = 1$. A possible realization of $\mathbf{NC0_{12}}(v)$ for this case exemplifies the second basic realization approach. Here the function result is a somewhat complicated function of the other six 12-neighbors. So we form an index on the two voxels, $\{v_2, v_{12}\}$, and then jump through a table of 4 pointers to code which realizes the simpler cases where eight neighbors of v are specified. E.g. for the $v_2 = v_{12} = 0$ subcase $\mathbf{NC0_{12}} = 1$ immediately; but for $v_2 = 0$, $v_{12} = 1$ $\mathbf{NC0_{12}} = 1$ only if $v_{10} = v_{11} = 1$. The goal in choosing these decompositions is to reduce the average number of neighbors of v which must be examined before reaching a decision. In a large number of cases for $\mathbf{NC1_{18}}$ and $\mathbf{Simple(18,12)}$ the decomposition of the functions in this manner is still rather complicated and recourse is taken to the third basic realization approach. Consider the case when $v_4 = 1$ and $v_5 = v_6 = v_7 = v_8 = v_9 = 0$. Partition the remaining $18 \setminus 12$–neighbors of v into an "upper plane" set $\{v_1, v_2, v_3, v_{13}, v_{14}, v_{15}\}$ and a "lower plane" set $\{v_{10}, v_{11}, v_{12}, v_{16}, v_{17}, v_{18}\}$. For the upper (lower) plane compute and store in a table the boolean function T_U (T_L) which is 0 iff the plane contains an 18-component of 1's which is not 18-connected to v_4. Then $\mathbf{NC1_{18}}(v) = 1$ iff $T_U = T_L = 1$. Using symmetries in this example one table suffices in the realization and the table is of size 32 bits, since v_{13} and v_{16} do not affect the result, i.e. there are only 5 voxels in each plane which need be considered. This realization approach tends to save on storage versus the second approach, but tends to be somewhat slower as the average number of voxel accesses is higher. Substantial use of this approach is made in our realizations of $\mathbf{NC1_{18}}$ and $\mathbf{Simple(18,12)}$.

5 Results and Conclusions

The new methods have been coded in GNU C and executed on SUN Sparc-10 workstations. The correctness of the approaches is verified by comparison with the fundamental component searching method using tree search and by

Table 1: Storage and average time for computations of topological functions.

Methods (18,12) Cases	Topological Functions Computed Simple(18, 12)	$NC1_{18}$	$NC0_{12}$	Genus	Storage (bytes)	Time (μs)
Toriwaki et al.[13]	√			√	6,588	9.57
Method 1	√	√	√		5,156	2.78
Method 2-Simple	√				38,648	1.87
Method 2-NC1		√			18,340	1.68
Method 2-NC0			√		23,660	1.53
(26,6) Cases	Simple(26, 6)	$NC1_{26}$	$NC0^{6}_{18}$	Genus		
TBL26-Simple[5]	√				48,928	1.47
TBL26-NC1[5]		√			38,764	1.38
TBL26-NC0[5]			√		28,392	1.45
Bertrand[1]	√	√	√		12,320	15.23

cross comparison to other realizations of other methods. For time and storage comparison we have realized the methods of Bertrand[1] and Toriwaki[13] within our milieu. We also compare to our best previously derived results for 26-6 images. [5] The comparative time and storage results are reported in Table 1. The reported time is the average user time used per evocation and the storage is the number of bytes used in the module realizing the given function(s). The check marks indicate which functions are realized in the module with the given time and storage complexities.

The new Method 1 gives all 3 functions with excellent storage complexity (the best yet reported) with good time results as compared to earlier FCC-based approaches. Using Method 2 realizations on individual functions we achieve a substantial decrease in time cost at the cost of substantially higher storage. We have not yet realized the combination of all 3 functions with our methods which (when done) should produce a combined storage less than the sum of the storage for the 3 reported realizations. Both new methods produce lower storage requirements than for comparable 26-6 realizations. But, time costs achieved with the current realizations are not as good as those in comparable 26-6 realizations. Our preliminary conclusion is that relatively fast FCC-based topological function realizations are available which have substantially lower storage than for comparable 26-6 realizations.

Acknowledgments

The authors enjoyed the thoughtful suggestions of the referees which improved the clarity of the presentation.

References

1. G. Bertrand, "On the computation of topological numbers," *Proc. 4th Conf. on Discrete Geom. for Comp. Imagery*, pp. 137-146, 1994.
2. G. Bertrand and G. Malandain, "A new characterization of three-dimensional simple points," *Patt. Recog. Lett.*, Vol. 15, pp. 169-175, 1994.
3. J.H. Conway and N.J.A. Sloane, *Sphere Packings, Lattices and Groups*, Springer-Verlag, Berlin, 1993, 2nd Ed.
4. K.J. Hafford and K. Preston, "Three-dimensional skeletonization of elongated solids," *Comp. Vision, Graphics, and Im. Proc.*, Vol. 27, pp. 78-91, 1984.
5. R.W. Hall and C.-Y. Hu, "Time-efficient computation of 3D topological functions," *Patt. Recog. Lett.*, Vol. 17, pp. 1017-1033,1996.
6. R.W. Hall and Ş. Küçük, "Parallel 3D shrinking algorithms using subfields notions," In *Proc. 11th IAPR Intl. Conf. on Patt. Recog.*, Vol. I, pp. 395-398, The Hague, The Netherlands, 1992.
7. T.Y. Kong, "On topology preservation in 2-D and 3-D thinning," *Int. J. of Patt. Recog. and Art. Intell.*, Vol. 9, pp.813-844, Oct. 1995.
8. T.Y. Kong and A. Rosenfeld, "Digital topology : introduction and survey," *Comp. Vision, Graphics Im. Proc.*, Vol. 48, pp.357-393, 1989.
9. S. Lobregt, P.W. Verbeek, and F.C.A. Groen, "Three-Dimensional skeletonization : Principle and algorithm," *IEEE Trans. Patt. Anal. Mach. Intell.*, PAMI-2, pp.75-77, 1980.
10. C.M. Ma, "On topology preservation in 3D thinning," *CVGIP: Image Understanding*, Vol. 59-3, pp.328-339, 1994.
11. A. McAndrew and C. Osborne, "Metrics on the face-centered cubic lattice," In *Vision Geometry*, Melter and Wu, eds., SPIE, Vol. 1832, pp. 49-60, Boston, MA, 1992.
12. Saha, P.K. and B.B. Chaudhuri, "Detection of 3-D simple points for topology preserving transformations with application to thinning," *IEEE Trans. Patt. Anal. Mach. Intell.*, PAMI-16, pp. 1028-1032, 1994.
13. J.-I. Toriwaki, S. Yokoi, T. Yonekura, and T. Fukumura, "Topological properties and topology-preserving transformation of a three-dimensional binary picture," *Proc. 6th IAPR Intl. Conf. on Patt. Recog.*, pp. 414-419, Munich, 1982.
14. Verbeek, P.W., F.C.A. Groen, H.A. Vrooman and B.J.H. Verwer (1985). Speeding up 3D binary image processing for robot vision. *SPIE Computer Vision for Robots*, SPIE Vol. 595, 233-238, Cannes, France.

PROPERTIES OF ZERNIKE AND LEGENDRE MOMENTS OF GRAY-SCALE IMAGES

TH.M. HUPKENS

Royal Netherlands Naval College, P.O. Box 10000, 1780 CA Den Helder, The Netherlands

Key words: *pattern recognition, image reconstruction*

In this paper several properties of Zernike and Legendre moments are discussed. Zernike and Legendre moments are very useful in pattern recognition, because of their ability to characterize digital images by only a few numbers. From a limited number of moments, an image can be constructed, which more or less resembles the original. It is shown that the reconstruction error for Zernike and Legendre moments, when using the same number of moments, is about the same. It is also shown that low-order Legendre and Zernike moments are very insensitive to noise.

1. Introduction

In order to make possible the automatic recognition of objects which are represented in digital images, it is feasible to store characteristic features of all applicable objects in a data base. We want to have as little features per object as possible, so these features should be very characteristic of the shape of the objects. In many cases so-called moments are used for this purpose. A big advantage of moments is that the complete image is used. Thus, the result is not very sensitive to small deviations or noise. If orthogonal moments are used, it becomes possible to reconstruct the original image from these moments. This property makes it easy to compare the 'sharpness' of several kinds of moments. It has been reported by Teh and Chin [2] that Zernike moments are better suited for characterizing objects than Legendre moments are, however this was tested for silhouettes only. Since Legendre moments, like Zernike moments, are not particularly well suited for silhouettes, the results might be different for gray-scale images.

2. Theory

2 a. Zernike moments

The Zernike polynomials V_{nk} ($n \geq 0$, $|k| \leq n$, $n - k$ even), are a complete set of orthogonal functions on the unit disk $r \leq 1$:

$$V_{nk}(r,\varphi) = R_{nk}(r)e^{ik\varphi}, \tag{1}$$

with

$$R_{nk}(r) = \sum_{s=0}^{\frac{n-|k|}{2}} (-1)^s \frac{(n-s)!}{s!(\frac{1}{2}(n+|k|)-s)!(\frac{1}{2}(n-|k|)-s)!} r^{n-2s} \qquad (2)$$

The Zernike functions satisfy the relation

$$\int_0^{2\pi}\int_0^1 V_{nl}^*(r,\theta)V_{m,k}(r,\theta)rdrd\theta = \frac{\pi}{n+1}\delta_{nm}\delta_{lk} \qquad (3)$$

A Zernike moment of *order* n and *repetition* k is defined as

$$A_{nk} = \frac{n+1}{\pi} \iint_{x^2+y^2 \leq 1} f(x,y)V^*{}_{nk}(x,y)dxdy \qquad (4)$$

Since $A_{n,-k} = A_{nk}^*$, we do not actually have to calculate Zernike moments with $k < 0$. However, the number of features is still equal to the number of moments defined by Eq. 1, because for $k > 0$, we have to store both the real and the imaginary part of the complex Zernike moments. It is more convenient to write the Zernike moments as a summation of geometrical moments M_{pq} (for $k >= 0$):

$$A_{nk} = \frac{n+1}{\pi} \sum_{\substack{p=k \\ n-p\ even}}^{n} \sum_{j=0}^{\frac{1}{2}(p-k)} \sum_{m=0}^{k} (-i)^k \binom{\frac{1}{2}(p-k)}{j} \binom{k}{m} B_{nkp} M_{p-2j-k+m,2j+k-m}$$

where (5)

$$B_{nkp} = (-1)^{\frac{1}{2}(n-p)} \frac{\left[\frac{1}{2}(n+p)\right]!}{\left[\frac{1}{2}(n-p)\right]!\left[\frac{1}{2}(k+p)\right]!\left[\frac{1}{2}(p-k)\right]!}$$

Note that Eq. 5 is essentially the same as the ‘closed Cartesian representation’ presented by Carpio and Malacara [4].

The partially reconstructed image is obtained by

$$\tilde{f}(x,y) = \sum_{n=0}^{\text{maximum order}} \sum_{k} A_{nk} V_{nk}(x,y) \qquad (6)$$

2 b. Legendre moments

A Legendre moment of order p + q for a two-dimensional continuous function *f(x, y)* is defined by

$$L_{pq} = (p+\tfrac{1}{2})(q+\tfrac{1}{2}) \int_{|x|\le 1} \int_{|y|\le 1} f(x,y) P_p(x) P_q(y)\,dx\,dy \tag{7}$$

For a two-dimensional digital image we have

$$L_{pq} = (p+\tfrac{1}{2})(q+\tfrac{1}{2}) \sum_i \sum_j f(x_i, y_j) \iint_{pixel\,(i,j)} P_p(x) P_q(y)\,dx\,dy \tag{8}$$

where the image is scaled to fit in the square $|x| \le 1$, $|y| \le 1$.
It is sometimes suggested [14] that the double integral in Eq. 8 should be calculated by numerical integration, but this method is very slow. It is much simpler to integrate the Legendre polynomials analytically. Suppose the primitive of $P_n(x)$ is the polynomial (of degree n+1) $H_n(x)$. The integral of a Legendre polynomial is:

$$\int P_n(x)\,dx = \frac{1}{n+1}\left[x P_n(x) - P_{n-1}(x)\right] + C \overset{\text{by definition}}{=} H_n(x) + C \tag{9}$$

This integral can be calculated by using the well-known recurrence relation for the two Legendre polynomials $P_n(x)$ and $P_{n-1}(x)$, but it is more convenient to derive a recurrence relation for the H-polynomials. We find:

$$\begin{aligned} &H_0(x) = x \\ &H_1(x) = \tfrac{1}{2}(x^2 - 1) \\ &(n+2) H_{n+1}(x) = x(2n+1) H_n(x) - (n-1) H_{n-1}(x) \end{aligned} \tag{10}$$

We now can rewrite Eq. 8:

$$L_{pq} = (p+\tfrac{1}{2})(q+\tfrac{1}{2}) \cdot$$

$$\sum_i \sum_j f(x_i, y_i)[H_p(x_i + \tfrac{1}{2}\Delta x) - H_p(x_i - \tfrac{1}{2}\Delta x)][H_q(y_j + \tfrac{1}{2}\Delta y) - H_q(y_j - \tfrac{1}{2}\Delta y)] \tag{11}$$

Since H_q is symmetrical for odd q and antisymmetrical for even q, only quarter of the polynomials have to be calculated.

A partially reconstructed image is obtained by

$$\tilde{f}(x,y) \approx \sum_{j=0}^{Max} \sum_{k=0}^{Max} L_{jk} P_j(x) P_k(y), \tag{12}$$

where Max is an arbitrarily chosen upper limit. If this series is truncated after only a few terms the global shape of the intensity function will be recovered. If more terms are used, more details of this function will be obtained.

3. Invariant features from Zernike moments

General methods to derive invariants from Zernike moments are presented in reference 10. It is obvious that the *modulus* of a Zernike moment is invariant for rotation about the Z-axis. Furthermore the real and imaginary part vary with the cosine and sine of k times the rotation angle. For high-resolution images, aliasing effects play only a minor role. This is shown in Fig. 1, where an overview of all Zernike moments of order 6 as a function of rotation angle is presented. The original image was rotated by a matrix multiplication over the indicated angle. Due to the high resolution (128 × 128) of the original image, aliasing effects hardly influence the results.

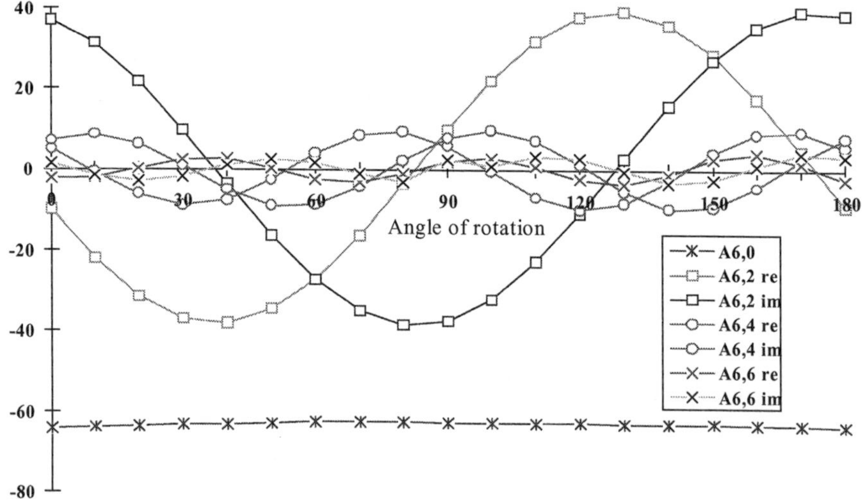

Fig. 1: Real and imaginary part of Zernike moments of order 6, calculated for a real image of 125 × 125 pixels.

It is sometimes suggested that scale invariance can be achieved by normalizing *f(x, y)* by using geometrical moments (see 8, 11, 12). This is only true, however, if *f(x, y)* is zero outside the unit circle *after* scaling. In practice this will not always be the case. If -on the other hand- the object described by *f(x, y)* becomes very small after scaling, many high order Zernike moments are necessary to describe the details accurately. In general one cannot know beforehand what will be the result of a scaling based on the geometrical moments, so this method is not very well suited for automatic recognition. It is easy to derive size-invariant features from Zernike moments, though, for instance $\mathrm{Im}(A_{nk})/\mathrm{Re}(A_{nk})$ is invariant under scale transformations. Instead of A_{nn} one could use $A_{nn}' = \dfrac{A_{nn}}{A_{00}^{\frac{1}{2}(n+2)}}$, (13)

which is scale-invariant. This is illustrated in Figure 2. It should be noted that the results presented here were obtained for a rather extreme situation. In the smallest image used, only about 113 pixels out of 512 × 512 pixels are not black. In practice it is often possible to do a rough scaling on the basis of other clues, such that the edges of the image are already close to the unit circle. If so, the effect of the normalization should be very small.

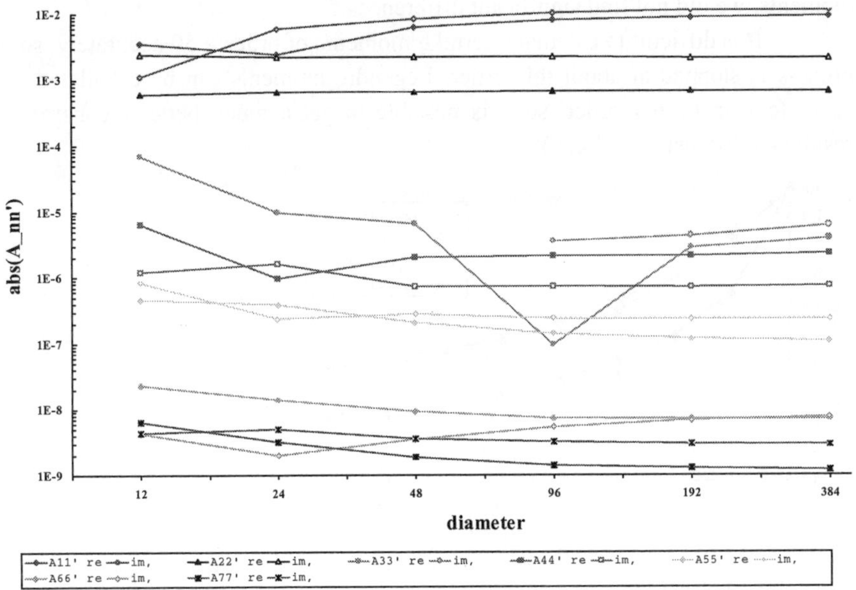

Fig. 2: The horizontal axis represents the diameter (number of pixels) of a circular image of a human face (after scaling), which was inserted at the center of a black 512 × 512 square.

4. Reconstruction

The quality of the Zernike and Legendre moments was evaluated by visual inspection of the partially reconstructed images and by comparing the reconstruction error ε.

The reconstruction error is defined by $\varepsilon = \sqrt{\dfrac{\sum_x \sum_y \left(\tilde{f}(x,y) - f(x,y)\right)^2}{\sum_x \sum_y f(x,y)^2}}$.

It should be noted that this measure not at all corresponds to the subjective impression of the reconstruction quality. The relative reconstruction error is defined as $\varepsilon/\varepsilon_0$, where ε_0 is the reconstruction error when only the zero-order moment is used. Typical results for two gray-scale images are shown in Figs 3 and 4. Each Zernike moment was counted as two independent features (real and imaginary part), except for the moments A_{n0}, which are always real. Although there sometimes were minor differences between the Zernike and Legendre moments, we did not find significant differences.

It is difficult to calculate Zernike moments of order > 50 accurately, so the process is stopped at about this order. Legendre moments can be calculated very accurately up to any order, so it is possible to get a much better reconstruction result (see for instance Fig. 6).

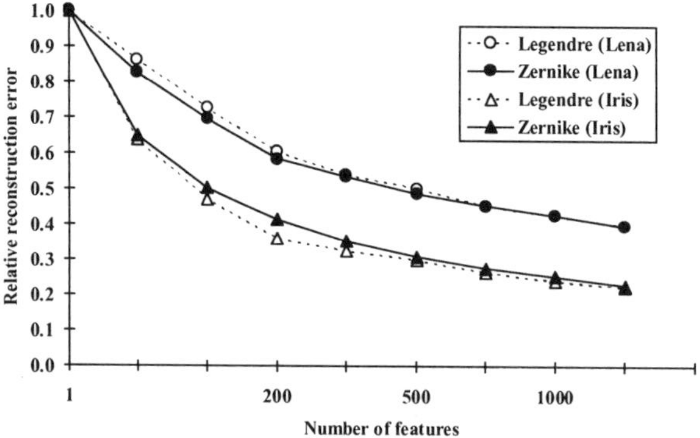

Fig. 3: Reconstruction error as a function of the number of features used, for Lena (64 × 64) and Iris (124 × 124), see also Fig. 4.

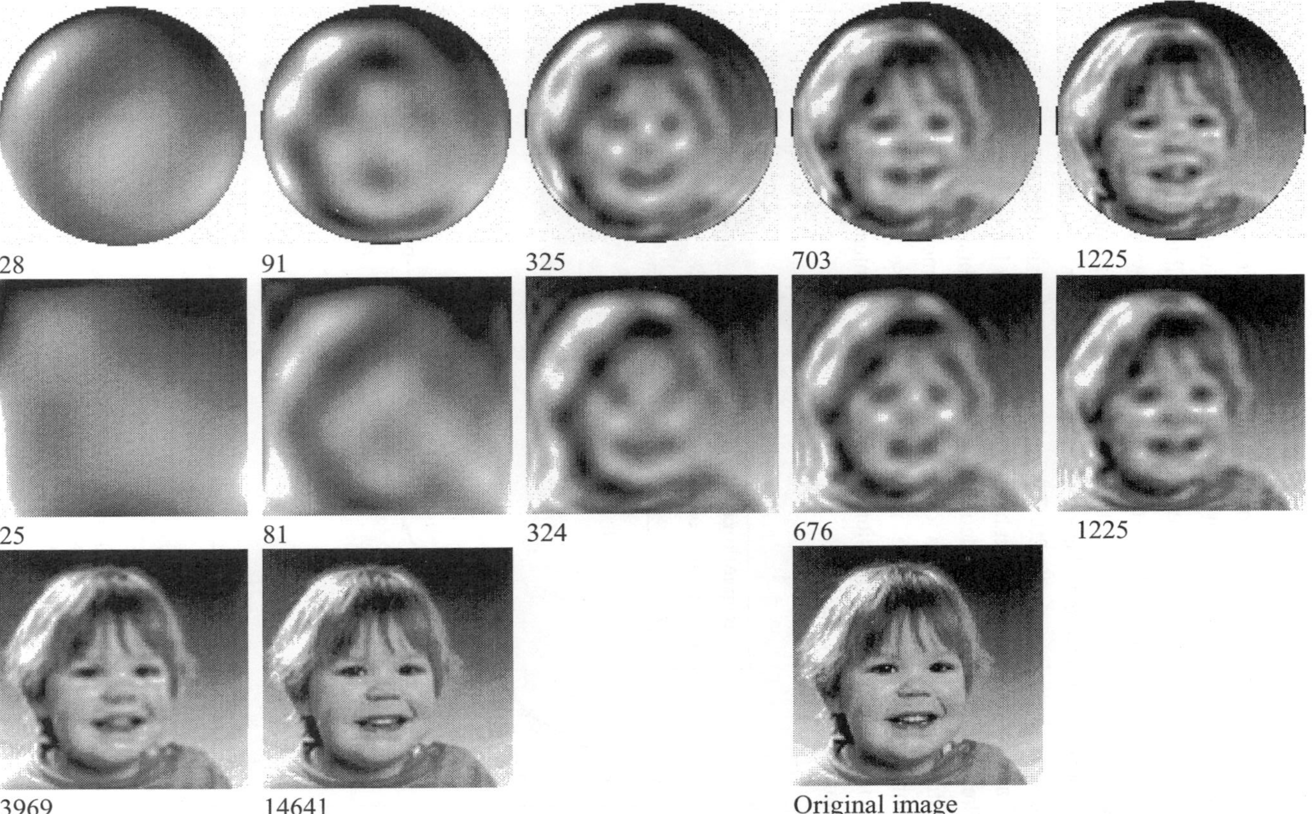

Fig. 4: Partially reconstructed images from Zernike moments (upper row) or Legendre moments (lower 2 rows). The total number of moments used is shown below the images.

5. Noisy gray-scale images

Gaussian noise was added to the original image. In order to simulate a few realistic situations, two kinds of gaussian noise were used, one with a constant standard deviation, the other with a standard deviation proportional to the square root of the original intensity of each pixel. An example of an image with added noise is shown in Fig. 5. After adding noise, the pixel intensities were rounded to integer values and negative values were replaced by zeros. A value of $\sigma = 20$ means that 67% of the noise is in the range -20..20. Typical results of the simulations are shown in Figs 5 and 6. The figures shown here, were obtained with Legendre moments, with Zernike moments almost identical results were obtained. Note that the reconstruction error does not go to zero if the number of moments used approaches the number of pixels in the image. This is because the digital image is approximated by a two-dimensional step function (the intensity is assumed to be constant over a pixel), see Eq. 8.

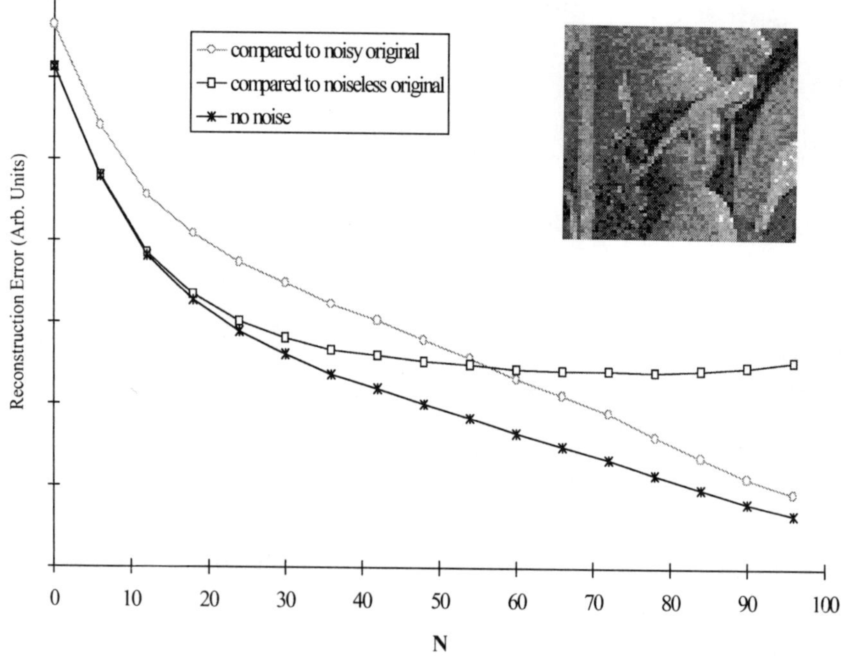

Fig. 5: Reconstruction error for a digital image of Lena, with added gaussian noise ($\sigma = 20$). Inset: Noisy Lena (64×64, 256 shades of gray). N is the highest degree of any Legendre polynomial used in the calculations; the corresponding number of moments is $(N + 1)^2$.

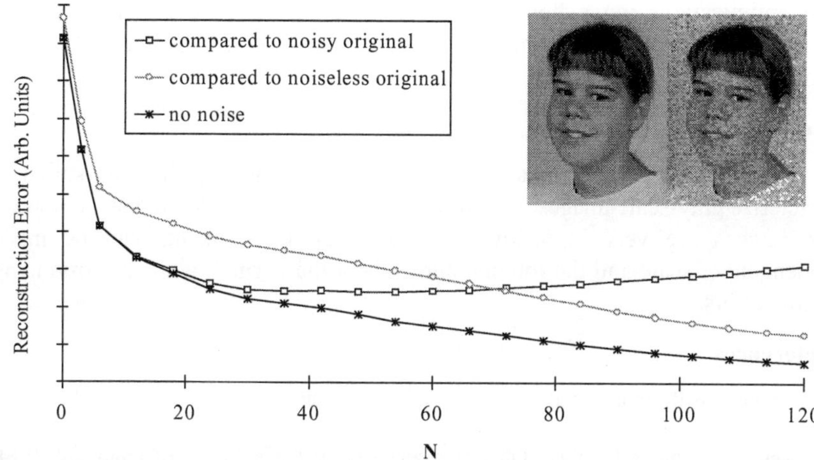

Fig. 6: Reconstruction error for a digital image of Irene, with added gaussian noise (σ proportional to the square root of the intensity). $(N + 1)^2$ Legendre moments were used. The original image and the original with added noise is shown in the inset.

With several other images and different noise levels, comparable results were obtained. It can be concluded that up to rather high orders, the reconstructed image resembles the noiseless image more than it resembles the noisy image. If the maximum order is not too high, there is hardly any difference between an image reconstructed using moments from the original with added noise, or from the noiseless original. Only if moments up to a high order are used, the reconstructed noisy image approximates the noisy original. If high resolution images are used, the noiseless original is even better approximated. The observed behavior can be explained as follows: all original images are rather smooth, so the intensity function can be fairly well approximated by a polynomial of a low degree. If noise is added, every modified pixel corresponds to a step in the intensity function, which can only be described by polynomials of a high degree.

6. Calculation speed

In many applications of Zernike or Legendre moments the calculation speed is important. The time needed to calculate Zernike moments can be reduced drastically by using the following recurrence relations:

$$\begin{aligned} \cos k\varphi &= 2\cos\varphi\,\cos(k-1)\varphi - \cos(k-2)\varphi \\ \sin k\varphi &= 2\cos\varphi\,\sin(k-1)\varphi - \sin(k-2)\varphi \quad , \\ r^{n} &= r.\,r^{n-1} \end{aligned} \tag{14}$$

For the calculation of Legendre moments the fast recurrence relation of Eq. 10 can be used. Almost a factor of four can be gained if (anti) symmetry is used. With these optimizations, on a home computer (Pentium 120), several hundreds of moments (or reconstruction from these moments) can by calculated for a 512 x 512 (!) image in only a few seconds.

7. Conclusion

It is shown that both Zernike and Legendre moments are equally well suited to characterize gray-scale images. Low order Zernike and Legendre moments of gray-scale images are very insensitive to noise. Zernike moments can be made independent of scale and the rotation angle about the normal, without introducing extreme errors.

8 References

[1] Teague, M.R. 'Image analysis via the general theory of moments', J. Opt. Soc. Am, Vol 70 (1980) 920

[2] Teh, C-H and R.T. Chin, 'On image analysis by the methods of moments', IEEE Transactions on pattern recognition and machine intelligence', Vol 4 (1988) 496

[3] Prokop, R.J. and A.P. Reeves, 'A Survey of Moment-Based Techniques for Unoccluded Object Representation and Recognition', CVPIG: Graphical Models and Image Processing, Vol 54 (1992) 438

[4] Carpio, M and D. Malacara, 'Closed cartesian representation of the Zernike polynomials', Optics Communications Vol 111 (1994) 514

[5] Prokop, R.J. and A.P. Reeves. 'A Survey of Moment-Based Techniques for Unoccluded Object Representation and Recognition', CVGIP: Graphical Models and Image Processing, Vol 54-5 (1992) 438

[6] Malacara, D, J.M. Carpio-Valadéz and J.J. Sánchez-Mondragón, 'Wavefront fitting with discrete orthogonal polynomials in a unit radius circle', Optical Engineering, Vol 29 (1990) 672

[7] Khotanzad A. and Y.H. Hong, 'Invariant Image Recognition by Zernike Moments', IEEE Transactions on Pattern Analysis and Machine Intelligence, Vol 12 (1990) 489

[8] Raveendran, P. and S. Omatu, 'Performance of an Optimal Subset of Zernike Features for Pattern Classification', Information Sciences, Vol 1 (1993) 133

[9] Sheng, Y and L. Shen, 'Orthogonal Fourier-Mellin moments for invariant pattern recognition', J. Opt. Soc. Am., Volume 11 (1994) 1748

[10] Belkasim, S.O., M. Shridhar and M. Ahmadi, 'Pattern recognition with moment invariants: a comparative study and new results', Pattern Recognition 24 (1991) 1117

[11] Boyce, J.F. and W.J. Hossack, 'Moment invariants for pattern recognition', Pattern Recognition Letters 1 (1983) 451

[12] Wood, J, 'Invariant pattern recognition: a review', Pattern Recognition 29 (1996) 1-17

[13] Ghosal, S and R. Mehrothra, 'Orthogonal moment operators for subpixel edge detection', Pattern Recognition 26 (1993) 295

[14] Gilge, M. 'Coding of arbitrarily shaped image segments using moment theory', Proceedings EUSIPCO-88 Vol 2 (1988) 855

GEOMETRIC COMPLEXITY OF SPATIAL CURVES

A. IMIYA
Dept. of Information and Computer Sciences, Chiba University
1-33 Yayoi-cho, Inage-ku, 263, Chiba Japan

The Fourier descriptor provides a method for extracting globally geometrical information from line drawings. Nevertheless, classical studies on the Fourier descriptor dealt with only a curve on a plane. This paper proposes a descriptor for a spatial line figure. We also define a rotation invariant complexity measure for a spatial curves.

1 Introduction

The Fourier descriptor provides a method for extracting globally geometrical information from a line-drawing form on a plane; that is, a curve reconstructed from low-frequency components of the Fourier descriptor roughly approximates the shape of the original curve. In this paper, we propose the Fourier descriptor for spatial curves, and define an entropylike complexity measure of a spatial curve that is invariant under similarity transformation.

Several types of Fourier descriptors have been proposed. A descriptor based on the natural equation of a planar curve [1] is applicable to both open curves and loops [2]. Several authors discussed similar types of descriptors and derived similar properties. Uesaka [2] introduced an entropylike complexity measure of a planar curve by the Fourier analysis of the natural equation of a curve. Réti and Czinege [3] defined a complex measure for a normalized curve whose length is unity by The total-power of the descriptor. Arkin *et al.* [4] defined a similarity measure for polygons which is derived by piecewise straight approximation of planar loops. These previous studies have dealt only with planar line figures [5].

Several knot theorists [6 7 8 9] defined energy functionals of a knot, which is a spatial closed curve. Some [8 9] restricted their attentions to a spatial n-gon from viewpoints of practical applications to biochemistry and DNA analysis. The other [6 7] considered continuous spatial curves. The energy functions of them are based on the "Coulomb's force" caused by electric charges which are distributed on some spatial curves. These energy functions are defined for prohibiting the self crossing of a spatial curve in the deformation and conformation processes of spatial curves. Furthermore, Milnor [10] dealt with the total curvature of a knot. These treatments studied for the classification of the number of knots using local minimums of the energy distribution.

Our method defines entropy of a spatial curve as a complexity measure of spatial shapes using the Fourier transform of the total curvature of a curve. In this paper, we examine possibilities for the application of the complexity measure like entropy to the indexing of the deformation operations for spatial curves through numerical examples.

2 Fourier Descriptor for Spatial Curves

Defining the orthogonal coordinate system x-y-z in $\mathbf{R}^3$, a vector in $\mathbf{R}^3$ is expressed by $x = (x, y, z)^\top$ where $\cdot^\top$ is the transpose of a vector. The inner product of vectors is defined by $\boldsymbol{x}^\top \boldsymbol{y}$ and the Euclidean distance between $\boldsymbol{x}$ and $\boldsymbol{y}$ is denoted by $|\boldsymbol{x} - \boldsymbol{y}|$ since we use the $|\cdot|$ for the standard norm in $\mathbf{R}^3$.

Setting S to be the length of a curve, a spatial line is denoted by

$$\boldsymbol{x}(s) = (x(s),\, y(s),\, z(s))^\top, \tag{1}$$

where $x(s)$, $y(s)$, and $z(s)$ are functions on the interval $[0, S]$. Setting $\dot{\boldsymbol{x}}(s)$ to be the derivative of $\boldsymbol{x}(s)$ with respect to s, a matrix $\boldsymbol{M}$ where

$$\boldsymbol{M} = \frac{1}{S}\int_0^S \dot{\boldsymbol{x}}(s)\dot{\boldsymbol{x}}(s)^\top ds \tag{2}$$

is the moment matrix of $\dot{\boldsymbol{x}}(s)$. For $n = 1, 2, 3$, let λ_n and $\boldsymbol{u}_n$ be the eigenvaluse and the eigenvector of $\boldsymbol{M}$ such that

$$\boldsymbol{M}\boldsymbol{u}_n = \lambda_n \boldsymbol{u}_n,\ |\boldsymbol{u}_n| = 1, \tag{3}$$

and

$$\lambda_1 \geq \lambda_2 \geq \lambda_3 \geq 0. \tag{4}$$

First we consider the case when $\lambda_n \neq 0$. Setting

$$\boldsymbol{U}^\top = (\boldsymbol{u}_1, \boldsymbol{u}_2, \boldsymbol{u}_3) \tag{5}$$

and

$$\boldsymbol{T} = \begin{pmatrix} 1 & i & 0 \\ 0 & 1 & i \\ i & 0 & 1 \end{pmatrix}, \tag{6}$$

we define a real vector

$$\begin{aligned} \dot{\boldsymbol{u}}(s) &= \boldsymbol{U}\dot{\boldsymbol{x}}(s) \\ &= (\xi_1(s), \xi_2(s), \xi_3(s))\top \end{aligned} \tag{7}$$

and a complex vector

$$\begin{aligned}\dot{\boldsymbol{v}}(s) &= \boldsymbol{T}\boldsymbol{U}\dot{\boldsymbol{x}}(s) \\ &= (\zeta_1(s), \zeta_2(s), \zeta_3(s))\top. \end{aligned} \tag{8}$$

Since $|\dot{\boldsymbol{u}}(s)| = 1$, the property $|\dot{\boldsymbol{v}}(s)|^2 = 2$ holds. Moreover, setting

$$\alpha_n(s) = \frac{\dot{\zeta}_n(s)}{|\dot{\zeta}_n(s)|} \tag{9}$$

and

$$a_n(k) = \frac{1}{S}\int_0^S \alpha_n(s) e^{-i2\pi \frac{s}{S} k} ds, \tag{10}$$

we define

$$\boldsymbol{a}(k) = (a_1(k), a_2(k), a_3(k))^\top. \tag{11}$$

We call $\{\boldsymbol{a}(k)\}_{k=-\infty}^{\infty}$ the Fourier descriptor for a spatial curve $\boldsymbol{x}(s)$.

3 Comlpexity of Spatial Curves

The Fourier descriptor satisfies the relations

$$\begin{aligned}\sum_{k=-\infty}^{\infty} |a_n(k)|^2 &= \frac{1}{S}\int_0^S |\alpha_n(s)|^2 ds = 1, \end{aligned} \tag{12}$$

$$\begin{aligned}\sum_{k=-\infty}^{\infty} |\boldsymbol{a}(k)|^2 &= \sum_{k=-\infty}^{\infty}\sum_{n=1}^{3} |a_n(k)|^2 = 3. \end{aligned} \tag{13}$$

Setting $p_n(k) = |a_n(k)|^2$, for $k = 0, 1, \cdots, \pm\infty$, vector $\boldsymbol{p}(k)$ such that

$$\boldsymbol{p}(k) = (\, p_1(k),\, p_2(k), p_3(k)\,)^\top \tag{14}$$

satisfies

$$\sum_{k=-\infty}^{\infty} p_n(k) = 1, \tag{15}$$

$$\sum_{k=-\infty}^{\infty} \boldsymbol{p}(k)^\top \overline{\boldsymbol{p}(k)} = 3. \tag{16}$$

Therefore, we define the complexity of a spatial curve as

$$\Gamma = -\frac{1}{3}\sum_{k=-\infty}^{\infty} \boldsymbol{p}(k)^{\top} \log \boldsymbol{p}(k), \tag{17}$$

where

$$\log \boldsymbol{p}(k) = (\log p_1(k), \log p_2(k), \log p_3(k)\,)^{\top}. \tag{18}$$

Setting

$$\Gamma_n = -\sum_{k=-\infty}^{\infty} p_n(k) \log p_n(k), \tag{19}$$

Eq. (17) implies that Γ is the average of Γ_n. For the complexities of spatial curves, we obtain the following theorem.

[**Theorem 1**] Γ is invariant under similarity transforms.

(*Proof*) Let $\boldsymbol{R}$, $\boldsymbol{t}$, and λ to be a 3×3 orthogonal matrix, a vector of three-dimensional Euclidean space, and a nonzero real number, respectively. For a curve $\boldsymbol{x}(s)$,

$$\boldsymbol{y}(\tau) = \lambda \boldsymbol{R}\boldsymbol{x}(s) + \boldsymbol{a} \tag{20}$$

is the result of a similarity transform. For $\tau = \lambda s$, since

$$\dot{\boldsymbol{y}}(\tau) = \boldsymbol{R}\dot{\boldsymbol{x}}(s) \tag{21}$$

we obtain the relation

$$\boldsymbol{N} = \boldsymbol{R}\boldsymbol{M}\boldsymbol{R}^{\top}, \tag{22}$$

setting

$$\boldsymbol{N} = \frac{1}{T}\int_0^T \dot{\boldsymbol{y}}(\tau)\dot{\boldsymbol{y}}(\tau)^{\top} d\tau. \tag{23}$$

Equation (22) implies that

$$\boldsymbol{N}\boldsymbol{R}\boldsymbol{u}_n = \lambda_n \boldsymbol{R}\boldsymbol{u}_n, \tag{24}$$

if $\boldsymbol{M}\boldsymbol{u}_n = \lambda_n \boldsymbol{u}_n$ for $n = 1, 2, 3$. Thus, for matrix $\boldsymbol{V}$ where

$$\boldsymbol{V}^{\top} = (\boldsymbol{R}\boldsymbol{u}_1, \boldsymbol{R}\boldsymbol{u}_2, \boldsymbol{R}\boldsymbol{u}_3) \tag{25}$$

we obtain $\boldsymbol{V} = \boldsymbol{U}\boldsymbol{R}$. Next, setting

$$\dot{\boldsymbol{v}}(\tau)' = (\zeta_1(\tau)', \zeta_2(\tau)', \zeta_3(\tau)')^{\top}, \;\; \dot{\boldsymbol{v}}(\tau)' = \boldsymbol{T}\boldsymbol{V}\dot{\boldsymbol{y}}(\tau) \tag{26}$$

we define

$$\boldsymbol{w}(\tau) = (\beta_1(\tau), \beta_2(\tau), \beta_3(\tau))^{\top} \tag{27}$$

where

$$\beta_n(\tau) = \frac{\dot{\zeta}_n(\tau)'}{|\dot{\zeta}_n(\tau)'|}. \tag{28}$$

Therefore, for

$$b_n(k) = \frac{1}{T}\int_0^T \beta_n(\tau) e^{-i2\pi\frac{\tau}{T}k} d\tau \tag{29}$$

we have the equality

$$b_n(k) = a_n(k). \tag{30}$$

This equality implies that $\boldsymbol{a}(k)$ and $\boldsymbol{p}(k)$ are invariant for a similarity transform. These properties conclude that Γ is invariant for a similarity transform.
(*Q.E.D.*)

4 Complexity of Planar Curves

Since Γ is rotation invariant, we can select that $\boldsymbol{u}_1 = (1,0,0)^\top$, $\boldsymbol{u}_2 = (0,1,0)^\top$, and $\boldsymbol{u}_3 = (0,0,1)^\top$. Because this selection of an orthogonal coordinate implies that $\boldsymbol{U}$ is the 3×3 identity matrix, we obtain

$$\dot{\boldsymbol{u}}(s) = (x(s) + iy(s), y(s) + iz(s), z(s) + ix(s))^\top. \tag{31}$$

This representation of a spatial curve concludes that the complexity of a spatial curve is the average of the complexities of three planar curves $(x(s), y(s), 0)^\top$, $(0, y(s), z(s))^\top$, and $(x(s), 0, z(s))^\top$ which are orthogonal projections of $\boldsymbol{x}(s)$ on to planes perpendicular to $(0,0,1)^\top$, $(1,0,0)^\top$, and $(0,1,0)^\top$, respectively.

In this section, we consider the cases when $\lambda_3 = 0$ and $\lambda_2 = \lambda_3 = 0$. First, if $\lambda_3 = 0$, $\dot{\boldsymbol{x}}(s)$ lies on a plane spanned by $\boldsymbol{u}_1$ and $\boldsymbol{u}_2$. This implies that $\boldsymbol{x}(s)$ also lies on the same plane. Second if $\lambda_2 = \lambda_3 = 0$, $\dot{\boldsymbol{x}}(s)$ lies on a line whose direction is $\boldsymbol{u}_1$. This implies that $\boldsymbol{x}(s)$ also lies on the same line. For both cases when $\lambda_3 = 0$ and $\lambda_2 = \lambda_3 = 0$, a curve lies on a plane. Therefore, we examine relations between the Fourier descriptor for planar curves and that for spatial curves. Therefor, for planar curves, it is possible to set $\boldsymbol{u}_1 = (1,0)^\top$ and $\boldsymbol{u}_2 = (0,1)^\top$.

Setting

$$\boldsymbol{x}(s) = (x(s),\ y(s))^\top, \tag{32}$$

to be a planar curve, we define the complex expression of a planar curve as

$$\boldsymbol{z}(s) = \left(x(s) + iy(s), i(\overline{x(s) + iy(s)})\right)^\top. \tag{33}$$

Therefore, setting

$$\cos\theta(s) + i\sin\theta(s) = \frac{\dot{x}(s) + i\dot{y}(s)}{|\dot{x}(s) + i\dot{y}(s)|}, \tag{34}$$

we obtain

$$\boldsymbol{s}(s) = (e^{i\theta(s)}, e^{i\frac{\pi}{4}}e^{-i\theta(s)})^\top. \tag{35}$$

Let ε be a constant which is 1 or -1 and $0 \le \phi \le 2\pi$. A 2×2 orthogonal matrix is defined by

$$\boldsymbol{R} = \begin{pmatrix} 1 & 0 \\ 0 & \varepsilon \end{pmatrix} \begin{pmatrix} \cos\phi & -\sin\phi \\ \sin\phi & \cos\phi \end{pmatrix}. \tag{36}$$

Since

$$\boldsymbol{R}\boldsymbol{s}(s) = (e^{i\phi}e^{i\theta(s)}, \varepsilon e^{i\phi}e^{i\frac{\pi}{4}}e^{-i\theta(s)})^\top, \tag{37}$$

the absolute value of each element of $\boldsymbol{s}(s)$ is rotation invariant.

Setting Γ_n to be a complexity defined by the n-th element of $\boldsymbol{s}(s)$, the relation $\Gamma_1 = \Gamma_2$ holds. Therefore, setting

$$\Gamma = \frac{1}{2}(\Gamma_1 + \Gamma_2), \tag{38}$$

we can define a complexity of a planar curve which is equivalent to that of Uesaka's definition.

5 Discrete Method for Spatial Curves

For an appropriate positive integer M, a point set $\{\boldsymbol{x}(m)\}_{m=0}^{M-1}$ such that

$$|\boldsymbol{x}(m+1) - \boldsymbol{x}(m)| = \frac{S}{M} \tag{39}$$

approximate $\boldsymbol{x}(s)$. Setting

$$\dot{\boldsymbol{x}}(m) = \boldsymbol{x}(m+1) - \boldsymbol{x}(m), \tag{40}$$

we define the moment matrix of $\dot{\boldsymbol{x}}(m)$ as

$$\boldsymbol{M} = \frac{1}{M}\sum_{m=0}^{M-1} \dot{\boldsymbol{x}}(m)\,\dot{\boldsymbol{x}}(m)^\top. \tag{41}$$

Moreover, denoting

$$\dot{\boldsymbol{v}}(m) = \boldsymbol{T}\boldsymbol{U}^\top\dot{\boldsymbol{x}}(m),\ m = 0, 1, \cdots, M-1 \tag{42}$$

we define

$$\frac{\dot{\zeta}_i(m+1)-\dot{\zeta}_i(m)}{\dot{\zeta}_i(m)-\dot{\zeta}_i(m-1)} = r_i(m)e^{i\alpha_i(m)}. \tag{43}$$

Next, for

$$\boldsymbol{A}(m) = \operatorname{diag}\left(\alpha_1(m), \alpha_2(m), \alpha_3(m)\right)^\top, \tag{44}$$

we define

$$\boldsymbol{F}(m) = \sum_{j=0}^{m} \boldsymbol{A}(j) \tag{45}$$

and

$$\boldsymbol{H}(k,m) = \exp\left(-i2\pi\frac{km}{M}\right). \tag{46}$$

We call a set of matrix $\{\boldsymbol{G}(k)\}_{k=0}^{M-1}$ which is defined by

$$\boldsymbol{G}(k) = \sum_{m=0}^{M-1} \boldsymbol{H}(k,m)\boldsymbol{F}(m) \tag{47}$$

the Fourier transform of $\{\boldsymbol{F}(m)\}_{m=0}^{M-1}$. The relation

$$\boldsymbol{G}(m) = \frac{1}{M}\sum_{k=0}^{M-1} \overline{\boldsymbol{H}(k,m)^\top \boldsymbol{F}(k)} \tag{48}$$

shows the inverse Fourier transform. Therefore, for $k = 0, 1, \cdots, M-1$,

$$\boldsymbol{P}(k) = \overline{\boldsymbol{G}(k)}\boldsymbol{G}(k)^\top \tag{49}$$

is the power spectrum of $\{\boldsymbol{F}(m)\}_{m=0}^{M-1}$.

Setting

$$\begin{aligned}
\exp\left[i\boldsymbol{F}(m)\right] &= \operatorname{diag}\left(e^{i\theta_1(m)}, e^{i\theta_2(m)}, e^{i\theta_3(m)}\right), && (50)\\
\boldsymbol{G}(m) &= \operatorname{diag}\left(f_1(m), f_2(m), f_3(m)\right), && (51)\\
\boldsymbol{P}(m) &= \operatorname{diag}\left(|f_1(m)|^2, |f_2(m)|^2, |f_3(m)|^2\right), && (52)\\
\log \boldsymbol{P}(m) &= \operatorname{diag}\left(\log|f_1(m)|^2, \log|f_2(m)|^2, \log|f_3(m)|^2\right), && (53)
\end{aligned}$$

we obtain the formula

$$\Gamma = -\frac{1}{3}tr\left[\sum_{m=0}^{M-1} \boldsymbol{P}(m)^\top \log \boldsymbol{P}(m)\right] \tag{54}$$

for the computation of Γ from sample points.

For a set of non-uniformly distributing sample points such that

$$|\boldsymbol{x}(s_{i+1}) - \boldsymbol{x}(s_i)| \neq \text{const.}, \tag{55}$$

where

$$0 = s_0 < s_1 < s_2 < \cdots < s_M = S, \tag{56}$$

setting

$$\dot{\boldsymbol{x}}_m = \frac{|\boldsymbol{x}(s_{i+1}) - \boldsymbol{x}(s_i)|}{\boldsymbol{x}(s_{i+1}) - \boldsymbol{x}(s_i)} \tag{57}$$

and

$$\dot{\boldsymbol{x}}(s) = \begin{cases} \dot{\boldsymbol{x}}_m, & \text{if } s \in (s_m, s_{m+1}] \\ 0, & \text{otherwise,} \end{cases} \tag{58}$$

a curve

$$\boldsymbol{x}(s) = \boldsymbol{x}(0) + \int_0^s \dot{\boldsymbol{x}}(\tau) d\tau \tag{59}$$

approximates the original curve.

6 A Numerical Example

Figure 1 illustrates $\Gamma(\theta)$ for a family of curves

$$\boldsymbol{x}_\theta(s) = (\cos s \cos \theta, \sin s \sin \theta, s \sin \theta)^\top, \ 0 \leq s \leq 2\pi, \tag{60}$$

where $\theta = \frac{\pi}{180}k$ such that $k = 0, 10, 20, 30, 40, 50, 60, 70, 80, 90$. These parameters show a family of curves yield by a series of deformations.

We approximated these curves by a point set $\{\boldsymbol{x}_\theta(2\pi\frac{m}{256})\}_{m=0}^{257}$. We computed $\Gamma(\theta)$ for this family of curves. Figure 2 shows $\boldsymbol{x}_\theta(s)$ for each k. In these examples, $\boldsymbol{x}_0(s)$ and $\boldsymbol{x}_{90}(s)$ are planar shapes. For $\boldsymbol{x}_0(s)$ and $\boldsymbol{x}_{90}(s)$, the ranks of the moment matrices are 2 and 1.

Figure 1 shows that $\Gamma(\theta)$ has local minimums for curves which are simple. In figure 2, a planar circles and a spatial line segment are examples of these curves. These curves only contain the low frequency components. Entropy determines a configuration space of spacial curves for the deformation of curves. Figure 1 shows that there exist the barriers among families of curves in the configuration space. The maximum peak between pair of families of curves might indicate a complexity for obtaining a curve from the other by the deformation.

7 Conclusions

We defined a complexity measure for spatial curves which is invariant under similarity transformations. This measure characterizes the complexity of spatial shapes. The classification of knots by our complexity is further research. For the classification of knots by entropy, it is desired to examine relations between the complexity measure and the winding number of the spatial curves, which determines the number of knots.

Acknowledgments

The final manuscript was prepared while the author was visiting Department of Applied Mathematics, University of Hamburg. The author express his thanks to Professor Ulrich Eckhardt and the faculties of the department for their hospitalities. While staying in Germany, the author was supported by Telecommunications Advancement Foundation.

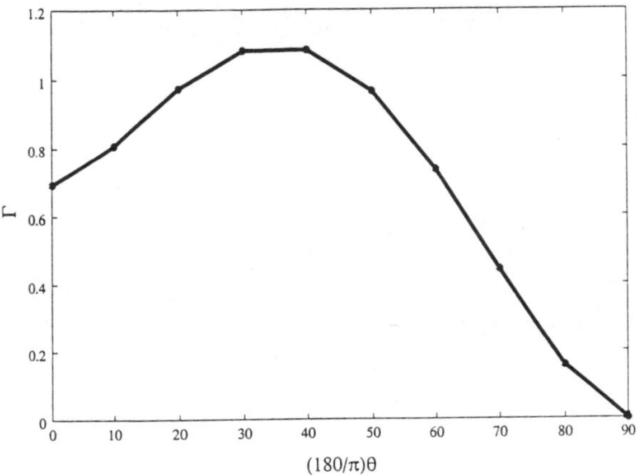

Figure 1: Γ for a family of curves.

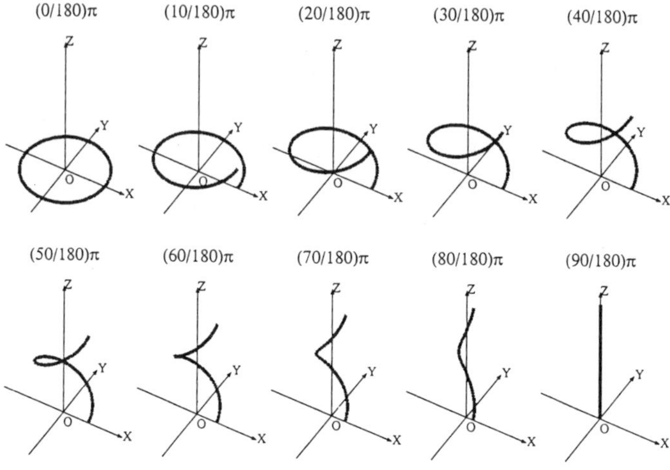

Figure 2: A family of curves.

References

1. H. W. Guggenheimer, *Differential Geometry*, (Dover, New York, 1963).
2. Y. Uesaka, *Science on form, proceedings of the first international symposium for science on form, S. Ishizaka, Y. Kato, R. Takai, and J. - I. Toriwaki eds.*, 405, (KTK Scientific Publishers, Tokyo, 1986).
3. T. Réti and I. Czinege, *Journal of Microscopy*, **156, Pt. 1**, 15, (1988).
4. E. M. Arkin, L. P. Chew, D. P. Huttenlocher, K. Kedem, and S. B. Mitchell, *IEEE Tr. PAMI*, PAMI-13, 209, (1991).
5. A. M. Bruckstein, N. Katzir, M. Lindenbaum, and M. Porat, "Differencial invariants of planar curves and recognizing partically occluded shapes," in C. Arcelli, L. P. Cordella, and G. Sanniti di Baja eds. *Visual Form-Analysis and Recognition*, 89, (Plenum Press, New York 1992).
6. J. O'hara, *Topology,* **30**, 241, (1991).
7. J. O'hara, *Topology and its Appli,* **48**, 147, (1992).
8. G. Buck and J. Simon, *Topology and its Appli.* **51**, 229, (1993).
9. G. Buck and J. Orloff, *Topology and its Appli.* **51**, 247, (1993).
10. J. W. Milnor, *Anal. Math.,* **52**, 248, (1950).

OBJECT CLASSIFICATION BASED ON CONTOURS WITH ELASTIC GRAPH MATCHING

EFTHIMIA KEFALEA
Institut für Neuroinformatik, Ruhr-Universität Bochum, 44780 Bochum, Germany

OLAF REHSE
Institut für Neuroinformatik, Ruhr-Universität Bochum, 44780 Bochum, Germany

CHRISTOPH VON DER MALSBURG
Institut für Neuroinformatik, Ruhr-Universität Bochum, 44780 Bochum, Germany
University of Southern California, Dept. of Computer Science and Section for Neurobiology, Los Angeles, CA 90089-2520, USA

We describe a system for the detection, classification and pose estimation of simple objects. The system is robust with respect to surface markings and cluttered background. Recognition is achieved by comparing the image to stored two-dimensional object views. Stored views are represented as labeled graphs and are derived automatically from images of blank object models. Graph nodes are labeled by edge information, graph edges by distance vectors in the image plane. Graphs emphasize occluding boundaries and inner object edges. These are identified by extracting local maxima in the Mallat wavelet transform of the image. Stored graphs are compared to test images by elastic matching. Our experiments demonstrate that the system is capable of fairly reliable shape classification and pose estimation of objects in natural scenes.

Keywords: computer vision, object recognition, Mallat wavelet transform.

1 Introduction

We present an approach to object classification in terms of shape. It contributes to our group's project of developing a service robot that can manipulate objects in natural environments and that can be trained by lay persons. The challenge is to reliably estimate object shape, position, size and pose as a basis for grasping, and to autonomously learn this capability from examples of new object types. During recognition the system has to be robust with respect to surface texture and to cluttered background.

Our system makes no attempt to derive three-dimensional shape directly from visual data. Previous work has shown that this is possible (see for instance [2]), although it turns out that it is difficult and requires availability of perfect contours as input [9] or visibility of certain object points (as pointed out in [12]), conditions which are rarely met in natural scenes. It is true that it would suffice to extract 3D information from clean training images, relying during later performance on stored shape information. However, we don't even attempt that here. In our robot system we plan to deduce all required shape information during grasping attempts, an approach already realized in simulation [11].

At present, we distinguish between four classes of shapes: cubes, bricks, spheres and cylinders. A particular challenge is the volume of raw data (pixel arrays), which obviously forces a great number of degrees of freedom on the system, and the great variability with which a particular object can appear in the image. We deal with the depth rotation problem by using a multiview approach based upon contour representations. This approach to object classification relies upon object-adapted representations from different viewpoints [7] and is motivated by results from psychophysics [1].

The system's knowledge about shape classes is described by model graphs, their nodes being labeled by sets of local features called *jets*. Jets represent edge information that is extracted from a small patch of an image by using the multiresolution analysis introduced by Mallat [4]. We describe the edge extraction and model graph creation of our system in sections 2.1 and 2.2, respectively.

Input images to be analysed are preprocessed in two steps. In the first step, we use the above mentioned Mallat method and in the second step a specific confidence-based algorithm introduced by us in [8]. In this way, we obtain a reliable edge interpretation of the scene. The preprocessing procedure of input images is discussed in section 2.3.

Our matching process is described in section 2.4. It is based on Elastic Graph Matching (EGM) described in[3], our present version being that described in [10]. EGM proceeds by comparing stored model graphs to the image in terms of similarities between stored jets and jets extracted from the image, adapting the location and size of model graphs until an optimum is found. EGM is a simple algorithmic caricature of Dynamic Link Maching, a neural model based on synchrony coding of feature binding and rapidly reversible synaptic plasticity [5].

We conclude with the results of our experiments in section 3 and a short discussion in section 4.

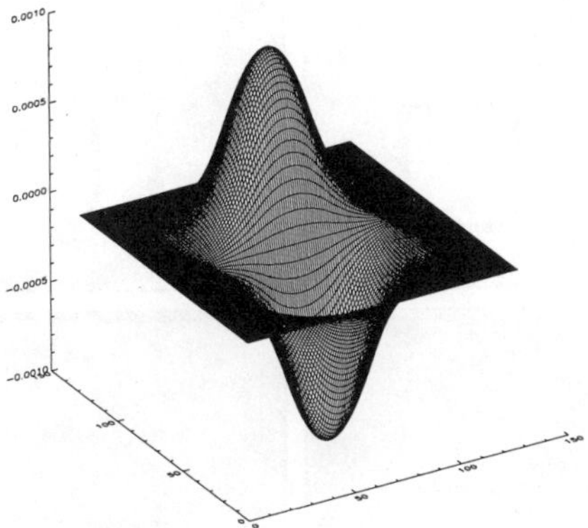

Figure 1: A two-dimensional Mallat filter in the spatial domain.

2 Description of the System

2.1 *Edge Extraction*

For the representation of objects the system employs *labeled model graphs.* A labeled graph $\mathcal{G}$ consists of N nodes positioned on contour points of the object at positions $\vec{x}_n$, $n = 1, ..., N$ and E edges between them. Edges connecting neighbouring nodes are labeled with distance vectors between node positions. Nodes are labeled with image information referring to features lying on the contour. These labels are called jets. They are derived from linear filter operations in the form of convolutions of the image $I(\vec{x})$ $(\vec{x} \in M^2; M := \{1, \ldots, r\})$ with filters $\psi_s^{(\nu)}(\vec{x})$

$$\vec{T}_{s_i}(\vec{x}) = I(\vec{x}) * \begin{pmatrix} \psi_{s_i}^{(\mathrm{h})}(\vec{x}) \\ \psi_{s_i}^{(\mathrm{v})}(\vec{x}) \end{pmatrix}$$

where $*$ represents a convolution, h and v stand for horizontal and vertical, and s_i $(s_i = s_0\, 2^i\,, i \in N)$ represents the width of a Gaussian the derivatives of which are used as filters. The absolute value $a_i(\vec{x}) = |\vec{T}_{s_i}(\vec{x})|$ and the angle $\varphi_i(\vec{x}) = \arctan \frac{T_{s_i}^{(\mathrm{h})}(\vec{x})}{T_{s_i}^{(\mathrm{v})}(\vec{x})}$ measure strength and orientation of an intensity change at scale s_i and position $\vec{x}$. Modulus Maxima positions mark local maxima of the strength a_i, representing precisely the trace of an edge. Fig. 1 shows a two-dimensional Mallat filter in the spatial domain. As we use 5 image

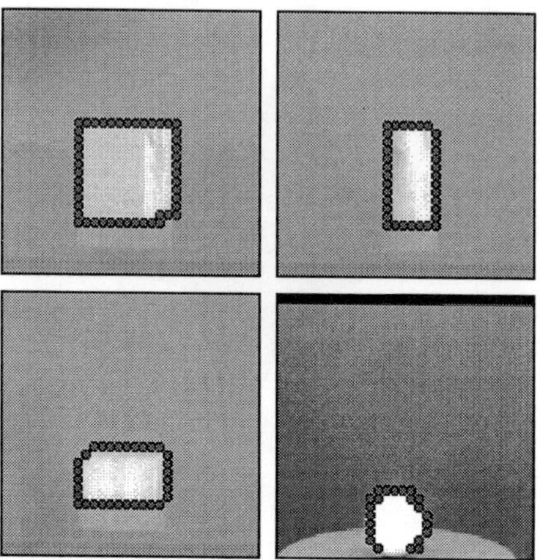

Figure 2: Views of different shape classes and their model graphs. Note that these are not test images, but examples of the system's knowledge about shape classes.

resolution levels, a feature vector coding local image information also called jet $\mathcal{J}$ is a collection of $2 \cdot 5$ values (a_i, φ_i), $i = 0, \ldots, 4$ with 0 denoting the highest frequency level.

2.2 Creation of Model Graphs

Model graphs represent the system's knowledge about shape classes. The system employs three different sizes of model graphs for each shape class. The structure of each model graph is object-adapted, its outline depending on object contours. Fig. 2 depicts model graphs superimposed on the original images.

Graphs of different views differ in geometry and local features. In order to be able to classify objects irrespective of viewpoint, we use a multiple-view approach. Due to the way we represent contour information, our system can recognize views of a shape class it has never seen before, by simply using a limited subset of all possible views. We employ a so-called *multigraph* structure. Each multigraph consists of a certain number of model graphs representing the same shape from different viewpoints. The procedure for creating such a multigraph is as follows:

We first create a discrete view sphere of an object. We then take object images by rotating the object according to Fig. 3 while having a constant object distance and varying angle θ. In $\theta-$direction we step with constant stepwidth from θ_{min} to θ_{max} taking n views. Furthermore, we instruct the system as

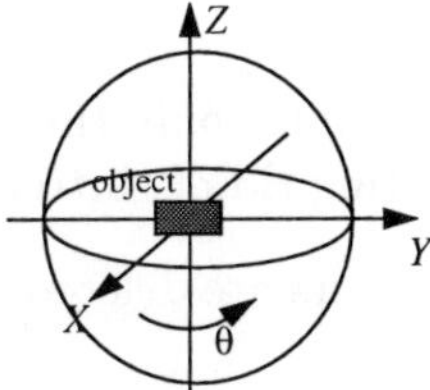

Figure 3: Sampling of the view sphere used for our multiple-view approach.

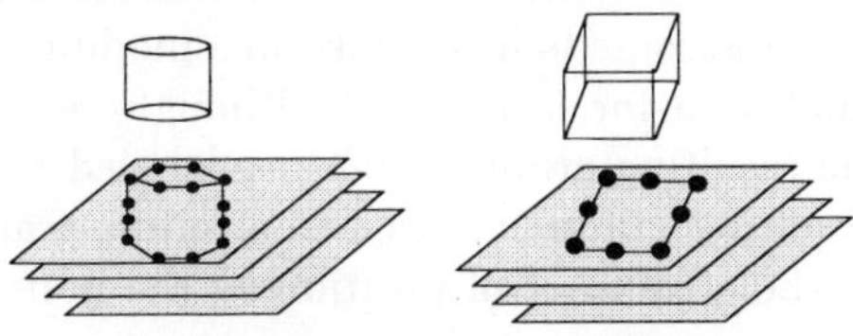

Figure 4: Each object is represented by multigraphs.

to which model graphs (representing different views) represent the same object, by simply giving identity labels to the corresponding model graphs (see Fig. 4). Since the labeling procedure is an external process, it needs no further computational time. This is an advantage of our approach in comparison to other multi-view object recognition systems, such as that described in [6].

Our gallery of models consists of simple wooden objects. We have four object classes: cubes, bricks, cylinders and spheres. Within each class there are objects of three different sizes. For each size there are 10 different views. These 30 graphs constitute the multigraph of that object. We recorded 8-bit grey-scale images of 128x128 pixels. Examples of our model gallery are given in Fig. 2.

To create a model graph a simple segmentation procedure is applied which requires a picture of the object. We transform this picture using the Mallat wavelet transform. All nodes on a square lattice of points with a spacing of 4 pixels are visited in the image. Each node has a maximum of eight neighbours. Nodes not lying on the object's contour are deleted according to the following procedure:

1. All nodes are deleted for which the average magnitude of the wavelet response at level 1 over a 4x4 square of pixels is below a given threshold value. In this way, contour nodes are favored over those positioned within the object or the background. This step leads to graphs corresponding

to connected regions.

2. Among the thus created graphs, only the one with the greatest number of nodes is kept (thus getting rid of clutter).

3. All nodes with ≥ 6 neighbours are deleted, as they presumably lie inside the object.

After these steps, all remaining nodes lie at or directly neighbouring to lines of local modulus maxima (computed at scale s_1). Some trivial precision adjustments of the nodes' positions may be fixed manually, in order to eliminate shadows or to have a node come to lie exactly on a modulus maximum. We still optimize the threshold value for each model, although we plan to eliminate this dependence. For the resulting graph, nodes are labeled with the jets (a_i, φ_i), $i = 0, \ldots, 4$. The resulting graph is stored as a model graph. This process of creating graphs has the advantage of positioning the nodes on the contour of objects.

2.3 Preprocessing of Input Images

Input test images, showing scenes which are unknown to the system, are preprocessed in two different steps. In a first step we use the multiresolutional analysis introduced by Mallat and described in section 2.1. Thus we obtain edge information, represented by the absolute values $a_i(\vec{x})$ and the orientation $\varphi_i(\vec{x})$ at different scales s_i. The filters extract all edges which represent contours, texture, shadows and noise. From these we have to separate object contours from all other edges. This is done by a "confidence-based" algorithm described in [8] by assigning a "confidence value" to every detected local edge element. Initially, this is equal to the absolute value of the filter outputs $a_i(\vec{x})$. The confidence values are then modified by a specific algorithm that emphasizes local edge elements which are part of a continuous curve. This proceeds on the assumption that object contours are the dominant structures of an image and that noise, shadows or texture edges are continuous only on a finer scale.

The algorithm which emphasizes continuous curves combines filter results of different scales by searching a counterpart at scale s_n for each edge element detected at a finer scale s_i $(i < n)$. Since there is no one-to-one mapping between edges at different scales, localization of edge information on coarser scales being imprecise, one has to search a local area for an appropriate counterpart. This is done with the help of a similarity function which measures the degree of the similarity between an edge at scale s_i and possible counterparts at scale s_n, taking in account strength and direction of the detected edges.

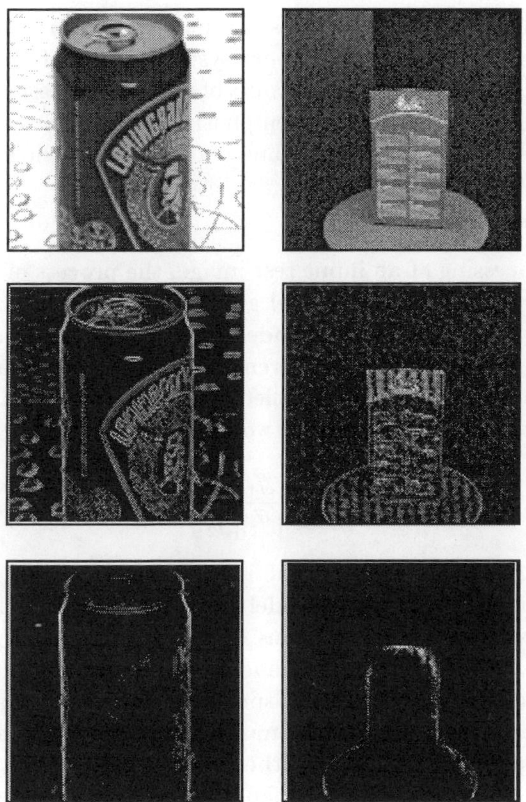

Figure 5: Preprocessing of images. First row: original grey level images. Second row: absolute value of Mallat filter results at scale s_0, interpreted as unmodified confidence values. Third row: Modified confidence values, emphazising the contours of the object, used as an input for the further processing steps. Note that the confidence values assigned to the filter results of higher scales s_i $(i > 0)$ can be modified in the same way.

The confidence values assigned to the edge elements at scale s_i are modified by multiplication with the similarity of the best fitting counterpart. By doing this, the confidence of only such local edge elements are emphazised which are also represented at a larger scale and thus belong to dominant structures in the image.

As the modified confidence values can help to obtain a more stable edge description of a scene, they are used in our system instead of the $a_i(\vec{x})$ extracted by Mallat filters. Fig. 5 shows some results of this preprocessing. It can be seen that the modified confidence values emphasize the contours as the dominant structures in the images while disturbing texture is weakened.

2.4 Elastic Graph Matching

After the preprocessing of an input test image, the process of finding optimal similarities between it and our model graphs follows. This process is called elastic graph matching (EGM). A model graph is compared node by node to jet information extracted at the current position of the input image. The function used to find similarities is called *similarity function* and is defined as the normalized scalar product of the two jets, $\vec{\mathcal{J}}_1$ and $\vec{\mathcal{J}}_2$,

$$\mathcal{T} = \frac{\vec{\mathcal{J}}_1 \cdot \vec{\mathcal{J}}_2}{|\vec{\mathcal{J}}_1||\vec{\mathcal{J}}_2|}.$$

The total similarity of the model graph is optimized by shifting and scaling it. The optimal similarity value for a model graph determines its fit to the image. In order to classify the object in terms of its shape we use the whole gallery of class models for matching. The model graph with the highest similarity determines the shape class but it also specifies the size and the position of the object within the image. Due to the multiview representation of our models, we also obtain a rough estimate of the object's orientation. The complete graph matching process used in this paper proceeds in two steps:

- First step: rough location of the object in the image. The graph remains undistorted. Object location corresponds to the position with maximal similarity between the model graph and the input image.

- Second step: adaptation of scale and improvement of location. The graph from the first step is allowed to vary in size by scaling it in the $x-$ and the $y-$direction by a common factor, shifting the position of the resulting graph by a few pixels to find maximal similarity. Since we are using model graphs of different sizes for each class, the scale factor always is between 0.8 and 2.0.

3 Results

We have tested our system with objects that are textured and the shape of which deviates from that of our stored model classes, see Fig. 6. We also used different backgrounds and natural scenes. For testing purposes we used 180 test images (natural and synthetic). In spite of varying illumination conditions, the system has been able to classify correctly 147 out of the 180 objects. Among these test scenes were also difficult cases containing several objects in one image, where the system had to find the dominant object in the scene. Some typical examples of the matching results are shown in Fig. 6. Recognition against complex background is difficult since parts of the background may be false targets and can easily be mistaken as parts of the object. By using the confidence-based preprocessing we were able to overcome this difficulty. Difficulties may also arise in cases where part of the object is occluded, as the last example in Fig. 6 where only the upper part of the can has been classified as a cylinder. Classification time on a Sparc-20 was 0.5-2 minutes per object, depending on the number of model graphs we used for matching. The preprocessing time is under 2.3 sec while matching with one modelgraph requires 1-1.5 sec.

In 103 out of 154 attempts (67%) the orientation of the object was estimated correctly. We plan to capture more views of each model in our gallery (at present only 10) in order to achieve better performance.

4 Discussion

Departing from the face recognition system described in [10] we here take up the challenge of classifying unknown objects in spite of varying surface markings and substantial rotation in depth. Central to our approach is our emphasis of object contours and our multiview representation. We intent to systematically explore the multiview approach in order to obtain a stable and robust representation for our models with a minimal amount of data. In the future we plan to improve segmentation by using relative motion and by recognizing occluding objects. We also plan to organize the recognition process in a hierarchical way: (i) identification of object position, size and orientation in the image, (ii) coarse shape classification, (iii) fine shape classification and (iv) refinement of pose estimation.

Acknowledgements

We wish to thank Christian Eckes for making available his segmentation algorithm for model graph creation. We thank also Laurenz Wiskott, Michael

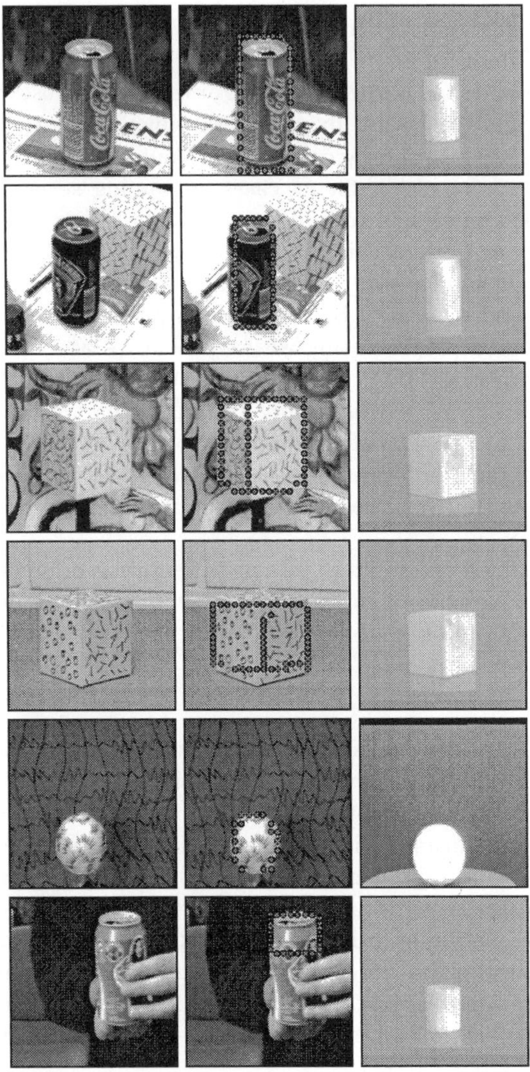

Figure 6: Examples of results of the matching procedure. The left column represents test objects, in the middle column the superimposed graphs are model graphs belonging to the objects shown in the right column.

Pötzsch and Thomas Maurer for fruitful discussions. This work was supported by the German Ministry for Science and Technology (grant 01IN504E9).

References

1. Biederman I., "Recognition by Components: A theory of human image understanding", *Psychological Review*, 94, pp. 115-147, 1987.
2. Havaldar P. and Medioni G., "Inference of Segmented, Volumetric Shape from Three Intensity Images", in *Proc. of the CVPR*, 1996.
3. Lades M., Vorbrüggen J.C., Buhmann J., Lange J., v.d. Malsburg C., Würtz R.P. and Konen W., "Distortion Invariant Object Recognition in the Dynamic Link Architecture", *IEEE Trans. on Computers* , 42(3), pp. 300-311, 1992.
4. Mallat S. and Zhong S., "Characterization of Signals from Multiscale Edges", *IEEE Trans. on PAMI* , 14(7), pp. 710-732, 1992.
5. v.d. Malsburg C., "The correlation theory of brain function", Intern. Rep., 81-2, MPI Biophysikalische Chemie, Göttingen, 1981. Repr. in E. Domany, J.L. van Hemmen, and K. Schulten, eds, *Models of Neural Networks II*, pp. 95-119. Springer, Berlin, 1994.
6. Poggio T. and Edelman S., "A network that learns to recognize three-dimensional objects", *Nature*, 343, pp. 263-266, 1990.
7. Reiser K., "Learning persistent structure", PhD thesis, Res. Report 584, Hughes Aircraft Co., 1991.
8. Rehse O., Pötzsch M. and v.d. Malsburg C.,"Edge Information: A Confidence Based Algorithm Emphazising Steady Curves", in *Proc. of Int. Conf. on Artificial Neural Networks*, pp. 851-856, Bochum 1996.
9. Ulupinar F. and Nevatia R.,"Perception of 3-D surfaces from 2-D contours", *IEEE Trans. on PAMI*, pp. 3-18, Jan. 1993.
10. Wiskott L., Fellous J.-M., Krüger N. and v.d. Malsburg C. ,"Face Recognition and Gender Determination", in *Proc. of the International Workshop on Automatic Face- and Gesture Recognition*, Zürich 1995.
11. Zadel S., "Ein lernfähiges, selbstorganisierendes System zum visuell gesteuerten Greifen bei Robotern", PhD thesis, VDI-Verlag, in preparation, Düsseldorf 1997.
12. Zerroug M. and Nevatia R., "Segmentation and Recovery of SHGCs from a Single Intensity Image", in *Proc. of the European Conference on Computer Vision*, pp. 319-340, Stockholm 1994.

SHAPE DECOMPOSITION BY TOPOLOGY

Y. KENMOCHI, A. IMIYA
Dept. of Information and Computer Sciences, Chiba University
1-33 Yayoi-cho, Inage-ku, Chiba 263, JAPAN

Shape decomposition is a fundamental method of extracting geometric features of objects. The decomposition of objects using geometric features is not sufficient for image representation with subpixel accuracy. This is because not only geometric structures but also topological structures of objects are variable and depend on the resolution of an image. In this paper, we define "dimensionalities" as new topological features. The term "dimensionality" comes from the dimensions of simplexes which are fundamental properties in classical combinatorial topology. First, we introduce a combinatorial shape description in 3-dimensional discrete space. Second, a method of shape decomposition using "dimensionalities" is presented.

1 Introduction

Shape decomposition is a fundamental method of extracting geometric features of objects [1]. A given object is divided into a collection of parts; the collection enables us to describe the given object as a collection of models which are precreated as fundamental shapes for the description of objects. The decomposition of objects into a collection of geometric parts is, however, insufficient for image representation with subpixel accuracy [2, 3]. This is because not only geometric properties but also topological properties of objects are variable and depend on the resolution of images. These topological properties are called "dimensionalities" in this paper. The term "dimensionality" comes from the dimensions of simplexes which are the basic properties in classical combinatorial topology [4].

In the first part of this paper, we introduce a combinatorial shape description in a 3-dimensional (3D) discrete space. We call the shape description a discrete complex which is taken from a term in combinatorial topology. We also show an algorithm for constructing a discrete complex from a given set of points in the 3D discrete space. A similar approach for discrete shape representation, which is called finite topology [5], exists. Since finite topology assumes that objects which are treated in a 3D discrete space are only 3D, dimensionalities of objects are only 3, whereas our shape description can include from 0 to 3 dimensionalities depending on the parts of represented objects. In the second part of this paper, a method of shape decomposition into nD parts of objects is presented using dimensionalities of each point. Each point has at least one kind of dimensionality, which can be from 0 to 3 in a 3D discrete space. A simple example of decomposing an object in the 3D discrete space is also illustrated.

2 Combinatorial Shape Description

This section gives an overview of a 3D shape description in a 3D discrete space using combinatorial topology. The details of combinatorial topology in a 3D discrete space are described in reference [6]. Setting $\mathbf{R}^3$ to be a 3D Euclidean space, a 3D discrete space $\mathbf{Z}^3$ is defined as a set of all points in $\mathbf{R}^3$ having integer coordinates. Denoting the Euclidean distance between two points, $\boldsymbol{x}$ and $\boldsymbol{y}$, by $\|\boldsymbol{x}-\boldsymbol{y}\|$, two types of neighborhoods of a point $\boldsymbol{x}$ in $\mathbf{Z}^3$ are defined as

$$N_m(\boldsymbol{x}) = \{\boldsymbol{y} \mid \|\boldsymbol{x}-\boldsymbol{y}\| \leq p,\ \boldsymbol{y} \in \mathbf{Z}^3\}, \tag{1}$$

where $m = 6$ or 26 corresponding to p which is 1 or $\sqrt{3}$. They are called 6- and 26-neighborhoods, respectively. One of the two neighborhoods must be assumed in $\mathbf{Z}^3$.

An nD discrete simplex is defined as a topological element which has an nD region in $\mathbf{Z}^3$, depending on each neighborhood. A discrete simplex consists of several points in $\mathbf{Z}^3$. If we embed these points of a discrete simplex in $\mathbf{R}^3$, then we can create the convex hull of these points in $\mathbf{R}^3$; the convex hull is called the embedded simplex. The dimension of a discrete simplex depends on the dimension of the region of its embedded simplex. Note that embedded simplexes do not include their boundary; in topological terms, they are relatively open in $\mathbf{R}^3$. The dimension can be from 0 to 3 in $\mathbf{Z}^3$. For each neighborhood, 0D discrete simplexes are regarded as isolated points in $\mathbf{Z}^3$. Discrete simplexes whose dimensions are more than 0 are obtained by the following recursive definition.

Definition 1 *An nD discrete simplex is defined as a set of points in $\mathbf{Z}^3$, such that the embedded simplex becomes one of nD minimum nonzero regions in $\mathbf{R}^3$ which are bounded by $(n-1)$D embedded simplexes.*

We abbreviate nD discrete simplexes as n-simplexes. An n-simplex which consists of k points, $\boldsymbol{x}_1, \boldsymbol{x}_2, \ldots, \boldsymbol{x}_k$, is represented by $[\boldsymbol{x}_1, \boldsymbol{x}_2, \ldots, \boldsymbol{x}_k]$.

For each of the 6- and 26-neighborhoods, n-simplexes are defined as shown in Fig. 1, where n is from 0 to 3. Let us consider discrete simplexes in the case of the 6-neighborhood. Embedded 1-simplexes in $\mathbf{R}^3$ are unit line segments because 1D regions in $\mathbf{R}^3$ are in lines; 1-simplexes become sets of two neighboring points which are regarded as endpoints of the line segments. Embedded 2-simplexes are unit squares bounded by four unit line segments which are 1-simplexes embedded in $\mathbf{R}^3$; 2-simplexes become sets of four points,

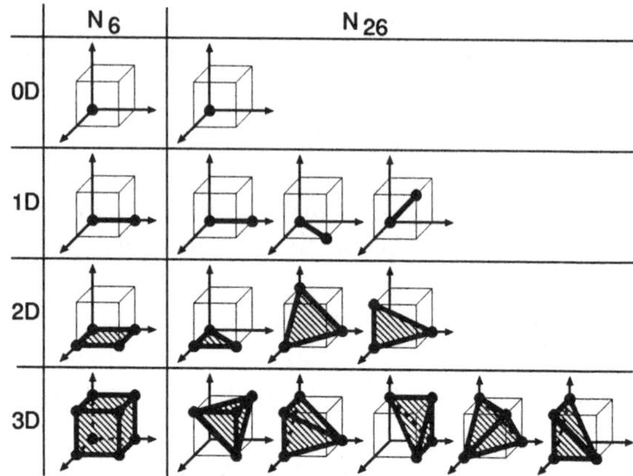

Figure 1: All possible discrete simplexes in $\mathbf{Z}^3$, whose shapes depend on the 6- or 26-neighborhood. We ignore congruent ones that differ from the discrete simplexes in this figure by translation and/or rotation.

each of which neighbors two other points. Embedded 3-simplexes are unit cubes bounded by unit squares which are 2-simplexes embedded in $\mathbf{R}^3$; 3-simplexes consist of sets of 8 points in $\mathbf{Z}^3$. Note that discrete simplexes shown in Fig. 1 are only counted if we ignore the congruent simplexes that differ from those in Fig. 1 by translation and rotation.

For an n-simplex, $[\boldsymbol{x}_1, \boldsymbol{x}_2, \ldots, \boldsymbol{x}_k]$, a function, $face([\boldsymbol{x}_1, \boldsymbol{x}_2, \ldots, \boldsymbol{x}_k])$, can be defined as a set of all discrete simplexes included in the n-simplex, whose dimensions are less than n. For instance, the faces of a 2-simplex are 0- and 1-simplexes. Using this function, discrete complexes, which are combinations of discrete simplexes, are defined in $\mathbf{Z}^3$.

Definition 2 *A discrete complex is defined by a finite set* $\mathbf{C}$ *of discrete simplexes satisfying the following two conditions.*

1. *If* $[a] \in \mathbf{C}$, $face([a]) \subseteq \mathbf{C}$.

2. *If* $[a_1], [a_2] \in \mathbf{C}$ *and* $|a_1| \cap |a_2| \neq \emptyset$, $[a_1] = [a_2]$,

where $[a]$ *and* $|a|$ *represent a discrete simplex and its embedded simplex, respectively.*

The dimension of a discrete complex is equivalent to the maximum dimension of its associated set of discrete simplexes. We abbreviate nD discrete complexes as n-complexes.

If every discrete simplex $[a]$ in $\mathbf{C}$ whose dimension is less than n satisfies

$$[a] \in face([b]), \tag{2}$$

where $[b]$ is one of the n-simplexes in $\mathbf{C}$, $\mathbf{C}$ is called pure. In addition to the pureness of complexes, $\mathbf{C}$ is called connected if, for any two elements $[a]$ and $[b]$ in $\mathbf{C}$, there exists a path between them:

$$[a_1] = [a], [a_2], \ldots, [a_n] = [b], \tag{3}$$

where $[a_i] \in \mathbf{C}$ for $i = 1, 2, \ldots, n$ and $[a_i] \cap [a_{i+1}] \neq \emptyset$ for $i = 1, 2, \ldots, n-1$.

If we embed all discrete simplexes included in a discrete complex into $\mathbf{R}^3$, a complex embedded in $\mathbf{R}^3$, which we call a body, can be obtained.

Definition 3 *The body of a discrete complex* $\mathbf{C}$ *is defined as*

$$\mathbf{B} = \bigcup_{[a] \in \mathbf{C}} |a|. \tag{4}$$

Obviously, bodies are sets in $\mathbf{R}^3$, not in $\mathbf{Z}^3$.

3 Construction of Discrete Complex

We assume that a subset $\mathbf{V}$ in $\mathbf{Z}^3$ is given. Every point in $\mathbf{V}$ is assigned a value of 1 while every point in the complement of $\mathbf{V}$ is assigned a value of 0. We call points whose values are 1 and 0 1-points and 0-points, respectively. This section presents a method of constructing a discrete complex from $\mathbf{V}$.

First, we create a discrete complex for each unit cube whose eight vertices are points in $\mathbf{Z}^3$ and side lengths are one. A discrete complex for each unit cube is created so that all points in the discrete complex are 1-points and that the region occupied by the discrete complex becomes maximum. The number of all possible patterns of 1- and 0-points in a unit cube is 23 if we ignore the congruent patterns that differ from them by rotation of the center of the unit cube. Tables 1 and 2 give discrete complexes for the 23 1-point patterns in a unit cube. Note that there can be several combinations of discrete simplexes for a 1-point pattern in a unit cube, even if the bodies of the discrete complexes for the 1-point pattern in a unit cube are equivalent, as shown in Fig. 2.

Next, we combine the discrete complexes for all unit cubes into a discrete complex without contradictions at the joints of two discrete complexes in adjacent unit cubes. According to reference [7], no contradiction occurs at any joint if we consider the 6-neighborhood. If we consider the 26-neighborhood, we join discrete complexes for all 1-point patterns, except for P4a, P5a, P6a, P6b and P7 in Table 2, first. Then, for each of these five patterns, we choose a discrete complex such that it can be joined to discrete complexes in adjacent unit cubes without contradictions among several candidates of discrete complexes whose combinations of discrete simplexes are different.

Figure 2: An example of two discrete complexes for a pattern, P6a, whose combinations of simplexes are not the same but whose bodies are equivalent.

Table 1: Discrete complexes in a unit cube corresponding to all 1- and 0-point patterns. The 6-neighborhood is assumed.

1-point number	discrete complex in a unit cube
0	P0
1	P1
2	P2a P2b P2c
3	P3a P3b P3c
4	P4a P4b P4c P4d P4e P4f P4g
5	P5a P5b P5c
6	P6a P6b P6c
7	P7
8	P8

a unit cube
● a 1-point

Table 2: Discrete complexes in a unit cube corresponding to all 1- and 0-point patterns. The 26-neighborhood is assumed.

1-point number	discrete complex in a unit cube
0	P0
1	P1
2	P2a P2b P2c
3	P3a P3b P3c
4	P4a P4b P4c P4d P4e P4f P4g
5	P5a P5b P5c
6	P6a P6b P6c
7	P7
8	P8

a unit cube
● a 1-point

The following two theorems are proved in reference [7].

Theorem 1 *For the 6-neighborhood, a discrete complex can be uniquely obtained from* $\mathbf{V}$.

Theorem 2 *For the 26-neighborhood, a discrete complex can be obtained from* $\mathbf{V}$. *Even if there exist several discrete complexes for* $\mathbf{V}$, *their bodies are always equivalent.*

Note that discrete complexes created from $\mathbf{V}$ may not be pure, because, for some 1-point patterns in a unit cube, any discrete simplexes whose dimensions can be from 0 to 3 are created according to Tables 1 and 2. In other words, there can exist 0-, 1- and 2-simplexes which are not included in any 3-simplex in a created 3-complex. Figure 3 illustrates examples of 3-complexes for the 6- and 26-neighborhoods.

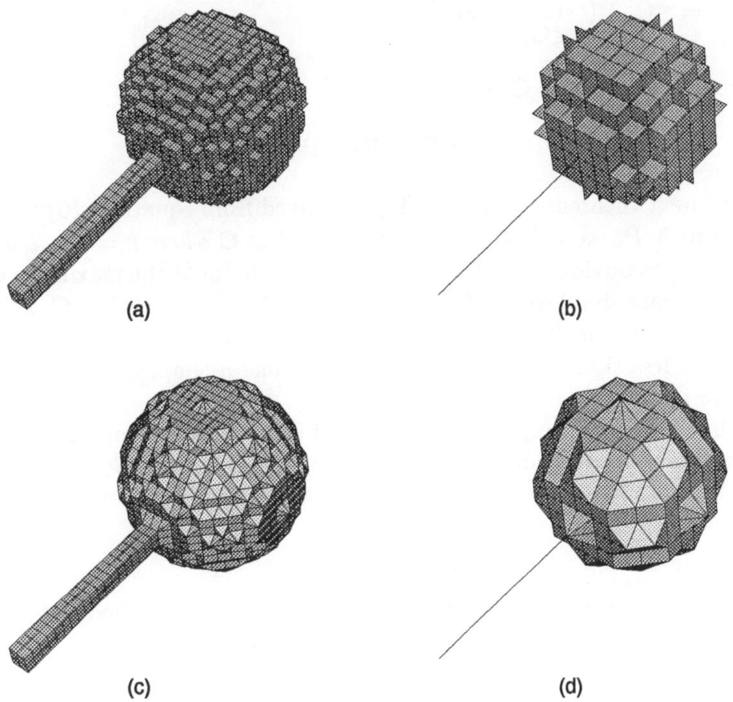

Figure 3: Examples of 3-complexes, (a) and (b) for the 6-neighborhood, and (c) and (d) for the 26-neighborhood. (a) and (c) are obtained from $\mathbf{V}_1$, and (b) and (d) are obtained from $\mathbf{V}_2$; $\mathbf{V}_2$ can be obatined from $\mathbf{V}_1$, such that the resolution of $\mathbf{V}_2$ is half that of $\mathbf{V}_1$.

4 Shape Decomposition

If a discrete complex $\mathbf{C}$ is obtained from a given subset $\mathbf{V}$ in $\mathbf{Z}^3$, we can divide $\mathbf{C}$ into four sets as

$$\mathbf{C} = \mathbf{C}_0 \cup \mathbf{C}_1 \cup \mathbf{C}_2 \cup \mathbf{C}_3, \tag{5}$$

where $\mathbf{C}_n$ is a set of all n-simplexes in $\mathbf{C}$. Obviously, $\mathbf{C}_n$ can be obtained from $\mathbf{C}$ without any calculations. Using these $\mathbf{C}_n$s, we can calculate $\mathbf{P}_n$ where $n = 0, 1, \ldots, 3$ consecutively as

$$\mathbf{P}_3 = \mathbf{C}_3 \cup (\bigcup_{[a]\in\mathbf{C}_3} face([a])), \tag{6}$$

$$\mathbf{P}_2 = \mathbf{C}'_2 \cup (\bigcup_{[a]\in\mathbf{C}'_2} face([a])) \quad \text{where} \quad \mathbf{C}'_2 = \mathbf{C}_2 \setminus (\bigcup_{[a]\in\mathbf{C}_3} face([a])), \tag{7}$$

$$\mathbf{P}_1 = \mathbf{C}'_1 \cup (\bigcup_{[a]\in\mathbf{C}'_1} face([a])) \quad \text{where} \quad \mathbf{C}'_1 = \mathbf{C}_1 \setminus (\bigcup_{[a]\in\mathbf{C}_2} face([a])), \tag{8}$$

$$\mathbf{P}_0 = \mathbf{C}_0 \setminus (\bigcup_{[a]\in\mathbf{C}_1} face([a])), \tag{9}$$

and we can decompose $\mathbf{C}$ to

$$\mathbf{C} = \mathbf{P}_0 \cup \mathbf{P}_1 \cup \mathbf{P}_2 \cup \mathbf{P}_3. \tag{10}$$

The next theorem concerning $\mathbf{P}_n$ is derived from equations (6) to (9).

Theorem 3 *$\mathbf{P}_n$ is a pure n-complex included in $\mathbf{C}$ where $n = 0, 1, 2, 3$.*

(Proof) It is obvious that $\mathbf{P}_n$ is an n-complex because the maximum dimension of discrete simplexes in $\mathbf{P}_n$ is n, and that $\mathbf{P}_n$ is included in $\mathbf{C}$, according to equations (6) to (9). In addition, every discrete simplex in $\mathbf{P}_n$, whose dimension is less than n, is included in at least one n-simplex in $\mathbf{P}_n$. Thus, $\mathbf{P}_n$ is a pure n-complex. *(Q.E.D.)*

Note that $\mathbf{P}_n$ can be empty. For instance, if $\mathbf{C}$ is a pure 3-complex, $\mathbf{P}_0$, $\mathbf{P}_1$ and $\mathbf{P}_2$ are empty because all discrete simplexes in $\mathbf{C}_0$, $\mathbf{C}_1$ and $\mathbf{C}_2$ are included in $\mathbf{C}_3$ as faces of 3-simplexes in $\mathbf{C}_3$. In other words, if $\mathbf{C}$ is a pure 3-complex,

$$\mathbf{P}_3 = \mathbf{C}. \tag{11}$$

Let $\mathbf{B}_n$ be the body of $\mathbf{P}_n$ where $n = 0, 1, 2, 3$; the body of $\mathbf{C}$, $\mathbf{B}$, is decomposed in a similar way to (10) as follows:

$$\mathbf{B} = \mathbf{B}_0 \cup \mathbf{B}_1 \cup \mathbf{B}_2 \cup \mathbf{B}_3. \tag{12}$$

According to Theorems 1 and 2, $\mathbf{B}$ is directly created from $\mathbf{V}$ and does not depend on $\mathbf{C}$. Thus, the next theorem is derived.

Theorem 4 $\mathbf{B}_n$ *is uniquely extracted from* $\mathbf{B}$ *depending on the given subset* $\mathbf{V}$ *in* $\mathbf{Z}^3$, *where* $n = 0, 1, 2, 3$.
(Proof) If we are concerned with the 6-neighborhood, a discrete complex $\mathbf{C}$ is uniquely constructed from $\mathbf{V}$ according to Theorem 1. Because every $\mathbf{C}_n$ is uniquely determined from $\mathbf{C}$, every $\mathbf{P}_n$ is also uniquely calculated following the equations. Thus, $\mathbf{B}_n$ is uniquely obtained. If we are concerned with the 26-neighborhood, $\mathbf{B}$ is uniquely obtained from $\mathbf{V}$ even if several discrete complexes can be constructed from $\mathbf{V}$ according to Theorem 2. If $\mathbf{B}$ has isolated points, these points must be included in $\mathbf{B}_0$, and $\mathbf{B}_0$ must not include any points other than these isolated points; $\mathbf{B}_0$ is obtained uniquely. If $\mathbf{B}$ has a series of line segments, these line segments must be included in $\mathbf{B}_1$, and $\mathbf{B}_1$ must not include any points other than the points on these line segments; $\mathbf{B}_1$ is also obtained uniquely. Similarly, if $\mathbf{B}$ has thin-wall-like parts, these parts must be included in $\mathbf{B}_2$, and $\mathbf{B}_2$ must not include any points other than points in the thin-wall-like parts; $\mathbf{B}_2$ is also obtained uniquely. The remaining parts of $\mathbf{B}$, which are not included in either $\mathbf{B}_0$, $\mathbf{B}_1$ or $\mathbf{B}_2$, are also uniquely obtained and the closure of the remaining parts becomes $\mathbf{B}_3$. *(Q.E.D.)*

Let $\mathbf{V}_n$ be a subset of $\mathbf{V}$, whose points are included in $\mathbf{B}_n$; $\mathbf{V}$ is also decomposed in a similar way to (10) as follows:

$$\mathbf{V} = \mathbf{V}_0 \cup \mathbf{V}_1 \cup \mathbf{V}_2 \cup \mathbf{V}_3. \tag{13}$$

Obviously, $\mathbf{V}_n$ can be determined from either $\mathbf{B}_n$ or $\mathbf{P}_n$ where $n = 0, 1, 2, 3$. Because $\mathbf{B}_n$ and $\mathbf{P}_n$ are uniquely extracted from $\mathbf{V}$ according to Theorem 4, $\mathbf{V}_n$ is also uniquely determined from $\mathbf{V}$.

5 Algorithm of Shape Decomposition

The previous section shows that we can decompose a given subset $\mathbf{V}$ in $\mathbf{Z}^3$ into the nD parts $\mathbf{V}_n$ where $n = 0, 1, 2, 3$ if a discrete complex $\mathbf{C}$ is already constructed from $\mathbf{V}$. In this section we demonstrate an algorithm for obtaining each $\mathbf{V}_n$ from $\mathbf{V}$ directly without converting $\mathbf{C}$ from $\mathbf{V}$.

Let $\mathbf{C}(\boldsymbol{x})$ be an n-complex constructed in the union of eight unit cubes, all of which include the point $\boldsymbol{x}$; $\mathbf{C}(\boldsymbol{x})$ can be decomposed into pure discrete complexes such as (10). Assuming that $\mathbf{P}_m(\boldsymbol{x})$ is a set of nonempty pure m-complexes in $\mathbf{C}(\boldsymbol{x})$ and that every m-simplex in $\mathbf{P}_m(\boldsymbol{x})$ includes $\boldsymbol{x}$ as one of the vertices of the m-simplex, it is said that $\boldsymbol{x}$ has the dimensionality m, where $m \leq n$. If $\boldsymbol{x}$ is included both in a 2-simplex in $\mathbf{P}_2(\boldsymbol{x})$ and in a 3-simplex in $\mathbf{P}_3(\boldsymbol{x})$, the dimensionalities of $\boldsymbol{x}$ are 2 and 3. Using the dimensionalities of points, objects of interest, which are given as subsets of $\mathbf{Z}^3$, can be decomposed following Algorithm 1.

Algorithm 1

input: *Finite nonempty subset* $\mathbf{V}$ *in* $\mathbf{Z}^3$.

output: *Decomposed objects* $\mathbf{V}_0, \mathbf{V}_1, \ldots, \mathbf{V}_3$.

begin

1. *Set* $\mathbf{V}_m = \emptyset$ *where* $m = 0, 1, 2, 3$.
2. *For each point* $\boldsymbol{x}$ *in* $\mathbf{V}$,
   - 2.1 *For each of eight unit cubes which include* $\boldsymbol{x}$, *look up the discrete complex in Table 1 or 2.*
   - 2.2 *Combine eight discrete complexes in the eight unit cubes into a discrete complex,* $\mathbf{C}(\boldsymbol{x})$.
   - 2.3 *Decompose* $\mathbf{C}(\boldsymbol{x})$ *into* $\boldsymbol{P}_m(\boldsymbol{x})$*s where* $m = 0, 1, 2, \ldots, 3$.
   - 2.4 *For* $m = 0, 1, 2, 3$, *if* $\boldsymbol{x} \in \mathbf{P}_m(\boldsymbol{x})$, *then add* $\boldsymbol{x}$ *to* $\mathbf{V}_m$

end

According to Tables 1 and 2, the number of possible patterns of discrete complexes in a unit cube is 23 both for the 6-neighborhood and for the 26-neighborhood, if we ignore discrete complexes which differ from those in the tables by rotation and/or translation. However, in Algorithm 1, we can precalculate discrete complexes for all 256 patterns of 1- and 0-points in a unit cube. This preprocessing for all 1- and 0-point patterns accelerates the computation of Step 2.1 in Algorithm 1.

Using Algorithm 1, we can decompose the 3-complex in Fig. 3 (d) into 1D and 3D parts. Every point in the 1D and 3D parts has dimensionality 1 and 3 respectively, and thus the joining point of the 1D and 3D parts has both dimensionalities, 1 and 3. Since every point in Fig. 3 (c) has dimensionality 3, the 3-complex cannot be decomposed into more than one part and contains no part except for the 3D part. The different results of decomposition between (c) and (d) in Fig. 3 is caused by the different resolutions of their object images.

If we compare Fig. 3 (a) with (c) and similarly (b) with (d), the results of shape decomposition are different, even if both are obtained from the same $\mathbf{V}_1$ and $\mathbf{V}_2$. This is caused by the different neighborhoods. According to Fig. 1, there are several shapes of discrete simplexes for the 26-neighborhood, whereas there is only one discrete simplex in each dimension for the 6-neighborhood. This implies that we can combine discrete simplexes for the 26-neighborhood more flexibly than for the 6-neighborhood and leads to the relation:

$$\mathbf{V}_3[6] \subseteq \mathbf{V}_3[26], \tag{14}$$

where $\mathbf{V}_3[m]$ is the 3D parts of $\mathbf{V}$ if we adopt the m-neighborhood. In Fig. 3, the relation (14) holds between (a) and (c), and between (b) and (d), respectively.

6 Conclusions

In this paper we introduced a combinatorial shape description in $\mathbf{Z}^3$ called a discrete complex which comes from a term in classical combinatorial topology. An algorithm for constructing a discrete complex from a given subset in $\mathbf{Z}^3$ was also presented. If a discrete complex is constructed from a given subset in $\mathbf{Z}^3$, the given subset is automatically decomposed into nD parts using topological structures of the discrete complex. We also showed an algorithm that directly extracts nD parts of the given finite subset in $\mathbf{Z}^3$ from the given subset, using the dimensionalities of each point. These nD parts are uniquely obtained.

References

[1] A. Held and K. Abe, "On the decomposition of binary shapes into meaningful parts", *Pattern Recognition*, vol. 27, no. 5, pp. 637-647, 1994.

[2] C. A. Berenstein, L. N. Kanal, D. Lavine and E. C. Olson, "A geometric approach to subpixel registration accuracy", *Computer Vision, Graphics, and Image Processing*, vol. 40, pp. 334-360, 1987.

[3] A. Imiya, "Subpixel superresolution and inversion of image pyramid", in *Proceedings of the Sixth International Conference on Artificial Intelligence and Information-Control Systems of Robots*, 1994, pp. 47-58.

[4] P. S. Aleksandrov, *Combinatorial Topology, Vol. 1*, Graylock Press, Rochester, N.Y., 1956.

[5] V. A. Kovalevsky, "Finite topology as applied to image analysis", *Computer Vision, Graphics, and Image Processing*, vol. 46, pp. 141-161, 1989.

[6] Y. Kenmochi, A. Imiya, and A. Ichikawa, "Discrete combinatorial geometry", to appear in *Pattern Recognition.*

[7] Y. Kenmochi, A. Imiya, and A. Ichikawa, "Boundary extraction of discrete objects", to appear in *Computer Vision and Image Understanding.*

PICTORIAL RELIEF

J.J. KOENDERINK
Helmholtz Instituut, Utrecht University, PO Box 80 000, 3508TA Utrecht, The Netherlands

When human observers look at pictures they are aware of both the picture surface and of a "pictorial space". Whereas the pictorial surface is only two-dimensional, pictorial space is three-dimensional: The additional "invented" dimension is "pictorial depth". Vision in depth is checked by the surfaces of opaque objects, the same applies to pictorial space. This gives rise to the notion of "pictorial relief". I study the structure of pictorial relief as a function of image structure ("pictorial cues") and viewing conditions. Often the images have been produced by some projection of a three-dimensional scene, vision then "reconstructs" the third dimension. In these cases the pictorial cues can be manipulated at the time of (*e.g.*) photographic exposure. Pictorial relief is expected to depend critically on this. I present examples.

1 Pictorial Relief: What is it?

It is a remarkable fact that the human observer is able to "look into" a photograph (say) and perceive not simply a planar surface covered with pigments in a certain simultaneous order, but—at the same time—a three-dimensional "pictorial space". Possibly man (or maybe the primates) are unique in the animal kingdom in this respect. Many observers have only a subsidiary awareness of the pictorial surface (they are of course aware of it witness the effective way they handle the material object "photograph") whereas their immediate experience tends to focus on the *content* of the photograph. In a way one has a "cue conflict" situation here: Binocular disparity, accommodation of the eye lens, movement parallax, haptic information, *etc.*, all inform the observer that the object is a planar one, whereas certain properties of the simultaneous order of pigments are apparently interpreted in terms of depth cues. Such cues are of the "monocular" type, *even when the observer happens to use both eyes.* Typical (and often important) depth cues are: Visual contour shape, cast shadow, shading, texture gradients, "familiarity", and so forth. Notice that the visual system never gets the cues *as such*, for instance, the "visual contour" is not immediately specified at all but has to be produced on the basis of the simultaneous order of pigments. One is dealing with an extremely sophisticated brain function here, in fact, modern computer methods are no match for the human observer in the overwhelming majority of cases. The human observer especially outperforms the artificial systems in pictures that represent (to the human observer that is!) rich, natural scenes, in which the cues are such a mess that no "shape from X"-algorithm even stands a chance of producing a tolerable result.

1.1 *Ways to Operationalize Pictorial Relief*

That the human observer possesses these remarkable competences has been common knowledge for ages. However, a scientific study of such abilities *in a realistic setting* had to wait until very recently. Many studies exist (more or less quantitatively since the early nineteenth century) for cases where the image structure was simplified to the point where one almost hesitates to talk of "pictures" at all. The reasons that so much work was done with such extremely poor stimuli (in terms of the structural complexity of the simultaneous order of pigments) have been various, but a recurring theme has to do with the firm conviction that true science progresses through a process of "going to the roots" of phenomena, that is to say, by the method of *reduction*. Indeed, the method of reduction has been vital in the successes of physics, chemistry and physiology. However, here one deals with problems of psychology and the method of stimulus reduction has yielded only scant and rather artificial knowledge that has turned out to bear hardly (if at all) on what goes on in the cases that interest one especially (observers looking at photographs of real scenes say). Moreover, the type of data gathered in experiments has been of a type that doesn't get one very far: Rather sparse data (for instance: the input is an image and the question is "is it a square", answer "no"), and not of the type that enables comparison with computer vision "shape–from–X" algorithms.

Is it actually *possible* to measure the geometrical structure of pictorial relief? After all pictorial relief is an experiential object that "exists in the head"—or rather, in consciousness. By "measuring structure" one would prefer to understand the quantitative measurement of geometrical attributes. For instance, if the pictorial surface is "curved", then what is its curvature (quantitatively) at such and so a location? People have generally doubted the possibility of such measurements, which is one reason why such data are not currently widely available despite over a century of serious scientific effort (most of the early laboratories in experimental psychology were founded by people associated with the laboratory of Wundt and are by now just over a century of age). However, I have (with my collaborators of course) found that such measurements are not only *possible*, but not at all hard to implement and I have by now experience with a variety of novel methods.

Notice that, since pictorial relief is an aspect of a person's consciousness, one has to find novel *operational definitions*. When you measure the temperature of water in a bucket you start with the assumption that there is something definite to measure and that the problem is to measure that something as precisely as possible. Here the situation is different. Although I don't doubt that consciousness *exists* (at least not in the case of myself, whereas I grant the possession of consciousness to my friends), it is not a scientific object. *There simply isn't a surface in the head that one has to measure as precisely as possible*, instead, *one defines "pictorial relief"* by the very method of measuring it. Thus the question: "have I perhaps made a measurement error?" is strictly meaningless. Moreover, suppose one had two methods and they gave different results, then the question "which one is (more) correct" is a meaningless one. For in order for the question to be meaningful there should exist a *real* pictorial relief against which to gauge the experimental results. Does this invalidate the whole enterprise? Not at all, it simply means that the study of pictorial relief involves all operationalizations that one can think of. It is quite likely that the set of different operationalizations itself will have a structure to it of course.

Here are two simple methods to study pictorial relief (by way of example: It is easy to think of others), they are quite different from each other, and each is capable of many interesting variations.

Consider how one performs measurements of a geometrical nature in general. One typical method is: One applies a gauge figure (template object) to the object to be gauged, and judges the *fit*. Examples are length (gauge figure a yardstick), hemicircularity (gauge figure a right angle), shape of a screw (gauge figure a template), and so forth. In many cases one can judge the fit of *the picture* of a gauge figure relative to *the picture* of an object: One can use this general, abstract principle in pictorial space. I have designed various gauge figures that allow one to measure, for instance, local surface attitude, sectional curvature, and others.

Another method is completely different in nature. When one says that one "perceives the shape" of an object in space one probably means something like that one would be able to compare the object to *itself* in another view. For instance, one recognizes a (familiar) person by the face in the *en face*, profile and three–quarter views. Consider *two or more* pictures of a single fiducial object. For instance, I might prepare the pictures by walking around the object in real space and snapping photographs from various viewpoints. Then, if I confront an observer with two pictures *and the observer sees them as two different views of a single object*, then that observer should be able to perform the following task with some confidence: One places a mark (for instance a red dot in the case of a graytone photograph) on the depiction in one image and asks the observer to put a mark on the other rendering at the corresponding location. Thus one collects correlations between pairs of points, one in each picture.

Both methods allow us to gather extensive amounts of data (one can let the observer judge the fit of the gauge figure at as many points as one pleases, likewise one may collect point–to–point correlations for as many locations as one fancies) of a geometrical nature. For instance, when one has dense data one may be able to actually estimate the pictorial surface with good spatial resolution (at least: good resolution in the picture plane, the "depth" resolution is an empirical fact that has to be awaited).

2 Gauging Pictorial Surface Attitude

A suitable gauge figure for pictorial attitude is *Tissot's indicatrix.* Tissot's indicatrix has been used to measure the deformation of cartographic projections: One draws a small circle on the globe and studies its shape on the map. This shape will in general be (approximately) elliptic. The orientation and eccentricity of this ellipse ("Tissot's indicatrix") specify the deformation of the projection very graphically. This is how I implement the gauge figure[1,5]: I present the (monochrome) picture on a computer screen. The pictures are regular photographs of real scenes. I superimpose an ellipse on the picture such that it is clearly a "Fremdkörper", for instance as a thin red curve. The size of the gauge figure is selected such that I have sufficient spatial resolution in the image plane and such that it is not larger than the area over which the spatial attitude of the pictorial surface changes appreciably. The observer is given control over the shape and orientation of the gauge figure, whereas the location and size are controlled by the experimenter. The observer is required to adjust the gauge figure so as to be perceived as a *circle painted on the surface of the object depicted.* Human observers find this a simple task and can reproduce settings very well when retested much later. They typically take a few seconds for a setting, and I routinely collect a thousand data points in an hour. Typically I sample the pictorial surface randomly in the course of a session, revisiting the same locations several times in the course of the session.

In the processing of the data I regard the ellipse as the projection of a circle, thus I may immediately find the corresponding surface attitude (slant and tilt). I typically obtain repeated samples of attitude at a few hundred locations, picked at the vertices of a planar triangulation of the pictorial surface (the observer is never aware of this!). In many cases (always if the picture depicts the surface of an opaque, smooth surface in real space) it turns out that these samples fit very well to the triangulation of a smooth surface in three dimensions. Violations of surface integrity are accounted for by the spread in repeated settings. Thus I obtain a true "pictorial relief".

3 Finding Picture Correspondences

The implementation of the second method turned out to be straightforward. The observer is confronted with two pictures, side to side, on a computer screen. A dot appears (random position) on one picture and the observer (using a mouse or trackball device) places a dot at the "corresponding location" in the other picture. Subjects find this a simple task and take only a few seconds for a setting. Again, one easily samples a thousand points in the course of an hour[9].

When the pictures are views of a single real object, the correspondences can be processed with conventional stereo algorithms to construct the "pictorial relief".

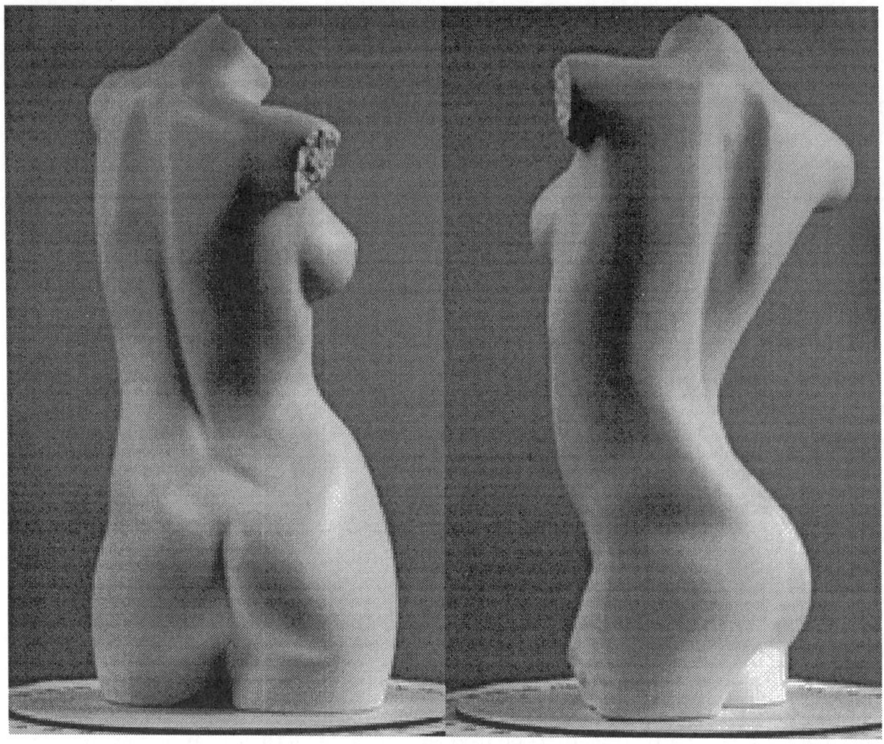

Figure 1: *The stimuli: On the left the stimulus used in the gauge figure task. On the right an image of the same object rotated by 90° about the vertical. Such pairs are used in the correspondence task: You may notice that it is a simple matter to find corresponding points in these images.*

4 Results of Attitude Measurements

I show a picture, the averaged settings (this also reveals the underlying triangulation), and the reconstructed pictorial relief for a certain case (figures 1 and 2). Clearly, one obtains a remarkable "reconstruction" of the real object, it is uncanningly like an instance of "inverse optics". However, there is of course no guarantee whatsoever that these results are like the real thing. It is necessary to distinguish sharply between:

— the uncertainty due to the scatter in repeated settings;

— the internal consistency (how well does the data conform to a surface (*any* surface)?

— how well does one subject reproduce a certain relief under variation of viewing conditions (time, familiarity, monocular versus binocular viewing, and so forth)?

— how well do different observers agree?
— how does the relief depend on the pictorial structure (for instance, the relevant parameters at the time of the exposure)?
— is the relief like the real thing (the issue of veridicality)?
Notice that the issue of veridicality is only one of a whole flock of questions and—in our opinion—not by far the most interesting one.

Figure 2: *Results from the gauge figure experiment. On the left an overview of the averaged settings, in the middle equal depth contours and on the right a profile view of the pictorial relief (the* veridical *contour is seen on the right in the previous figure).*

I state summarily that:
— the result is systematically different from the real thing,
— the differences depend on viewing conditions and on the pictorial structure,
— observers produce reliefs that are typically more alike among each other than they are to the real thing,
— moreover, observers typically reproduce their results very precisely, even after a considerable period of time.

The influence of viewing conditions is very systematic[2,3,4] and in full agreement with prior notions (dating all the way from Leonardo and exploited in image viewers by the German optical industry at the turn of this century):

Refief depends on the conditions only with regard to *amplitude.* All results are (depth–) scaled versions of each other. One obtains increased relief by looking monocularly from the correct perspective center. Oblique viewing and looking binocularly both decrease the amplitude of the pictorial relief.

The influence of the circumstances at the time of exposure is also of much interest. One obtains qualitatively different pictorial reliefs by, for instance, displacing a key light source. Here one traces the direct influence of the nature of the input data on the "shape–from–X" algorithms run in the brain of the human observer[7,8]!

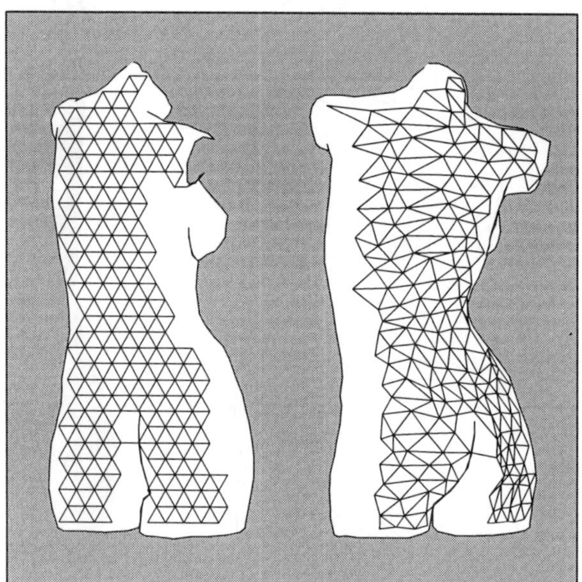

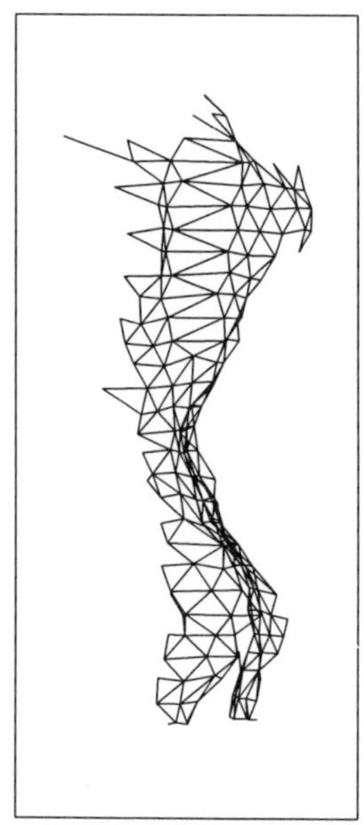

Figure 3: *Results from the correspondence task. On the right of the left panel the average correspondences for a turn of* 45° *about the vertical. In the right panel a profile view of the reconstructed pictorial relief.*

5 Results from picture correspondences

I show the pictorial correspondences for the same stimulus compared with the image of the same object, but rotated over 45° about the vertical (figures 1 and 3). Such images look quite different at first blush (compare the left and right picture in figure 1, where the rotation is 90°). I find that though observers are very bad at estimating the viewpoints under which pictures were actually taken, their correspondences are sufficiently precise to *reconstruct* these viewpoints with considerable precision! That people can actually perform the task is indeed remarkable since it cannot be done on the basis of mere *image structure.* Apparently observers reconstruct pictorial surfaces and perform the task *in three–dimensional pictorial space.* Their precision depends on the inherent ambiguities, for instance, for cylinders they are lousy in the direction transverse to the generators, for spherical surfaces they rely completely on remote "anchor points" if these are present in the pictures (figure 4).

It proves to be possible to predict the correspondences rather well from attitude measurements on any single image. Although these are different operationalizations of "pictorial relief", and thus—as I have argued before—actually *different* pictorial reliefs, it turns out to be the case that the tasks apparently involve a single "internal representation". Apparently I am zooming in on a more or less well defined aspect of the observer's consciousness here.

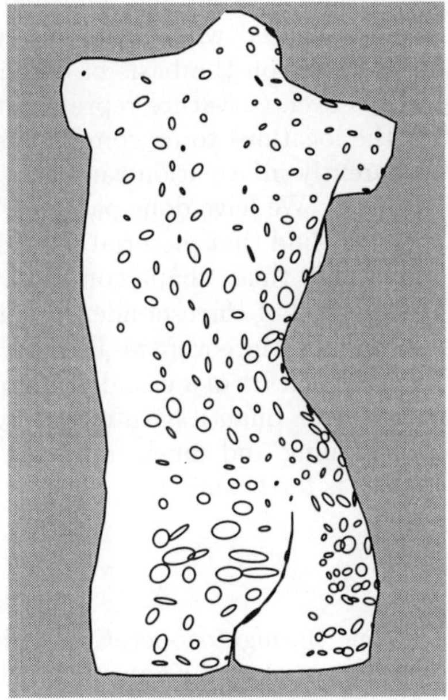

Figure 4: *Covariance ellipses for the correspondence task.*

6 Conclusions

I have shown that it is very well possible to measure pictorial relief in such a way that one gathers extensive data of a quantitative, geometrical nature. I have also shown a few results that illustrate how such methods can be used to probe the human observer's consciousness in such a way that the results can be compared with the great variety of machine algorithms that are presently available. I expect methods such as these (I only presented a pair of examples here, a great variety of methods can be readily developed) to soon dominate the experimental psychology concerned with pictorial perception, especially in its interaction with computer vision and image processing. Such a paradigm shift is indeed sorely needed because computer vision/image processing and experimental psychology have been mutually isolated for too long by their idiosyncratic methods and conceptualizations that make either field a closed book to the other.

By now there exist several studies in which these methods have been applied: The influences of the viewing mode (monocular, binocular, synoptic, frontal versus oblique) on pictorial relief have been quantified, both in pictorial relief and for real three–dimensional objects[2,3,4]. The influence of cue combination has been studied for shading, contour and binocular disparity[4,7,8]. Surface attitude probing has been compared with depth discrimination[5,6]. We find that observers are unlikely to act on the basis of depth maps, probably they use surface attitude, perhaps even curvature representations. Depth discrimination deteriorates when the locations to be compared straddle a ridge or rut of the pictorial relief: Apparently information can be integrated quantitatively only over simple slope districts. We have done parametric studies of cue variation in the case of shading. We find that pictorial relief depends systematically on the direction of illumination[8], thus "shape constancy" pertains only in the first approximation[7]. The method of correspondences has been compared with the method of attitude sampling. Moreover, we used the method of correspondences to probe the in–depth structure of a visual contour, a subject that—until now—had not been studied with quantitative methods. As remarked above, such results are only a beginning and much improved understanding of the human perception of "relief" is forthcoming.

Acknowledgments

This work could only be done through cooperation with several other people. Here I mention Andrea van Doorn, Astrid Kappers, Jim Todd, Joe Lappin, Mitsuo Kawato and Frank Pollick. Part of the work reported here was done in a Human Frontiers in Science Program sponsored by the Japanese government. We also gratefully acknowledge support from the Advanced Telecommunications Research Laboratories (ATR), Kyoto, Japan.

References

1. J J Koenderink and A J van Doorn *Perception & Psychophysics* **52**, 487–496 (1992)
2. J J Koenderink A J van Doorn and A M L Kappers *Perception* **23**, 583–594 (1994)

3. J J Koenderink A J van Doorn and A M L Kappers *Perception* **24**, 115–126 (1995)
4. J Todd J J Koenderink A J van Doorn and A M L Kappers *Journal of Experimental Psychology: Human Perception and Performance* **22**, 695–706 (1996)
5. J J Koenderink and A J van Doorn *Image and Vision Computing* **13**, 321–334 (1995)
6. J J Koenderink A J van Doorn and A M L Kappers *Perception & Psychophysics* **58**, 163–173 (1996)
7. J J Koenderink A J van Doorn C Christou and J S Lappin *Perception* **25**, 155–164 (1996)
8. J J Koenderink A J van Doorn C Christou and J S Lappin *Perception* **25**, 1009–1026 (1996)
9. J J Koenderink A M L Kappers F E Pollick and M Kawato *Perception & Psychophysics*, in press

ROBUST OBJECT LOCALIZATION FROM SEGMENTED RANGE IMAGES BY MATCHING INTRINSIC LINE FEATURES

P. KOHLHEPP
Forschungszentrum Karlsruhe - Technik und Umwelt, Institut für Angewandte Informatik Postfach 3640, 76021 Karlsruhe, Germany, E-mail: kohlhepp@iai.fzk.de

E. HOFFMANN
Forschungszentrum Informatik (FZI) - Abt. Technische Expertensysteme und Robotik Haid- und Neustr. 10-14,76131 Karlsruhe, Germany, E-mail: ehoffman@fzi.de

Locating 3-D rigid objects reliably from segmented range images in the presence of occlusion, noise, or discrepancies between image and model is important for many applications. While surface features work perfectly for matching, point and line features are still needed for locating. Fast, non-iterative locating methods usually require accurate point correspondences, and do not tolerate significant occlusion. We present a new method to decide which features are object-intrinsic for a given matching hypothesis. To get precise point correspondences, we apply an extension of Arkin's shape similarity metric to multiple intrinsic 3-D contour sections. The metric is robust with respect to segmentation errors. As features, we use the surface patch boundaries, but the method could be applied to other line features. We demonstrate some experience from a gantry robot test site equipped with time-of-flight laser scanners.

1 Introduction

Locating multiple, possibly occluded objects in a *range image* remains a key problem in computer vision and is essential for robotic applications like recycling and dismantling, inspection, digital cartography, medical or virtual reality applications. It means to identify each object instance in the image by a suitable model description, and to find a 3-D transformation $\boldsymbol{T}=(R,T)$ - rotation R, translation T - that aligns the image with the model or with another image by minimizing the sum of Euclidean distances between matching features [1].

The methods differ in the object representations (global ones, or local feature graph based ones), and the kind of features (e.g. points, lines, surfaces). In general, surface features are more robust towards measurement noise and greatly reduce computational cost by data reduction. Only *maximal homogeneous* surface patches [2] bounded by distance, normal vector, or curvature jumps, in contrast to *minimal planar* patches [3], will yield *stable* constraints for matching. Least square methods are available for estimating $\boldsymbol{T}$ from corresponding feature sets such as normal or axis vectors, e.g. the singular value decomposition or Horn's unit quaternion method [1,3,6]. With maximal patches, however, too few features on each object may be visible to determine $\boldsymbol{T}$, in particular in a restricted top-down sensor view. While *surfaces* work perfectly for *deciding* the correct object type, *points* or *lines* are still needed for *location computation*. They are obtained from the *segmented surface boundaries.* However, great care has to be taken applying correspondence-based locating methods to points and lines:

- *Finding intrinsic features*: which parts of the image boundaries make features intrinsic to the object itself, must map onto corresponding model boundaries and are therefore relevant to localization, and which ones are artifacts created by the scene view, by occlusion or noise?
- *Finding precise correspondences*: ***T*** is sensitive to how well point distances are preserved, depending on *representation* and *discretization.* A circular boundary may be approximated by an irregular polygon with notches. Part of the effort devoted to minimize correspondence errors may be adverse to optimal surface alignment. Earlier work [2] has shown that tree-search for corresponding points, comparing neighboring *edges*, fails to locate even seemingly simple scenes.

The paper develops rules and methods for detecting intrinsic features as part of the interpretation tree. For locating occluded objects, a new, two-stage approach is proposed: Arkin's shape similarity metric [8] and contour matching will yield an initial rotation and precise point correspondences first, from which the final object location is then computed directly. The metric compares polygonal *shapes*, instead of comparing *representations* (*edges*). This makes it robust towards discretization noise, and general enough to handle smooth objects without requiring a parametric representation. We extend the metric to 3-D contours and their intrinsic subsections.

For lack of space, we only mention recently proposed iterative algorithms [7,11,12] which *avoid* the correspondence problem, but have other disadvantages, mainly in real-time applications. Using surface function approximations such as bi-cubic splines, quadrics, super-quadrics or hyper-quadrics [4,5] does not seem to help much in solving the location problem, either.

In chapter 2, the geometric representation will be briefly reviewed. Chapter 3 covers the location methods. Chapter 4 presents preliminary experimental results, and chapter 5 gives a short conclusion.

2 Geometric representation

Our experimental system SOMBRERO (**s**urface **o**riented **m**odel **b**uilding for the **re**construction and **r**ecognition of **o**bjects) employs the same kind of boundary representation to images (2.5-D scene views) and 3-D models, comprising surfaces, attributes and relations. The main difference concerns the relations: a scene description may explicitly state an occlusion relation between surfaces whereas a model allows only view-independent neighborhood relations. Brep's are efficiently recognized and automatically derived from pixel data. Tab.1 summarizes the geometry model, and fig. 1 the data flow. For details we refer to [2].

Surface_type results from a global, learning classification of each surface by the predominant value in the *curvature_histogram* of K-/H-sign combinations [9].

Approximation denotes the coefficients of an implicit function approximation (quadric). *Boundary_description* represents a closed 3-D contour by a sequence of straight line or circular edges. *Relation_class* specifies a neighborhood or occlusion relation between adjacent surfaces, or a relation between objects. *Arguments* denotes the related surface-id's or object-id's. *Transition_edge* specifies an edge in 3-D space forming the transition between the surfaces. *Transition_attribute* characterizes a relation numerically (e.g. by an included angle), and *transition_type* takes the following values:

:JUMP_COVERING (f1,f2)	f1 occludes f2 (discontinuity of distance map)
:JUMP_COVERED (f1,f2)	f1 occluded by f2 (discontinuity of distance map)
:CUT_HARD_CONCAVE (f1,f2)	concave crease between planar surfaces f1, f2
:CUT_HARD_CONVEX (f1,f2)	convex crease between planar surfaces f1, f2
:CUT_ROUND_CONCAVE (f1,f2)	concave crease between curved surfaces f1, f2
:CUT_ROUND_CONVEX (f1,f2)	convex crease between curved surfaces f1, f2
:CUT_SMOOTH (f1, f2)	curvature transition between curved surfaces

Scene /object description	
class	*(for objects only)*
centre_ of_gravity	
extent	
volume	
list of surface identifiers	
list of surface descriptions	
list of relation descriptions	

Table 1: Summary of geometry model

Surface Description
surface_type
surface_area
extent
centre_of_gravity
approximation
curvature_histogram
direction_vector
list of boundary_descriptions

Relation Description
relation_class
arguments
transition_edge
transition_attribute
transition_type

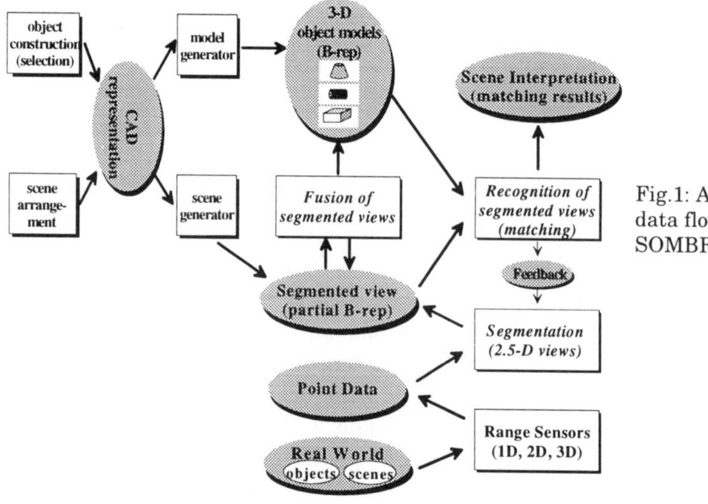

Fig.1: Architecture and data flow in SOMBRERO

3 Localization

3.1 Intrinsic boundary parts

The following definition states whether an observed image surface boundary may be *used* for object localization:

***Def.1** (Intrinsic boundary part):* An image surface boundary (part) b is *intrinsic* iff the pose transformation $(R,T)^{-1}$ for the object instance b belongs to must map b onto a surface boundary of the matching object model, within certain distance tolerances.

Since (R,T) is *unknown*, equivalent conditions are needed to *detect* intrinsic boundaries from the data. This depends on the *segmentation conditions* for bounded surfaces, the *object configuration* in the scene, and, in case of smoothly curved surfaces, even the *viewpoint*. The first step is to seek an *explanation* for each boundary part (edge) *by a relation* (3-D *transition edge*) to other surfaces.

***Def.2** (Explained boundary part):* An edge b_e of an image surface boundary b is *explained* by a relation $\boldsymbol{R}$ iff there exists a tuple t for this surface whose edge e is almost *parallel* and *close* to b_e and *overlaps* most of b_e, and there is no other relation $\boldsymbol{R'}$ meeting these criteria to a higher degree.

For the segmentation conditions of model objects and images, we assume *maximal* surface patches not separable into disjoint parts by occlusion, crease, or curvature transitions. Also, each image surface must belong to a single object. Part of a surface boundary may arise from occlusion, yet not be detectable as a COVERED jump edge. A closer look at the explaining relation is then needed: do the related surfaces belong to a single rigid object or to different objects, and is there an attribute preserving (*invariant*) relation in the model? The hypothetical grouping of surfaces to object instances is controlled by the interpretation tree. Different hypotheses may produce different intrinsic features and therefore different location results which, again, are used to verify or defeat the hypothesis. For polyhedral scenes with planar surfaces, a simple and strong condition is obtained:

***Rule 1** (for planar surfaces)*
A boundary edge b_e of a planar image surface is intrinsic iff it is explained by a COVERING relation, or by a convex crease, or by an invariant concave crease $\in$ {CUT_HARD_CONCAVE, CUT_ROUND_CONCAVE, CUT_SMOOTH} to a neighboring image surface of the same scene object instance.

This rule is justified by example cases without giving a formal proof. Notches in boundaries caused by missing data or segmentation noise are not explained and can be excluded, exploiting the redundant edge information. So are occluded (viewpoint dependent, COVERED) boundaries. However, occluding boundaries (COVERING) of *planar* surfaces are always intrinsic. There must exist a corresponding convex crease to an (invisible) image surface of the same object, and, according to the segmentation conditions, a locatable boundary of a model surface explained by the crease. The same holds for a convex crease visible in the image, no matter if its angle is preserved in the model and if there is just one object or two objects lying flush. However, a boundary explained by a concave crease may arise from occlusion by another object and it is intrinsic only if the related surfaces lie on the same object and have a matching model relation (see fig. 2a).

Things get slightly more complicated for smooth surfaces and transitions. In particular, an occluding boundary with the surface tangential plane nearly parallel to the sensor viewing direction, is occluded at the same time (the surface occludes an unknown part of itself). A matching model boundary may not exist (fig. 2b). The viewing direction of the sensor is required to make a decision:

> ***Rule 2** (for curved surfaces)*
> A boundary edge b_e of a curved image surface is intrinsic iff it is explained by a non-self-occluding COVERING relation, or by any invariant relation $\in$ {CUT_HARD_CONCAVE, CUT_ROUND_CONCAVE, CUT_HARD_CONVEX, CUT_ROUND_CONVEX, CUT_SMOOTH} to another image surface of the same object instance.

Note that boundaries explained by convex transitions need no longer be intrinsic. Consider the convex surface F1 in fig. 2b, partially occluded by a wedge-shaped object (surface F2) lying on top. The occluded part of the boundary of F1 appears as a convex crease (CUT_ROUND_CONVEX), where we would expect a COVERED relation, but it is not a stable model boundary imposed by a segmentation condition, such as a curvature transition.

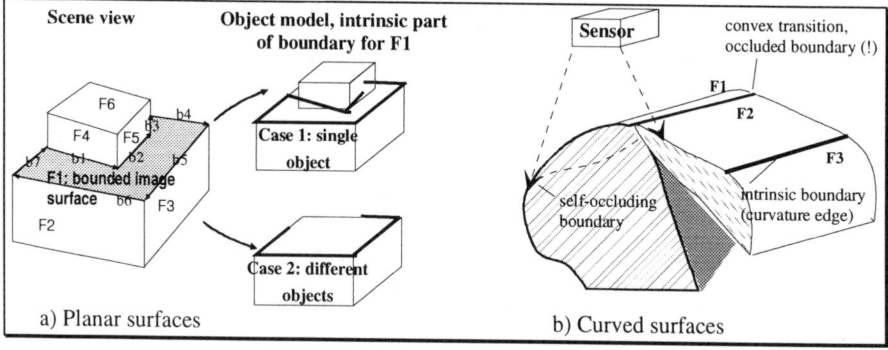

Fig. 2: Examples and counterexamples of intrinsic surface boundaries

3.2 Locating surfaces by matching intrinsic boundaries

3.2.1 The Arkin metric for 2-D polygonal contours

A 2-D contour A can be represented by its *turning function* $\psi_A(t)$: the accumulated turning angle ψ at any contour point, counted from an arbitrary reference point O, versus the accumulated arc length t [8]. The perimeter of the contour is normalized to 1. For a simple closed contour $\psi_A(1)= \psi_A(0)\pm 2\pi$ always holds. $\psi_A(t)$ offers many advantages for constructing a contour distance function:

- for polygons, it is a step function (the jumps correspond to the polygon vertices)
- by definition, it is invariant under translation and scaling of the polygon
- rotation of the polygon corresponds to a vertical (angular) shift $\Delta\psi$
- a change of the origin O corresponds to a horizontal (arc length) shift Δt.

For polygons A and B, the distance between the turning functions $\psi_A(t)$, $\psi_B(t)$, minimized with respect to all possible vertical shifts $\Delta\psi$ and horizontal shifts Δt (rotations and choices of reference O), defines a distance metric:

$$d(A,B):=[\min_{\Delta\psi,\Delta t\in[0,1]} D^{A,B}(\Delta\psi,\Delta t)]^{1/2},$$

$$D^{A,B}(\Delta\psi,\Delta t):=\int_0^1(\psi_A(s+\Delta t)-\psi_B(s)+\Delta\psi)^2 ds \qquad (1)$$

For fixed value Δt, the optimizing value $\Delta\psi^*(\Delta t)$ is directly computable by

$$\Delta\psi^*(\Delta t)=\int_0^1\psi_A(s)ds-\int_0^1\psi_B(s)ds-2\pi\Delta t \qquad (2)$$

In order to minimize $d(A,B)$ it suffices to find the value $\Delta t\in[0,1]$ that minimizes the function

$$D^{A,B}(\Delta\psi^*(\Delta t),\Delta t):=\int_0^1(\psi_A(s+\Delta t)-\psi_B(s))^2 ds-[\Delta\psi^*(\Delta t)]^2 \qquad (3)$$

This is a piecewise linear function of Δt - a sum of rectangular areas whose width changes linearly with Δt. The slope of $D^{A,B}$ changes at 'critical events' where the total ordering of the vertices in A and B changes, i.e. where any 2 polygon vertices are superimposed. Therefore, $D^{A,B}$ has to be computed only for the mn superpositions of vertices which can be done in $O(mn(m+n))$ time. Arkin et. al. also give an incremental (updating) algorithm achieving run time $O(mn\log(mn))$.

3.2.2 Multiple intrinsic contour parts

Contour matching will be applied to the intrinsic, non-occluded parts of boundaries only. For matching an image boundary BS of length l_S to a model boundary BM of length l_M, the integral bounds in (*1-3*) need to be adjusted and the $\psi_M(t)$ function to be extended for $t>l_M$, since image contours are not necessarily closed. Boundary sizes are relevant for recognition. Implicit scaling of all contour lengths to 1 is impossible, since the total arc length including the occluded parts is not known. For very noisy image contours we introduced a *scale factor n* telling explicitly how to scale the image arc length for comparison with the model. For fixed Δt and n, a best value $\Delta\psi^*(\Delta t, n)$ can be computed by a formula similar to (2).

In general, *several* intrinsic parts $BS_1,...,BS_k$ of a closed image contour BS are to be simultaneously matched to a single model contour BM. Minimizing the distance between each BS_i and BM independently will result in a large number of 'optimal' partial matches (Δt_i, $\Delta\psi_i$) but will fail to produce a global, consistent solution which is highly constrained:

1. the *order* in which the BS_i appear on BM is *known* from BS and fixed
2. the angular shift (*rotation*) $\Delta\psi^*$ with respect to BM must be *identical* for all BS_i
3. different BS_i must map onto *disjoint* sections of BM.

We incorporate the constraints 1 and 2 and connect each BS_i with its successor BS_{i+1} by a fictitious straight line segment L_i to form a single closed contour $\overline{BS} := BS_1 \bullet \cdots \bullet BS_k$. The contributions of the L_i-intervals in the distance function are set to 0. Of course, the placements of the BS_i sections on BM are not fixed relative to each other. Since they should not overlap (constraint 3), the relative horizontal shifts Δt_{i+1}-Δt_i may vary between 0 and the difference in arc length between BM and $\overline{BS}$. For each such placement $(\Delta t_1,.. ,\Delta t_k)$ the *single* optimal angular shift $\Delta\psi^*(\Delta t_1,.., \Delta t_k)$ is obtained by a formula similar to (2). Minimizing over all admissible $\Delta t_1,.. ,\Delta t_k$ - each Δt_i still represents a critical event for BS_i and BM - can be best achieved using the incremental algorithm in [8] where the critical events are pre-sorted in increasing order of horizontal shifts. For lack of space, details are omitted here.

3.2.3 Signatures of 3-D space curves

We will now generalize the representation of 2-D polygons to discretized 3-D space curves, using signatures of turning angle and torsion angle. The motion of a smooth 3-D space curve $\underline{r}:[a,b]\to\Re^3$, $\underline{r}(s):= (x(s),y(s),z(s))^T$ with unit tangent vector $\underline{t}(s)=\underline{r}'(s)$, unit normal vector $\underline{n}(s)$, and binormal vector $\underline{b}(s):= \underline{t}(s)\times\underline{n}(s)$, is described by the Frenet-Serret differential equations [10]

$$\dot{\underline{t}}(s) = \kappa(s)\cdot\underline{n}(s) \qquad \dot{\underline{b}}(s) = -\tau(s)\cdot\underline{n}(s) \qquad \dot{\underline{n}}(s) = \tau(s)\cdot\underline{b}(s) - \kappa(s)\cdot\underline{t}(s) \qquad (4)$$

For a given pair of continuous curvature and torsion functions, $\kappa:[a,b]\to\Re$, $\tau:[a,b]\to\Re$, a curve of arc length $(b-a)$ having κ,τ as curvature and torsion functions is uniquely determined up to a rotation and a translation in 3-D space.

For a 3-D polygon $\boldsymbol{P}$ with vertices $\boldsymbol{p}_0,...,\boldsymbol{p}_N$ we define a discrete version of the above differential equations, using a recurrence relation and discrete curvature and torsion angles (see fig.3):

$$s_i := \|p_{i+1} - p_i\| \quad S_i := \sum_{j=0}^{i} s_j \quad \underline{t}_i := (p_{i+1} - p_i)/s_i \tag{5a}$$

$$(\underline{b}_{i+1}, \underline{n}_{i+1}) := \begin{cases} (\underline{b}_i, \underline{n}_i) & \textit{if} \quad \underline{t}_i \underline{t}_{i+1} \approx 1 \quad (5b) \\ (\underline{b}_i, \underline{b}_i \times \underline{t}_{i+1}) & \textit{if} \quad \underline{b}_i (\underline{t}_i \times \underline{t}_{i+1}) \approx -1 \quad (5c) \\ (\underline{t}_i \times \underline{t}_{i+1}, (\underline{t}_i \times \underline{t}_{i+1}) \times \underline{t}_{i+1}) & \textit{otherwise} \quad (5d) \end{cases}$$

$\kappa_i \in (-\pi, \pi]$:= included turning angle $\angle(\underline{t}_{i-1}, \underline{t}_i)$ within the plane $\underline{b}_i(\underline{x}-p_i)=0$
$\tau_i \in (-\pi, \pi]$:= included torsion angle $\angle(\underline{b}_{i-1}, \underline{b}_i)$ within the plane $\underline{t}_i(\underline{x}-p_i)=0$.

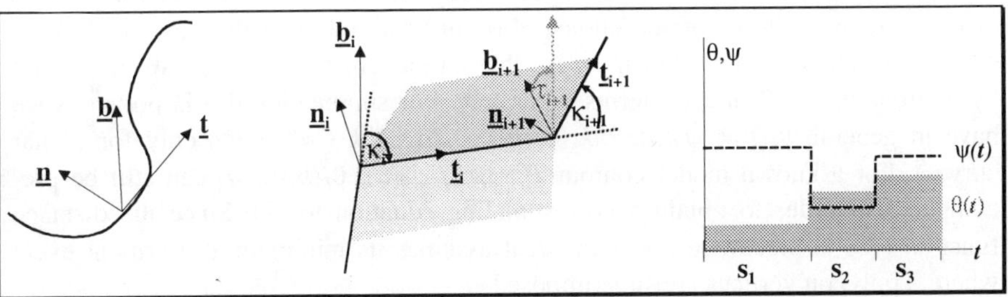

Fig. 3: Tangent, normal, and binormal vectors for a 3-D space curve (left), for a 3-D polygon (centre), and shape signature (right)

We define as the shape signatures of a discrete 3-D polygon $\boldsymbol{P}$ the accumulated turning and torsion angles. They are piecewise constant functions of the arc length s:

$$\psi_P : [a, b] \rightarrow \Re, \qquad \psi_P(s) := \sum_{S_i \le s} \kappa_i \tag{6a}$$

$$\theta_P : [a, b] \rightarrow \Re, \qquad \theta_P(s) := \sum_{S_i \le s} \tau_i \tag{6b}$$

For open or closed polygons $\boldsymbol{P}$ in Euclidean space, the functions ψ_P , θ_P are uniquely and well defined. The definition *(5c)* keeps the vector $\underline{b}_i$ from arbitrarily being flung nearly 180° around at points where the curve changes from locally convex to locally concave. The definition (5b) prevents a straight line from ambiguously being represented as a twisted line. (5b)-(5d) essentially insure uniqueness as well as continuity of the representation: small changes in polygon vertices will result in small changes in the angle representation. For a planar curve $\boldsymbol{P}$ with 2-D shape signature ψ we have: $\psi_P \equiv \psi$, $\theta_P \equiv 0$.

Given two piecewise constant functions ψ_P, θ_P and a coordinate frame at the starting position, a 3-D space curve having ψ_P, θ_P as its shape signature is uniquely determined by solving the recurrence relation, as in the continuous case by solving the Frenet-Serret equations. The distance measure

$$d(A,B) = [\min_{\Delta\psi,\Delta\theta,\Delta t \in [a,b]} D^{A,B}(\Delta\psi,\Delta\theta,\Delta t)]^{1/2} \tag{7a}$$

$$D^{A,B}(\Delta\psi,\Delta\theta,\Delta t) := \int_a^b [(\psi_A(s+\Delta t) - \psi_B(s) + \Delta\psi)^2 + (\theta_A(s+\Delta t) - \theta_B(s) + \Delta\theta)^2]ds \tag{7b}$$

defines a metric between 3-D polygons. The values of $\Delta\psi$, $\Delta\theta$, Δt minimizing $d(A,B)$ correspond to an offset (choice of origin) and a 3-D rotation by which the 2 contours optimally match. For *fixed* Δt, the optimal shift values $\Delta\psi$, $\Delta\theta$ are found by minimizing the 2 integral terms separately. For simple closed 3-D polygons we have in general $\psi_P(b) \neq \psi_P(a) \pm 2\pi k$, $\theta_P(b) \neq \theta_P(a) \pm 2\pi k$ ("=" holds only for planar curves). For a known model contour $\boldsymbol{P}$, $\psi_P(b)-\psi_P(a)$, $\theta_P(b)-\theta_P(a)$ can still be precomputed in order to obtain a corresponding equation to *(2)*. Since the distance function *(7b)* is piecewise linear in Δt, it assumes its minimum at a critical event where 2 polygon vertices are superimposed.

3.2.4 Sampling point correspondences

From $\psi(s)$ matching, a rigid 3-D transformation (R_0, T_0) between image and model contour may be directly obtained: compute R_0 from the angular shifts $\Delta\psi^*$, $\Delta\theta^*$, and take T_0 as the translation that maps the 2 polygon vertices of the critical event, say $\underline{p}_S$, $\underline{p}_M$, onto each other. However, (R_0, T_0) is not the final transformation we are looking for. In general, $\psi(s)$ matching cannot produce the translation for optimal alignment in Euclidean space (fig.4): the $\psi(s)$ representation is *invariant* to 3-D shifts! Instead, *corresponding points* may be obtained directly from the $\psi(s)$ diagram, by *sampling* image and model contours at *equal arc length intervals*, starting from the pair $(\underline{p}_S, \underline{p}_M)$. Again, this may not lead to optimal, distance preserving correspondences, as fig. 4 shows. Better correspondences are obtained by assigning to each sampled image point of an intrinsic contour section the closest point on the model contour transformed by (R_0, T_0).

Locating is invoked in SOMBRERO as soon as possible, to discard implausible matching hypotheses ('*matching by locating*' [3]), and, conversely, it requires a hypothesis to extract the intrinsic boundaries. A matching hypothesis for a single object contains a list of surface pairs $((S_1,M_1),...,(S_k,M_k))$ and their boundaries. From all the corresponding boundary points the final transformation $\boldsymbol{T}$ is estimated by Horn's algorithm. The surface quadric approximations are used as well, for location verification. We refer to an extended version of the paper for details of the correspondence sampling and the localization algorithms.

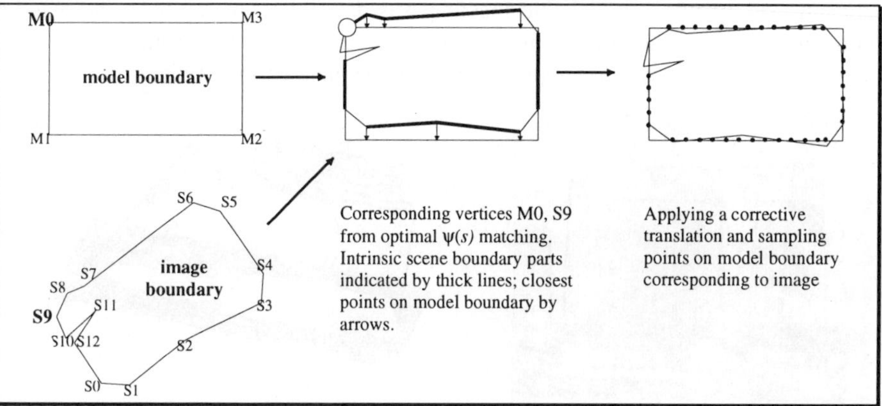

Fig. 4: Finding point correspondences (illustrated by 2-D contour example)

4 Experimental results

Object recognition and localization have been implemented using Allegro Common Lisp 4.2 with CLIM 2.0, and applied to about 15 simulated and real range images. Fig.5a shows an aerial-like view of a synthetic house block scene, fig.5b a high-noise image collected by a time-of-flight laser scanner (LADAR 2-D) mounted to a gantry robot and looking 'top-down'. Fig. 5c,e show the results of locating house blocks. Light grey lines represent boundaries of unrecognized surfaces, e.g. the pyramid-like tower peak for which no suitable model was provided. Dark grey lines indicate surfaces that have been recognized but not located, such as the 'road level' background surface: its outer boundary, the image border, is not explained by any surface relation, and its 3 inner boundaries are occluded by the house blocks. The orientation angle errors are less than 2° and are due to segmentation inaccuracies.

In the LADAR scene only the chest and barrel were recognized and located (fig.5d,f). No models were provided for the clamping bolts (F8, F9). The hypothesis generation tentatively assigned the splinter surfaces F4-F7 to the chest object, but rejected it during hypothesis verification. The orientation angle error is about 1° and the alignment errors between image and model surfaces are well below the measurement errors of the laser scanner (±30mm). Viewing the fact that only a coarse and fuzzy segmented boundary was available for locating, accuracy is very good. About 80% of the top boundary of the chest are explained by surface relations and are intrinsic (in fig.5d these edges are indicated as thick lines). By rule 1 in 3.1, the convex transitions between F1 and F4-F7 which do not belong to a real object can still be used for locating the chest. Only 45% of the top surface of the barrel are explained, and part of them are occluded. The cylindrical mantle of the barrel has self-occluding boundaries parallel to the viewing direction of the sensor. They are not intrinsic by rule 2 in 3.1. No location was directly estimated from the mantle boundary. Rather, the algorithm estimates the transformation from the flat top surface, and uses the quadric approximation of the mantle to verify it.

Fig. 5a: Synthetic house block scene (100x100)

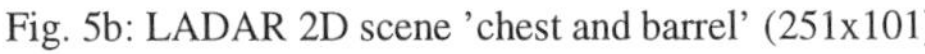

Fig. 5b: LADAR 2D scene 'chest and barrel' (251x101)

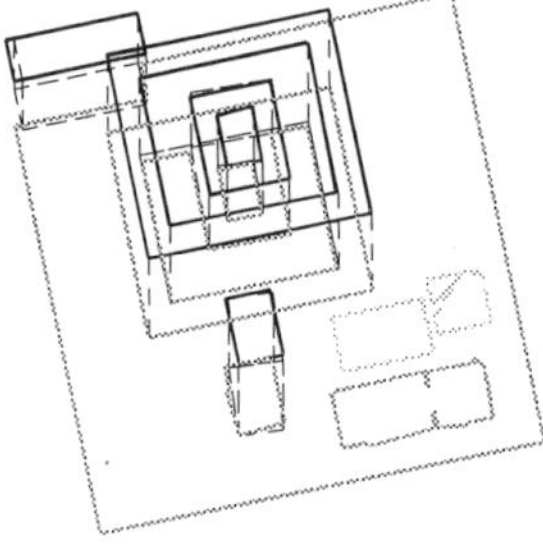

Fig. 5c: Locating the house block scene (wire diagram, surface boundaries extracted from segmentation output)

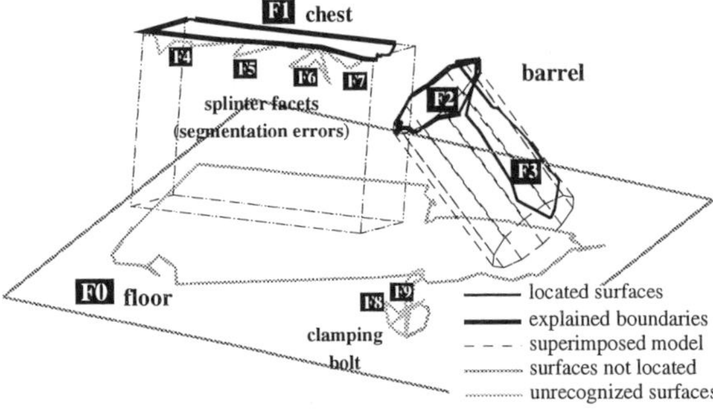

Fig. 5d: Locating the 'chest and barrel' scene (wire diagram, surface boundaries extracted from segmentation output)

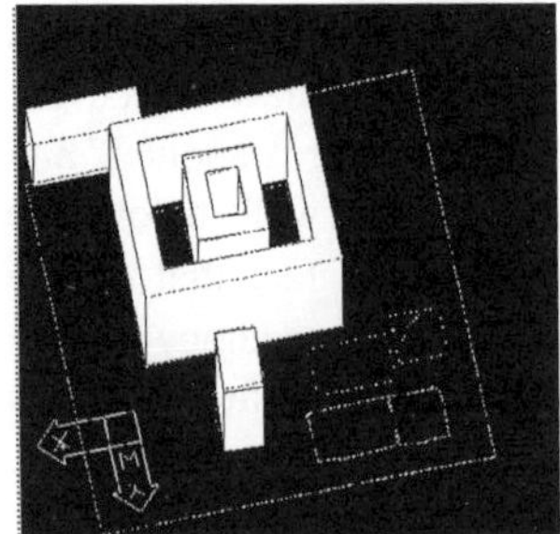

Fig. 5e: House block scene, solid model superimposed

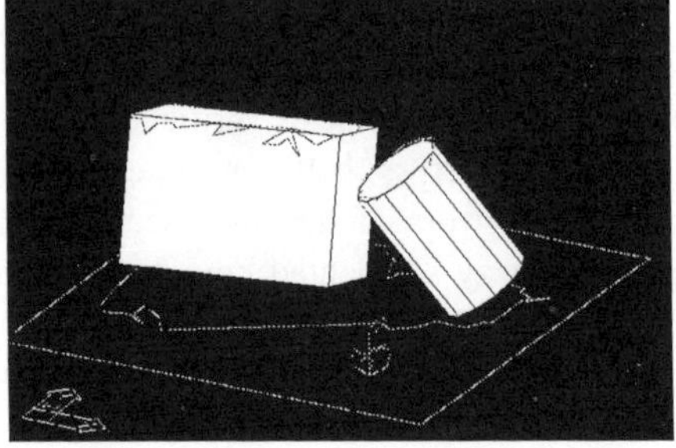

Fig. 5f: Chest-and-barrel scene, solid model superimposed

5 Conclusion

Boundary representations are powerful models for range image analysis. However, estimating a rigid transformation from surface normal vector pairs or boundary point pairs may in practice fail for several reasons: the limited number of surfaces visible, the failure to distinguish relevant from irrelevant boundary information, and the discretization noise introduced by segmentation.

The new locating method proposed copes with coarse, segmented boundary information from partially occluded laser scanner images. By extracting the intrinsic subsections of surface boundaries and applying a 3-D extension of Arkin's contour metric, precise point correspondences are sampled, from which a location may be directly calculated by least squares methods. CAD model object and noisy image may differ in discretization and resolution, as was shown by a few examples. The geometry model could be enhanced by additional intrinsic line features than just boundaries. E.g. crest lines could be easily computed from the curvatures.

References

[1] B.Sabata, J.K.Aggarwal, *Estimation of Motion from a Pair of Range Images: A review*, CVGIP: Image Understanding 54(3), Nov. 1991, pp. 309-324

[2] P.Kohlhepp, A.Hanczak, Li Gang, *The generation, recognition and consistent fusion of partial boundary representations from range images*, Sensor Fusion VII, Boston, Mass., Oct 31- Nov 4, 1994

[3] O.D.Faugeras, M.Hebert, *The Representation, Recognition, and Locating of 3-D Objects*, In: The International Journal of Robotics Research 5(3), 1986, pp.27-52

[4] T.E.Boult, A.D.Gross, *Recovery of superquadrics from 3-D information*, SPIE Intelligent Robots and Computer Vision, Vol. 848, 1987

[5] S.Kumar, S.Han, D.Goldgof, K.Bowyer, *On Recovering Hyperquadrics from Range Data*, IEEE Trans. PAMI 17(11), 1995, pp. 1079-1083

[6] B.K.P.Horn, *Closed-form solution of absolute orientation using unit quaternions*, J.Opt.Soc.Am. 4(4), 1987, pp. 629-642

[7] P.J.Besl, D.N.McKay, *A Method for Registration of 3-D Shapes*, IEEE Trans. PAMI 14(2), 1992, pp. 239-256

[8] E.Arkin, L.Chew, D.Huttenlocher, K.Kedem, J.Mitchell, *An Efficiently Computable Metric for Comparing Polygonal Shapes*, IEEE Trans. PAMI 13, 1991, pp. 209-216

[9] P.J.Besl, *Surfaces in range image understanding*, Springer Series in Perception Engineering, Ed. R.C.Jain, Springer, New York, 1988

[10] A.W.Nutbourne, R.R.Martin, *Differential Geometry Applied to Curve and Surface Design*, Ellis Horwood Ltd, 1988

[11] R.Begevin, M.Soucy, H.Gagnon, D.Laurendeau, *Towards a General Multi-View Registration Technique*, IEEE Trans. PAMI 18(5), 1996, pp.540-547

[12] M.Soucy, D.Laurendeau, *A General Surface Approach to the Integration of a Set of Range Views*, IEEE Trans. PAMI 17(4), 1995, pp.344-358

EVALUATION OF FINITE DIFFERENCE ALGORITHMS FOR A LINEAR SHAPE-FROM-SHADING PROBLEM

R. KOZERA

Department of Computer Science, The University of Western Australia, Nedlands 6907 W.A., Australia

R. KLETTE

Tamaki Campus, Computer Science Department, The Auckland University, Private Bag 92019, Auckland, New Zealand

We analyse finite difference based algorithms for the recovery of object shape from a single shading pattern generated under the assumption of a linear reflectance map. They operate on a rectangular discrete image (or part of it) and use the height of the sought-after surface along a curve in the image (image boundary) as initial data.

1 Introduction

In this paper, we present some results concerning the shape-from-shading problem in which the reflectance map is *linear*. Such a special case arises *e.g.* in the study of the maria of the moon (see [1, Subsections 10.9 and 11.1.2]). If a small portion of a surface, described by the graph of a function u, having reflectivity properties approximated by a linear reflectance map, is illuminated by a distant point source of unit power in direction $(a_1, a_2, -1)$, then the corresponding image $\mathcal{E}(x_1, x_2)$ satisfies a *linear image irradiance equation* of the following form

$$\left(a_1\frac{\partial u}{\partial x_1}(x_1,x_2)+a_2\frac{\partial u}{\partial x_2}(x_1,x_2)+1\right)(a_1^2+a_2^2+1)^{-1/2}=\mathcal{E}(x_1,x_2), \quad (1)$$

over $\Omega = \{(x,y) \in \mathbf{R}^2 : \mathcal{E}(x_1,x_2) > 0\}$. Letting $E(x_1,x_2) = \mathcal{E}(x_1,x_2)(a_1^2 + a_2^2+1)^{1/2} - 1$, one can rewrite (1) as a *transformed* linear image irradiance equation

$$a_1\frac{\partial u}{\partial x_1}(x_1,x_2)+a_2\frac{\partial u}{\partial x_2}(x_1,x_2)=E(x_1,x_2). \quad (2)$$

In this paper we evaluate some finite difference based algorithms for the equation (2). The original idea of this work is an extension of Kozera's work [3], where the finite difference scheme, based on central difference derivative approximations, is discussed. We continue here, to investigate the issue of the stability and the convergence of different algorithms based on the combination of the forward and backward derivative approximations. Convergence, stability, and domain of influence, will be considered here as algorithmic features and used in this paper for evaluating shape reconstruction algorithms based on finite difference schemes. Critical to our approach is the assumption that u is given along some (not necessarily smooth) initial curve γ in the image (image boundary). The algorithms provide the numerical solution of the following Cauchy problem (for $u \in C(\bar{\Omega}) \cap C^2(\Omega)$) considered over a rectangle Ω:

$$L(u(x_1, x_2)) = E(x_1, x_2) \tag{3a}$$

$$u(x_1, 0) = f(x_1) \quad 0 \le x_1 \le a, \text{ for } \operatorname{sgn}(a_1 a_2) \ge 0, \tag{3b}$$

$$u(x_1, b) = f(x_1) \quad 0 \le x_1 \le a, \text{ for } \operatorname{sgn}(a_1 a_2) < 0, \tag{3c}$$

$$u(0, x_2) = g(x_2) \quad 0 \le x_2 \le b; \tag{3d}$$

here $Lu = a_1 u_{x_1} + a_2 u_{x_2}$, and functions $f \in C([0,a]) \cap C^2((0,a))$ and $g \in C([0,b]) \cap C^2((0,b))$ satisfy $f(0) = g(0)$, $E \in C^2(\overline{\Omega})$, and a_1 and a_2 are constants such that $(a_1, a_2) \neq (0,0)$. To simplify consideration we will assume that $\operatorname{sgn}(a_1 a_2) \ge 0$ and $a_2 \neq 0$ and therefore only the case $(3)(a,b,d)$ will be considered (the others are analogous). For extended version of this paper, an interested reader is referred to Kozera and Klette [4,5] (submitted as Alexander von Humboldt Research project in 1993). A general information about shape-from-shading problem can also be found *e.g.* in [1] or Klette *et al.* [2].

2 Basic Notions and Theory for Finite Difference Schemes

We recall first some basic notions and results from the theory of finite difference method applied to PDE (see Van der Houwen [6, Chapter 1]).

Assume that an interval $[0,T]$ and a domain $G \subset \mathbf{R}$ together with its boundary Γ and $\bar{G} = G \cup \Gamma$ are given and that $(E_0(\bar{G}), \|\ \|_{E_0})$, $(E(\bar{G}), \|\ \|_{\bar{G}})$, $(E(\Gamma), \|\ \|_G)$, and $(E(G), \|\ \|_G)$ are linear normed spaces of scalar (vector) functions, defined respectively, on the set of points $\bar{G}$, $\bar{G} \times [0,T]$, $\Gamma \times [0,T]$, and $G \times [0,T]$. Consider now the following problem

$$U_t(x,t) + D(x,t)U_x(x,t) = H(x,t), \quad U(\Gamma \times [0,T]) = \Psi(\Gamma), \quad \text{and } U(x,0) = U_0(x), \tag{4}$$

where $(x,t) \in G \times [0,T]$, the scalar functions $U_0 \in E_0(\bar{G})$, $\Psi \in E(\Gamma)$, and the vector function $F(x,t) = (H(x,t), D(x,t)) \in E(G)$.

A problem of finding the inverse of a given mapping $\mathcal{L} : D_{\mathcal{L}} \to \Delta_{\mathcal{L}}$ of an unknown function $U \in D_L = (E(\bar{G}), \|\ \|_{\bar{G}})$ onto a known element $(U_0, F, \Psi) \in \Delta_{\mathcal{L}} = (E_0(\bar{G}) \times E(G) \times E(\Gamma), \|\ \|_\times)$, where $\|(U_0, F, \Psi)\|_\times = \|U_0\|_{E_0} + \|F\|_G + \|\Psi\|_\Gamma$, will be called ***initial boundary value problem***.

The initial boundary value problem $\mathcal{L}U = (U_0, F, \Psi)$ is said to be *well-posed* with respect to the norms in $E(\bar{G})$ and in $E_0(\bar{G}) \times E(G) \times E(\Gamma)$ if $\mathcal{L}$ has a unique inverse $\mathcal{L}^{-1}$ which is continuous at the point (U_0, F, Ψ).

We shall now introduce the definition of the *uniform grid sequence*. We replace the continuous interval $[0, T]$ by a discrete set of points $[t_0 = 0, t_1, t_2, \ldots, t_M = T]$, where $t_{i+1} - t_i = \Delta t$ (for each $i \in [0, \ldots, M-1]$) and $M\Delta t = T$, together with a finite set of points $\Gamma_{\Delta t} \subset \Gamma$ such that the distance between two consecutive points in the X-axis direction satisfies $\Delta x = \mathcal{N}(\Delta t)$ and $N\mathcal{N}(\Delta t) = \mu(G)$, where $\mu(G)$ denotes the measure of G. These three sets of points constitute *a grid* or *net* $Q_{\Delta t}$ in $\bar{G} \times [0, T]$ *i.e.* $Q_{\Delta t} = \bar{G}_{\Delta t} \times \{t_k\}_{k=0}^{N}$, where $\bar{G}_{\Delta t} = G_{\Delta t} \cup \Gamma_{\Delta t}$. We assume that *a sequence of nets* $Q_{\Delta t}$ is defined in such a way that $\lim_{\Delta t \to 0^+} Q_{\Delta t}$ is dense in $\bar{G} \times [0, T]$. The last requirement is satisfied when $\lim_{\Delta t \to 0^+} \mathcal{N}(\Delta t) = 0$. Furthermore, we introduce the corresponding normed grid spaces

$$(E_0(\bar{G}_{\Delta t}), \|\ \|_{E_{0\Delta t}}), \quad (E(\bar{G}_{\Delta t}), \|\ \|_{\bar{G}_{\Delta t}}), \quad (E(\Gamma_{\Delta t}), \|\ \|_{\Gamma_{\Delta t}}), \quad (E(G_{\Delta t}), \|\ \|_{G_{\Delta t}}) \tag{5}$$

defined on the sets $\bar{G}_{\Delta t}$, $\bar{G}_{\Delta t} \times \{t_k\}_{k=0}^{N}$, $\Gamma_{\Delta t} \times \{t_k\}_{k=0}^{N}$, and $G_{\Delta t} \times \{t_k\}_{k=0}^{N}$, respectively. The elements of these spaces are called *net functions* and will be denoted by lower case letters u_0, u, ψ, and f. A mapping $\mathcal{R}_{\Delta t}$ of an unknown net function u of $(E(\bar{G}_{\Delta t}), \|\ \|_{\bar{G}_{\Delta t}})$ into the known element (u_0, f, ψ) of $(E_0(\bar{G}_{\Delta t}) \times E(G_{\Delta t}) \times E(\Gamma_{\Delta t}), \|\ \|_{\Delta t_\times})$, where $\|(u_0, f, \psi)\|_{\Delta t_\times} = \|u_0\|_{E_{0\Delta t}} + \|f\|_{G_{\Delta t}} + \|\psi\|_{\Gamma_{\Delta t}}$ is defined for each net $Q_{\Delta t}$, will be called *a finite difference scheme.* Difference schemes can be described by the equation $\mathcal{R}_{\Delta t} u = (u_0, f, \psi)$, with the domain and range of $\mathcal{R}_{\Delta t}$ denoted by $D_{\mathcal{R}\Delta t}$ (called as *a discrete domain of influence*) and $\Delta_{\mathcal{R}\Delta t}$, respectively. It will be assumed that both $D_{\mathcal{R}\Delta t}$ and $\Delta_{\mathcal{R}\Delta t}$ are linear spaces and $\mathcal{R}_{\Delta t}$ has *a unique inverse* $\mathcal{R}_{\Delta t}^{-1}$, which is *continuous* in $D_{\mathcal{R}\Delta t}$ for every $\Delta t \neq 0$. We can also define a set $D_I \subset \Omega$ called *a domain of influence* as $D_I = cl\,(\bigcup D_{\mathcal{R}\Delta t})$ which clearly depends on a given initial boundary value problem, grid sequence and associated finite difference scheme.

Let us now introduce the *discretisation operator* $[\ ]_{d(\Delta t)}$ which transforms a function $U \in E(\bar{G})$ to its discrete analogue $[U]_{d(\Delta t)}$ defined as U reduced to the domain of the net $Q_{\Delta t}$. In the same manner we can define discretised elements $[U_0]_{d(\Delta t)} \in E_0(\bar{G}_{\Delta t})$, $[F]_{d(\Delta t)} \in E(G_{\Delta t})$, and $[\Psi]_{d(\Delta t)} \in E(\Gamma_{\Delta t})$. In this paper we shall use the convention: $[U]_{d(\Delta t)} = u$, $[U_0]_{d(\Delta t)} = u_0$, $[F]_{d(\Delta t)} = f$, and $[\Psi]_{d(\Delta t)} = \psi$, where $f = (h, d)$. Moreover, it is also assumed that the norms on the grid sequence $\{Q_{\Delta t}\}_{\Delta t}$ *match* the corresponding norms from the related *"continuous spaces" i.e.*

$$\|u\|_{\bar{G}_{\Delta t}} \to \|U\|_{\bar{G}}, \quad \|u_0\|_{E_{0\Delta t}} \to \|U_0\|_{E_0}, \quad \|f\|_{G_{\Delta t}} \to \|F\|_{G}, \quad \|\psi\|_{\Gamma_{\Delta t}} \to \|\Psi\|_{\Gamma}, \tag{6}$$

as $\Delta t \to 0$. We shall now introduce the basic definitions. Assume now that $\widetilde{U}$ is a solution to the initial boundary value problem $\mathcal{L}\widetilde{U} = (U_0, F, \Psi)$, and that u is a solution to the corresponding discrete problem

$$\mathcal{R}_{\Delta t} u = (u_0, f, \psi). \tag{7}$$

If $\mathcal{R}_{\Delta t}$ is to be a good approximation of $\mathcal{L}$ we should expect that the function $\widetilde{u} = [\widetilde{U}]_{d(\Delta t)}$, for some element $(\widetilde{u}_0, \widetilde{f}, \widetilde{\psi})$, satisfies a finite difference equation $\mathcal{R}_{\Delta t}\widetilde{u} = (\widetilde{u}_0, \widetilde{f}, \widetilde{\psi})$ which closely relates to (7). The value $\|[\mathcal{L}\widetilde{U}]_{d(\Delta t)} - \mathcal{R}_{\Delta t}\widetilde{u}\|_{\Delta t_\times}$ is called the *error of approximation.* The value $\|u - \widetilde{u}\|_{\bar{G}_{\Delta t}}$ is in turn called *the discretisation error.*

Definition 1 *We say that a difference scheme is consistent with an initial boundary value problem if the error of approximation converges to zero as* $\Delta t \to 0$. *We say also that a difference scheme is convergent to the solution u (if it exists) if the discretisation error converges to zero as* $\Delta t \to 0$.

Finally, we shall define a notion of stability for the linear difference schemes in the sense of Rjabenki and Filippov (see also [6]).

Definition 2 *A linear difference scheme is R-F stable if operators* $\{\mathcal{R}_{\Delta t}^{-1}\}$ *are uniformly bounded as* $\Delta t \to 0$.

Combining the Definition 5.3 and 6.2 with the Theorem 5.1 (see Van der Houwen [6]) we have the following:

Theorem 1 *A consistent and R-F stable finite-difference scheme is convergent to the solution of* $\mathcal{L}\widetilde{U} = (U_0, F, \Psi)$ *(if such solution exists).*

Of course, for a Cauchy problem (3)(a,b,d), we have $T = b$, $x_2 = t$, $G = (0, a)$, $\Gamma \doteq \{0\}$, $U_0(x_1) = f(x_1)$, $\Psi(\Gamma) = g(x_2)$, $H(x_1, x_2) = (1/a_2)E(x_1, x_2)$, and $D(x_1, x_2) = (a_1/a_2)$. The corresponding normed spaces are assumed to be here as follows:

$$E_0(\bar{G}) = \{U_0 : [0, a] \to \mathbf{R} : U_0 \in C([0, a]) \cap C^2((0, a))\}$$

with $\|U_0\|_{E_0} = max_{x_1 \in [0,a]} |U_0(x_1)|$, (here $\widetilde{a} = (a_1/a_2)$ and $x = (x_1, x_2)$)

$$E(\bar{G}) = \{(E, \widetilde{a}) : [0, a] \times [0, b] \to \mathbf{R}^2 : E, \widetilde{a} \in C([0, a] \times [0, b]) \cap C^2((0, a) \times (0, b))\}$$

with $\|(E, \widetilde{a})\|_{\bar{G}} = max_{x \in [0,a]\times[0,b]} |E(x)| + max_{x \in [0,a]\times[0,b]} |\widetilde{a}(x)|$,

$$E(\Gamma) = \{g : \{0\} \times [0, b] \to \mathbf{R} : g \in C(\{0\} \times [0, b]) \cap C^2(\{0\} \times (0, b))\}$$

with $\|g\|_G = max_{x_2 \in [0,b]} |g(0, x_2)|$, and

$$E(G) = \{U : (0, a) \times [0, b] \to \mathbf{R} : U \in C([0, a] \times [0, b]) \cap C^2((0, a) \times (0, b))\}$$

with $\|U\|_G = max_{(x_1,x_2) \in [0,a]\times[0,b]} |U(x_1, x_2)|$.

In a similar manner we introduce discrete analogues of the above defined normed spaces which satisfy *compatibility conditions* (6).

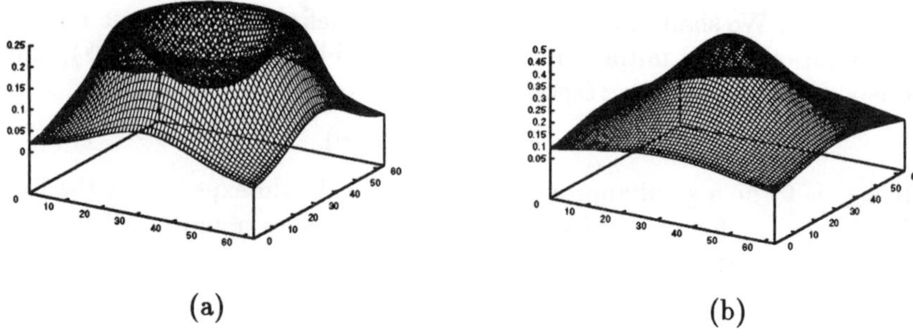

(a) (b)

Figure 1: (a) The graph of the function $u_v(x,y) = (1/(4(1+(1-x^2-y^2)^2)))$ being a volcano-like surface. (b) The graph of the function $u_m(x,y) = (1/(2(1+x^2+y^2)^2))$ being a mountain-like surface.

3 Evaluation of Different Finite-Difference Schemes

We assume now that $\Delta x_2 = (b/M)$, $\Delta x_1 = (a/M)$ (where $M \in [0,1,\ldots,\infty]$; so $M = N$), $((a_1\Delta x_2)/(a_2\mathcal{N}(\Delta x_2))) = const$, and that a function u is a C^2 solution to (2), and lastly that problem (3) is well-posed (see [4,5]).

3.1 Forward-Forward Finite Difference Approximation

Applying *forward difference* approximations together with Taylor's formula yields

$$\left.\frac{\partial u}{\partial x_1}\right|_j^n = \frac{u_{j+1}^n - u_j^n}{\Delta x_1} + O(\Delta x_1) \quad \text{and} \quad \left.\frac{\partial u}{\partial x_2}\right|_j^n = \frac{u_j^{n+1} - u_j^n}{\Delta x_2} + O(\Delta x_2), \quad (8)$$

for any $j,n \in \{1,\ldots,M-1\}$; here u_j^n, $\left.\frac{\partial u}{\partial x_1}\right|_j^n$, and $\left.\frac{\partial u}{\partial x_2}\right|_j^n$ denote the values of u, $\frac{\partial u}{\partial x_1}$, and $\frac{\partial u}{\partial x_2}$, respectively, at the point (x_{1j}, x_{2n}) in the grid; Δx_1 and Δx_2 denote the distances between grid points in the respective directions; M denotes the density of the grid. By substituting (8) into (2) at each point (x_{1j}, x_{2n}), we get

$$a_1\frac{u_{j+1}^n - u_j^n}{\Delta x_1} + a_2\frac{u_j^{n+1} - u_j^n}{\Delta x_2} + O(\Delta x_1, \Delta x_2) = E_j^n. \quad (9)$$

Denoting by v an approximate of u, we obtain from (9) the following

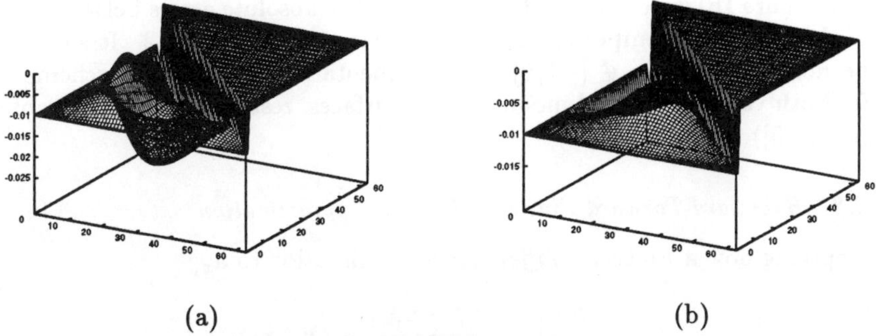

(a) (b)

Figure 2: (a) The absolute error between volcano-like and computed surface for the forward-forward scheme. (b) The absolute error between mountain-like and computed surface for the forward-forward scheme.

sequential two-level *explicit* scheme

$$v_j^{n+1} = \left(1 + \frac{a_1 \Delta x_2}{a_2 \Delta x_1}\right) v_j^n - \frac{a_1 \Delta x_2}{a_2 \Delta x_1} v_{j+1}^n + \frac{\Delta x_2}{a_2} E_j^n \tag{10}$$

with $j, n \in \{1, \ldots, M-1\}$. The following result can be established (for a full proof see [4,5]):

Theorem 2 *Consider the problem* (3) *over a rectangle* Ω. *Let* $\alpha = (a_1 \Delta x_2)(a_2 \Delta x_1)^{-1}$ *be a fixed constant. Then, numerical scheme* (10) *is R-F stable, if and only if* $-1 \le \alpha \le 0$. *Consequently (by Th. 1), for* $-1 \le \alpha \le 0$, *the sequence of functions* $\{u_{\Delta x_2}\}$ *(where each* $u_{\Delta x_2}$ *is a solution of* (10) *with* Δx_2 *temporarily fixed) is convergent to the solution of the Cauchy problem* (3), *while* $\Delta x_2 \to 0$.

As mentioned before, given an initial boundary value problem (3), the scheme (10) recovers the unknown shape over a domain of influence which, for $a_1 \neq 0$ and $M = N$, coincides with

$$D_I = \{(x_1, x_2) \in \mathbf{R}^2 : 0 \le x_1 \le a, \text{ and } 0 \le x_2 \le (-b/a)x_1 + b\}, \tag{11}$$

and for $a_1 = 0$ with the entire $\bar{\Omega}$.

The algorithm (10) has been tested on a number of commonly encountered shapes. For example, with $\Delta x_1/\Delta x_2 = 1.0$, $a_1 = -0.5$, and $a_2 = 1.0$, and thus $\alpha = -0.5$, the volcano-like surface represented by the graph of the function $u_v(x,y) = (1/(4(1+(1-x^2-y^2)^2)))$ (see Figure 1a) and for the mountain-like surface represented by the graph of the function $u_m(x,y) = (1/(2(1+x^2+y^2)^2))$

(see Figure 1b) were taken as test surfaces. The absolute errors between heights of the ideal and computed surfaces are presented in Figure 2. It should also be noted that for $\alpha \notin [-1,0]$ an implementation of numerical scheme (10), for both volcano-like and mountain-like surfaces, resulted in instability of (10) (see [4, 5]).

3.2 Backward-Forward Finite Difference Approximation

Applying now a *backward difference* approximation to u_{x_1}

$$\left.\frac{\partial u}{\partial x_1}\right|_j^n = \frac{u_j^n - u_{j-1}^n}{\Delta x_1} + O(\Delta x_1),$$

and a *forward difference* approximation to u_{x_2} leads to the corresponding two-level *explicit* finite difference scheme

$$v_j^{n+1} = \left(1 - \frac{a_1 \Delta x_2}{a_2 \Delta x_1}\right) v_j^n + \frac{a_1 \Delta x_2}{a_2 \Delta x_1} v_{j-1}^n + \frac{\Delta x_2}{a_2} E_j^n, \tag{12}$$

with $j, n \in \{1, \ldots, M-1\}$. The following stability and convergence result for above finite difference scheme is true (for a full proof see [4, 5]).

Theorem 3 *Consider the problem* (3) *over a rectangle* Ω. *Let* $\alpha = (a_1 \Delta x_2)(a_2 \Delta x_1)^{-1}$ *be a fixed constant. Then, numerical scheme* (12) *is R-F stable, if and only if* $0 \le \alpha \le 1$. *Consequently (by Th.* 1*), for* $0 \le \alpha \le 1$, *the sequence of functions* $\{u_{\Delta x_2}\}$ *(where each* $u_{\Delta x_2}$ *is a solution of* (12) *with* Δx_2 *temporarily fixed) is convergent to the solution of the Cauchy problem* (3), *while* $\Delta x_2 \to 0$.

The domain of influence of scheme (12) coincides with $\bar{\Omega}$, for arbitrary α. Thus, given the criterion of deriving a global shape reconstruction algorithm, it is clear that (12) provides a better reconstruction means as opposed to (10).

The algorithm (12) has been tested for the same shapes as in the previous case. With $\Delta x_1 / \Delta x_2 = 1.0$, $a_1 = 0.5$, and $a_2 = 1.0$, and thus $\alpha = 0.5$, the absolute errors between heights of the ideal and computed surfaces are presented in Figure 3.

3.3 Forward-Backward Finite Difference Approximation

Applying now a *forward difference* approximation to u_{x_1} and a *backward difference* approximation to u_{x_2} leads to the following two-level *explicit horizontal* scheme

$$v_{j+1}^n = \left(1 - \frac{a_2 \Delta x_1}{a_1 \Delta x_2}\right) v_j^n + \frac{a_2 \Delta x_1}{a_1 \Delta x_2} v_j^{n-1} + \frac{\Delta x_1}{a_1} E_j^n, \tag{13}$$

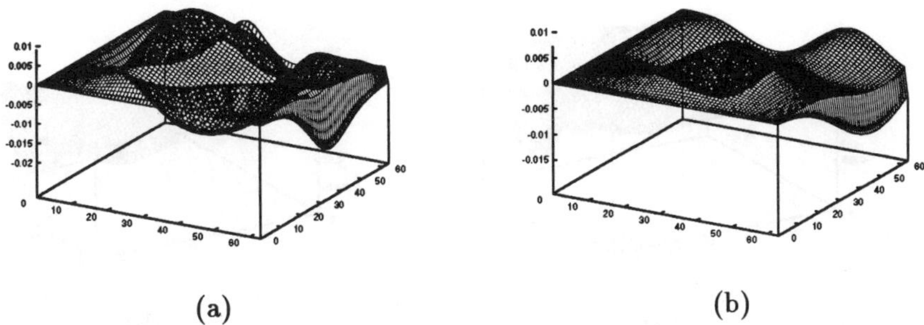

Figure 3: (a) The absolute error between volcano-like and computed surface for the backward-forward scheme. (b) The absolute error between mountain-like and computed surface for the backward-forward scheme.

(for $a_1 \neq 0$), or otherwise to the following *vertical* two-level *explicit* scheme

$$v_j^n = v_j^{n-1} + \frac{\Delta x_2}{a_2} E_j^n, \tag{14}$$

with $j, n \in \{1, \dots, M-1\}$. Observe that for the scheme (13) the role of increment step Δt is played by Δx_1 (if we do not want to deal with *implicit schemes*). Clearly, the shape reconstruction proceeds here sequentially along X_1-axis direction (opposite to the so far presented cases). In a natural way, the boundary condition is represented by the function $f(x_1)$ and the corresponding initial condition by the function $g(x_2)$. We shall present now the next convergence result for the schemes (13) and (14) (for a full proof see [4,5]).

Theorem 4 *Consider the problem* (3) *over a rectangle* Ω. *Let* $\tilde{\alpha} = (a_2 \Delta x_1)(a_1 \Delta x_2)^{-1}$ *be a fixed constant. Then, numerical scheme* (13) *is R-F stable, if and only if* $0 \leq \tilde{\alpha} \leq 1$. *Consequently (by Th.* 1*), for* $0 \leq \tilde{\alpha} \leq 1$, *the sequence of functions* $\{u_{\Delta x_1}\}$ *(where each* $u_{\Delta x_1}$ *is a solution of* (13) *with* Δx_1 *temporarily fixed) is convergent to the solution of the Cauchy problem* (3), *while* $\Delta x_1 \to 0$. *Moreover, numerical scheme* (14) *is R-F stable and its sequence of computed solutions* $\{u_{\Delta x_2}\}$ *converges to the solution of the corresponding Cauchy problem* (3), *while* $\Delta x_2 \to 0$.

For both schemes the corresponding domains of influence coincide with $\bar{\Omega}$. We discuss here only the performance of the scheme (14). It has been tested for the same sample surfaces as in the previous cases. With $\Delta x_1 / \Delta x_2 = 1.0$, $a_1 = 1.0$, and $a_2 = 0.5$, and thus $\tilde{\alpha} = 0.5$, the absolute errors between heights of the ideal and computed surfaces are presented in Figure 4.

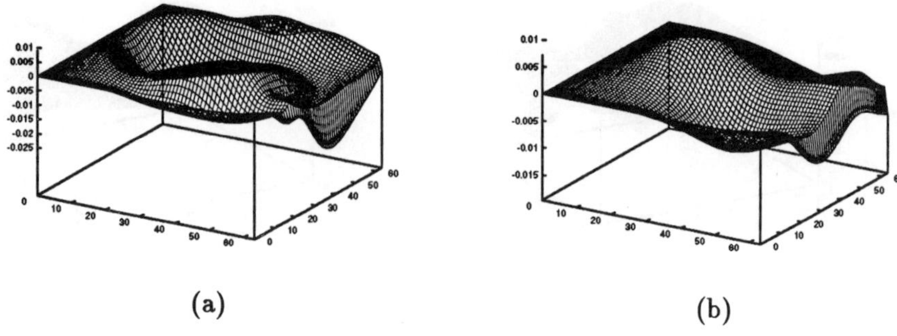

(a) (b)

Figure 4: (a) The absolute error between volcano-like and computed surface for the forward-backward scheme. (b) The absolute error between mountain-like and computed surface for the forward-backward scheme.

3.4 Backward-Backward Finite Difference Approximation

Applying now *backward difference* approximation for both derivatives u_{x_1} and u_{x_2} we arrive at the following two-level *implicit* scheme

$$v_j^n = \frac{1}{1+\alpha} v_j^{n-1} + \frac{\alpha}{1+\alpha} v_{j-1}^n + \frac{\Delta x_2}{a_2(1+\alpha)} E_j^n \tag{15}$$

(for $\alpha \neq -1$), or otherwise at the following two-level *explicit* scheme

$$v_{j-1}^n = u_j^{n-1} + \frac{\Delta x_2}{a_2} E_j^n, \tag{16}$$

with $j, n \in \{1, \ldots, M-1\}$ and $\alpha = (a_1 \Delta x_2 / a_2 \Delta x_1)$.

It is clear that, as opposed to the last subsection, (15) cannot be reduced to the explicit iterative form by a mere change of the "recovery direction". This can be achieved by using another approach (see Subsection 3.4 in [4, 5]). The following result for schemes (15) and (16) is proved in [4, 5].

Theorem 5 *Consider the problem* (3) *over a rectangle* Ω. *Let* $\alpha = (a_1 \Delta x_2)(a_2 \Delta x_1)^{-1}$ *be a fixed constant. Then, numerical scheme* (15) *is R-F stable, if and only if* $\alpha \geq 0$. *Consequently (by Th.* 1*), for* $\alpha \geq 0$, *the sequence of functions* $\{u_{\Delta x_2}\}$ *(where each* $u_{\Delta x_2}$ *is a solution of* (15) *with* Δx_2 *temporarily fixed) is convergent to the solution of the Cauchy problem* (3), *while* $\Delta x_2 \to 0$. *Moreover, numerical scheme* (16) *is R-F stable and its sequence of computed solutions* $\{u_{\Delta x_2}\}$ *converges to the solution of the corresponding Cauchy problem* (3), *while* $\Delta x_2 \to 0$.

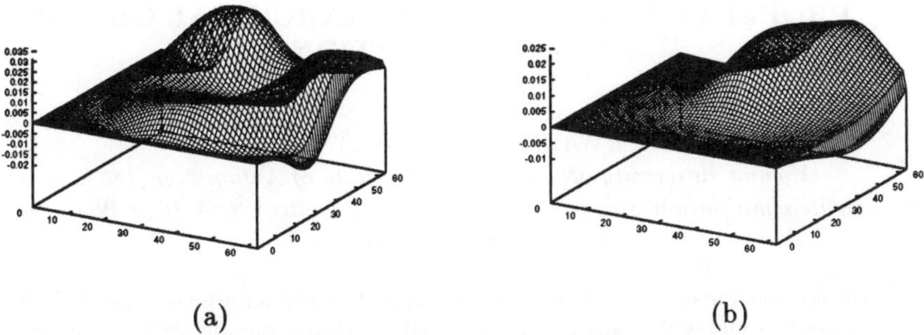

Figure 5: (a) The absolute error between volcano-like and computed surface for the backward-backward scheme. (b) The absolute error between mountain-like and computed surface for the backward-backward scheme.

The domain of influence for the scheme (15) covers the entire $\bar{\Omega}$, whereas for the scheme (16) coincides with (11). With $\Delta x_1/\Delta x_2 = 1.0$, $a_1 = 0.5$, and $a_2 = 1.0$, and thus $\alpha = 0.5$, and entry functions as before the absolute errors between heights of the ideal and computed surfaces are presented in Figure 5.

Acknowledgments

The support within the Deutsche Forschungsgemeinschaft Project and Alexander von Humboldt Fellowship Project is also acknowledged by both authors.

References

1. B.K.P. Horn, *Robot Vision*, (McGraw-Hill, New York, Cambridge M.A., 1986).
2. R. Klette *et al.*, in German *Computer Vision - Raümliche Information aus Digitalen Bildern*, (Verlag Vieweg, Wiesbaden/Braunschweig, 1996).
3. R. Kozera in *Proc. CAIP'95*, ed. V. Hlavac and R. Sara (Lecture Notes in Computer Science, Sringer Verlag, Prague, 1995).
4. R. Kozera and R. Klette, *Machine Graphics and Vision*, to appear.
5. R. Kozera and R. Klette, *Technical Report 96-18*, Technische Universität Berlin, Fachbereich Informatik, Berlin (1996).
6. P.J. Van der Houwen, *Finite Difference Methods for Solving Partial Differential Equations*, (Mathematical Centre Tract 20, Matchematisch Centrum Amsterdam, 1968).

PROPERTY PRESERVING HIERARCHICAL GRAPH TRANSFORMATIONS

WALTER G. KROPATSCH
Vienna University of Technology, Institute of Automation 183/2
Pattern Recognition and Image Processing Group, Treitlstr.3, A-1040 Wien, Austria
email: krw@prip.tuwien.ac.at

Minsky and Papert proved in 1969 that connectivity of an arbitrary pixel set X cannot be computed locally in general. Their theorem essentially depends on their two stage architecture. The present paper introduces a pyramidal strategy to solve similar complex problems with the major difference that the data are not organized in a regular grid but in planar graphs and that the repeated transformations depend adaptively on the data. The algorithm is demonstrated by two examples: (1) Finding connected boundary segments and how they are connected with each other; (2) Given two arbitrary non-intersecting curves in an image determine whether two marks 'x' are placed on the same or on different curves. In both cases computational complexity depends on $\log|X|$. It is made possible by controlling the contraction process in a way that does not destroy the desired global property.

1 Introduction

The analysis of shapes often involves checking properties like connectivity, convexity, circularity, arrangement of curvature extrema along the boundary etc. (see Nagy [1] for many other shape extraction methods). Minsky and Papert[2] describe such properties formally by predicates $\psi(X)$ of a subset X of pixels belonging to the shape. Our approach allows the domain of X to be any subset of regions of a partition of the continuous image plane I. A given shape boundary intersects the partition cells $X \subset I$ which we shortly call boundary segments.

The connectivity predicate $\psi_{\text{CONNECTED}}(X) = true$ if the set of boundary segments X is connected in the image I. Checking the connectivity of a set X involves finding connected paths between any pair of elements in X. This is a difficult task even for humans. A simplified psychological test lead to conjectures about the type of visual routines used in human perception. The image contains two separate curves and two marks 'X', placed on the same or on different curves (Fig. 1). The two curves $C_1, C_2 \subset I$ do not intersect each other but may have complicated intertwinned shapes. The task is to decide, as rapidly as possible, whether the two Xs are on the same curve expressed by $\psi_{xx}(X) = true$ or on different curves, $\psi_{xx}(X) = false$.

Psychophysical experiments [3] suggest that people can trace curves internally at high speed, and that curve tracing is a 'visual routine'. Fig. 1(a)

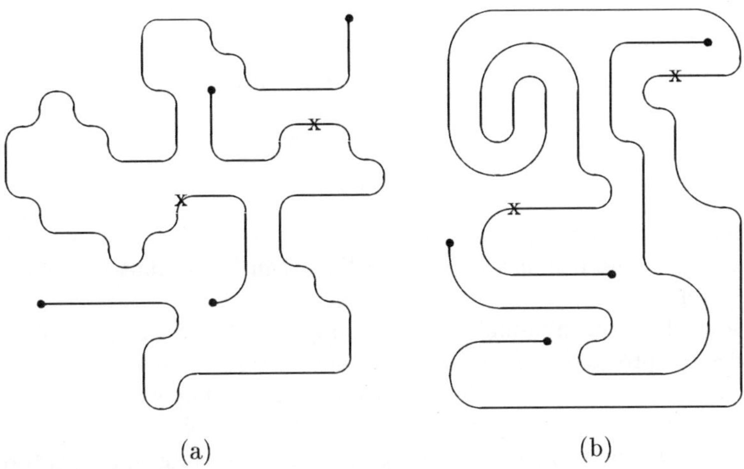

Figure 1: Are the 2 x on the same curve?

approximates the configuration of the experiments used by Jolicoeur [3]. Sequential curve tracing was hypothesized from their experiments because (1) 'more time was required ... when longer distances along the curve separated the two curves' and because (2) 'response times were slower, on average, for "different" trials than for "same" trials'.

The complexity of the task is related to a principle problem of $\psi_{\text{CONNECTED}}$ as pointed out by Minsky and Papert [2]: *'$\psi_{\text{CONNECTED}}$ is not conjunctively local of any order.'* They assume a two stage computation: in stage I many properties are computed in parallel and each individual property accesses maximally $k < n = |X|$ elements of X; Stage II combines all results of stage I in a simple way (e.g. by logical AND). The above theorem refers to this two stage computation scheme and it means that the computational complexity of computing the connectivity of an arbitrary set $X \subset I$ needs $\mathcal{O}(|X|)$ steps.

In this paper we show a computational solution that needs less complex computations. In our case one computation stage consists in a transformation $\tau : X \mapsto X'$ that reduces the data size by a factor $\lambda > 1$

$$|X'| < |X|/\lambda \tag{1}$$

while the reduced data set X' preserves the property to compute:

$$\psi(X') = \psi(X) \tag{2}$$

The application of τ can be repeated on the reduced data set X' until any further reduction would destroy property ψ. Assume that $X^{(n)} = \tau^n(X)$ is the result after n repetitions. From (1) follows that the overall size reduction is bounded by $\lambda^n < \frac{|X|}{|X^{(n)}|}$ and also the number n of repetitions:

$$n < \frac{\log |X| - \log |X^{(n)}|}{\log \lambda} \tag{3}$$

Together with constraints (1) and (2) and the assumption that τ needs only local parallel computations $\psi(X) = \psi(X^{(n)})$ can be computed in $\mathcal{O}(\log |X|)$ parallel steps.

Classical regular pyramids [4] possess property (1), but, in general, counter examples for property (2) can be constructed [5]. It has been demonstrated [6] that adaptive pyramids in which transformation τ depends on the data X overcome the problem. The price to pay is the loss of regularity. Section 2 shortly reviews the transition from regular pixel grids to graph structures and the specific transformation τ to contract graphs: dual graph contraction. Then selection rules are described (in section 3) that preserve the connectivity of the boundary based shape representation. Section 4 relates the efficiency of the method with results from psychophysical experiments. The conclusion summarizes the paper and gives an outlook to several related issues.

2 From Pixels to Graphs

Fig. 2 illustrates how a pixel grid can be represented by a neighborhood graph $G(V, E)$ and its dual face graph $\overline{G}(F, \overline{E})$. Vertices V correspond to pixels, geometrical properties like coordinates or gray value are stored as attributes. Vertices containing curve information will be called cells to highlight this fact. Two vertices are joined by an edge if the corresponding pixels are neighbors[a]. The faces of the dual graph are placed inside the square formed by 4 vertices. Two faces are joined by a dual edge if the corresponding squares are adjacent in G. There is a one-to-one relationship between E and $\overline{E}$. This graph representation extends the scope to any tesselation of the image plane.

Dual graph contraction $(G', \overline{G'}) = C[(G, \overline{G}), (S, N)]$ is the transformation τ that reduces the size of the pair of dual graphs using contraction kernels (S, N) as parameters [6]. Contraction kernels can be any spanning subgraph of G without cycle. The roots of the forest (V, N) are called surviving vertices and they constitute the vertices of the contracted graph $G', V' = S \subset V$. The contraction process contracts all edges N into the root in V', edges E' are established in G' if the two surviving endpoints are connected in G by a

[a] 4-neighbors are used because they make G planar.

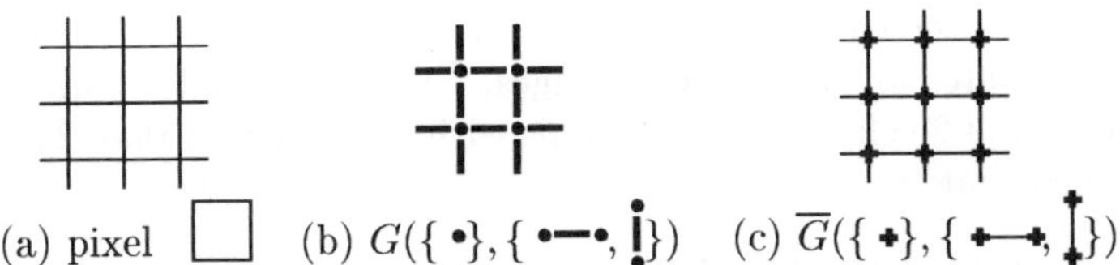

Figure 2: (a) pixel grid, (b) neighborhood graph $G(V, E)$, (c) dual face graph $\overline{G}(F, \overline{E})$

connecting path consisting of two branches of the two contraction kernels and one edge $e \in E \setminus N$ which is called a bridge. We shall control this process by a data dependent selection of the contraction kernels such that the predicate ψ is preserved.

The stack of successively reduced graphs $((G_0, \overline{G_0}), (G_1, \overline{G_1}), \ldots, (G_n, \overline{G_n}))$, $G_0 = G$, is called a dual irregular pyramid. Any number of contraction kernels can be combined together in an equivalent contraction kernel (ECK) that contracts the base graph G directly into the top graph. Every tree of the ECK spans the complete receptive field of its root vertex i.e. all vertices of V_0 that have been contracted into this root.

3 Connectivity Preserving Boundary Contraction

The following solution combines the concepts of curve relation and dual irregular pyramid. In contrast to the irregular curve pyramid [7], here, the cells where the curves are represented are contracted and not the dual graph. Like in the regular curve pyramid [8], curve and cell may be related by several cell classes:

0-cell ... denotes an empty cell (no curve within the receptive field)

2-cell ... one single curve crosses the receptive field; it enters and exits the cell at two particular boundary segments (e.g. across two edges $e_1, e_2 \in E$).

1-cell ... a curve ends in this cell (a filled circle marks 1-cells in the figures); it enters the cell at a particular boundary segment.

***-cell ...** a cell where more than one curves meet. [b]

Fig. 3(a) overlays a pixel grid and a curve network. In a first phase all cells in the base (squares in Fig. 3(a)) are assigned to one of the four cell-classes. A simple algorithm starts with edges between 4-adjacent pixels: If a curve

[b] Since both $\psi_{\text{CONNECTED}}$ and ψ_{xx} do not need any differentiation between different types of crossings, it is considered also as the end of all curves that meet there.

crosses the edge the edge receives an attribute 1 otherwise 0. Then all pixels sum the attributes of their incident edges. Sums 0, 1, and 2 correspond the 0-cell, 1-cell, and 2-cell, respectively, cells with a sum higher than 2 are *-cells. It is assumed that

1. the cell classes are consistent, i.e. if a curve crosses a boundary segment both cells adjacent to this segment are in the correct class;
2. all curves are well distinguishable in the base, e.g. there are no more than one single curve in one single cell of the base (except at *-cells).

3.1 Selecting the Contraction Kernels

Fig. 3b,c,d illustrate three successive contractions. Since contraction of vertices corresponds to merging receptive fields these are drawn as closed lines. Root vertices are indicated by circles.

Selection rules: 1-cells and *-cells must always survive. *-cells are not allowed to have children. This prevents the area of unclear information [c] from growing. Branches of contraction kernels follow the curves if possible and are selected in following order: 1-cell, 2-cell, 0-cell. Receptive fields of contracted edges merge and collect the information from the individual parts:

1. A 1-cell can merge with its adjacent 2-cell (this is the only neighbor connected to the 1-cell by an edge with attribute 1), then with any adjacent 0-cell and will become an 1-cell again;
2. a 2-cell can merge with both adjacent 2-cells (connecting edges must have attribute 1!) or with any adjacent 0-cell and remains a 2-cell;
3. a 0-cell can merge with any adjacent cell and remains a 0-cell only if it is merged with another 0-cell.

Random selection (like in adaptive pyramids [9]) applies whenever the above rules do not determine the contraction kernels completely. If surviving cells form a maximum independent set connecting paths have at least length two and hence cells along boundaries are reduced by a factor $\lambda > 2$.

During contraction the bridges of connecting paths inherite their attribute to the new edge. It can be easily verified that the above merging rules preserve the consistency between edge attributes and cell classes, i.e. the sum of attributes of incident edges determine the class of cells. When a 1-cell meets another 1-cell (the other end!) we have found a complete curve segment.

---

[c] Curves may intersect or may be just close to each other.

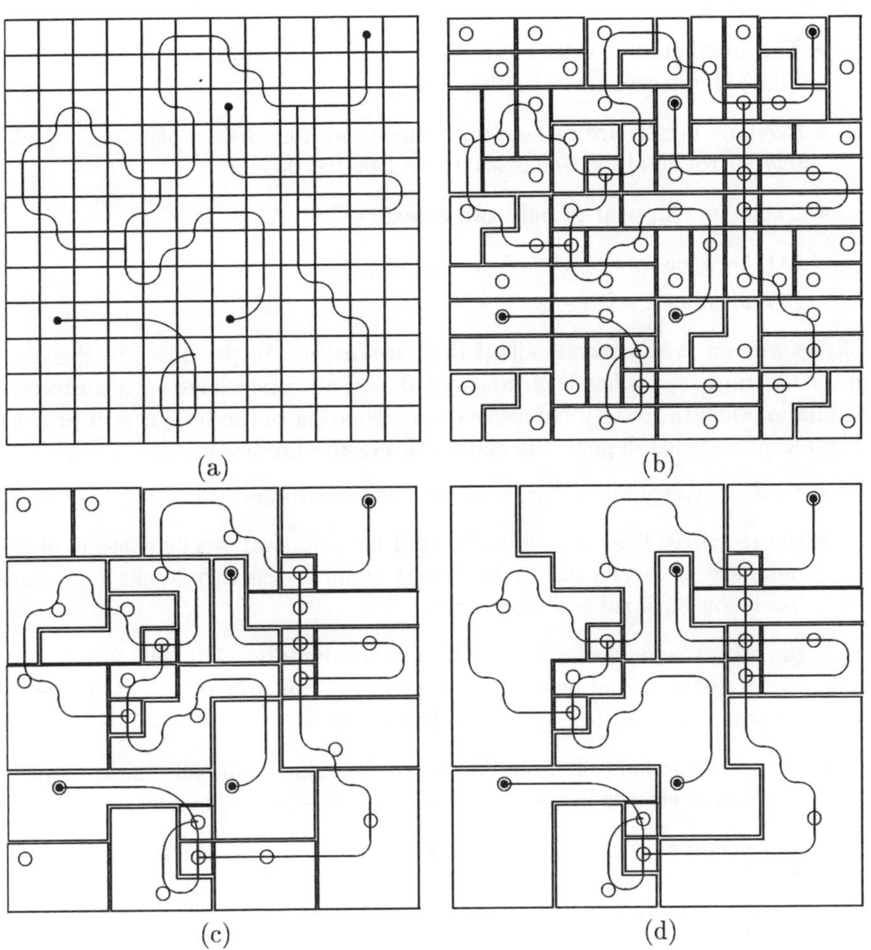

Figure 3: Three step boundary contraction preserving $\psi_{CONNECTED}$

3.2 The Final Graph

Above selection criteria determine the parameters with which we dually contract the graphs until no further contraction is possible. The resulting graph has following properties (verify in Fig. 3d):

- The number of 1-cells (4 in Fig. 3d) and the number of *-cells (7 in Fig. 3d) correspond to the base graph.
- No more 0-cells are present with one exception: An empty area completely surrounded by *-cells leaves an isolated 0-cell.
- 2-cells may appear in only two cases:
  (a) between two *-cells (7 in Fig. 3d), or
  (b) forming a self-loop.

Curves remain in separated cells if they are distinct in the base. In this final graph all empty space has been contracted, and all curves have been contracted to minimal length, but all connectivity information of the base is still present. The receptive fields depend the cell classes in the top level:

- *-cells correspond to *-cells in the base one-to-one;
- the receptive field of a 2-cell located between two *-cells consists of the sequence of 2-cells in the base that connect the two *-cells plus some 0-cells on both sides of the curve;
- the receptive field of a 2-cell self-loop accumulates all 2-cells forming the closed curve in the base, the complete interior area of 0-cells if there is no other curve inside, and some 0-cells outside;
- the receptive field of two adjacent 1-cells collects all cells the corresponding curve crosses in the base plus some 0-cells at the sides;
- the receptive field of a 1-cell adjacent to a *-cell is the complete set of 2-cells that connect the 1-cell in the base with the other *-cell plus some 0-cells at the sides.

The method finds a topologically correct ($\psi_{\text{CONNECTED}}(G) = \psi_{\text{CONNECTED}}(G_{(n)})$) and minimal description for all possible (planar) configurations of curves as complicated the layout may be, as long as the sampling allows discrimination of curves in the base. Even strange cases as space filling curves can be treated since the receptive fields may have arbitrary shapes as long as they are planar and connected. In those cases there exist spanning trees covering the curve that can serve as kernels for contraction.

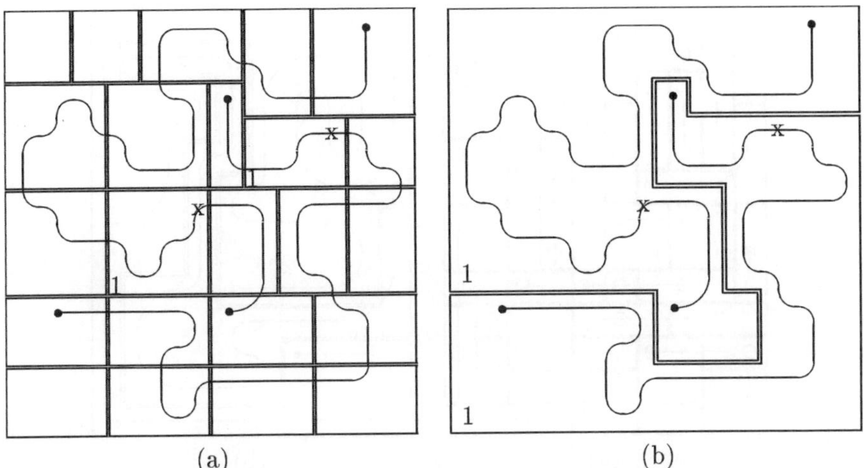

Figure 4: Step 1 and 3 of boundary contraction preserving $\psi_{xx} = false$.

4 Contracting Two Xs On a Curve

We use 0-, 1-, and 2-cells as introduced for computing $\psi_{\text{CONNECTED}}$, *-cells do not appear in the 2x problem. X-marks can be implemented as additional numeric labels of cells, e.g. label(2-cell)=$k, k \in \{0, 1, 2, ...\}$ if k x-marks are found in the receptive field of the 2-cell. Labels greater than 0 are displayed in figures 4 and 5 in the left bottom corner of the box delineating the receptive field. All cells are filled with the appropriate labels in the base. It is assumed that, in addition to the two consistency conditions for $\psi_{\text{CONNECTED}}$, the two x-marks are correctly detected and entered as label(cell)=1.

Contraction proceeds as in the general case with following additions: If two 2-cells or 1-cells are merged their labels are summed. The two curves remain in two separated cells if they are distinct in the base. Note that dual graphs need not be considered in this case because we know that the image contains two separate curves and, consequently, no cycles can appear that give rise to faces in the final result. The second example of Figure 1(b) leads to $\psi_{xx} = true$ after four contractions (Fig. 5(a)-(d)).

Our proposal offers a computational solution to this problem that needs $\mathcal{O}(\log(curvelength))$ parallel steps. This is consistent with experimental observations: if both x are on the "same" curve, the response can be given after the time needed to contract the arc in between both x whereas the "different"-response needs at least the shorter curve to be completely contracted.

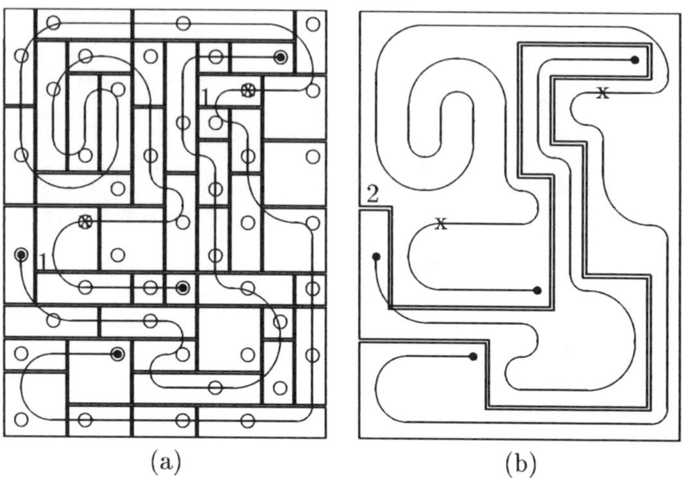

Figure 5: Steps 1 and 4 of example "same" with $\psi_{xx} = true$

5 Conclusion and Outlook

Dual graph contraction transforms graphs into a hierarchy of smaller graphs without destroying properties like connectivity: $\psi_{\text{CONNECTED}}$and ψ_{xx} can be computed in $\mathcal{O}(\log|X|)$ steps. Hierarchical aggregation replaces sequential search and speeds up the computational complexity.

The generality of the approach lies in a clear separation between the contraction process and the choice of control parameters that can be adapted to many different predicates ψ. The efficiency is based on the fact that the contraction can reduce the data by a factor $\lambda > 1$ without loosing any piece of information necessary for computing the predicate ψ.

The presented contour segmentation complements the universal region segmentation [6]. Both partition the image plane completely but in a different way: Contours remain in the interior of ECK in the contour segmentation, whereas they separate regions in the region segmentation. Regions in the contour segmentation are split among the contour segments that surround them. The bridges of the contour segmentation that fall inside a region form a sort of axis of the region.

Acknowledgments

The author thanks Jean-Michel Jolion and Horst Bischof for contributing several ideas. Part of the work was supported by the Austrian National Fonds zur Förderung der wissenschaftlichen Forschung under grant S7002-MAT.

References

1. George Nagy. An Induced Taxonomy of Visual Form. In Carlo Arcelli, Luigi P. Cordella, and Gabriella Sanniti di Baja, editors, *2nd Intl. Workshop on Visual Form*, pages 410–419, Capri, Italy, June 1994.
2. Marvin Lee Minsky and Seymour A. Papert. *Perceptrons: An Introduction to computational geometry.* The MIT Press, expanded edition, 1988.
3. Pierre Jolicoeur, Shimon Ullman, and Marilynn Mackay. Curve tracing: A possible basic operation in the perception of spatial relations. *Memory & Cognition*, 14(2):129–140, 1986.
4. Jean-Michel Jolion and Azriel Rosenfeld. *A Pyramid Framework for Early Vision.* Kluwer Academic Publishers, 1994.
5. M. Bister, J. Cornelis, and Azriel Rosenfeld. A critical view of pyramid segmentation algorithms. *Pattern Recognition Letters*, Vol. 11(No. 9):pp. 605–617, September 1990.
6. Walter G. Kropatsch and Souheil BenYacoub. A revision of pyramid segmentation. In Walter G. Kropatsch, editor, *13th International Conference on Pattern Recognition*, volume II, pages 477–481. IEEE Comp.Soc., 1996.
7. Walter G. Kropatsch and Dieter Willersinn. Parallel line grouping in irregular curve pyramids. In *Proceedings Computer Vision and Pattern Recognition - CVPR'93*, pages 784–785. IEEE Comp.Soc.Press, 1993.
8. Walter G. Kropatsch. Curve Representations in Multiple Resolutions. *Pattern Recognition Letters*, Vol. 6(No. 3):pp.179–184, August 1987.
9. Jean-Michel Jolion and Annick Montanvert. The adaptive pyramid, a framework for 2D image analysis. *Computer Vision, Graphics, and Image Processing: Image Understanding*, 55(3):pp.339–348, May 1992.

INFERRED DESCRIPTIONS IN TERMS OF CURVES, REGIONS AND JUNCTIONS FROM SPARSE, NOISY BINARY DATA

MI-SUEN LEE GERARD MEDIONI
Institute for Robotics and Intelligence Systems,
University of Southern California,
Los Angeles, CA 90230, USA
E-mail: misuen, medioni@iris.usc.edu

We present a unified computational framework to generate descriptions in terms of regions, curves, and labelled junctions, from sparse, noisy, binary data in 2-D. Each input site can be a point, a point with an associated tangent direction, a point with an associated tangent vector, or any combination of the above. The methodology is grounded on two elements: tensor calculus for representation, and non-linear voting for communication: each input site communicates its information (a tensor) to its neighborhood through a predefined (tensor) field, and therefore casts a (tensor) vote. Each site collects all the votes cast at its location and encodes them into a new tensor. A local, parallel routine such as a modified marching squares process then simultaneously detects junctions, curves and region boundaries. The proposed approach is very different from traditional variational approaches, as it is non-iterative. Furthermore, the only free parameter is the size of the neighborhood, related to the scale. We illustrate the approach with results on a variety of images, then present the straightforward extension to the case where the input consists of 3-D features, and outline further applications.

1 Introduction

Our research goal is to develop a unified computational framework for the inference of viewer-centered descriptions in terms of curves, regions and junctions in the scene from noisy oriented or non-oriented binary data, without invoking specific object or scene model. By introducing the use of a computational technique called ***tensor voting*** as communication framework, a robust, non-iterative, and threshold-free method is devised to achieve this goal.

Notice that for any scene description method to be useful in real application, it has to be able to handle the presence of multiple structures, and the interaction between them, in any noisy, irregularly clustered data set. It is therefore necessary to address the issues of interpolation, discontinuity detection, and outlier identification when designing such a method. Most previous works on region inference from dot clusters and curve inference from oriented or non-oriented data take either the fit-and-split or the fit-and-merge approach, attacking the 3 subproblems in a sequential manner. These divide-and-conquer approaches result in iterative algorithms which require parameter tuning.

Recently a number of non-iterative method have been developed for 2-D curve completion that involve the computation of a measurement for every image point which signifies the presence of perceptually significant structures. Among them, Guy and Medioni[4] have introduced a salient structure estimation technique called vector voting that is able to handle the tasks of interpolation, discontinuity detection, and outlier identification simultaneously. They have obtained impressive results for the inference of multiple undirected curves and illusory contours. While other methods[7][11] give equally good results, it is the potential for generalization that make Guy and Medioni's approach promising. Applying the same methodology to surface inference, they have obtained exciting results[5] in 3-D.

Inspired by Guy and Medioni's work, we attempt to derive a general salient structure estimator that interpolates, detects discontinuities, and identifies outliers ***simultaneously*** using non-linear voting. We introduce the use of a construct called ***saliency tensor*** which is able to signal the presence of a salient structure, or a discontinuity, or a outlier at any location. The design of the saliency tensor is based on the observation that a discontinuity is indicated by the disagreement in curve orientation estimation. As orientations are represented by vectors, it is therefore the *variations* in the vector estimation that signify a discontinuity, which can be captured by a (second order symmetric) tensor. On the other hand, outliers can be detected by insufficient support in the estimation of curve orientation, and therefore can be signified by the size of the votes which we called saliency. Combining the efficiency of voting with the strength of tensor representation, we develop a salient structure inference engine which make use of tensor voting to extract salient junctions, curves, and regions from any noisy combination of non-oriented points, oriented points, and oriented points with associated polarity in a unified way. Figure 1.1(b) depicts the results of applying our method to the dot clusters given in Figure 1.1(a).

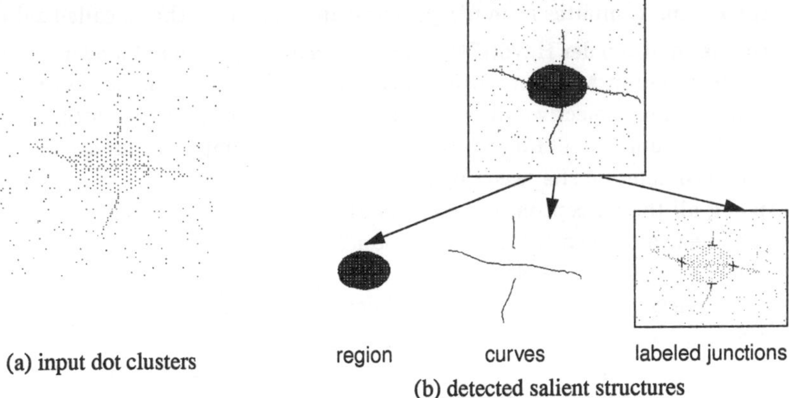

(a) input dot clusters

(b) detected salient structures

Figure 1.1 Salient features automatically detected by the method

In this paper, a review of previous work on curve and region inference is given in section 2. Our unifying tensorial framework for salient structure inference is presented in section 3. Section 4 illustrates the simultaneous inference of junctions, curves and regions using our salient structure inference engine with results on point and line data, dot clusters, and illusory figures. Section 5 concludes this paper with a discussion on extending the methodology to 3-D and outlining further application.

2 Previous Work

The inference of curves and regions from sparse noisy data is traditionally studied in the field of perceptual grouping. Based on the type of input, we can classify previous works into 3 areas, namely, dot clustering, line grouping, and illusory contour inference.

Zucker and Hummel[12] were the first to address the problem of dot clustering, which they cast as an optimzation problem. Other methods (a summary can be found in [1]) take a similar approach, either implement the relaxation process as merging degenerate partitions of the same label class, or dividing a mixed partition into separate label classes.

In the area of line grouping, Dolan and Weiss[2] have demonstrated a hierarchical approach to 2-D curve inference from oriented binary data represented by unit length tangent segments. Parent and Zucker[9] have presented an iterative relaxation labelling algorithm for curve inference where local kernels are used to estimate tangent and curvature.

Recently a number of methods have been developed for curve completion that involve the computation of a map in which perceptually significant structures are highlighted. Sha'ashua and Ullman[10] have proposed an incremental optimization scheme that computes from noisy, sparse line segments the so-called saliency map. Heitger and von der Heydt[7] has presented a computational model for recovering illusory contours by computing convolutions of keypoint images with anisotropic, orientation selective filters. William and Jacobs[11] has attempted to compute the completion of illusory contours, on the assumption that the prior distribution of completion shape can be modeled as a random walk.

Among all the perceptual grouping methods, Guy and Medioni's work is the only non-linear approach that is able to handle point, line segments, and illusory figure inputs, altough individually.

Extending Guy and Medioni's methodology, our tensorial framework of salient structure inference broadens the original method significantly. It augments the non-linear voting approach with a mathematical foundation which accounts for many heuristic measures in the original work, unifies the representation of different features and the inference of various structures, and allows us to incorporate ***polarity*** for the inference of regions.

3 Salient Structure Inference Engine

The building block of our computational framework for inferring salient structure is the procedure that simultaneously interpolates smooth surfaces or surface borders, identifies discontinuities, and detects outliers, which we called the *salient structure inference engine*. The input to this procedure are local estimates of orientation associated with a directed or undirected tangent. Multiple orientation estimations are allowed for each location. Typical input include the combined responses obtained by applying orientation selective filters to a greyscale image, or dots in a binary image. The output of this procedure is a salient integrated description for the input that compose of labeled junctions and directed or undirected curves.

In the following, we first outline the mechanism of our salient structure inference engine in section 3.1. We then define the saliency tensor in section 3.2. The details of tensor voting and voting interpretation are given in section 3.3. Polarity is being incorporated into the tensor framework in section 3.4. The process of integrating individual salient structures is described in section 3.5. Section 3.6 summarize the time complexity of this procedure.

In this paper, scalars are denoted by italic letters, e.g. l, tensors are denoted by bold capital letters, e.g. $\boldsymbol{T}$, vectors are denoted by bold lower-case letters, e.g. $\boldsymbol{e}$. The unit length vector for $\boldsymbol{e}$ is denoted as $\hat{\mathbf{e}}$.

3.1 Overview of the inference engine

Our salient structure inference engine is a non-iterative procedure that makes use of tensor voting to infer salient geometric structures from local features. Figure 3.1 illustrates the mechanisms of this engine. In practice, the domain space is digitized into discrete cells. We use a construct call a saliency tensor, to be defined in section 3.2, to encode the saliency of various surface features such as points, curve elements and surface path elements. Local feature detectors provide an initial local measure of surface features. The engine then encodes the input into a sparse saliency tensor field. Saliency inference is achieved by allowing the elements in the tensor field to communicate through voting. A voting function specifies the voter's estimation of local orientation/discontinuity and its saliency regarding the collecting site, and is represented by tensor fields. The vote accumulator uses the information collected to update the saliency tensor at locations with features and establish those at previously empty locations. From the densified saliency tensor field, the vote interpreter produces saliency maps for various features from which salient structures can be extracted. By taking into account the different properties of different features, the integrator locally combines the features into a consistent salient structure. Once the generic saliency inference engine is defined, it can be used to perform many tasks, simply by changing the voting function.

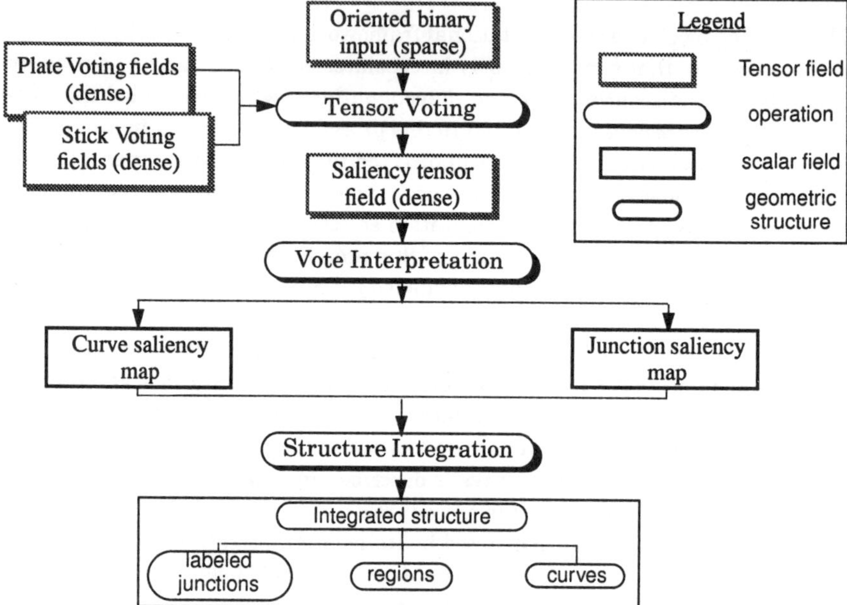

Figure 3.1 Flowchart of the Salient Structure Inference Engine

3.2 *Saliency Tensor*

The design of the saliency tensor is based on observation that discontinuity is indicated by the variation of orientation when estimating curve locally. Intuitively, the variation of orientation can be captured by an ellipse in 2-D. Note that the *shape* of the ellipse describes the orientation variation, and its *size* encodes saliency. One way to represent an ellipse is to use the distribution of points on the ellipse as described by the covariance matrix. By decomposing a covariance matrix $\boldsymbol{S}$ into its eigenvalues λ_1, λ_2 and eigenvectors $\hat{\boldsymbol{e}}_1$, $\hat{\boldsymbol{e}}_2$, we can rewrite $\boldsymbol{S}$ as:

$$\boldsymbol{S} = \begin{bmatrix}\hat{\boldsymbol{e}}_1 & \hat{\boldsymbol{e}}_2\end{bmatrix}\begin{bmatrix}\lambda_1 & 0 \\ 0 & \lambda_2\end{bmatrix}\begin{bmatrix}\hat{\boldsymbol{e}}_1^T \\ \hat{\boldsymbol{e}}_2^T\end{bmatrix} \tag{2.1}$$

Thus, $\boldsymbol{S} = \lambda_1\hat{\boldsymbol{e}}_1\hat{\boldsymbol{e}}_1^T + \lambda_2\hat{\boldsymbol{e}}_2\hat{\boldsymbol{e}}_2^T$ where $\lambda_1 \geq \lambda_2$ and $\hat{\boldsymbol{e}}_1$ and $\hat{\boldsymbol{e}}_2$ are the eigenvectors correspond to λ_1 and λ_2 respectively. The eigenvectors correspond to the principal directions of the ellipse and the eigenvalues encode the size and shape of the ellipse, as shown in Figure 3.2. $\boldsymbol{S}$ is a *linear* combination of outer product tensors and, therefore a tensor.

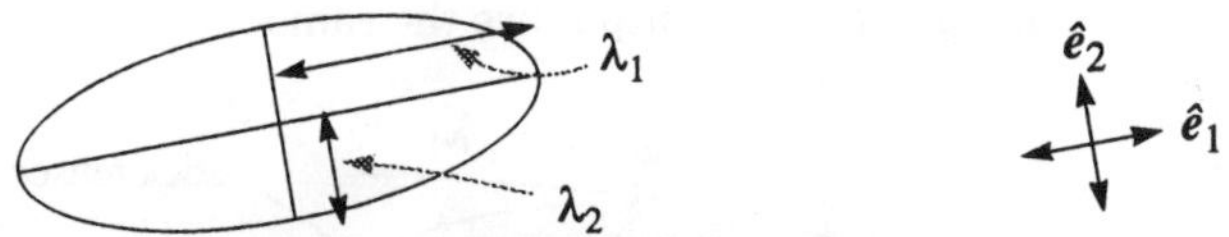

Figure 3.2 An ellipse and the eigensystem

This tensor representation of orientation/discontinuity estimation and its saliency allows the identification of features, such as points or curves elements, and the description of the underlying structure, such as tangents, to be computed at the same time. Figure 3.3 shows the shape of the saliency tensors for various features under curve inference.

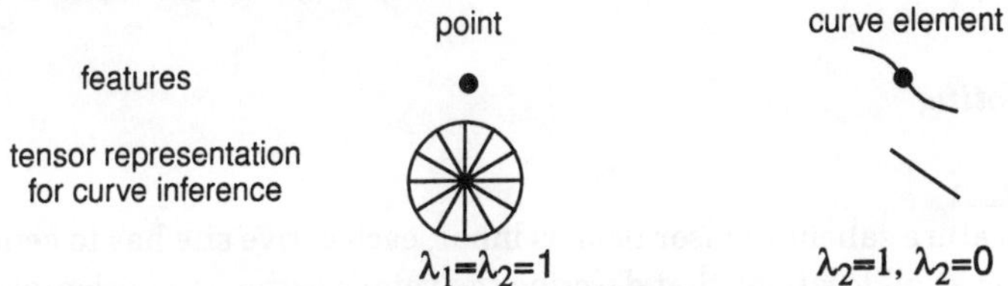

Figure 3.3 Input saliency tensors

Every saliency tensor, denoted as $\boldsymbol{T}(\lambda_1,\lambda_2,\theta)$, thus has 3 parameters, where θ is the angle of rotation. This saliency tensor is sufficient to describe feature saliency for undirected curves. When dealing with boundaries of regions, we need to associate a polarity to the feature orientation to distinguish the inside from the outside. Polarity saliency, which relates the polarity of the feature and its significance, will be dealt with in section 3.4.

Notice that all the tensors shown in Figure 3.3 are of the proper shape of either a stick or a plate. In general, a saliency tensor $\boldsymbol{S}$ can be anywhere in between these cases, but the spectrum theorem[3] allow us to state that any tensor can be expressed as a *linear* combination of these 2 cases, i.e.

$$\boldsymbol{S} = (\lambda_1 - \lambda_2)\hat{e}_1\hat{e}_1^T + \lambda_2(\hat{e}_1\hat{e}_1^T + \hat{e}_2\hat{e}_2^T) \tag{2.2}$$

where $\hat{e}_1\hat{e}_1^{\mathrm{T}}$ describes a stick and $(\hat{e}_1\hat{e}_1^{\mathrm{T}}+\hat{e}_2\hat{e}_2^{\mathrm{T}})$ describes a plate. Figure 3.4 shows the shape of a general saliency tensor as described by the stick and plate components. A typical example of a general tensor is one that represents the orientation estimates at a corner. Using orientation selective filters, multiple orientations $\hat{\boldsymbol{u}}_i$ can be detected at corner points with strength s_i. We can use the tensor sum $\Sigma s_i^2\hat{\boldsymbol{u}}_i\hat{\boldsymbol{u}}_i^{\mathrm{T}}$ to compute the distribution of the orientation estimates. The addition of

2 saliency tensors simply combines the distribution of the orientation estimates and the saliencies. This linearity of the saliency tensor enables us to combines votes and represent result efficiently. Also, since the input to this voting process can be represented by saliency tensors, our saliency inference is a closed operation whose input, processing token and output are the same.

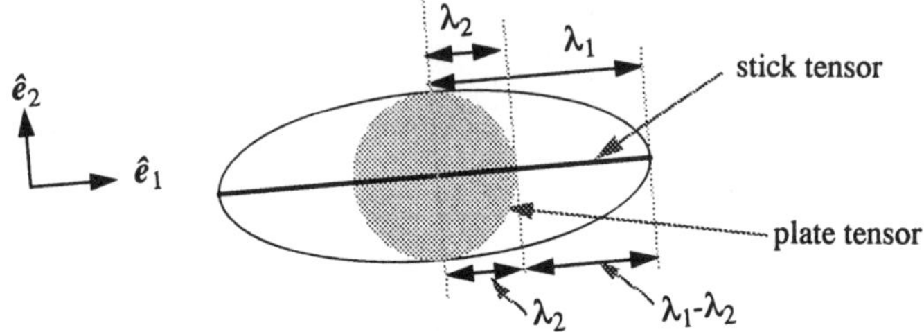

Figure 3.4 Decomposition of a general saliency tensor

3.3 Tensor Voting

The voting function

Given a sparse feature saliency tensor field as input, each active site has to generate a tensor value at all locations that describe the voter's estimate of orientation at the location, and the saliency of the estimation. The value of the tensor vote cast at a given location is given by the voting function $V(S,p)$ which characterize the structure to be detected, where p is the vector joining the voting site p_v and the receiving site p_s, and S is the tensor at p_v. Since all orientations are of equal significance, the voting function should be independent of the principal directions of the voting saliency tensor S. As the immediate goal of voting is to interpolate smooth surfaces or surface borders, the influence of a voter must be smooth and therefore decrease with distance. Moreover, votes for neighboring collectors must be of similar strength and shape. Thus, although the voting function has infinite extent, in practice, it disappears at a predefined distance from the voter. While the voting function should take into account the orientation estimates of the voter, it is only necessary to consider each of the voter's orientation estimate individually and then use their combined effect for voting.

Representing the voting function by discrete tensor fields

We describe, in the following, two properties of the voting function that allow us to implement this tensor voting efficiently by using a convolution-like operation.

The first property expresses the requirement that the voting function is independent of the principal directions of the voting saliency tensor. For any voting saliency tensor $S = T(\lambda_1,\lambda_2,\theta)$, the vote $V(S,p)$ for a site p from the voter is:

$$V(T(\lambda_1, \lambda_2, \theta), p) = V(R_\theta R_\theta^{-1} T(\lambda_1, \lambda_2, \theta) R_\theta^{-T} R_\theta^T, R_\theta R_\theta^{-1} p)$$
$$= R_\theta V(T(\lambda_1, \lambda_2 0), R_\theta^{-1} p) R_\theta^T \quad (2.3)$$

The second property is due to linearity of the saliency tensor. Recall that every saliency tensor can be interpreted as being a linear combination of a stick and a plate as described in equation (2.2). If the voting function is linear with respect to the saliency tensor S, every vote can be decomposed into two components as:

$$V(S, p) = (\lambda_1 - \lambda_2) V(\hat{e}_1 \hat{e}_1^T, p) + \lambda_2 V(\hat{e}_1 \hat{e}_1^T + \hat{e}_2 \hat{e}_2^T, p)$$
$$= (\lambda_1 - \lambda_2) V(S_1, p) + \lambda_2 V(S_2, p) \quad (2.4)$$

where $S_1 = T(1,0,\theta)$, and $S_2 = T(1,1,\theta)$. Notice that S_1 a stick tensor and S_2 is a plate tensor. Consequently, rather than dealing with infinitely many shapes of voting saliency tensors, we only need to handle two shapes of saliency tensors. Applying (2.3) to (2.4),

$$V(S, p) = (\lambda_1 - \lambda_2) R_\theta V(T(1, 0, 0), R_\theta^{-1} p) R_\theta^T + \lambda_2 R_\theta V(T(1, 1, 0), R_\theta^{-1} p) R_\theta^T \quad (2.5)$$

This means that any voting function linear in S can be characterized by two saliency tensor fields, namely $V_1(p) = V(T(1,0,0),p)$, the vote field cast by a stick tensor, and $V_2(p) = V(T(1,1,0),p)$, the vote field cast by a plate tensor.

This would seem to imply that we need to define 2 different tensor fields for each voting operation, one for the stick and one for the plate. This is indeed what Guy and Medioni [4] did. They defined, from first principles, these 2 fields. Thanks to our tensorial framework, we can instead derive the plate tensor *directly* from the stick tensor votes. Since we only need to consider each of the voter's orientation estimates individually, V_2 in fact can be obtained from V_1 as:

$$V_2(p) = \int_0^\pi R_\theta V_1(R_\theta^{-1} p) R_\theta^T d\theta \quad (2.6)$$

The voting process

Given the saliency tensor fields which specify the voting function, for each input site saliency tensor, voting thus proceeds by aligning each voting field with the principal directions of the voting saliency tensor and centering the fields at the corresponding location. Each tensor contribution is weighted as described in equation (2.2). This process is similar to a convolution with a mask, except that the output is *tensor* instead of scalar. Votes are accumulated by tensor addition. As a result, all sites, with or without feature initially, are treated equally during the inference.

Vote interpretation

After all the input site saliency tensors have cast their votes, the vote interpreter builds feature saliency maps from the now densified saliency tensor field by computing the eigensystem of the saliency tensor at each site. According to equation (2.2), each saliency tensor can be broken down into two components,

$(\lambda_1-\lambda_2)\hat{e}_1\hat{e}_1^T$ corresponds to an orientation, and $\lambda_2(\hat{e}_1\hat{e}_1^T+\hat{e}_2\hat{e}_2^T)$ corresponds to an isotropic junction. For curve inference, the curve saliency therefore is measured by $(\lambda_1-\lambda_2)$, with tangent estimated as $\hat{e}_1$, and the junction saliency is measured by λ_2. It is interesting that with perfect orientation data, this tensor representation of saliency feature inference produces feature saliency measurements identical to those derived by Guy and Medioni[4] from intuition.

The voting function is smooth, so structures are located at the *local maxima* of the corresponding feature saliency map. The vote interpreter hence can extract features by non-maxima suppression on the feature saliency map. To extract structures represented by oriented salient features, we use the methods developed in [6]. Note that a maximal curve is usually not an iso-contour. By definition, the first derivative will change sign as we move normal to the curve. By expressing a maximal curve as a zero-crossing curve, a local iso-contour marching process [8] can be used for the extraction process.

3.4 *Incorporating polarity*

So far, we have only considered the inference of undirected curves from undirected features. However, in real applications, we often deal with bounded regions. Computationally, it is economical to represent regions differentially, that is by their boundaries. By following the contour of a region, one knows which is the inside versus the outside. The simplest encoding for region therefore is to associate a polarity, which denotes the inside of the object, with each curve element along the region boundary. It is precisely this polarity information that is being expressed in the output of an edge detector, where the polarity of the directed edgel indicates which side is darker. As shown later, ignoring this information may be harmful. We therefore need to augment our representation scheme to express this knowledge, and to use it to perform directed curve and region grouping.

In the spirit of our methodology, we attempt to establish at every site in the domain space a measure we called polarity saliency which relates the possibility of having a directed curve passing through the site. In particular, a site close to two parallel features with opposite polarities should have low polarity saliency, although the undirected curve saliency will be high.

3.4.1 *Encoding polarity*

Figure 3.5 depicts the situation where the voter has the polarity information. Since polarity is only defined for directed features, it is necessary to associate polarity only with the stick component of the saliency tensor. Thus, a scalar value from -1 to 1 encodes polarity saliency. The sign of this value indicates which side of the stick component of the tensor is the intended direction. The size of this value measures the degree of polarization at a site. Initially, all sites with features have polarity saliency of -1, 0, or 1 only.

Figure 3.5 Encoding Polarity Saliency

To propagate this polarity information, we need to modify the voting function accordingly. Note that polarity does not change along a path or a surface. Hence, to incorporate polarity into the voting function, we only need to assign either -1 or 1 to each stick tensor vote as polarity saliency, which is determined by the polarity of the voter and the estimated connection between the stick component of the voter and the site.

3.4.2 Inferring directed feature saliency

Once votes are collected, directed curve saliency map can be computed by combining polarity saliency with undirected curve saliency.

Since polarity is associated with an orientation, we need to take the orientation into account when we infer polarity saliency. Note that despite this association between polarity and orientation, they are independent of each other, and thus are inferred separately. An intuitive way to determine polarity is to compute the vector sum $u(x, y) = \sum_i v_i(x, y)$ of these directed votes $v_i(x,y)$'s at every site (x,y). The length of the resulting vector gives the degree of polarization and the resulting direction relates the indented polarity. We thus assign to every site a polarity saliency $PS(x,y)$ as:

$$PS(x, y) = \mathrm{sgn}(u(x, y) \bullet \hat{e}_1(x, y))|u(x, y)| \quad (3.1)$$

where $\hat{e}_1(x,y)$ is the major direction of the saliency tensor obtained at site (x,y).

Directed curve elements are those which have both high undirected curve saliency and polarity saliency. The natural way to measure directed curve saliency hence is to take the product of the undirected curve saliency and the polarity saliency. Once the directed curve saliency map is computed, region boundaries can be extracted by the method described in section 3.3.

3.5 Structure Integration

Our salient structure inference engine is able to report junctions where estimation of an orientation fails and extraction of curve should stop. Since the process is designed for the estimation of curves, it only detects, but does not precisely localize junctions. In order to link multiple curves together properly, junctions need to be correctly located and labeled. To rectify junction location and compute junction label, we need to start with the only reliable source of information, that is, the salient curves. For each location with a high junction saliency value, salient curves are identified and allowed to grow locally. The growing process can easily be accomplished by tensor voting. Junction is then located and labeled by computing the intersection of the grown smooth structures. The junction information in turn enables us to identify disconnected curve that needs to be reconnected. This local process only adds a constant factor to the total processing time.

3.6 Complexity

The efficiency of the salient structure inference engine is determined by the complexity of each of the 3 subprocesses in the engine. Tensor voting requires $O(Cn)$ operation, where n is the number of input features, and C the size of the tensor field. The size of C depends on the scale of the voting function and is usually much smaller than the size of the domain space, m. It is therefore the density of the input features that determines the speed of tensor voting. Since the number of input features are usually sparse, the total number of operations in tensor voting is normally a few times the size of the domain space.

In vote interpretation, the saliency tensor in each location of the domain space is decomposed into its eigensystem, which takes $O(1)$ for each of the m elements in the domain space. The maximal curve extraction process[8] only takes $O(m)$. Therefore the complexity of vote interpretation is $O(m)$.

Since the process of structure integration only recompute the structures for some of the input features, its complexity is bounded by that of the first tensor voting process, that is, $O(Cn)$.

In summary, the time complexity of the salient structure inference engine is $O(Cn+m)$, where C is the size of the tensor fields specifying the voting function, n is the number of input features, and m is the size of the domain space.

4 Salient Structure Inference

Having defined the salient structure inference engine, we proceed to describe how to apply it to infer salient curves, regions and junctions in 2-D. An overview of the algorithm is depicted in Figure 4.1. Given any combination of points, curve elements, or directed curve elements, curves and regions are inferred independently and simultaneously. To make use of the salient structure inference engine, we need to define a voting function for estimating tangents at every site, whose derivation is given in section 4.1. In order to deal with the clustering of non-oriented data where local estimation of tangent and polarity is not immediate, we define a procedure which make use of the salient structure inference engine to identify points, and the corresponding polarities, on region boundaries. Once all the polarity information is available, directed curves can be inferred using the voting function defined for curve inference, which is described in section 4.2. After the salient curves, regions and junctions are extracted individually, the structure integrator locally combines them into a consistent salient structure using the procedure presented in section 3.5.

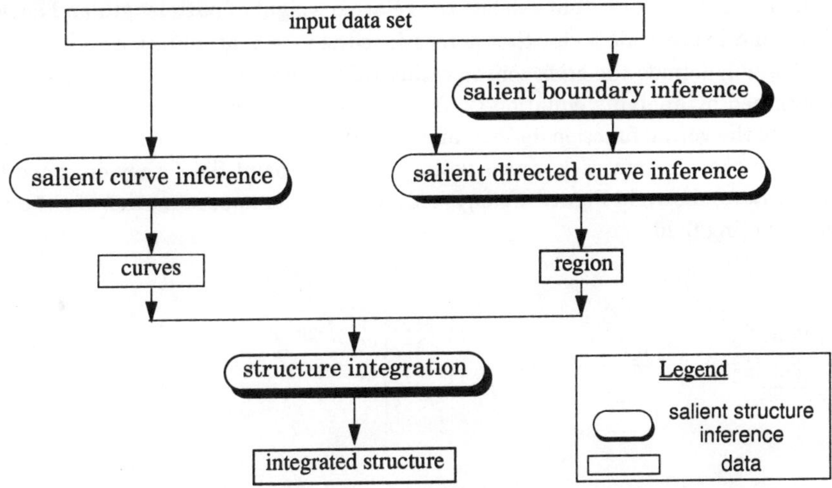

Figure 4.1 Overview of our 2-D salient structure inference method

4.1 Curve inference

In this section, we detail the inference of undirected curves from both points and curve elements input using the salient structure inference engine. While the salient structure inference engine defined in above performs structure inference efficiently, it is the definition of the voting function that determines the effectiveness of the inference. For curve inference, the voting function specifies how curve orientation is estimated by a voting feature regarding each location in the domain space. Since the orientations of the votes should change gradually in a local neighborhood, any curve element with an orientation, say θ, must be connected to points in a local neighborhood through non-crossing, C_1-continuous paths with initial orientations equal to θ. From a energy consumption point of view, circular path, which is the only C_1-continuous path that has constant curvature and is defined for all pairs of points and orientations, is preferred over other smooth paths.

Besides the orientation of the votes, the voting function also specifies the saliency of the votes. As stated in the beginning of section 3.3, the influence of a voter must be smooth, and decreases with distance. Moreover, low curvature is preferred over high curvature. We use the Gaussian function to model the decay *DF* of voter's influence with path length *s* and curvature ρ as:

$$DF(s, \rho) = e^{-\left(\frac{s^2 + c\rho^2}{\sigma^2}\right)} \tag{3.1}$$

where *c* is the constant that reflects the relative weight of path length and curvature and σ is the scale factor that determines the rate of attenuation.

Having defined the stick tensor voting field, the voting field for plate tensors is obtained by applying equation (2.6). Figure 4.2 depicts the voting fields correspond to the voting function defined in above. While the extension field in [4] is exactly the same as our stick tensor voting field, the "point field" they designed for point voters, shown in Figure 4.2(c), is only a first-order approximation of our plate tensor voting field.

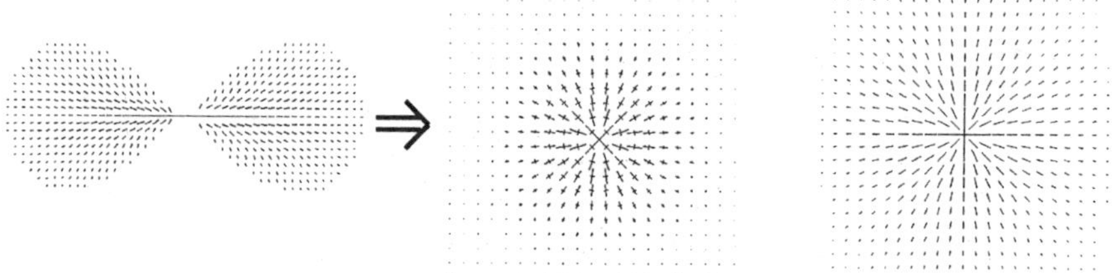

(a) stick tensor voting field (b) plate tensor voting field (c) "point field"

Figure 4.2 Voting fields for stick and plate voters vs. "point field"

Applying the voting function defined in above, we have obtained results on noisy data, one of which is shown in Figure 4.3.

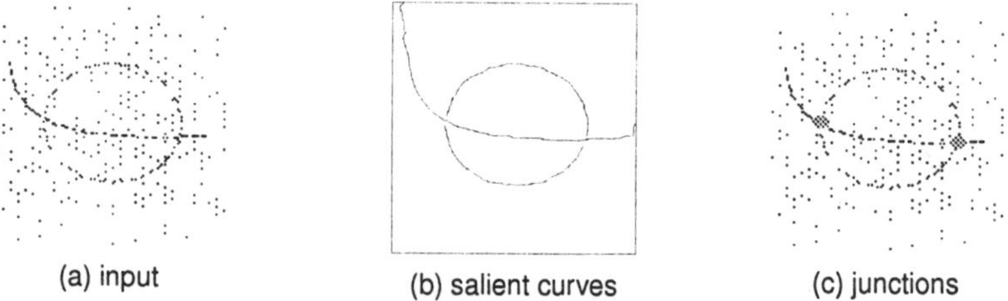

(a) input (b) salient curves (c) junctions

Figure 4.3 An example of curve inference

4.2 *Region inference*

Directed curve inference

Using the voting function defined in above, together with the inference of polarity saliency described in section 3.4, directed curves are inferred in a similar manner as the undirected curves. To illustrate the importance of polarity in directed curve inference, we consider the salient structure inference for a pair of filled circles and that for a pair of empty circles. Figure 4.4(b) shows the resulting directed curve saliency map for the pair of the directed circles that describe the filled circle in Figure 4.4(a). Compare to the curve saliency map shown in Figure 4.4(d) obtained for a pair of empty circles in Figure 4.4(a), the high agreement between the circles, which is acceptable for the empty circle pair but not the filled circle pair, is eliminated by properly incorporating the polarity information.

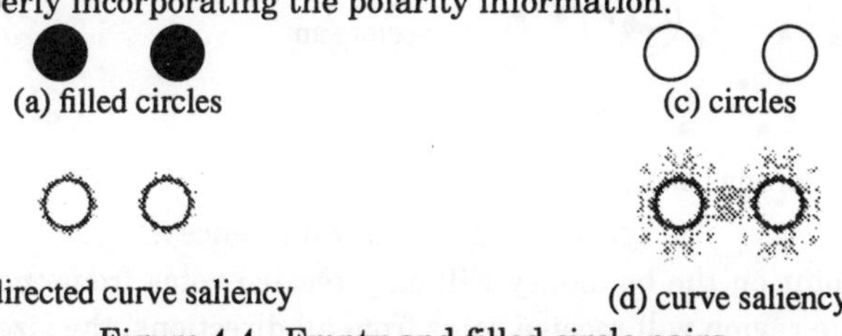

Figure 4.4 Empty and filled circle pairs

An interesting effect of handling polarity and curve saliency separately is that they can be combined to detect structures other than directed curves. Consider a line in 2-D. We can treat it as a region bounded by a contour with two straight portions very close to each other, as shown in Figure 4.5. In fact, this is the way most edge detectors represent a line. The two straight portions of such contour are parallel but of opposite polarities, and thus produces high orientation saliency but low polarity saliency for the site in between the contour. We therefore can recover the line by locating the local minima in the directed curve saliency map. Hence polarized and unpolarized features can be handled uniformly in our framework of salient structure inference.

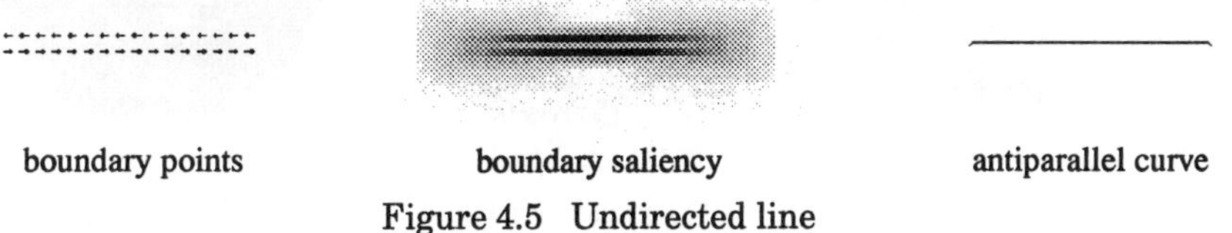

Figure 4.5 Undirected line

Dealing with dot clusters

While the incorporation of polarity allows us to infer regions properly, this polarity information is not always available. When data are sparse and irregular, local boundary detection becomes hard. A typical example is shown in Figure 4.7(a). Since boundary detection is about locating discontinuities, it is possible to use the salient structure inference engine to detect points on the boundary. In the spirit of our methodology, we again seek to compute at every location in the domain space a measure we call boundary saliency which relates the possibility of having the site being on the boundary of a region. A boundary point has the property that most of its neighbors are on one side. We therefore can identify boundary points by computing the directional distribution of neighbors at every data point, as illustrated in Figure 4.6(a). This local discontinuity estimation is similar to the orientation estimation for salient structure inference. We depict in Figure 4.6(b) the corresponding voting field which uses the Gaussian decay function.

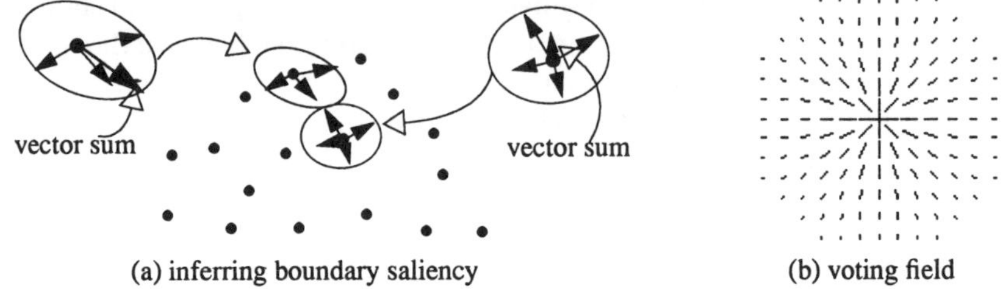

(a) inferring boundary saliency (b) voting field

Figure 4.6 Boundary inference

Since a point on the boundary will only receive votes from one side while a point inside the region will receive votes from all directions, the size of the vector sum of the polarized votes should indicate the "boundariness" of a point, that is, the boundary saliency. On the other hand, the direction of the resulting vector relates the polarity information at the site. Figure 4.7(b) presents the result of this boundary inference on the 2-D data set depicted in Figure 4.7(a). Observe that

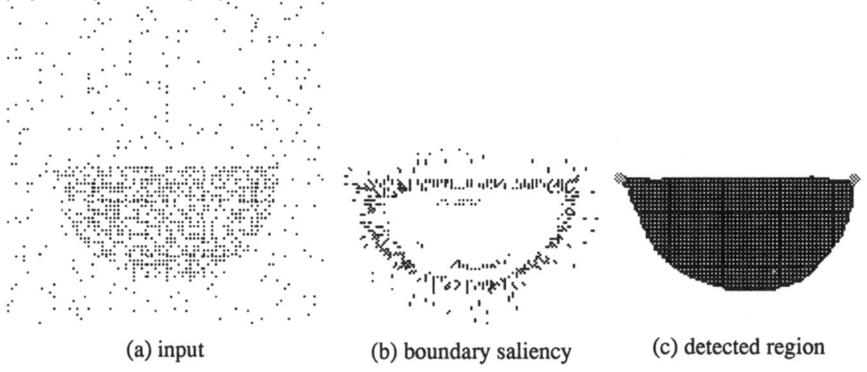

(a) input (b) boundary saliency (c) detected region

Figure 4.7 Region Inference

points are not labeled in absolute terms as borders or non-borders, but are presented with reservations as indicated by the boundary saliencies.

Having obtained the polarity information and identified the boundary points, the inference of region can proceed as described in above by using the boundary saliencies as the initial point saliency. Figure 4.7(c) depicts the resulting region inferred from the boundary points shown in Figure 4.7(b). Note that we not only find the region, but also accurately find the corners.

4.3 Other examples of salient structure inference

Figure 1.1(b) and Figure 4.8(b) show the result of applying our salient structure inference algorithm to the dot clusters in Figure 1.1(a) and Figure 4.8(a) respectively. As in all perceptual tasks, the detection of regions from sparse dot clusters are scale dependent. In this case, scale is determined by the density of points inside the region. The point set shown in Figure 4.8 is a typical example that consists of regions of multiple scales. When the scale of the boundary voting function is larger than that of the region, the boundary so detected are badly located. When the scale of the boundary voting function is smaller than that of the region, the boundary is not detected at all. We believe this problem has to be solved by using multiple scales in detection.

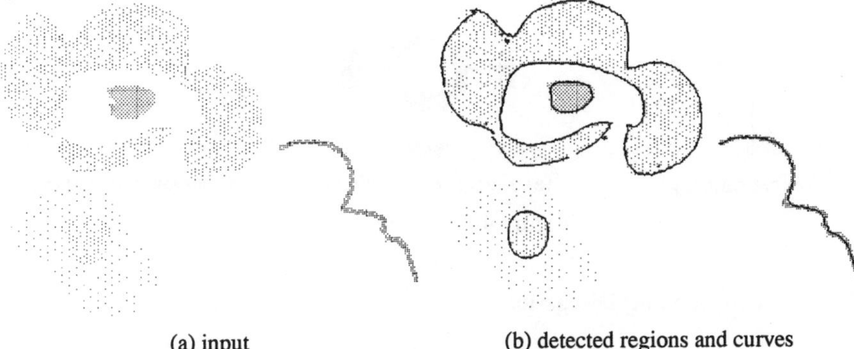

(a) input (b) detected regions and curves

Figure 4.8 Sparsely distributed point set

We have also applied our salient structure inference algorithm to the four-armed Ehrenstein figure shown in Figure 1.1(a). For illusory figures like this, the inference task is to extract contours which are perceivable, but not detectable from the input signal. The rationale behind such perception is that lines usually do not end abruptly, and that they are most likely being occluded by a region. In our framework, illusory contour can easily be inferred by considering the possible shape, that is, the orientation, of the occluding contour at each endpoint. Following the arguments in [6], the probability of a line being intersected by a region contour at an angle θ is proportional to $\sin\theta$. Since this information is only relevant for region boundary inference, we encode it in the polarity portion of the vote. The resulting polarized voting field for illusory contour inference is shown in Figure 4.9(a). To infer illusory contour from the four-armed Ehrenstein figure (shown in Figure 4.9(b)), we first detect the endpoints by applying the boundary detector described in above. Using the boundary saliency value (highlighted in Figure 4.9(c)) as the weight for the polarity votes, we obtain the disc contour when polarity is considered, which is highlighted in the directed curve saliency map (Figure 4.9(e)), the 4 underlying lines when polarity is ignored, which is highlighted in the curve saliency map(Figure 4.9(f)). The junctions between the region and the lines are further verify by the structure integrator in the salient structure inference engine.

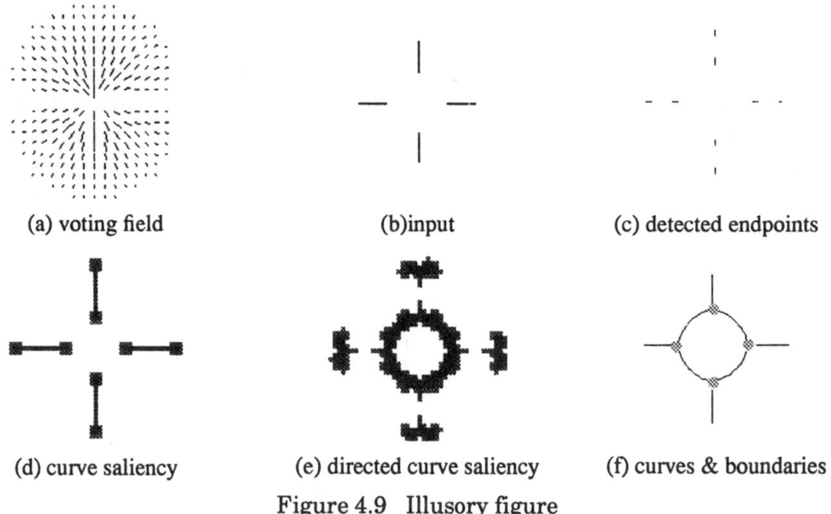

(a) voting field (b)input (c) detected endpoints

(d) curve saliency (e) directed curve saliency (f) curves & boundaries

Figure 4.9 Illusory figure

5 Conclusion and Discussion

We have presented a unifying computational framework for the inference of multiple salient junctions, curves and regions from sparse noisy data. The methodology make use of a technique called tensor voting, which combines the efficiency of non-linear voting and the strength of tensor representation, to allow simultaneous detection of discontinuities and outliers while interpolating curves and region boundaries. The proposed method is non-iterative, requires no initial guess and thresholding, and the only free parameter is scale.

While we have only shown examples in 2-D, this methodology can easily be extend to 3-D by using tensors of dimension 3. A 3-D tensor has the shape of an ellipsoid which can be decomposed into 3 components according to the eigensystem of the tensor. Figure 5.1 depicts an example of salient structure inference in 3-D using this methodology.

Notice that the problem of inferring salient structures from noisy data in fact is common among many computer vision tasks, we believe our approach can be used to solve a number of mid-level vision problems. We have applied our method to compute shape descriptions from local disparity measurements in shape from stereo and image irradiance in shape from shading and have obtained some promising results. Other potential applications includes image segmentation using

(a) one view of the 3-D inputs

(b) junction curve

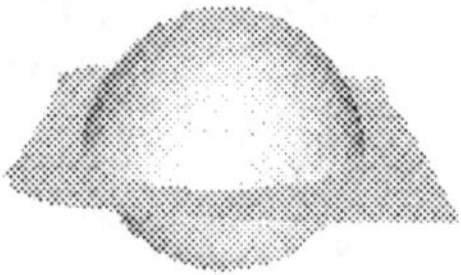

(c) salient structures

Figure 5.1 An example of surface inference

edge and polarity information obtained by edge detectors, and shape from motion using local estimation of optical flow in image sequences.

References

[1] N. Ahuja and M. Tuceryan, "Extraction of early perceptual structure in dot patterns: integrating region, boundary, and component Gestalt", *Computer Vision, Graphics and Image Processing*, vol. 48, 1989, pp. 304-356.

[2] J. Dolan and R. Weiss, "Perceptual Grouping of Curved Lines", *Proc. Image Understanding Workshop*, 1989, pp. 1135-1145.

[3] G.H. Granlund and Knutsson, *Signal Processing for Computer Vision*, Kluwer Academic Publishers, 1995.

[4] G. Guy and G. Medioni, "Inferring Global Perceptual Contours from Local Features", *Int. J. of Computer Vision*, vol. 20, no. 1/2, 1996, pp. 113-133.

[5] G. Guy and G. Medioni, "Inference of Surfaces, 3D Curves and Junctions from Sparse 3-D Data", *Proc. IEEE Symposium on Computer Vision*, Coral Gable, 1995, pp. 599-604.

[6] G. Guy, *Inference of Multiple Curves and Surfaces from Sparse Data*, Ph.D. dissertation, Technical Report IRIS-96-345, Institute for Robotics and Intelligent Systems, University of Southern California.

[7] F. Heitger and R. von der Heydt, "A Computational Model of Neural Contour Processing: Figure-Ground Segregation and Illusory Contours", *Proc. Int. Conf. Computer Vision*, 1993, pp. 32-40.

[8] W.E. Lorensen and H.E. Cline, "Marching Cubes: A High Resolution 3-D Surface Reconstruction Algorithm", *Computer Graphics*, vol. 21, no. 4, 1987.

[9] P. Parent and S.W. Zucker, "Trace Inference, Curvature Consistency, and Curve Detection", *IEEE Trans. Pattern Analysis and Machine Intelligence*, vol. 11, no.8, 1989, pp. 823-839.

[10] A. Sha'ashua and S. Ullman, "Structural Saliency: the Detection of Globally Salient Structures using a Locally Connected Network", *Proc. Int. Conf. on Computer Vision*, 1988, pp.321-327.

[11] L.R. Williams and D. Jacobs, "Stochastic Completion Fields: A Neural Model of Illusory Contour Shape and Salience", *Proc. Int. Conf. Computer Vision*, 1995,pp. 408-415.

[12] S.W. Zucker and R.A. Hummel, "Toward a Low-Level Description of Dot Clusters: Labeling Edge, Interior, and Noise Points", *Computer Vision, Graphics, and Image Processing*, vol. 9, no.3, 1979, pp.213-234.

IMPLICIT POLYNOMIAL BASED GEOMETRIC SHAPE MODELING AND RECOGNITION*

ZHIBIN LEI, DAVID B. COOPER
Division of Engineering, Brown University, Providence, RI 02912

This paper presents a brief overview and focuses on two key aspects of a technology for representing and recognizing complicated 2D and 3D shapes subject to partial occlusion and missing data, based on implicit polynomials. The two key aspects are new concepts and results for fast, robust, repeatable fitting of implicit polynomials to data, and new approaches to representing and recognizing complicated shapes based on these polynomials. This representation is built around ***signature curves of vector valued algebraic invariants*** which permit a recognition machine to start anywhere in a shape data set, choose a data patch of appropriate length, fit an implicit polynomial to the patch, and recognize the shape or index into a database by comparing algebraic invariants of the polynomial with those stored in the signature curves. Fitting and recognition or indexing can be multiscale. This technology can also be applied to curves obtained from shape data, such as Kimia's shocks and time to shock-formation [1], and our set-of-curves representation for generalized cylinders [2].

1 IP Shape Modeling And Recognition: An Overview

Shape modeling for what purpose? Shape model development should depend on the intended use. In this paper, we are interested in shape models for the purposes of machine recognition of shapes and shape-based indexing into databases for 2D curve and 3D surface shapes, and shape models that have good representation power and are easy to manipulate for animation and deformation in computer graphics or virtual reality. Desirable characteristics for the first two uses are low computational cost and low error rate. Of interest are both the case of specific rigid or articulated objects, and the more difficult case of specific deformable objects or determining the class association of a shape in the data. This paper presents a brief overview and focuses on two key aspects of a technology for representing and recognizing or indexing complicated 2D and 3D shapes subject to partial occlusion and missing data, based on implicit polynomials. *The two key aspects are new concepts and results for fast, robust, repeatable fitting of implicit polynomials to data, and new approaches to invariantly representing and recognizing complicated shapes based on these polynomials.*

Implicit polynomial planar curves and 3D surfaces can be thought of as extensions of quadric curves and surfaces to polynomials of higher de-

*Acknowledgement: This work was partially supported by NSF Grant # IRI-9224963

gree that can represent much more complicated shapes. An implicit polynomial $2D$ curve of degree d is the set of points (x, y) where the polynomial $f(x, y) = \Sigma_{i,j\geq 0, i+j\leq d} a_{ij} x^i y^j$ is 0 [3,4,5,6]. (3D implicit polynomial surfaces are the set of points (x, y, z) where the polynomial $f(x, y, z)$ is 0.) For 2D shape modeling, implicit polynomial curves can be used to represent an object's silhouette boundary, and can also be used to represent internal structure in an object image as well; the latter would result from discontinuities in the albedo of a surface due to patterns on the surface or from the intersection of two surfaces having the same albedos but having normal vectors, near the intersection, that make different angles with the illuminating light rays. The curves in question do not have to be closed, and they can intersect one another. The 3D data to be represented can result from 3D reconstruction based on two or more images and use of stereo algorithms [7,8,9,10], if the cameras are calibrated, or structure and motion estimation algorithms if the cameras are uncalibrated [11,12,13,14,15,10,16,17,18,19]. Or the 3D data can come from LADAR, or mechanical sensing, etc.. The first two images in Figure 1 are 3D implicit polynomial surface fits to sensed data for a dog's heart and a human nose.

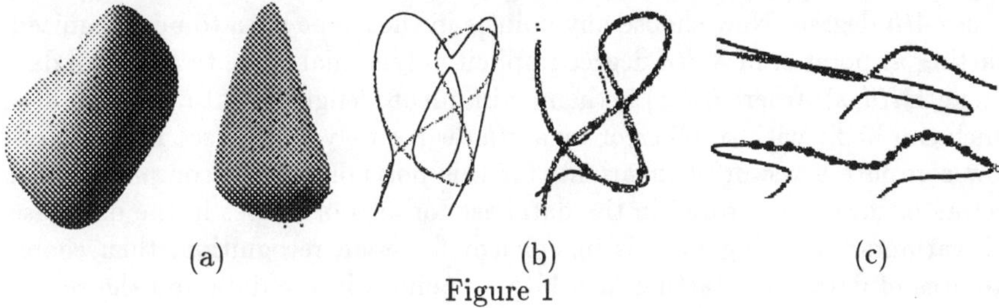

(a) (b) (c)

Figure 1

Of great importance for shape recognition is the availability of *invariants* of these polynomials. An algebraic invariant of a polynomial is a function $g(\underline{a})$, of the coefficient vector $\underline{a}$ of a polynomial, that is invariant to certain transformations of the curve (or surface), e.g., Euclidean, affine, or projective transformations [20,21], which arise when the camera/object relative geometry is arbitrary. These invariants are *generalized* shape descriptors. Examples of these invariants that we have discovered and used are Euclidean and affine self-invariants [22,23,24,25] for an implicit polynomial curve or 3D surface, and the affine mutual-invariants [26,27,2] for pairs of implicit polynomial curves. The latter are important when it is desired to capture the joint shape in a pair or in a larger number of implicit polynomial curves. An example of an affine self-invariant is: $6 * a_{22}^3 - 27 * a_{13} * a_{22} * a_{31} + 81 * a_{04} * a_{31}^2 + 81 * a_{13}^2 * a_{40} - 216 * a_{04} * a_{22} * a_{40}$. A mutual-invariant of two implicit polynomials is defined similarly and it is a function of coefficient vectors of the two polynomials. Examples of $3D$ invariants can be found in [22,24]. These invariants have been shown to be robust to noisy data, and somewhat robust to missing data, e.g., due to partial occlusion [24,27,2]. The technology for 3D surfaces is the same as for 2D curves. No other representation has these important features! *Bayesian Object recognition* for *simple objects* are implemented in [24,27,15]. To summarize, what is the shape recognition procedure and why is it among the best possible approaches to recognition?

Recognition procedure: 1. For simple shapes. Fit a single implicit polynomial 2D curve (or 3D surface) to each shape in the database — typically we use $4th$ degree implicit polynomials. Compute a vector of a few invariants for each of these implicit polynomials and store the vector of invariants as a feature vector for the object in the database. Typically, we use 3-6 invariants. To recognize new shape data, fit an implicit polynomial 2D curve (3D surface) to the data, compute a vector of invariants for this curve, and compare this vector of invariants with each of those stored in the database. Recognition is determined by the object in the database for which the stored vector of invariants is most like the measured vector of invariants. 2. For complicated shapes — *one approach.* Choose a degree d for the polynomials — typically we use $4th$ degree. Now choose any point s in the shape data to be recognized. Starting at point s, fit a dth degree implicit polynomial curve to an arc of data of length $l(d, s)$, where $l(d, s)$ is the maximum arc-length of data, starting at s, which can be fit with small error by a dth degree polynomial (see Figure 4(e)). Now compute a vector of invariants for this polynomial and compare it with vectors of invariants stored in the database for arcs of shapes in the database. If invariants for a single arc is insufficient for good recognition, then choose two arcs of data, one starting at arbitrary point s in the data and the second starting at point s' which is where the first arc ends and which has arc-length $l(d, s')$. Then compute a vector of *mutual invariants* for this pair of patches of polynomials, and compare this vector of mutual invariants with vectors of mutual invariants stored for shapes in the database.

Unusually powerful features of this approach: 1. We now have fast, robust approaches to fitting polynomials of degrees up to $16th$ or so, such that the geometry of the fitted curve with respect to the data is invariant with Euclidean transformations of the data and is meaningful and stable for affine transformations of the data. Typically, a $4th$ degree curve can be fit in a few milliseconds on a SPARC 10. Then recognition for simple shapes is very fast because it involves only the comparison of the measured vector of invariants with a vector of invariants stored for each object in the database. Hence, the computational cost of the complete recognition procedure is probably close to the minimum possible. 2. The data along the shape does not have to be connected; it can be sparse and can have gaps. The data does not have to be closed; it can represent only a portion of a shape boundary. **3.** For complicated shapes and for partially occluded shapes, recognition is in terms of a vector of invariants for a polynomial that is fit to a visible arc of data, or by a vector of mutual invariants for two or more arcs of visible data. This recognition becomes possible because of our new concept of stored representation which is our *signature curves of invariants.* This is conceptually possible because we now have a way of choosing the length $l(d, t)$ for an arc starting at point t in the data to be recognized such that the arc will correspond to an arc for the corresponding object in the database. It is computationally possible because of our low computational cost fitting algorithms. **4.** The shape modeling and recognition technology for 3D objects based on 3D implicit polynomial surfaces is exactly the same as the preceding technology for 2D curves.

Other applications: 1. These approaches can be applied to other representation, e.g., to representing and recognizing skeletons. We also have a representation for 3D generalized cylinders as a family of curves which can be represented as a family of implicit polynomial curves and recognized by their mutual invariants, even in the presence of partial occlusion [27,2]. 2. The technology for 2D curve recognition is ideally suitable for ultrafast shape indexing into pictorial databases. 3. Fast indexing into video databases may be possible by 3D surface reconstruction from a video clip, and then 3D surface representation and recognition using 3D implicit polynomial surfaces [15].

2 Robust IP Fitting Procedures

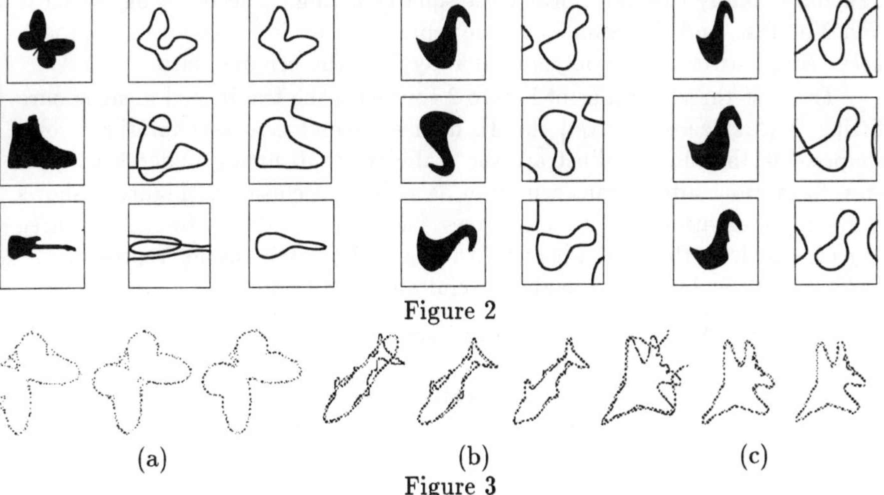

Figure 2

(a) (b) (c)

Figure 3

Two new approaches, *the 3 level-set method* (3L) [28], and *linear programming* (LP) [29], were developed for fitting $2D$ curves to data in the plane (and extend directly to $3D$ surface fitting to range data). Both yield very stable fits, i.e., the geometry of the fitted curve with respect to the data is highly stable under translations and rotations, as well as under general linear transformations. The LP algorithm uses linear programming to find an implicit polynomial that fits a chosen set of control points (often a select number of data points) within a distance ϵ, if a representation can satisfy the constraints. Control points can be chosen either automatically, or interactively, thereby permitting either the machine, or the user, to control the quality of the fit over various regions as desired. Images 3 and 5 in Figure 1 are data on which are overlaid $4th$ degree polynomial fits produced by one of the good current fitting algorithms. images 4 and 6 are arbitrarily chosen control points and the LP implicit polynomial fits to the data and satisfying constraints at the control points. The (3L) algorithm results in curves which are smooth, physically meaningful representations of the data, even when the fitting polynomial is chosen to be of lower degree than what is necessary to represent the data precisely, and the computation time is orders of magnitude less than for presently used methods. The (3L) method easily fits polynomials of degree 14 or 16. The remarkable stability of the (3L) representation comes from augmenting the data to be fit, Figure 4(a), by two additional data sets, each set at a distance c inside and outside the original data set, respectively. A new data set is now created with the data set taking values 0 at the original data points and taking values c and $-c$ on the new outer and inner curves, respectively. Then an *explicit polynomial* is fit to this new data simply through linear least squares fitting. The resulting fitting is lightning fast, and the stability in the representation is because this approach keeps singularities in the polynomial away from the original data.

The first three columns of Figure 2 compares the traditional mean square fitting [30] (first zero set) and the 3L fitting (second zero set) for three solid shapes. 4-7th columns illustrate the stability of 3L fitting under Euclidean transformation, affine transformation as well as occlusions. Figure 3 shows curve representations for fits of degrees $4, 8, 12$, respectively, to each of three objects. This is the case where a $4th$ degree IP curve cannot represent the data accurately, but can provide a useful approximation.

3 Invariant Matching and Signature Curves

If an object boundary is too complicated to be represented by a dth degree implicit polynomial, preliminary recognition, to eliminate a large number of possible candidates, can be realized by approximating a complex shape with a $4th$ degree polynomial; the new fitting algorithms described in previous section makes this possible for the first time. However, in order to then realize more refined recognition or in order to handle partial occlusion, our approach is to choose a number of patches of the boundary of an object, approximate each such patch well by an implicit polynomial, compute a vector of invariants for each polynomial and perhaps a vector of mutual invariants for each pair of polynomials in a selected subset of pairs, and recognize the object by matching these measured invariants against invariants stored in the database. The way this handles partial occlusion is that one or more patches measured in the data will be of the true object, and hence useful for object recognition through comparison with patches stored in the database (see Figure 3(e)). Patches that lie entirely or partially on an occluding boundary will not have invariants that match with those stored in the database for the true object. Conceptually, this is a terrific approach for handling partial occlusion and model-based object/background segmentation; in practice,there are a number of difficulties. The serious difficulty is having a patch stored in the database, for the true object, that corresponds to the patch to be recognized in the data. Our proposed solution is what we call *signature vector-curves* or just *signature curves* which we now describe.

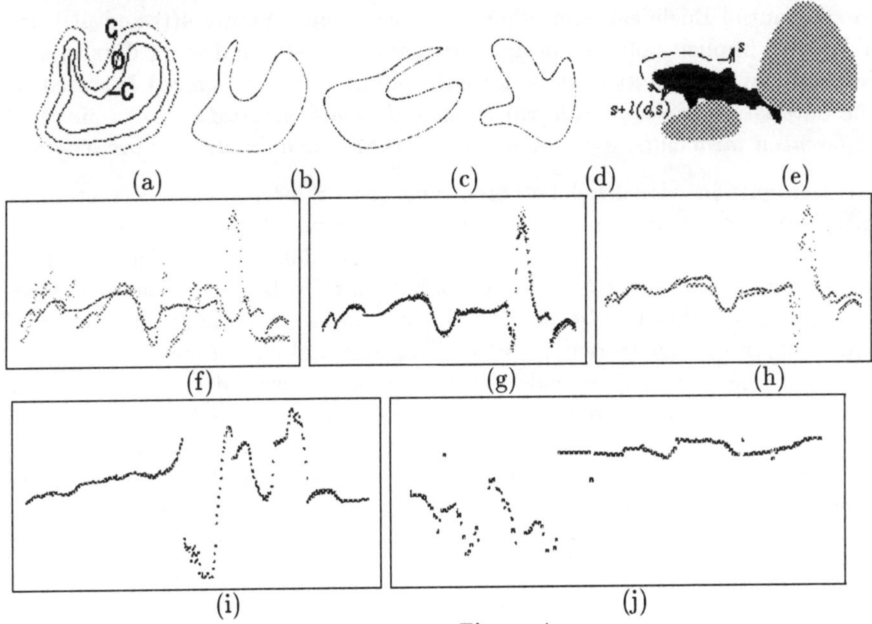

Figure 4

This is a solution to a long standing problem in computer vision, namely, decomposing a complex shape into *patches or parts* such that the extraction of a patch or part in the data and its use in object recognition is of low computational cost. The following is possible because the fitting procedure we use is computationally fast, so that fittings can be done for 10-50 patches of curve data with little computation. We build a database for shape recognition or shape-based indexing as follows. Fix the polynomial degree d. Let s denote arc length and therefore specify location along an object boundary curve from some start point. For each location s, fit a dth degree implicit polynomial to a boundary patch of length $l(d,s)$ starting at s. Length $l(d,s)$ is chosen to be the largest length boundary patch that can be well approximated by a dth degree implicit polynomial (Figure 4(e)). Now compute a vector $\underline{v}(s)$ of invariants for this boundary patch. We call $\underline{v}(s)$, this vector-valued function of s, the signature curve for the object. Figure 4 illustrates the idea of signature curves. The middle curve in Figure 4(a), marked O, shows a shape. Figure 4(b) and 4(c) are the Euclidean and affine transformations of this shape. Figure 4(d) is another free-form shape. Figure 4(f) shows the signature curves for one invariant of second degree implicit polynomials for the shape 4(a) and 4(d). Figure 4(g) shows the signature curves for 4(a) and 4(b), and Figure 4(h) shows the signature curves for 4(a) and 4(c), illustrating their invariance to substantial Euclidean and affine transformations. Figure 4(i) and 4(j) are 4th degree implicit polynomial signature curves for 4(a) and shark data in 4(e) respectively. A *signature curve* for each object to be recognized is stored in the database. *The approach can be viewed as a generalization of a curve of differential invariants, e.g., a curve of curvature as a function of arc length.*

Recognition is realized by comparing one or more measured vectors of invariants for one or more patches of curve data with the *signature curve* for an object in the database. Hence, for each curve data patch of length $l(d,t)$, beginning at some point t on an object boundary to be used in indexing, the vector of invariants for the patch will have the same value as the vector of invariants in the signature curve at some a priori unknown point s, where s in the signature curve corresponds to t in the data curve. *What is crucial and conceptually beautiful here is that this works because our method for choosing $l(d,s)$, the appropriate length for a boundary patch, is Euclidean and affine invariant, so for each data patch for an object, there will be a corresponding boundary patch used in computing the signature curve in the database even if the object data has undergone an arbitrary Euclidean or affine transformation.* Thus, a pair of corresponding patches, one in the data and one used in the database, may be of different arc-lengths! *The very nice feature of this approach is that choosing an appropriate patch for indexing is computationally trivial, there is no complicated search for any special structure!* Recognition is very fast — certainly fast enough for indexing into a database because checking for whether a point on the signature curve has the same value as the vector of invariants for a measured data patch is computationally fast.

What values should be used for polynomial degree d? A larger d permits a larger $l(d,s)$ which results in a data patch having more shape structure and therefore more shape discriminating power for indexing. Then one or two such patches might suffice for indexing, whereas a greater number would be needed if smaller d is used. However, if partial occlusion is a serious problem, then smaller values of $l(d,s)$ may be preferred, which means smaller values for d should be used. Good shape discrimination can be achieved for small values of d by using mutual invariants for pairs of polynomials fit to pairs of data patches. Also, the relative merits of small versus large values of d need to be studied for assessing required computational cost.

Multi-scale invariant choice of patch arc-length. In this section, data patch arc-length for representation by a dth degree polynomial was chosen to be the maximum such that the polynomial would fit the data with small error. By a multiscale representation, we mean approximation of a patch of data by a polynomial of degree d which is smaller than necessary for providing a small error fit, the purpose being to represent the data with fewer parameters. Therefore, given polynomial degree d and location s on an object boundary, how should the arc-length of a patch starting at s be chosen such that the arc-length is greater than $l(d,s)$ but the portion of the shape covered by the patch is invariant to Euclidean or affine transformations? One solution to this problem is choose the arc-length such that the patch is fit with small error by a polynomial of degree d', where $d' > d$, e.g., $d' = 6$, and then fit the resulting patch with a dth degree polynomial, e.g., $d = 4$.

Shape Decomposition into Blobs and Generalized Cylinders. In representing the 2D silhouette or the 3D surface of a human or a horse, we would model the head and torso with implicit polynomials, but it does not seem to make sense to do this for the arms or legs and the tail. Rather, we would model these as 2D or 3D generalized cylinders, i.e., an axis and width along the axis in the direction perpendicular to the axis in the case of the 2D silhouettes, and an axis and cross section curve, as a function of arc-length along the axis, in a plane perpendicular to the axis in the case of 3D data. This 2D representation and the 3D representation can each be given in terms of a set of implicit polynomial curves and their self and mutual invariants [2].

References

1. B.B. Kimia, A.R. Tannenbaum, and S.W. Zucker. Shapes, shocks, and deformations, i: The components of shape and the reaction-diffusion space. *IJCV*,

Auguest 1995.
2. D. B. Cooper and Z. Lei. *Object Representation in Computer Vision*, chapter On representation and invariant recognition of complex objects based on patches and parts, pages 139–153. Springer Lecture Notes in Computer Science Series, 1995.
3. G. Taubin. Estimation of planar curves, surfaces and nonplanar space curves defined by implicit equations, with applications to edge and range image segmentation. *IEEE Transactions on Pattern Analysis and Machine Intelligence*, November 1991.
4. J. Ponce, A. Hoogs, and D.J. Kriegman. On using cad models to compute the pose of curved 3d objects. *CVGIP: Image Understanding*, March 1992.
5. C.M. Hoffmann. Implicit curves and surfaces in cagd. *IEEE Computer Graphics and applications*, January 1993.
6. D. Moore and J. Warren. Approximation of dense scattered data using algebraic surfaces. Technical Report COMP TR91-135, Department of Computer Science, Rice University, P.Ø. Box 1892, Houston, TX 77251-1892, October 1990.
7. B. Cernuschi-Frias, D. B. Cooper, and Y. P. Hung. Toward a model-based bayesian theory for estimating and recognizing parametrized 3-d objects using two or more images taken from different positions. *IEEE PAMI*, 11(10):1028–1052, 1989.
8. Y.P. Hung, D.B. Cooper, and B. Cernuschi-Frias. Toward a model-based bayesian thoery for estimating and recognizing parametrized 3-d objects using two or more images taken from different positions. *IJCV*, 6(2):105–132, 1991.
9. R. M. Bolle, D. B. Cooper, Y. P. Hung, and P. N. Belhumeur. On optimally combining pieces of information, with applications to estimating 3d complex-object position from range data. *IEEE PAMI*, 8(5):1028–1052, 1989.
10. O. D. Faugeras. *Three-dimensional computer vision: a geometric viewpoint.* MIT Press, 1993.
11. D. Weinshall and C. Tomasi. Linear and incremental acquisition of invariant shape model from image sequences. *IEEE PAMI*, 17(5):512–517, 1995.
12. C. Tomasi and T. Kanade. Shape and motion from image streams under orthography: a factorization method. *IJCV*, 9(2):137–154, 1992.
13. Conrad J. Poelman and Takeo Kanade. A paraperspective factorization method for shape and motion recovery. Technical Report CMU//CS-92-208, Carnegie Mellon University, School of Computer Science, October 1992.
14. C.Y. Lee and D.B. Cooper. Structure from motion: a region based approach using affine transformations and moment invariants. In *IEEE Conf. on Robotics and Automation*, 1993.
15. Z. Lei and Y.T. Lin. 3d shape inferencing and modeling for semantic video retrieval. In *Multimedia Storage and Archiving Systems*, Boston, MA, November 1996.
16. L.S. Shapiro, A. Zisserman, and M. Brady. 3d motion recovery via affine epipolar geometry. *International Journal of Computer Vision*, 16:147–182,

1995.
17. C.J. Taylor and D. J. Kriegman. Structure and motion from line segments in multiple images. *IEEE PAMI*, 17(11):1021–1032, 1995.
18. A. Shashua. Projective structure from uncalibrated images:structure from motion and recognition. *IEEE Transactions on Pattern Analysis and Machine Intelligence*, 16(8):778–790, 1994.
19. R. Mohr. Projective geometry and computer vision. In C. H. Chen, L. F. Pau, and P. S. P. Wang, editors, *Handbook of pattern recognition and computer vision*. World Scientific publishing Company, 1995.
20. J. L. Mundy and A. Zisserman, editors. *Geometric Invariance in Computer Vision*. MIT Press, Cambridge, MA, 1992.
21. J. L. Mundy, A. Zisserman, and D. Forsyth, editors. *Applications of invariance in computer vision: second joint European-US workshop, Ponta Delgada, Azores, Portugal, October 9–14, 1993: proceedings*, volume 825, New York, NY, USA, 1994. Springer-Verlag Inc.
22. D. Keren, J. Subrahmonia, and D.B. Cooper. *Applications of Invariance in Computer Vision*, chapter Integrating algebraic curves and surfaces, algebraic invariants and Bayesian methods for 2D and 3D object recognition. Springer Verlag, 1994.
23. G. Taubin and D.B. Cooper. *Symbolic and Numerical Computation for Artificial Intelligence*, chapter 2D and 3D object recognition and positioning with algebraic invariants and covariants. Academic Press, NYC, 1992.
24. J. Subrahmonia, D.B. Cooper, and D. Keren. Practical reliable bayesian recognition of 2d and 3d objects using implicit polynomials and algebraic invariants. *IEEE Transactions on Pattern Analysis and Machine Intelligence*, pages 505–519, May 1996.
25. H. Civi, C. Christopher, and A. Ercil. Applications of the classical theory of invariants in computer vision. In *Proceedings, National Conf. on Signal Processing and Applications*, April 1996.
26. M. Barzohar, D. Keren, and D. B. Cooper. Recognizing groups of curves based on new affine mutual geometric invariants, with applications to recognizing intersecting roads in aerial images. In *12th International Conference on Pattern Recognition*, October 1994.
27. Z. Lei, D. Keren, and D.B. Cooper. Computationally fast bayesian recognition of complex objects based on mutual algebraic invariants. In *IEEE International Conference on Image Processing*, pages 635–638, Washington, D.C., October 1995.
28. Z. Lei, M.M. Blane, and D.B. Cooper. 3l fitting of higher degree implicit polynomials. In *Third IEEE Workshop on Applications of Computer Vision*, Sarasota, FL, December 1996.
29. Z. Lei and D.B. Cooper. New, faster, more controlled fitting of implicit polynomial 2d curves and 3d surfaces to data. In *Proceedings, Computer Vision and Pattern Recognition*, San Francisco, CA, June 1996.
30. V. Pratt. Direct least squares fitting of algebraic surfaces. *Computer Graphics*

SYMMETRY, CAUSALITY, MIND

MICHAEL LEYTON

Department of Psychology, Busch Campus,
Rutgers University,
New Brunswick, NJ 08903. USA
E-mail: leyton@ruccs.rutgers.edu

1 Introduction

We argue that current approaches to defining and investigating perception are founded on ideas that necessarily prevent these approaches from discovering the basic regularities governing the perceptual system. We develop a substantially different approach and show how this approach actually produces these basic regularities. We argue that all current frameworks fail to make use of the following profound point: Perception is, fundamentally, a form of *memory;* i.e. memory of causal events in the environment. Thus, we ground our theory of perception on a theory of memory. Our theory of memory is based on the following four principles all of which are centered on the construct *symmetry:*

ASYMMETRY PRINCIPLE: *An asymmetry in the present is understood as having originated from a past symmetry.*

SYMMETRY PRINCIPLE: *A symmetry in the present is understood as having always existed.*

SECOND SYSTEM PRINCIPLE: *Increased asymmetry over time can occur in a system only if the system has a causal interaction with a second system.*

MAXIMAL GAIN RULE: *Use the Asymmetry Principle in such a way that it gains maximal symmetry.*

In addition, we need this distinction: In the inference of history from the present,

external inference concerns **intra**-state asymmetries

internal inference concerns **inter**-state asymmetries

2 Causality and Computational Vision

Whereas the central recovered construct of contemporary computational vision is the *surface,* we argue that this construct should be replaced by that of *causality.* In our theoretical system, everything is *memory,* and something becomes memory when it is causally explained. In particular, the entire purpose of perception is to convert the retinal stimulus into memory.

We argue that perception structures this memory into two overall layers; i.e. layers that are phases of causal interactions. These phases are presented as the first and second arrows from left to right in Fig 1. They are, respectively, as follows:

Phase 1: Object Interactions → Environmental Memory

The first phase is indicated by the number 1 in Fig 1. That is, the past consists of the interactions of environmental objects with each other; e.g. rock hitting rock, foot kicking garbage can, hand crushing paper. (We exclude only those objects, photons, that constitute illumination.) These causal interactions leave environmental memory; e.g. geological formations, dented garbage cans, crushed paper, etc. In fact, we will propose later that *everything* in the environment is perceptually defined as the memory of causal interactions.

Phase 2: Environmental Memory → Retinal Memory

The second phase is indicated by the number 2 in Fig 1. The objects that produce illumination, i.e. the photons, interact with environmental memory, and proceed to interact with the retina, thus creating retinal memory.

The first phase will be called *environment-formation* and the second phase will be called *image-formation.*

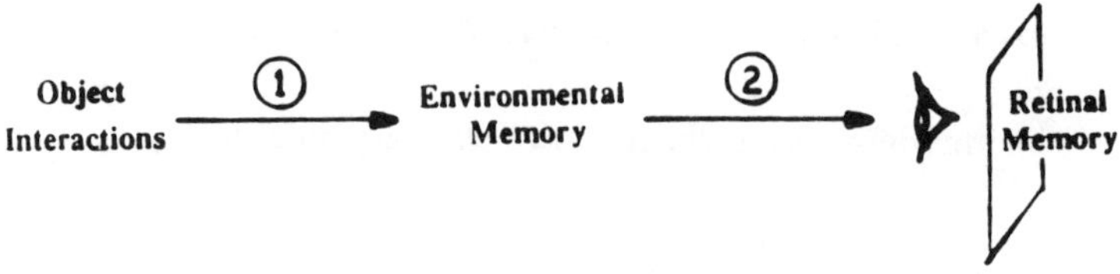
Object
Interactions
①
Environmental
Memory
②
Retinal
Memory

Fig 1

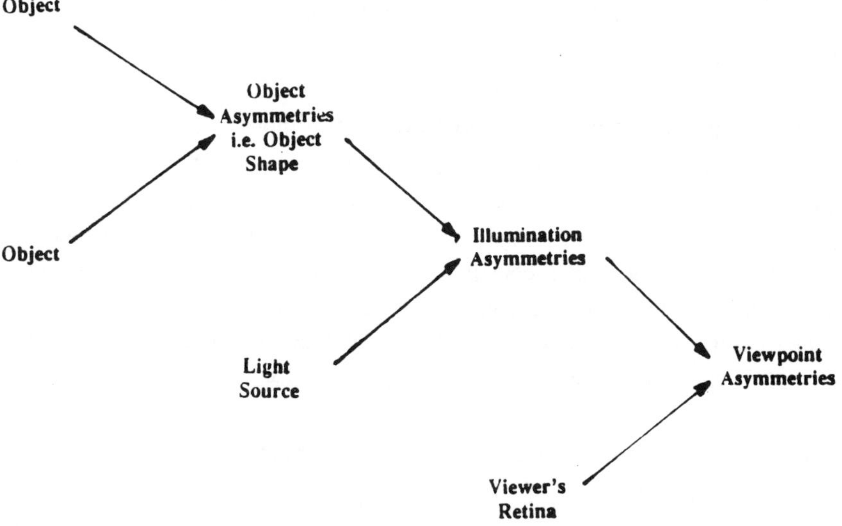
Object
Object
Object
Asymmetries
i.e. Object
Shape
Illumination
Asymmetries
Light
Source
Viewpoint
Asymmetries
Viewer's
Retina

Fig 2

It is important now to observe that contemporary computational vision is concerned basically with phase 2, i.e. the phase called image-formation, in which illumination projects the environmental structure onto the retina. In particular, the various recovery modules - Shape-from-Shading, Shape-from-Texture, Shape-from-Contour, etc. - are concerned purely with this phase.

3 Three Layers of Asymmetry

The entire two-phase history described above involves three types of causal interactions which occur successively at the beginning, middle, and end of that history. Each introduces a new set of asymmetries into the history. Thus the image on the retina has three layers of asymmetry, as follows:

(1) Object asymmetries. Environment-formation processes create the shapes of objects in the environment; e.g. geological shapes, dented garbage cans, torn shirts, crushed newspapers, etc. By Leyton [7], the shapes of these objects are a set of asymmetries, because any shape is a set of asymmetries.

(2) Illumination asymmetries. Light interacting with an environmental object introduces a variation in brightness across the object. This brightness variation is an extra layer of asymmetry that is added to the surface of the object. That is, the surface is already asymmetric by virtue of its shape, as created by the environment-formation processes; but, in this new stage, the illumination asymmetries are then "painted" onto these surface asymmetries.

(3) Projective asymmetries. Light, having left the environmental objects, projects onto the retina, creating an additional type of asymmetry: the *viewpoint asymmetries.* For example, a cube - which has equal edges in the 3D enviroment - projects to a 2D image in which several of its edges are necessarily unequal.

It is important to observe that, in accord with the Second System Principle (section 1), each of these layers of asymmetry is created by an interaction with an additional system. In (1), the object asymmetries are created by objects interacting with each other; e.g. rock hitting rock, foot kicking garbage-can, hands compressing paper. In (2), the illumination asymmetries are created by the interaction of the object shapes with a new system, the light rays. In (3), the viewpoint asymmetries are created when the light rays, reflected from the objects, interact with a new system, the viewer's retina. These successive interactions are diagrammed in Fig 2. There are three successive pairs of converging arrows, from left to right, corresponding to the three stages. In each pair, the two arrows are converging because they represent the fact that two systems are brought together in an interaction. The lower arrow, in each pair, introduces the new system in each case.

4 The Reinterpretation Thesis

In the last section we argued that there are three successive types of causal interactions in the history leading up to the retinal image, and that these interactions leave three layers of asymmetry on the image. We now propose that an image *is* a collection of asymmetries:

IMAGE-IS-ASYMMETRY THESIS. *(1) The image is best characterized as a collection of asymmetries. (2) All perception should be regarded as the recovery of causal-history from these asymmetries.*

It is in this way that the image is converted into memory.

The domain considered by current computational vision is the image-formation phase. Thus we will reinterpret the main principles and results, of current computational vision, within the framework we are developing here, showing that it is only by using this framework that one can discover that those principles and results are manifestations of much deeper regularities in the visual system.

Current computational vision, being concerned with the image-formation phase, takes, as its main problem, the recovery of surface structure; i.e. the recovery of the *shape* of the environment. For example, surface structure (shape) is recovered from image cues such as shading, texture, contour, stereo, motion. Correspondingly, researchers speak of recovery problems, such as, Shape-from-Shading, Shape-from-Texture, Shape-from-Contour, Shape-from-Stereo, Shape-from-Motion. We shall argue the following:

REINTERPRETATION THESIS. *(1) Each of the major image cues of computational vision - shading, texture, contour, stereo, motion, etc - is a type of* **asymmetry.** *(2) Each of the associated major recovery procedures - Shape-from-Shading, Shape-from-Texture, Shape-from-Contour, Shape-from-Stereo, Shape-from-Motion, etc - is the recovery of* **history from an asymmetry;** *i.e. an instantiation of the* **Asymmetry Principle.**

5 Shape-from-Texture

We are now going to illustrate this thesis with Shape-from-Texture. The other Shape-from-x problems follow the same type of argument.

Shape-from-Texture concerns the third causal interaction in the causal chain shown in Fig 2, i.e., it concerns the third layer of asymmetries described in section 3. This layer consists of two types of asymmetries as follows:

5.1 Compression

Consider a plane consisting of a square grid. Now let us imagine that this grid is slanted with respect to the viewer, with the bottom nearest the viewer and the top furthest away. We shall call this condition, *vertical slant.*

Let us, for the moment assume that viewer receives and image of the grid via *parallel projection.* As a result of the vertical slant of the grid, the horizontal lines will be be vertically compressed together in the image.

Note however that the vertical grid-lines are not compressed together horizonatally. This is because there is no slant in the horizontal direction. We are therefore led to the following conclusion: *The slanting of a plane with respect to the retina causes the following* **asymmetry** *in the retinal image: Compression occurs in the direction of slant and no compression occurs in the perpendicular direction.*

5.2 Scaling

Now let us take into account the fact that, in human perception, rays converge because projection takes place via a point-like lens. The compression effect described above still occurs; but an additional asymmetry is introduced due to the converging process: *Objects of equal size in the environment become unequal in size, in the image, in a manner that depends on their distance from the viewer.* We will call this the *scaling* effect.

5.3 The Total Asymmetry

The asymmetry created by the projection process is a sum of the asymmetry that constitutes the compression effect and the asymmetry that constitutes the scaling effect.

Having examined the asymmetries added by the projection process, let us now consider Shape-from-Texture.

5.4 *Texture and Uniformity*

Texture is generally understood to be the repeated occurrence of some visual primitive over some region. Thus, a texture consists of a two-level structure

(1) a primitive

(2) a placement structure; i.e. a structure that determines where the primitives are placed.

Each of these levels has its own organization. In projecting an this repetitive texture onto the retina, the texture becomes compressed and scaled in the manner described above. The recovery of Shape-from-Texture consists of removing the compression and scaling from the image and returning the texture to its uniform environmental state, i.e., its repetitious structure.

5.5 *Shape-from-Texture as a Memory Problem*

We shall now argue that these standard concepts from computational vision are, on a deeper level, examples of our theory of causal inference.

We have seen that the recovery of shape from texture works by the assumption, in the visual system, that compression and scaling of texture in the image correspond to a uniform texture in the environment. However, the inference of the visual system, in going from the non-uniform image texture to the uniform environmental texture, is a process of going backward in time; i.e. recovering the *past.* Therefore, the assumption of a uniform texture in the environment is an instantiation of our *Asymmetry Principle* which states that an asymmetry in the present is assumed to have arisen from a symmetry in the past.

A wealth of different methods have been developed, in the literature, for recovering Shape-from-Texture. Examination of each of these methods, however, reveals that each is based on a uniformity assumption; i.e. an assumption that the texture was uniform prior to projection. Each method concentrates on a different structural aspect of the notion of texture and designates that aspect to be uniform prior to the projection process. Each method is therefore an example of the Asymmetry Principle, because each is an assumption that an asymmetry in the present arose from a symmetry in the past.

For example, let us merely list the uniformity assumptions made in the first few years of Shape-from-Texture research:

(1) Uniform Density (Gibson, [3]). Non-uniform density of texture elements, in the image, is assumed to have arisen from uniform density of texture elements, in the environment.

(2) Uniform Boundary-Lengths (Aloimonos, [1]). Texture elements with non-uniform boundary-lengths, in the image, are assumed to have arisen from texture elements with uniform boundary-lengths, in the environment.

(3) Uniform Spatial Frequency (Bajcsy & Lieberman, [2]). Non-uniform spatial frequency, across the image, is assumed to have arisen from uniform spatial frequency, across the environmental surface.

(4) Uniform-Sized Texture Elements (Stevens, [9]). Texture elements of non-uniform size, in the image, are assumed to have arisen from texture elements of uniform size, in the environment.

(5) Uniform Spacing (Kender, [6]). Texture elements with non-uniform spacing, in the image, are assumed to have arisen from texture elements of uniform spacing, in the environment (in fact, a square grid).

(6) Uniform Tangent Direction (Witkin, [10]). For irregular texture elements, such as blotches, the tangents to each boundary point on the element have an arbitrary direction, i.e. there is uniform statistical probability across the range of possible directions. Non-uniform distribution of directions, in the image, is assumed to have arisen from uniform distribution, in the environment.

(7) Symmetric Texture Element (Ikeuchi, [4]). Non-symmetric texture elements, in the image, are assumed to have arisen from symmetric ones, in the environment.

In conclusion, we observe that, even though each of the above uniformity assumptions concerns a different structural factor, each is nevertheless an instantiation of the *Asymmetry Principle;* that is, each is the assumption that an asymmetry in the present originated from a symmetry in the past.

5.6 Assumption Diversity

At different phases in the history of computational vision, there has been controversy concerning which uniformity assumption is correct. Each uniformity assumption was often introduced by a researcher who also argued that some previous uniformity assumption cannot be valid (e.g. Witkin, [10]).

However, we shall now see that, in fact, there are logically only two possible uniformity assumptions, and the many uniformity assumptions, in the literature, are each examples of only these two. This, in turn, will let us more fully understand the fundamental role of the Asymmetry Principle in Shape-from-Texture. The two types of uniformity assumption follow from the two types of effects that the projection process has on texture: *compression* and *scaling.* Let us consider these again:

Compression. This causes squashing along one direction and leaves the perpendicular direction unchanged. Because compression alters the length-to-width ratio, it destroys any *rotational symmetry* in the original environmental surface (rotational symmetry means indistinguishability under rotations).

Scaling. Scaling causes squashing in all radial directions into a point, by an equal amount on each of these radial directions. Thus its effect can be observed only if it occurs in different amounts at different positions across image. For example, in the case of the vertically slanted square grid, scaling has occurred in increasing amounts towards the top. Thus, to have evidence that scaling took place, one has to translate an element at some position in the image (e.g. at the bottom) to another position (e.g. the top) and see whether it is the same size as the element at the second position. If it is not, then a *translational symmetry* has been lost (translational symmetry means indistinguishability under translations).

Each of the seven uniformity assumptions listed in the previous section is an example of one of these two assumptions: rotational symmetry or translational symmetry. In fact, the first five listed are examples of translational symmetry, and the last two are examples of rotational symmetry. Note that the last two are the statistical and deterministic versions, respectively, of the same assumption.

6 The Theoretical and Methodological Role of Uniformity Assumptions

In Leyton [7], we have shown that the recovery of environment-formation is based on the same fundamental rules as the recovery of image-formation.

Recovery of the image-formation phase is impossible without recovery of the previous environment-formation phase.

That is, the researcher might argue that, while it is demonstrably true that the visual system recovers the image-formation phase - otherwise one would not *see* the environment - it is not at all obvious that the recovery of environment-formation takes place, or in particular that it is part of perception.

It is here that we produce an argument that we believe is the most damaging to the theoretical structure of contemporary computational vision. In order to show that the mind does indeed recover the environment-formation phase, and that this is part of perception, we will show that it is impossible to carry out the recovery of the image-formation phase without the recovery of the environment-formation phase; that is, we will now demonstrate the validity of the above proposal (bold print). Thus we will show that even the limited program of contemporary computational vision cannot be properly carried out without the recovery of environment-formation.

To do this we will need to examine still further the contemporary use of uniformity assumptions in the analysis of the image-formation phase. As we said earlier, current computational vision believes that every Shape-from-x module uses a uniformity assumption, and, indeed, every alternative solution to the same Shape-from-x problem, e.g. the seven alternative solutions listed for Shape-from-Texture, uses a uniformity assumption. No one can avoid a uniformity assumption. Why?

Given the previous analysis, the answer is now obvious. A uniformity assumption is always of this form: Assume that some asymmetry in the image arose from some symmetry in the environment. That is, a uniformity assumption is always an instantiation of our Asymmetry Principle for the recovery of the past.

However, even though uniformity assumptions are always included in computational vision, they are viewed as peripheral adjuncts to the theory, mere extras that are brought in at the last minute to make the computation tractable. Essentially, a computational analysis always proceeds by going through the following three-stage research program:

> (Stage 1) One establishes first a theory of the environment independent of the observer.
>
> (Stage 2) One then establishes a theory of how the environment is projected onto the observer's retina to create the image.

> (Stage 3) One establishes finally a theory of how the observer-independent environment can be recovered from the image.

Near the end of this program, one discovers that if one attempts to solve Stage 3 by using only what has emerged at Stages 1 and 2, then Stage 3 is intractable. This is because the image, being only an impoverished representation of the environment, does not possess enough information to extract the environment. So one is forced to resort to a unformity assumption. Suddenly, one's computation becomes tractable.

However, the analysis we have provided implies a very different view. Whereas, according to computational vision, research begins with the theory of the environment (Stage 1), and progresses through the subsequent stages only to resort to a uniformity assumption at the last moment, according to our analysis, the uniformity assumption *is* the theory of the environment. It *is* Stage 1.

How could this be the case? To answer this, recall that, according to our analysis, each uniformity assumption is an instantiation of the Asymmetry Principle; i.e. an asymmetry in the image is explained as having arisen from a symmetry in the environment. Thus, the uniformity assumption is a statement about the structure of the environment, i.e. that it is symmetrical in a certain way. Furthermore, since the uniformity assumption is a statement about how the environment was structured *prior* to its projection onto the retina, the uniformity assumption is about the *environment independent of the observer*. This means that the uniformity assumption is a crucial component of Stage 1 of the research program, not an adjunct to Stage 3. It is part of the foundation on which the subsequent research stages are built.

This issue must be fully understood because, as we shall see, when it is fully understood, it ends the immense diversity of rules that dominates and confuses computational vision today - a condition that we shall argue prevents computational vision arriving at genuine laws of perception.

In order to understand the role of uniformity assumptions, let us now involve another issue.

It is usually supposed in the literature that one uniformity assumption will eventually prove itself to be better than the others. This view is challenged by the argument of the present paper. To see this, let us return, for example, to Witkin's [10] method for Shape-from-Texture. Witkin's method is based on the observation that an oblique image of an *irregular coastline* causes the coastline to gain a regularity: the directions in the coastline become aligned more with the direction of slant. Thus Witkin suggests that, when one is presented with the image, the appropriate inference rule is to hypothesize an environmental coastline in which the bias has been removed; i.e. in which randomness is maximized.

Now, Witkin argues that this uniformity assumption is better than the uniformity assumption proposed by Gibson, which is that non-uniform *density* in the image arises from uniform density in the environment; e.g. given an image of the American flag waving in the wind, the stripes, which have varying density across the image, arose from stripes of uniform density in the environment.

We argue that Witkin is incorrect in proposing that one of the uniformity assumptions is better than the other. They are of equal value. Witkin's uniformity assumption works for images of irregular coastlines, and Gibson's uniformity assumption works for images of American flags. They both *fail* when they are applied to the image handled by the other. For example, Witkin's fails when applied to the American flag because Witkin requires that bias in directionality be removed in recovering the environmental structure, and the American flag in the environment, being striped, represents the strongest possible directional bias.

Thus, we see that Witkin's uniformity assumption implies that one kind of environment is responsible for the image, and Gibson's implies that another kind of environment is responsible for the image. In fact, as we argued earlier, the uniformity assumption, in each case, *is* the specification of the type of environment that is involved.

Now, we were going to attack the environmental modularity and consequent computational and research modularity that underlies contemporary computational vision; i.e attack the view that the environment is divided into a set of independent domains and correspondingly the computational system must be divided into a set of independent subsystems, and research can therefore be carried out as a set of independent problems (see Leyton, [8] for a full discussion of the different kinds of modularity). However, we seem, in contradiction to our argument, to have arrived at a modularity position due to the uniformity assumptions, thus: We have argued that each uniformity assumption is the specification of a different environment, one that excludes the existence of an alternative environment; e.g. an environment that is like a coastline excludes an environment that is like an American flag. This mutual exclusion of environments seems to imply that research can be carried out in independent units.

However, this conclusion is not correct, and it is extremely important to examine why it is not correct because such an examination leads to a much deeper understanding of the visual process.

Let us consider what would happen if one used Witkin's and Gibson's uniformity assumptions in each other's environmental situations. Thus consider first what would happen if one tried to use Witkin's uniformity assumption on an image of an American flag, and tried to explain it as having arisen from an irregular coastline. One would, in particular, be trying to explain smooth lines in the image as having arisen from irregular lines in the environment. To do this, one would have to assume that the environmental lines were not only intrinsically irregular but that they had been drawn on an extremely irregular surface, and that the irregularities in the surface exactly fitted the irregularities in the lines so that, when projected, the latter resulted in smooth lines in the image.

Now the reader might at first think that such a situation is excluded by the Non-Accidentalness Rule of Kanade [5], which states essentially that a regularity in the image should not be assumed to be the result of some unlikely accident of projection. However, even if one decides to use this rule, one would have to extend the non-accidentalness to exclude the unlikely and highly complicated process in which the creation of the surface irregularity had been exactly coordinated, point by point, with the creation of the line irregularity so that the former exactly compensated for the latter. This means that one would have make reference to the history of the surface *prior* to the image-formation process. That is, considerations of image-formation are not enough; one is forced to consider environment-formation.

Non-accidentalness is not in fact the issue. To see this, consider the reverse situation - that in which one used the Gibson uniformity assumption on an image of an irregular coastline, and tried to explain the coastline as the projection of part of an American flag. The Non-Accidentalness Rule would now be irrelevant because one would be trying to explain irregularity in the image. Now, to explain the irregular image coastline as a projection, for example, of a pair of smooth parallel lines on the environmental flag, one would have to conjecture that the flag had been made very crumpled and then squeezed at the sides so that the two lines met at their ends and formed a closed coastline. That is, one would have to assume a complex environment-formation process.

Let us take stock: In both, the use of the Witkin assumption on a Gibson-type image, and the use of the Gibson assumption on a Witkin-type image, one is forced to conjecture an immensely complicated environmental history prior to the image-formation phase. We propose therefore that the reason why one does not use these uniformity assumptions in the "wrong" situations is that one avoids conjecturing immensely complicated environment-formation histories.

The first important thing that this argument shows is that, in order to select the appropriate uniformity assumption, perception has to create a model of the environment-formation phase; i.e. the history *prior* to image-formation. That is, considerations of image-formation are not enough.

The second important thing that this argument shows is that modularity is inappropriate in perception. To see this observe first that a single rule excludes the inappropriate use of the Witkin and the Gibson uniformity assumptions. The rule is simply this: *Minimize the conjectured history.* We shall call the rule, the History Minimization Principle. Observe that to decide between using the Witkin and Gibson assumptions in a situation, one requires minimizing only the environment-formation phase, because this phase is the only variable across the two cases; i.e. the image-formation phase (projection) is the same in the two situations.

The History Minimization Principle, like our other principles, is based on the concept of *symmetry.* It is the requirement that the conjectured history contains as little distinguishability as possible. More precisely, the conjectured history must be as translationally symmetric as possible, across time. Detailed structural aspects of the principle have been studied in Leyton [7].

Now, the way in which the History Minimization Principle excludes the complex scenarios mentioned above is that it ensures that the residual asymmetry that has not been explained in the image-formation phase, i.e. the asymmetry left to be explained in the environment-formation phase, is as small as possible. This means that the History Minimization Principle has, as a corollary, the Maximal Gain Rule, given at the beginning of the paper.

In particular, one should use the Asymmetry Principle, in the image-formation phase, in such a way that it gains maximal symmetry for the use of the Asymmetry Principle in the environment-formation phase.

In fact, the single rule, the Maximal Gain Rule, replaces the large set of uniformity assumptions which contemporary computational vision believes is part of the visual system. To see this, note first that the uniformity assumptions, being independent, are used in a modular form. Let us therefore contrast the use of our single rule with the current approach that is based on modularity and the associated use of many uniformity assumptions. A workable use of the modularity approach would be as follows: Different uniformity assumptions are needed for different environmental contexts. Therefore, extra computation is required, *prior* to the use of a uniformity assumption, in order to establish the environmental context and thus to select the appropriate uniformity assumption.

In contrast, the Maximal Gain Rule does not require establishing the environmental context. It requires merely that the Asymmetry Principle is used such that causal history be minimized. According to this view, there is no such thing as an appropriate environmental context. There is history that needs to be minimized. In that history, asymmetries are converted into symmetries backwards in time. The selection of the order in which these asymmetries are symmetrized is determined by the Maximal Gain Rule.

7 What is the Environment?

The considerations of the previous section allow us now to understand what an "environment" is. We have argued that perception is the use of four principles - the Asymmetry Principle, the Symmetry Principle, the Second System Principle, and the Maximal Gain Rule - that together determine a single process: the conversion of asymmetries to symmetries backward in time. According to this view, what could be called the "environment" is the particular order chosen to convert the asymmetries back to symmetries - an order which, as we saw at the end of previous section, is determined by the Maximal Gain Rule. That is, the environment is the minimal order in which image asymmetries can be changed back to symmetries; e.g. this minimal order defines the environment to be either an American flag or a geographical outline.

It is worth understanding this more fully, and to do so we must clarify further the nature of the Second System Principle. This principle states that, if a system undergoes a change from symmetry to asymmetry, in the forward time direction, then a second system must have been involved. What we must be clear on now is that the sole explanatory role of the second system is that this system brings with it an extra set of asymmetries not contained in the first system alone. These asymmetries are, so to speak, passed on to the first system in the causal interaction. For example, consider the Shape-from-Shading problem. A non-uniform light flux reaching the retina is assumed to have been a uniform light flux at some time in the past. In accord with the Second System Principle, the change from symmetry to asymmetry in the light flux is explained by the introduction of a second system, a surface. The role of the surface is this: The surface has a collection of asymmetries, e.g. it is undulating. In a causal interaction, these asymmetries are passed on to the light flux. (More fully, the new asymmetries introduced by the second system include those introduced by the *relationship* between the two systems.)

One can now explain, in a deep way, why Gibson and contemporary computational vision claim that *the* crucial aspect of the environment that the perceptual system attempts to recover is *surface structure;* i.e. what computational vision calls *shape.* The claim is usually justified by saying that shape is the primary aspect of the environment with which human beings interact on the level of scale on which they live. However, according to our argument, this is not correct. No matter on which level of scale human beings were to live, shape would always be what they would attempt to recover. The reason is this: As we argue in Leyton [7], shape and asymmetry are literally the same thing. Thus, in accord with the Second System Principle, the recovery of environmental shape is the recovery of the asymmetry that, as a second system, introduced asymmetry into the stimulus energy.

This means that, on whatever level of scale human beings were to live, when presented with an asymmetric system, e.g. the stimulus array, they would attempt to "undo" its asymmetry by postulating that it arose from a symmetrical past state in which it interacted with a second system that was asymmetrical. Furthermore, that second system would itself be explained as having arisen from a symmetrical past state in which it interacted with a third system that was asymmetrical, and so on. Each additional system would be what one would call "shape" because it would be a set of asymmetries.

Therefore, according to our rules, at each stage backwards in time, perception recovers two things: a symmetrized version of a given system and an asymmetrical additional system. This argument defines the real meaning of the term *environment:* An environment is the set of symmetries and asymmetries that are pulled apart in the successive causal interactions inferred backwards in time by our four inference rules.

Acknowledgments

I wish to thank Chuck Schmidt and Stacy Marsella for feedback on this paper.

References

1. J. Aloimonos, 1988, Shape from texture. *Biological Cybernetics.* 345-360
2. R. Bajcsy, & L. Lieberman, 1976, Texture gradient as a depth cue. *Computer Graphics and Image Processing, 5,* 52-67
3. J.J. Gibson, 1950, *The Perception of the Visual World.* Boston, Mass: Houghton Mifflin.
4. K. Ikeuchi, (1984) Shape from regular patterns. *Artificial Intelligence, 22,* 49-75

5. T. Kanade, 1981, Recovery of the three-dimensional shape of an object from a single view. In J.M. Brady (Ed), *Computer Vision,*

6. J.R. Kender, 1979, *Shape from Texture.* PhD Thesis, CMU.

7. M. Leyton, 1992, *Symmetry, Causality, Mind.* Cambridge, Mass: MIT Press.

8. M. Leyton, M. (In press) New Foundations for Perception.

9. K.A. Stevens, 1981, The information content of texture gradients. *Biological Cybernetics.* 95-105

10. A.P. Witkin, 1981, Recovering surface shape and orientation from texture. In J.M. Brady (Ed), *Computer Vision,* New York: North Holland.

RECOGNITION OF A GIVEN POLYHEDRAL OBJECT IN A SINGLE PERSPECTIVE IMAGE USING A VANISHING PSEUDO INVARIANT

G. MAROLA
Dipartimento di Ingegneria dell'Informazione
Facoltà di Ingegneria
Via Diotisalvi, 2 - 56126 Pisa- Italy
E-mail: marola@pimac2.iet.unipi.it

A.VACCARELLI
Istituto di Elaborazione della Informazione -CNR
Via S.Maria, 46 - 56126 Pisa- Italy
E-mail: vaccarelli@iei.pi.cnr.it

In this paper we use a pseudo perspective invariant for detecting a given three dimensional object in a single perspective view of a scene. It is a matrix determinant that vanishes when a 2D pattern is matched with the corresponding 3D one. This approach allows to handle very simple expressions and does not require iterative solution of non linear equations. The method has been tested in several conditions, using either synthetic or real images. The proposed method is advantageous in terms of processing time and is particularly fit to be implemented in real-time application, such as mobile robots. The possibility of recognizing an object from a single perspective view, without calibrating camera, appears very attractive.

1 Introduction

A fundamental problem in computer vision is the identification of the shape of a given object in an image, as it changes with position, orientation, and with intrinsic parameters of the camera. The 2D optical image of an object is highly dependent on the position of the imaging device. If a perspective projection is assumed, the expressions relating 2D and 3D lengths, areas and angles are quite complex and, as a consequence, they complicate the processing of inverting the perspective projection transformation. This problem can be alleviated if intrinsic characteristics (features) of the object, not depending on the position of observation, are introduced. These features, known as perspective invariants, remain unaffected by perspective transformation and can be used to perform object recognition in the 2D image, regardless of the viewing point.

In literature, various kinds of invariants are described, for example cross-ratios, Fourier descriptors, moment invariants, affine invariants under perspective transformation [1-3], etc.. They can be used successfully depending on the hypothesis and on the constraints imposed in a particular problem. However, even if the invariant approach is a powerful tool and investigation about invariants is still a topic of interest, in most cases the problem of perspective inversion cannot be solved by means of the known invariants.

In this paper we propose a sort of perspective invariant, which is a set of 2D and 3D parameters arranged in a matrix, whose determinant vanishes when a 2D pattern is matched with the corresponding 3D one. This approach allows to handle very simple expressions and does not require iterative solution of non linear equations.

In Sect. 2 we introduce a generalization of the perspective invariants, which will be devoted to set up the matching problem between a 2D and the corresponding 3D pattern in a polyhedral object. In Section 3 a vanishing pseudo invariant is defined. In Sect. 4 some example of the application of the proposed procedure is described and finally, in Section 5 some conclusions are drawn, evidencing advantages and limits of this approach.

2 A generalization of perspective invariants for identifying a pattern in a single perspective view.

In the literature a perspective invariant I is defined as a function of a given set of points {P} in a 3D object that is not affected by a perspective projection T, applied to the object itself. This can be formalized as follows:

$$I(T\{P\})=I(\{P\}) \tag{2.1}$$

that can be rewritten as:

$$I(T\{P\})-I(\{P\})=0 \tag{2.2}$$

The left hand side of the above expression is a vanishing function of the original set of points {P} and of the transformed set T{P}:

$$D(T,I)= I(T\{P\})-I(\{P\}) \tag{2.3}$$

However, if we consider D instead of I as the invariant of the transform T applied to {P}, we can introduce a broad class of functions of T and {P}, assuming a more complicated expression f(T{P},{P}) in which T{P} and {P} are intermixed together in some complicated manner, instead of the simple form I(T{P})-I({P}) in which T{P} and {P} appear separately. The vanishing of the above functions can be used to verify if there is a possible perspective correspondence T between object and image. For example, in this work we define a function D whose vanishing allows to test whether a set of segments of a 2D image is or not a perspective view of a certain 3D polyhedral object in order to perform object recognition. The proposed method is effective and simple and does not require the solution of non-linear equations.

3 The definition of the vanishing pseudo invariant

Let us consider the segment P_1P_2 in the 3D space and its perspective projection Q_1Q_2 on the image plane shown in Fig.1.

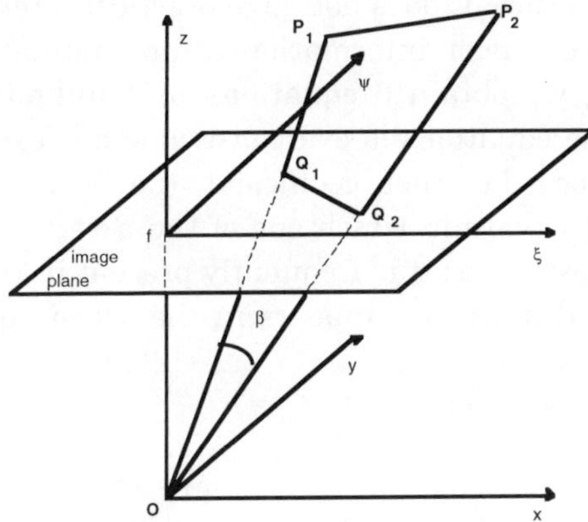

Fig.1: A 3D segment P_1P_2 and its perspective projection Q_1Q_2 on the image plane.

By observing Fig.1, the following geometrical relationship can be written

$$(P_1P_2)^2 = (OP_1)^2 + (OP_2)^2 - 2(OP_1)(OP_2)\cos(\beta)$$

with

$$\beta = P_1\hat{O}P_2 = Q_1\hat{O}Q_2 \tag{3.1}$$

where the distance P_1P_2 is known, being measured on the 3D object. The term $\cos(\beta)$ can be obtained by a similar relationship written for the segment Q_1Q_2, measured on the 2D image:

$$(Q_1Q_2)^2 = (OQ_1)^2 + (OQ_2)^2 - 2(OQ_1)(OQ_2)\cos(\beta) \tag{3.2}$$

where:

$$(Q_1Q_2)^2 = (\xi_p\text{-}\xi_q)^2+(\psi_p\text{-}\psi_q)^2$$
$$(OQ_1)^2 = \xi_p{}^2+\psi_p{}^2 + f^2$$
$$(OQ_2)^2 = \xi_q{}^2+\psi_q{}^2 + f^2$$

being (ξ_p,ψ_p) and (ξ_q,ψ_q) the co-ordinates of the point P and Q, respectively, in the image plane and f the known focal length of the viewing device. In this problem the unknowns are OP_1 and OP_2 and, once they are computed, the exact location of 3D object in the space is obtained.

Let us now consider the complete set of segments linking n vertexes. By applying the relation (3.1) to each segment, we can write 3(n-2) equations with n unknowns. Though the case n=3 is often considered in literature, it does not have practical interest, as only three vertexes give a very poor information to discriminate among several objects. For n=4, we obtain 6 equations in 4 unknowns. The system comprised of these equations is overconstrained; it can be solved if two conditions are imposed on their coefficients (i.e. on 2D and 3D data). Let us now consider the case in which one of the n vertexes is hidden; it is particularly interesting, as it is frequently present in real scenes. In this case, an additional unknown appears in the set of equations obtained from relation (3.1).

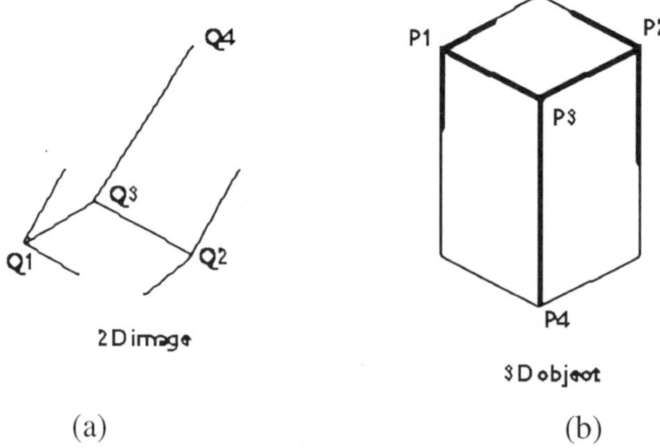

Fig. 2: The case of n=4 with one vertex (P4) hidden: (a) 2D image; (b) 3D object.

The pattern depicted in Fig. 2(a) is a perspective projection of the 3D pattern evidenced in Fig. 2(b). The vertex P_4 (corresponding to Q_4 in

2D image) could be hidden by another object or could have been extracted not correctly from the image. The segment corresponding to the hidden vertex is shortened by a factor λ, as shown in Fig. 2. By considering the factor λ as a further unknown of the problem, we can write, now, the following 6 equations in 5 unknowns (see Fig.3)

$$x_1^2 + x_2^2 - 2x_1x_2c_{12} = a_{12}^2 \quad (3.3a)$$

$$x_1^2 + x_3^2 - 2x_1x_3c_{13} = a_{13}^2 \quad (3.3b)$$

$$x_1^2 + x_4^2 - 2x_1x_4c_{14} = a_{13}^2 + \lambda^2 a_{34}^2 + \lambda(a_{14}^2 - a_{13}^2 - a_{34}^2) \quad (3.3c)$$

$$x_2^2 + x_3^2 - 2x_2x_3c_{23} = a_{23}^2 \quad (3.3d)$$

$$x_2^2 + x_4^2 - 2x_2x_4c_{24} = a_{23}^2 + \lambda^2 a_{34}^2 + \lambda(a_{24}^2 - a_{23}^2 - a_{34}^2) \quad (3.3e)$$

$$x_3^2 + x_4^2 - 2x_3x_4c_{34} = \lambda^2 a_{34}^2 \quad (3.3f)$$

where x_i (i=1,...,4) are the unknown distances of the vertexes P_i from the origin O; c_{ij} (i,j=1,...,4) are the cosines of the angles $P_i\hat{O}P_j$ and a_{ij} (i,j=1,...,4) are the lengths of the segments P_iP_j. As we have supposed that P_4 is hidden, it has been substituted by P'_4. and the auxiliary unknown λ has been introduced.

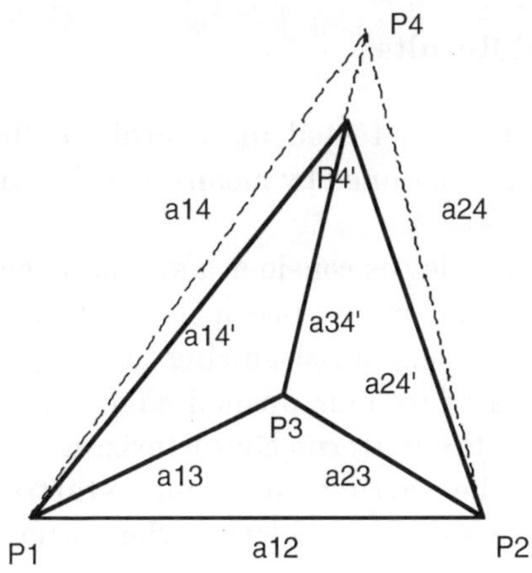

Fig.3: The geometrical 3D structure where the distances a_{ij} among the four vertexes are known.

As we have 6 equations and 5 unknowns, the condition to be imposed on the coefficients to obtain a solution is only one. In general, this means that the above system of equations is overconstrained; hence it can not have any solution and the correspondence between the 2D image and 3D model can not exist. However, when the above correspondence does exist, this introduces a condition on coefficients, which allows the system to be solved. The existence of is condition can be verified by dropping the unknowns x_1, x_2, x_3, x_4 and λ one at a time. This procedure can be carried out analytically by using the Sylvester's resultant and it is detailed in the Appendix (Sect. 6).

Regardless of the used method, the final result is a determinant of 16th order. If the determinant vanishes (i.e. the condition on the data is satisfied), the hypothesized correspondence between the 2D pattern, comprised of 4 vertexes P_i, and the 3D object is verified. Note that this determinant is a function both of the $\{P_i\}$ four 3D points and of their perspective projection $T\{P_i\}$ on the viewing plane and, hence, it has quite the form and the properties of the function D described at the beginning of this section.

Moreover in this case the algebraic equations, obtained while dropping the unknowns from Eqs. (3), allow to locate exactly the object in the 3D space.

4 Experimental Results

The method has been tested in several conditions, using either synthetic or real images obtained by means of a TV camera with a known focal length.

As a first example, let us consider a synthetic perspective view of a pyramid partially occluded by two prisms is displayed in Fig. 4. Here, we have considered the problem of recognizing the shape of the pyramid, by using the coordinates of its four dashed edges as a 3D database (see Fig.4a). The choice of the patterns characterizing an object is a setting problem, that must be carried out before starting the recognizing procedure. In the case we are considering, the pattern has been selected as it carries significant topological information about the shape of the pyramid. Two possible matches have been found, using a graph-isomorphism based search procedure (for details on this procedure see [4]). The first one, shown in Fig.4b, has been correctly accepted as true even if the edge PA is partially missing, as the found value of the determinant D is very small. On the contrary, the correspondence hypothesized in Fig.4c has been correctly rejected, being the corresponding value of the determinant very high.

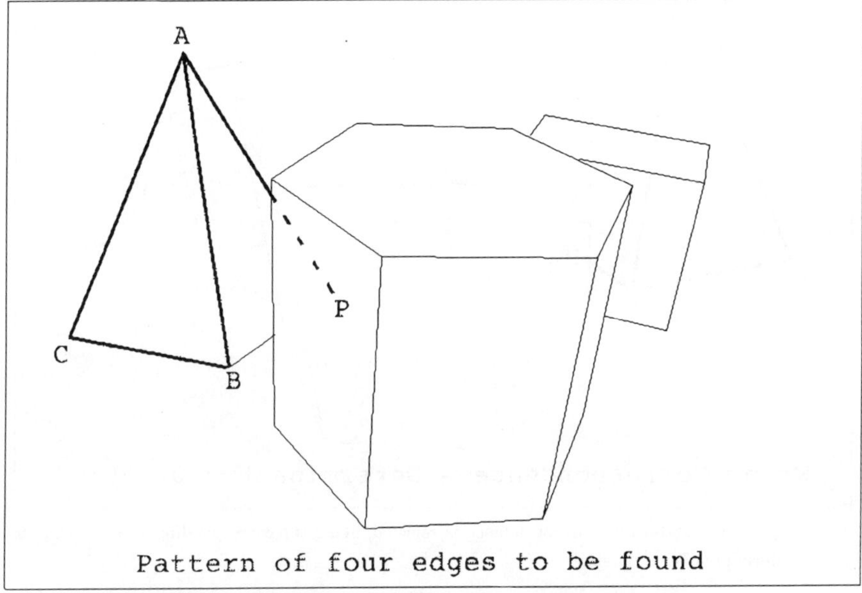

Fig.4a: a synthetic perspective view of a pyramid partially occluded by two prisms.

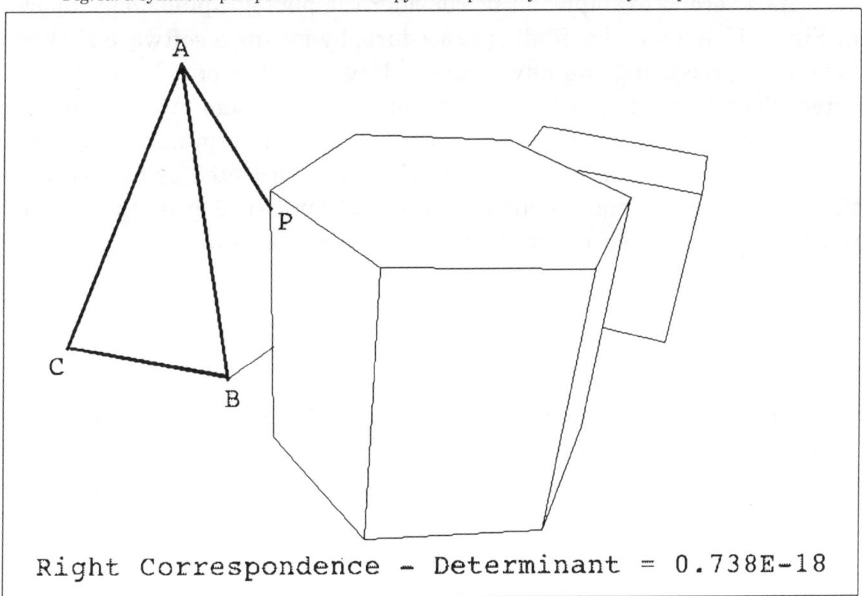

Fig.4b: A possible matches. It is accepted as true as the found value of the determinant D is very small.

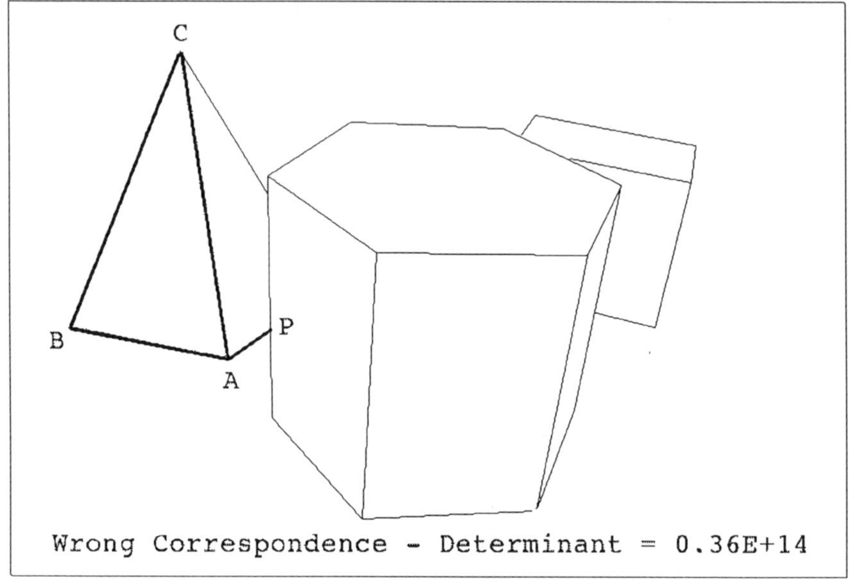

Fig.4c: A hypothesized correspondence is rejected, being the corresponding value of the determinant D very high.

As a second example, let us consider the photographic image shown in Fig. 5. Using an edge finding procedure, by means a software package for image processing, we have found a large number of polygonal set of three edges connecting sets of four points: three of them are evidenced in Fig.5. The A and B sets give rise to a value of the determinant ranging in the 10^{-3}- 10^{-5} interval and therefore they were accepted as belonging to the spark-plug or, equivalently, to the tool for twisting it. Instead the wrong set C has been rejected having given rise to a determinant value >>1.

5 Conclusions

The proposed method allows to perform object recognition simply by verifying if a given algebraic function of the 3D database and of the viewed image assumes a zero value, without the need to solve non-linear equations using iterative methods. This is an advantage in terms of processing time and makes this approach fit to be implemented in real-time application, such as robotics. For example, a mobile robot, navigating in a partially structured environment, could perform its camera calibration by recognizing some object present in the environment, without requiring special marks.

The most relevant limit could be the number of vertices necessary to obtain a simple solution of the equations. However, in practical cases, a pattern comprised of 4 vertices is easy to be found in an object and can carry enough information to perform recognition.

Fig.5: A real image where the evidenced sets (A,B and C) have been tested with the method: A and B has been accepted and C rejected

6 Appendix

We start from the Equations (3.3). After a simple algebra, we drop out the λ unknown thus obtaining the following dour equations in the four unknowns x_1, x_2, x_3 and x_4:

$$(- x_1x_4c_{14} - 2\,x_3^2 + x_1x_3c_{13} + x_3x_4c_{34})(a_{24} - a_{23} - a_{34}) =$$

$$= (- x_2x_4c_{24} - 2x_3^2 + x_2x_3c_{23} + x_3x_4c_{34})\,(a_{14} - a_{13} - a_{34}) \qquad (3.4a)$$

$$(x_1^2 + x_2^2 - x_1x_2c_{12})\, a_{13} = (x_1^2 + x_3^2 - x_1x_3c_{13})\, a_{12} \tag{3.4b}$$

$$(x_1^2 + x_2^2 - x_1x_2c_{12})\, a_{23} = (x_2^2 + x_3^2 - x_2x_3c_{23})\, a_{12} \tag{3.4c}$$

$$\begin{aligned} &a_{23}\, a_{34}\, (- x_1x_4c_{14} - 2\, x_3^2 + x_1x_3c_{13} + x_3x_4c_{34})\\ &\quad (-x_2x_4c_{24} - 2x_3^2 + x_2x_3c_{23} + x_3x_4c_{34}) =\\ &\quad =(a_{14} - a_{13} - a_{34})(a_{24} - a_{23} - a_{34})\, (x_2^2 + x_3^2 - x_2x_3c_{23})\\ &\quad (x_3^2 + x_4^2 - x_3x_4c_{34}) \end{aligned} \tag{3.4d}$$

The x_1 unknown can be obtained easily from Eq. (3.4a), so that dropping it out from the remaining three equations we have three homogeneous equations in the three unknowns x_2, x_3 and x_4. Hence, by using the new variables $y = x_2/x_3$ and $z = x_4/x_3$ we obtain three polynomial equations in the form (i=1,2,3):

$$\begin{aligned} &(A_{i2}z^2+A_{i1}z+A_{i0})y^2+(B_{i2}z^2+B_{i1}z+B_{i0})y+\\ &\quad +(C_{i2}z^2+C_{i1}z+C_{i0}) = 0 \end{aligned} \tag{3.5}$$

whose coefficients A_{ij}, B_{ij} and C_{ij} are functions both of the 2D image and of the 3D object.

Finally, by dropping out the y and z unknowns (using for example the Sylvester resultant) we obtain a (16x16) determinant, whose vanishing is a necessary and sufficient condition for the existence of a solution of the given system of equations i.e. for the correspondence between the 2D image and the 3D object.

7 References

[1] K.Arbter, W.E.Snyder, H. Burkhardt, G.Hirzinger, "Application of affine invariant Fourier descriptors to recognition of 3-D objects", *IEEE Trans. Pattern Anal. Machine Intell.*, PAMI-12, 1990, 640-646.

[2] F.A. Sadjadi, E.L. Hall, "Three-Dimensional moment invariants", *IEEE Trans. Pattern Anal. Machine Intell.*, PAMI-2, 1980, 27-136.

[3] Lamdan Y., Schwartz J.T., Wolfson H.J., "Affine invariant model-based object recognition", *IEEE Trans. on Robotics Automation* 6(5), 1990, 578-589.

[4] G. Marola and A. Vaccarelli, "An Algebraic Method for Recognition of Polyhedral Objects from a Single Image", *Pattern Recognition*, vol. 27, no. 10, 1994

DIMENSIONALITY REDUCTION FOR FACE RECOGNITION

ALEIX MARTÍNEZ, JORDI VITRIÀ
Computer Vision Center - Universitat Autònoma de Barcelona
Edifici O, 08193 Bellaterra (Barcelona) - Spain
aleix, jordi@cvc.uab.es

An image of a face depends not only on its shape, but also on the viewpoint, illumination conditions, and facial expression. In this paper, the representation capabilities of the derivatives of the gaussian filters are studied, and it is discussed which representation is better to choose in each case. Since this representation is defined in a high-dimensional space, a dimensionality reduction method is necessary if further studies are to be done. For that reason the MultiDimensional Scaling (MDS) method is proposed; the results are also compared with the Principal Components Analysis (PCA) method. In order to analyse the results a neural network is built which shows that using only one sample per person the system can achieve positive identification results up to 96% when changes in facial expression and viewpoint position are present, and up to 67% when changes in illumination and viewpoint position are present.

1 Introduction

For a long time, the dimensionality reduction problem has been studied from many different points of view. There are several reasons for that: *(a)* it is very difficult to work on high-dimensional spaces, *(b)* not all the dimensions have relevant data, many of them can be noise, *(c)* the number of samples we have to use on learning algorithms are normally proportional to the dimensionality of the input data.

In this paper, two computational experiments about dimensionality reduction are presented. Both are related to the task of face recognition, although some results could be extended to a general object recognition purpose (specially to natural objects). The first experiment deals with the similarity of faces when they change facial expressions, whereas the second one is concerned to the changes in illumination direction.

2 Dimensionality Reduction

Turk and Pentland [8], showed that the use of PCA (Principal Components Analysis) on face images (what they have called *eigenfaces*) is useful for face recognition. However, when PCA is used, we have no idea of the number of dimensions the face-space should have; that is, which is the minimum number of dimensions that allows us to have the same vector's behavior as the original high-dimensional ones. In fact, there is not any analysis tool which can help us to find the best (not even near the best) minimum dimensional space needed. So as to find a solution, some rules of thumb had been proposed (i.e. Murase and Nayar [5]), but none of them has neither a general solution nor a mathematical support; that means, one must use a *generate-and-test* method and this is clearly not the best way for solving the problem. Further studies on this field are complex for that reason. We have used MDS to determine the real dimensionality of the data, independently from the dimension of the original representation space.

2.1 What is MDS?, and Which is the Dimensionality of the Data?

Supose you are given a map showing the location of several cities in a specific country, and are asked to construct a table of distances between these cities. That is a simple matter to fill in any entry. But, now, consider the reverse problem, where you are given the table of distances and asked to produce the map. In essence, MDS is a method for solving this inverse problem although many problems can arise. On one hand, the data usually contain considerable errors or *noise*. On the other hand, it is seldom known in advance if a simple two-dimensional map will be adequate or if three, four or even more dimensions are needed. Thus, how can we decide when a projection is good and when it is not?.

When the distance data is projected to an *n-dimensional* space, it is obvious that some error is introduced. This error is named *stress*, and can be calculated in many different ways. Perhaps the most common one is the *f-stress* which is defined as:

$$\sqrt{\frac{\sum_i \sum_j (f(\delta_{ij}) - d_{ij})^2}{scale\ factor}} \tag{1}$$

where d_{ij} are the original distances and $f(\delta_{ij})$ the ones obtained from the new data projection [3].

There are two methods which allow us to select the dimensionality. The first one uses heuristic rules: stress values lower than 0.1 mean quite good approximations, lower than 0.05 are good, and lower than 0.025 are very good. The second one is statistical [7,3], whereas here, we simply give an extremely brief indication. The given data are scaled in several dimensionalities (normally from one to five) and the stress plotted as a function of dimensionality (as shown in figure 3).This plot is then compared with similar plots derived by Monte Carlo techniques for synthetic data in which the true dimensionality and the true error level are known. By finding the Monte Carlo plot which best matches our data plot, we infer the dimensionality of that known data.

2.2 Shape representation: Gaussian filters

In order to extract visual information from images, we use gaussian derivatives (at different scales and orientations), a well-known basis functions for natural images [6,5]. In such a way we hypothesize that the gaussian filters responses remap the image space in a manner that makes similar objects (such as differents views of the same 3D object) closer each other, and dissimilar objects further apart. To test this hypothesis human faces are used.

Different representations have been tested: *(i)* pixel values, *(ii)* gaussian filter, *(iii)-(vi)* first, second, third and fourth derivatives of the gaussian, *(vii)* first and third derivative together, *(viii)* second and fourth, *(ix)* all four together, and *(x)* the *eigenfaces* projection (which will be shown for comparison).

2.3 Face Data Base

Two different face data bases are used, one for each experiment. On the first experiment six images of six different people were taken (that is, 36 images, three males, two females and a boy). The different images of each person varied in viewing position and facial expression. On the second experiment six images of three different people were used (that is, 18 images, two females and a male). All of them varying on viewing position and illumination conditions but none of them on facial expression. Some examples can be seen in figure 1. Each image was of 256×256 pixels 8 bits per pixel. To avoid background influences **only** the face part of the image was used (see figure 2).

Figure 1: Some examples of our data bases.

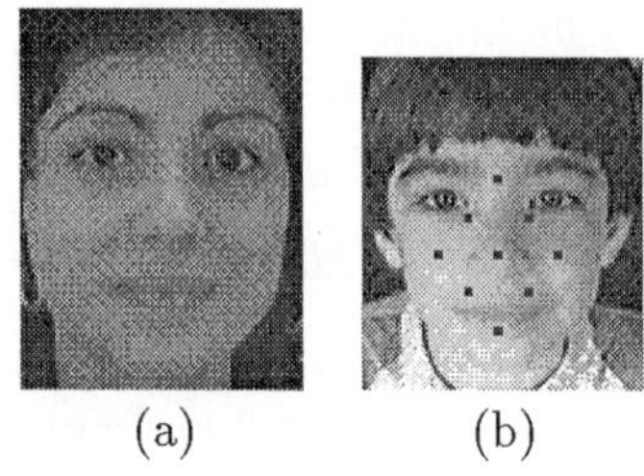

Figure 2: (a) Only the face part of the image is used; (b) the mask (grid) being used.

3 Computational Experiments

In the following experiments we aim to reduce the dimensionality of shape representation. As suggested before, we base this definition on the utility of the representation for recognizing 3D objects.

3.1 Experiment 1: Facial expression analysis

The first step in this experiment consists of extracting the information filters (from *(i)* to *(ix)*) using the mask shown in figure 1 and constructing an *n-dimensional* vector with the information of all nine point; that is, $V_i = (p_{i,1}, p_{i,2}, ..., p_{i,9})$, where i is the face being used and p_{ik} the response of the filter used on the point k of the mask. Then, using these *n-dimensional* vectors we create a matrix of distances among all of them (named the *dissimilarity matrix*) which will be used for the MDS algorithm to remap the data into a one, two, three, four, five and six dimensional space. After that, a graphic of the stress values (obtained on each dimension) is created. Then, by finding the Monte Carlo plot which best matches it [7], we decide at which dimensionality the data can be reduced. An example of this process can be appreciated in figure 3(a).

Applying this process to each case we found that the best dimensional choose is: *(i)* 4-dimensional, *(ii)* 2-dimensional, *(iii)* 5-dimensional, *(iv)* 5-dimensional, *(v)* 6-dimensional, *(vi)* 6-dimensional, *(vii)* 6-dimensional, *(viii)* 6-dimensional and *(ix)* 6-dimensional. But, now, in order to analyse these results, some analysis tools have to be defined.

Data analysis: Two different ways of analysis are proposed. The first one consist of (*manually*) evaluating the clustering of the points belonging to the different faces by viewing the first two components of each n-dimensional space in a 2D plot. Obviously, this is not an objective way of clustering or, at least, not enough. So as to find a better, numerical analysis tool, we have

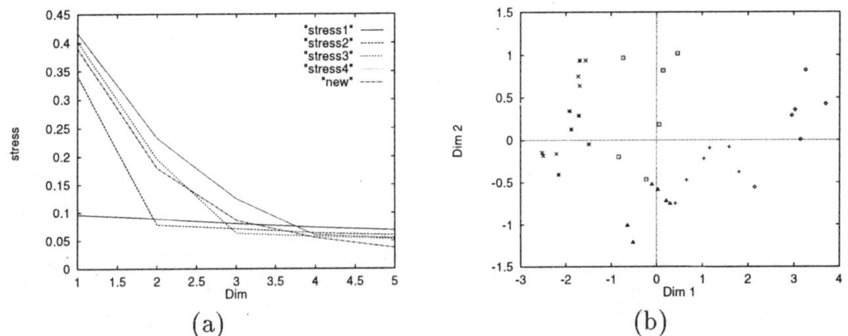

(a) (b)

Figure 3: (a) Pixels results: Clearly the best match is made at either three or fourth dimensional stress function.(b) 2D plot of the pixel response.

built a neural network (base on the Backpropagation algorithm) which might help us on that purpose.

The results of the 2D space projection can be appreciated in figure 4 for gaussian and derivatives responses, and in figure 3(b) for pixel clasification. The symbols used in the 2D graphiques are specified in figure 5. It is easy to appreciate that the pixel configuration has the worst classification, whereas the fourth derivative seems to have the best one. Although, good classification results were also obtained using both the second and fourth together, and all fourth together, it is obvious that they use more information (than if we only use the fourth derivative). Thus, a priory, there would not be any reason for using them.

Anyhow, let us study how well our neural network classify using these differents representations. On that purpose a neural network of three layers (based on the Backpropagation learning algorithm) was used. The first layer has as many inputs as dimensions. The second (or hidden) layer always uses twelve neurons. At last, the third one, has six outputs (one for each person). A *winner-take-all* mechanism is applied at the output layer; that is, the neuron that has higher output value is reassigned to one whereas the others are reassigned to zero.

As said before, one of the main advantages of dimensionality reduction is that only few data examples have to be used (in the training step) in order to learn from that representation. But, *how many samples will we need once those dimensionality reductions have been done?*. We have tested our neural network using three, two and only one sample per face and found that, **using only one sample per face, the net is able to overcome with very good, promising results**. The rate results are shown in figure 6(a).

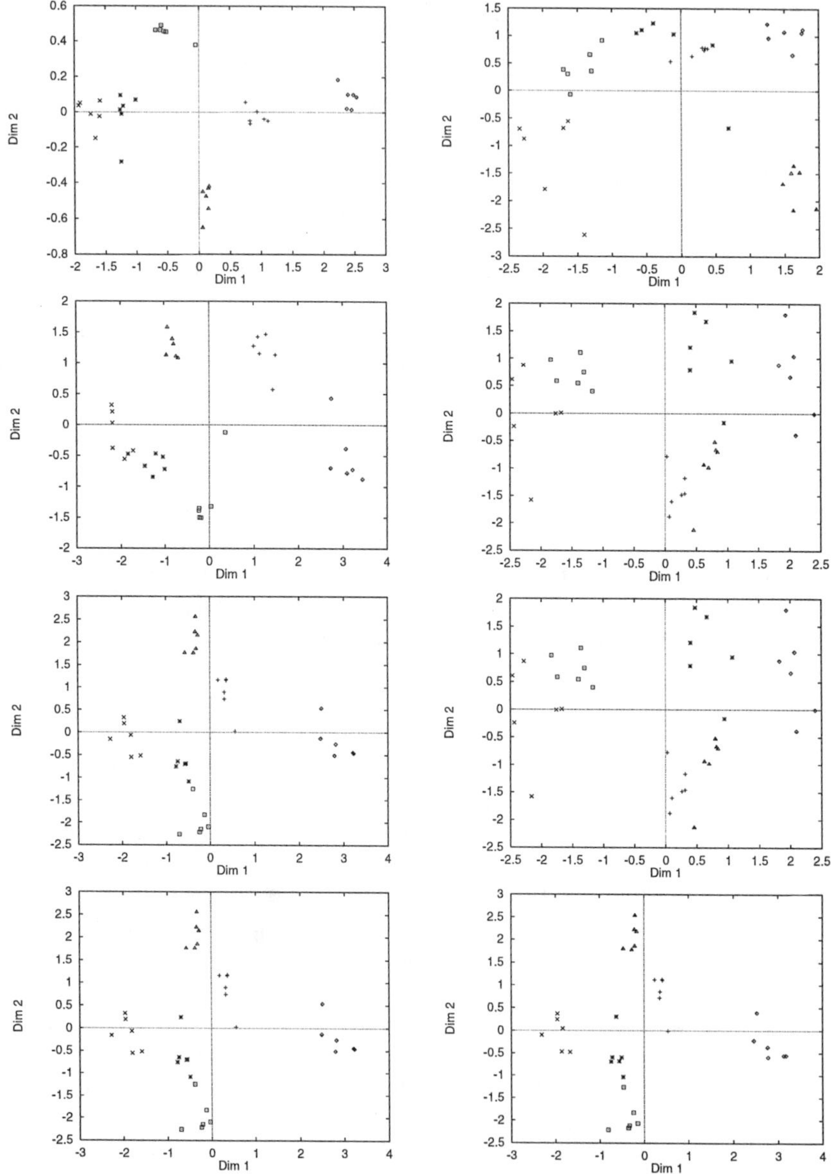

Figure 4: Different 2D plots of the faces. From up to down and left to right: gaussian filter, first, second, third and fourth derivatives of gaussian filters, first and third derivatives together, second and four together, and, all fourth derivatives together.

Figure 5: Symbols of each person's face.

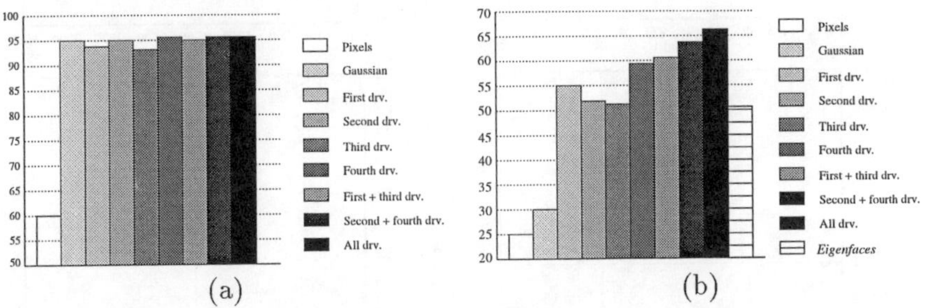

Figure 6: Identification rate (using only one face per person). (a) Results of the first experiment. (b) Results of the second experiment.

So far, we have seen that only using the gaussian filter we are able to recognize faces with a very large degree of accuracy. Thus, why should we use derivatives if they do not overcome with much better results?. It seems clear that if there are illumination changes, the derivatives will get better results than the gaussian filter since their responses are not so much illumination dependent. The second experiment is aimed to this issue.

3.2 Experiment 2: Illumination analysis

In order to study the influence of change in illumination direction, we will repeat the same experiment proposed before but using the second face data base. By doing the same process as before we found that the best dimensional chosen is (in each case): *(i)* 4-dimensional, *(ii)* 3-dimensional, *(iii)* 4-dimensional, *(iv)* 5-dimensional, *(v)* 5-dimensional, *(vi)* 6-dimensional, *(vii)* 5-dimensional, *(viii)* 6-dimensional and *(ix)* 6-dimensional. Some results of the 2D projections are shown in figure 7 (simbols are shown in figure 8), whereas the face identification rate is shown in figure 6(b).

It seems clear, now, that the best results are obatined when all four derivatives are used. However, by using the second and fourth derivatives the results obtained are also quite good. It must be pointed out that the first derivative

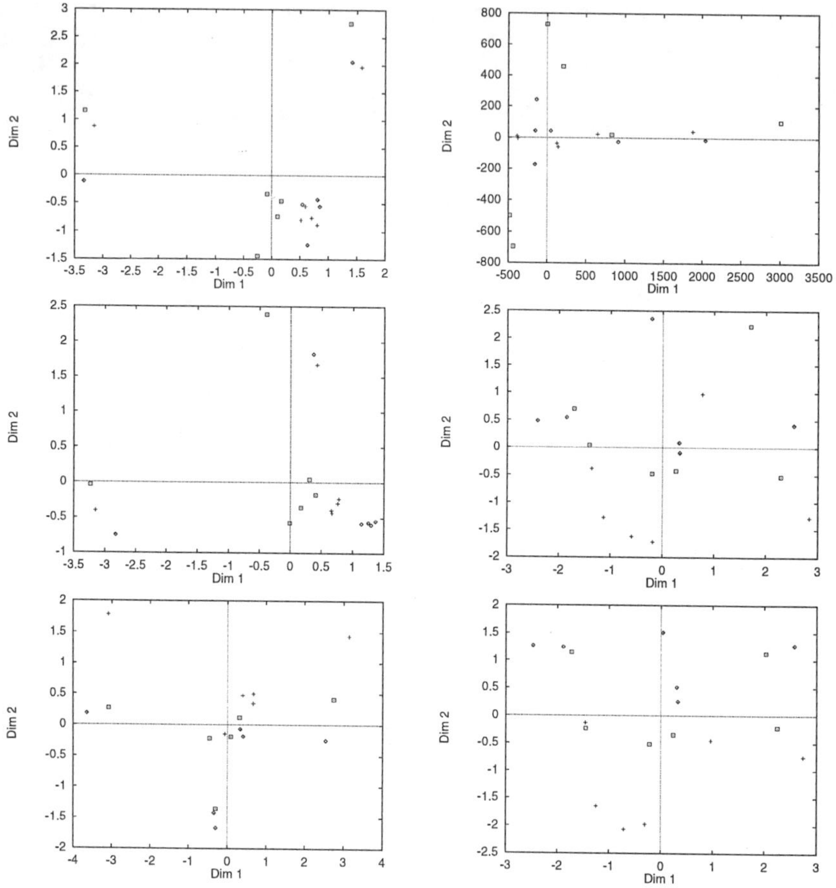

Figure 7: From up to down and left to rigth: pixel responses, *eigenfaces*, gaussian filter, all fourth derivatives together, firts and third derivatives together, and, second and fourth derivatives together

Figure 8: Symbols of each person's face (in the second data base).

response has better results than the second and the third derivatives. This is why the first derivative has responses at the boundaries of the object's shape and that seems to be less illumination dependent than the other ones (as has been suggested by many authors). Nevertheless, the fourth derivative cope with even better results than the first. It is also clear, that the gaussian filter cannot cope with good results when the illumination problem arises.

In addition, the results of *eigenfaces* (using the eight first *eigenvectors*) are shown for comparision. Although they have a very good result compared with the pixels and gaussian filters (remind that *eigenfaces* only uses the pixel values), they are using much more information; that is, whereas all of our representations only use the nine convolutions showed in figure 1, the *eigenfaces* uses all the pixels of the image.

4 Discussion and Conclusions

In the experiments described in this paper, we have shown that the derivatives of the gaussian filter remaps the raw data in a manner that: *(a)* make different views of the same face be more similar to each other than two views of different faces, *(b)* facial expressions do not affect the classification capabilities of these filters, and *(c)* these *receptive-fields* representation is useful for dimensionality reduction.

That last point is very important since the number of samples a learning algorithm needs, depends on the dimensionality of the input data. As higher dimensionality is used, more samples are needed. In the first experiment we have shown that by using only one sample per face we are able to recognize faces with a very high degree of accuracy (around 96%). However, when illumination changes are presents, the face recognition rate decreases (around 67%). Anyhow, the gaussian derivative filters still remaps the data in a way which help to the face identification algorithm. And, although it is clear that further image processing should be done in order to increase the correct identification degree[4], we have shown that gaussian derivatives filters can help at this problem. Moreover, better results than the *eigenfaces* are obtained when only one sample is used in the face identification neural network.

The other important point to be mentioned here is the complexity of the face identification algorithm. Pay attention to the low computational-cost of these filters. Only nine convolutions are needed in each case (that costs much less than one second in a Sun Sparc IPX). Then, the dimensionality reduction is needed. There are two steps on that process. The first one when the dimensionality reduction is made on the face training set (which cost around three second for 36 images). And, the second one, when a new face image arrive and has to be projected into that space (which cost, using a least square method, less than one second).

Acknowledgments

First off all, we would like to thanks at all the CVC staff for they patience when the face data base was created. Especially to the people who have appeared in this report: Craig, Anna, Jordi, Gemma, Xavi and Dina. We also thanks the help of Maria Vanrell for her explanations about MDS and SPSS environment. Finally, we wish to acknowledge Joan Carbó who has been working in the face recognition project during all this last year. This research was supported in part by grant TAP94-0401 from CICYT.

References

1. Y. Adini, Y. Moses and S. Ullman. *Face Recognition: the Problem of Compensating for Changes in Illumination Direction.* CS-TR93-21, Weizmann Inst. Scie., 1993.
2. G.M. Davies, H. Ellis and J. Shepherd (Editors). *Perceiving and Recognizing Faces.* Academic Press, 1981.
3. J.B. Kruskal and M. Wish. *Multidimensional Scaling.* SAGE University Paper, 1978.
4. A. Martínez and J. Vitrià. *A First Step Towards a Low-Dimensional Face Representation Space.* CVC Tech.Rep. #20, 1997.
5. H. Murase and S. Nasyar. *Visual Learning and Recognition of 3-D Objects from Appearance.* Int. J. of Computer Vision, 14, pp.5-24, 1995.
6. R.Rao and D. Ballard . *An active architecture based on iconic representation.* Artificial Intelligence, 78, pp.461-505, 1995.
7. I. Spence and J. Graef. *The Determination of the Underlying Dimensionality of an Empirically Obtained Matrix of Proximities.* Multivariate Behav. Res. 9, pp.331-342, 1974.
8. M. Turk and A. Pentland. *Eigenfaces for Recognition.* J'l Cog. Neuroscience, 1991.
9. Y. Weiss and S. Edelman. *Representation of similarity as a goal of early visual processing.* CS-TR94-09, Weizmann Inst. Scie., 1994.

COUPLED SEGMENTATION AND RECONSTRUCTION OF UNDERWATER 3D ACOUSTIC IMAGES USING CONFIDENCE INFORMATION

VITTORIO MURINO
Department of Mathematics and Computer Science
University of Udine
Via delle Scienze 206, 33100 Udine, Italy
E-mail : swan@dimi.uniud.it

ANDREA TRUCCO
Department of Biophysical and Electronic Engineering
University of Genova
Via all'Opera Pia 11A, 16145 Genova, Italy
E-mail : fragola@dibe.unige.it

This paper describes a technique for the integration of confidence information using a Markov Random Fields approach to improve the reconstruction and segmentation processes of three-dimensional acoustical images. Acoustical echoes are arranged by a beamforming process to generate two images. In either image, each pixel represents the distance (range) from the sensor plane and the related confidence of the measure, respectively. Unfortunately, this kind of images are plagued by several problems due to the nature of the signal and to the related sensing system, thus heavily affecting data quality. In the proposed algorithm, range and confidence images are modelled as Markov Random Fields whose associated probability distributions are specified by a single energy functional. Two different energy functions are devised to exploit both types of data in order to perform the coupled reconstruction and segmentation of the acoustic images in terms of edges and regions. Optimal final estimates of the 3D and confidence images are obtained by minimizing the energy functional by using simulated annealing.

1 Introduction

Acoustic systems used to "sense" underwater environments are increasing their importance due to the limited capacity of optical devices used for similar objectives. Moreover, acoustic systems have an important and useful implicit property as compared with simple optical cameras, that is, they allow to directly recover three-dimensional (3D) information about the scene considered. Unfortunately, these types of sensors produce data of bad visual quality (very noisy and at poorer resolution) than those produced by optical cameras, although range capability is larger, so making their use largely diffuse for many underwater applications.

This paper aims at proposing a novel methodology to improve the reconstruction and segmentation of acoustic 3D images integrating in the same framework two kinds of information, an actual range image and a confidence image associated each other point by point and denoting the reliability of each depth estimate. Beamforming (BF) is the most widely used technique to form 3D acoustic images [1,2]. BF is also used to derive, associated with a dense range image, a reliability measure for each depth estimate, namely the "confidence" of each 3D measure [3]. Unfortunately, this approach exhibits two critical problems, speckle noise due to the coherence of the acoustical signal [4], and side lobes due to the non-ideal sensor characteristics (beam power pattern) [1].

To perform coupled reconstruction and segmentation, depth and confidence maps are modelled as Markov Random Fields (MRFs) [5], whose associated single energy function has been devised to include the confidence information in the reconstruction process to reduce the physical effects due to speckle and side lobe so as to obtain a good segmented image, too.

The MRF approach [6] was previously addressed in the literature for range image segmentation and fusion of range and intensity images [7,8]. Specific literature on acoustical images address several issues linked to segmentation [9,10], restoration of side scan sonar images by using Simulated Annealing and Iterative Conditional Modes [9], reconstruction of sea bed bathymetric data [10] by using the Graduated Non-Convexity minimization method. However, a very few works deal with the reconstruction and segmentation of underwater acoustic images and none of them addresses these tasks in a cooperative way making explicit use of confidence information.

The problem of reconstruction of acoustic data extracted by a multibeam system was already addressed by the authors in [11,12] and these works were the first attempts to explicitly processing both kinds of data. In [12], it is proposed an energy functional jointly considering the dual information in such a way that, only those pixels belonging to the range image showing high confidence are retained, whereas the range values were assumed unreliable in those pixels showing low confidence. In [11], this mechanism is evolved in the definition of a different functional which takes into account the physical significance of the coupling between range and confidence images.

In the present work, we investigate and compare reconstruction and segmentation processes performed by MRFs using different energy functionals, each one actively embedding confidence data. The energy functionals includes prior and observation (sensor) knowledge for the confidence and range fields adequately revised to account for the problem at hand. In particular, to introduce the segmentation in the joint process, two energy functions are proposed related to the segmentation of the images in edges (1st case) and regions (2nd case), respectively. The energy function related to the edge-based segmentation has been classically defined as a summation of potential functions defined over the possible edge clique configurations [5,6]. Instead, the region-based segmentation is directly derived by the confidence field and the related energy terms aim at enhancing those points whose value shows the presence of an echo backscattered from an object, while weakening those points derived by clutters. The energy terms related to reconstruction allow to integrate, in an intelligent way, the current reliability and segmentation information to improve final reconstruction results. In general, in both cases, the estimated confidence values and current segmentation results operate to both reinforce the closeness to observation constraint and to prevent smoothing at the object boundaries.

The paper is organized as follows. In Section 2, the process of image formation is described and modelled. In Section 3, the MRF approach is presented, with special emphasis on the energy functional formulations. In Section 4, results are presented and conclusions are drawn.

2 The Acoustic Acquisition Process

Beamforming (BF) is a technique aimed at estimating signals coming from a fixed steering direction, while attenuating those coming from other directions [1]. BF produces a set of so called beam signals, $bs_{\mathbf{u}}(t)$, each one steered in a different direction $\mathbf{u}$. The directivity characteristic, i.e., the beam pattern [1], presents a main lobe in the direction $\mathbf{u}$, in which the array is steered, and side lobes of minor, but not negligible, magnitudes that cause the generation of artifacts degrading useful information. Typically, the envelope, $b_{\mathbf{u}}(t)$, of a beam signal is extracted containing a replica of the insonification pulse backscattered by an object present in the steering direction sunk in spurious information due to side lobes and noise.

A common method to detect the distance of the scattering object is to look for the maximum peak of the beam signal envelope [2]. Denoting by t^* the time instant at which the maximum peak occurs, the related distance, R^*, is easily measurable from the geometry of the system. A suitable and simple measure of confidence, s^*, can be the amplitude of the maximum peak, that is, $s^* = b_{\mathbf{u}}(t^*)$. From these considerations, for each steering direction $\mathbf{u}$, a triplet ($\mathbf{u}$, R^*, s^*) can be extracted and two orthoscopic images parallel to the plane of the array can be derived, i.e., a range image $z^* = f(x^*,y^*)$ and a confidence image $s^* = g(x^*,y^*)$. Largest z^* values are related to white pixels and vice versa (see Fig. 1(a)) using a linear relation in between. Confidence information is normalized between 0 and 1 (denoting 1 as maximum confidence) and visualized in a negative way (see Fig. 1(b)).

Confidence data derived from the maximum peak amplitudes can be used in several ways. The simplest and, probably, most common way is to consider as valid only the z^* points whose related confidence values s^* are above a fixed threshold. In general, the highest side-lobe elevation determines the threshold to be used. Unfortunately, this simple and fast procedure removes side lobe effects together with many correct points whose confidence values are low due to speckle noise.

Speckle [4] is the main noise source affecting the imaging system, causing a non-deterministic magnitude of backscattered echoes. In this paper, a Gaussian distribution is adopted as a probability density function for the peak values of the beam envelopes, due to the roughness of typical man-made submerged objects considered [2,11]. The noise variance, related to the roughness characteristics of the surface, is estimated taking into account such physical properties [4]. Concerning the range map, an additive Gaussian noise model has been considered as well, like typically assumed for range images [5].

3 The MRF-Based Integration Methods

An MRF is defined on a lattice field of random variables in which the probability of a specific realization is given by a Gibbs distribution (Hammersley-Clifford theorem [5]). The energy function associated with such distribution can be computed by summing only *local* contributions with respect to a neighbourhood system defined on the lattice. Therefore, the energy minimization leads to the optimal estimate in a probabilistic sense. For a complete definition of an MRF the reader can refer to [5].

2.1 First case : Edge-based segmentation

For the definition of the single energy functions to perform the reconstruction and segmentation processes, let us consider $Y = (Y_s, Y_z)$ (i.e., the observable random field pair) as input data, where Y_s is related to the $M \times M$ confidence image S and Y_z is related to the $M \times M$ range image Z to be estimated, respectively. A line field L is also considered representing a dual lattice with respect to the field S [5,6]. This is an $M \times M$ binary map where each pixel may assume the value 1 or 0 according whether it is labelled as an edge point or not. We regard Z, S and L as sample realizations of an MRF for a given neighbourhood system, then, the process of coupled reconstruction and segmentation lies in estimating the true fields Z, S and L given the noisy input image pair Y.

Therefore, under the assumption of additive i.i.d. (independent, identically-distributed) Gaussian noise for the two maps and using the Hammerslay-Clifford equivalence and the Bayes criterion, we can write as usual the a-posteriori joint energy function (related to the a-posteriori probability [5]) as the sum of several terms:

$$E(Z,S,L/Y_z,Y_s)=\sum_{i\in Z}\sum_{j\in N_i}\left\{(z_i-z_j)^2(1-l_{ij})+\sigma_z^{-2}(z_i-y_{z_i})^2 V(s_i)\right\}+ \\ +\sum_{i\in S}\left\{(s_i-s_{i,t}(N_{l_i}))^2+\sigma_s^{-2}(s_i-y_{s_i})^2\right\}+\sum_{i\in L}\sum_{c\in C}V_c(l_i) \quad (1)$$

where i is a generic pixel site, z_i and s_i are the values to be estimated related to the depth field Z and confidence field S, respectively, y_{z_i} and y_{s_i} are the actual value of the pixel i of the observation fields Y_z and Y_s, respectively, and N_i is the neighbourhood of the pixel i (on fields Z, S and L).

The first and third term of the RHS of Eq. (1) represent the a-priori models for the field Z and S, respectively, while the second and fourth term represent the sensor models for the same two fields. The last term is related to the line field only. The line process is related to the S field. Actually, classical potential functions V_c have been devised for each edge configuration associated to the clique c belonging to the whole set of possible cliques C, considering a 2nd order neighbourhood system [5,6]. It should be noted that the definition of such functions is problem dependent, hence, heuristics has been used to assign these values.

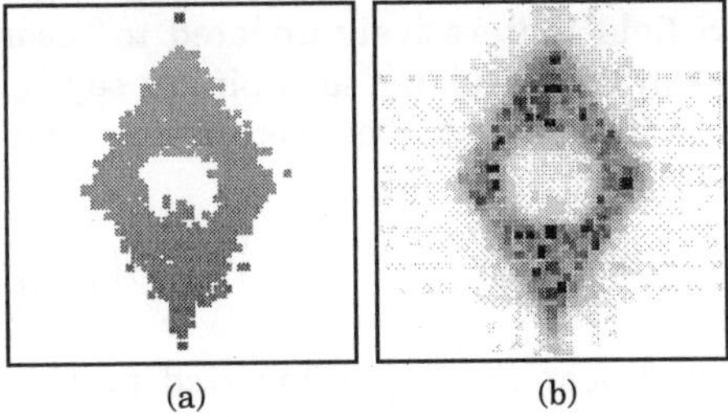

(a) (b)

Fig. 1 : Images resulting from the beamforming process and peak detection: (a) noisy range image Z retaining only z^* points whose associated confidence value s^* is over an arbitrary threshold TH = 20 (manually chosen); (b) noisy confidence image S.

The prior energy term for Z is the weak membrane model. The function l_{ij} is just introduced to prevent smoothing at object boundaries, assuming value 1 if an edge point is present between sites i and j, and zero otherwise. The sensor energy term for Z is related to the closeness to the observations. The modulating function $V(\cdot)$ aims at reinforcing or weakening this contribution, taking the form:

$$V(s_i) = \sqrt{s_i} \qquad \forall\, i \in S \tag{2}$$

It reaches the maximum value, equal to 1, if the confidence of the pixel z_i is 1, stressing the data compatibility constraint.

The restoration of the field S are mainly guided by the third and fourth terms of the RHS of Eq. (1). It should be noted that the Z estimates would not have to affect the sensor model for the field S, and the prior knowledge should force the confidence image to become binary, i.e., 1 (maximum confidence) where an object is present, and 0 otherwise. Therefore, the prior model for S (third term) is devoted to force the field to be binary. The value $s_{i,t}$ can be 0 or 1 on the basis of the number of neighbourhood pixels whose value is larger than a fixed threshold T_c set on the basis of the side lobe level. It is equal to 1 if most of the pixels in the neighbourhood of s_i are above the threshold T_c, and is equal to 0 otherwise. All of the neighbouring pixels are considered except those having an edge point between s_i and its neighbours. On the basis of this level, it is possible to calculate the attenuation of the beam signals due to the side lobes, likely allowing to separate confident from non-confident pixels. For the sensor model of S, the usual Gaussian model is adopted.

2.2 *Second case : Region-based segmentation*

In this case, the line field L is missing and only a coupled field (Z,S) is considered. The coupled reconstruction and segmentation process takes advantage of the particular restoration performed on the S field. In other words, since the S field is iteratively updated to become a binary field, the final estimate can be considered as a binary segmentation in regions of the scene, i.e., to discriminate between objects and background. The global energy function is :

$$E(Z,S/Y_z,Y_s) = \sum_{i\in Z,S}\sum_{j\in N_i}\left(z_i - z_j\right)^2 \cdot r_i(N_i) + \sigma_z^{-2}\left(z_i - y_{z_i}\right)^2 V(s_i) + \left(s_i - s_{i,t}\right)^2 + \sigma_s^{-2}\left(s_i - y_{s_i}\right)^2 \tag{3}$$

Actually, a nonlinear term r_i is inserted to separate zones where local confidence was very likely low or high and zones where local confidence is uncertain. For each site s_i, the number of pixels belonging to its neighbourhood set, s_j, having a value larger and less than a threshold T_c are stored, respectively. The term r_i is equal to 1 only if these two values are much different. In this way, when a generic point z_i has a clear local (related to the associated neighbourhood system of s_i) high or low confidence, smoothness is allowed as such point is likely derived from an object surface or background. If local confidence is not reliably high or low, no smoothness is performed as such point likely belongs to a boundary. The other energy terms remain unchanged.

The minimization of the global energy function is performed using the simulated annealing [13] procedure in which the fields Z and S (and L in the first case) evolve iteratively in a set of sample configurations in order to achieve the optimal ones. The fields are changed according to a process similar to the dual process of restoration and edge-extraction (grey-level and line fields) performed in [6]. For all of the fields, a Gibbs sampler is used [5].

4 Results and Conclusions

The proposed algorithm was tested on real and simulated acoustic 3D images. The adopted simulator [14] is widely accepted as the correct mode of generation of acoustic images, as it makes it possible to generate very realistic images of slightly rough objects affected by speckle noise.

The synthetic example consists of a single but quite complicated object for an acoustic imaging process: it is an inclined rhomb with a circular inside hole. The distance of the rhomb from the array ranges from 4.5 m to 4.7 m and the main diagonal is 1.1 m. Inside the rhomb, a circular hole with a radius of 0.2 m is present. The proposed algorithms aim at obtaining object representations that are as equal as possible to the ideal ones shown in Figs. 2(a) and 2(b), starting from the noisy images in Fig. 1(a) and Fig. 1(b).

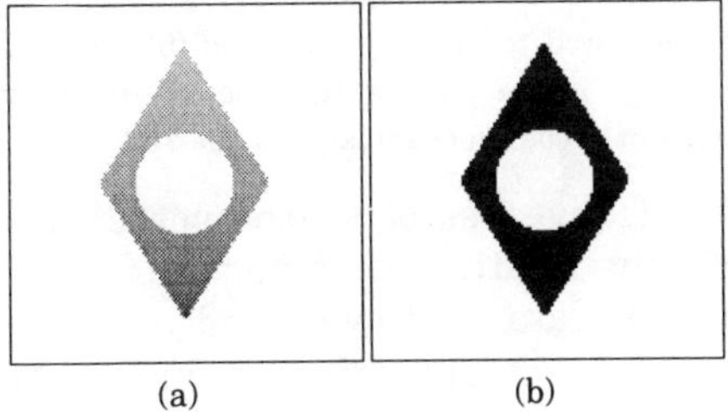

(a) (b)

Fig. 2 : (a) Ideal range image; (b) ideal confidence image.

A range image containing as valid points z^* only those associated with confidence values s^* above a fixed threshold arbitrarily chosen has been used as initial Z image, as shown in Fig. 1(a). In other words, the initial Z configuration is obtained by preprocessing the rough data as usually made in acoustic systems. We would like to stress that the value of such a heuristically set threshold, chosen in a completely arbitrary way (e.g., the operator cuts arbitrarily the signal values below such threshold in order to understand the scene), does not affect the goodness of the final estimations but only the convergence period of the algorithm. The proposed MRF algorithm works on 128×128 8-bit per pixel images using a 1st order neighbourhood set for the fields S and Z, and a 2nd order set for the field L. The confidence threshold was fixed in accordance with the highest side lobe level equal to -13 dB. Then, the threshold T_c was fixed equal to 22% of the average of the 100 highest values of confidence.

Figures 3(a), (b) and (c) show the reconstructed range image, the restored confidence image, and the edge image, respectively, for the 1st case. The result is three-fold: first, the algorithm removes holes and side-lobe effects from inside and outside objects, respectively; second, the final confidence map is a binary image that separates confident points from non-confident ones, and, third, an edge structure of the scene is obtained. Figures 3(d) and 3(e) show the reconstructed range image and the segmented confidence image, respectively, for the 2nd case. One can notice that the segmentation is quite good while the reconstruction of the map Z presents a poor visual quality. However, the mean square error is similar and the bad appearance is probably due to the poor smoothness performed inside the object. This is probably due to the simplicity of the function modelling the proposed region process.

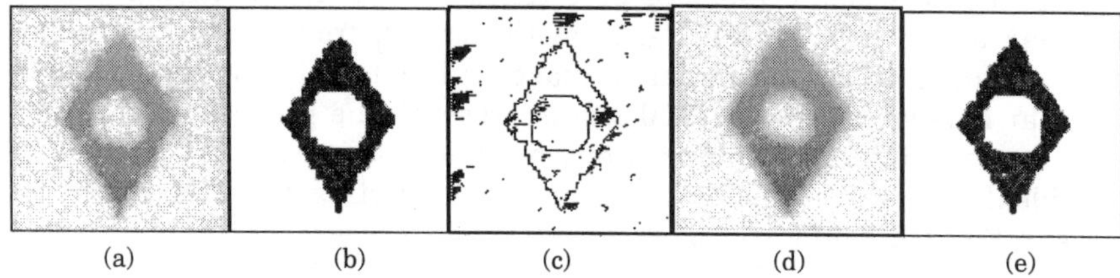

(a) (b) (c) (d) (e)

Fig. 3 : (a) Final reconstructed range image and (b) restored confidence image and (c) resulting edge image for the 1st case; (d) final reconstructed range image and (e) segmented confidence image for the 2nd case.

To verify the effectiveness of the proposed algorithms, the mean square error (*MSE*), the relative percentage *MSE* (*RMSE*) between the actual and estimated Z data, and over- and under-segmentation errors have been considered. Our algorithms achieve errors one order of magnitude smaller than the errors achieved with the simple threshold method and an MRF-based method applied directly on the Z field without using confidence. It should be noticed that applying the proposed algorithm using the ideal confidence map (see Fig. 2(b)) leads to an error even smaller, so proving the actual utility of using and restoring confidence information.

Finally, we consider a real example of a scene composed of two anchor chains and a little round object (8 cm in diameter) placed from 3 to 7 m far from the array. The images were acquired with an acoustic camera Echoscope 1600, i.e., a real-time 3D camera. In Figs. 4(a) and

4(b), one can see the actual range and confidence images composed of 128 $\times$128 pixels covering an area of 3.2$\times$3.2 m^2. The two anchor chains appears like two narrow rectangles with different orientations and distances with respect to the array plane and the round object is placed between them and closer to the array. One can notice that these real images are similar to those synthetically generated, thus proving the goodness of the simulation algorithm used. Figures 4(c), 4(d) and 4(e) show the final reconstructed, restored, and segmented images, respectively, using the energy related to the 1st case, while 4(f) and 4(g) show the results for the 2nd case. As expected, our algorithm works quite well with real data: the chains are well identified, like the little round object located between them. Cluttering data inserted by side lobe effects above the round object location are correctly removed and the 3D scene structure seems well determined.

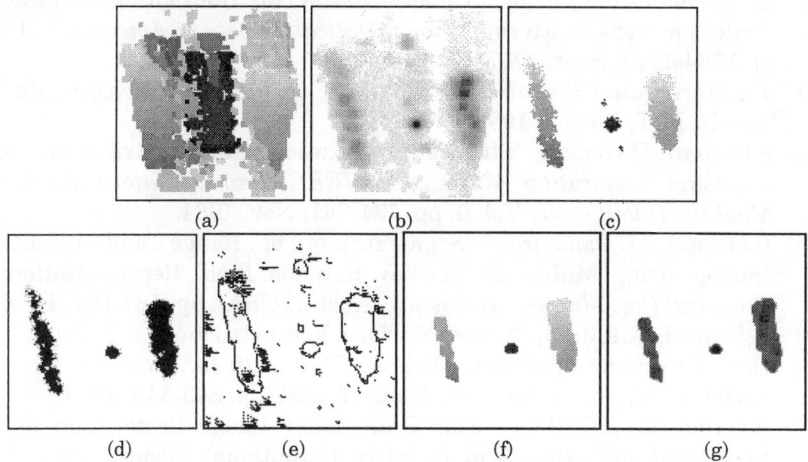

Fig. 4 : Results related to the real scene: (a) input noisy range image, (b) input noisy confidence image; (c) final reconstructed range image (1st case); (d) restored confidence image (1st case); (e) edge image (1st case) (f) final reconstructed range image (2nd case); (g) segmented confidence image (2nd case).

In conclusion, we presented a probabilistic methodology for the integration of confidence information aimed at the reconstruction and segmentation of underwater 3D acoustic images. Two MRF-based processes are proposed considering the coupled reconstruction of the range image Z and the segmentation of the confidence image S in edge and regions, respectively, performed at the same time. Owing to the MRF approach, confidence information is actively used leading to a better reconstruction as compared with other methods operating on the same degraded acoustical data. The final segmentation of the confidence image allows to discriminate between object(s) and background making it possible an easy recovering of the shape for subsequent higher level tasks like object recognition.

References

[1] R.O.Nielsen, *Sonar Signal Processing*, Boston: Artech House, 1991.

[2] M.Okino, Y.Higashi, "Measurement of Seabed Topography by Multibeam Sonar Using CFFT", *IEEE Jour. Oceanic Engineering*, Vol. 11, pp. 474-479, Oct. 1986.

[3] V.Murino, A.Trucco, "Acoustic Image Improvement by Confidence Levels", *Proc. IEEE Ultrasonics Symp.*, Cannes (France), pp. 1367-1370, Nov. 1994.

[4] E.Jakeman, R.J.Tough, "Generalized *K* distribution: a statistical model for weak scattering", *Jour. Optical Society of America*, Vol. 4, pp.1764-1772, Sept. 1987.

[5] J.L.Marroquin, *Probabilistic Solution of Inverse Problems,* Ph.D. Thesis, MIT, Boston, 1985.

[6] S.Geman, D.Geman, "Stochastic relaxation, Gibbs distribution, and Bayesian restoration of images", *IEEE Trans. Pattern Analysis Machine Intelligence,* Vol. 6, pp. 721-741, Nov. 1984.

[7] B.Günsel, E.Panayirci, "Segmentation of Range and Intensity Images using Multiscale Markov Random Field Representations", *Proc. Int. Conf. Image Processing,* Austin (USA), pp. 187-191, 1994.

[8] B.Günsel, A.K.Jain, "Visual Surface Reconstruction and Boundary Detection using Stochastic Models", *Proc. 11th Int. Conf. on Pattern Recognition*, The Hague (The Netherlands), pp. 343-346, 1994.

[9] R.S.Beattie, S.C.Elder, "Side Scan Sonar Image Restoration using Simulated Annealing and Iterative Conditional Modes", *Proc. Int. Conf. Sonar Signal Proc.*, Loughborough (UK), pp. 161-167, 1995.

[10] S.Show, J.Arnold, "Automated Error Detection in Multibeam Bathymetry Data", *Proc. IEEE OCEANS '93*, Victoria (Canada), Vol. II, pp. 89-94, 1993.

[11] V.Murino, E.Frumento, F.Gabino, "Restoration of noisy underwater acoustic images using Markov Random Fields", in *Lecture Notes in Computer Science n. 974,* Berlin: Springer, pp. 355-360, 1995.

[12] V.Murino, "Acoustic Image Reconstruction by Markov Random Fields", *Electronics Letters*, Vol. 32, N. 7, pp. 697-698, March 1996.

[13] S.Kirkpatrick, C.D.Gellatt Jr., M.P.Vecchi., "Optimization by simulated annealing", *Science*, Vol. 220, No. 4598, pp. 671-680, 1983.

[14] T.L.Henderson, S.G.Lacker, "Seafloor Profiling by a Wideband Sonar: Simulaton, Frequency-Response, Optimization and Results of Brief Sea Test", *IEEE J. Ocean. Eng.*, Vol. 14, pp. 94-107, Jan. 1989.

FIGURE-GROUND SEGMENTATION AS A STEP TOWARDS DERIVING OBJECT PROPERTIES

PETER NORDLUND, JAN-OLOF EKLUNDH
Computational Vision and Active Perception Laboratory (CVAP)
Department of Numerical Analysis and Computing Science
Royal Institute of Technology, S-100 44 Stockholm, Sweden
Email: petern@nada.kth.se

Abstract

In this paper we discuss how figure-ground segmentation can be important in deriving object properties such as shape. Our approach is based on a conjunction of motion and depth. The main idea is to produce a 2-dimensional histogram with depth in one dimension and horizontal motion in the other. This histogram is then analyzed. The most significant peaks in the histogram are backprojected to the image to produce an object mask. This object mask is maintained over time.

Keywords: stereo disparity, image motion, scale-space, segmentation, cue-integration

1 Introduction

Research in biological vision aims at understanding the principles of vision as they manifest themselves in nature. Seeing creatures trivially have functioning vision systems, so the question is "how" these work, not "if". In computer vision, on the other hand, the goal is to develop artifacts, namely machine based vision systems or components of them. Then it becomes a major concern to design approaches that work. This is an issue at the level of a single algorithm for computing a certain characteristic, which in turn could be useful in a more complex vision system solving a particular task. It is certainly crucial when we try to design machine vision systems that are capable of performing tasks of, say, recognition, or guiding a mobile robot or robot manipulator.

Areas such as the study of visual shape have produced sophisticated theories of local and global shape representation and computation, see e.g. Koenderink [1], or Arcelli et al. [2] for examples. Such theories have been applied successfully for instance in the context of scene reconstruction and in the computation of local shape characteristics. However, in cognitive or high-level tasks such as object recognition and robot manipulation only simple models have been applied, as e.g. in recognition where leading work like that of

Brooks [3], Zerroug and Nevatia [4], Dickinson and Metaxas [5], and Pentland and Sclaroff [6], relies on models which are rather simple. These approaches may well be developed to deal with more sophisticated models in the future. Moreover, in the case of object recognition approaches that combine methods using shape with view-based techniques are emerging, see e.g. Ullman [7] for a discussion.

In this paper we will discuss figure-ground segmentation as a level that could bridge the gap between existing advanced theories for deriving scene characteristics of e.g. shape and their application to cognitive tasks such as object recognition. If a system could segment out a target in the world by some basic and perhaps coarse methods, and without knowing what it is, it might be easier for the ensuing processes to perform their tasks. In fact, many shape analysis models are concerned with single objects, and hence such a mechanism is indeed a prerequisite for them to apply in real scenes. Before going into the details it should be mentioned that although we presume an active observer, the main assumption used is that we consider a dynamic 3-dimensional world.

1.1 Related work

There is a host of work in which various aspects of what we propose have been considered. Nordlund [8] contains a detailed discussion on this. Examples are given by the work by Milanese [9], Clark and Yuille [10] and Maki [11] on fusing different features and Bülthoff and Mallot [12] for the particular case of shape reconstruction.

The problems of cue integration and figure-ground segmentation in biological systems are addressed in e.g. [13, 14, 15, 16].

The systems perspective that we advocate and its implications is considered by Hager [17]: "The *task* the system must carry out determines what information is needed and to what level of refinement.". An experimental system containing three components: image processing, tracking and motion, and fusion and planning is presented in [17], which states that the problem can be seen as information gathering. Since the computational resources are limited, the solution is not to run all possible algorithms at the same time and fuse all the output data. The solution is to *select* which algorithms to run. Moreover, the concept of *information cost* is discussed more extensively in [17, pp 60].

By letting included algorithms produce some kind of reliability measure the selection process could be facilitated. A method to switch between different features, depending on the value of a significance measure, to obtain a better texture segmentation is presented by Porter and Canagarajah [18]. The importance of having included algorithms signaling success or failure is pointed out by Firby [19], where a robot control architecture is described. Toyama and Hager [20] present a layered architecture for robust tracking. The topmost layer performs the highest precision tracking. The layers below have less precision. After a tracking cycle, control moves up or down the framework depending of the success of tracking during the previous cycle. The authors stress the importance of mechanisms for algorithm failure detection. This is necessary for the transitions between the layers.

2 Our approach

The problem of figure ground segmentation can be regarded as consisting of two steps:

1. The (partial) selection of the location of the object/figure of interest. This forms an initial attention step.
2. Refining and maintaining this initial selection to achieve "good" figure ground segmentation. This forms maintenance of attention. (In case of a moving object, this could be seen as a more or less robust tracking, while gathering useful information/characteristics.)

In this paper we focus on the second step. As cues to attention we use in particular motion and binocular disparities. Attentional selection is handled with simple heuristics such as selecting the closest moving target. However, we stress that it is important to link these two steps together, i.e. once the selection has taken place (step 1), the maintenance (step 2) knows what formed the initial selection.

At the heart of our proposed solution lies *identification*. By this we mean to determine what the characteristics of the object are, i.e. what identifies it. Natural elements of this identification are of course what formed the initial attention. However we argue that is is not enough for maintenance and refinement of the figure ground segmentation. In general more characteristics are needed for this. In our paper we will present a number of central issues in our proposed approach. These can be listed as follows:

- Finding the characteristics of an object.
- Defining and determining measures of reliability of the algorithms telling if they can be trusted or not.
- Fusing of or choosing between cues based on reliability measures.

- Combining cues both by strong and weak coupling.
- Using consistency over time.

These issues will now be discussed in subsequent order.

2.1 Cue Combination

In the work on attention, Nakayama and Silverman [13] pointed out that humans can perform parallel search over stereoscopic disparity and either color or motion. The authors suggest that retinal disparity has priority over visual stimulus dimensions, cf. Bülthoff and Mallot [12].

Figure-ground segmentation could benefit from combining a depth cue in parallel to other cues, since the depth of an object is independent of most of other characteristics of it, such as color and texture. In our approach we have chosen binocular disparity[a] as the depth cue to use, capitalizing on the existence of algorithms with reasonable robustness and complexity computing a dense depth-map,(see e.g. Maki et al. [21]).

Our suggestion is to combine depth with some other cue as a first step towards the figure-ground segmentation. This could be motivated by the fact that practically all objects we are interested in have a small extent in depth compared to the particular depth at which they are observed.

2.2 Reliability measures

Single algorithms based on specific cues will, as pointed out above, not suffice for a seeing robot. Such a system should have several redundant algorithms running in parallel to handle the variability and changes in its environment. It should in fact also be able to detect algorithm failures and then switch between algorithms in a proper way. To integrate the algorithms, both by switching between different algorithms and by fusing their output the algorithms need a common representation. As the common representation for the different algorithms we have chosen a segmentation mask. This is a binary image where the figure-ground segmentation already has been performed to single out the interesting object.

Strategies for deciding whether an algorithm is applicable or not has so far attracted limited attention, both because it is a difficult problem and because few practical attempts to use computer vision algorithms in a system-context

---

[a] We use intrinsic camera calibration, a parallel camera geometry but no extrinsic calibration, so we obtain only relative depth. From now on we use the term ***depth***.

have been made. As noted earlier Toyama and Hager [20] and Firby [19] briefly touch upon this problem.

There are several reasons why we can't expect algorithms to always give proper results. First the required data may be difficult to observe due to noise or extreme imaging conditions. Then the algorithm will give uncertain results. A somewhat different case occurs when the assumptions that the algorithm build upon are not valid at all, for instance when the required features are absent, or when the model assumption are violated. Many algorithms for computing disparities or optic flow and obviously also for shape-from-texture need texture to work (see e.g. Karu et al. [22]). If an area in the image is textured or not may easily be detected (up to some accuracy not defined here) by some gradient-based measure. This provides a way of introducing uncertainties. However, it is worse to handle violations of assumptions. A shape-from-texture algorithm that assumes that textures are isotropic can be fooled by anisotropic textures, for instance if a receding pattern is painted on a planar surface. Another concrete example of failures that are hard to detect is false matchings in a stereo-algorithm, e.g. when having repetitive patterns in the image.

A well-designed figure-ground segmentation system should calculate reliability measures at many different stages of the segmentation. An example of an early stage reliability measure is the saliency of a region based on the prominence of the corresponding peak in a multidimensional histogram. Reliability measures can also be calculated at much later stages. We have found it convenient to work with the compactness of the resulting segmentation mask as a measure[b]. One example of how to compute a compactness measure can be the area/perimeter ratio. If the mask is dissolving or if the boundary is getting irregular that reliability measure decreases.

Reliability for secondary algorithms Highly specialized algorithms will only give useful output when their assumptions are valid, which occurs seldom. Therefore, they can be applied in conjunction with a "cuing"[c] or primary algorithm which is working under more general conditions. If the secondary

[b]Usually decisions based on lower level reliability measures have already been taken before we end up with this measure.

[c]The cuing algorithm can be seen as the primary algorithm, usually with a more robust behavior than secondary algorithms. Compare with the ideas by Bülthoff and Mallot [12]. The term "secondary" is not used with strictly the same meaning here, as in [12]. The cuing algorithm defines area of interest in the image, bounding boxes of interesting objects etc. that may be used by the secondary algorithm. If an algorithm is cuing or secondary could be context dependent. That is: for a mobile robot one algorithm could be cuing in one particular situation, while another algorithm is cuing in another situation.

algorithm produces results that coincide well with the cuing algorithm this gives a high reliability for the secondary algorithm. The fact that more than one algorithm supports the same hypothesis increases the reliability of all involved algorithms. Of course the reliability increases if the algorithms continue to coincide over time.

When the reliability of the cuing algorithm goes below some threshold the secondary algorithm may take over the segmentation and become the cuing algorithm. Strategies of those kinds have been applied in our experiments.

2.3 Weakly coupled systems vs. strongly coupled systems

Clark and Yuille [10, p 103–104], introduce these terms. They state: "Weakly coupled fusion is characterized by the combination of the outputs of independent information sources. Each module operates independently of the others" and "Strongly coupled data fusion involves alteration of the prior constraints (either the image formation model, prior model, or system model) used by a information processing module by the output of another module or sets of modules."

Using strong coupling when segmenting has both benefits and drawbacks. The information obtained from a segmentation step exploiting strong coupling between several cues is usually more informative compared to a segmentation using only one cue. On the other hand, if one of the cues turn out to be totally wrong due to some shortcoming of the algorithm, that whole segmentation step can be ruined if strong coupling is used.

Using weak coupling between several cues when segmenting gives less information from each included component, but if one algorithm fails (indicated by its low reliability measure), the system can more robustly recover by relying on backup from the other algorithms included.

2.4 The segmentation mask and consistency over time

The segmentation mask has been introduced to allow integration of algorithms that provide output in different representations. It also allows a check for determining consistency over time, which in many cases is more informative and reliable than spatial consistency. A particular case occurs when the segmented target is moving and become occluded. By continuously observing characteristics of the tracked object, i.e. inside the segmentation mask, such as e.g. depth and motion and also shape we can detect when something extraordinary happens to the temporal update, thus detecting events like occlusion.

There are basically three reasons to why a sudden change in the computed velocity of the tracked object could occur:

- A real sudden change in the velocity of the tracked object.
- A false match, (plain mismatching).
- The tracked object gets occluded, (thus quite likely creating a false match).

In the first case the mask will still have approximately the same size and continuous but not smooth motion over time. In the second case the mask motion will probably be discontinuous. In the third case the mask area will decrease rapidly. Applying these cases and including various measures of reliability in each algorithm we use consistency over time as an essential additional criterion to obtain overall systems performance.

3 Description of algorithms

First the early modules used in our experiments are described briefly, then the algorithms will be described. We first describe the preattentive cues used.

3.1 Attentional mechanisms, starting up segmentation masks

This paper does not address on the problem of which attentional mechanism to use. Attention could come from bottom up processes such as motion detection, or from top down processes such as external information of where to look. This is very much a task-dependent problem, and it is fairly easy to exchange the attentional mechanism in our framework.

In our experiments so far we have used criteria such as focusing on the closest target and keeping attention fixed for a certain number of frames. This make sense in many applications, e.g. for a moving robot.

3.2 Binocular disparity

Relative depth, that plays a central role in our model, is derived from a dense disparity map. As disparity estimator we employ a phase-based stereo algorithm which has the advantages of low computational cost, stability against varying lighting condition and especially of allowing good direct localization of the estimated disparity. The disparity estimation algorithm is described in [21]. For a comparison with an algorithm described in [23, chap 2-3], see Figure 5.

3.3 Motion disparity

By applying the stereo algorithm to consecutive image frames instead of to a stereo image pair, information of horizontal image motion can be obtained. In our experimental implementation, the use of the motion disparity cue is only in one dimension, along the horizontal direction, because by doing so this early module can share identical input with the binocular disparity module.

To use only horizontal motion can be motivated from the fact that most motions are performed over a ground plane. Most people, vehicles and creatures are bound to the ground plane. In such situations it is not a severe limitation to disregard vertical motion.

3.4 Gray scale blobs

As an example of spatial features we have chosen gray-scale-blobs. One could think of other spatial features such as different texture segmentation algorithms, color, or some simple gray-scale thresholding techniques.

The gray-scale-blobs are used for texture segmentation. This can be done as follows. We assume that blobs of a common size belong together. A segmentation mask coming from depth-motion segmentation provides a region of interest centered around this mask. In the region of interest the blob size is histogrammed and the distinct peaks in the histogram are found. After classifying blobs we run a convex hull algorithm for the blob class that agrees best with the blob size statistics inside the depth-motion mask. The mask resulting from the convex hull algorithm is then compared with the depth-motion mask. When the two masks have a support-measure (will be described in Section 3.8) above a threshold the blob-segmentation algorithm is considered to have succeeded. For experimental results, see [8].

3.5 2-D histogramming of depth and motion

After obtaining dense depth and motion images with respective confidence images produced by the phase-based disparity algorithm, a weighted 2-D histogram is produced. By not having fixed ranges on the histogram, but actually adapting the ranges from frame to frame based on statistics from the motion and depth calculations the computational resources can be exploited more efficiently. It has turned out to be very important how to select the ranges of the histogram axes to get a both a good computational efficiency and a good end result. By having a small grid in the histogram the subsequent scale-space analysis can be sufficiently speed up. We have chosen to exclude a certain percentage of the lowest and highest values from the motion and depth images respectively.

The confidence values C_M and C_D for motion and depth are used for weighting in the histogramming in the following way:

If depth D with corresponding confidence C_D and motion M with confidence C_M belongs to bin B_{ij} in the histogram, then we add $\sqrt{C_D C_M}$ to bin B_{ij}.

3.6 Analyzing the histogram

Peaks in the histogram reflect areas in the image which have consistent depth and motion. To decide which peaks that are significant can be viewed as a scale-space problem. Lindeberg [24] has proposed a method to handle this problem based on "The Scale-Space Primal Sketch", which has been used here. This method is a multiscale method which detect peaks at different scales. The detected peaks are given a significance measure and the peaks are also tracked over scale.

This method can give rise to one single fine scale peak located fully inside one coarser scale peak. We have chosen to disregard those fine scale peaks. We also disregard peaks with the ratio: blob-area/blob-bounding-box-area, below a threshold. This is mainly done to get rid of blobs appearing as edge effects in the corners of the histogram grid.

Detected peaks with a significance measure above a threshold are used for focus of attention and are backprojected into the original image thus creating masks.

3.7 Tracking objects over time, maintaining segmentation masks

After attending an object, the object characteristics are observed (here we use the depth-motion blob of the object). The tracking of an object is made in two different domains:

- The blobs in the depth-motion histogram
- The 2-D image[d]

These domains are coupled together in a heuristic scheme explained below:

[d] We have just arbitrarily chosen to work in the left image.

The blobs in the depth-motion histogram The tracking is mainly performed in the depth-motion histogram using an α-β-tracker [25] on the blob centroid $(\bar{D}, \bar{M})$. The predicted centroid is denoted $(\bar{D}^p, \bar{M}^p)$. To verify that the matching proceeds in a normal way a consistency check is made by backprojecting the blob to produce a segmentation mask S_t, at time t, in the 2-D image. The matching will be explained in more detail below.

The 2-D image Corresponding to the 2-D image there is an accumulated segmentation mask A_{t-1} from the previous time-instant, $t-1$. The current mask image[e] S_t, has the value 1 for the object and -1 for the background. The motion between consecutive frames are only a few pixels in our experiments, so we have chosen a simple update-scheme for the accumulated object mask A_t. A^*_{t-1} is just A_{t-1} but with a translating compensation the distance according to the motion component of the centroid of the depth-motion blob. We just let the mask S_t be added to the accumulated object mask by the following formula, operating pixelwise:

$$A_t = A^*_{t-1} + S_t$$

$$\text{if} \quad A_t > K_1, \quad A_t = K_1$$

$$\text{if} \quad A_t < K_2, \quad A_t = K_2$$

where K_1 and K_2 are constants. In our experiments K_1 was set to 3 and K_2 to -2. This scheme gives the object mask some hysteresis, since we consider $A_t > 0$ to belong to the object mask and $A_t \leq 0$ to belong to the background. The consequence of the fact that pixels not belonging to the object can get as low value as K_2 is that a "bad" mask updating the object mask, will not affect the appearance of the object mask until the bad appearance has been present for at least $K_2 + 1$ consecutive frames.

As a last step we compute some descriptors for the masks A_t and S_t to be used for the matching. We compute an ellipse with the descriptors, centroid in both x and y direction, major axis, minor axis and angle. Below denoted for A_t:[f] $A_{\bar{x}}$, $A_{\bar{y}}$, A_{min}, A_{maj}, A_{ang}, and in a corresponding way for S_t.

Given the region Ω defining the object mask[g] in A_t (and S_t respectively),

---

[e] We run a connected component algorithm on the backprojection and keep only the largest connected area, to get rid of spurious areas erroneously backprojected.

[f] We from now on drop the t subscript when it is not necessary for clarity.

[g] I.e.: pixels with values > 0.

the image coordinates x, y:

$$\sigma = \sum_{(x,y)\in\Omega} 1, \quad A_{\bar{x}} = \bar{x} = \frac{1}{\sigma}\sum_{(x,y)\in\Omega} x, \quad A_{\bar{y}} = \bar{y} = \frac{1}{\sigma}\sum_{(x,y)\in\Omega} y$$

$$\mu_{xx} = \frac{1}{\sigma}\sum_{(x,y)\in\Omega}(x-\bar{x})^2, \qquad \mu_{yy} = \frac{1}{\sigma}\sum_{(x,y)\in\Omega}(y-\bar{y})^2$$

$$\mu_{xy} = \frac{1}{\sigma}\sum_{(x,y)\in\Omega}(x-\bar{x})(y-\bar{y})$$

$$A_{maj} = \left[8\left(\mu_{xx}+\mu_{yy}+[(\mu_{xx}-\mu_{yy})^2+4\mu_{xy}^2]^{1/2}\right)\right]^{1/2}$$

$$A_{min} = \left[8\left(\mu_{xx}+\mu_{yy}-[(\mu_{xx}-\mu_{yy})^2+4\mu_{xy}^2]^{1/2}\right)\right]^{1/2}$$

$$A_{ang} = tan^{-1}\left[\frac{-2\mu_{xy}}{\mu_{xx}-\mu_{yy}+[(\mu_{xx}-\mu_{yy})^2+4\mu_{xy}^2]^{1/2}}\right]$$

Matching Matching of the tracked object on a frame-to-frame basis could be done in many different more or less computationally demanding ways. The matching consists of two steps. In both steps we compute a weighted distance measure, but with different weights.

On all of the descriptors mentioned above we apply α-β-trackers. The predicted values are denoted with a superscript ^{p}, so the predicted value of A_{maj} is A^p_{maj}, and so on.

The distance measure looks as follows:

$$w_1(\bar{M}-\bar{M}^p)^2 + w_2(\bar{D}-\bar{D}^p)^2 + w_3(S_{\bar{x}}-A^p_{\bar{x}})^2 + w_4(S_{\bar{y}}-A^p_{\bar{y}})^2 + \\ w_5(S_{maj}-A^p_{maj})^2 + w_6(S_{min}-A^p_{min})^2 + w_7(S_{ang}-A^p_{ang})^2$$

In the first step w_1 and w_2 are much higher than the rest of the weights, thus raising the significance of a good depth-motion blob match. All matching candidates with a distance over a threshold are disregarded in this step. In the second matching/verification step the significance of the segmentation mask descriptors are raised, and if below a threshold, the candidate with shortest distance is chosen as a match. If no distance is below the threshold the tracked object is considered lost, the main hypothesis is that the object has been occluded, and a predict mode is entered. In this mode the depth-motion blob centroid is used to predict where the object will appear after the occlusion has ceased.

3.8 Reliability measure

In some experiments we have used a compactness measure defined as: the mask area divided by the sum of 8-connected perimeter pixels in the binary object mask. The lower this measure is, the more compact the mask is. As mentioned in Section 2.2 the temporal aspect could also be taken into account.

Switching to a secondary algorithm When using a secondary algorithm producing its own binary object mask S_{alg2}, we calculate a support measure *Suppmes* for this mask relative to the original algorithms mask S_{alg1} as a normalized sum of pixels after performing a pixelwise xor operation:

$$Suppmes = \frac{\sum S_{alg1} + \sum S_{alg2}}{\sum (S_{alg1} \oplus S_{alg2})}$$

If this support measure has been high for a while and suddenly the cuing algorithm gets below a threshold, this is an indication for switching to having the secondary backup algorithm as cuing.

In our experiments we have set the threshold manually. Crowley [26] defines a confidence factor of a more general nature. Confidence is computed as a probability using a sample set of correct detections. We have not yet explored any such measure. Such a method seems to be good for setting thresholds in complex systems. For experimental results, see [8].

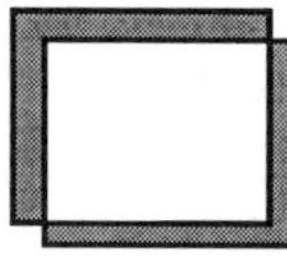

Figure 1: Given two rectangular masks, if they overlap perfect, the Support measure will go to infinity. In this example the rectangles do not fit perfectly. The area marked with gray graphically illustrates the denominator of the support measure *Suppmes*.

4 Experiments

We illustrate the ideas presented above by some experimental results. More experiments including such that test the performance of the approaches are given in Nordlund [8].

The experiments were performed with the head-eye system constructed by Pahlavan [27]. This head-eye system has now been mounted on a mobile platform.

All images have been acquired at a frame-rate of 25 Hz using a MaxVideo 200 as frame-grabber. From one of the cameras[h] only one interlace is used, this gives us images of the size 366×287 pixels, and a shutter speed of 1/50 second. The lens used is a zoom lens[i], set to the widest viewing angle: 657 pixels focal length, or 31° and 24.6° viewing angle in the horizontal and vertical direction respectively.

The first experiment is performed on an image sequence of three people moving at different depth. The camera is stationary. This experiment illustrates the performance of the depth-motion based segmentation step when one target becomes occluded. In Figure 2 every 8th frame of the original sequence is shown.

Figure 2: Original sequence. Left camera in the top row, right camera in the bottom row (every 8th frame is shown).

The tracking of the person getting occluded can successfully be maintained since there is a filter[j] predicting the object characteristics depth and motion, In Figures 3 and 4 backprojected histogram blobs are shown.

For comparison we have replaced our simple algorithm for computing disparities with a computationally more expensive technique [23, chap 2-3]. The results presented in Figure 5 show that overall systems performance hardly improves.

[h] The robot head is equipped with 2 CCIR cameras, Philips LDH 670.

[i] Camera lenses:Ernitec, model M12Z6. Manufacturers specifications: Focal length 12.5-75 mm, max aperture: F1.2, horizontal angle of view for 2/3" chip: 6°7'−38°7', (Max angle of view we practically can use is 31° horizontally).

[j] An α-β-tracker [25].

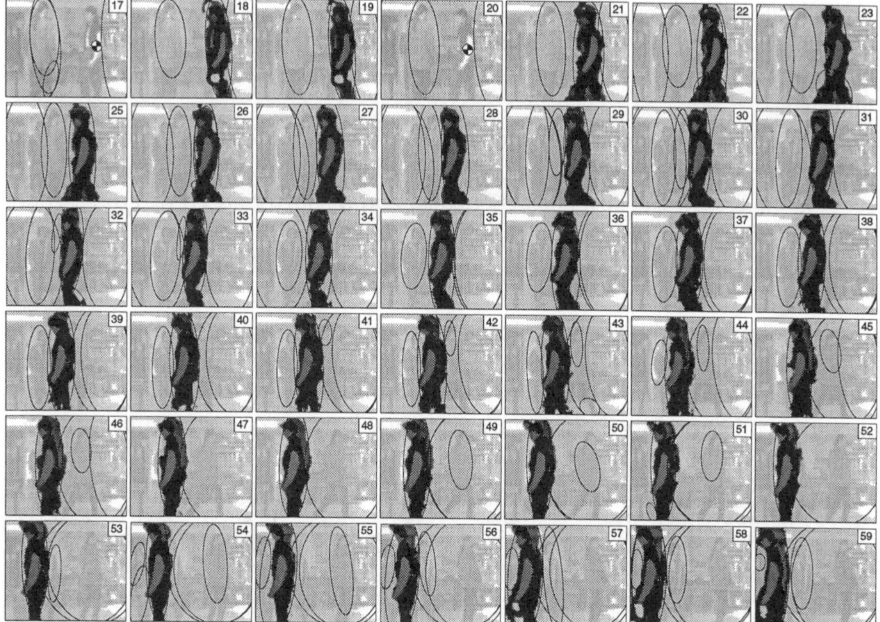

Figure 3: Example of backprojected and tracked blobs. All backprojected blobs in each frame are visualized by an ellipse representing their second-order moment. The updated tracking mask is shown in black. In some frames there is a black/white circle showing the predicted centroid of the tracking mask, when the tracking update fails. Frame number is indicated in upper right corner.

Figure 6 finally show results on a simpler object and with a moving observer (panning camera). In these cases it actually turns out that a too simple background can pose problems, here due to reflections.

5 Discussion

In the paper we have considered figure-ground segmentation as a step towards applying higher level visual analysis of objects, such as shape analysis or recognition. We have applied a systems perspective based on multiple cues and especially used 3-dimensional information as a primary source of information. The goal is to combine this approach with techniques for deriving properties of e.g. shape of these segmented objects.

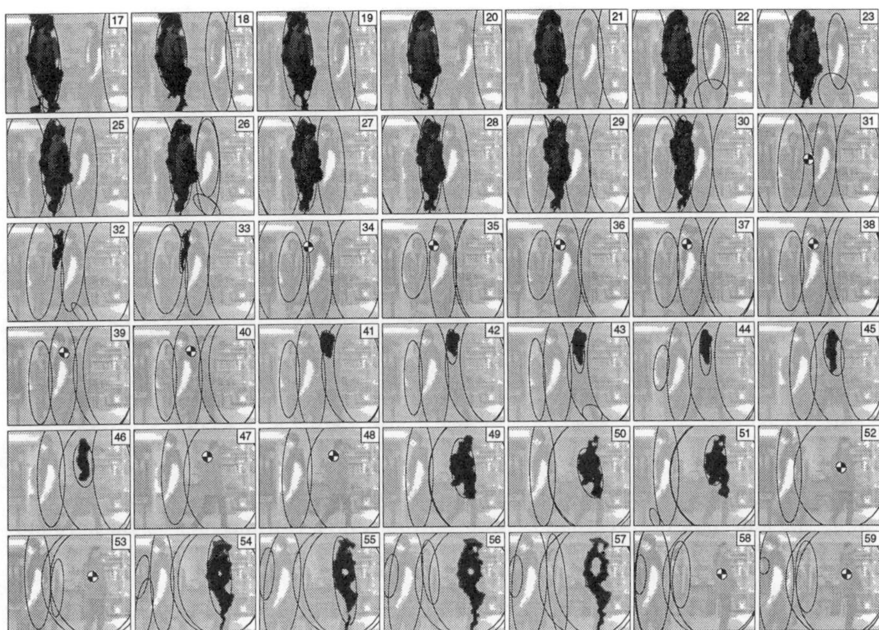

Figure 4: Example of backprojected and tracked blobs. Observe that the tracking is maintained although the tracked person gets occluded. All backprojected blobs in each frame are visualized by an ellipse representing their second-order moment. The updated tracking mask is shown in black. In some frames there is a black/white circle showing the predicted centroid of the tracking mask, when the tracking update fails. Frame number is indicated in upper right corner.

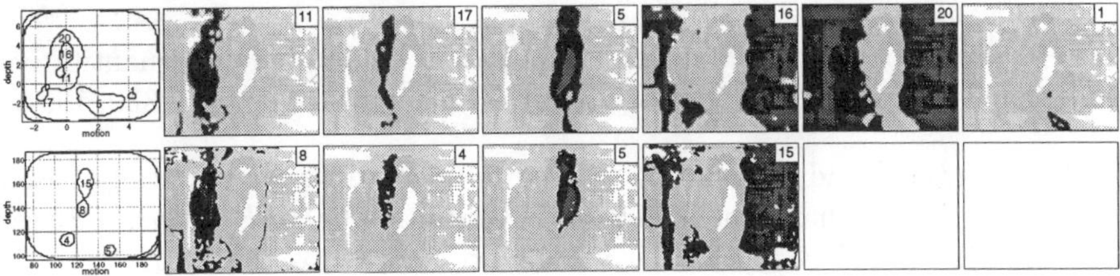

Figure 5: Compare backprojected blobs. Top row: Segmentation using algorithm by Maki [21]. Bottom row: Segmentation using algorithm by Westelius [23].

References

[1] J. J. Koenderink, *Solid Shape.* Cambridge, Massachusetts: MIT Press, 1990.

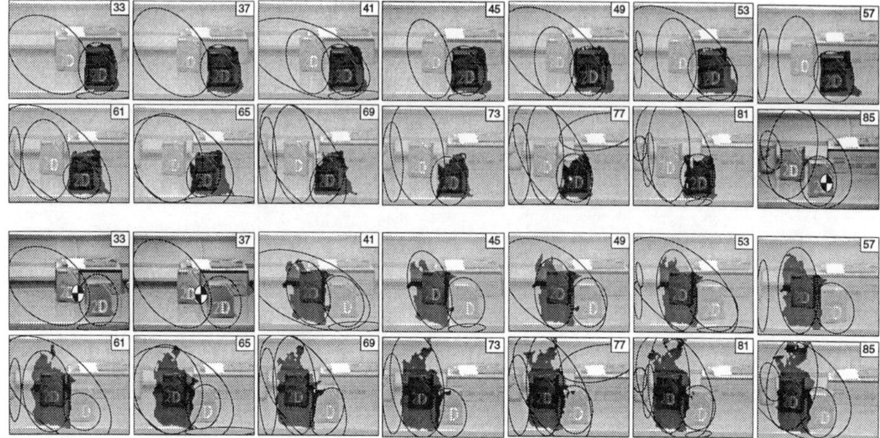

Figure 6: Example of tracked blobs. Diskette boxes, uniform background. Two top rows: tracking box in foreground. Two bottom rows: tracking box in background. Frame number is indicated in upper right corner.

[2] C. Arcelli, L. P. Cordella, and G., eds., *Visual Form: Analysis and Recognition.* New York: Plenum Press, 1992.

[3] R. A. Brooks, "Symbolic reasoning among 3-d models and 2-d images," *J. of Artificial Intelligence*, vol. 17, no. 1–3, pp. 285–348, 1981.

[4] M. Zerroug and R. Nevatia, "Volumetric descriptions from a single intensity image," *Int. J. of Computer Vision*, vol. 20, pp. 11–42, 1996.

[5] S. Dickinson and D. Metaxas, "Integrating qualitative and quantitative shape recovery," *Int. J. of Computer Vision*, vol. 13, pp. 311–330, 1994.

[6] A. Pentland and S. Sclaroff, "Closed-form solutions for physically based shape based shape modelling and recognition," *IEEE Trans. Pattern Analysis and Machine Intell.*, vol. 13, no. 7, pp. 715–729, 1991.

[7] S. Ullman, *High-level Vision.* Cambridge, Massachusetts: MIT Press, 1991.

[8] P. Nordlund, "Maintenance of figure-ground segmentation by cue-selection," Tech. Rep. ISRN KTH/NA/P--97/05--SE, Dept. of Numerical Analysis and Computing Science, KTH, Stockholm, Sweden, Apr. 1997.

[9] R. Milanese, *Detecting Salient Regions in an Image: From Biological Evidence to Computer Implementation.* PhD thesis, Dept. of Computer Science, Univ of Geneva, Switzerland, Dec. 1993.

[10] J. J. Clark and A. L. Yuille, *Data Fusion for Sensory Information Processing Systems.* Dordrecht, Netherlands: Kluwer Academic Publishers, 1990. ISBN 0-7923-9120-9.

[11] A. Maki, *Stereo Vision in Attentive Scene Analysis.* Ph. D. dissertation, Dept. of Numerical Analysis and Computing Science, KTH, Stockholm, Sweden, Mar. 1996. ISRN KTH/NA/P--96/07--SE.

[12] H. H. Bülthoff and H. A. Mallot, "Interaction of different modules in depth perception," in *Proc. 1st International Conference on Computer Vision,* (London, England), pp. 295–305, June 1987.

[13] K. Nakayama and G. H. Silverman, "Serial and parallel processing of visual feature conjunctions," *Nature,* vol. 320, pp. 264–265, 1986.

[14] S. Grossberg, "A solution of the figure-ground problem for biological vision," *Neural Networks,* vol. 6, no. 4, pp. 463–483, 1993.

[15] S. Grossberg and L. Wyse, "A neural network architechture for figure-ground separation of connected scenic figures," *Neural Networks,* vol. 4, no. 6, pp. 723–742, 1991.

[16] L. T. Maloney and M. S. Landy, "A statistical framework for robust fusion of depth information," in *Proc. of the SPIE: Visual Communication and Image Processing IV* (W. A. Pearlman, ed.), vol. 1199, (Philadelphia, Pennsylvania), pp. 1154–1163, Nov. 1989.

[17] G. D. Hager, *Task-Directed Sensor Fusion and Planning. A Computational Approach.* Dordrecht, Netherlands: Kluwer Academic Publishers, 1990. ISBN 0-7923-9108-X.

[18] R. Porter and N. Canagarajah, "A robust automatic clustering scheme for image segmentation using wavelets," in *Proc. 2nd Asian Conference on Computer Vision* (E. K. Teo, ed.), vol. 2, (Singapore), pp. 76–80, Dec. 1995.

[19] R. J. Firby, "Building symbolic primitives with continuous control routines," in *First International Conference on AI Planning Systems,* (College Park MD), June 1992.

[20] K. Toyama and G. D. Hager, "Incremental focus of attention for robust visual tracking," in *Proc. IEEE Comp. Soc. Conf. on Computer Vision and Pattern Recognition, 1996*, (San Francisco, California), pp. 189–195, IEEE Computer Society Press, June 1996.

[21] A. Maki, T. Uhlin, and J.-O. Eklundh, "Phase-based disparity estimation in binocular tracking," in *Proc. 8th Scandinavian Conference on Image Analysis* (K. H. K. A. Høgdra, B. Braathen, ed.), (Tromsø, Norway), pp. 1145–1152, Norwegian Society for Image Processing and Pattern Recognition, May 1993.

[22] K. Karu, A. K. Jain, and R. M. Bolle, "Is there any texture in the image?," in *Proc. 13th International Conference on Pattern Recognition*, vol. II, (Vienna, Austria), pp. 770–774, IEEE Computer Society Press, Aug. 1996.

[23] C.-J. Westelius, *Focus of Attention and Gaze Control for Robot Vision.* Ph. D. dissertation, Linköping University, Sweden, May 1995.

[24] T. Lindeberg, "Detecting salient blob-like image structures and their scales with a scale-space primal sketch: A method for focus-of-attention," *Int. J. of Computer Vision*, vol. 11, no. 3, pp. 283–318, 1993. Also ISRN KTH/NA/P--93/33--SE.

[25] R. Deriche and O. Faugeras, "Tracking line segments," in *Proc. 1st European Conference on Computer Vision* (O. Faugeras, ed.), vol. 427 of *Lecture Notes in Computer Science*, (Antibes, France), pp. 259–268, Springer Verlag, Berlin, Apr. 1990.

[26] J. L. Crowley, "Multi-modal tracking for video compression," in *Proc. IEEE Comp. Soc. Conf. on Computer Vision and Pattern Recognition, 1997*, (San Juan, Puerto Rico), IEEE Computer Society Press, June 1997. (To appear).

[27] K. Pahlavan, *Active Robot Vision and Primary Ocular Processes.* Ph. D. dissertation, Dept. of Numerical Analysis and Computing Science, KTH, Stockholm, Sweden, May 1993. ISRN KTH/NA/P--93/16--SE.

EFFICIENCY OF SIMPLE SHAPE DESCRIPTORS

M. PEURA, J. IIVARINEN
Helsinki University of Technology
Laboratory of Computer and Information Science
P.O. Box 2200 FIN-02015 HUT, Finland

Characterizing objects by their shape is a critical part in many computer vision applications. Several theoretically interesting approaches exist which, however, remain computationally too expensive. The goal of this paper is to emphasize the value of primitive shape descriptors. A set of simple descriptors is used as a feature vector in order to group similar objects together. Each descriptor is discussed separately and discriminatory power of their combination is demonstrated on irregular sample objects. The advantages of using simple shape descriptors are obvious: faster calculation and more general applicability. Sometimes "general applicability" implies poor performance in a specific application. A neural network method (Self-Organizing Map) is used in adapting a system to an application-specific shape space. The results of the experiments are good. It is shown that fairly simple shape descriptors can be flexibly used in complex recognition tasks involving irregular objects.

1 Introduction

Shape descriptors have been actively studied [7, 11] as an alternative to the approaches involving texture and colour distribution. Intuitively, using only the contour of an object instead of the whole area would imply a square-root proportional saving in calculations. This is practically true although there does not always exist analog counterparts between 1D and 2D operations. For example, one can hardly adapt textural features to contours whereas orientation of an object can be derived using either area or contour.

The underlying practical justification for the descriptors presented in this paper is the fact that a significant amount of information is contained in the contour of an object. In practical situations, variation of contours produced by 3D objects cause severe problems. Moreover, occlusion of contours due to overlapping objects may turn shape descriptors worthless. In this paper, contours of objects are assumed to be given in a representative pose. In other words, practical problems in image acquisition such as illumination and viewing angle are assumed to be solved.

Shape descriptors that use the contour of an object include the following techniques. Moment-based techniques have been used in object recognition since 1962 [4]. Moments derived from the contour of an object were used by Dubani et al. [1], and Gupta and Srinath [3]. Zahn and Roskies [12] used the

Fourier coefficients of a contour as shape descriptors. The chord distribution of a contour was proposed by Smith and Jain [10]. A scale-space technique to form a description for plane curves was proposed by Mokhtarian and Mackworth [9]. Evans et al. [2] proposed pairwise geometric histograms as shape descriptors. Iivarinen and Visa [5] proposed chain code histograms for irregular shape recognition.

We claim that one often applies too sophisticated methods in practical problems. For instance, why use Fourier descriptors unless objects really originate from a periodic process? We propose that one should hold to basic shape descriptors whenever possible. Our suggestion is based on the following simple aspects.

It is desired to find a method that is both simple and generally applicable. This truism is sometimes forgotten. For example, increasing computational resources allow us to see a planar contour of N pixels as a 2N-dimensional vector. Certainly, this does not imply that the phenomenon producing that contour be that complex.

Each descriptor should be semantically simple. It is safe to start designing descriptors by considering how human beings would describe objects. Some transformations, though motivated by mathematical properties such as reversibility, contradict this aim. Primitive descriptors such as *compactness* and *elongatedness* are revised in Sec. 2.

Combining descriptors should introduce a new perspective. It is expected that combinations of descriptors will provide new, more complex but still explicable descriptions. For example, if an object is nearly circular but not compact it must be ragged or star-like.

Some correlation between descriptors is acceptable. Clearly, descriptors are designed to detect possibly *different* properties. However, for a particular limited data set two descriptors might essentially measure the same quantity. For example, if all the contours in a data set are relatively simple and *smooth*, values of elongation and compactness will strongly correlate. On the other hand, no derived properties mentioned in above would appear if elementary descriptors were strictly orthogonal.

A general approach might need adjustment in applications. A set of measurements produces a vector, which is an instance of the current "application space". Redundancy within the elements can be removed by standard methods such as principal component analysis. We propose *Self-Organizing Map* (Sec. 3) because of its feasibility for visualization.

2 Simple shape descriptors

In this section, five simple shape descriptors are revised (Fig. 1). Variations of most of them have been widely used in object recognition [11]. The notations used here on are listed in Table 1.

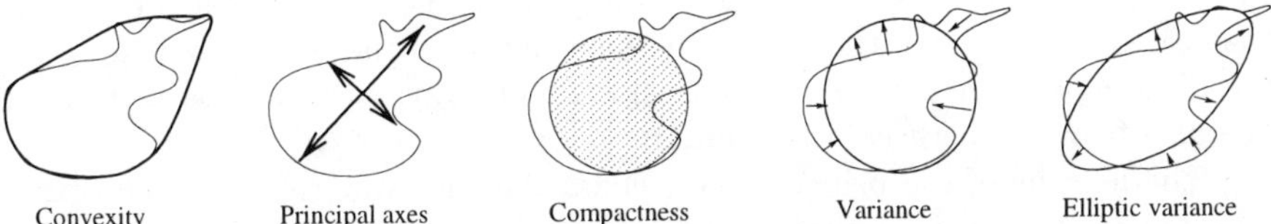

Figure 1: Five simple shape descriptors.

$\boldsymbol{p}_i = \begin{pmatrix} x_i \\ y_i \end{pmatrix}$	contour point
$\boldsymbol{p} = \{\boldsymbol{p}_i\}, i = 1 \ldots N$	contour
$\mathcal{A}$	area
$\mathcal{P}$	perimeter
$\|\|\cdot\|\|$	vector length
$\boldsymbol{\mu} = \frac{1}{N}\sum_i \boldsymbol{p}_i$	centroid
$\mu_r = \frac{1}{N}\sum_i \|\|\boldsymbol{p}_i - \boldsymbol{\mu}\|\|$	mean radius
$\boldsymbol{C} = \frac{1}{N}\sum_i (\boldsymbol{p}_i - \boldsymbol{\mu})(\boldsymbol{p}_i - \boldsymbol{\mu})^\top$	covariance matrix
λ, $\exists \boldsymbol{e} : \boldsymbol{Ce} = \lambda \boldsymbol{e}$	eigenvalue of $\boldsymbol{C}$
$\boldsymbol{e}$	eigenvector of $\boldsymbol{C}$

Table 1: Notations.

2.1 Convexity

A convex hull is the minimal convex covering of an object. It can be thought as an elastic ribbon stretched around the contour of an object. A straightforward measure for convexity can thus be defined as the ratio of perimeters of the convex hull and the original contour,

$$conv = \frac{\mathcal{P}_{convexhull}}{\mathcal{P}}. \tag{1}$$

The algorithm for constructing a convex hull involves traversing the contour and minimizing turn angle in each step. The straightforward implementation of *conv* requires $\mathcal{O}(N^2)$ calculation steps. Algorithms of linear complexity has been reported as well [8].

2.2 *Ratio of principal axes*

Principal axes of a given object can be uniquely defined as the segments of lines that cross each other orthogonally in the centroid of the object and represent the directions with zero cross-correlation. This way, a contour is seen as an instance from a statistical distribution.

The lengths of the principal axes equal the eigenvalues $\lambda_{1,2}$ of the covariance matrix $\boldsymbol{C}$ of a contour (Table 1). Let us denote the elements of $\boldsymbol{C}$ as

$$\boldsymbol{C} = \begin{pmatrix} c_{xx} & c_{xy} \\ c_{yx} & c_{yy} \end{pmatrix}. \tag{2}$$

The ratio of principal axes is a reasonable measure of elongation and can be calculated directly:

$$prax = \frac{c_{yy} + c_{xx} - \sqrt{(c_{yy} + c_{xx})^2 - 4(c_{xx}c_{yy} - c_{xy}^2)}}{c_{yy} + c_{xx} + \sqrt{(c_{yy} + c_{xx})^2 - 4(c_{xx}c_{yy} - c_{xy}^2)}}. \tag{3}$$

The calculation of actual eigenvectors $\boldsymbol{e}_{1,2}$ or eigenvalues $\lambda_{1,2}$ remain unnecessary – they could be calculated with a further effort equal to that of *prax* itself. Thus, the computational effort for *prax* is small – it requires only $\mathcal{O}(N)$ steps.

2.3 *Compactness*

Compactness is often defined as the ratio of the squared perimeter and the area of an object. It reaches the minimum $\frac{(2\pi r)^2}{\pi r^2} = 2\pi$ in a circular object and approaches infinity in thin, complex objects. The measure applied in this paper is the ratio of the perimeter of a circle with equal area as the original object and the original perimeter, i.e.,

$$comp = \frac{\mathcal{P}_{circle}}{\mathcal{P}} = \frac{2\sqrt{\mathcal{A}\pi}}{\mathcal{P}}, \; \mathcal{A}_{circle} = \mathcal{A}. \tag{4}$$

The calculation of the area $\mathcal{A}$ requires a single traversal of the contour [11]. The same applies for the contour length $\mathcal{P}$ and consequently, *comp* can be calculated in $\mathcal{O}(N)$ operations.

2.4 Circular variance

Sometimes a shape should be compared against a template. Clearly, a circle must be one of the simplest and most general possible choices. The proportional mean-squared error with respect to solid circle, or circular variance, can be defined

$$cvar = \frac{1}{N\mu_r^2}\sum_i(||\boldsymbol{p}_i - \boldsymbol{\mu}|| - \mu_r)^2. \tag{5}$$

Thus, *cvar* gives zero for a perfect circle and increases along shape complexity and elongation. *cvar* requires $\mathcal{O}(N)$ calculation steps.

2.5 Elliptic variance

Starting from *cvar*, a natural choice to increase the degrees of freedom is to allow elongation, i.e., to fit an ellipse and measure the mapping error. Intuitively, it seems logical to find an ellipse having an equal covariance matrix, $C_{ellipse} = C$. It is practically effective to apply the inverse approach yielding

$$evar = \frac{1}{N\mu_{rC}}\sum_i(\sqrt{(\boldsymbol{p}_i - \boldsymbol{\mu})^\top \boldsymbol{C}^{-1}(\boldsymbol{p}_i - \boldsymbol{\mu})} - \mu_{rC})^2, \tag{6}$$

$$\mu_{rC} = \frac{1}{N}\sum_i\sqrt{(\boldsymbol{p}_i - \boldsymbol{\mu})^\top \boldsymbol{C}^{-1}(\boldsymbol{p}_i - \boldsymbol{\mu})}$$

Despite the apparent complexity *evar* requires $\mathcal{O}(N)$ calculation steps.

3 Experiments

The shape descriptors listed in the previous section were applied to a set of irregular shapes. More specifically, a five-element *feature vector* was extracted for each sample. The sample set consisted of 79 contours originating from an industrial quality control process. The covariance matrix for the descriptors is given in Table 2.

As may be expected, *conv* and *comp* as well as *prax* and *cvar* have high covariances. On the other hand, *conv* and *prax* seem to be independent properties in involved samples. It should be noticed that the given covariance values apply only to this particular set of samples. Further considerations are presented in the discussion.

The feature vectors were further used to train the Self-Organizing Map [6]. A result is shown in Fig. 2. The consistent and continuos organization of the shapes meets the eye. Circularity dominates the lower left corner of the

	conv	*prax*	*comp*	*cvar*	*evar*
conv	100	0	83	-10	-35
prax	0	100	45	-85	-39
comp	83	45	100	-58	-63
cvar	-10	-85	-58	100	73
evar	-35	-39	-63	73	100

Table 2: Scaled covariance matrix of the descriptors applied to a sample set.

map and elongated shapes the upper right corner. Moreover, smooth contours tend to be at the left and rough ones at right hand side of the figure. The transformations between different types of shapes are smooth which in fact is an essential property of Self-Organizing Maps. The banana-like shapes should be noticed to the right of the center in Fig. 2: none of the elementary descriptors alone detects this property but their combination does.

4 Discussion

There is a direct and intuitive trade-off in developing faster and simpler feature descriptors. Many proposed shape descriptors rely on the assumption that statistical measures, no matter how cryptic they might be, produce similar values for similar objects. However, one should pay attention to possible loss of information when applying descriptors with unclear semantic meaning: a descriptor might perform many-to-one mapping, thus failing in a classification task. Counter-examples exist as well. Hu showed that an infinite set of moments can be used to reconstruct an image [4]. It is, however, difficult to find verbal descriptions for high-level moments involved.

The descriptors listed in this paper have each a comprehensible explanation and can be applied separately in practical applications. Consequently, the authors studied visually the distributions of all the 10 possible descriptor pairs. It seems probable that three or even two of the reviewed descriptors will suffice to obtain reasonable classification performance. However, this assumption applies only for this data set — the distribution of values is inevitably case-dependent.

The Self-Organizing Map is an ideal tool in exploring structure of high-dimensional data. It produces a non-linear topology-preserving mapping from a data space to the two-dimensional space. This means that the Self-Organizing Map resolves the internal dimensionality of data. For example, the contours in Fig. 2, which were ordered by SOM according to five descriptors, seem to have

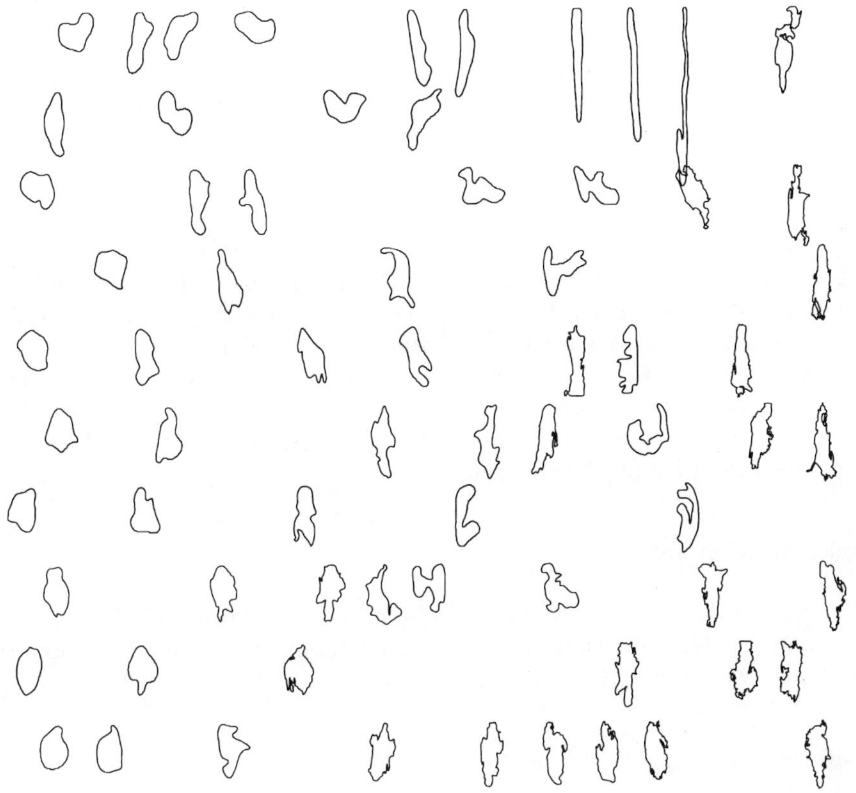

Figure 2: Sample contours on a Self-Organizing Map.

roughly three dimensions, elongation, smoothness and bending. This property is reflected also in the two remarkable covariances (*conv*,*comp*) and (*prax*,*cvar*) in Table 2.

There are many practical shortcuts that can be used to speed up the computation. For example, both $\mathcal{A}$ and $\mathcal{P}$ might have been calculated in a former stage of a process, and the computational effort for *comp* becomes negligible. The covariance matrix $\boldsymbol{C}$, which is needed in *prax* and in *evar*, has to be calculated only once. Thus, as far as calculational effort is considered, it is nearly equivalent to calculate just two or all the five descriptors. The authors recommend using all the five descriptors when little prior knowledge of applied shapes is available.

One can expect that the five descriptors apply also to more regular objects such as contours of tools or fauna. However, they might be of no use in the context of objects with loose or elastic parts such as with chromosomes, or in the context of objects with contours containing little information for recognition, as in the case of human faces.

5 Conclusions

The recognition power of five classical shape descriptors, which use only the contour of an object, was illustrated and discussed. The usefulness of the descriptors was pointed out in terms of computational effort, understandability, and cooperative power. The samples of the experiment were highly irregular, thus indicating general applicability of the discussed descriptor set. The future work involves comparing other shape descriptors to ones described here and experimenting with regular objects.

Acknowledgment

The authors wish to thank Dr. Ari Visa from Helsinki University of Technology for many helpful discussions and Mr. Juhani Rauhamaa from ABB Industry Oy for providing an interesting problem.

References

[1] S. A. Dubani, K. J. Breeding, and R. B. McGhee, "Aircraft identification by moment invariants", *IEEE Transactions on Computers*, C-26:39–46, 1977.

[2] A. C. Evans, N. A. Thacker, and J. E. W. Mayhew, "Pairwise representations of shape", In *Proceedings of the 11th IAPR International Conference on Pattern Recognition*, volume 1, pages 133–136, The Hague, The Netherlands, August 30 – September 3, 1992.

[3] L. Gupta and M. D. Srinath, "Contour sequence moments for the classification of closed planar shapes", *Pattern Recognition*, 20(3):267–272, 1987.

[4] M.-K. Hu, "Visual pattern recognition by moment invariants", *IRE Transactions on Information Theory*, IT-8:179–187, 1962.

[5] J. Iivarinen and A. Visa, "Shape recognition of irregular objects", In *Proceedings of SPIE Vol. 2904, Intelligent Robots and Computer Vision XV: Algorithms, Techniques, Active Vision, and Materials Handling*, Boston, USA, November 19-21 1996.

[6] T. Kohonen, *Self-Organizing Maps.* Springer-Verlag, 1995.

[7] S. Marshall, "Review of shape coding techniques", *Image and Vision Computing*, 7(4):281–294, November 1989.

[8] A. Melkman, "On-line construction of the convex hull of a simple polyline", *Information Processing Letters*, 25(1):11-12, 1987.

[9] F. Mokhtarian and A. Mackworth, "Scale-based description and recognition of planar curves and two-dimensional shapes", *IEEE Transactions on Pattern Analysis and Machine Intelligence*, PAMI-8(1):34–43, January 1986.

[10] S. P. Smith and A. K. Jain, "Chord distributions for shape matching", *Computer Graphics and Image Processing*, 20:259–271, 1982.

[11] M. Sonka, V. Hlavac, and R. Boyle, *Image Processing, Analysis and Machine Vision.* Chapman & Hall Computing, 1993.

[12] C. T. Zahn and R. Z. Roskies, "Fourier descriptors for plane closed curves", *IEEE Transactions on Computers*, C-21(3):269–281, March 1972.

EXTRACTING SHAPE ELEMENTS BY PERCEPTUAL PATTERN DETECTION

P. PULITI, G.TASCINI, P. ZINGARETTI
Istituto di Informatica, University of Ancona, Via Brecce Bianche , 60131 Ancona, Italy
{puliti, tascini, zinga}@inform.unian.it

The paper presents an approach to the extraction of shape elements that attempts to solve the problem of imperfect data produced by state-of-the-art edge detectors. The method reduces the transition gap in the flow of information between edge points and contours by the use of the connectivity-code intermediate representation and of saliency-enhancing operations derived from the psychology field. This intermediate representation is particularly useful in the description of those patterns that are perceived by the human with more evidence of all others and constitute singularities in contours, such as points of line cotermination. Starting from a grey level image and after a series of perceptual processes, the system detects salient contour elements, mainly lines and junctions, by processing the connectivity code patterns. By filtering these connectivity maps the "line-supports", regions with common features, that is similar connectivity codes, are extracted. Then, all pixels of a line-support are interpolated by a single line. The result supplies a good segmentation of the original grey level image and seems to constitute a very promising basis for both the focus of attention and the high-level processing.

1 Introduction

In machine vision the extraction of contours from an image is important because it provides useful information for segmenting images into meaningful regions. The usefulness of extracted contours is related to the ability of handling them by computer with enough flexibility in order to cover any shape concept, like line drawing, skeleton, or closed boundary. An approach is to extract a series of edge points belonging to a boundary: the edge points are firstly detected by sensing where pixel intensity, colour or range, changes abruptly, and then are linked into lines or contours. These edges are normally organised in contours using information present in the data themselves and a set of perceptual grouping rules which are domain independent.

Problems exist with local edge operators. They are widely known and mainly related to the possibly small spatial extent of the operator relative to the events they are designed to detect, and to the deviation of actual image data from assumed models. For example, a significant variation in edge contrast along a line due to a changing background behind an occluding surface prevents the extraction of a single line. In addition, edge maps resulting from application of a local edge detector cannot always provide perceptually meaningful lines and curves because missing, misplaced, and extraneous edges are often detected. These edge maps are also very dense and unable to distinguish among boundary edges, shadows, and reflectance and orientation changes in surface.

Related to the mandatory initial edge detection, techniques have been proposed to aggregate local information into global line-like structures after discarding unimportant or redundant information. These include Hough transform [3], that was generalised to detect nonlinear boundaries and specific shapes [1], edge tracking and contour following [9], relaxation algorithms [7], hierarchical-refinement techniques [5] and high-level model-based processes.

The Hough transform may be considered one of the most popular method that was initially developed to detect the existence of analytically defined shapes, such as lines, circles or ellipses. After computing the edge strength at each pixel, border pixels can be selected either by setting a threshold or choosing all the local maxima in the edge image [3]. The generalised Hough transform of Ballard [1] is able to detect the shape of an object with an arbitrary size and orientation, but, even if attractive, it departs from edge points and requires the complete specification of the exact shape of the target object. Therefore, the Hough transform allows the detection of objets with complex, but predetermined, shapes. In addition, the Hough transform suffers from various other problems: computational expensiveness; difficulty in selecting optimal quantization of the parameter space; inability in the proximity evaluation (that is, it does not discriminate between points belonging another straight line and noise with the same orientation); inaccuracy near junctions or parallel lines for methods based on edge orientation.

From another side, also methods for shape extraction based on perceptual grouping have some problems: they lack of an effective implementation and have the problem of combining the results when different criteria give different results.

In this paper we present a system for extracting shape elements, mainly lines and junctions, that attempts to solve the problem of imperfect data produced by state-of-the-art edge detectors. The system reduces the transition gap in the flow of information between edge points and contours by the use of the connectivity-code intermediate representation, and of saliency-enhancing operators derived from the psychology field.

To facilitate the definition of shape elements Burns et al. [2] already proposed the construction of an intermediate representation of edge/line information through which high-level interpretation mechanisms have efficient access to relevant lines. In this paper we adopt their idea of an intermediate representation. So we to do not link edge points directly into contours, but we pass through the connectivity-code intermediate representation. We also introduce low-level perceptual processing and an intermediate representation that is very useful in the description of those particular patterns that are perceived by the human with more evidence of all others and constitute singularities in contours, such as points of line cotermination.

The paper is organised as follows. In Section 2 we describe the perceptual processing operations applied both to edge points and to patterns of our intermediate representation. In Section 3 we define the connectivity code and outline the processing that leads to its computation and to the extraction of salient contour parts. Results are illustrated in Section 4 and some conclusions are reported in Section 5.

2 Perceptual Processing

The most popular form of perceptual processing is perceptual grouping [6]. The purpose of perceptual grouping is to take into account the edges that are detected and aggregate them into more perceptually meaningful structures, such as line segments. Laws of perceptual grouping, like proximity, connectivity and similarity in orientation, contrast, and intensity, may be used for linking line segments in contours.

Even if perceptual grouping implementation will depend to some degree on the size of features that are being extracted, local perceptual processing can be considered domain independent. Moreover, local processing is particularly advantageous at the early stages because it is potentially massively parallel (even if it has the disadvantage that information in a small neighbourhood is not always reliable in a more global context).

Our approach to perceptual processing is based on a series of assumptions related to a series of observations and consists in the following operations: 1) processing of contrast sensitivity based on the nonlinear response of the human eye to intensity changes; 2) processing of interactions among edges with their subsequent reinforcement or inhibition; 3) processing of patterns based on their perceived contrast.

As to the first point, it is known [10] that the adaptive ability of the human eye does not correspond to an accurate judgement of absolute brightness. The contrast sensitivity depends on the surround intensity and can be expressed by the Weber function, given by $\Delta I/I$, where ΔI is the intensity difference from the background intensity I. Even if the Weber function is nearly constant over a wide range of intensities (Weber region), the binarization of the edge maps resulting from application of a directional edge detector (e.g., Sobel) on the basis of a global threshold, fitted for the Weber region, cannot be also effective for the De Vries-Rose and saturation regions. So we binarize the edge maps by determining local thresholds on the basis of the perceptual contrast as in [11].

Psychovisual studies by Helmholtz [4] demonstrated that the human visual system attributes importance to both edges and interactions between edges. From here the hypothesis that the human perception can distinguish edges according more to their location than to their intensity. In the well known binocular experiment of

Helmholtz we have two images representing one a cross and another the texture: the resulting image cannot be constructed by a uniform combination of the two images. Helmholtz explained this process by inhibitory mechanisms and, more in general, he defined the "normal use of eyes" as the activities of selective attention and of sensation sharpening that result from a perceptive learning process. In this sense, the intention of moving eyes causes a mechanism that inhibits the scene movements producing the stability of the perceptive world, despite of the variability of the retinal images. According to this theory, each entity interacts with each other in an inhibitory way. For example, the more closely two edges stand, the more severely their intensities are weakened, and in the neighbourhood of weak edges, strong edges dominate; this domination will diminish gradually as a function of the distance from the stronger edge. To face these aspects we have implemented a second perceptual processing operator, a Helmholtzian transformation [14] that, after the detection of the stronger edges and the computation of the minimum distances of each edge pixel from these ones, applies an inhibition function, based on Helmholtz's principle of progressive inhibition, to the gradient intensity of each pixel.

The third perceptual processing operation is motivated by Walters' psychophysical experiments aiming at showing how the perceptual significance of patterns could be derived from a variation in the perceived contrast. For instance the local length of lines and the relationship between the ends of lines correlate with the differences in the perceived contrast. This may be explained by the fact that the human visual system preferentially processes these patterns by an automatic shift of attention. Another interesting aspect of her research is that parallel lines have a lower perceived contrast than single, long line segments. This fact can be explained by the perceptual organisation theory [6] which assumes the existence of a hierarchy of visual features and, consequently, the existence of many perceptually significant dimensions. Parallelism, as a more global property, could belong to a different dimension with respect to the local features that correlate with the higher perceived contrast. In this way, parallel lines, which have been successfully used in Computer Vision [8], are perceptually significant but at a stage, or a processing module, different from that of the end-connectedness. We have applied Walters' hierarchy of perceptual relevance of patterns to the modelling of the attraction field of each connectivity code, our intermediate representation, in the processing aiming at the extraction of "line-supports" (see Section 3).

3 Line and Contour Extraction

In most edge and line extraction algorithms, the magnitude of the intensity change is used in some manner as a measure of the importance of the local edge. On the contrary, edge orientation carries important information about the set of pixels that participate in the intensity variation that underlies the straight line, particularly its spatial extent. So in the construction of our intermediate representation we have considered both the local gradient magnitude (measured over a small local window) and the local gradient orientation, which will vary relatively little apart from near junctions.

Firstly an edge detection is applied to the original grey level image using directional kernels. The resulting multilevel edge maps, one for each orientation, are submitted to a multilevel thresholding in which binarization thresholds are perceptually determined on the basis of the Weber function. In practice, we have implemented a filter by which the noise components due to perceptually weak edges are partially removed. The filter evaluates the perceptual contrast in each edge-pixel on the basis of the mean intensity in its neighbourhood, and assumes four different thresholds, one for each region of the contrast curve: constant, De Vries-Rose, Weber and saturation region [11].

Then further perceptual processing relies on the application of a Helmholtzian transformation that, taking into account the distance among residual edges on binarized edge maps, attenuates or enhances gradient intensities in original multilevel edge maps [14]. In particular, the Helmholtzian transformation excites the local perceptual power of strong edges and inhibits the weaker edges near them, but, at the same time, leaves unchanged the textural pattern far from them. The goal of this module is to create a perceptual feature map by implementing inhibitory/excitatory mechanisms to outline the perceptual strength of edges. An example of excitatory interaction may be represented by the reconstruction of broken line segments, while an example of inhibitory interaction is represented by the attenuation that strong edges exert on neighbouring weak edges.

At this point the connectivity-code intermediate representation, a specialised tool to identify a neighbouring pattern, is computed by considering both multilevel and binarized edge maps [13]. The main assumption in the use of the connectivity code is that in each window there are only coded the most significant edge or junction orientations. If we use a 3x3 neighbourhood, ordered as shown in Fig. 1a, we have 2^8 possible codes with only two intensity possibilities for each neighbouring pixel: equal to or less than the intensity of the central pixel, greater than the intensity of the central pixel. In the connectivity maps, which are a representation at higher level than edge maps, each node corresponds to a different pattern of short line segments. The connectivity code emphasises local edge distributions; for example, points with parallel micro-edges have a connectivity code different from corner or crossing points. In addition, this intermediate representation limits the use of domain specific knowledge at the early stages of visual data organisation, and reduces the amount of data to be processed at higher levels. A symbolic representation of the connectivity-code patterns corresponding to the black pixels inside the shaded box of Fig. 3 is shown in Fig. 4. Here each pixel location is expanded to show pattern symbols. We can see the typical cotermination patterns and how the accumulation of different patterns near junctions fades going away.

While the connectivity codes give a good representation of the edges in the neighbourhood of each pixel, it should be noted that an algorithm for line and contour extraction based on the tracking, pixel by pixel, of these codes is destined to fail due to the presence of junctions, which break the line-code sequence, and of thick edges. Instead, the connectivity code assigned to each pixel can be regarded as the source of an attraction field; that is, each pixel generates a field in the direction where a connection with other edge pixels is more probable to occur. In addition, we reinforce these directional and local fields on the basis of Walters' hierarchy on perceived contrast [8]. Then, we extract connected regions ("line-supports") with common features, that is, similar connectivity codes, by a filtering process. Finally, all pixels of a line-support are interpolated by a single line, which will be compared and adjusted with previously extracted lines.

There are two problems in the previous procedure for line extraction. Both are due to the discrete nature of the connectivity code. Firstly, according to whether the filtering operation for the extraction of line-supports for a north-north-east line, for example, is based on one (68) or three (68, 36, 66) connectivity codes (see Fig. 1b) there may be too short or too many extracted lines, respectively. To avoid these problems the detection of quasi-vertical lines is allowed not only by the code 68, but also by all codes corresponding to orientations slightly different from the vertical: 36, 66, 72 and 132. The second problem is related to the extraction of the more accurate straight line for each detected line-support. We have analysed various solutions on the basis of a trade-off between computational costs and accuracy. In fact, an additional benefit related to the extraction of line-supports is that other aspects of the line, such as contrast and width, can be more accurately measured.

4 Results

In Fig. 5 the results of all processing steps applied to the well known "Lena" grey level image of Fig. 2 are shown. Fig. 4 represents the connectivity codes for the pixels inside the shaded box of Fig. 3, in which the black pixels correspond to points of the standard image "Lena" that have a connectivity code greater than 0. In particular, in Fig. 3 it can be noticed how the Helmholtzian transformation eliminates most of the texture edges normally present in correspondence of the ornament of the hat.

Fig. 5 shows the result of the line extraction process performed passing through the line-support detection (the sum of all line-supports gives the black pixels represented in Fig. 3) and the computation of a line for each line-support region. In particular, there were obtained 399 lines with an average length of about 20 pixels. It should also be noted that, as it could be perceivable from a screen representation, the lines in Fig. 5 preserve the intensity gradient for each pixel, so giving a greater relevance to particulars.

Finally, extracted lines could be subsequently processed to obtain longer lines. On the contrary, for the present, we have only filtered them by considering lines that have a length greater than 12. The result of this filtering are the 185 lines shown in Fig. 6, which constitute a very promising basis for focus of attention and high-level processing.

It is our opinion that further improvements of the above results are possible acting at all vision levels. In particular, a more complex inhibition function of the Helmholtzian transformation could be used, the modelling of the attraction field could integrate more psychovisual and psychophysical aspects, and the grouping of the extracted lines could be performed at a perceptually higher level, for example to obtain longer lines. A relevant aspect of our approach is that it seems very suitable for including these enhancements.

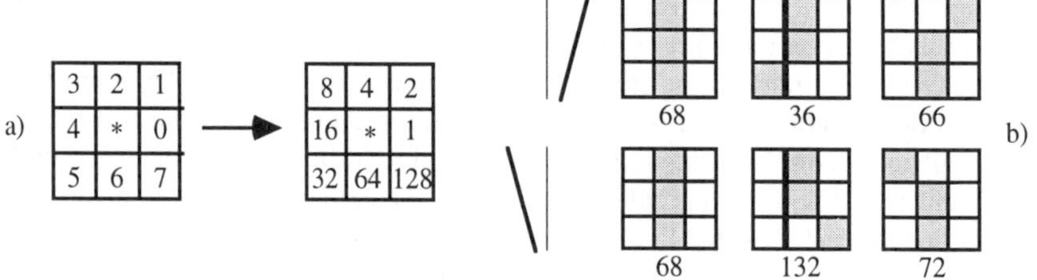

Fig. 1. Connectivity code: a) pixel order and weights, b) codes for quasi-vertical segments.

Fig. 2. The standard grey level image "Lena".

Fig. 3. Line-supports for image "Lena".

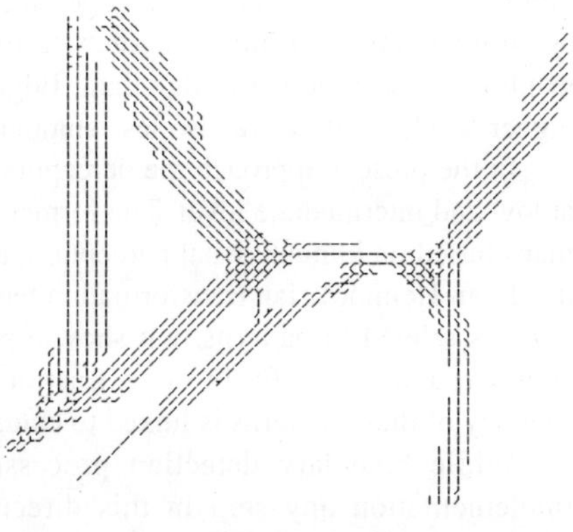

Fig. 4. Connectivity codes for the pixels inside the shaded box of Fig. 3.

Fig. 5. Lines extracted from image "Lena".

Fig. 6. Lines longer than 12 pixels.

5 Conclusions

Edges can be considered at different levels in the visual hierarchy: at low level as pixels which are treated independently and as unrelated in a computed edge map; at intermediate level as connected edge pixels lying on the same segment; at high level as components of primitives, such as line or curve segments, used in generating symbolic descriptions of edge data. Edges at low level are less stable than ones at higher level, but they are also less computationally expensive.

In the present approach the perceptual processing of edges has been applied both at low and intermediate level. The former concerns an automatic thresholding of edge maps based on human visual perception, and the reinforcement or inhibition of edges due to an Helmholtzian transformation based on neighbourhood edge processing. The latter is related to patterns that show a perceptual relevance, in terms of perceived contrast, and are useful in the extraction of salient contour parts. In particular, the saliency of these patterns is linked to cotermination shapes.

While boundary detection processes suffer from the lack of an effective implementation any step in this direction is actually important. Our approach attempts to introduce a generally implementable manner for contour elements which is based on a perceptual extraction of shape elements, that is, line segments and polylines. In particular, our strategy of forming an intermediate representation to facilitate the definition of shape elements avoids the use of domain specific knowledge at the early stages of visual data organisation, allows the localisation of attention on perceptually salient elements, and reduces the amount of data to be processed at higher levels.

In conclusion, the method presented in this paper, starting from a grey level image and after a series of perceptual processes, first allows to extract connectivity-code patterns and then to detect salient contour elements. The results, like those presented in Figg. 5 and 6, supply a good segmentation of the original grey level image and seem to constitute a very promising basis for both focus of attention and high-level processing.

References

[1] D.H. Ballard, "Generalizing the Hough transform to detect arbitrary shapes", *Pattern Recognition*, vol. 13, n. 2, pp. 111-122, 1981.

[2] J.B. Burns, A.R. Hanson, E.M. Riseman, "Extracting straight lines", *IEEE Trans. on PAMI*, vol. 8, n. 4, pp. 425-455, 1986.

[3] R.O. Duda, P.E. Hart, "Use of the Hough transformation to detect lines and curves in picture", *Comm. ACM*, vol. 15, n. 1, pp. 11-15, 1972.

[4] H. Helmholtz, *Treatise on Physiological Optics: The Perceptions of Vision*, vol. III (J. Southall, Ed.), The Optical Society of America, 1925.

[5] T.H. Hong, M. Shneier, R.L. Hartley, A. Rosenfeld, "Using pyramids to detect good continuation", *IEEE Trans. on Systems, Mans and Cybernetics*, vol. 13, n. 4, pp. 631-635, 1983.

[6] D.G. Lowe, *Perceptual Organization and Visual Recognition*, Kluwer Academic, Boston, 1986.

[7] J. Matas, J. Kittler, "Junction detection using probabilistic relaxation", *Image and Vision Computing*, vol. 11, n. 4, pp. 197-202, 1993.

[8] R. Mohan, R. Nevatia, "Perceptual Organization for Scene Segmentation and Description", *IEEE Trans. PAMI*, vol. 14, n. 6, pp. 616-635, 1992.

[9] R. Nevatia, K. Babu, "Linear feature extraction and description", *Computer Graphics and Image Processing*, vol. 13, pp. 257-269, 1980.

[10] W.K. Pratt, *Digital Image Processing*, Wiley, New York, pp. 21-43, 1991.

[11] D.C. Tseng, M.Y. Huang, "Automatic thresholding based on human visual perception", *Image and Vision Computing*, vol. 11, n. 9, pp. 539-548, 1993.

[12] D. Walters, "Selection of Image Primitives for General-Purpose Visual Processing", *Computer Vision and Image Processing*, vol. 37, pp. 261-298, 1987.

[13] P. Zingaretti, A. Carbonaro, G. Tascini, "Modelli di interazione percettiva tra feature", *V Convegno AI*IA*, Atti del gruppo di lavoro Percezione, Napoli, 1996.

[14] P. Zingaretti, F. Marchegiani, P. Puliti, "Perceptually motivated model generation for template matching", in *Machine learning and perception*, Tascini, Esposito, Roberto, Zingaretti eds, World Scientific, Singapore, vol. 23, pp. 125-134, 1996.

SKELETONIZATION METHOD FOR AUTOMATED MYOCARDIAL SPECT QUANTIFICATION

D. SCELLIER
ERIM,centre J.Perrin,Médecine Nucléaire,BP 392, 63011 Clermont-Ferrand Cedex.France. E-mail:didier.scellier@cjp.u-clermont.fr

Z. AKTOUF
ESIEE,labo PSI,cité Descartes,BP 99, 93162 Noisy-Le-Grand Cedex.France. E-mail:aktoufz@esiee.fr

J.Y. BOIRE
ERIM,rue Montalembert,BP 184, 63005 Clermont-Ferrand Cedex.France. E-mail:j-yves.boire@cjp.u-clermont1.fr

G. BERTRAND
ESIEE,labo PSI,cité Descartes,BP 99, 93162 Noisy-Le-Grand Cedex.France. E-mail:bertrang@esiee.fr

J. MAUBLANT
ERIM,centre J.Perrin,Médecine Nucléaire,BP 392, 63011 Clermont-Ferrand Cedex.France. E-mail:jean.maublant@cjp.u-clermont.fr

We have previously described a new method to automatically detect and quantitate the myocardial distribution of a radiotracer in Single Photon Emission Computed Tomography (SPECT) lying on the application of skeletonization process [1]. This method is based on the fitting of the morphological skeleton of the left ventricle to a truncated bullet model. When the skeleton is interrupted by one or several defects related to a cardiac disease, these defects are filled according to the theoretical model. After completion, a fuzzy logic algorithm is applied using the skeleton (quench function) to generate a functional image representing the *degree of belonging to the myocardium* for each pixel. Being displayed with a higher contrast than on the original scintigraphic image, the myocardium can be much easily segmented, allowing an automatic quantification of its activity. In this paper, we will present a new method of skeletonization which has the originality to be 2D and 3D topology preserving in order to fit with the 3D theoretical model of the myocardium and the fuzzy algorithm which is applied in the 2D space.

1 Introduction

Single Photon Emission Computed Tomography (SPECT) of the left ventricular (LV) myocardium provides a 3D-image of the injected radiotracer distribution, which mostly reflects myocardial blood flow. Usually, the reconstructed transverse sections are automatically reoriented in order to display the LV in a standard orientation (Fig. 1). Areas with decreased uptake correspond either to ischemia (if hypoactive) or infarction (if defects). It is important for the diagnosis to be able to recognize their size, location and depth. Quantifying the activity implies to involve the entire myocardium which includes the normal areas as well as those with a low level of activity. We have developed an automatic method which can deal with this difficulty and in which the skeleton of the LV is used. The normal myocardial areas are extracted by segmentation with a fixed threshold at 50% of the maximum within the object. The level of this threshold ($\pm 5\%$) has no really effect on the resulting skeleton. Then the defects within the skeleton are filled in conformity with a truncated bullet model. The completed skeleton is associated with a fuzzy logic algorithm to generate a functional image with a high contrast and no apparent defect which provides a mask for segmentation of the entire myocardium. To locate and quantify the relative distribution of activity, the selected myocardium is partitioned into 18 sectors [2].

The paper is organized as follow: in the next section, we will briefly describe the general method for the automated SPECT quantification of the myocardium. Then, we will discuss the choice and the advantages of our new skeletonization method which we present more formally in the following section. Finally, we will compare the results obtained from our method and the Lantuejoul 3D skeleton.

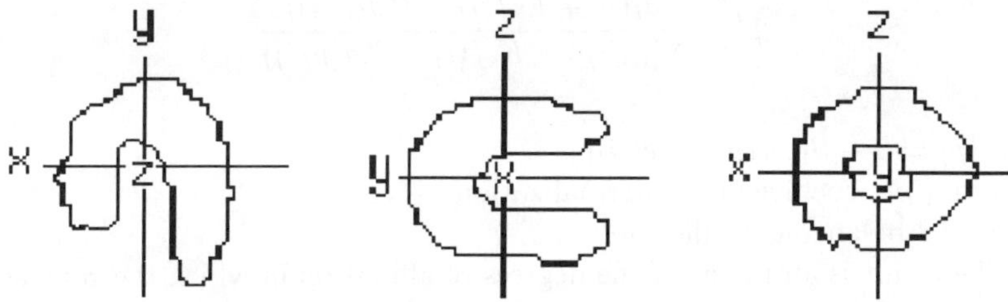

Figure 1: Outlines of a normal reoriented left ventricle on orthogonal sections

2 General requirements for a suited skeleton

Once it has been obtained, the skeleton must fulfill a number of requirements in order to allow the processing to proceed.

1)The skeleton should have the same general shape than the LV myocardium and it should preserve the homotopy.

2)In case of defects, the skeleton is necessarily discontinuous. The missing segments are filled in conformity with the theoretical model of a truncated bullet [3]. The truncated bullet is an oriented ellipsoid of revolution. The cylinder is truncated using a statistical model from normal data base. The distance mapping for each skeleton points is used in the cost function, so as to give more weight to the points of the skeleton close to the defects.
3)Fuzzy logic is introduced to process ambiguous areas in the 3D-object. In myocardial SPECT, these areas are represented by the hypoactive pixels which activity is between normal and defect values. Instead of defining each pixel i as belonging or not belonging to object X (binary logic case), i is set with a value belonging to the $[0, 1]$ interval (fuzzy logic case), which defines his *degree of belonging* to the object X [4]. The skeleton and the edge of the frame could be used like the object X because their degree of belonging are respectively equal to 1 and 0.

To compute the degree of belonging to the myocardium, from each point, beams are thrown in the eight discrete directions. Four input data are considered: activity level at fuzzy point ($act(p)$), activity level at no fuzzy point ($act(i)$), distance between fuzzy point 'p' and no fuzzy point 'i' ($d(p/i)$), and value of the distance mapping at skeleton point ($f(i)$).

The association of this four data gives the degree of belonging for each fuzzy point(see [1]).

$$\mu' = \frac{\mu_i(p) + K.f(i) - P.d(p/i))}{\sum(\mu_i(p) + K.f(i) - P.d(p/i))} \tag{1}$$

with :

$\mu_i(p) = \alpha - \beta|act(p) - act(i)|$

α and β : coefficients of normalization

K, P : balancing coefficients

The result is an image of the degrees of affiliation in which the contrast is increased and the apparent level of activity of the defects is attenuated. local thresholds applied to this image provides the binary LV.

3 Resulting requirement

The algorithm is applied on a set of 2D images. The 3D object is obtained with the superposition of this set. The skeletonization method must be better a three-dimensional method:
1)The theoretical model is define in the three-dimensional space.
2)With 2D skeletonization methods, little branches ("barbule") appear on the skeleton and generates a morphologic incompatibility between the skeleton and

the true myocardium aspect (Fig. 2). These branches are not really "barbule" because it is the logical result of a 2D LV thinning. Fuzzy segmentation algorithm assumes that the skeleton is morphological like the initial object. All skeletonization process applied in 2D do not permit to consider the object in its supposed shape. Therefore, to preserve the three-dimensional morphology of the myocardium, a three-dimensional process must be used to thin the LV.

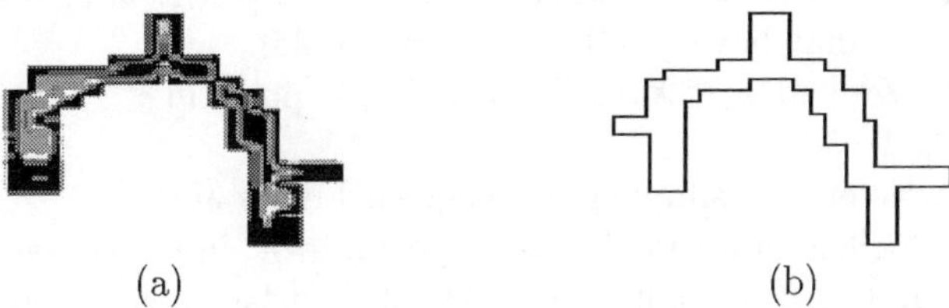

(a) (b)

Figure 2: 2D skeletons obtained from the distance mapping (a), and an homotopic thinning method (b).

The skeleton is obtained, and fitting to a model as described in the part 2. The added points in conformity with the theoretical model are set to 1 (for defects localization). The fuzzy algorithm must be only applied to a connected skeleton. The skeleton must be connected in the 2D space, because the degree of affiliation is calculated by measuring the discrete distance separating the considered point and the skeleton point on the nearest side. A disconnection in the skeleton generates distance errors. This problem seems to be solved when the skeleton is filled in conformity with its bullet model. But added points are sets to one (to locate defects), and an unconnected area instead of a normal area generates false degree of belonging to the myocardium for the points near to this area.

Therefore,the skeletonization process must also preserve the 2D topology.

4 Skeletonization method : Description

The myocardium skeleton is computed in order to have a 3D surface representing the organ. The skeletonization process consists in removing points without modifying the topology of the image. Such points are called *simple points.*

In 3D, in order to check if a point is simple or not, we use the caracterisation based upon the topological numbers[5]. To give the definition of these numbers, we need to introduce the following notations:

-$N_n(x)$ stands for the n-neighborhood of x. We denote $N_n^*(x) = N_n(x) \setminus \{x\}$.

-Let $X \subset \mathbf{Z^3}$, we denote $X_n^x = N_n^* \cap X$.

-The set of all n-connected components of X is denoted $C_n(X)$.
-The set of all n-connected components of X adjacent to x is denoted $C_n^x(X)$.

The topological numbers relative to $X \subset \mathbf{Z^3}$ and $x \in X$ are the two numbers:
$T_6(x, X) = \#C_6^x(X_{18}^x)$ and $T_{26}(x, X) = \#C_{26}^x(X_{26}^x)$

If we use the n-connectivity for X and the $\overline{n}$-connectivity for $\overline{X}$, $T_n(x, X)$ and $T_{\overline{n}}(x, \overline{X})$ are considered for describing the topological characteristics of the point x. We may have $(n, \overline{n})$=(26, 6) or (6, 26).

Let $X \subset \mathbf{Z^3}$ and $x \in X$, x is an n-simple point iff : $T_n(x, X) = 1$ and $T_{\overline{n}}(x, \overline{X}) = 1$.

An example of a 26-simple point is given Figure 3(a).

The topological numbers play an important role in the characterization of curve points and surface points[6]. For example, surface points may be detected with $T \geq 2$ as shown figure 3(b) using the 26-connectivity for X. Since a skeleton of an object consists on curves and surfaces, the topological numbers are also used to detect the end points during a skeletonization process.

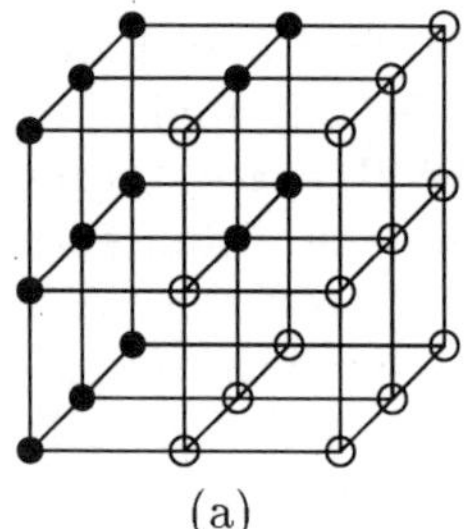

(a)

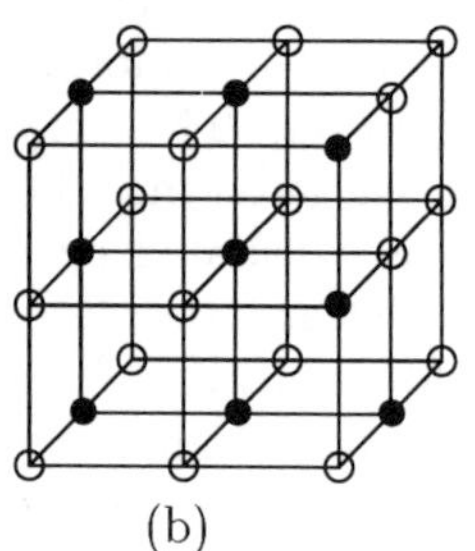

(b)

Figure 3: Examples of neighborhoods : The points of X are represented by full circles and the points of $\overline{X}$ by empty circles.

A classical 3D skeletonization algorithm does not preserve the 2D topology. In fact:

1) It may remove all the points of a 2D slice if they are all simple in the 3D case: On Fig 6, we can see that the slices numbered 26, 27, 28, 40 and 41 are empty while in the original image (Fig 5) these slices contain points which are set to 1.

2) It may increase the number of connected components in a 2D slice: On Fig 4, we represent a 3D object and its surface skeleton. The original object is composed by horizontal slices containing one connected component whereas some horizontal slices of the 3D surface skeleton are composed by two connected components.

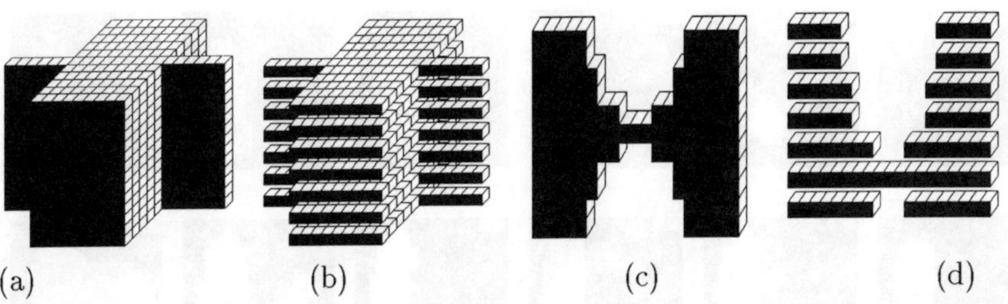

Figure 4: (a) : A 3D-image. (b) : Some 2D slices of (a). (c) : Surface skeleton of (a). (d) : some 2D slices of (c).

To apply the fuzzy algorithm, a 3D skeleton, also connected in the 2D case is needed. For this purpose, we have implemented a parallel thinning algorithm which allows the preservation of the 3D as well as the 2D topological properties of the binary image. It computes the 3D skeleton of the myocardium and keeps the connectivity unchanged at each slice of the organ.

The algorithm we used is based upon the strategy of subfield [7] : The cubic grid is divided into 8 subfieds which are activated sequentially. The points belonging to the same subfield are suppressed in parallel if they are simple in both the 2D and the 3D case. To obtain a 3D-surface skeleton, we keep the points which appear as surface and curve points. The result of this algorithm is shown on Fig. 7 in which we can see that the 2D topology is preserved.

5 RESULTS

Our skeletonization algorithm is applied to the automatic myocardial SPECT quantification program and compared with the 3D Lantuejoul skeleton used in [3] which does not preserve the 2D topology.

The final 3D binary LV obtained by superposition of 2D slices treated with the fuzzy logic approach is finally partitioned into 18 sectors. The spatially corresponding mean activity inside each sector is expressed in percentage of the sector with maximal activity [2]. The sectors with a value higher than 80% were usually considered as normal, whereas those lower than 60% as a defect, and the remaining as hypoactive. Programs have been applied to three patients, one patient without defect, one patient with an hypoactive area, and one patient with a large defect. The difference between the two methods is measured as described in [8] and shown on Fig 8. For all patients, most of the sectors are well classified. For the patient without defect, there is no mean lower than 80%, for patient with an hypoactive area, no mean is lower than 60%, and for the patient

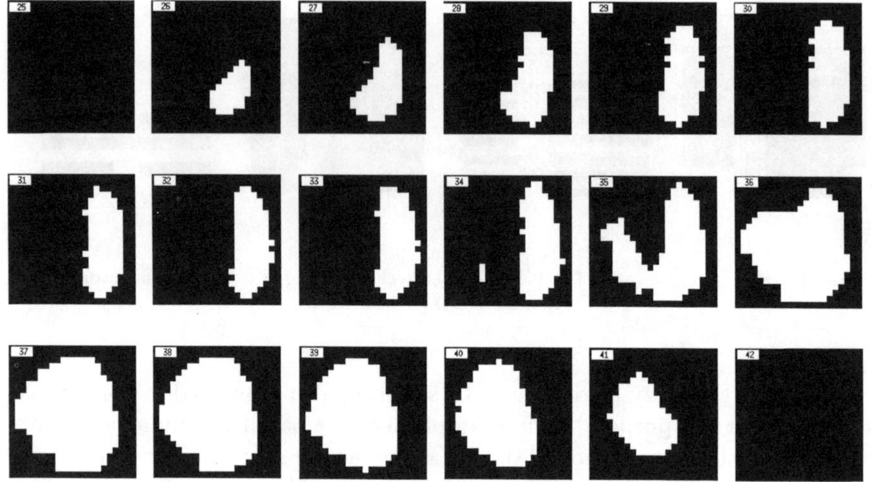

Figure 5: Original image of the myocardium.

with a defect area, the distribution is largely spread, well below 60%. There is no contradiction between the two methods for a global classification. When we consider the difference between the means, we see that the Lantuejoul method overestimates the sectorial activity for the patients without defect, and with an hypoactive area. For the patient with a large defect, the Lantuejoul method underestimates the sectorial activity. When looking at the final results of the quantification program, our new approach of skeletonization provided mean values which are more accurate than the Lantuejoul algorithm with regard to the visual interpretation from clinical expert.

6 CONCLUSION

When a skeletonization method does not preserve the 2D topology, for a normal patient, or a patient with hypoactive area, points have to be added in normal parts of the skeleton. When that skeleton is used in view of a fuzzy logic algorithm, these points alter the calculation of the degree of belonging. The result is a poorly completed binary left ventricle. A 3D method is necessary to preserve the 3D aspect of the LV. A fuzzy logic algorithm applied to the 3D space was developed, but the execution time was too long (17min in 3D versus 4min in 2D on Sophy NXT from SNVI industry). A 3D skeletonization method which preserves the 2D topology was presented. It solves all problems

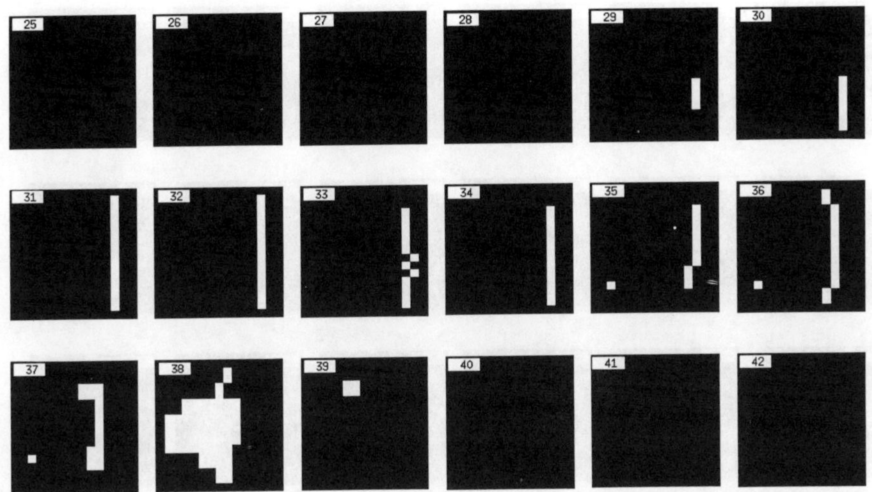

Figure 6: 3D-surface skeleton of the myocardium using the subfield method.

presented in the first part. This method developed for our application could be used for all applications in which it is necessary to use a 2D and 3D object.

References

1. D. Scellier, J.Y. Boire, J. Maublant, and A. Veyre. Fuzzy logic for the segmentation of myocardial tomoscintigraphic images. *18th Annual International Conference of the IEEE Engineering in Medecine and Bioology Society*, Oct-Nov 1996.
2. D. Scellier, J. Maublant, J.Y. Boire, F. Jousse, J.C. Cauvin, and A. Veyre. Quantification automatique et analyse sectorielle d'images temp pour la localisation des zones pathologiques du myocarde. *XXXIVe Colloque de médecine nucléaire de langue française Monté-Carlo*, 19, No7/9:415, Oct-Nov 1995.
3. J.C. Cauvin, J.Y. Boire, J. Maublant, J.M. Bonny, M. Zanca, and A. Veyre. Automatic detection of the left ventricular myocardium long axis and center in thallium-201 single photon emission computed tomography. *Eur. J. Nucl. Med.,*, 19:1032–1037, December 1992.
4. P. Fauroux, J.P. Fillard, and A. Artus. A new approach to fuzzy partition for image segmentation. In *Proceeding of the annual international protocol conference of the IEEE engineering in medecine and biology so-*

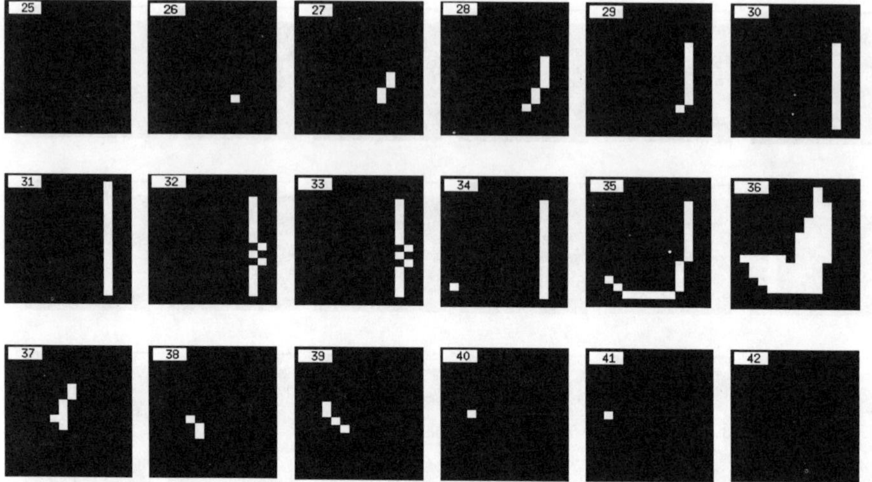

Figure 7: Surface skeleton of the myocardium using the subfield method preserving the 2D and the 3D topology.

ciety, volume 14, part 5 to 7, pages 1922–1923, Oct-Nov 1992.

5. G. Bertrand and G. Malandain. A new characterization of 3d simple points. *Pattern Recognition Letter*, 15:169–175, 1994.
6. G. Bertrand and G. Malandain. A new topological classification of points in 3d images. *Proc. European Conf. on Computer Vision*, pages 710–714, 1992.
7. G. Bertrand and Z. Aktouf. A 3d thinning algorithm using subfields. *Proc. SPIE Conf. on Vision Geometry III*, 2356(2):113–124, 1994.
8. M.J. Bland and D.G. Altman. Statistical methods for assessing agreement between two methods of clinical measurement. *The Lancet*, pages 307–310, February 1986.

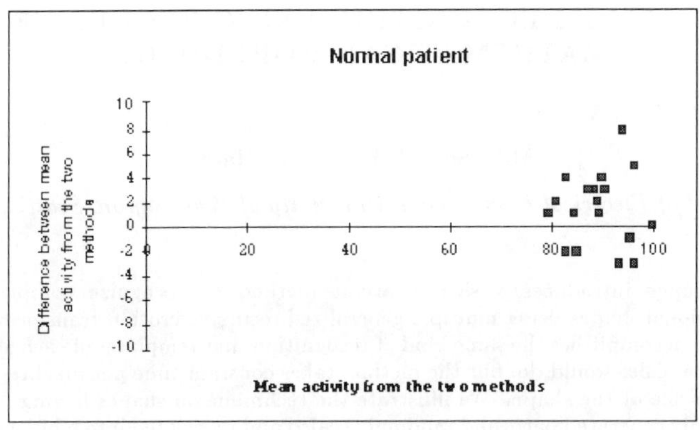

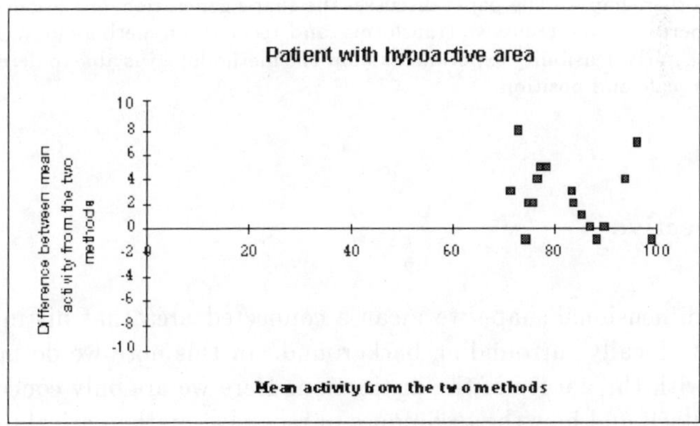

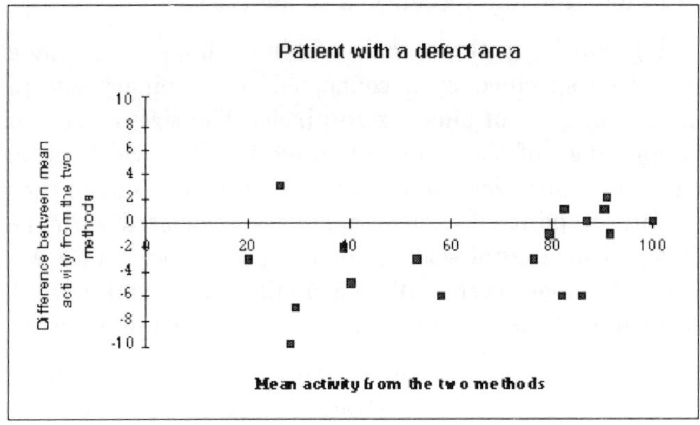

Figure 8: Difference against mean between the two methods.

SHAPE RECOGNITION USING RECURSIVE MATHEMATICAL MORPHOLOGY

Mike Schauf, Robert M. Haralick

Department of Electrical Engineering, University of Washington, Seattle, WA 98195

This paper introduces a size invariant method to recognize complex two-dimensional shapes using multiple generalized recursive erosion transforms. The method accomplishes the same kind of recognition that templates of each shape at multiple scales would do, but the method takes constant time per pixel regardless of the scale of the shape. We illustrate the technique on shapes having multiple randomly generated parts and randomly scaled and translated into a binary image having other shapes. The paper discusses the shape generation, image generation, image perturbation, recursive transforms, and recognition methodology. Results from the initial feasibility experiments show the methodology is able to detect each model's scale and position.

1 Perspective

By a two-dimensional shape we mean a connected area that distinguishes itself from its locally surrounding background. In this note we do not concern ourselves with the nature of the distinction. Here we are only concerned with the shape itself and how the techniques of recursive mathematical morphology can be used to describe and recognize a shape class.

Our setting will be in the domain of binary images. A shape prototype description will be specified by a connected set of binary one pixels and a spatially surrounding set of binary zero pixels. The size of the prototype will be in the high range of the scales of interest. The width of the spatially surrounding set of binary zero pixels is considered to be one of the parameters of the shape prototype itself. The shape class associated with the prototype will be the set of all digital scalings of the prototype. Since we are in the domain of digital images, there will be a smallest scale and it will be the scale for which the thinnest part of the shape is at least two pixels wide.

A shape prototype consists of primitive shape parts translated and rotated with respect to one another and constrained so that the resulting shape prototype is a connected set. The primitives used in the feasibility study reported here consist of circles, rectangles, triangles, sectors, lines, and parallelograms.

2 Recursive Erosion Transform

The erosion of an image A by a structuring element B is the set of all translated origins of the structuring element B where B can be wholly placed in A. The definition of erosion is defined below

The erosion of A by a structuring element B is denoted by $A \ominus B$ and is defined

$$A \ominus B = \{x \in E^n \mid \cap_{b \in B} A_{-b}\}$$

As an example take the image and structuring element in Fig. 1

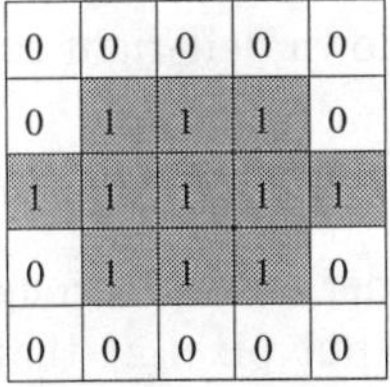

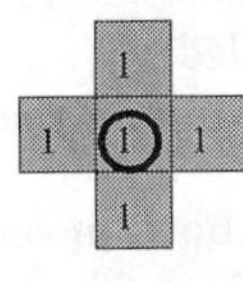

Figure 1: On the left is the binary image and on the right is a cross-shaped structuring element.

The positions where the cross-shaped structuring element can be wholly placed in the image can be seen in Fig. 2 and the resulted erosion is seen in Fig. 3.

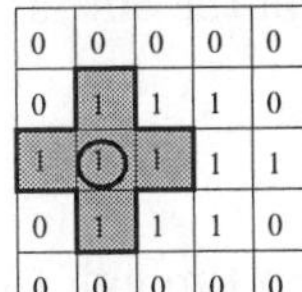

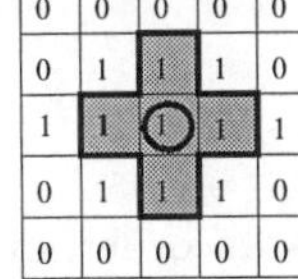

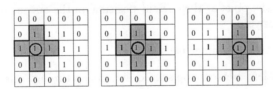

Figure 2: The structuring element can be wholly covered in the three locations shown.

The erosion transform is found by eroding the image and each erosion result by the structuring element B over and over again ($A \ominus B \ominus B \ldots$) until nothing is left in the result. The number of times a pixel 1 value remains at a coordinate in each erosion result is the value for that coordinate in the erosion transform.

Rather than do the erosions over and over again and count the number of times a pixel appears in the result, recursive morphology simplifies the erosion transform into two passes. First the structuring element is broken into two

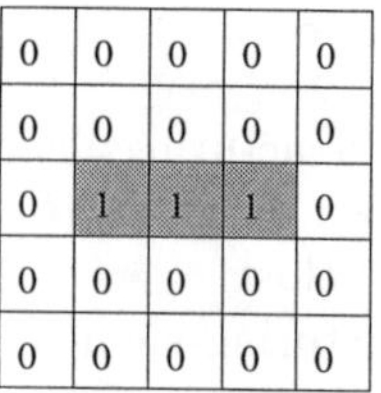

Figure 3: The resulting erosion.

parts, that is before the origin in top-down, left-right scan order, called y, and that which is after, called z.

The algorithm for finding the erosion transform is listed as follows.

1. In left-right, top-bottom scan order, sweep through the input image. If a pixel value of 0, define the output pixel at that position to have the value 0. If a pixel has a value of 1 than do the following.
   - translate the structuring element y to the current position on the output image
   - find the values of the output image pixels for each of the locations in the translated structuring element y
   - select the minimum of the values and add 1
   - give the pixel at the current position on the output image this minimum value
2. Call the resulting image G
3. In a right-left, bottom-top scan order, sweep through the image G.
   - translate the structuring element z to the current position on the output image
   - find the values of the pixels of G for each of the locations in the translated structuring element and add 1
   - find the value of G at the current position
   - place in the current position of G the minimum value of all the values

Fig. 4 shows the first pass and second pass result of the erosion transform using the image and structuring element in Fig. 1.

0	0	0	0	0
0	1	1	1	0
1	2	2	2	1
0	1	2	3	0
0	0	0	0	0

0	0	0	0	0
0	1	1	1	0
1	2	2	2	1
0	1	1	1	0
0	0	0	0	0

Figure 4: On the left is the first pass of the image in Fig. 1 using the cross structuring element and on the right is the second pass and final erosion transform result.

3 Methodology

The scale invariance recognition is based on the following idea: the erosion transform of any scale of a shape prototype will result in a scaled version of the original erosion transform. For example if we were to scale a shape prototype to half size, the erosion transform of the scaled shape will result in a same shaped erosion transform as the original but half the size and the maximum value of the erosion transform will be half that of the original. And proceeding away from the location of the maximum value, the values of the erosion transform will ramp down in the same way as in the original. The key to using the erosion transform for recognition is the fact the position of the scaled original maximum transform value from the center of the model is the scale of the maximum original transform value.

For an example, Fig. 5 is a possible result of an erosion transform of two scaled models. The larger is the outline of the erosion transform of the model and the smaller is the outline of the erosion transform of the model scaled by .5. An X marks the maximum value position of both transforms. As can be seen the global maximum of the original transform is twice that of the scaled transform and the positions also have the same scale.

Using structuring elements that span all directions results in different transforms and can provide information about each of the different shape classes.

One problem with this methodology is the need for a preprocessing noise removal step. This is because any perturbation of the image will result in changes in the erosion transform. The changes could be very large, for example if the perturbation introduces a hole in the middle of a shape. Since the maximum values are mostly in the middle of the erosion transform, noise on the outside of the model will have just a slight effect on the positions and values. But if the maximum is on the edge of the model, it likely will be

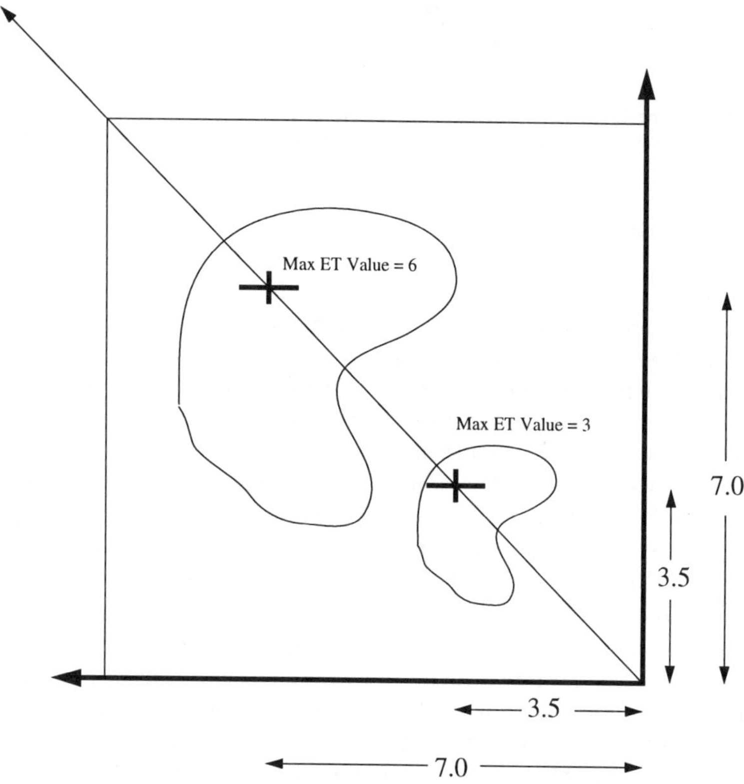

Figure 5: In this figure the shape prototype is the larger of the two objects and its maximum ET value is marked with a cross. The center of the shape prototype is at the origin. The smaller shape is a .5 scaled version of the shape prototype with its center also at the origin. It can be seen that the result from scaling is that the max ET value in the scaled model ET is also scaled .5 and it's coordinates are also scaled by .5.

affected. Fig. 6 and Fig. 7 shows an example of this. In Fig. 7 it can be seen that the maximum erosion transform value is different resulting from just two added pixels.

0	0	0	0	0
0	1	1	1	0
1	1	1	1	1
0	1	1	1	0
0	0	0	0	0

0	0	1	0	0
0	1	1	1	0
1	1	1	1	1
0	1	1	1	0
0	0	1	0	0

Figure 6: The figure on the left is the image from Fig 1. The central figure is the image from Fig. 1. with a pixel of noise added above and below.

0	0	0	0	0
0	1	1	1	0
1	2	2	2	1
0	1	1	1	0
0	0	0	0	0

0	0	1	0	0
0	1	2	1	0
1	2	3	2	1
0	1	2	1	0
0	0	1	0	0

Figure 7: The figure on the left is the erosion of the image from Fig 1 without noise. On the right is the erosion transform of the image with added noise.

To account for these possibilities, the algorithm was formed to include the case of this happening. It was decided that matching scales had to be within one of the scale candidate, and the position of the maximum had to be within five pixel places of the scaled maximum pixel position.

3.1 Algorithm

The algorithm for shape detection has an offline and an online part. The offline part consists of doing the following for each of the shape prototypes:

1. Calculate the recursive erosion transform of the shape prototype using the first structuring element.
2. Mask the first primitive with the model and select the maximum values.
3. Run a connected components on the results of step 2 and select the coordinate that is the center of all the maximum pixel positions.

4. Record in the training data the center position of the masked maximum transform value relative to the center of the model along with the maximum value.

5. Repeat steps 2 through 5 for every primitive in the model.

6. Calculate the recursive erosion transform of the first model using all the other structuring elements and repeat steps 2 through 6.

The offline part produces the training data for the recognition stage. The traning data consists of the x and y coordinates of the central maximum pixel location relative to the center of the shape prototype and the maximum value of the erosion transform.

The online recognition algorithm consists of the following steps.

1. Starting with the image's erosion transform from the first structuring element, find the maximum value and select the first position in the image that has that maximum value in left-right top-down raster scan order.

2. To find a scale candidate, divide the maximum value in the image erosion transform by the maximum value found in the erosition transform of the first shape prototype.

3. Find the model's center candidate by subtracting the scaled coordinates of the maximum transform value in the shape prototype from the position of the maximum erosion transform value in the image.

4. Now with a possible center and scale of the model, check to see if indeed the scaled shape prototype exists by going to each scaled position where the masked erosion transform value was at a maximum for each primitive and calculate the scale. If the scale for each position is the same as the candidate scale, then with respect to the structuring element, we can hypothesize that a scaled version of the shape prototype exits centered at the location.

5. Keeping the center candidate and scale candidate, repeat step 5 using the image erosion transforms for the rest of the structuring elements and the training data of the first shape prototype with each respective structuring element.

6. If there are a sufficient number of times for which we cannot reject the hypothesis that the shape matches we assert the hypothesis of a shape

match and record its scale and position. Then we determine the bounding box for the scaled shape prototype and use it to mask out all those pixels in the bounding box.

7. If there are not a sufficient number of times for which we cannot reject the hypothesis that the shape matches, steps 3 through 7 are repeated for the next shape prototype.

8. Finally repeat the entire process on the remainder of the image.

The algorithm is based on the fact that the maximum value in the image erosion transform must be a scale of the maximum value of the erosion transform of one of the shape prototypes. This is so because of the characteristic of the erosion transform and the fact that the scaled shapes on the image do not touch. Knowing this we can divide the maximum value in the image erosion transform by the maximum value in each shape prototype's erosion transform to get candidates for scale. With scale we can now calculate the center of the scaled model since the position of the maximum value is just the scale of the position of the maximum value of the shape prototype. Then we check to see if the shape class does exist there by going out to each scaled maximum masked position and checking if it has the same scale there as the scale just calculated.

4 Testing and Results

Testing the feasibility of the method requires the generation of primitives, shape prototypes, and images of perturbed scaled and translated shape prototypes. This is described in the following sections.

4.1 Shape Generation

A shape prototype is composed of a set of primitives. Each primitive is mildly constrained so that its digital image bears a reasonable resemblance to the continuous primitive ideal. The line primitives must be at least five pixel wide and at least five pixels long. The triangles and parallelograms must have vertex angles greater than 30 degrees and each side must be at least 30 pixels long. The circles and sectors must have a radius of at least 30 pixels long and the sector must have an angle greater than 30 degrees. Finally the sides of rectangles must be at least 30 pixels long.

The shape prototype is constrained so that the set of its constituting primitives form a connected set with the overlap constrained to between each pair of connecting primitives constrained to be less than 5%. Overlap between a pair of connecting primitives is measured as the area of the union of the primitives divided by the sum of the areas of the primitives.

4.2 Image Generation

Image generation requires scaling the shape prototypes and randomly placing them in the image so that they do not overlap with any other shape already in the image. For this feasibility study, the image size is 512 by 512 and the scales are randomly generated between .33 and 1.

4.3 Image Perturbation

1. For each foreground pixel, f_i, compute the pixel's distance from the nearest background pixel. Let this distance be $d(f_i)$.

2. For each background pixel, b_i, compute the pixel's distance from the nearest foreground pixel. Let this distance be $d(b_i)$.

3. For each foreground pixel, compute the probability of switching to a background pixel,

$$P(0|d(f_i), foreground, c_0, \alpha_0, \alpha) = c_0 + \alpha_0 e^{-\alpha d^2(f_i)}$$

   Generate a random number between 0 and 1 and flip the pixel to a background pixel (0) depending on whether the random number is lower or higher than the pixel-switching probability.

4. For each background pixel, compute the probability of switching to a foreground pixel,

$$P(1|d(b_i), background, c_0, \beta_0, \beta) = c_0 + \beta_0 e^{-\beta d^2(b_i)}$$

   Generate a random number between 0 and 1 and flip the pixel to a foreground pixel (1) depending on whether the random number is lower or higher than the pixel-switching probability.

5. Perform a morphological closing of the resultant image with a disk structuring element of diameter $stElSize$. This introduces a correlation amongst neighboring pixels.

4.4 Feasibility Test

It was decided that there would be four different models each 256 by 256. Each model consisted of randomly generated primitives placed at random positions, making sure each was slightly overlapped to another. Than with four different models, four different images were generated randomly placing the four different models in the image at randomly generated scales between .3 and 1. Training data was obtained from the models and images and later the software was run on each of the images.

Fig 8 shows the four different models generated and Figures 9, 10, 11, and 12 show the four generated images.

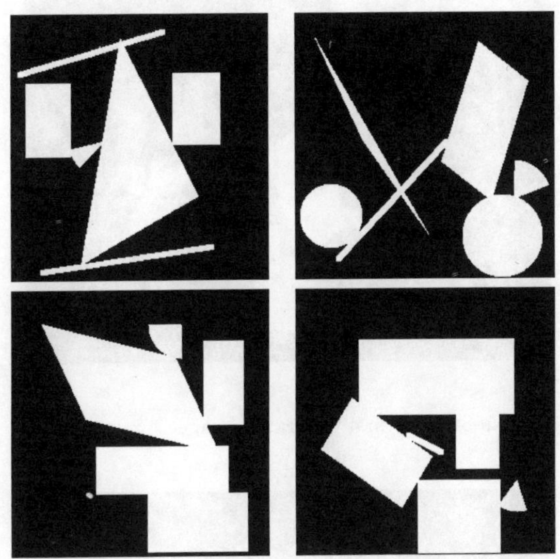

Figure 8: The four randomly generated models for testing

Fig. 13 shows the 14 different structuring elements.

The erosion transform of model one and image one with the eleventh structuring element is shown in Fig. 2.

We ran two experiments in which each there were 14 different noise perturbations of each image. The results of the experiments are summarized in Tables 1-5.

5 Further Work

The reported study is only a feasibility study. To refine the method for operational use would require a proper statistical treatment of the estimation and scale and the way in which the matching takes place. We discuss this in the next subsection. Also, it would be reasonable to use the locally surrounding binary 0 pixels of each shape prototype in the same way that the binary 1 pix-

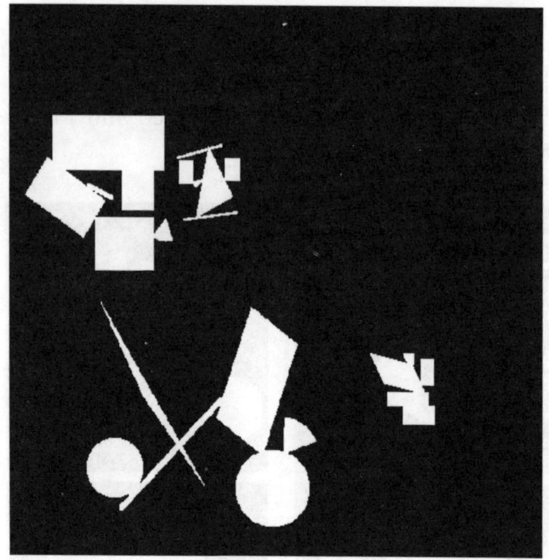

Figure 9: The first generated image

Figure 10: The second generated image

Figure 11: The third generated image

Figure 12: The fourth generated image

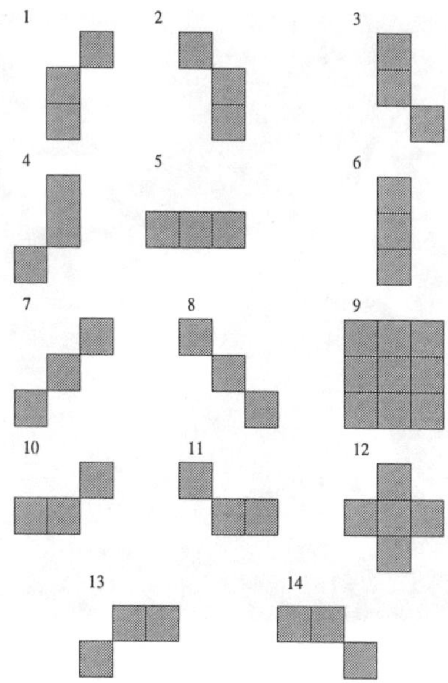

Figure 13: The 14 different structuring elements used for the erosion transforms

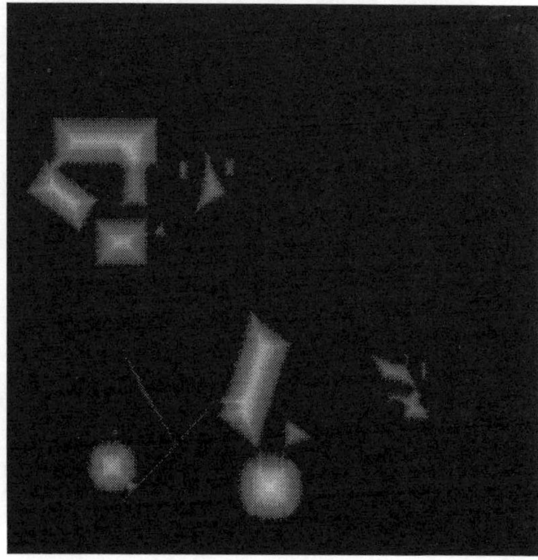

Figure 14: Erosion transform of the first image by the eleventh structuring element

Table 1: Recognition Results from Ideal Images

Image 1

Model	Position (r,c)	Scale
Model 1	(127.36, 160.00)	0.31
Model 2	(276.86, 74.71)	0.90
Model 3	(321.24, 346.21)	0.31
Model 4	(102.93, 15.21)	0.70

Image 2

Model	Position (r,c)	Scale
Model 1	(92.00, 307.46)	0.92
Model 2	(32.58, 133.50)	0.55
Model 3	(186.85, 86.92)	0.85
Model 4	no model	

Image 3

Model	Position (r,c)	Scale
Model 1	(91.86, 42.93)	0.77
Model 2	(309.08, 19.15)	0.65
Model 3	(183.00, 216.21)	0.85
Model 4	(13.00, 287.43)	0.45

Image 4

Model	Position (r,c)	Scale
Model 1	(57.23, 351.54)	0.40
Model 2	(108.43, 75.86)	0.87
Model 3	(328.00, 185.25)	0.46
Model 4	(313.71, 19.79)	0.45

Table 2: Recognition Results from Degraded Images

Image 1

Model	Position (r,c)	Scale
Model 1	(127.00, 160.00)	0.31
Model 2	(276.64, 74.50)	0.90
Model 3	(321.33, 346.67)	0.30
Model 4	(102.67, 15.60)	0.70

Image 2

Model	Position (r,c)	Scale
Model 1	(91.71, 306.71)	0.93
Model 2	(32.29, 132.93)	0.55
Model 3	(187.00, 86.50)	0.83
Model 4	no model	

Image 3

Model	Position (r,c)	Scale
Model 1	(92.14, 43.86)	0.76
Model 2	(308.92, 18.92)	0.65
Model 3	(183.14, 216.43)	0.85
Model 4	(13.08, 287.46)	0.45

Image 4

Model	Position (r,c)	Scale
Model 1	(57.23, 351.62)	0.40
Model 2	(108.36, 75.86)	0.87
Model 3	(327.83, 185.16)	0.46
Model 4	(313.45, 19.79)	0.45

Table 3: Ground Truth Image Data

Image 1

Model	**Position (r,c)**	Scale
Model 1	(129, 161)	0.30
Model 2	(276, 74)	0.90
Model 3	(322, 347)	0.30
Model 4	(103, 15)	0.70

Image 2

Model	Position (r,c)	Scale
Model 1	(91, 306)	0.93
Model 2	(33, 134)	0.54
Model 3	(187,86)	0.83
Model 4	no model	

Image 3

Model	Position (r,c)	Scale
Model 1	(91, 44)	0.76
Model 2	(310, 20)	0.64
Model 3	(183, 216)	0.85
Model 4	(13, 287)	0.82

Image 4

Model	Position (r,c)	Scale
Model 1	(58, 352)	0.39
Model 2	(107, 75)	0.87
Model 3	(329, 186)	0.45
Model 4	(314, 21)	0.44

Table 4: Shape Recognition Statistics for the Degraded Images

Image 1

Model	Cor Det	False Alarm	Mis Det
Model 1	14	0	0
Model 2	14	0	0
Model 3	14	0	0
Model 4	14	0	0

Image 2

Model	Cor Det	False Alarm	Mis Det
Model 1	13	0	1
Model 2	12	0	2
Model 3	13	0	1
Model 4	no model		

Image 3

Model	Cor Det	False Alarm	Mis Det
Model 1	14	0	0
Model 2	13	0	1
Model 3	14	0	0
Model 4	14	0	0

Image 4

Model	Cor Det	False Alarm	Mis Det
Model 1	13	0	1
Model 2	14	0	0
Model 3	12	0	2
Model 4	14	0	0

Table 5: Shape Recognition Statistics for the Degraded Images

Image 1

Models	Cor Det	False Alarm	Mis Det
Model 1	10	0	4
Model 2	14	0	0
Model 3	3	0	11
Model 4	10	0	4

Image 2

Models	Cor Det	False Alarm	Mis Det
Model 1	14	0	0
Model 2	14	0	0
Model 3	14	0	0
Model 4	no model		

Image 3

Models	Cor Det	False Alarm	Mis Det
Model 1	14	0	0
Model 2	13	0	1
Model 3	14	0	0
Model 4	13	0	1

Image 4

Models	Cor Det	False Alarm	Mis Det
Model 1	13	0	1
Model 2	14	0	0
Model 3	12	0	2
Model 4	11	0	3

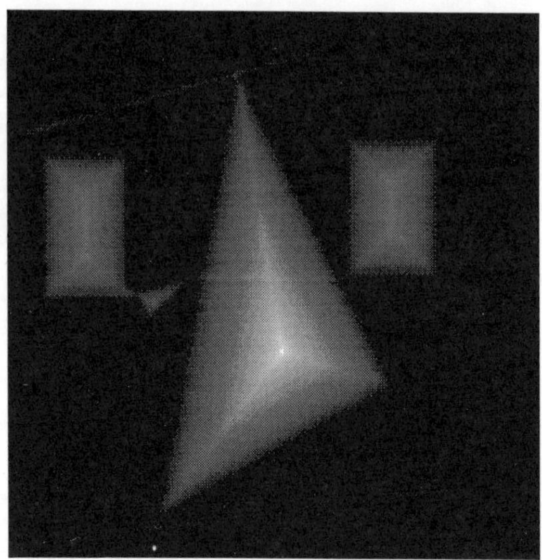

Figure 15: Erosion transform of the first shape prototype by the eleventh structuring element.

els are used. Both these improvements would undoubtedly change the results reported from being close to perfect to being very close to perfect.

5.1 Scale Estimation

Let $\mu_1, \ldots, \mu_N$ be a fixed ordering of the 3×1 mean position-maximum-value vectors and $\Sigma_1, \ldots, \Sigma_N$ be the covariances of a given shape prototype. The first two components of each μ are the row column coordinates of a maxima of an erosion transform and the third component is the value of the maxima. The row column coordinates are specified with respect to the origin of the shape prototype. The ordering is determined by a fixed rule associated with the shape prototype and depends on the position of the maxima and from which structuring element the maxima comes about.

Let $x_1, \ldots, x_N$ be the same fixed ordering resulting from a noisy observation of a scaling of the shape prototype. Let s be the unknown scale parameter. We model the noisy observations the following way:

$$x_n = s\mu_n + \psi_n$$

where ψ_n has a Normal$(0,\Sigma_n)$ distribution and ψ_m is independent of ψ_n for $m \neq n$.

To estimate the value for s, we find that value which maximizes $P(s \mid x_1, \ldots, x_N)$. This is equivalent to obtaining an s that minimizes

$$\sum_{n=1}^{N}(x_n - s\mu)'\Sigma^{-1}(x_n - s\mu) - 2logP(s)$$

We take the prior probability $P(s)$ to be Normal(μ, σ^2).
In this case, we seek the s that minimizes

$$\sum_{n=1}^{N}(x_n - s\mu)'\Sigma^{-1}(x_n - s\mu) + (s-\mu)^2/\sigma^2$$

Differentiating with respect to s, collecting terms together and solving for s results in

$$s = \frac{A + \mu/\sigma^2}{B + 1/\sigma^2}$$

where

$$A = \sum_{n=1}^{N} \mu'\Sigma^{-1}x_n$$

$$B = \sum_{n=1}^{N} \mu'\Sigma^{-1}\mu$$

6 Conclusion

The feasibility study has four steps consisting of shape prototype generation, image generation, image perturbation, and recognition. The insight of the entire method was the use of the recursively computed erosion transform knowing that the erosion transform of a scaled model has a maximum erosion transform value and position proportional to the maximum erosion transform and position of the original shape prototype. And that proportion is the scale. Testing this methodology resulted in correctly detected position and scales of four different shape prototypes randomly placed in 4 images.

1. Haralick, Robert, (1991) Computer & Robot Vision, Vol. 1, Chapter 5 "Mathematical Morphology." Addison Wesley, New York.
2. Kanungo, Tapas, (1995) DDM Users Manual, University of Washington, Seattle, WA.

ACTIVE SHAPE FOCUSING

J.A. SCHNABEL[a], S.R. ARRIDGE[b]
Department of Computer Science, University College London, Gower Street, London WC1E 6BT, United Kingdom

In this work a new hierarchical tool for shape description is presented, combining geometric differential image invariants in scale-space, and active contour models. This tool allows to perform quantitative and qualitative shape studies at multiple levels of image detail, exploring the *scale* or image resolution as an extra degree of freedom. Using scale-space continuity, the global object shape can be detected at a coarse or low level of image detail (corresponding to high image scales), and finer shape characteristics are localized at higher levels of detail (corresponding to low image scales). A new method named *active shape focusing* has been developed for the extraction of shapes at a large set of scales using an active contour model whose energy function is regularized with respect to scale and geometric differential image invariants. The resulting set of shapes is formulated as a *hierarchical shape stack* which is evaluated and described for each scale level with a large set of shape descriptors in order to obtain and analyse shape changes across scales. We demonstrate the applicability of the technique with a set of fractal images at different levels of fractal resolution.

Keywords: Shape analysis, hierarchical shape stack, scale-space, fractals, focusing, active contour models.

1 Introduction

Multi-scale techniques in shape extraction and analysis have recently attracted much interest [1,2], as they allow to investigate shape characteristics at multiple scales rather than at a single scale, thus exploring the extra scale degree of freedom. This scheme allows to extract global shape characteristics from blurred versions of a shape, and to localize finer details in lower scale versions. Multi-scale image segmentation integrates image scale-space information into this process, ranging from *edge focusing*[3] over a *hyperstack* technique based on heuristic root labelling of image scale-spaces [4] to *level-set evolution* processes based on implicit formulations of iso-intensity image curves [5].

The technique for *active shape focusing* presented in this work combines image data driven approaches with multi-scale contour representation and description techniques. Using the concept of active contour models [6], scale-space continuity is applied in order to extract and describe shapes at a large set of

[a] J.Schnabel@cs.ucl.ac.uk
[b] S.Arridge@cs.ucl.ac.uk

scales. Additionally, local geometric image invariants in scale-space [7] are incorporated into the model, leading to robust shape regularization with respect to scale and underlying geometric image structure.

The remaining paper is organized as follows: First, we briefly review the concepts of multi-scale techniques, fractals and active contour models. Then we present the technique for active shape focusing and its application to a fractal structure of known shape and dimension in order to demonstrate the applicability of this method to various shape metrics across scales, and discuss the results.

1.1 Multi-Scale Image Processing

The concept of scale-space as introduced by Witkin [1] is a means to obtain a hierarchical signal description in form of *finger prints.* Mokhtarian and Mackworth [2] have extended this approach by introducing the *curvature scale space* of shapes, leading to a hierarchical shape representation based on points of inflexion across scales. However, these multi-scale shape-based techniques operate on binary shapes, making a prior shape extraction necessary and possibly dependent on the scale used for the initial shape extraction.

Multi-scale segmentation techniques, e.g. using *edge-focusing* as developed by Bergholm [3], enable to extract a shape robustly by finding a coarse estimate at low levels of image detail, which is then subsequently refined for increasing levels of detail. However, only the shape obtained at the lowest scale level is taken as the segmentation result, while the implicit segmentation results obtained at intermediate and higher levels of image scale are discarded.

Local image structure can be revealed by convolution $\otimes$ of the image luminance function $L(\mathbf{x})$ with the Gaussian kernel $G(\mathbf{x};\sigma)$,

$$G(\mathbf{x};\sigma) = \frac{1}{(2\pi\sigma^2)^{n/2}} e^{\frac{-\mathbf{x}^2}{2\sigma^2}} , \tag{1}$$

where σ is the scale or width of the scaling operator. A thus constructed continuous scale-space $L(\mathbf{x};\sigma) = G(\mathbf{x};\sigma) \otimes L(\mathbf{x})$ enables local image analysis in a robust way, while at the same time global features are captured through the extra scale degree of freedom. An improved description uses higher order multi-scale differential invariants [7]. For the purpose of this work, we concentrate on the notion of edges in terms of the smoothed image gradient L_w, the ridges of that gradient magnitude, denoted by $R(L_w^2)$, and the curvature of the smoothed image isophotes (contours of constant grey levels) which is given by $-L_{vv}/L_w$. These terms are here expressed in a local gauge coordinate system (v, w), where v points along the tangential direction of the image isophotes,

Figure 1: Different fractal resolution levels of the von Koch curve or *snowflake*, with a fractal dimension of $\log 4/\log 3 \approx 1.2618$. For each fractal scale step, a triangular *island* of side length $l/3$, l being the side length of the previous step, is connected to each side.

and w expresses the image gradient direction, being normal to the isophotes. For vanishing gradients, the $-L_{vv}/L_w$ operator becomes numerically unstable, so lower limits to the partial derivatives need to be set [8]. In 2D, the isophote image curvature is thus computed by

$$-\frac{L_{vv}}{L_w} = \frac{(L_x+\epsilon)^2 L_{yy} + (L_y+\epsilon)^2 L_{xx} - 2L_x L_y L_{xy}}{((L_x+\epsilon)^2 + (L_y+\epsilon)^2)^{3/2}}\,, \tag{2}$$

where ϵ is a stabilizer. For $\epsilon = 1$ and low values of L_x and L_y, this expression approaches the Laplacian $\Delta L = L_{xx} + L_{yy}$.

1.2 Fractal Shapes

A related topic to scale-space representations is Mandelbrot's [9] fractal theory which introduces the mathematical description of scale-invariant, self-similar structures, and the relationship between measured quantity (e.g. perimeter, area or volume) and the scale in which that quantity is measured. This relationship is characterized by a scalar called *fractal dimension*, which can be found by measuring the perimeter of the fractal structure with different *yardsticks* scaled down by a ratio ς to obtain measurements of scaled subsets of the fractal structure, each being identical to the overall structure in all aspects. The fractal dimension D is then given by the relation $P(\varsigma) = \frac{1}{\varsigma^D}$. An example of such a structure is the von Koch curve or *snowflake*, which is constructed by repeatedly replacing the sides of the curve by scaled versions of itself. The initiator for generation step $n = 0$ and the subsequent generations are shown in figure 1.

1.3 Active Contour Models

Active contour models, originally presented by Kass, Witkin and Terzopoulos [6], are a powerful model-based segmentation tool combining geometry and physics with approximation and estimation theory. The parameterized contour model $\mathbf{v}(s)$ is constrained by internal and external forces via an associated energy functional:

$$\mathcal{E}(\mathbf{v}(s)) = \mathcal{S}(\mathbf{v}(s)) + \mathcal{P}(\mathbf{v}(s)) = \int_0^1 S(\mathbf{v}(s))ds + \int_0^1 P(\mathbf{v}(s))ds \quad (3)$$

The internal energy $\mathcal{S}$ controls the autonomous shape of the contour in terms of its elasticity $\mathbf{v}_s(s)$ and bending $\mathbf{v}_{ss}(s)$, whereas the external term $\mathcal{P}$ attracts the contour to image features like edges. Typically, the negative squared gradient magnitude $-L_w^2$ is chosen as the feature potential. The deformation of the model is handled as an energy minimization process, e.g. using variational calculus [6]. In the following, we present our technique for active shape focusing based on a modified, scale-based active contour model.

2 Active Shape Focusing

We have developed a modified active contour model which provides a matching mechanism between the internal contour curvature and the underlying curvature of the image isophotes [10]. This mechanism enables the extraction of highly curved and convoluted shapes. Additionally, the model is attracted to the image intensity gradient magnitude, and a distance transform of the gradient magnitude ridges R_D creates an additional attraction potential. We use a B-spline parameterization, which is normally only used for the final contour interpolation, for a continuous optimization of the chosen energy functional:

$$\begin{aligned} \mathcal{E}(\mathbf{v}(s)) \; = \; & \int_0^1 \alpha_1 \|\mathbf{v}_s(s)\|^2 ds + \int_0^1 \alpha_2 \left\| \mathbf{v}_{ss}(s) \pm \frac{L_{vv}}{L_w} \right\|^2 ds \mp \\ & \int_0^1 \alpha_3 L_w^2 \left(\frac{\nabla L}{L_w} \cdot \mathbf{n}(s) \right)^m ds \mp \int_0^1 \alpha_4 R_D^2(L_w) \left(\frac{\nabla L}{L_w} \cdot \mathbf{n}(s) \right)^m ds \end{aligned} \quad (4)$$

The sign of the isophote image curvature (term 2), the gradient magnitude potential (term 3) and the ridge potential (term 4) depend on the chosen spline normal direction $\mathbf{n}(s)$ and the image contrast, and terms 3 and 4 are weighted with the alignment of the gradient direction with the spline normal direction. Optimization is carried out using a modified, non-sequential *Greedy* algorithm, originally developed by Williams and Shah [11]. The choice of the fixed weighting parameters α_i (with $\alpha_1 = 0.00001$, $\alpha_2 = 1$, $\alpha_3 = 1$, and $\alpha_4 = 0.1$) reflects that the main emphasis of the energy potential lies in the curvature matching and the attraction to the gradient magnitude for robust shape extraction, with a slightly lower attraction to the associated ridge potential due to its higher steepness. An adaptive resampling technique, eliminating redundant points and inserting points if needed, allows for a very low elasticity influence.

We have found that fixing the weighting parameters $\alpha_i(s)$ to constant terms α_i does not restrict the performance of this model. The elasticity influence, which is also implicitly defined by the spline representation, becomes automatically larger if the spline control points shift together at finer scales during the resampling process, thus preventing the formation of uncontrolled discontinuities. However, corners and curvature discontinuities of the image isophotes can still be reliably detected by this model due to the adjustment of the curvature properties of the model to the underlying isophote characteristics. The model is very robust towards noise and initialization due to the scale-space approach, as slowly focusing the model down prevents the tracking of spurious edges and noise, locking to the global shape outline at a high scale.

The active shape focusing process is performed as a series of implicit shape extractions or regularizations with respect to scale. Starting at a high initial scale, an initial circular or ellipse-shaped estimate is optimized using the presented active contour model. Choosing the following scale sampling schedule,

$$\sigma_i = \sigma_0 f_\sigma^i \qquad \text{with} \qquad f_\sigma = \left(\frac{\sigma_{n-1}}{\sigma_0}\right) , \tag{5}$$

f_σ being the scale change factor, the shape is subsequently regularized for lower levels of image scale, using the resulting shape of the previous, next higher scale level as an initial estimate, forming a hierarchical shape stack with n entries [12]. As for high scales, only few contour points are needed for a coarse approximation of the shape, with an increasing number of necessary points when the shape becomes more complex at increasing levels of detail, a similar sampling schedule for the contour resolution in terms of the distance between the contour points was chosen. This also reflects the increasing confidence in the *locality* [5] of the shape, while continuously adjusting the contour resolution to the underlying image resolution.

Having thus obtained a multi-scale, hierarchical shape stack, we can evaluate the shapes at all levels σ_i in terms of global and local shape metrics to derive shape changes across scales.

3 Results and Discussion

We have applied our technique for active shape focusing to the von Koch curve as a true fractal structure (figure 1). The resulting shape stacks have been triangulated and surface rendered using the Visualization Toolkit [13] (figure 2). The results for global shape measurements across scales are shown in figure 3.

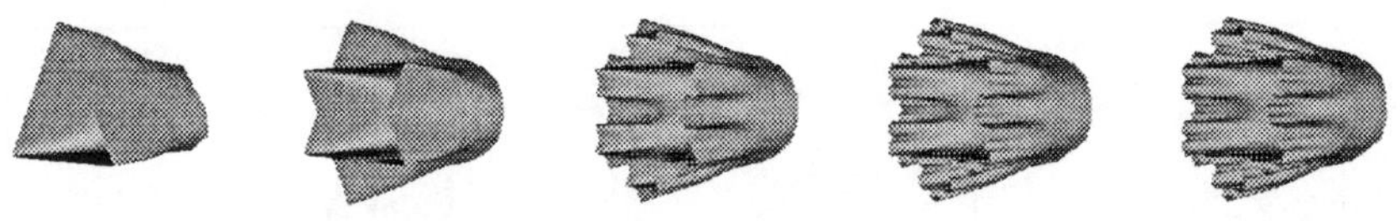

Figure 2: Rendered hierarchical shape stacks obtained by the active shape focusing technique of the images in figure 1 (for fractal generations $n = 0..4$).

The shape area, perimeter and compactness all increase for decreasing scales to compensate for the shrinking caused by the smoothing process[14] and because of the increasing complexity of the objects. The ranking of the metrics in terms of their size corresponds to the fractal resolution of the objects. It should be noted, however, that the limited image resolution causes problems when detecting structures of higher fractal generation, leading to an underestimation of area and perimeter at lower scales. This is especially obvious when noticing the slight drop in area in figure 3 for some of the curves at the lowest image scale.

Since smaller details are introduced for higher fractal generations, the distance between the metrics decreases for increasing generations. All distance measurements show a decreasing deviation of the shape from the reference shape for decreasing scales. However, since the Hausdorff distance[15] measures rather the worst than the average mismatch, this metric leads to a discontinuous shape metric with respect to scale. The Chamfer distance[16] measures the distance to the *closest* rather than the *corresponding* contour points only. Hence the order of the size of these distance measures does not correspond to the order of the fractal generations or fractal resolution levels, which could have been expected when looking at the other global quantifiers. The triangulated distance, defined via triangulating the reference shape with each of the higher scale shapes and measuring the distances of the minimum edge-length vertices, seems to be a more applicable shape distance measurement in this respect because it minimizes over all connecting vertex distances.

This effect can also be observed when mapping the local, pointwise distance metrics (figure 4). The curvature mapping (also shown in figure 4) shows an increase of curvature over scale for convoluted parts of the fractal shapes, which allows to visually perceive the increasing complexity of the fractal shapes for increasing fractal generations. Colour animations of these results are available on the World Wide Web[c].

[c]URL: `http://www.cs.ucl.ac.uk/staff/J.Schnabel/conferences/iwvf3/`

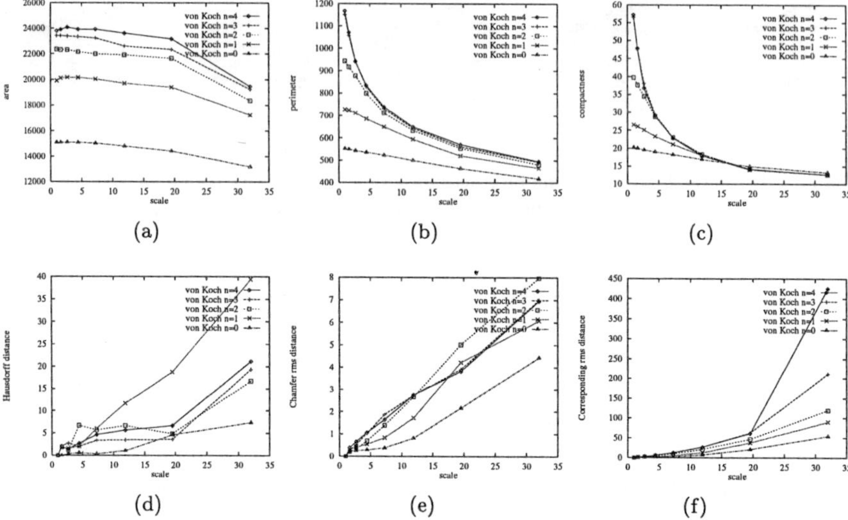

Figure 3: Global shape measurements for the von Koch curve across scales: (a) Area. (b) Perimeter. (c) Compactness. (d) Hausdorff distance. (e) Root-mean-squared Chamfer distance. (f) Triangulated distance. Distance metrics are relative to the reference shape.

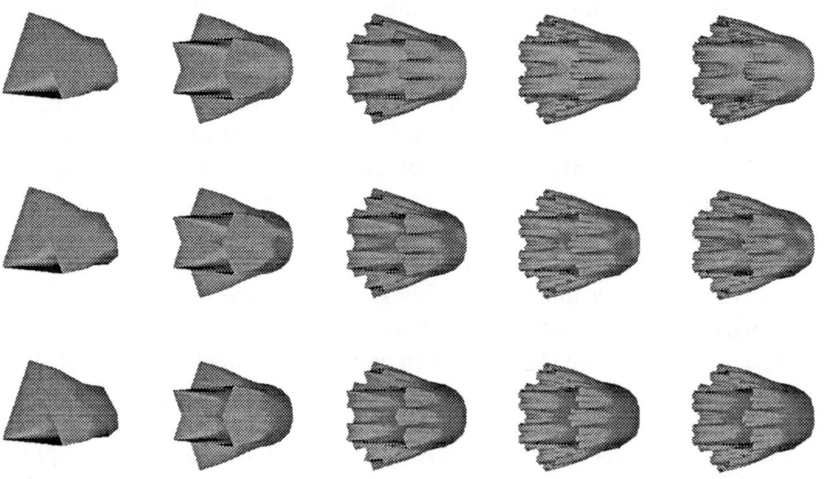

Figure 4: Grey-scale mapped local shape descriptors, from top to bottom: curvature, root-mean-squared Chamfer distance, and triangulated distance, for increasing levels of fractal generations (from left to right).

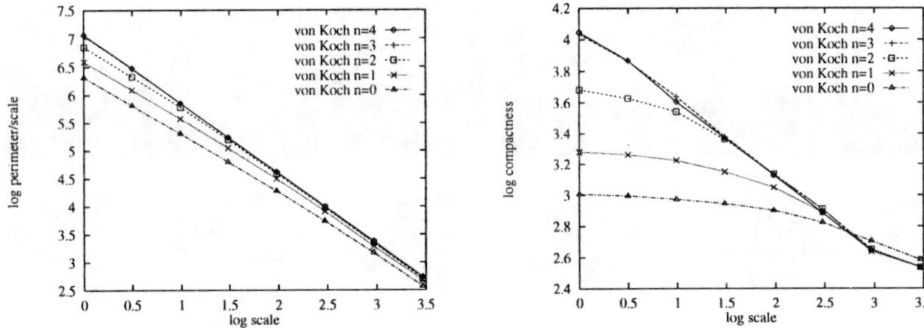

Figure 5: Log-log plot of the scaled perimeter against scale (left) and for the compactness against scale (right) for the von Koch curve.

Figure 3 indicates that there is deeper, fractal relationship between perimeter and scale, given the exponential increase of perimeter for decreasing scales. Investigating this in a log-log plot for the scaled perimeter against the image scale at which the perimeter measurement has been obtained (figure 5) shows a true linear relationship for the higher fractal generation curves, while for lower fractal generations this linear relationship only holds at higher scales. This is because the fractal curves do not have any additional structure below their internal fractal resolution, thus below the image scale corresponding to the respective fractal scale (side length of the constructing triangle), the increase of the perimeter is only controlled by compensating for the shrinking caused by smoothing, and not by focusing to a more detailed structure. The measurement of the negative slope s_p can be obtained by performing a linear regression and estimating the slope within the appropriate range of *fractal* scales:

$$\log(p(\sigma_i)/\sigma_i) = -s_p * \log(\sigma_i) + \log(const) \ , \qquad (6)$$

recovering the fractal dimension with an estimate of $s_p = 1.25$ (the true fractal dimension being $log(4)/log(3) \approx 1.26$) for all fractal resolution levels. Another interesting relationship can be found in the log-log plot of the dimensionless compactness (defined as perimeter^2/area) against scale (figure 5), allowing to estimate a negative slope of $s_c = 0.46$ in the respective range of fractal scales for all curves. Both quantities will need to be further investigated in terms of their relationship to the known fractal dimension of the curves at zero scale, the limited image resolution (*partial pixel effect*), the shrinking effect due to smoothing, and appropriate distance measures and metrics in scale-space. Additionally, the obtained shape metrics need to be put into relation with existing theoretical expressions of perimeter and area (and hence compactness) for derivatives of planar curves with respect to scale[14].

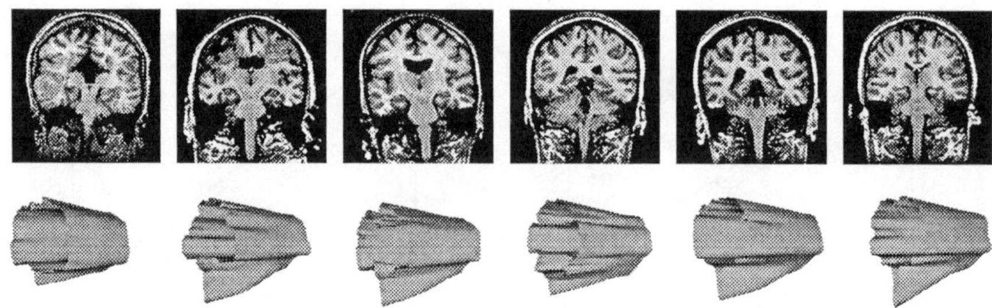

Figure 6: Upper row: Magnetic resonance images showing brain slices of four patients with epilepsy(left four columns), and two controls with normal shape variations (right two columns). Lower row: Corresponding hierarchical shape stacks.

4 Summary and Outlook

A tool for active shape focusing and description, based on a multi-scale active contour model and geometric differential invariants, has been developed. It allows to accurately track and quantify shapes across scales. In particular its ability to localize highly curved parts has been demonstrated for fractal images. A new fractal measurement obtained by estimating the slope of the log-log plot of the scaled perimeter and the compactness against scale has been formulated and successfully tested on fractal shapes for its validity. It is expected that these measurements can help to describe the complexity of shapes as well as their fractal behaviour and scale ranges. Current work includes the application of the presented tool to medical imaging for the quantification of grey-matter deformations in neurological diseases (figure 6) [17], as well as the application to non-linear scale-spaces.

References

[1] A. Witkin. Scale–space filtering. In *Proc. International Joint Conference on Artificial Intelligence*, pages 1019–1022, 1983.

[2] F. Mokhtarian and A.K. Mackworth. A theory of multiscale, curvature-based shape representation for planar curves. *IEEE Transactions on Pattern Analysis and Machine Intelligence*, 14(8):789–805, 1992.

[3] F. Bergholm. Edge focusing. *IEEE Transactions on Pattern Analysis and Machine Intelligence*, 9(6):726–741, 1987.

[4] K.L. Vincken, A.S.E. Koster, and M.A. Viergever. Probabilistic multiscale image segmentation. *IEEE Transactions on Pattern Analysis and Machine Intelligence*, 19(2):109–120, 1997.

[5] R. Whitaker. Volumetric deformable models: active blobs. In *Proc. 3rd International Conference Visualization in Biomedical Computing (VBC'94)*, pages 121–134, 1994.

[6] M. Kass, A. Witkin, and D. Terzopoulos. Snakes: Active contour models. In *Proc. 1st International Conference on Computer Vision (ICCV'87)*, pages 259–268. IEEE Computer Society, 1987.

[7] B.M. ter Haar Romeny, L.M.J. Florack, J.J. Koenderink, and M.A. Viergever. Scale-space: Its natural operators and differential invariants. In *Information Processing in Medical Imaging: Proc. 12th International Conference (IPMI'91)*, pages 239–255. 1991.

[8] G. Gerig, G. Szekely, G. Israel, and M. Berger. Detection and characterization of unsharp blobs by curve evolution. In *Information Processing in Medical Imaging: Proc. 14th International Conference (IPMI'95)*, pages 165–176. 1995.

[9] B.B. Mandelbrot. *The Fractal Geometry of Nature.* W.H. Freeman and Co., 1982.

[10] J.A. Schnabel and S.R. Arridge. Active contour models for shape description using multi-scale differential invariants. In *Proc. 6th British Machine Vision Conference (BMVC'95)*, volume 1, pages 197–206, 1995.

[11] D.J. Williams and M. Shah. A fast algorithm for active contours and curvature estimation. *Computer Vision, Graphics, and Image Processing: Image Understanding*, 55(1):14–26, 1992.

[12] J.A. Schnabel and S.R. Arridge. Hierarchical shape description of MR brain images based on active contour models and multi-scale differential invariants. In *16th Leeds Annual Statistical Research (LASR) Workshop: Image Fusion and Shape Variability Techniques*, pages 36–43, 1996.

[13] W. Schroeder, K. Martin, and B. Lorensen. *The Visualization Toolkit.* Prentice Hall, 1996.

[14] M. Gage and R.S. Hamilton. The heat equation shrinking convex plane curves. *Journal of Differential Geometry*, 23:69–96, 1986.

[15] D.P. Huttenlocher, G.A. Klanderman, and W.J. Rucklidge. Comparing images using the Hausdorff distance. *IEEE Transactions on Pattern Analysis and Machine Intelligence*, 15(9):850–863, 1993.

[16] G. Borgefors. Distance transformations in digital images. *Computer Vision, Graphics, and Image Processing*, 34:344–371, 1986.

[17] J.A. Schnabel and S.R. Arridge. Multi-scale active shape description. In *Scale-Space'97 - 1st International Conference on Scale-Space Theory in Computer Vision*, Lecture Notes in Computer Science. Springer Verlag, 1997. In press.

CUBE, CUBE-OCTAHEDRON OR RHOMBODODECAHEDRON AS BASES FOR 3-D SHAPE DESCRIPTIONS

J. SERRA
Centre de Morphologie Mathématique - Ecole des Mines de Paris
35, rue Saint-Honoré - 77305 Fontainebleau (FRANCE)

The digital three dimensional objects are usually generated on cubic grids, or in case of anisotropy, on rectangular parallelepiped ones (e.g. stack of sections, confocal microscopy, N.M.R., etc.). In the following it is assumed that, after possible pre-treatment, the data are cubic. Then three digital spheres may be chosen, namely cubes, cube-octahedra or rhombododecahedra. They do not share the same advantages. The cube seems to be more natural. However, the cube-octahedron grid exhibits unit edges of a unique length. Moreover, the size of the elementary ball being smaller (13 pixels, versus 27 for the cube), the computations which involve a range of the successive sizes (i.e. distance function, skeleton, ultimate erosion) are treated more finely. Concerning anisotropies now, the best approach is that based on the rhombododecahedron. First, because this polyhedron is obtained by Minkowski addition of the four diagonals of the cube, which can be considered individually (e.g. chord distribution); second, because its twelve faces are identical. Finally, since the rhombododecahedra partition the space, digital change in resolution can be performed. These comparative properties are illustrated on an example of isolated objects (biological cells) and another of texture (expended polymer), by means of an implementation on standard microcomputer.

1 Introduction

In image processing, 3-D treatments appeared during the 80's for both analysis and synthesis purposes. In the present paper, we concentrate on analysis of images, or more precisely, of stacks of binary images. These piles of sections are nowadays currently produced macroscopically (e.g. NMR), or at microscopical scales (e.g. confocal microscopes). They produce experimental data on 3-D rasters which tend to be cubic. Downstream, these computerized data are binarized by some techniques we will not consider here. These binary data constitute, by definition, sets in $\mathbb{Z}^3$, as well as estimations of sets of $\mathbb{R}^3$. How to access them? How to extend to the 3-D space the usual 2-D notions of sizes, directions, distances, connectivity, homotopy, etc.? This is what we would like to develop hereafter. What follows is basically a tutorial; however the space graph approach for homotopy and decomposition of cube-octahedra are new results (as far as I know). A survey of literature shows that in 3D morphology, the two places that have been producing the most substantial series of results, and for a long time, are the pattern recognition section, at Delft University of Technology (see in particular P.W. Verbeek [1][2], J.C. Mullikin [3], Jonker [4]) and the Centre de Morphologie Mathématique, at the Ecole des Mines de Paris (see in particular Serra [5], Meyer [6] [7], Gratin [8], Gesbert et al. [9]).

2 Three dimensional grids

By grid, we do not only mean a regular distribution of points in the the 3-D space, but also a definition of the elementary edges, faces, and polyhedra associated with these points. The three crystallographic grids we find below derive from the cube, and are constructed as follows

i/ cubic grid, which is generated by translations of a unit cube made of 8 vertices;

ii/ the centred cubic grid (cc grid) where the centres of the cubes are added to the vertices of the previous grid;

iii/ the face-centred cubic grid (fcc grid) where the centres of the faces are added to the vertices of the cubic grid.

A comprehensive comparison of these grids can be found in F. Meyer's study [6].

2.1 Interplane distances

In the last two grids, the vertices generate square grids in the horizontal planes, and in vertical projection the vertices of plane No n occupy the centres of the squares in plane No $n-1$. We shall say that these horizontal plane are *staggered.* If a stands for the spacing between voxels in the horizontal planes, then the interplane vertical spacing is equal to $a/2$ in the cc case, and to $a\sqrt{2}/2$ in the fcc one.

2.2 First neighbors

Every vertex has

- 6 first neighbors in the cubic case
- 8 first neighbors in the cc case
- 12 first neighbors in the fcc case

Geometrically speaking, when point x is located at the centre of the $3{\times}3{\times}3$ cube, its projections

- on the faces of the cube provide the cubic neighbors
- on the vertices the cc-neighbors
- and on the edges the fcc-neighbors

Fig. (1) illustrates this point. One can see, also, that the first neighbors generate the smallest isotropic centred polyhedron of the grid, i.e. a 7-voxel tetrahedron (cubic case) a 9-voxel cube (cc-grid) a 13-voxel cube-octahedron (fcc grid). Denote them by the generic symbol B, and the nth iteration of B by B_n, i.e.

$$B_n = B \oplus B \quad ... \quad \oplus B \qquad n \text{ times} ,$$

with $B_0 =$ Identity. From the implication $n \geq p \Rightarrow B_n \geq B_p \quad n,p$ non negative integers, from the equality $B_n B_p = B_{n+p}$, and from the symmetry of B we draw (proposition 2.4 in Serra [10]) that the 3-D raster of points turns out to be a metric space (in three different ways, according to the grid), where the smallest isotropic centred polyhedron is the unit ball.

3 Elementary edges, faces, and polyhedra

In order to complete the definition of the grids, we will introduce now elementary edges, faces and polyhedra. Edges are necessary to define paths, hence connectivity. Faces and polyhedra are required to introduce notions such as Euler-Poincare number for example, or more generally, to introduce the graph approach.

3.1 Cubic grid

As elementary edges, the best candidates are obviously the closest neighbors (in the Euclidean sense), i.e. those of fig. (1). However, they are not so numerous, in the cubic and in the cc case, in particular, which leads to poor connections. For example, in the cubic grid, the extremities of the various diagonals are not connected, we meet here a circumstance similar to that which led to the 8 and 4-connectivities in the 2-D grid. For the same reason, the authors who focused on the cubic grid, such as A. Rosenfeld [11], [12] or K.S. Fu [13], at the beginning of the 80's, introduced the 26- and the 6-connectivity on the cubic grid. When the foreground X is 26-connected, then the background X^c

is 6-connected and vice-versa. In other words, a voxel $x \in X$ admits, as edge partners, all those voxels $y \in X$ that pertain to the cube $C : 3 \times 3 \times 3$ centred at x. Coming back to fig. (1b), we now have to take into account not only the centres of the cube faces, but also the 12 middle points of its edges, and its 8 vertices. Such an extension of the connectivity for X is possible only when the connectivity on X^c remains restricted to the six closest neighbors. If not, we should run the risk of over crossings of diagonals of $1's$ and of $0's$, so the faces should be undefined.This dissymmetrical connectivity brings into play a second digital metric, where cube $3 \times 3 \times 3$ is the unit ball. In particular, the boundary of set X^c is

$$\delta X^c = X^c \backslash X^c \ominus C$$

whereas the boundary of set X is defined via the unit tetrahedra T:

$$\delta X = X \backslash X \ominus C$$

We draw from this last equation that $\delta X \ominus T = \emptyset$, and from the previous one that $\delta X^c \ominus C = \emptyset$. The boundary of X is thinner, but it may comprise zones of a thickness 2, and of course lines or fine tubes.

Note also that, unlike tetrahedron T, cube C admits a Steiner decomposition into three orthogonal segments of three voxels length each. Consequently, the dilation $X \oplus nC$ is obtained as the product of three linear dilations of size $2n$ in the three directions of the grid.

3.2 cc grid

The cc grid call very similar comments, but now with staggered horizontal planes. The low number of the first neighbors (i.e. 8) of each voxel suggests to add the second neighbors, in number of six (see fig.1). This results in the unit rhombododecahedron R shown in fig. (2), which exhibits 15 vertices (including the centre), 12 rhomb faces, identical up to a rotation, and 24 edges whose common length is the first neighbor distance.

Just as previously, with the cubic grid, the adjunction of 2nd neighbors complicate the situation, for they cannot be added simultaneously to the $1's$ and $0's$. This results in a 14-connectivity for the grains versus a 8-connectivity for the pores. By comparison with the cubic case, the connectivity contrast between foreground and background is reduced, but it remains.

Again, as previously, a new metric is provided, namely that of the rhombododecahedron. In this metric, the isotropic dilations can be decomposed into segment dilations, since R admits a Steiner decomposition into the four diagonals of the cube $(2,2,2)$, i.e.

$$R = \begin{pmatrix} 1 & \cdot \\ \cdot & 0 \end{pmatrix} \oplus \begin{pmatrix} 0 & \cdot \\ \cdot & 1 \end{pmatrix} \oplus \begin{pmatrix} \cdot & -1 \\ 0 & \cdot \end{pmatrix} \oplus \begin{pmatrix} \cdot & 0 \\ -1 & \cdot \end{pmatrix} \tag{1}$$

where -1, 0, 1 indicate the level of the plane, and where the origin is always assigned to the point of plane 0 [10].

3.3 fcc grid

With the fcc grid, things become simpler [6][8]. We still are in a grid where the odd horizontal planes have been shifted by $(a/2, a/2, 0)$ from the cubic spacing, but now each voxel x admits 14 nearest neighbors, at a distance $a\sqrt{2}/2$. They form the unit cube-octahedron D, of figure (2), centred at point x. Geometrically speaking, such a high number of first neighbors means that the shape of D is a better approximation of the Euclidean sphere, than those of the cube C and the rhombododecahedron R.

As far as connections are concerned, it becomes cumbersome to resort to 2nd neighbors. Therefore there no longer is a risk of diagonal overcrossing. The existence of an edge no longer depends on the phase under study but exclusively on the intersection between grid and sets: two neighbors $1's$ define an edge in set X, two neighbors $0's$ an edge in set X^c.

Finally X and X^c are treated by the same balls D_n, but the latter cannot be decomposed into Minkowski sum of segments, unlike C and R.

3.4 Conclusion

As a conclusion, three reasons argue in favor of the fcc grid, namely

1/ the shape of the cube-octahedron D provides a better approximation of the unit Euclidean sphere, than C or R (isotropic dilations, skeletons, distance functions, etc. will seem more "Euclidean") ;

2/ D is more condensed: 13 points on 3 consecutive planes (D) are more economic than 15 points on 5 planes (R), or 27 on 3 planes. D leads to thinner boundaries, to finer ultimate erosions, etc. and requires less logical tests in its implementation.

3/ In the fcc grid, the connectivity is based on the first neighbors only, which allows a common approach for grains and for pores (in cubic grid, when one decides to attribute *a priori* more than four possible neighbors to the $1's$ than to the $0's$, a rather severe assumption is made, which holds, paradoxically, on the convexity of the *pores*. Most often, both grains and pores exhibit concave and convex portions, and the 26/6-connectivity assumption is just irrelevant).

Facing these advantages, the weakness of the fcc grid is the staggered organization of its successive horizontal planes. However, is it really a drawback? This is the question we will examine now.

4 Directions

In this section, we analyse how the directions, hence the shapes, are modified when embedding the digital 3-D grids into the Euclidean space. First of all a brief (and last) reminder on our three polyhedra is provided.

4.1 Equidistributed directions in $\mathbb{R}^3$ and in $\mathbb{Z}^3$

In $\mathbb{R}^2$, we can subdivide the unit disc in as many equal arcs as we want. In $\mathbb{R}^3$, unfortunately, such nice simplicity vanishes: given an arbitrary integer n, one cannot find in general n equidistributed directions on the unit sphere, i.e. one cannot partition this sphere into n solid angles which would derive from one another by rotations (a question related to the famous five Platonian polyhedra). Indeed, the 3-D space may be partitioned only into 2, 4, 6, 8, 12 and 20 equal solid angles. The first two partitions are too poor and the last one hardly reachable by small digital polyhedra. The partitions into 6, 8 and 12 angles are those seen from the centre of a cube, an octahedron and a rhombododecahedron respectively, whose faces are windows.

A second and less known result is the following. The axes of these 6, 8 and 12 solid angles coincide with the vectors from a voxel to its 6, 8 and 12 first neighbors in the cubic, cc and fcc grids respectively

These results directly extend to digital grids. For example, in the cubic grid, there are three sets of equi-angular directions, namely

i/ the three basic directions of the grid;

ii/ the four directions involved in eq. 1, which are also the edges directions of the rhombododecahedron;

iii/ the six following directions

$$\begin{pmatrix} 0 & 1 \\ \cdot & \cdot \end{pmatrix};\begin{pmatrix} 0 & -1 \\ \cdot & \cdot \end{pmatrix};\begin{pmatrix} 0 & \cdot \\ 1 & \cdot \end{pmatrix};\begin{pmatrix} 0 & \cdot \\ -1 & \cdot \end{pmatrix};\begin{pmatrix} \cdot & 0 \\ 0 & \cdot \end{pmatrix};\begin{pmatrix} 0 & \cdot \\ \cdot & 0 \end{pmatrix} \quad (2)$$

which correspond to the edge directions of the cube-octahedron.

Note that the dilation of the first three unit vectors (i) generate the unit cube ($2 \times 2 \times 2$), that of the four ones (ii) produces the rhombododecahedron (cf. eq. 1), and that of the six vectors of (eq. 2) the tetrakaidecahedron (but not the cube-octahedron...). In addition, each of these three Steiner polyhedra generates by translation a partition of the 3-D space $\mathbb{R}^3$ or $\mathbb{Z}^3$. The tetrakaidecahedron (fig. 2), a sort of Steiner version of the cube-octahedron, is unfortunately too thick for digital purposes (voxels distributed over five successive planes for the unit size).

As for the cube-octahedron itself, if it cannot be obtained by dilating segments, it admits, however, a decomposition into the Minkowski sum of two tetrahedra. For example

$$\begin{matrix} 0 & 1,-1 & 0 \\ 1,-1 & 0 & 1,-1 \\ 0 & 1,-1 & 0 \end{matrix} = \begin{pmatrix} 0 & -1 \\ -1 & 0 \end{pmatrix} \oplus \begin{pmatrix} 0 & +1 \\ +1 & 0 \end{pmatrix} \qquad (3)$$

4.2 Digital fcc grids, virtual staggering

How to produce a stack of staggered square grids, or, equivalently, how to produce a digital unit cube-octahedron? An easy way is to favor the diagonal horizontal directions, as in (Eq. 3). The staggering structure is created automatically, since each of the two diagonal subgrid appears, alternatively, in the successive horizontal planes. The negative counterpart is that half of the voxels only are taken into account. For example, the dilation of (Eq. 3) produces neither the central points at levels +1 and -1, nor the middle points of the sides at level zero. We may always add these points, in order to complete the basic cube-octahedron, but then

i/ We increase the elementary size from 13 up to 19 voxels, hence we become less accurate in delineating boundaries, ultimate erosions, skeletons, etc.

ii/ We lose the advantage of a unique type of edges, which governs homotopy and connectedness properties.

iii/ We do not know what to do with the amount of information carried by the non used voxels.

An alternative solution should consist in interpolating one horizontal grid every two planes. This would add a computational step, but above all, it seems "fiddled": how to weight the four horizontal neighbors, versus the two vertical ones? How to display the resulting grid? etc. Therefore, we propose neither to move nor to remove or even modify, any voxel of the cubic initial data, and to consider each even plane, *as it is*, as being staggered. According as the central plane is odd or even, we then obtain one of the two elementary polyhedra of fig. 3.

	first plane			second plane			third plane		
1	1	.	.	1	.	1	1	.	
1	1	.	1	1	1	1	1	.	a/
.	.	.	.	1	.	.	.	.	
.	.	.	.	1	.	.	.	.	
.	1	1	1	1	1	.	1	1	b/
.	1	1	.	1	.	.	1	1	

Fig. 3 : *Decomposition of the unit cube-octahedraon in a cubic raster, in order to simulate the staggered structure (a: odd central plane, b: even central plane.*

Such a *virtual staggering* is similar to that used in $\mathbb{Z}^2$, when one generates a hexagonal grid from a square raster. In both cases, the irregularity of the unit polyhedron (resp. polygon) is self-compensated by iteration. In other words, the mappings which bring into play sequences of successive sizes, such as distance functions, medial axes, granulometries, sequential alternated filters, etc. are treated by means of *actual* digital cube-octahedra (resp. hexagons), (see fig. 5).

5 Space graphs and measurements

From now on, we consider sets of points in $\mathbb{Z}^3$, that model the voxels associated with physical objects of the three dimensional space. Sets are given capital letters (X, A, B...), and points small letters.

One find a rather important literature on digital surface description, and calculus, for 3-D sets [2][6][9][11][14][15]. If one has in mind to bridge the gap between digital and continuous spaces, i.e. to provide a Euclidean meaning with digital measurements, the techniques based on digital boundary measurement (i.e. volume difference between dilate and object, or object and eroded set) are not acceptable, and one must deal with stereology [6][9][15][16]. Below we follow this approach (note that [2] turns out to be an improvement of the classical stereological method). Moreover we are not exclusively interested in surface area, but more generally in digital estimators of "good" Euclidean measurements.

5.1 Reminder on the genus of a surface

The theory of Euclidean surfaces is classical, and dates back to the beginning of the 20th century (R. Poincaré). The comment below derives from [17], more information can be found in general documents such as Encyclopedia Britannica.

In $\mathbb{R}^n$, a *closed orientable surface* is topologically equivalent to a sphere with an even number $2p$ of holes (made by removing discs) which have been connected in pairs by p *handles* (shaped like the surface of half of a doughnut). A *closed non orientable surface* is topologically equivalent to a sphere which has had a certain number q of discs replaced by *cross-caps*. The numbers p and q are said to be the genus of the surface not being closed means that some discs have been removed and the hole left open. A torus is a sphere with one handle; a Möbius strip is a sphere with one cross-cap and one "hole" ; a Klein bottle is a sphere with two cross-caps; a cylinder is a sphere with two "holes". In general, the Euler-Poincaré number of a surface is equal to $2 - 2p - q - r$, where p is the number of handles, q is the number of cross-caps (zero for an orientable surface), and r is the number of holes (or boundary curves). The Euler Poincaré number of the union of disjoint surfaces is the sum of each of them.

5.2 Euler-Poincaré number and space graphs

Here, a convenient set model is the class of all finite unions of compact convex sets. This class, called "the convex ring of $\mathbb{R}^n$" allows to elaborate a theory about measurements (Hadwiger theorem below), and on the other hand lends to digitization (space graphs below). In this framework, a deep property of Euler-Poincaré number is stated by the following theorem [18].

Theorem 1 *(Hadwiger): the only functional defined on the convex ring in* $\mathbb{R}^n$*, of degree zero, invariant under displacements,* C*-additive and constant for the compact convex sets, is the Euler-Poincaré number* ν.

This topological number ν allows to bridge the gap between Euclidean and digital spaces, since it can be equivalently defined in both modes when we interpret it in terms of graphs. In two dimensions, ν is classically expressed via planar graphs. In $\mathbb{R}^3$, a *space graph* is

i/ a set X of *points* ;

ii/ a collection E of *edges*, i.e. of lines homotopic to the segment [0,1]. Both extremities of each edge belong to X, and two edges may possibly meet at their extremities only;

iii/ a collection F of faces, i.e. of surfaces homotopic to the closed unit disc. The contours of the faces are exclusively edges, and two faces may possibly intersect along edges only;

iv) a collection P of blocks, i.e. the connected components of the space that remain when all points, edges and faces of a space graph have been removed.

The space graph is *the* turning point between Euclidean and digital spaces, for the questions investigated here. Defined in $\mathbb{R}^3$, it may also be reinterpreted in $\mathbb{Z}^3$, and the derived relations (e.g. Eq. 4) are meaningful in both spaces.

One proves by induction [5, p. 229], that when set X is finite, or at least locally finite, the Euler-Poincaré constant $\nu(Y)$ set $Y = X \cup E \cup F$ formed by the points, the edges and the faces of X is equal to (4):

$$\nu(Y) = N(vertices) + N(faces) - N(edges) - N(blocks) \tag{4}$$

Seen from a digital point of view, the problem consists now in associating space graphs with the set of points in $\mathbb{Z}^3$. Then, clearly, embedding such graphs in $\mathbb{R}^3$ allows a digital interpretation of their Euler-Poincaré numbers.

Various examples of such "polyhedrizations" are described in literature. The probably oldest one [19] deals with cubic grid and provides an algorithm for $\nu(Y)$ from (Eq 4). According to the choice of connectivities other cubic graph are possible [12][13]. The literature about the rhombododecahedric graphs is undoubtedly more reduced [5][9]. An excellent study on the topological properties of the cubic grid, due to G. Bertrand, will be found in [20]. The last reference also gives a solution to Eq. 4 for the graphs on cc grid. We focus here on the most interesting case, namely the space graphs over fcc grid.

In the fcc case, the graph edges associated with a set X are the pairs of neighboring points of X, the faces are the elementary triangles generated by three (two by two) neighbors, and the blocks are the resulting tetrahedra and octahedra. Unlike the triangles, the elementary squares do not constitute faces in the graph structure, and, for this reason, the elementary pyramids are no longer blocks. Finally, all these definitions are also valid, by duality, to X^c, i.e. to the set of 0's

When applied to a cfc graph X, relation (Eq. 4) reduces to the six configurations drawn in fig. 4.

Note that unlike the number of particles, number ν is a local *measurement*: one needs only small neighborhoods around best points to estimate it statistically.

5.3 Minkowski measures

Euler-Poincaré number, that we have just introduced in the three-dimensional cases, is indeed defined by induction in any $\mathbb{R}^k$. In particular:

- for $k = 0$, the space is reduced to one point and $\nu_0(X) = 1$ iff X is this point;

- for $k = 1$, $\nu_1(X)$ equals the number of segments of X;

- for $k = 2$, $\nu_2(X)$ equals the number of particles of X minus their holes.

Consider now a 3-D Euclidean set X, and a subspace $S(x,\omega)$ of location x and orientation ω. Take the cross section $X \cap S(x,\omega)$ and integrate its ν_k-constant over the displacements, i.e. in x and in ω. According to Hadwiger's theorem, we then obtain the only functionals to be invariant under displacements, c-additive, homogeneous of degree $n-k$, and continuous for the compact convex sets, namely (up to a multiplicative constant):

$$\begin{array}{llcll} \textit{volume} & v(X) & = & \int_{\mathbb{R}^3} \nu_0 \left(X \cap \{x\}\right)\, dx & (5) \\ \textit{surface area} & \frac{1}{4}s(X) & = & \frac{1}{4\pi} \int_{4\pi} d\omega \int_{\pi\omega} \nu_1 \left[X \cap \Delta\left(x,\omega\right)\right]\, dx & (6) \\ \textit{mean caliper} & d(X) & = & \frac{1}{4\pi} d\omega \int_{4\pi} d\omega \int_{-\infty}^{+\infty} \nu_2 \left[X \cap \Pi\left(x,\omega\right)\right]\, dx & (7) \end{array}$$

At first glance, the notation seems heavy; in fact, it is extremely meaningful. In (Eq. 6) for example, ω indicates a direction on the unit sphere, and $\Delta(x,\omega)$ a test line of direction ω passing through point x. The first sum integrates over a plane Π_ω, orthogonal as ω, as the foot x of $\Delta(x,\omega)$ spans Π_ω. The second integral, in $d\omega$ is nothing but a rotation averaging (similar comment for Eq 7). The meaning of these relations is clearly stereological. For example, the surface area, a 3-D concept, turns out to reduce to a sum of number of intercepts, i.e. a typically 1-D notion.

When set X admits at each point of its surface a mean curvature C and a total curvature C', then mean caliper and Euler-Poincaré number take another geometric interpretation, since

$$2\pi d(X) = \int_{\delta X} C\, ds \qquad \text{and} \qquad 4\pi\nu_3(X) = \int_{\delta X} C'\, ds$$

The three relations (Eq. 5) to (Eq. 7) attribute a *Euclidean* meaning to *digital* data (we meet again the turning point aspect of space graphs). By discretization, (Eq. 5) becomes

$$v * (X) = (\text{Number of voxels of } X) \times v_0$$

where $v_0 = a^3$ (cubic grid) or $a^{3/4}$ (fcc grid) or $a^{3/2}$ (cc grid).
Similarly, (Eq. 6) is written

$$s^*\,(X) = (\text{average number of intercepts}) \times 2a^2\sqrt{2}$$

where the averaging is taken over the six directions of (Eq. 2), in the cubic grid. Since estimate $s^*\,(X)$ concerns the Euclidean surface $s(X)$, it differs from the facets areas of the digital set X. For example, here, a facet of a zero thickness counts twice.

5.4 *Other measurements*

Being stereological is not an exclusive property of Minkowski functionals. Here are two instructive counter examples.

Roughness: Assume that δX admits curvatures everywhere, and let $F(l)$ be the combined chord distribution of X and X^c. Then, near the origin we have [21]

$$F(l) = \frac{l^2}{16}\left[-C' + 3\int_{\delta X} C^2 ds\right]$$

In particular, when X is a physical relief, the term C' vanishes, and the slope of the intercepts density near the origin is proportional to the average of the square mean curvature C^2. It was taken advantage of this descriptor to study road surfaces from profiles.

3-D contacts: Consider a random packing of spheres of radius R, and a cross section through it. The spheres becomes discs, and the distribution of the shortest distances between discs follows a law

$$F(l) \simeq 1.438 \quad n_c(lR)^{1/2}$$

where n_c is the number of contacts between spheres per unit volume [22]. This law, which governs some modes of thermic and electric permeabilities, has been experimentally verified J-P. Jernot.

Both above measurements are invariant under displacement, homogeneous, continuous on convex sets, but, unlike Minkowski functional, do fulfill the c-additivity condition

$$\mu(X \cup X) + \mu(X \cap X') = \mu(X) + \mu(X')$$

which is not essential here.

6 Increasing operations and their residues

As soon as spheres and lines (in a set of directions) are digitally defined, it becomes easy to implement isotropic and linear dilations and erosions, hence openings, closings, granulometries, and all usual morphological filters.

Similarly, the residuals associated with distance function, i.e. skeletons (in the sense of "erosions\openings"), conditional bisectors, and ultimate erosions derive directly.

Examples of fig. 5 illustrate this point.

7 Thinnings, thickenings, and homotopy

After the measurements, the second use of the space graphs concerns thinnings and thickenings, and more particularly, those operators that preserve homotopy.

Given two erosions ε_1 and $\varepsilon_2 : \mathcal{P}(E) \to (E)$, one defines the hit-or-miss transformation as [5]:

$$X \to \varepsilon_1(X) \cap \varepsilon_2(X^c) \qquad\qquad X \subset E$$

Then, set X is *thinned* by $(\varepsilon_1, \varepsilon_2)$ when its hit-or-miss transform is subtracted, and it is *thickened* when added. If θ and τ stand for thinning and thickening operators respectively, we have

$$\theta(X) = X \cap [\varepsilon_1(X) \cap \varepsilon_2(X^c)]^c$$
$$\tau(X) = X \cup [\varepsilon_1(X) \cap \varepsilon_2(X^c)]$$

Unlike erosion and dilation, thinning and thickening may satisfy constraints for homotopy preservation. In two dimensions comprehensive studies have been performed on this subject by C. Arcelli and G. Sanniti di Baja, in Naples, for the square grid [see among others 23], and by J. Serra for the hexagonal one [5]. In three dimensions, for the cubic grid the most important achievements are due to the Delft school, namely S. Lobregt et al. [24], and more recently P. Jonker [4]. One may mention also some pioneer work by T. Yf and K.S. Fu [13]. Concerning fcc grid, the results are considerably more limited, however some attempts by P. Bhanu Prasad and P. Jernot [25], and by J.H. Kimberly and K. Preston [26] may be indicated. A general comment on all these 3D analyses, is that each of them proposes a unique algorithm, whose genesis is never explicited and whose justification is provided by one or two examples.

Now, in 3D, just as in 2D, the homotopy of a bounded set X, may be represented as a tree. Starting from the background, one first considers all the connected components δX_i of δX that are adjacent to the background. They form the first level of the tree. With each of them is associated a genus. Some δX_i enclose inside areas. If Y_i is the inside of a δX_i, Y_i may contain in turn boundaries of X, say $\delta Y_{i,j}$; each of them admits a certain genus, etc. The collection of the $\delta Y_{i,j}$ form the branches of the tree that derives from Y_i ; ... and so on.

Two sets are homotopic when their homotopy trees are identical, and a mapping $X \to \psi(X)$ is homotopic when for all X, $\psi(X)$ is homotopic to X.

From now on, we limit ourselves to the neighborhood mappings. They are not the only ones able to preserve homotopy, but the simplest ones in the translation invariant approach. In such a case, each pixel is compared with a neighborhood, which is always the same modulo a translation, and the pixel is kept or removed according to the configuration of the neighborhood. We find again the thinning operator.

Such thinning will be homotopic when by changing $1 \rightarrow 0$ we do not locally modify the genus of the boundaries. Since it holds on boundary, such a condition is symmetrical for X and X^c; i.e. the change must not open a hole, neither create a new particle; must not generate a donut of grains or of pores, neither suppress a grain or a pore, etc. On the fcc grid, the neighborhood of size one around a voxel x admits all the edges involved in the unit cube-octahedron $D(x)$ centred at point x. But since the squares are *not* faces, this neighborhood exhibits six pyramidal hollows, as shown in fig. 6a.

On the unit cube-octahedral sphere $\delta D(x)$ (i.e. $D(x)$ minus its centre x), the only admissible configurations of 1's and 0's are those which result in a simply connected component of 1's, say T_1 and also of 0's, say T_0. One easily verifies that the other ones may change homotopy.

A convenient way to group and classify the admissible configurations consists in taking for $T_1(x)$ one point, these two connected point, and three, etc. of $\delta D(x)$, considering the neighbors of $T_1(x)$ on $\delta D(x)$ as a no man's land, and taking for $T_0(x)$ the remaining voxels of $\delta D(x)$. This technique is right if the obtained T_0 is simply connected (which is always true), and if the neighbors of T_0 on δD coincide with those of T_1 (which is not always true, so we have to exclude some neighborhoods).

We finally obtain five candidate configurations, up to rotations and complement, where T_1 is successively

- 1 point $= H_1$
- 2 extremities of one edge $= K_1$
- 3 consecutive summits of a hexagonal section $= L_1$
- 3 summits of a triangular face $= M_1$ (fig. 7)
- 4 summits of an elementary square $= N_1$ (fig. 7)

Moreover, the above conditions are necessary, but not sufficient. If the four summits of a square on $D(x)$ are 0's, then by changing the centre x of $D(x)$ from 1 to 0 one generates a hole in the pores. Therefore in all cases where such a square may arise one must replace the hollow by the octahedron which fills it, i.e. add some of the supplementary point that change fig. 6a into fig. 6b.

Such a completion is not necessary for the first and last above cases (involving H_1 and N_1), but needed for the three other ones. After having completed correctly the structuring elements, one obtains five pores $H = (H_1, H_0)$, $K = (K_1, K_0)$, $L = (L_1, L_0)$, $M = (M_1, M_0)$ and $N = (N_1, N_0)$. Just as in 2D, one can list the geometrical meaning of the corresponding thinnings.

H : for a simply connected particle, thins it down to one point, and thickens it up to its convex hull; it acts independently on disjoint particles, but in thinning only.

K and L : thin the sets down to lines; L but not K is symmetrical under complementation.

M and N : thin the sets down to sheets ; both are symmetrical for the complement.

Their geometrical interpretations are true up to some pathological configurations (just as in 2D, see [5] p. 396 for ex.), which fortunately rarely occur. The above interpretations are drawn from the consideration of the invariant blocs, faces and edges in each thinning.

It would be long and tedious to develop all the structuring elements involved in each operator. More briefly, we indicate in fig. (7), the two configurations M and N, in a perspective display. For the former, some external 1's and 0's have to be added.

8 References

[1] P.W. Verbeek, H.A. Vrooman and L.J. van Vliet, "Low level image processing by max-min filters", *Signal Process.,* vol. 15, pp. 249-258, 1988.

[2] J.C. Mullikin and P.W. Verbeek, "Surface area estimation of digitized planes", *Bioimaging,* vol. 1, pp. 6-16, 1993.

[3] J.C. Mullikin, *Discrete and Continuous Methods for Three Dimensional Image Analysis*, Delft: Univ. Press, 1993.

[4] P.P. Jonker, "Parallel processing in computer vision and collision free path planning of autonomous systems", in *26th ISATA*, 1993.

[5] J. Serra, *Image Analysis and Mathematical Morphology,* London: Acad. Press, 1982.

[6] F. Meyer, "Mathematical Morphology: from two dimensions to three dimensions", *J. of Micr.,* vol. 165, pp. 5-29, 1992.

[7] C. Gratin and F. Meyer, "Mathematical Morphology in three dimensions", *Acta Stereol.* vol. 11, pp. 551-558, 1991.

[8] C. Gratin, *De la représentation des images en traitement morphologique d'images tridimensionnelles,* PhD thesis, Ecole des Mines de Paris, 1993.

[9] S. Gesbert, C.V. Howard, D. Jeulin and F. Meyer, "The use of basic morphological operations for 3D biological image analysis", *Trans. Roy. Microsc. Soc.*, vol. 1, pp. 293-296, 1990.

[10] J. Serra, "Mathematical Morphology for Boolean lattices", in *Image Analysis and Mathematical Morphology,* vol. 2, J. Serra (ed.), London: Acad. Press, 1988.

[11] D.G. Morgenhaler and A. Rosenfeld, "Surfaces in three-dimensional digital images", *Information and Control,* vol. 51, pp. 227-247, 1981.

[12] T. Kong and A. Rosenfeld, "Digital topology: Introduction and survey", *Comp. Vis. Image Proc.*, vol. 48, pp. 357-393, 1984.

[13] Y.F. Tsao and K.S. Fu, "A parallel thinning algorithm for 3-D pictures", *Comp. Graph. Image Proc.*, vol. 17, pp. 315-331, 1981.

[14] J. Mukkerjee and B.N. Chatterji, "Segmentation of three-dimensional surfaces", *Pattern Rec. Letters,* vol. 11, pp. 215-223, 1990.

[15] V.C. Howard and K. Sandau, "Measuring the surface area of a cell by the method of the spatial grid with a CSLM", *J. of Micr.,* vol. 165, pp. 183-188, 1992.

[16] P. Bhanu Prasad, J.P. Jernot, M. Coster, J.L. Chermant, "Analyse morphologique tridimensionnelle des matériaux condensés", *in Proc. PIXIM,* 1988, pp. 31-42.

[17] James and James, *Mathematics Dictionary,* Van Nostrand, 1982.

[18] H. Hadwiger, *Vorsesungen über Inhalt, Oberfläche und Isoperimetrie,* Springer, 1957.

[19] J. Serra, "Introduction à la Morphologie Mathématique", *Cahiers du CMM,* Ecole des Mines de Paris, 1969.

[20] G. Bertrand, "Simple points, topological numbers and geodesic neighborhoods in cubic grids", *Pattern Rec. Letters,* vol. 15, pp. 1003-1012, 1994.

[21] J. Serra, "Descriptors of flatness and roughness", *J. of Micr.*, vol. 134, pp. 227-243, 1984.

[22] Y. Pomeau and J. Serra, "Contacts in random packings of spheres", *J. of Micr.*, vol. 138, pp. 179-187, 1985.

[23] C. Arcelli and G. Saniti di Baja, "Width-independent fast thinning algorithms", *IEEE Trans. Pattern Anal. Machine Intell.,* vol. 7, pp. 463-474, 1985.

[24] S. Lobregt, P.W. Verbeek and F.A. Groen, "Three dimensional skeletonization: Principle and algorithm", *IEEE Trans. Pattern Anal. Machine Intell.,* vol. 1, pp. 75-77, 1980.

[25] P. Bhanu Prasad and J.P. Jernot, "Three dimensional homotopic thinning of digitized sets", *Acta Stereol.,* vol. 9, pp. 235-241, 1990.

[26] J.H. Kimberly and K. Preston, "Three dimensional skeletonization on elongated solids", *CVGIP*, vol. 27, pp. 78-91, 1984.

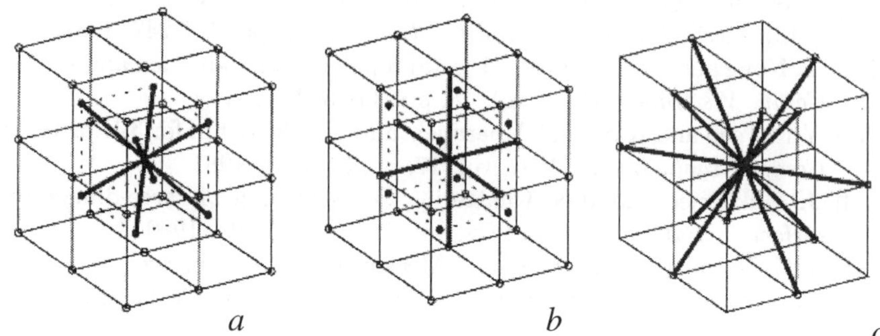

Fig 1 (a) Eight neighbours for the centred cubic grid, (b) six neighbours for the cubic grid, (c) twelve neighbours for the face-centred grid.

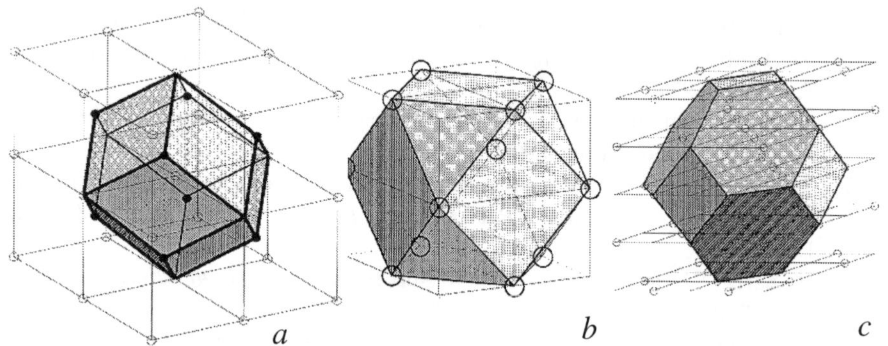

Fig 2 (a) Rhombododecahedron, (b) Cube-octahedron , (c) Tetrakaidecahedron

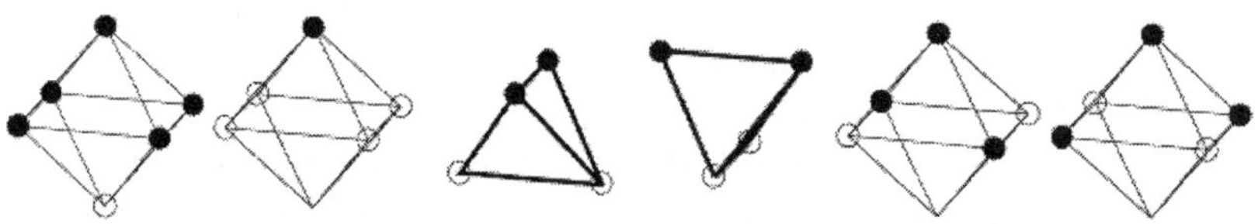

Fig 4 The six structuring elements necessary to compute Euler-Poincaré number on the fcc grid. The occurrences of each of them are computed, and added, first two ones positively, and the four last ones negatively (from F.Meyer[6]).

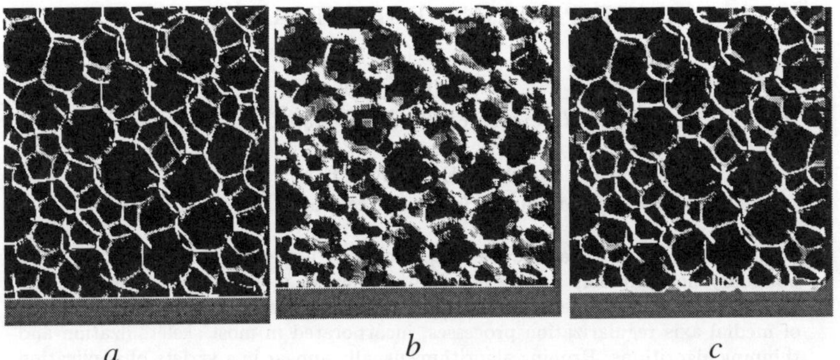

Fig 5 (a) Moss of expanded Polystyrene, (b) cube-octahedral dilation of size 8, (c) cube-octahedral opening of size 8 (the 3-D image originates from a CMM study for Shell Company).

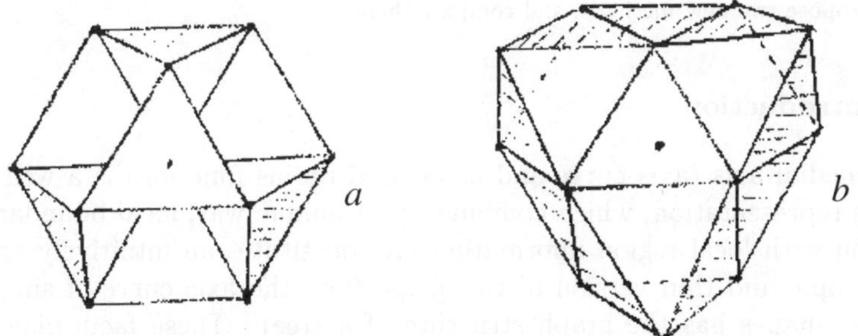

Fig 6 (a) Space graph associated with unit cube-octahedron , (b) Filling of the hollows of fig 8a

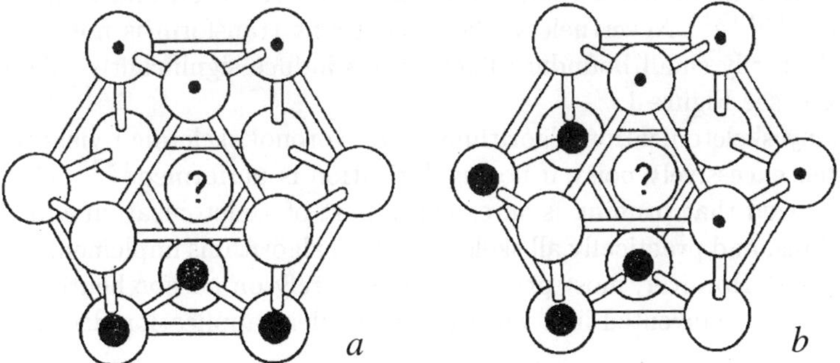

Fig 7 (a) and (b): Two candidate configurations for cube-octahedral thinning (from Bhanou-Prasad and Jernot). For configuration a), three 0's have to be added in the upper plane, and three 1's in the lower plane, following fig 8b

RATE PRUNING FOR MEDIAL AXES

D. SHAKED[a]
Hewlett Packard Israel Science Center, Technion City, Haifa 32000, Israel.

A.M. BRUCKSTEIN
Department of Computer Science, Technion, Haifa 32000, Israel.

The medial axis is an attractive shape feature, however its high sensitivity to boundary noise hinders its use in many applications. In order to overcome the sensitivity problem some regularization has to be performed. Pruning is a family of medial axis regularization processes, incorporated in most skeletonization and thinning algorithms. Pruning algorithms usually appear in a variety of application dependent formulations, and seemingly different algorithms are in fact equivalent. In this paper we suggest the rate pruning paradigm as a standard for pruning methods. The proposed paradigm is a framework in which it is easy to analyze, compare and tailor new pruning methods. We analyze existing pruning methods, propose two new methods, and compare them.

1 Introduction

The medial axis (axis curve and associated radius function) is a well defined shape representation, which combines, in a unique way, local boundary information with local region information. It constitutes an intuitively appealing homotopic and thin version of the shape (i.e. the axis curve of simply connected shapes has the graph structure of a tree). These facts may explain why despite frequent shifts in methods and paradigms, the medial axis has constantly maintained a central role in computer vision and shape analysis research.[6,13,1,19,18] Nevertheless, the medial axis transform is not continuous, and arbitrarily small boundary fluctuations induce significantly different medial axes, see Figure 1.

Many skeletonization algorithms (e.g. Voronoi skeletons) yield axes that are often excessively noisy if no regularization is performed.[4,8,16] Therefore it is recognized that pruning is an essential part of skeletonization and thinning algorithms, and practically all skeletonization algorithms implement some type of pruning. However, most pruning methods rely on ad-hoc heuristics, which are too often reinvented in a variety of equivalent application driven formulations.

Practically all pruning methods are based on an intrinsic significance measure for axis points. Variability in significance measures is the major source for variability in pruning methods. A secondary source of variability follows from

[a]Work done while at the Department of Electrical Engineering in the Technion.

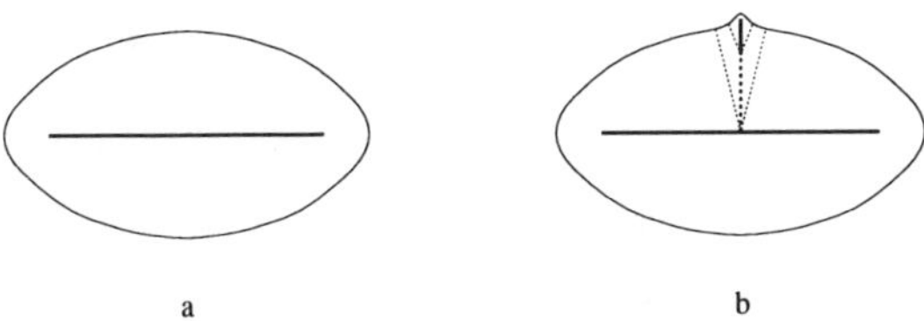

Figure 1: Small boundary fluctuations result in significant changes of the medial axis.

different pruning paradigms, i.e. different ways to incorporate the intrinsic significance measures in the pruning process.

The main goal of this paper is to introduce a standard framework for pruning methods, which consists of a specific pruning paradigm and a standard terminology for significance measures. A terminology consistent across all applications will surely enhance the flow of information and enable comparison of different pruning methods. In this paper we also suggest two new pruning methods. The suggested methods provide an example of how the proposed paradigm helps to tailor and analyze new pruning methods.

In Section 2 we briefly review pruning methods. In Section 3 we suggest the standard pruning paradigm and terminology. Using the proposed framework, we introduce two new pruning methods in Section 4, and analyze them in Section 5. We summarize in Section 6.

2 Existing Pruning Methods

The significance measure used by the earlier pruning methods [6,10,13] is the propagation velocity V_p of the symmetry axis in the Prairie Fire Model, see Figure 2. V_p may be easily shown to depend on the angle ϕ between the tangents at the corresponding boundary points.

$$V_p = \frac{V_f}{\cos\frac{\phi}{2}} \tag{1}$$

The classical pruning paradigm, applied in most methods using propagation velocity as significance measure [6,10,11,13] is the threshold paradigm: All axis points whose significance measure is low are deleted. Such prunings may however result in disconnected axes, as can be seen in Figure 1b, where the dotted axis corresponds to low propagation velocity.

Paradigms preserving axis connectivity were also suggested, in which pruning is activated from the end points of the axis branches as long as a certain condition is satisfied (e.g. while the significance measure is decreasing or while

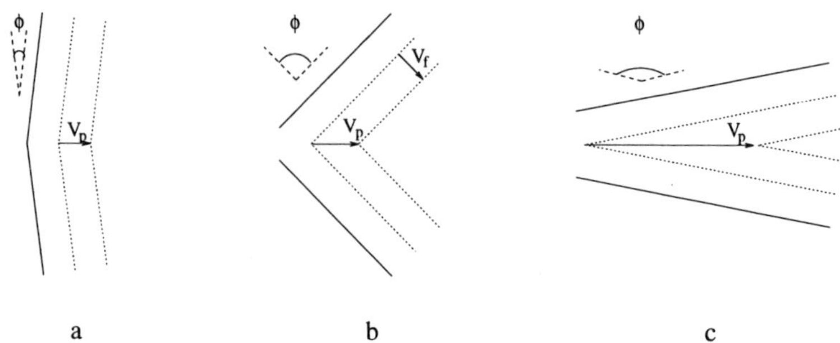

Figure 2: Propagation velocity depends on the angle between the generating boundaries.

it is below a threshold [2,4]). Using those paradigms, the pruned axis is connected, however, pruning is not continuous, and arbitrarily small changes in the threshold of the significance measure may induce large changes in the pruned axis, see Figure 3.

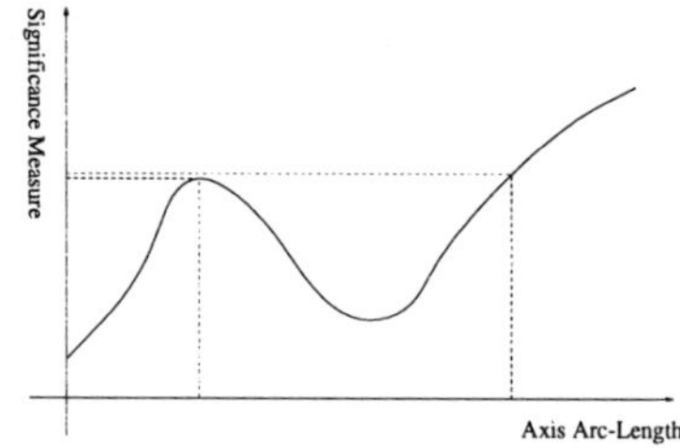

Figure 3: Two close threshold levels result in significantly different pruning locations.

A different significance measure is the maximal thickness of the implied erosion.[3,8,14,20] The effect of pruning on the shape is a loss of a localized layer near the boundary (the gray area in Figure 4), as if the shape has been locally eroded. Thus, a possible pruning measure is the maximal thickness of the eroded layer induced by pruning. Note that in axis segments resulting from boundary perturbations, extensive pruning results in a limited loss of shape contents.

The *erosion thickness* significance measure was used in several application dependent formulations: The erosion thickness of a point q on an axis with end point p, is

$$R(p) + d(p,q) - R(q) \tag{2}$$

where $R(\cdot)$ is the radius function on the axis, and $d(p,q)$ the distance between points p and q, see Figure 4. Note that this significance measure is monotone (the radius function $R(q)$ can never increase as much as the distance function d, see references [6,19,22]). Hence, the threshold paradigm can be applied with no danger of disconnection.

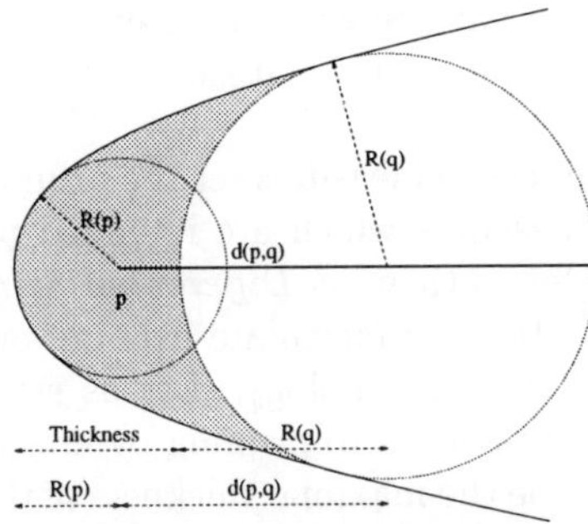

Figure 4: The erosion thickness significance measure.

A different significance measure is related to the length ratio of the axis and the boundary it unfolds: Noisy axis branches may be characterized by the small amount of boundary they unfold, see e.g. Figure 1b. Ogniewicz [15,16,17] suggests a set of significance measures for which the thresholding approach does not disconnect the axis. All the suggested measures are variations of the boundary/axis length ratio measure i.e. the amount of boundary unfolded by an axis segment.

3 Rate Pruning

In this section we propose a unified terminology for pruning methods. We present the *rate pruning paradigm* and advocate a specific terminology for significance measures. We also translate some existing pruning methods into the proposed framework and terminology.

Rate pruning is a parallel process "melting" the axis simultaneously from all its end points. The pruning velocity, or pruning rate, at each axis end point is inversely proportional to the local significance measure. The duration of pruning parameterizes its degree. Thus, instead, of setting a threshold on axial significance the significance measure cues local pruning rate. A high significance measure indicates that pruning should be slow, whereas a low significance measure indicates fast pruning.

Pruning of an axis segment terminates when it reaches and annihilates into a junction. The remaining two segments at the junction are then merged. Thus, rate pruning assures connected and continuous pruning regardless of the incorporated significance measures.

To unify pruning methods, it is necessary to use standard terminology to specify the significance measures. We propose formulating significance measures in terms of local axis parameters. These include the value of the radius function and its derivatives, and local features of the axis curve, like for example its curvature.

In rate pruning, significance measures set the pruning rate. We distinguish them from significance measures which are intended to be used in threshold based paradigms, and refer to them as *Differential Significance Measures.*

In the rest of this section we formulate existing pruning methods within the proposed framework and terminology. Let us start with the differential significance measure corresponding to pruning by erosion thickness: Given an axis segment, what would be the maximal thickness of the erosion layer induced by deleting a Δ long segment off its end? In Figure 4 assume $q = p+\Delta$. If Δ is small enough, we may approximate $R(p) = R(q-\Delta) = R(q) - \Delta \cdot R_a(q)$, where $R_a = \frac{\partial R}{\partial a}$. Replacing $d(p,q) = \Delta$ in Eq. 2 we get that the thickness is $\Delta \cdot (1 - R_a(q))$. Hence the differential significance measure corresponding to erosion thickness pruning is

$$1 - R_a \tag{3}$$

Note that [7,19,22] since $R_a \leq 1$ the differential significance measure is non negative.

In the basic boundary/axis length ratio pruning suggested by Ogniewicz et al.,[16,17] the significance of an axis point is the length of the shortest boundary segment connecting its two generating points. The differential significance measure corresponding to this method was already proposed by Blum and Nagel [7], and it was shown [23] to be

$$2R_a \frac{1 - R_a^2 - RR_{aa}}{\sqrt{1 - R_a^2}} \tag{4}$$

4 New Pruning Methods

We would have liked to call this section "improved pruning methods" but we can not since there are no globally accepted quality criteria for pruning. We suggest the following pruning methods because they provide an example of how rate pruning may help in understanding and tailoring new pruning methods. Furthermore, the heuristics and performance of the proposed methods may be deemed better than those of existing methods for certain applications.

Using rate pruning we can impose the *pruned area* as a significance measure.[5,9,23] The corresponding differential significance measure is the shaded area of the crescent in Figure 4, which may be approximated[23] by the area of the rectangle whose height and width are the height $2R\sqrt{1-R_a^2}$, and maximal thickness $(1-R_a)$ of the crescent. The proposed erosion area significance measure is therefore

$$2R\sqrt{1-R_a^2}\cdot(1-R_a) \tag{5}$$

A different pruning method is derived from the curvature flow smoothing[12] which seems recently to gain a position of preferred shape smoothing method. Suppose the boundary of a given shape evolves under a given differential flow. The changing boundary induces a constant change in the shape and its medial axis. Although smooth boundary evolution does not guarantee smooth axis evolution, discontinuities in the axial description are localized both in space and time. In reference[21] a framework has been suggested to translate differential boundary evolution rules to evolution rules of the axis description. Evolving axes are described by a large set of rules: A curve evolution rule for the axis curve, a rule for the radius function, and boundary rules for both the axis curve and the radius function at free axis end points as well as at junctions.

We derive the proposed pruning method from the translation of curvature flow to axial evolution rules. Since in pruning the only operation is deletion of axis end points, we implement only the boundary condition for free axis end points. It may be shown[21] that when the boundary evolves under curvature flow, axis end points are pruned at a rate proportional to $-\frac{1}{R_{aa}R^2}$. In reference[23] it was shown that the rate is, as required, non negative, and that a corresponding differential significance measure is

$$R(1-R_a) \tag{6}$$

It is interesting to note that this significance measure is, in some sense, half the way between the erosion thickness and erosion area significance measures in Eqs. 3, 5.

5 Simulation Results

In this section we compare simulation results from different pruning methods: Erosion thickness (ET), boundary/axis length ratio (LR), erosion area (EA), and boundary smoothing based pruning (BS). In our opinion, optimal smoothing can not be truly determined, mainly because human understanding of "good smoothing" is almost always context dependent. Thus the goal of this section is to point out the different interpretations of smoothing implied by the various pruning methods, rather then to find "the best" method.

We applied the four pruning methods to two shapes: Man and Square, see Figure 5. In Figure 6 we show the first pruning hierarchy for each of the methods (pruning hierarchies were presented by Ogniewicz [16,17]).

Figure 5: The two original shapes Man and Square, with axes superimposed.

The ET and LR methods are scale independent, consequently elongated shape protrusions are considered significant no matter how narrow they may be. This might be considered good in a shapes like the man shape of Figure 5a, where relatively small protrusions have contextual meanings of hands and fingers. In context-free shapes as the square shape of Figure 5b the same feature might be considered a disadvantage.

The difference between the EA and BS methods is usually unnoticeable. In some sense the EA method prunes faster (EA differential significance measure is always smaller than the BS measure since $|R_a| < 1$). The higher pruning rate brought about the pruning of the axis segments corresponding to the base of the man shape by the EA method.

We observe that in the LR method occasional groupings of noisy axis branches may seem significant. Note that the unpruned noisy axis branches in the LR pruning of the square shape in Figure 6 are roots of such groupings. If some of those branches would have terminated in junctions with the main axis rather then joining together before they meet the main axis, all of them would have been deleted.

6 Summary

The medial axis is an attractive shape feature, however its high sensitivity to boundary noise hinders its use in many applications. In order to overcome this sensitivity some regularization has to be performed. Pruning methods

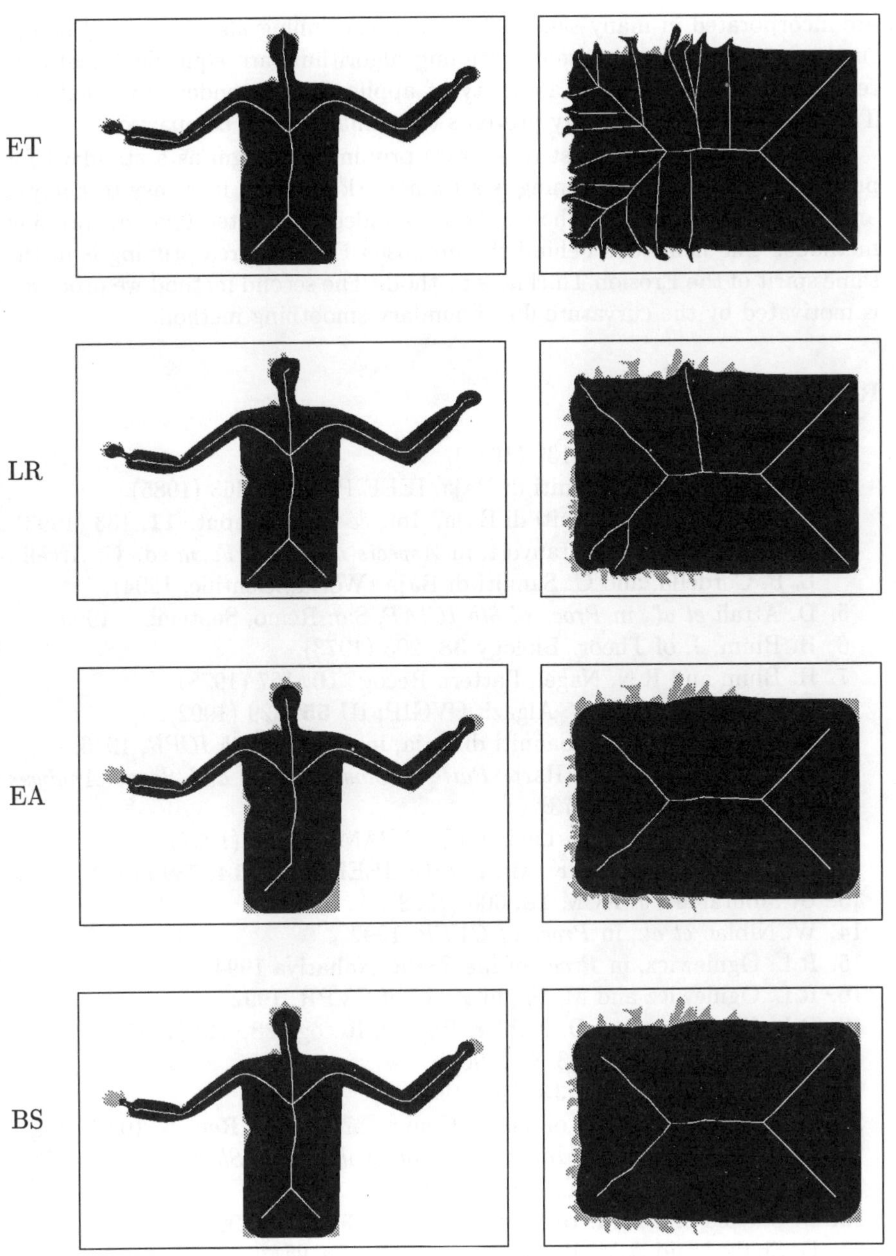

Figure 6: First pruning hierarchy, pruning large scale details of 10% and unpruning up to small scale details of 2%.

are incorporated in many skeletonization and thinning algorithms. Although they may seem different, many pruning algorithms are equivalent methods reinvented and restated in a variety of application dependent formulations. The inconsistent terminology prevents their analysis and comparison.

In this paper we suggested the rate pruning paradigm as a standard for pruning methods. Rate pruning is a framework in which it is easy to analyze and tailor new pruning methods. We have indeed suggested two new pruning methods: The heuristics behind the proposed Erosion Area pruning is in the same spirit of the Erosion Thickness method. The second method we proposed is motivated by the curvature flow boundary smoothing method.

References

1. C. Arcelli, CGIP **17**, 130 (1981).
2. C. Arcelli and G. Sanniti di Baja, IEEE PAMI **7**, 463 (1985).
3. C. Arcelli and G. Sanniti di Baja, Im. & Vis. Comput. **11**, 163 (1993).
4. D. Attali and A. Montanvert, in *Aspects of Visual Form* ed. C. Arcelli, L. P. Cordella, and G. Sanniti di Baja (World Scientific, 1994).
5. D. Attali *et al.*, in *Proc. of 8th ICIAP*, San Remo, September 1995.
6. H. Blum, J. of Theor. Biology **38**, 205 (1973).
7. H. Blum and R.N. Nagel, Pattern Recog. **10**, 167 (1978).
8. J.W. Brandt and V.R. Algazi, CVGIP: IU **55**, 329 (1992).
9. L.P. Cordella and G. Sanniti di Baja, in *Proc. of 8th ICPR*, 1986.
10. R.O. Duda and P.E. Hart, *Pattern Classification and Scene Analysis* (Wiley, New York, 1973).
11. F. Leymarie and M.D. Levine, IEEE PAMI **14**, 56 (1992).
12. F. Mokhtarian and A.K. Mackworth, IEEE PAMI **14**, 789 (1992).
13. U. Montanari, J. ACM **18**, 600 (1968).
14. W. Niblac *et al.*, in *Proc. of CVPR*, 1992.
15. R.L. Ogniewicz, in *Proc. of the SSPR*, Nahariya 1994.
16. R.L. Ogniewicz and M. Ilg, in Proc. of CVPR, 1992.
17. R.L. Ogniewicz and O. Kübler, Pattern Recog. **28**, 343 (1995).
18. J. Ponce, CVGIP **52**, 328 (1990).
19. A. Rosenfeld, CVGIP **33**, 156 (1986).
20. G. Sanniti di Baja, J. of Visual Comm. and Image Rep. **5**, 107 (1994).
21. D. Shaked, *Symmetry Invariance and Evolution in Shape Analysis*, PhD Thesis, Technion, Haifa, Israel, 1995.
22. D. Shaked and A.M. Bruckstein, CVIU **63**, 367 (1996).
23. D. Shaked and A.M. Bruckstein, *CIS Report 9511*, Technion, May 1995, accepted to *CVIU*.

SHAPE RECOGNITION USING INVARIANT UNARY AND BINARY RELATIONS

Z Shao and J Kittler
Centre for Vision, Speech and Signal Processing,
School of Electronic Engineering, Information Technology and Mathematics
University of Surrey, Guildford GU2 5XH, United Kingdom
emails: {Z.Shao,J.Kittler}@ee.surrey.ac.uk

The problem of transformation invariant object recognition is considered. We develop a projective transformation invariant representation for both scene and model which facilitates an attributed relational graph object matching based only on unary and binary relations. The unary and binary measurements used for matching are derived from sets of reference points such as corners and bi-tangent points which are stable under the various transformations considered. Each set of reference points is used to generate a distinct barycentric coordinate basis system associated with one node of the object graph representation. We show that barycentric coordinates of the reference image points can be made invariant under any arbitrary projective transformation. For the object and scene representation we use the barycentric coordinates of the reference points, together with auxiliary measurements such as colour and texture as the node's unary measurements. For binary measurements we use the product of the barycentric coordinate system for one node with the inverse of the barycentric coordinate system associated with another node. The unary and binary relations provide an orthogonal decomposition of the shape being matched. They are used in a relaxation process to detect instances of objects consistent with a given model.

1 Introduction

Transformation invariant object recognition is a problem that has long been pursued by computer vision researchers. Assuming rigid objects, when the scene that contains an object to be recognised is projected onto the imaging plane, the projected image of the object is related to its model by a projective transformation. In this paper we develop a projective invariant representation for both scene and model in the context of model based vision. The aim of the proposed representation is to facilitate an attributed relational graph object matching based on only unary and binary relations.

An arc of an ARG can connect more than two nodes, in which case it represents a high order relation between the matching entities and the ARG is in fact a hyper-graph. Many researchers have considered transformation invariant constraints being such high order relations [2,3,4].

Random hyper-graph matching is an NP complete problem. Recently there have been some developments in solving the problem of Attributed Relational

Graph matching in polynomial time. In this context relaxation labelling deserves a particular mention. However even now we are still not able to enforce general high order relational constraints in these algorithms because of the high computational cost, with the only exception of objects arranged in a lattice structure where the correspondence problem does not arise. In this paper, we show that it is possible to derive an appropriate set of unary and binary measurements capable of representing the global transformation constraint and thus to eliminate the necessity of using high order relations in the first place.

The paper is organised as follows. In the next section we recollect common projective transformations to which our representation should be invariant. In Section 3 we propose unary and binary measurements that are invariant to specified projective transformations. The use of the proposed representation in shape matching is demonstrated in Section 4. Section 5 offers a summary of the presented work and conclusions.

2 Projective Transforms

We commence by demonstrating how to generate a projective invariant ARG representation of object shape. In particular, this representation will only consist of unary and binary measurements.

Formally we define our second order ARG as a quadruple $G = (N, E, f, g)$, with N being a set of nodes and $E \subset \{(i,j)|i \in N, j \in N\}$ being a set of arcs. $f : N \to X$ is a function over N representing the unary measurements associated with the nodes, where X denotes the vector space of unary measurements; $g : E \to A$ is a function representing a binary measurement associated with each arc of the graph, and A is the vector space of the binary relational measurements. With N defined purely for labelling purposes, shape information contained in the ARG description manifests itself mainly through the unary and binary measurements. Therefore, our major task is to develop unary and binary measurements that suit the projective invariant requirement.

We represent an arbitrary 2D image point $p = (p_x, p_y)$ with its homogeneous coordinate

$$P = \begin{pmatrix} P_x & P_y & P_z \end{pmatrix} \tag{1}$$

where $p_x = P_x/P_z$ and $p_y = P_y/P_z$. Therefore we can represent a projective transform from point p to p' with a linear transform between their homogeneous coordinates:

$$P' = PT \tag{2}$$

Since a linear transform in the 3D homogeneous coordinate system corresponds to a projection between two 2D coordinate systems ([1], Chapter 1), matrix T

can be used to represent a wide class of 2D projections including affine and perspective transforms [1,8,10]. To illustrate our approach, we will concentrate on the *affine* projection. *Affine transform* which includes scaling and shear transform, is represented by

$$T_a = \begin{pmatrix} r_1 & r_2 & 0 \\ r_3 & r_4 & 0 \\ t_x & t_y & 1 \end{pmatrix} \tag{3}$$

where r_1, r_2, r_3 and r_4 together describe rotation, scaling and shear, and t_x, t_y represent translation. It preserves parallelism as well and has six degrees of freedom.

In the following section we shall derive the unary and binary measures for the affine case and compare our approach with the conventional methods.

3 Projective Invariant Unary and Binary Measures

3.1 A general form of projective invariant unary and binary measurements based on point features

We develop our binary and unary measurements based on a set of reference points. These points are supposed to be detectable under projective transforms described above. For example, corners (large curvature extrema) as well as *bi-tangent* points around concavities [11] are stable under all these transforms. Given a set of reference points, it is possible to generate a *basis matrix* :

$$B = \begin{pmatrix} B_{11} & B_{12} & \dots & B_{1n} \\ B_{21} & B_{22} & \dots & B_{2n} \\ \dots & \dots & \dots & \dots \\ B_{m1} & B_{m2} & \dots & B_{mn} \end{pmatrix} \tag{4}$$

Provided the basis matrix B is square and non-singular, we can define the *barycentric coordinates* of image point P with basis B as

$$C_B(P) = PB^{-1} \tag{5}$$

Suppose we apply an arbitrary projective transform T to point P and the basis. Then the barycentric coordinates of the transformed point are:

$$C_{B'}(P') = C_{BT}(PT) = (PT)(BT)^{-1} = PTT^{-1}B^{-1} = PB^{-1} = C_B(P) \tag{6}$$

Therefore we conclude that the barycentric coordinates are invariant to arbitrary projective transform T if

1. one can find a basis matrix B for an arbitrary image without the knowledge of the projection, i.e. image features used to construct the basis matrix B must be invariant and detectable under arbitrary projection;
2. B is *non-singular*;
3. basis B from one image and the corresponding basis B' obtained for the projection of the image should be related to each other by the multiplication of the transformation matrix T, i.e. $B' = BT$. In group representation theory terms, T is a representation of the underlying transformation group and B is transformed as a *vector*.

The first condition is presumably satisfied when we generate a basis matrix using salient image features that are invariant to the projection, e.g. colours, sharp corners, bi-tangent points etc. In the next subsection, we will illustrate how to derive a basis matrix for projections that satisfy conditions 2 and 3.

Let us now construct unary and binary relations using the basis representation. Suppose a node (a local shape primitive) V_i contains n points $(P_1, \dots P_n)$, and the basis of the node is B_i. The barycentric coordinates of these points (together with the measurements such as colour, intensity associated with these points) can be used jointly as the unary measurements of the node :

$$X_i = (C_{B_i}(P_1), C_{B_i}(P_2) \dots C_{B_i}(P_n),) \tag{7}$$

If for each j, $C_{B_i}(P_j)$ is calculated from a common basis B_i, then X_i describes the shape of the segment irrespective of the projection it undergoes. Note that for 2D transforms up to affine, the basis matrices are 3x3, and our invariant measurements $C_{B_i}(P_j)$, $j = 1 \dots n$ are 3 dimensional vectors. However the three components of each $C_{B_i}(P_j)$ are not independent from each other. In practice, only two out of these three numbers are needed to describe the point.

For binary measurements, we use the barycentric coordinate of the basis B_i of node V_i in relation to the basis B_j of the node V_j i.e.

$$A_{ij} = B_i {B_j}^{-1} \tag{8}$$

It can be proved that this measurement A_{ij} is also an invariant to arbitrary transformation T if both bases, measured from the same rigid object the features belong to, undergo the same transformation. Both unary and binary features are derived from the same basis matrix. While X_i describes the intra-node features, A_{ij} describe the inter-node relations. X_i and A_{ij} together give an *orthogonal decomposition* of the shape data into binary and unary measures.

The global constraint that requires all the matched nodes to undergo the same transform is embedded in the binary measure A_{ij} when we expand the neighbourhood of the node V_i to all V_js ($j \neq i$) in the model. Suppose two nodes V_i with B_i and V_j with B_j in model G, correspond to two nodes V'_p with B'_q and V'_q with B'_q in scene G'. It is easy to see that the matched pairs (V_i, V'_p) and (V_j, V'_q) respectively determine two possible underlying transformations T_{ip} and T_{jq} from the model to the scene :

$$B'_p = B_i T_{ip} \tag{9}$$

$$B'_q = B_j T_{jq} \tag{10}$$

From 9, 10 and 8, we see that if one observes binary measurement A_{ij} between V_i and V_j and A'_{pq} between V'_p and V'_q then

$$A'_{pq} = B'_p {B'_q}^{-1} = B_i T_{ip} (B_j T_{jq})^{-1} = A_{ij} \ , \ iff \ T_{ip} = T_{jq} \tag{11}$$

$$T_{ip} = {B_i}^{-1} B'_p = (A_{ij} B_j)^{-1} A'_{pq} B'_q = T_{jq} \ , \ iff \ A'_{pq} = A'_{ij} \tag{12}$$

Equation 11 and 12 tell us that if the binary measurements in the two images are the same (i.e. $A'_{pq} = A_{ij}$), so should the underlying transformations between the pairs of features i.e. $T_{ip} = T_{jq}$, and vice versa. Also if T_{ip} and T_{jq} are different, our binary measures from the two images must be different too. Therefore binary measurement A_{ij} expresses the compatibility of a pair of labelling with respect to the common projective transform constraint.

Equations 7 and 8 provide a general framework for deriving the invariant measurements. Now we will demonstrate how to obtain the appropriate basis matrix from a given set of reference points.

3.2 Basis matrices for affine transform

For the affine transform shown in 3, given three none collinear reference points (a, b), (c, d) and (e, f), the proposed basis matrix is :

$$B_a = \begin{pmatrix} a & b & 1 \\ c & d & 1 \\ e & f & 1 \end{pmatrix} \tag{13}$$

It is easy to see that Condition 2 holds, since B_a is always invertible when the three reference points in the basis are not collinear. Also we can prove that B_a is a valid basis for affine transformation by expanding $B_a T_a$ and showing that the basis matrix undergoes the same transformation as any arbitrary point (x, y). In fact, since each reference point is transformed independently by T_a and B_a is arranged as an ensemble of coordinates of the three reference points, condition $B'_a = B_a T_a$ always holds.

Substituting 13 and 1 into 5 and simplifying, we have an affine invariant representation for arbitrary point $(x, y, 1)$ in the image : (relative to an ordered set of reference points)

$$(C_x, C_y, C_z) = \frac{\begin{pmatrix} x & y & 1 \end{pmatrix}}{ad + cf + eb - af - cb - ed} \begin{pmatrix} d-f & f-b & b-d \\ e-c & a-e & c-a \\ cf-ed & eb-af & ad-cb \end{pmatrix} \tag{14}$$

Basis of the form 13 has been proposed in[12] as a feature for geometric hashing and some also used it for matching by back projection. Here we use it as a tool for developing affine invariant relational description. Note that $C_x + C_y + C_z = 1$, therefore we choose (C_y, C_z) as our invariant representation of point.

In summary, we have shown how to use barycentric coordinates and reference points to develop unary and binary projective invariants. We showed how to derive a set of invariant measures from the generic concept of barycentric coordinate and provided a set of conditions that must be satisfied in order to use the invariant formula. The advantages of our approach are as follows :

1. It is applicable to all common projective transforms.

2. Invariant measures we developed have a number of desirable qualities. They decompose the data orthogonally into binary and unary relations. They are simple and elegant to allow efficient computation and easy analysis.

3. Most importantly, we have demonstrated a way of capturing global geometric transformation constraint using only binary relations and in this way we make it possible to use deterministic ARG matching algorithms for shape matching under complex projective transforms.

4. Our approach is based solely on salient reference points. Using the proposed unary invariant measurements, we can represent and reconstruct arbitrary measurements associated with a node, be it an unparameterised contour or a group of scattered regions. The nodes of our ARG representation can virtually be anything, not just line segments.

In practice the reference points from which we build the basis are obtained from the image using some salient features such as inflections on curves[7], largest inscribed triangles[12] and bi-tangent points around concavities. As the detection of these points is not noise free, the basis matrix also suffers from some kind of error, and it becomes difficult to analyse when the error of our invariant representation of the data point P does not only depend on

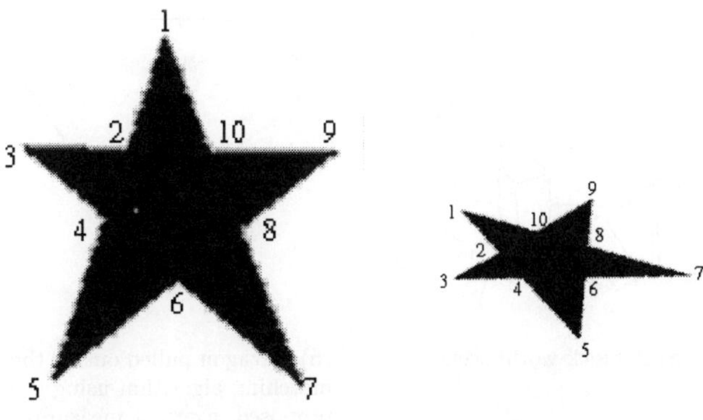

(a) Reference points are labelled with $i = 1 \dots 10$

(b) Reference points correspond to those in the model

Figure 1: Model of "star" for testing our binary measure

its positioning error in the Cartesian system but also on that of the reference points. For affine basis (13), there is some work directed towards finding the sensitivity of invariant measurement in relation with the choice of the reference points e.g. [12]. But in our problem, we are constrained to the choices of reference points which are not only invariant to the transformation, but also a locally detectable and applicable to objects with arbitrary convexities and concavities. In practice, we chose a combination of *bi-tangent* and maximum average FB/saliency points [9] as the reference points for the above reason.

4 Experiment

We demonstrate the proposed methodology on the star image in Figure 1.a. It contains a group of $n = 10$ feature points from which we construct $n - 1$ nodes with basis $B_i(p_{i-1}, p_i, p_{i+2}), i = 1 \dots n-1$. The image is matched to its affine transformed version shown in Figure 1.b . For binary measurements, we need to take two sets of reference points from each image, each set containing 3 points for an affine basis. The two sets may share at most two points with each other, therefore in practice, it is sufficient to have an ordered list of four points to obtain a binary measure. Table 1 shows that binary relations $A_{1,i} = B_i {B_1}^{-1}, i = 2 \dots n-1$ are identical in both images (i.e. they are invariant to affine transform.) Moreover, the binary relations are identical

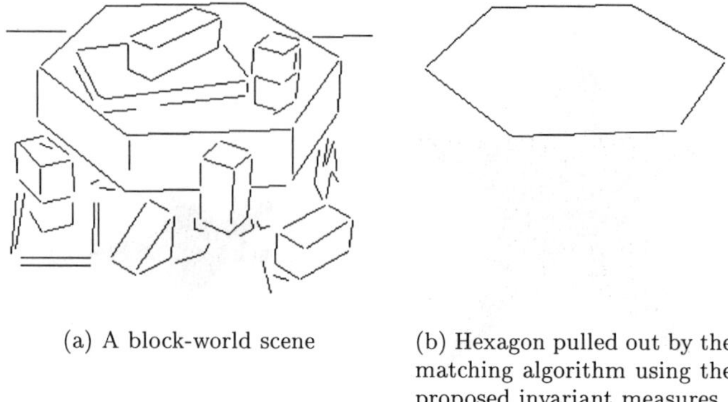

(a) A block-world scene

(b) Hexagon pulled out by the matching algorithm using the proposed invariant measures

Figure 2: Experiment 1 : Matching a Hexagon under Affine Transform

only if the two nodes correspond to each other. The binary relation $A_{1,i}$ never yields the same value for different i unless the nodes completely overlap in the image. This is the case even when the object contains symmetric features (such as nodes $(1, 2, 3)$ and $(1, 10, 9)$ etc. in this "star" figure).

The second experiment demonstrates a matching problem solved using ARG representations with the proposed affine invariant binary and unary measures. The scene contains a hexagonal face under a perspective projection in a cluttered background. The system correctly identifies the object of interest using the proposed approach.

5 Conclusions

The problem of transformation invariant object recognition was studied. We developed a projective transformation invariant representation for both scene and model which facilitates an attributed relational graph object matching based only on unary and binary relations. The unary and binary measurements used for matching are derived from sets of reference points such as corners and bi-tangent points which are stable under the various transformations considered. Each set of reference points is used to generate a distinct barycentric coordinate basis system associated with one node of the object graph representation. We showed that barycentric coordinates of the reference image points can be made invariant under any arbitrary projective transfor-

Table 1: Comparison of binary measurements $A_{1,i}$ of the model and of the scene ($i = 2\ldots5$)

node triplet $(i-1, i, i+1)$	binary measures from model	binary measures from scene
(1,2,3)	$\begin{pmatrix} 0.00 & 0.00 & -1.17 \\ 1.00 & -0.00 & 0.02 \\ 0.00 & 1.00 & 2.15 \end{pmatrix}$	$\begin{pmatrix} -0.00 & -0.00 & -1.16 \\ 1.00 & -0.00 & 0.04 \\ 0.00 & 1.00 & 2.11 \end{pmatrix}$
(3,2,1)	$\begin{pmatrix} -1.17 & 0.00 & 0.00 \\ 0.02 & -0.00 & 1.00 \\ 2.15 & 1.00 & 0.00 \end{pmatrix}$	$\begin{pmatrix} -1.16 & -0.00 & -0.00 \\ 0.04 & -0.00 & 1.00 \\ 2.11 & 1.00 & 0.00 \end{pmatrix}$
(2,3,4)	$\begin{pmatrix} 0.00 & -1.17 & 0.04 \\ -0.00 & 0.02 & -0.66 \\ 1.00 & 2.15 & 1.62 \end{pmatrix}$	$\begin{pmatrix} -0.00 & -1.16 & 0.07 \\ -0.00 & 0.04 & -0.64 \\ 1.00 & 2.11 & 1.57 \end{pmatrix}$
(4,3,2)	$\begin{pmatrix} 0.04 & -1.17 & 0.00 \\ -0.66 & 0.02 & -0.00 \\ 1.62 & 2.15 & 1.00 \end{pmatrix}$	$\begin{pmatrix} 0.07 & -1.16 & -0.00 \\ -0.64 & 0.04 & -0.00 \\ 1.57 & 2.11 & 1.00 \end{pmatrix}$
(3,4,5)	$\begin{pmatrix} -1.17 & 0.04 & 0.10 \\ 0.02 & -0.66 & -2.16 \\ 2.15 & 1.62 & 3.06 \end{pmatrix}$	$\begin{pmatrix} -1.16 & 0.07 & 0.21 \\ 0.04 & -0.64 & -2.03 \\ 2.11 & 1.57 & 2.82 \end{pmatrix}$
(5,4,3)	$\begin{pmatrix} 0.10 & 0.04 & -1.17 \\ -2.16 & -0.66 & 0.02 \\ 3.06 & 1.62 & 2.15 \end{pmatrix}$	$\begin{pmatrix} 0.21 & 0.07 & -1.16 \\ -2.03 & -0.64 & 0.04 \\ 2.82 & 1.57 & 2.11 \end{pmatrix}$
(1,10,9)	$\begin{pmatrix} 0.00 & 1.00 & 2.40 \\ 1.00 & 0.00 & -0.05 \\ 0.00 & 0.00 & -1.35 \end{pmatrix}$	$\begin{pmatrix} -0.00 & 1.00 & 2.49 \\ 1.00 & -0.00 & -0.03 \\ 0.00 & 0.00 & -1.46 \end{pmatrix}$

mation. The conditions that must hold for a basis to be valid were stated. We illustrated how the barycentric coordinate systems can be constructed for the affine and perspective transformations.

For the object and scene representation we use the barycentric coordinates of the reference points, together with auxiliary measurements such as colour and texture as the node's unary measurements. For binary measurements we use the product of the barycentric coordinate system for one node with the inverse of the barycentric coordinate system associated with another node. The unary and binary relations provide an orthogonal decomposition of the shape being matched. They are used in a relaxation process to detect instances of objects consistent with a given model.

We demonstrated the proposed methodology of projective transformation invariant object recognition on two examples. In the first example the representation technique is illustrated on the problem of matching a star shape under affine transformation. We showed experimentally that the unary and binary relations derived are invariant. The second example demonstrated the proposed approach as a tool for 3D object recognition. The aim was to recognise 3D objects in terms of planar faces. A hexagonal model shape was hypothesised in the image. The only instance of the hypothesised model was successfully recovered.

Acknowledgements

Financial support was provided by Esprit Project 'RETINA'.

1. T. H. Reiss *Recognizing objects using invariant features* Dissertation, Trinity College, University of London, Aug. 1992
2. C. Lee, T. Huang *Finding point correspondences and determining motion of a rigid object from two weak perspective views.* CVGIP Vol.52, pp.309-327, 1990
3. D. Yang and J. Kittler *MFT based discrete relaxation for matching high order relational structures* . ICPR-B, pp.219-223, 1994
4. G. Sudhir, S. Banerjee and A. Zisserman, *Finding point correspondences in motion sequences preserving affine structure.* BMVC 93, pp.359-368, BMVA Press 1993
5. J.Y.Wang and F. S. Cohen *Part I : 3-D object recognition and shape estimation from image contours using B-splines, shape invariant matching, and neural network.* IEEE T-PAMI, Vol.16, No.1, pp.1-12 Jan. 1994
6. F.S.Cohen and J.Y.Wang, *Part II : 3-D object recognition and shape estimation from image contours using B-splines, shape invariant matching, and neural network.* IEEE T-PAMI, Vol.16, No.1, pp.13-23 Jan. 1994
7. T.Pavlidis, *Application of splines to shape description.* Visual Forms – Analysis and Recognition, Proceedings of International Workshop on Visual Form, pp.431, May. 1991
8. M. E. Mortenson *Geometric Modelling.* pp. 366-369, John Wiley, 1985
9. M.A.Fischler, H.Wolf. *Locating Perceptually Salient Points on Planar Curves.* IEEE PAMI-16, No.2, pp.131, Feb. 1994.
10. J. D. Foley, A. van Dam, S. K. Feiner and J. F. Hughes *Computer Graphics Principles and Practice.* pp.203-222, pp.253-271, Addison-Wesley, 1990.
11. D. Forsyth, J. L. Mundy, A. Zisserman, C. Coelho, A. Heller and C. Rothwell *Invariant descriptors for 3-D object recognition and pose.* IEEE PAMI Vol.13, pp.971-991, 1991
12. C. Gotsman *On the most robust affine basis* PRL 14, pp.647-650, 1993
13. Z. Shao and J. Kittler, *Fuzzy Non-iterative ARG Labelling with Multiple Interpretations.* ICPR-96 B, 1996

SALIENCY REGIONS AS A BASIS FOR OBJECT RECOGNITION

ALI SHOKOUFANDEH
Department of Computer Science, Rutgers University, New Brunswick, NJ 08903

IVAN MARSIC
Department of Electrical and Computer Engineering, Rutgers University, New Brunswick, NJ 08903

SVEN DICKINSON
Department of Computer Science and Center for Cognitive Science, Rutgers University, New Brunswick, NJ 08903

We introduce a novel view-based object representation, called the *saliency map graph (SMG)*, which captures the salient regions of an object view at multiple scales using a wavelet transform. This compact representation is highly invariant to translation, rotation (image and depth), and scaling, and offers the locality of representation required for occluded object recognition. To compare two saliency map graphs, we introduce two graph similarity algorithms. The first computes the topological similarity between two SMG's, providing a coarse-level matching of two graphs. The second computes the geometrical similarity between two SMG's, providing a fine-level matching of two graphs. We test and compare these two algorithms on a large database of model object views.

1 Introduction

The view-based approach to 3-D object recognition represents an object as a collection of 2-D views, sometimes called aspects or characteristic views. The advantage of such an approach is that it avoids having to construct a 3-D model of an object as well as having to make 3-D inferences from 2-D features. Most approaches to view-based modeling represent each view as a collection of extracted features, such as extracted line segments, curves, corners, line groups, regions, or surfaces, e.g., [11]. In contrast to the feature-based approaches, whose success requires reliable segmentation, a number of image-based view-based recognition systems have emerged [7,4,9]. Although these image-based approaches have been shown to work on natural objects, they are sensitive to (one or more of) illumination changes, scaling, image rotation, depth rotation, or occlusion.

Coarse-to-fine image descriptions have much support in the computer vision community, e.g., [1,5]. Most of these have been developed for attention purposes and, as a result, lose the detailed shape information required for object recognition. In a top-down recognition system, Rao et al. use correlation to compare a multiscale saliency map of the target object with a multiscale saliency map of the image in order to fixate on the object [8]. Crowley presented an approach which is related to the approach presented in this paper, in which circular features are detected in a Laplacian pyramid [2]. The resulting features are linked to form a tree, with the similarity of two trees defined as the similarity of paths through the tree.

In this paper, we present a multiscale view-based representation of 3-D objects that, on one hand, avoids the need for complex feature extraction, such as lines, curves, or regions, while on the other hand, provides the locality of representation necessary to support occluded object recognition as well as invariance to minor changes in both illumination and shape. In computing a representation for a 2-D image (whether model image or image to be recognized), a multiscale wavelet transform is applied to the image, resulting in a hierarchical saliency map of the image. This saliency map is represented as a hierarchical graph structure, called the *saliency map graph*, that encodes both the topological and geometrical information found in the saliency map.

The similarity between a test image and a model image is defined as the similarity between their respective saliency map graphs. We address the problem of matching two saliency map graphs, leading to two matching algorithms. The first algorithm finds the best mapping between two saliency map graphs in terms of their topological structure, while the second algorithm factors in the geometry of the two graphs. In each case, we present an evaluation function that determines the overall quality of the match, i.e., the similarity of the two graphs. We demonstrate and evaluate our image representation and our two matching algorithms using the Columbia University COIL image database.

2 A Scale-Space Saliency Representation of an Image

The scale-space image representation that we have selected is based on a multiscale wavelet transform [10]. The advantage of the wavelet decomposition lies in its effective time (space)–frequency (scale) localization. In the output of the transform, the salient shape of small objects is best captured by small wavelets, while the converse is true for large objects. Searching from finer to coarser scales, we select the *characteristic scale* which captures the most efficient encoding of an object's salient shape; above the chosen scale, extraneous information is encoded, while below the chosen scale, the object is overly blurred. The region defining the object at the chosen scale is called the *scale-space cell* (SSC). Our procedure for detecting the SSC's in an image consists of the following four summarized steps [6], while Figure 1 illustrates the invariance of the SSC's.

Step 1—Wavelet Transform: Compute the wavelet pyramid of an image with ℓ dyadic scales using oriented quadrature bandpass filters tuned to 16 different orientations, i.e. $\Theta = 0°, 22.5°, 45°, ..., 337.5°$. See [10] for a detailed derivation and description of computing the wavelet pyramid using steerable basis filters.

Step 2—Local Energies: Compute the oriented local energies using the equation:

$$E(\Theta, s, x, y) = \left[G^{\Theta}(s, x, y)\right]^2 + \left[H^{\Theta}(s, x, y)\right]^2 \qquad (1)$$

where $G^{\Theta}(s, x, y)$ and $H^{\Theta}(s, x, y)$ are the outputs of a quadrature pair of analyzing wavelet filters at the scale-space coordinate (s, x, y), oriented at the angle Θ. For each image point, 16 different oriented local energies are computed.

Step 3—Saliency Maps: Compute ℓ saliency maps. The saliency of each particular SSC is computed using the convolution:

$$\text{saliency SSC}(s, x, y) = \sum_{\Theta} \left[E(\Theta, s, x, y) * \vartheta(\Theta, x, y)\right] \qquad (2)$$

where $\vartheta(\Theta, x, y)$ is the filter kernel obtained by computing the sum of the squared impulse responses of the two analyzing wavelet filters $G^{\Theta}(s, x, y)$ and $H^{\Theta}(s, x, y)$.

Step 4—Peaks in Saliency Maps: Moving from finer to coarser scales at every location, we select the first saliency map for which a peak (local maximum) at that location exceeds a given threshold. By using a series of oriented 1-D filters to detect the characteristic scale, we can detect objects that are not perfectly circular in shape. For example, if a non-circular shape's variation in diameter does not reach neighboring scales above or below the current scale, then a circularly-symmetric filter, such as that used by Crowley [2], will give a weak response for the shape. In our approach, however, the 1-D filters are slightly adjusted in width (bounded by neighboring scales). The result is a cluster of oriented peaks from which we compute the 2-D shape's location as the centroid of these peaks. The salience of the 2-D shape is computed as the sum of the oriented saliencies of the oriented peaks near this centroid. Finally, we apply a non-maximum suppression process to eliminate closely overlapping salient SSC's at each scale.

The computed saliency map can be represented as a hierarchical graph with nodes representing saliency regions and specifying region location (in the image), region size, region saliency, and scale level. More formally, we define the Saliency Map Graph (SMG) to be a directed acyclic graph $G = (V, E)$,

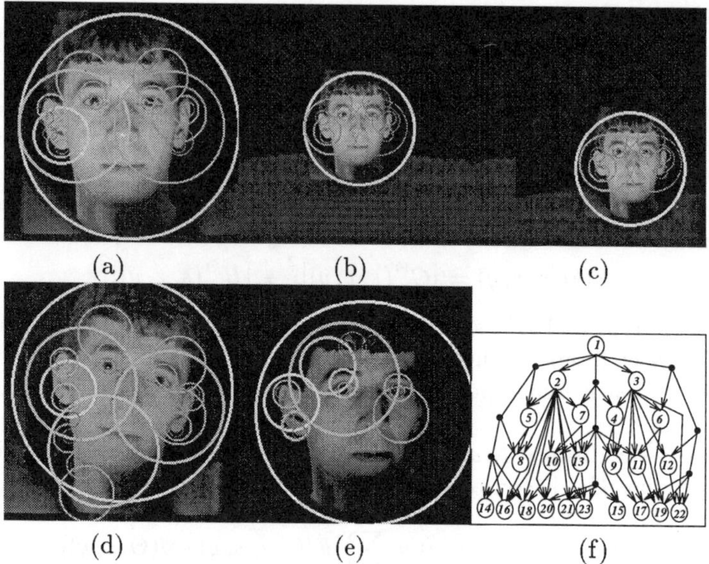

Figure 1: Extracting the most salient SSC's in an image: (a) original image and its saliency map; (b) scale invariance; (c) translation invariance; (d) image rotation invariance; (e) invariance to rotation in depth (illuminated left side of face exhibits little change in its saliency map); and (f) the saliency map graph (SMG) of the original image in (a).

with each saliency region r_i having a vertex v_i in V. (v_i, v_j) is a directed edge in E if and only if the scale level of region r_i is less than the scale level of region r_j, and the center of the region r_j lies in the interior of the region r_i. All the edges of G will therefore be directed from vertices at a coarser scale to vertices at a finer scale, as shown in Figure 1 (lower-right). Finally, to construct the database of object views, a set of views is obtained for each object from a fixed number of viewpoints (e.g., a regularly sampled tessellation of a viewing sphere centered at the object). For each view, the Saliency Map Graph is computed and stored in the database.

3 Matching Two Saliency Map Graphs

We propose two methods for computing the similarity of two SMG's. In the first method, we compare only the topological or structural similarity of the graphs, a weaker distance measure designed to support limited object deformation invariance. In the second method, we take advantage of the geometrical information encoded in an SMG and strengthen the similarity measure to ensure geometric consistency, a stronger distance measure designed to support subclass or instance matching.

Let us first formulate our matching problem. Two graphs $G = (V, E)$ and $G' = (V', E')$ are said to be isomorphic if there exists a bijection $f : V \to V'$ satisfying, for all $x, y \in V$, $(x, y) \in E \Leftrightarrow (f(x), f(y)) \in E'$. To compute the similarity of two SMG's, we consider a generalization of the graph isomorphism problem, which we will call the *SMG similarity problem*: Given two SMG's $G_1 = (V_1, E_1)$ and $G_2 = (V_2, E_2)$, let $f : V_1 \to V_2$ be any partial mapping, and let $\mathcal{E}$ be an appropriately-defined error function. We say that a partial mapping f is feasible if $f(x) = y$ implies that there are parents p_x of x and p_y of y, such that $f(p_x) = p_y$. Our goal is therefore to find a feasible mapping f which minimizes $\mathcal{E}(f)$.

3.1 Choosing a Suitable Error Function

The requirement of feasibility assures that the partial mapping preserves the path structure between G_1 and G_2. The error function incorporates two components: 1) the similarity of mapped nodes in terms of their topology, geometry, and salience; and 2) the degree to which model nodes are excluded from the mapping. Given two SMG's, $G_1 = (V_1, E_1)$ and $G_2 = (V_2, E_2)$, and a partial mapping, $f : V_1 \to V_2$, we define the mapping matrix $M(f)$ between G_1 and G_2, to be a $|V_1| \times |V_2|$, $\{0, 1\}$-matrix with $M_{u,v}$ equal to 1 if $u \in V_1$, $v \in V_2$ and $u = f(v)$, and 0 otherwise. Since f is a bijective mapping, $\sum_{v \in V_2} M_{u,v} \leq 1$ for all $u \in V_1$, and $\sum_{u \in V_1} M_{u,v} \leq 1$ for all $v \in V_2$. Given this formulation of the mapping f, we define its error to be:

$$\mathcal{E}(f) = \varepsilon \sum_{u \in V_1, v \in V_2} M_{u,v}\ \omega(u, v)\ |s(u) - s(v)| + (1 - \varepsilon) \sum_{u \in V_1, f(u) = \emptyset} s(u) \quad (3)$$

where $\varepsilon = |\mathbf{1}^t M(f)\mathbf{1}|/(|V_1| + |V_2|)$ represents the fraction of matched vertices ($\mathbf{1}$ denotes the identity vector), $f(.) = \emptyset$ for unmatched vertices, and $s(.)$ represents region saliency. For the SMG topological similarity, Section 3.2, $\omega(.,.)$ is always one, while for the SMG geometrical similarity, Section 3.3, it denotes the Euclidean distance between the regions.[a]

3.2 A Matching Algorithm Based on Topological Similarity

In this section, we describe an algorithm which finds an approximate solution to the SMG similarity problem. The focus of the algorithm is to find a minimum

[a] For perfect similarity $\mathcal{E}(f) = 0$, while $\mathcal{E}(f)$ will be $\sum_{u \in V_1} s(u)$ if there is no match.

weight matching between vertices of G_1 and G_2 which lie at the same level. Our algorithm proceeds in phases, beginning at level 1. At the i-th phase, the algorithm considers the sets A_i and B_i of vertices at the i-th level of the graphs G_1 and G_2, respectively. Using the algorithm of [3], we construct a maximum cardinality, minimum weight matching M_i in the bipartite graph $\mathcal{G}_i(A_i, B_i, E_i)$ whose edge set E_i contains edges of the form (u, v), with each edge satisfying one of the following constraints: (1) $i = 1$; (2) neither u or v has a parent in G_1 and G_2; or (3) both u and v have at least one matched parent of depth less that i. We define the weight of the edge (u, v) to be $|s(u) - s(v)|$. For two SMG's on n vertices and ℓ scales, the algorithm terminates after ℓ phases. The partial mapping M of SMG's can be simply computed as the union of all M_i's. The error of the mapping M can be computed using Eq. 3. Finally, the complexity of each phase is dominated by the matching algorithm, which is $O(n^2\sqrt{n \log\log n})$ [3] per scale, implying a total complexity of $O(\ell n^2\sqrt{n \log\log n})$.

3.3 A Matching Algorithm Based on Geometric Similarity

The SMGBM similarity captures the structural similarity of two SMG's in terms of their general topology but ignores their geometric properties. In this section, we introduce a second measure, called SMG Similarity using an Affine Transformation (SMGAT), that exploits SMG geometry, e.g., relative positions of the regions. Given $G_1 = (V_1, E_1)$ and $G_2 = (V_2, E_2)$, the algorithm will hypothesize a correspondence between three regions of G_1, say (r_1, r_2, r_3), and three regions (r'_1, r'_2, r'_3) of G_2. The mapping $\{(r_1 \leftrightarrow r'_1), (r_2 \leftrightarrow r'_2), (r_3 \leftrightarrow r'_3)\}$ will be considered as a basis for alignment if it satisfies: (1) each pair r_i and r'_i lie at the same level, and (2) $(r_i, r_j) \in E_1$ if and only if $(r'_i, r'_j) \in E_2$, implying that corresponding regions have the same adjacency structure. Next, we determine the affine transformation (A, b) that aligns the mapped triples, by solving the following system for $a_{i,j}, \forall i, j \in \{1, 2\}$, b_1, and b_2:

$$\begin{cases} x_{r_i} a_{1,1} + y_{r_i} a_{1,2} + b_1 = x_{r'_i}, \; i = 1, 2, 3 \\ x_{r_j} a_{2,1} + y_{r_j} a_{2,2} + b_2 = y_{r'_j}, \; j = 1, 2, 3 \end{cases} \quad (4)$$

A new graph G' will be formed by applying the affine transformation (A, b) to regions in G_1 . Next, a matching between the regions of G' and G_2 will be found. However, instead of matching regions based on similarity of their saliency, regions are mapped based on minimum Euclidean distance between them.[b] In a series of steps, SMGAT constructs weighted bipartite graphs $\mathcal{G}_i =$

[b]Given two regions u and v, their distance $d(u, v)$ can be defined as the distance between their centers, i.e. $d(u, v) = \sqrt{(x_u - x_v)^2 + (y_u - y_v)^2}$.

(A_i, B_i, E_i) for each level i of the two SMG's, where A_i and B_i represent the i-th level vertices of G' and G_2, respectively. The constraints on edges in E_i are identical to those in the SMGBM algorithm, with edge (u, v) having weight $d(u, v)$. A maximum cardinality, minimum weight matching M_i is found for each $\mathcal{G}_i$, their union for all i defines the mapping $f_{(A,b)}$ (corresponding to the transformation (A, b)), and the error $\mathcal{E}(f_{(A,b)})$ is computed using Eq. 3. The algorithm proceeds to the next region triple and finally chooses the triple with minimum error. As with the SMGBM algorithm, the complexity for the SMGAT algorithm is dominated by solving the bipartite matching problems, resulting in a complexity of $O(\ell n^2 \sqrt{n \log \log n})$ per region triple. In the worst case, i.e., when both saliency map graphs have only one level, there are $O(n^6)$ possible transformations.

4 Experiments

To illustrate our approach to shape representation and matching, we apply it to a database of model object views generated by Murase and Nayar at Columbia University. Views of each of the 20 objects are taken from a fixed elevation every 5 degrees (72 views per object), for a total of 1440 model views. The top row of images in Figure 2 shows three adjacent model views for one of the objects (piggy bank) plus one model view for each of two other objects (bulb socket and cup). The second row shows the computed saliency maps for each of the five images, while the third row shows the corresponding saliency map graphs. The time to compute the saliency map averaged 156 seconds/image on a Sun Sparc 20, but can be reduced to real-time on a system with hardware support for convolution, e.g., a Datacube MV200. The average time to compute the distance between two SMG's is 50 ms using SMGBM, and 1.1 second using SMGAT (an average of 15 nodes per SMG).

To illustrate the matching of an unoccluded image to the database, we compare the middle piggy bank image (Figure 2(b)) to the remaining images in the database. Table 1 shows the distance of the test image to the other images in Figure 2; the two other piggy bank images (Figures 2 (a) and (c)) were the closest matching views in the entire database. Table 1 also illustrates the difference between the two matching algorithms. SMGBM is a weaker matching algorithm, searching for a topological match between two SMG's. SMGAT, on the other hand, is more restrictive, searching for a geometrical match between the two SMG's. For similar views, the two algorithms are comparable; however, as two views diverge in appearance, their similarity as computed by SMGAT diverges more rapidly than their SMGBM similarity.

To illustrate the matching of an occluded image to the database, we com-

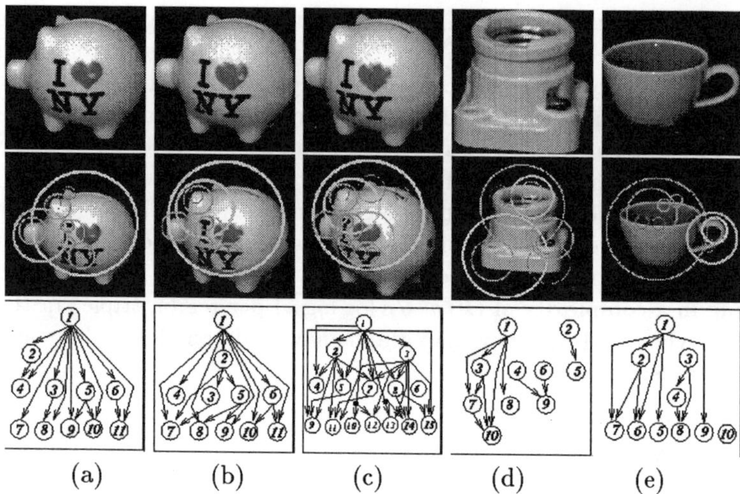

Figure 2: A sample of views from the database: top row represents original images, second row represents saliency maps, while third row represents saliency map graphs.

Algorithm	2(a)	2(c)	2(d)	2(e)
SMGBM	9.57	10.06	14.58	23.25
SMGAT	8.91	12.27	46.30	43.83

Table 1: Distance of Figure 2(b) to other images in Figure 2

pare an image containing the piggy bank occluded by the bulb socket, as shown in Figure 3. Table 2 shows the distance of the test image to the other images in Figure 2. In a labeling task, the subgraph matching the closest model view would be removed from the graph and the procedure applied to the remaining subgraph. Thus, the first three columns in Table 2 represent the distance between the test image SMG and the three piggy bank images (closest three model views in database), while the last two columns in Table 2 represent the distance between the test image SMG and the socket and cup images after removing that portion of the test image SMG that matched the piggy bank. The socket in Figure 2(d) was the closest view in the database.

5 Conclusions

Our saliency map graph offers a stable, multiscale representation of an image that not only captures the salient image structure, but provides the locality of representation required to support occluded object recognition. We have

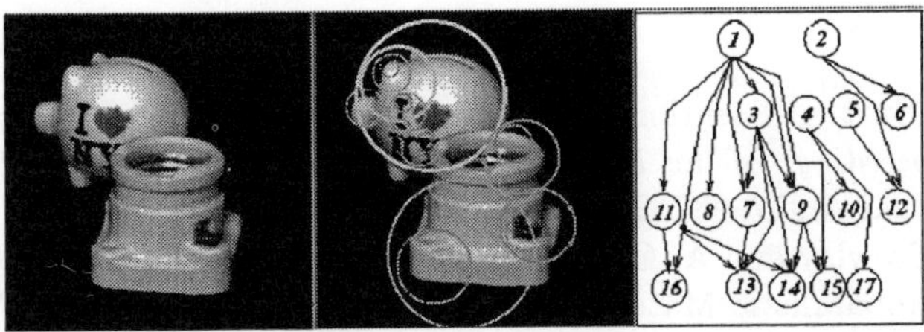

Figure 3: Occluded Object Matching: (a) original image; (b) saliency map; and (c) saliency map graph

Algorithm	2(a)	2(b)	2(c)	2(d)	2(e)
SMGBM	16.02	5.15	15.93	8.64	18.58
SMGAT	51.61	19.31	54.33	18.74	37.34

Table 2: Distance of Figure 3(a) to other images in Figure 2. The first three columns show the three closest views in the entire database, while last two show the distance to the remaining views in Figure 2, after the subgraph corresponding to the best-matching pig view was removed.

presented two graph matching algorithms, SMGBM and SMGAT, that offer an effective mechanism for comparing the topological and geometric structure, respectively, of a test image SMG and a database image SMG. Our graph matching formulation is applicable to any multiscale image representation, e.g., a Laplacian pyramid, which can be mapped to a vertex-weighted, directed acyclic graph. We are currently embedding our matching algorithms in an object recognition system that uses SMG subgraphs as an indexing structure.

The approach is not without its limitations. For example, we currently assume that similar objects have similar layer structure. In addition, we have not addressed the problem of how to select a model view, for matching, from among a large database of mode views. Finally, in using Nayar's COIL database, we have not been able to extensively evaluate the invariance of our representation to changes in lighting, scale, etc.

6 Acknowledgements

We gratefully acknowledge Columbia University's Shree Nayar for providing us with the database of model views. We also gratefully acknowledge the support of the National Science Foundation.

7 References

1. P. J. Burt. Attention Mechanisms for Vision in a Dynamic World. In *Proceedings of the International Conference on Pattern Recognition, Vol.1*, pages 977–987, The Hague, The Netherlands, 1988.
2. J. L. Crowley and A. C. Sanderson. Multiple Resolution Representation and Probabilistic Matching of 2–D Gray–Scale Shape. *IEEE Transactions on Pattern Analysis and Machine Intelligence*, 9(1):113–121, January 1987.
3. M. G. H. N. Gabow and D. Williamson. An efficient approximate algorithm for survivable network design problems. *Proc. of the Third MPS Conference on Integer Programming and Combinatorial Optimization*, pages 57–74, 1993.
4. A. Leonardis and H. Bischoff. Dealing with occlusions in the eigenspace approach. In *Proceedings, IEEE Conference on Computer Vision and Pattern Recognition*, pages 453–458, San Francisco, CA, June 1996.
5. T. Lindeberg. Detecting Salient Blob–Like Image Structures and Their Scales With a Scale–Space Primal Sketch—A Method for Focus–of–Attention. *International Journal of Computer Vision*, 11(3):283–318, December 1993.
6. I. Marsic. Data–Driven Shifts of Attention in Wavelet Scale Space. Technical Report CAIP–TR–166, CAIP Center, Rutgers University, Piscataway, NJ, September 1993.
7. H. Murase and S. Nayar. Visual learning and recognition of 3-D objects from appearance. *International Journal of Computer Vision*, 14:5–24, 1995.
8. R. P. N. Rao, G. J. Zelinsky, M. M. Hayhoe, and D. H. Ballard. Modeling Saccadic Targeting in Visual Search. In D. Touretzky, M. Mozer, and M. Hasselmo, editors, *Advances in Neural Information Processing Systems 8*, pages 830–836. MIT Press, Cambridge, MA, 1996.
9. C. Schmid and R. Mohr. Combining greyvalue invariants with local constraints for object recognition. In *Proceedings, IEEE Conference on Computer Vision and Pattern Recognition*, pages 872–877, San Francisco, CA, June 1996.
10. E. Simoncelli, W. Freeman, E. Adelson, and D. Heeger. Shiftable multiscale transforms. *IEEE Transactions on Information Theory*, 38(2):587–607, 1992.
11. S. Ullman and R. Basri. Recognition by linear combinations of models. *IEEE Transactions on Pattern Analysis and Machine Intelligence*, 13(10):992–1006, October 1991.

SHAPE PERCEPTION, SHOCKS AND WIGGLES

KALEEM SIDDIQI
Center for Computational Vision & Control, Yale University
New Haven, CT 06520-8285, USA

BENJAMIN B. KIMIA
Division of Engineering, Brown University
Providence, RI 02912, USA

ALLEN TANNENBAUM
Department of Electrical Engineering, University of Minnesota
Minneapolis, MN 55455, USA

STEVEN W. ZUCKER
Center for Computational Vision & Control, Yale University
New Haven, CT 06520-8285, USA

We earlier introduced an approach to categorical shape description based on the singularities (shocks) of curve evolution equations. The approach relates to many techniques in computer vision, such as Blum's grassfire transform, but since the motivation was abstract, it is not clear that it should also relate to human perception. We now report that this shock-based computational model can account for recent psychophysical data collected by Christina Burbeck and Steve Pizer. In these experiments subjects were asked to estimate the local centers of stimuli consisting of rectangles with "wiggles" (sides modulated by sinusoids). Since the experiments were motivated by their "core" model, in which the scale at which boundary detail is represented is proportional to object width, we conclude that such properties are also implicit in shock-based shape descriptions.

1 Shocks and the Shape Triangle

Observing that shapes that are slight deformations of one another appear similar, Kimia *et al.* proposed the following evolution equation for visual shape analysis [2,1]:

$$\boxed{\begin{cases} \mathcal{C}_t & = (\beta_0 - \beta_1 \kappa)\mathcal{N} \\ \mathcal{C}(s,0) & = \mathcal{C}_0(s). \end{cases}} \tag{1}$$

Here $\mathcal{C}$ is the vector of curve coordinates, $\mathcal{N}$ is the outward normal, s is the path parameter, t is the time duration (magnitude) of the deformation, and β_0, β_1 are constants. The space of all such deformations is spanned by the ratio β_0/β_1 and time t, constituting the two axes of the *reaction-diffusion space.* When $\beta_1 = 0$ the equation is equivalent to the grassfire transformation of Blum, or

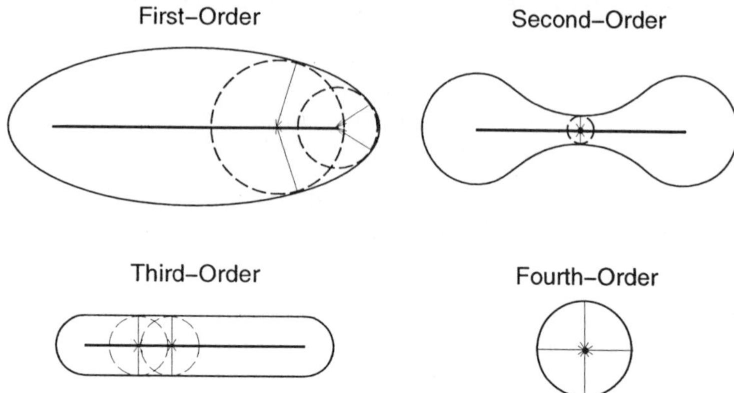

Figure 1: This figure illustrates the four types of shocks that arise in the reaction-diffusion space [1].

to Huygen's principle [3,1]; when β_1 is large, it becomes a geometric heat equation. In this paper, we shall only be interested in the former case, under which the equation is hyperbolic and four types of *shocks* [4], or entropy-satisfying singularities, can form (Figure 1): 1) A FIRST-ORDER SHOCK is a discontinuity in orientation of the shape's boundary; 2) A SECOND-ORDER SHOCK is formed when two distinct non-neighboring boundary points collide, but none of their immediate neighbors collapse together; 3) A THIRD-ORDER SHOCK is formed when two distinct non-neighboring boundary points collide, such that the neighboring boundary points also collapse together[a]; and 4) A FOURTH-ORDER SHOCK is formed when a closed boundary collapses onto a single point. To get an intuitive feel for the shock types consider the numerical simulation of a dumbbell shape evolving under constant inward motion, Figure 2. Note the emergence of a qualitative description of the shape as that of two parts separated at a "neck" (second-order shock), with each part consisting of three "protrusions" (first-order shock groups) merging onto a "seed" (fourth-order shock).

Such generic perceptual shape classes have lead to the metaphor of a shape triangle, where three distinct processes compete with one another to explain shape [5], Figure 3 (left). The sides of the triangle reflect this competition and

[a] Whereas third-order shocks are not generic they merit a distinct classification for several computational reasons as well as their psychophysical relevance [5]. Consider the abundance of biological and man-made objects with symmetric "bend-like" components, *e.g.*, fingers of a hand, limbs, legs of a table, branches of a tree, *etc.*

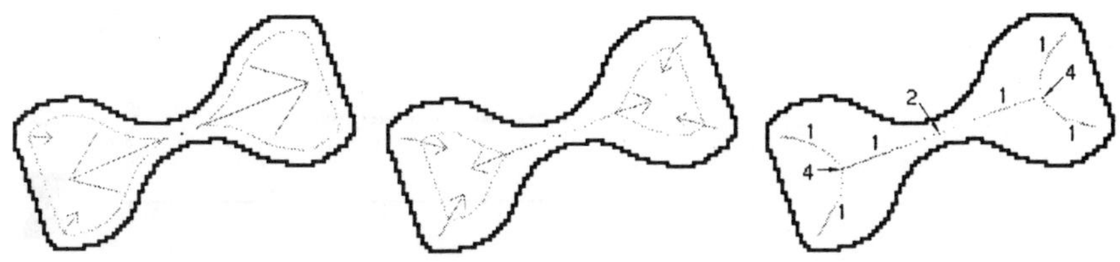

Figure 2: The detection of shocks for a dumbbell shape undergoing constant inward motion, taken from [6]. Each sub-figure is a snapshot of the evolution in time, with the outline of the original shape shown in black, the evolved curve overlayed within, and the arrows representing velocity vectors for the current first-order shocks.

capture the tension between object composition (parts), boundary deformation (protrusions) and region deformation (bends). When one considers the *parts-protrusions* continuum and plots the time till formation of the second-order shock under constant inward motion, normalized by the time till annihilation of the shape, Figure 3 (right), a curious connection is unearthed. The ratio is a measure of local width versus global width, and provides a metric for the perceptual distance of the shape from the "parts" node along this axis.

Now, note that intermediate shapes along the *bends-protrusions* continuum closely resemble wiggles. The term "wiggle" appropriately describes not only the sinusoidal nature of the boundary modulation, but also its perceived effect on the object's central axis [7]. In the context of the shape triangle, for thin objects placed close to the "bends" node the axis is seen to wiggle, for thicker objects placed close to the "protrusions" node the axis is perceived to be straight. Within the shock-based framework, such effects are reflected in the geometry of the high-order shocks that arise, Figure 6. We are formally led to the following prediction:

Prediction 1 *The perceived center of a "wiggle" along a horizontal line in alignment with a sinusoidal peak coincides with a high-order shock[b] that forms under constant inward motion.*

The psychophysical experiments of Burbeck *et al.*, introduced next, involved precisely the above class of shapes.

[b]Type 3 or 4 for in-phase sinusoids, and type 2 for out-of-phase ones (mirror symmetric shapes).

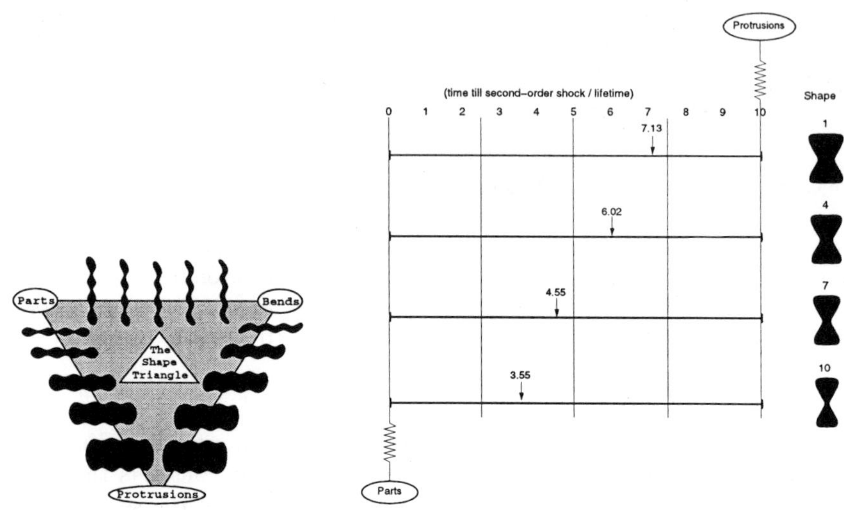

Figure 3: LEFT: The sides of the shape triangle represent continua of shapes; the extremes correspond to the "parts", "protrusions" and "bends" nodes [5]. RIGHT: Using the shock detection algorithm in [6], we plot the time till formation of the second-order shock (for constant inward motion), normalized by the lifetime of the shape, for samples of the "bow-tie" stimuli used in [5]. Observe the increase in this ratio in moving from the *parts* node (shape 10) to the *protrusions* node (shape 1).

2 Wiggles

Pizer *et al.* [8,9,7] have developed an alternative approach to visual shape analysis called the *core* model. Underlying the formulation of the core model is the hypothesis that the scale at which the human visual system integrates local boundary information towards the formation of more global object representations is proportional to object width. Psychophysical examinations of Weber's Law for separation discrimination support this proposal [10]. Arguing that the same mechanism explains the attenuation of edge modulation effects with width, Burbeck *et al.* have recently reported on an elegant set of psychophysical experiments where subjects were required to bisect elongated stimuli with wiggly sides. In the following we present their main findings. As predicted above, we will later demonstrate a strong correlation between these findings and computational results obtained from a shock-based description of the wiggles.

The stimuli consisted of rectangles subtending 4 degrees of visual arc in

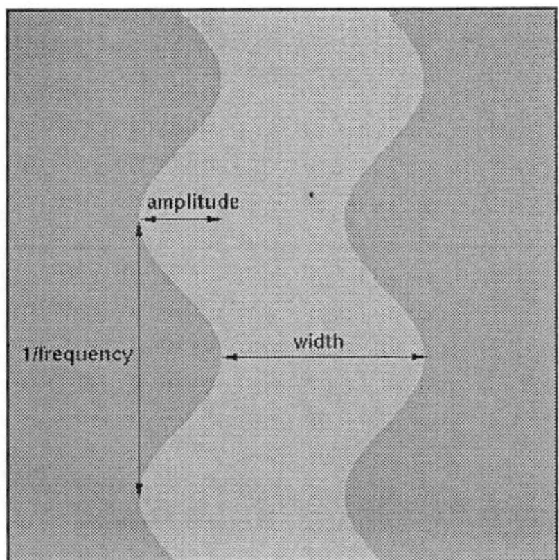

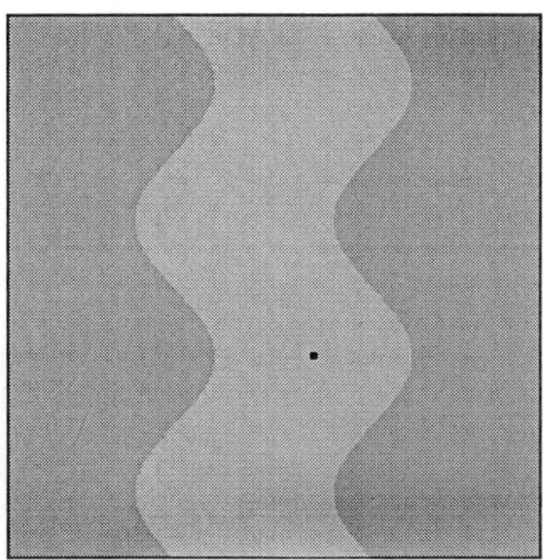

Figure 4: LEFT: The geometry of a "wiggle" stimulus. RIGHT: Is the dot to the left or to the right of the object's center?

height, with sinusoidal edge modulation, Figure 4 (left). Two widths were considered (0.75° and 1.5°) and for each width there were 6 edge modulation frequencies ($0.25, 0.5, 1, 2, 4, 8$ cycles/o) and 2 edge modulation amplitudes (20% and 40% of object width). A black probe dot appeared near the center of each stimulus, in horizontal alignment with a sinusoidal peak. The subject was asked to indicate "whether the probe dot appeared to be left or right of the center of the object, as measured along a horizontal line through the dot."[c] As a sample experiment view the stimulus on the right of Figure 4 for a period of one second from a distance of 1.5 meters. You are likely to judge the dot to be to the right of the object's center. It may surprise you to find that it actually lies midway between the boundaries on either side, as can be verified by placing a ruler across the figure. In fact, despite instructions to make a local judgement your visual system is biased towards acquiring edge information across a more global spatial extent.

Burbeck and Pizer quantified this effect of edge modulation on the perceived center by varying the horizontal position of the probe dot and subjecting the data to probit analysis. The center of the object was inferred as the 50% point on the best-fitting probit function[d], and the *bisection threshold* was defined as the variance of this function. The *perceived central modulation* was

[c]See[7] for further details.

[d]The location at which a subject is statistically equally likely to judge the probe dot to be to the left or to the right of the object's center.

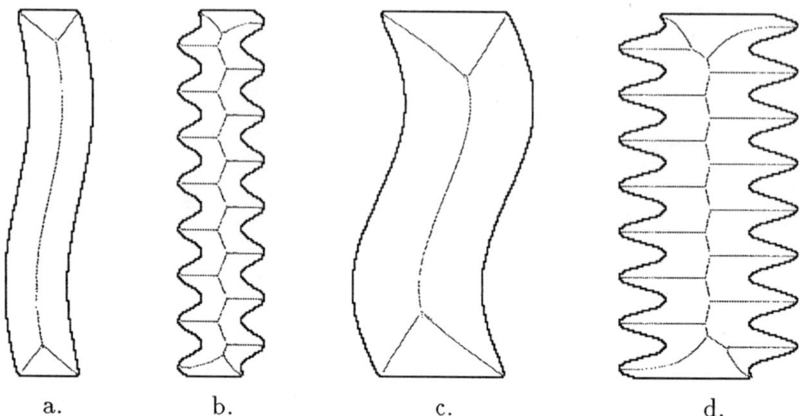

Figure 5: The shock-based description of selected 40% amplitude modulation stimuli used in [7]. a) 0.75 degree width, 0.25 cycles/degree edge modulation; b) 0.75 degree object, 2.0 cycles/degree edge modulation; c) 1.5 degree object, 0.25 cycles/degree edge modulation; d) 1.5 degree object, 2.0 cycles/degree edge modulation.

then obtained as the horizontal displacement between the perceived centers in alignment with left and right sinusoidal peaks. The main findings were:

Result 1 *For a fixed edge modulation frequency the perceived central modulation decreases with increasing object width.*

Result 2 *For a fixed object width the perceived central modulation decreases with increasing edge modulation frequency.*

These results appear to be consistent with our earlier prediction. Specifically, if the perceived centers of the wiggle stimuli inferred by Burbeck *et al.* coincide with high-order shocks, *the central modulation computed as the horizontal displacement between fourth-order shocks in alignment with successive left and right sinusoidal peaks, Figure 6, should agree with the psychophysical data.* Thus in the following section we compare computational results obtained using the shock detection algorithm of [6] with Burbeck *et al.*'s data.

3 Results and Discussion

We computed shock-based representations for all 24 wiggles using the algorithm in [6]. Results for selected stimuli are shown in Figure 5, with the geometry of the high-order shocks explained in Figure 6. As striking evidence in favor of our hypothesis, consider the computed central modulations overlayed as solid lines on the original observer data taken from [7], in Figure 7. We note

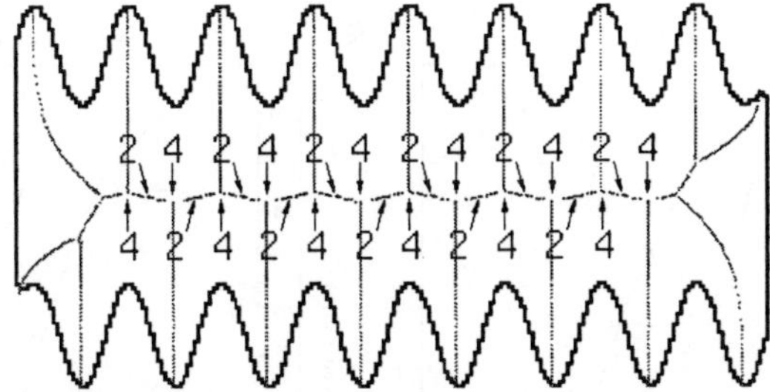

Figure 6: Shape (d) from Figure 5 is rotated and second-order and fourth-order shocks are labeled (all other shocks are first-order). Note that the fourth-order shocks are in alignment with the sinusoidal peaks.

that the discrepancy between the data for the two observers is greater than that between any single observer and the computational prediction. Hence the predicted central modulations indicate an "average" observer's data (unfortunately psychophysical data for more observers was not available).

Whereas the core and the shock-based representation are motivated from quite different points of view, the strong overlap between computational and psychophysical results for each model points to an intimate connection between the two. A precise mathematical comparison is beyond the scope of this paper. Instead, we identify the qualitative connections that have emerged.

First, the "fuzziness" of the core model, whereby the width of the core scales with object width, is paralleled by the ratio of a shock's formation time to the lifetime of the shape, a measure of local width/global width. This property is also reflected in the "bisection-threshold" or variance of the perceived centers in Burbeck *et al.*'s psychophysical experiments. Underlying this notion is the concept that the scale at which boundaries should interact to form more global object models is proportional to the spatial extent across which they communicate.

Second, the effects of edge modulation on perceived centers for the wiggle stimuli can be explained by both models. We submit that the shock-based predictions are clearer, the only relevant parameter being the location of the relevant high-order shocks. The core model is mathematically quite complex, and its simulation requires the proper choice of a number of parameters [8]. However, to put this comparison in proper context, we note that the algorithm for the core is designed to infer medialness directly from grey level images; a non-trivial task. On the other hand, the framework for shocks assumes that a foreground binary shape has already been segmented, an assumption

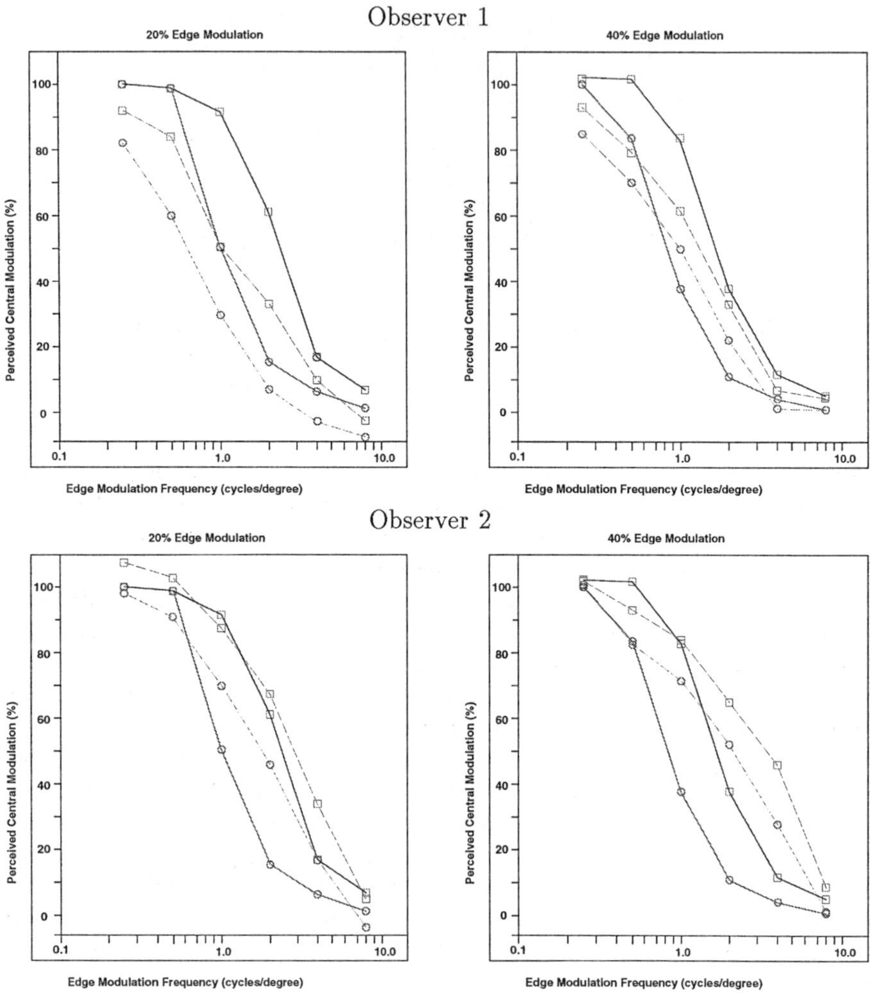

Figure 7: Central modulations computed from shock-based descriptions (solid lines) are overlayed on the observer data (dashed lines) reproduced from [7]. The central modulations are expressed as a percentage of the edge modulation amplitude and are plotted against edge modulation frequency for amplitudes of 20% of the object width (left) and 40% of the object width (right). Results for the wider 1.5° object are depicted by the circles and for the narrower 0.75° object by the squares.

which although not unreasonable for the synthetic wiggle stimuli, is certainly a limitation for more complicated images. Both models support medial-axis like representations for shape; see[11] for recent work on this topic. It is indeed gratifying that they are further quantifiably consistent with human performance involving shape.

Acknowledgments

This work was supported by grants from the Natural Sciences and Engineering Research Council of Canada, from the National Science Foundation, from the Air Force Office of Scientific Research and from the Army Research Office. We thank Christina Burbeck, Steve Pizer and Xiaofei Wang for fruitful discussions and for supplying us with the wiggle stimuli, and the reviewers for their helpful comments.

References

1. B. B. Kimia, A. Tannenbaum, and S. W. Zucker. Shape, shocks, and deformations I: The components of two-dimensional shape and the reaction-diffusion space. *Int. Journal of Computer Vision*, 15:189–224, 1995.
2. B. B. Kimia, A. Tannenbaum, and S. W. Zucker. Toward a computational theory of shape: An overview. *Proceedings of the First European Conference on Computer Vision*, pages 402–407, 1990.
3. R. Brockett and P. Maragos. Evolution equations for continuous-scale morphology. In *Proceedings of the IEEE Conference on Acoustics, Speech and Signal Processing*, San Francisco, CA, March 1992.
4. Peter D. Lax. Shock waves and entropy. In *Contributions to Nonlinear Functional Analysis*, pages 603–634, New York, 1971. Academic Press.
5. Benjamin B. Kimia, Allen R. Tannenbaum, and Steven W. Zucker. The shape triangle: Parts, protrusions, and bends. In *Aspects of Visual Form Processing*, pages 307–323. World Scientific, June 1994.
6. Kaleem Siddiqi and Benjamin B. Kimia. A shock grammar for recognition. In *IEEE Conference on Computer Vision and Pattern Recognition*, pages 507–513, June 1996.
7. Christina A. Burbeck, Stephen M. Pizer, Bryan S. Morse, Dan Ariely, Gal S. Zauberman, and Jannick Rolland. Linking object boundaries at scale: A common mechanism for size and shape judgements. *Vision Research*, In press, 1996.
8. Bryan S. Morse, Stephen M. Pizer, and Christina A. Burbeck. General shape and specific detail: Context-dependent use of scale in determining

visual form. In *Aspects of Visual Form Processing*, pages 374–383. World Scientific, June 1994.

9. Christina A. Burbeck and Stephen M. Pizer. Object representation by cores: Identifying and representing primitive spatial regions. *Vision Research*, 35:1917–1930, 1995.
10. Christina Burbeck and S. Hadden. Scaled position integration areas: Accounting for weber's law for separation. *Journal of the Optical Society of America A*, 10(1):5–15, 1993.
11. Carlo Arcelli, Luigi P. Cordella, and Gabriella Sanniti di Baja, editors. *Aspects of Visual Form Processing.* World Scientific, June 1994.

SHAPE DESCRIPTION AND SEGMENTATION IN 2 AND 3 DIMENSIONS BY POLYNOMIAL EXPANSION

ÖRJAN SMEDBY
Department of Diagnostic Radiology, Uppsala University Hospital
SE-751 85 Uppsala, Sweden
E-mail Orjan.Smedby@radiol.uu.se

GUNILLA BORGEFORS
Centre for Image Analysis, Swedish University for Agricultural Sciences
Lägerhyddsvägen 17
SE-752 37 Uppsala, Sweden

Based on the theory of Fourier descriptors as a tool for studying 2D shape, this study aims at creating a theory for 3D shape description with polynomials. Parametrizing the unit circle with arc length, one can approximate the distance from the origin in each direction with a trigonometric sum (Fourier expansion). If, instead, Cartesian coordinates are used to parametrize the circle, a polynomial of corresponding degree is obtained. 3D shape can be studied by approximating the distance by a polynomial in the Cartesian coordinates of a point on the unit sphere. The coefficients of this polynomial may be calculated with inner products defined by surface integrals over the unit sphere. Using spherical harmonic polynomials, a unique expansion with adaptable accuracy is obtained. Preliminary empirical computations are presented. Since the algorithms for polynomial expansion of the boundary are linear, they are easily generalized to segmentation algorithms for non-binary images.

1 Introduction

Modern imaging methods, in particular in biomedical applications, to an increasing extent yield volume images, i.e., truly 3-dimensional data sets. This makes traditional image analysis methods inadequate for many situations. In two dimensions, Fourier expansion of the boundary is a useful technique to describe the shape of many objects [1,2]. The Fourier coefficients offer a unique representation of the shape with variable accuracy (determined by the number of terms) and a measure of similarity between shapes, which may be useful e.g. for classification of objects. With some modification, the representation can be made invariant for translation, rotation and linear scaling [2].

In its usual formulation, the theory relies on identifying the image plane with the plane of complex numbers or on representing the boundary with a periodic function in one variable. This makes generalization to higher dimensions difficult. However, much of the theory can be given an alternative formulation involving a global polynomial model. The objective of this study is to to develop such an alternative formulation of the theory, which is more easily generalized to 3 dimensions.

2 The similarity measure

Our first objective is to define a measure of resemblance between objects. Suppose that the object is centered around the origin. Consider the function D assigning to each point on the unit sphere S (or in the 2D case the unit circle T) — i.e. a direction vector — the distance from the origin to the object boundary in the corresponding direction. Sets that can be described in this manner are called star-shaped.

If the orientation problem is not taken into account, the likeness between two objects described by such functions D_1 and D_2 can be defined with the normalized inner product of the function space $L^2(S)$:

$$Li(D_1, D_2) = \frac{\langle D_1 | D_2 \rangle}{\|D_1\| \cdot \|D_2\|} = \frac{\langle D_1 | D_2 \rangle}{\sqrt{\langle D_1 | D_1 \rangle} \cdot \sqrt{\langle D_2 | D_2 \rangle}} \tag{1}$$

where $\langle f | g \rangle$ denotes the inner product (see below).

To compare objects that may differ in orientation, a measure of similarity is then defined by

$$Sim(D_1, D_2) = \sup_{\mathbf{A} \in \mathbf{SO}(3)} Li(D_1 \circ \mathbf{A}, D_2) \tag{2}$$

i.e., the greatest likeness that can be obtained by rotating one of the objects with an orthonormal matrix $\mathbf{A}$.

Numerically, the computation of this similarity measure amounts to an optimization problem with few parameters (3 degrees of freedom). However, with objects defined by 3D data sets, each rotation and inner product calculation involves substantial computational work, which will be reduced by the more condensed representation introduced below.

3 Parametrization and shape representation

A 2D Case

The parametrization of the unit circle can be made in several ways. For Fourier expansion, one uses the arc length t along the circle, resulting in a periodic function:

$$D(t) = a_0^0 + a_1^0 \cos t + a_1^1 \sin t + a_2^0 \cos 2t + a_2^1 \sin 2t + a_3^0 \cos 3t + a_3^1 \sin 3t + \ldots \tag{3}$$

However, both cos kt and sin kt can be expressed as polynomials in cos t and sin t

of degree k. Introducing the Cartesian coordinates of the direction vector, u=cos t and v=sin t, we obtain a polynomial expansion

$$D(u,v) = b_0^0 + b_1^0 u + b_1^1 v + b_2^0 u^2 + b_2^1 uv + b_2^2 v^2 + \ldots \tag{4}$$

To include the frequency range up to cos nt and sin nt, we let the polynomial have degree n. This representation is not unique, as the polynomials in u and v are not linearly independent on the unit circle ($v^2 = 1 - u^2$, $u^2 v = v - v^3$ etc.).

According to a theorem in functional analysis (Stone-Weierstrass), every continuos function D can be uniformly approximated with a polynomial[3]. If the object is smooth enough (has a boundary of class C^1), then the expansion in Eq. (4) converges uniformly to D.

The simplest way to obtain a unique representation is the following: every term of degree $k \le n-2$ is substituted with two terms of degree $k+2$ by multiplying with $u^2 + v^2$, which is identical to 1 on the unit circle. Thus one can eliminate (recursively) all terms except those of degree $n-1$ and n.

A different unique representation (with the original coefficients a_k^j) can be obtained with orthogonal polynomials, e.g.

$$\begin{aligned} D(u,v) = a_0^0 + a_1^0 T_1^0(u,v) + a_1^1 T_1^1(u,v) + a_2^0 T_2^0(u,v) + a_2^1 T_2^1(u,v) + \\ + a_3^0 T_3^0(u,v) + a_3^1 T_3^1(u,v) + \ldots \end{aligned} \tag{5}$$

where $T_k^0(u,v) = \cos kt = T_k(u)$ (Chebyshev polynomial of degree k)[4] and

$$T_k^1(u,v) = \sin kt = T_k(K_k^0 u + K_k^1 v),\ \ K_k^0 = \cos\frac{\pi}{2k},\ \ K_k^1 = \sin\frac{\pi}{2k}$$

The orthogonality of the polynomials will simplify the computation of the coefficients a_k^j (see below). The polynomials T_k^j may also be calculated recursively.

B 3D Case

In analogy with above, we approximate D with a polynomial in u, v and w, i.e. the Cartesian coordinates of the direction vector:

$$D(u,v,w) = b_0^0 + b_1^0 u + b_1^1 v + b_1^2 w + b_2^0 u^2 + b_2^1 uv + b_2^2 v^2 + b_2^3 uw + \ldots \tag{6}$$

Just as in the 2D case, one may include terms up to a given degree in order to study the shape of the object more or less in detail.

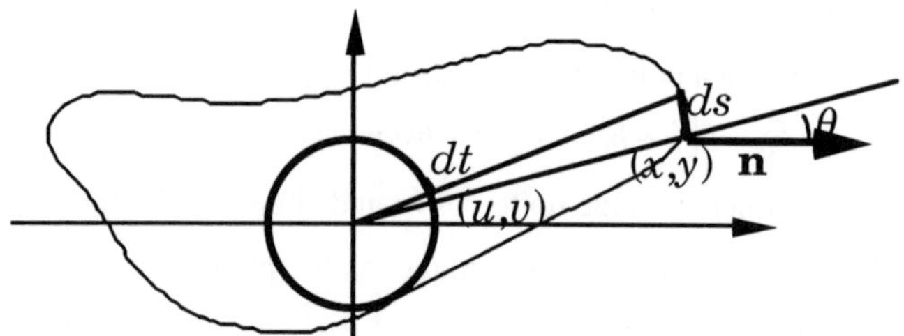

Fig. 1. Integration on unit circle and object boundary in 2D.

4 Computation of coefficients – continuous

A 2D Case

To compute the coefficients of the polynomials, one can employ the inner product in $L^2(T)$, defined by a curve integral with a normalizing factor:

$$\langle f | g \rangle = \frac{1}{2\pi} \int_T f(\mathbf{u})\, g(\mathbf{u})\, dt \tag{7}$$

With orthonormal polynomials, this becomes particularly easy:

$$a_k^j = \left\langle T_k^j \middle| D \right\rangle = \frac{1}{2\pi} \int_T T_k^j(u,v)\, D(u,v)\, dt = \frac{1}{2\pi} \int_T T_k^j(\mathbf{u})\, D(\mathbf{u})\, dt \tag{8}$$

Here, $(u,v) = \mathbf{u}$ and dt denote points and curve elements on the unit circle, whereas $(x,y) = \mathbf{x}$ and ds are points and curve elements on the boundary ∂B (Fig. 1).

The integral above may be rewritten as an integral over ∂B, taking into account that $Ddt = \cos\theta\, ds$, where θ is the angle between the radius and the outer normal of the curve:

$$a_k^j = \frac{1}{2\pi} \int_T T_k^j(u,v)\, D(u,v)\, dt = \frac{1}{2\pi} \int_{\partial B} T_k^j \left(\frac{x}{\sqrt{x^2+y^2}}, \frac{y}{\sqrt{x^2+y^2}} \right) \cos\theta\, ds \tag{9}$$

Introducing the notation $\mathbf{u}(\mathbf{x}) = \frac{1}{|\mathbf{x}|}\mathbf{x}$, this equation becomes

$$a_k^j = \frac{1}{2\pi} \int_T T_k^j(\mathbf{u})\, D(\mathbf{u})\, dt = \frac{1}{2\pi} \int_{\partial B} T_k^j(\mathbf{u}(\mathbf{x}))\, \mathbf{u}(\mathbf{x}) \cdot \mathbf{n}\, ds \tag{10}$$

B 3D Case

In this case, the inner product (in $L^2(S)$) is defined by a normalized surface integral over S:

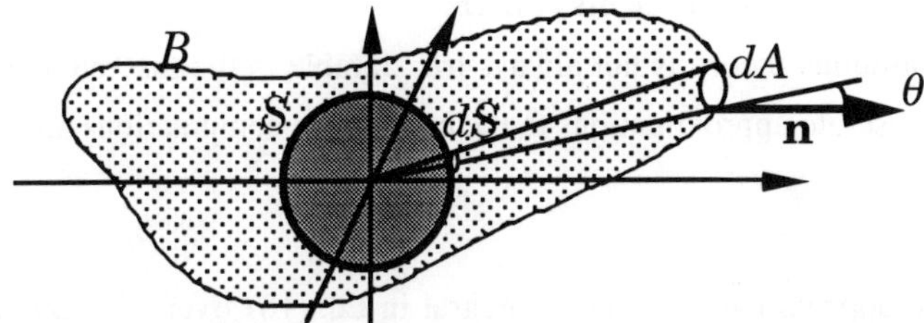

Fig. 2 Integration on unit sphere and object boundary in 3D.

$$\langle f|g\rangle = \frac{1}{4\pi}\int_S f(\mathbf{u})\, g(\mathbf{u})\, dS \tag{11}$$

A complete set of orthonormal polynomials with respect to this inner product is given by the spherical harmonic polynomials[5]. It can be shown that every function f in $L^2(S)$ — and thus every continuous function on S — has a unique representation in the form

$$f(\mathbf{u}) = p_0(\mathbf{u}) + p_1(\mathbf{u}) + p_2(\mathbf{u}) + \ldots \tag{12}$$

where $p_k(\mathbf{u})$ is a homogeneous harmonic polynomial of degree k and the series converges in L^2 norm.

For each degree k, let $\left\{S_k^1(\mathbf{u}), S_k^2(\mathbf{u}), \ldots, S_k^{n_k}(\mathbf{u})\right\}$ be an orthonormal basis for the n_k-dimensional vector space of homogeneous harmonic polynomials of degree k restricted to S. How such a basis can be explicitly constructed is shown in [5]. We thus have:

$$f(\mathbf{u}) = \sum_{k=1}^{\infty} p_k(\mathbf{u}) = \sum_{k=1}^{\infty}\sum_{j=1}^{n_k} c_k^j S_k^j(\mathbf{u}) \tag{13}$$

The coefficients in this expansion may be computed from

$$c_k^j = \left\langle S_k^j \middle| D \right\rangle = \frac{1}{4\pi}\int_S S_k^j(u,v,w)\, D(u,v,w)\, dS = \frac{1}{4\pi}\int_S S_k^j(\mathbf{u})\, D(\mathbf{u})\, dS \tag{14}$$

This time, though, the surface element dA of ∂B is given by $\cos\theta\, dA = D^2\, dS$ (Fig. 2). This gives (15)

$$c_k^j = \frac{1}{4\pi}\int_S S_k^j(\mathbf{u})\, D(\mathbf{u})\, dS = \frac{1}{4\pi}\int_{\partial B} \frac{S_k^j(\mathbf{u}(\mathbf{x}))}{D(\mathbf{u}(\mathbf{x}))}\, \mathbf{u}(\mathbf{x})\cdot\mathbf{n}\, dA = \frac{1}{4\pi}\int_{\partial B} \frac{S_k^j(u,v,w)}{D(u,v,w)} \cos\theta\, d$$

5 Computation of coefficients – discrete

Although continuous theory is not always transferable to the discrete context, it is natural to try discrete approximations to the continuous computations above.

A 2D Case

Our goal is to approximate the curve integral in Eq. (10) over ∂B from a discrete binary image. To avoid depending on a specific parametrization of ∂B, we calculate the integral by summing over the entire plane, while weighting by scalar multiplication in each point with a vector **W** corresponding to **n**ds, i.e. the arc length ds on ∂B, multiplied with the normal vector, which can have only eight directions. Table 1 shows how the vector **W** may be constructed from a 2×2 neighborhood. As the xy-values used for further computations do not have to be integers, each edge element between two pixels here gives two contributions to **W**, located at each end of the edge, where the coordinates differ from the center of the pixel by $\frac{1}{2}$.

Table 1. Examples of computation of the weighted normal vector.

Neighborhood	Normals of edge elements	Weighting vector (**W**)
	0	0
	$\left(\frac{1}{2},0\right)$ $\left(\frac{1}{2},0\right)$	(1,0)
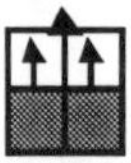	$\left(0,\frac{1}{2}\right)$ $\left(0,\frac{1}{2}\right)$	(0,1)
	$\left(\frac{1}{2},0\right)$ $\left(0,\frac{1}{2}\right)$	$\left(\frac{1}{2},\frac{1}{2}\right)$
	$\left(\frac{1}{2},0\right)$ $\left(0,\frac{1}{2}\right)$	$\left(\frac{1}{2},\frac{1}{2}\right)$
	0	0

The explicit formula for computing **W** from the binary image B is

$$\mathbf{W}\left(x+\frac{1}{2},y+\frac{1}{2}\right)=\frac{1}{2}\big(B(x,y)+B(x,y+1)-B(x+1,y)-B(x+1,y+1), \\ B(x,y)+B(x+1,y)-B(x,y+1)-B(x+1,y+1)\big) \tag{16}$$

Thus the discrete approximation of Eq. (10) will be

$$a_k^j=\frac{1}{2\pi}\sum T_k^j(\mathbf{u}(\mathbf{x}))\,\mathbf{u}(\mathbf{x})\cdot\mathbf{W}(\mathbf{x}) \tag{17}$$

where the sum is extended over the entire image plane.

B 3D Case

For discrete computation of the surface integral Eq. (15), we use a 2×2×2 mask to obtain $\mathbf{W}(\mathbf{x})$ as a 3D vector-valued gradient image, in analogy with Eq. (16). The algorithm for calculating c_k^j becomes:

$$c_k^j=\frac{1}{2\pi}\sum\frac{S_k^j(\mathbf{u}(\mathbf{x}))}{|\mathbf{x}|}\mathbf{u}(\mathbf{x})\cdot\mathbf{W}(\mathbf{x})=\frac{1}{2\pi}\sum\frac{S_k^j\left(\frac{1}{|\mathbf{x}|}\mathbf{x}\right)}{|\mathbf{x}|^2}\mathbf{x}\cdot\mathbf{W}(\mathbf{x}) \tag{18}$$

where the summation is carried out over the entire *xyz*-space.

6 Further development: segmentation

The theory presented above is based on a binary image $B(\mathbf{x})$. It may, however, be of interest to investigate what will happen if the image is only "approximately binary", i.e. if it consists of one region with values close to 0 and one region with values close to 1. This is a common situation in image segmentation, if the gray-values are first suitably rescaled.

Since the formulas for computing the coefficients a_k^j and c_k^j (the gradient calculation and the summations in Eqs. (17) and (18)) are linear, they may be applied to gray-scale images. After appropriate rescaling, this will result in a polynomial defining a position for the border in every direction from the origin. This detected contour or surface will depend only on gradient information in the radial direction. It is reasonable to assume that, if $B(\mathbf{x})$ in some sense resembles a certain binary image, then the contour computed in this way will also resemble the contour in the binary image.

7 Preliminary experimental results

The 2D version of the described technique has been applied to a few synthetic binary and gray-scale images, and the results are shown in Fig. 3. The computed contours of the binary images clearly approach the true position of the boundary as the degree of the polynomial increases. For the gray-scale images, the polynomial contours with lowest degree (n=4) are fairly close to the polynomial contours of the corresponding binary images. With higher degree, artifacts from the noise are introduced, and at degree 16, the polynomials do not yield any meaningful information.

An experiment with 3D shapes is illustrated in Fig. 4. The computation was carried out in Mathematica (Wolfram Research, Inc., Champaign, IL, USA) using publicly available code for the spherical harmonic polynomials[5]. The input image was a binary representation of an octahedron. At degree 2, a spherical shape was obtained. At degree 6, the general shape of the octahedron can be discerned, and at degree 12, a closer resemblance is seen.

8 Discussion

The increasing use of volume images, in particular in medical applications, motivates the development of theory to describe shape in 3 dimensions. Whereas splines often give good approximations locally, relatively few attempts have been made to apply a global analytical description to the shape of 3D objects in image data. One occasionally used approach is the use of superquadrics[6,7]. Spherical harmonics have been employed to model 3D shape in a few previous studies in the fields of image analysis, organic chemistry and virology[7,8,9].

The proposed method offers a concise representation of shape in 2D and 3D and allows similarity computations (as in Eq. 2) to be made with reasonable efforts, once the inner products of the basis functions have been tabulated. Just as with 2D Fourier descriptors, the accuracy of the description may be adjusted by the number of terms included in the expansion. The main limitation is that the objects studied must be star-shaped. Assigning a 3-dimensional position vector rather than a radial distance to each point on the sphere, Székely *et al*[8]. have been able to describe a much wider range of objects, at the price, however, of a rather complicated and computationally intensive optimization procedure in the parametrization step.

In addition to shape description, our algorithms may be applied to segmentation problems, if low accuracy (low degree of the polynomial) is sufficient. However, a considerable theoretical effort remains to establish resemblance criteria between gray-scale images and computed shapes. Other possible ways to apply the shape description to segmentation include polynomial expansion after thresholding and parametric optimization using some resemblance criterion. A natural continuation of the work presented in this paper will be to to evaluate our method in comparison with alternative solutions for similar problems, e.g. deformable contours (snakes) and surfaces [7,8,10].

9 Acknowledgment

The authors are indebted to Christer Kiselman for advice concerning the mathematical theory and to H. Azadali and I. Berglund for computational assistance.

10 References

1. C. T. Zahn and R. Z. Roskies, "Fourier descriptors for plane closed curves", *IEEE Transactions on Computers*, vol. C-21, pp. 269–281, 1972.
2. G. H. Granlund, "Fourier preprocessing for hand print character recognition", *IEEE Transactions on Computers*, vol. C-22, pp. 195–201, 1972.
3. Rudin W. *Functional Analysis*. McGraw-Hill, 1973.
4. *Encyclopedic Dictionary of Mathematics*, vol. I–IV. Cambridge, Massachusetts: The MIT Press, 1986.
5. S. Axler, P. Bourdon and W. Ramey, *Harmonic Function Theory*, New York: Springer-Verlag, 1992.
6. A. Gupta and R. Bajcsy, "Volumetric segmentation of range images of 3D objects using superquadric models", *CVGIP: Image Understanding*, vol. 58, pp. 302-26, 1993.
7. H. Staib and J. S. Duncan, "Deformable Fourier models for surface finding in 3D images", in *SPIE Proceedings, VBC'92*, 1992, pp. 90–104.
8. G. Székely *et al.*, "Segmentation of 2-D and 3-D objects from MRI volume data using constrained elastic deformations of flexible Fourier contour and surface models.", *Medical Image Analysis*, vol. 1, pp. 19–34, 1996.
9. B. S. Duncan and A. J. Olson, "Approximation and characterization of molecular surfaces", *Biopolymers*, vol. 33, pp. 219-29, 1993.
10. M. Kass, A. Witkin and D. Terzopoulos, "Snakes: active contour models", *International Journal of Computer Vision*, vol. 1, pp. 321–331, 1987.

n=4 n=8 n=16

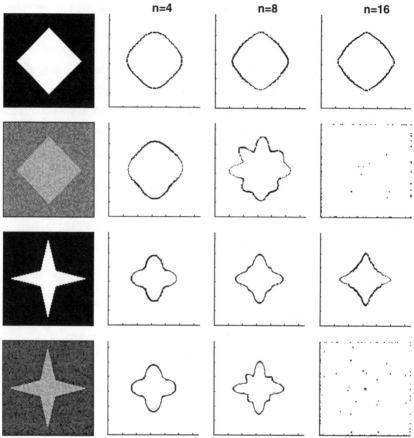

Fig. 3 Examples of 2D images with computed polynomial boundaries of 3 different degrees.

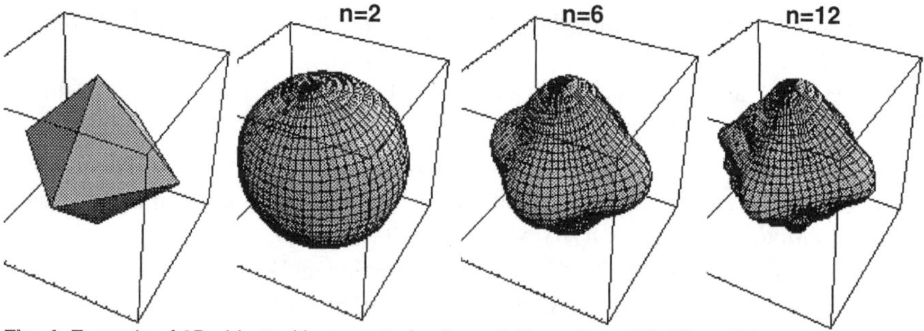

Fig. 4 Example of 3D object with computed polynomial boundary of 3 different degrees.

NEGATIVE SHAPE FEATURES FOR IMAGE DATABASES CONSISTING OF GEOGRAPHIC SYMBOLS

AYA SOFFER
Computer Science and EE Department
University of Maryland Baltimore County
Baltimore, MD 21250 and
CESDIS, Goddard Space Flight Center
E-mail: soffer@cs.umbc.edu

HANAN SAMET
Computer Science Department and
Center for Automation Research and
Institute for Advanced Computer Science
University of Maryland at College Park
College Park, Maryland 20742
E-mail: hjs@umiacs.umd.edu

Abstract

A method for representing geographic symbols for storage and retrieval in an image database is presented. Symbols are characterized by a collection of features that describe their shape. Many of these geographic symbols are composed of a circle (or rectangle) enclosing one or more small shapes. A new representation of such symbols based on their interior with the shapes considered as holes, termed a *negative symbol*, is described. A set of shape features used to characterize geographic symbols is presented. These features are appropriate for symbols that are represented by their negation as well as for symbols that are composed of only one part and thus are not represented by their negation. Negative symbols along with these features have been used successfully to index maps in a map image database system. Results of experiments testing the accuracy of the database using these features are given.

1 Introduction

Consider a database containing a large number of images each composed of several symbols that have some meaning (e.g., the symbol on a paper map that represents a museum). Such images are called *symbolic images* and their domain includes maps, engineering drawings, and floor plans. For example, suppose that we wish to find all of the images in the database that contain a particular symbol. There are generally two methods of achieving this capability. In the first method, termed *classification*, each symbol in each image is classified (i.e., it is replaced by its symbolic meaning). In the second method, termed ***abstraction***, each symbol is represented by some properties of its visual representation (e.g., shape, length, connectivity, genus, etc.) termed a *feature vector*. Classification can potentially be performed using template matching. However, template matching is limited to cases where all instances of the same symbol have the same scale and orientation. Therefore, classification should be performed using a more robust method such as statistical pattern recognition based on some descriptive features of the symbols. In both methods for storing images it is desirable to represent a symbol by a small number of numeric descriptors.

In our work, we concentrate on databases consisting of images that contain geographic symbols. These images could be, for example, the symbol layer of a tourist map. An interesting characteristic of such symbols is that many of them tend to be composed of a circle (or rectangle) enclosing one or more small shapes (e.g., the beach and hotel symbols in Figure 1 which shows the geographic symbols that we have studied along with their semantic meaning). Ideally, we would like to represent each symbol in the database with only one feature vector in order to simplify the search process at query time. Therefore, for symbols that are composed of several shapes, we must select one of these shapes to represent it. This may lead to ambiguity and as a result we may not be able to distinguish between some symbols. In order to overcome this problem, we propose to represent such symbols by the interior of the circle with the small shapes considered as holes in this object (termed a *negative symbol*). For example, the "beach" symbol in Figure 1 would be represented by the interior of a circle with the two wiggly lines as holes.

Most image databases treat images as a whole and index them on the basis of color and texture [7, 8, 14]. However, shape features have also been used [1, 11]. In all of these cases the objects that are being indexed based on shape are assumed to be simple (i.e., composed of only one part). Most research in map recognition has concentrated on skeletonization and vectorization methods [15]. Some research has been done on separating the layers of scanned maps [13]. Recognizing geographic symbols in the context of map recognition has also been considered [5, 16]. The methods employed in these studies are either very computationally expensive or require the user to explicitly build a semantic model that is used to perform the classification of map objects. Thus, these methods are not applicable in the context of an image database.

In this paper, we study the appropriateness of using the negative symbol representation. In addition, we describe a set of shape features that can be used to characterize symbols represented by their negation as well as symbols that are only composed of one part and thus are not represented by their

Figure 1: Geographic symbols and their semantic meaning.

negation (termed *positive symbols*). These features should be easy to compute since we need to calculate them for a large number of images. Furthermore, the number of features should be relatively small in order to facilitate efficient comparison of features. Finally, these features should be effective in discriminating between different geographic symbols. We have used negative symbols along with these features to successfully index maps in a map image database system that we have developed [10]. In this paper, we assume that we are using the classification approach to storing images. That is, we are classifying the geographic symbols as the map images are input to the system. However, these same features can also be stored directly in the database if using the abstraction method [12].

The rest of this paper is organized as follows. Section 2 presents an overview of the symbol recognition method that we used. Section 3 motivates our use of negative symbols. Section 4 describes the shape features that we use to represent geographic symbols. Section 5 discusses the implementation and experimental results. Section 6 contains concluding remarks.

2 Overview of Symbol Recognition Method

Figure 2 is an overview of the method. The symbol layer of the map is scanned. Next, segmentation is performed which identifies the individual symbols to be classified. Features are extracted for each individual symbol. Finally, each symbol is classified. In our system, segmentation is performed via a connected

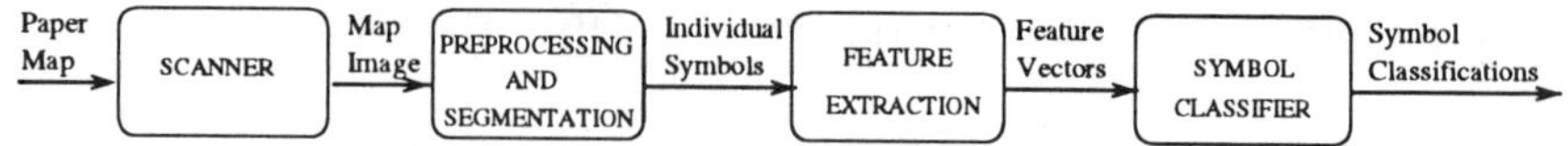

Figure 2: Block diagram of symbol classification system

component labeling algorithm. This results in a labeled image in which each pixel has a region number as its value.

As mentioned above, complex map symbols are represented by the interior of the symbol with the enclosed shapes considered as holes. This enables us to represent symbols such as the beach symbol that are composed of more than one piece by only one connected component. Our system assumes that the symbols may be distinguished from each other by just one connected component using this method.

Symbols are classified based on the shape features that are computed for the connected component using a *weighted bounded several-nearest neighbor classifier* [2]. This classifier makes use of a training set with several representative feature vectors for each symbol. We construct an initial training set library by analyzing the legend and inserting the feature vector of the connected component that was chosen to represent each symbol into the training set. The training set is later expanded by adding feature vectors of symbols that are identified by the user as having been erroneously classified. For more details about this process, see [10].

3 Why Use Negative Symbols?

We encountered several problems when using only positive symbols. We use Figure 3, a typical image used in our application, to illustrate the difficulties with positive symbols. Recall, that our goal is to represent each symbol by only one feature vector in order to simplify the search process at query time.

The main problem with positive symbols is ambiguity. For example, using only positive symbols we cannot distinguish between the hotel ◙ symbol and the youth hostel ▪ symbol. If we choose to represent the hotel ◙ by the square inside the circle, then there is no difference between it and the youth hostel ▪ symbol. The circle cannot represent the hotel ◙ either, as it is common to many symbols. However, using negative symbols the hotel ◙ is represented by a circle with a square cut out of it and the youth hostel ▪ is represented by a square, and thus we can distinguish between the two. Another source of ambiguity is that using positive symbols we cannot distinguish between a letter that is enclosed in a circle, and is thus a legend symbol, and a letter that

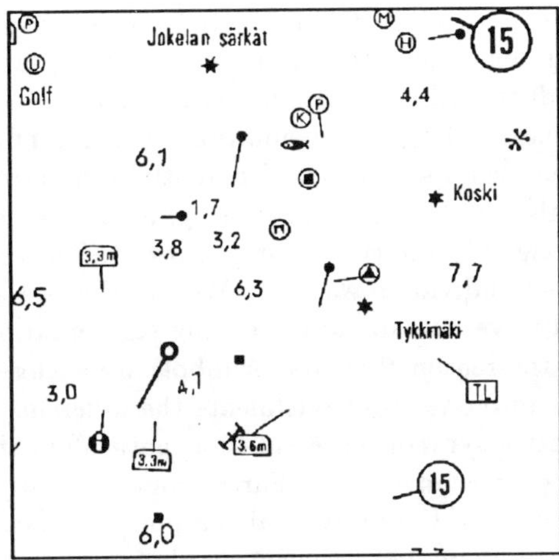

Figure 3: Example map tile

is part of a word. For example, we cannot distinguish between the symbol for cafe Ⓚ and the "K" in the word "Kuski" (see Figure 3). However, using negative symbols the cafe Ⓚ is represented by a circle with a "K" cut out of it, and thus the "K" in the word "Kuski" will not be erroneously considered a cafe Ⓚ .

It is worth noting that if we were to represent symbols by more than one region, we would encounter additional problems using positive symbols. For example, we could represent the hotel ◉ as a combination of a square and a circle. However, we would then need to also model the topological layout (that is, that the square is inside the circle). The database search process would need to verify this at query time, and as a result searching would be much more complex. In addition, if two symbols touch each other (e.g., ⓀⓅ), then the two circles would be considered one region and we could not recognize either symbol. However, this is not a concern when using negative symbols. Although the circles touch, the interiors do not, and thus we have two separate regions and this problem does not arise.

As part of the segmentation process, we set a threshold for the minimal acceptable size of a segment. Any segment (i.e., connected component) that is smaller than this threshold is not considered a potential symbol. When using positive symbols, this threshold has to be smaller than when using negative symbols since a symbol may be represented by a relatively small component. For example, we could represent the beach ⊖ symbol by one of the waves ~ .

The size of the wave ⌒ is relatively small. In order to ensure that we do not discard it during segmentation, the minimal size for acceptable segments needs to be relatively small as well. As a result, each image contains more segments and thus the database is larger. In addition, a larger number of segments that do not represent valid symbols will potentially be erroneously classified as valid symbols (false hits). Using negative symbols, the beach symbol is represented by a circle with the two waves ⌒ cut out. The size of this region is much larger than each individual wave ⌒. We can thus set a higher threshold and each individual wave ⌒ is discarded during segmentation.

To summarize, the reason that map symbols are enclosed in a circle is to group several pieces into one and to delineate the difference between symbols and text. The negative symbol representation naturally captures this grouping using only one connected region. Furthermore, the size of this region is large relative to the size of the individual components that make up the positive symbol, and thus many non-relevant symbols can be filtered out during segmentation by use of a simple threshold.

4 Shape Feature Selection

The selection of the particular shape features that are used to characterize the symbols is one of the most important factors in achieving high recognition rates. Numerous shape features have been described in the literature (e.g., [6]). These features are generally either based on the boundary or interior representation of the object. The boundary-based shape features capture the "jaggedness" and complexity of the object. In order to use these features, the object is usually approximized by a polygon. Measurements such as the number of sides, the relative length of these sides, and the angles between the sides of the polygonal approximation are then used to describe the shape of the object. Since we are performing symbol recognition as part of the input process of an image database, we wanted to keep the computation as simple and quick as possible. Thus, we did not use such features.

The features that we use are all based on the interior representation of the symbols as output by the connected component labeling process. Recall that each symbol is represented by one of its connected components. In particular, in the case of complex symbols, this component is the negation of the symbol (i.e., the interior of the circle). Figure 4 demonstrates this process for an example symbol. The symbol has three regions after connected component labeling. Region 3, which is the interior of the circle with the letter "H" cut out is selected to represent this symbol. The shape features that we compute approximate the boundary complexity and the shape regularity of the symbol's

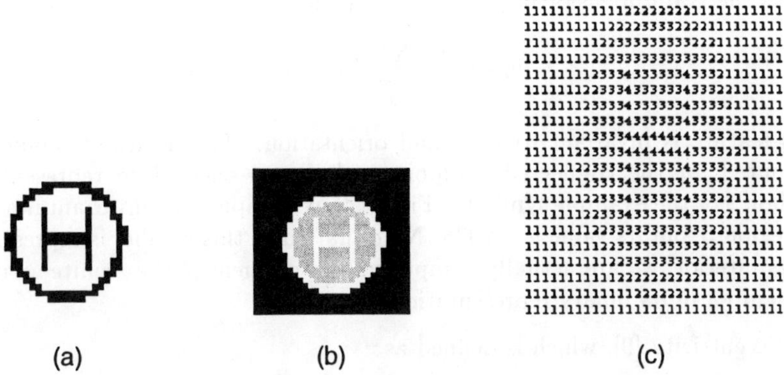

Figure 4: Processing one example symbol: (a) Binary representation of the symbol. (b) Symbol after connected component labeling. Each region has a different color. (c) Bit map of the symbol after connected component labeling. Region 3 is selected to represent this symbol.

representative component based on the area of this component, the perimeter of the component, and the major and minor axes of the component. In addition to these global features, we also compute some local features pertaining to holes in the component. We define a hole as a region that is enclosed in another region either vertically or horizontally. These features are required in order to distinguish between symbols that are represented by their negation. The global shape is very similar for all of these components as they are all basically circles. The discriminating factor between them is the shape of the holes. Note that all of the features that we compute require only one pass over the image following connected component labeling. We use the following shape features. F_1: First invariant moment [4], which is defined as

$$M_1 = \mu_{20} + \mu_{02}.$$

Here μ_{pq} is the central moment given by

$$\mu_{pq} = \sum_i \sum_j (i - \overline{x})^p (j - \overline{y})^q I(i,j),$$

where $I(i,j)$ is the intensity (grey level) at point (i,j) in image I, and $\overline{x}$ and $\overline{y}$ are defined as follows:

$$\overline{x} = \frac{m_{10}}{m_{00}} \qquad \overline{y} = \frac{m_{01}}{m_{00}}.$$

m_{pq} is the two-dimensional $(p+q)$th order moment and is defined as

$$m_{pq} = \sum_i \sum_j i^p j^q I(i,j).$$

This feature is invariant to scale and orientation. The invariant moment is computed for the connected component that was selected to represent the symbol. For the example symbol in Figure 4, we compute the invariant moment for region 3 and its value is 0.2078. Note that since this symbol is represented by its interior, we are actually computing the moment of the "white" part of the symbol in its binary representation.

F_2: Eccentricity [9], which is defined as

$$E = \frac{|D - W|}{D},$$

where W and D are the length of the minor and major axis of the component. Eccentricity is a measure of the elongation of the symbol. It is 0 for a square and approaches 1 for elongated shapes. Eccentricity is useful for characterizing positive symbols (i.e, symbols not represented by their negation) such as the scenic view symbol in Figure 1. However, it does not discriminate well between negative symbols since the length of the axes is not affected by the holes in their representative component, and eccentricity will thus have similar values for all such symbols. For the example symbol in Figure 4 which is represented by region 3: width = 15, height = 16, and thus eccentricity = 0.9375.

F_3: Circularity [3], which is defined as

$$C = \frac{P^2}{4\pi A},$$

where P is the perimeter of the component, and A is its area. Circularity equals 1 for a circle and takes on larger values for distortions therefrom. It is useful for characterizing both positive and negative symbols. The area and perimeter of negative symbols is computed for the component that represents the interior in effect measuring the "white" region in the binary representation of the symbol. For the example symbol, area = 175, perimeter = 92, and thus circularity = 3.848.

F_4: Rectangularity, which is defined as

$$PB = \frac{A}{A_{bb}},$$

where A is the area of the component, and A_{bb} is the area of the minimal rectangle enclosing the component. Rectangularity equals 1 for a rectangle and approaches 0 for least rectangular shape. If the bounding box is restricted to being parallel to the axes, then this feature is not invariant to rotation. Rectangularity is not very effective for negative symbols since the bounding box is not affected by the hole area. However, since the component area is affected by the hole area, there will be some variation in rectangularity between negative symbols. For the example symbol, area = 175, bounding box area = 240, and thus rectangularity = 0.729.

F_5: Hole area ratio, which is defined as

$$HAR = \frac{A_h}{A},$$

where A is the area of the component and A_h is the total area of all holes in the component. Hole area ratio is most effective in discriminating between symbols that have big holes (e.g., the first aid station ⊕ symbol) and symbols with small holes (e.g., the beach ⊜ symbol). For the example symbol, area = 175, hole area = 32, and thus hole area ratio = 0.18.

F_6: Horizontal gaps ratio, which is defined as

$$HGR = \frac{HG^2}{A},$$

where A is the area of the component, and HG is the number of horizontal gaps in the component (i.e., the number of pixels in the object whose right neighbor is a hole). This feature discriminates among symbols based on the shape of the holes themselves. For the example symbol, area = 175, horizontal gaps = 18, and thus horizontal gaps ratio = 1.85.

F_7: Vertical gaps ratio, which is defined as

$$\mathrm{V}GR = \frac{VG^2}{A},$$

where A is the area of the component, and VG is the number of vertical gaps in the component (i.e., the number of pixels in the object whose bottom neighbor is a hole). It has the same characteristics as the horizontal gaps ratio. For the example symbol, area = 175, vertical gaps = 8, and thus vertical gaps ratio = 0.366.

5 Implementation and Experiments

The shape features described above were incorporated into the feature extractor of a map image database system developed by us [10]. Using these shape features, the system was tested on the red sign layer of the GT3 map of Finland. The scale of the map is 1:200,000. The layer was scanned at 240dpi. Figure 3 shows the extracted red sign layer. An initial training set containing 22 symbols was constructed from the legend. 60 tiles were used to expand the training set to 100 samples. The remaining tiles were processed automatically.

In the context of an image database, the classifier is evaluated in terms of the accuracy of the results of a query requesting images that contain particular symbols. We evaluated the accuracy using two error types that are commonly used in document analysis studies. A type I error occurs when an image that meets the query specification was not retrieved by the system (a miss), and a type II error occurs when an image that the system retrieved for a given query does not meet the query specification (a false hit). Note that type I and type II errors correspond to the recall and precision metrics, respectively, used in information retrieval experiments.

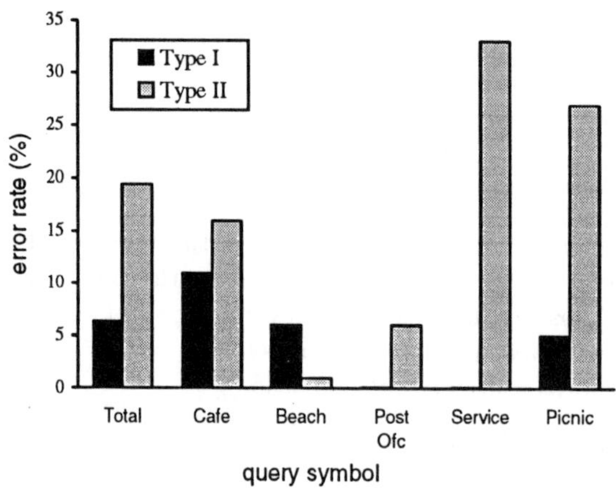

Figure 5: Type I and type II error rates.

We computed the error rates by querying the database for all tiles containing each symbol in our application. Type II error rates were calculated by counting how many results did not meet the query specification for each symbol. The total type II error rate is the total number of incorrect results (over all symbols) divided by the total number of results. Type I errors, were calculated by determining which tiles contain each symbol, and checking whether any result tiles were missed. We did this for 50 tiles (out of the 425 tiles) chosen at random and for each one of the symbols. Type I error rates were computed for each symbol in addition to a total type I error rate which is the total number of missed results divided by the total number of results we should have had.

Figure 5 reports the total type I and type II error rates, as well as these error rates for a few of the symbols. The total type I error rate was 6% (i.e., 94% of the tiles that should have been retrieved were in fact retrieved by the system). The rates varied from 0% for the post office Ⓟ symbol to 11% for the cafe Ⓚ symbol. The total type II error rate was 19% (i.e., 81% of the tiles that were retrieved did in fact contain the desired symbol). It varied from 1% for the beach ⊜ symbol to 33% for the service station Ⓗ symbol. We attribute the variance in the error rates between different symbols to the ability of the system to distinguish between them based on the selection of shape features, the classification method, and the content of the training set used for classification. Although the results that we report here are for one particular training set, we experimented with various configurations, and these results were consistent in all cases. In order to achieve lower error rates, more features would most likely be required.

6 Concluding Remarks

Representing geographic symbols that are composed of more than one component by their negation was effective for distinguishing between such symbols. The experimental results showed that with the particular shape features that were used, we can on average retrieve 94% of the required images. We are currently analyzing the effects of the individual features both analytically via principal component analysis, and empirically by using subsets of the features for classification. In addition, we plan to explore whether using additional features such as higher order moments, minimum bending energy of the curvature, and other curvature-based features will improve the accuracy. Furthermore, for symbols that are represented by their negation we need to investigate other features that can characterize the shape and the distribution of the holes as an aggregate that are invariant to scale and orientation (e.g., average circularity and eccentricity of the holes).

Acknowledgements

We are grateful to Karttakeskus, Map Center, Helsinki, Finland for providing us the map data. The support of USRA/CESDIS and NASA Goddard Space Flight Center is gratefully acknowledged. The support of the National Science Foundation under GrantIRI-92-16970 is gratefully acknowledged.

References

[1] A. Del Bimbo and P. Pala. Image indexing using shape-based visual fetaures. In *Proceedings of the 13th International Conference on Pattern Recognition*, volume III, pages 351–355, Vienna, Austria, August 1996.

[2] J.L. Blue, G.T. Candela, P.J. Grother, R. Chellappa, and C.L. Wilson. Evaluation of pattern classifiers for fingerprints and OCR applications. *Pattern Recognition*, 27(4):485–501, April 1994.

[3] S.B. Gray. Local properties of binary images in two dimensions. *IEEE Transactions on Computers*, C-20(5):551–561, May 1971.

[4] M.K. Hu. Visual pattern recognition by moment invariants. *IRE Transactions on Information Theory*, IT-8(2):179–187, February 1962.

[5] R. Kasturi and J. Alemany. Information extraction from images of paper-based maps. *IEEE Transactions on Software Engineering*, 14(5):671–675, May 1988.

[6] M.D. Levine. *Vision in Man and Machine*. McGraw-Hill, New York, 1982.

[7] W. Niblack, R. Barber, W. Equitz, M. Flickner, E. Glasman, D. Petkovic, and P. Yanker. The QBIC project: Querying images by content using color, texture, and shape. In *Proceeding of the SPIE, Storage and Retrieval of Image and Video Databases*, volume 1908, pages 173–187, San Jose, CA, February 1993.

[8] A. Pentland, R. W. Picard, and S. Sclaroff. Photobook: Content-based manipulation of image databases. In *Proceeding of the SPIE, Storage and Retrieval of Image and Video Databases II*, volume 2185, pages 34–47, San Jose, CA, February 1994.

[9] A. Rosenfeld and J.L. Pfaltz. Distance functions on digital pictures. *Pattern Recognition*, 1(1):33–61, July 1968.

[10] H. Samet and A. Soffer. MARCO: MAp Retrieval by COntent. *IEEE Transactions on Pattern Analysis and Machine Intelligence*, 18(8):783–798, August 1996.

[11] S. Sclaroff. Encoding deformable shape categories for efficient content-based search. In A. W. M. Smeulders and R. Jain, editors, *Proceedings of the 13th International Conference on Pattern Recognition*, pages 107–114, Amsterdam, The Netherlands, August 1996.

[12] A. Soffer and H. Samet. Retrieval by content in symbolic-image databases. In *Proceedings of the SPIE, Storage and Retrieval of Still Image and Video Databases IV*, volume 2670, pages 144–155, San Jose, CA, February 1996.

[13] S. Suzuki and T. Yamada. MARIS: Map recognition input system. *Pattern Recognition*, 23(8):919–933, August 1990.

[14] M. Swain. Interactive indexing into image databases. In *Proceeding of the SPIE, Storage and Retrieval for Image and Video Databases*, volume 1908, pages 95–103, San Jose, CA, February 1993.

[15] N. Tanaka, T. Kamimura, and J. Tsukumo. Development of a map vectorization method involving a shape reforming process. In *Proceedings of the Second International Conference on Document Analysis and Recognition*, pages 680–683, Tsukuba Science City, Japan, October 1993.

[16] H. Yamada, K. Yamamoto, and K. Hosokawa. Directional mathematical morphology and reformalized hough transformation for analysis of topographic maps. *IEEE Transactions on Pattern Analysis and Machine Intelligence*, 15(4):380–387, April 1993.

INTERPENETRATING WAVES AND MULTIPLE GENERATION SHOCKS VIA THE CEDT*

HÜSEYIN TEK
LEMS, Brown University, RI 02906, USA

FREDERIC LEYMARIE
Thomson-CSF/Syseca, S2IG/GIIS Dept., Malakoff 92247 Cedex, France

BENJAMIN B. KIMIA
LEMS, Brown University, RI 02906, USA

The extraction of symmetries as quench points of propagating orientation elements from edge maps of grey scale images for object recognition is faced with fundamental theoretical and computational challenges. The theoretical issues arise since object symmetries are drastically altered due to missing edges (gaps), introduction of new parts and occluders, and spurious edges. While the *full* symmetry set retains much of the original figure's symmetries and as a result is less sensitive to such changes, it brings to bear many unintuitive branches, thus requiring further selection for object recognition. In this paper, we view the full symmetry set as the superposition of shocks arising from *multiple generations of waves*: the quenching points of the waves from the initial edge map constitute the first generation of shocks. A second generation of waves initiated at these points, simulate interpenetrating waves and generate a second generation of shocks, and so on until no further shocks can be formed. This view of the full symmetry set supports a *selective* continuation of waves, *e.g.,* at shock loops to remove spurious edges, and at shock-hypothesized limbs to partition shape and close boundary gaps. This selective continuation of waves brings out relevant symmetries, but avoids the ambiguity of the full symmetry set. The computational challenge is addressed by a framework based on the Contour-based Euclidean Distance Transform (CEDT) for shock detection, classification, labeling, as well as for simulating interpenetrating waves and multiple generation shocks described above. The key feature of CEDT that makes this possible is the explicit simultaneous propagation of orientation and distance, as well as additional features, *e.g. labels.* In addition, CEDT is exact and of very low numerical complexity. The results for a number of illustrative examples indicate the suitability of this framework for the recovery of object symmetries from real imagery.

1 Introduction

The versatility of symmetry-based representations for object recognition from unsegmented *real* imagery is seriously challenged by at least three fundamental theoretical issues. First, the extraction of symmetries is ill-conditioned in that the removal of a small portion of the boundary introduces a large change in

*This research was supported by funding from NSF and the Whitaker Foundation.

the object symmetry, Figure 1a. Second, the changes induced on the object's visible boundary by an occluder, or as result of changes in the visibility of a part, induce large changes in the object symmetry, Figure 1b. Finally, spurious edges due to surface markings, texture edges, specularity highlights, noise, *etc.* alter the underlying object symmetry, Figure 1c. Thus, symmetries recovered in a straightforward fashion from edge responses from real images often contain *(i)* additional skeletal points due to gaps; *(ii)* missing skeletal points due to occluders and parts; and *(iii)* distorted symmetries due to spurious elements, such that the resulting skeletons are not recognizable, nor lead to figure/ground segmentation. These difficulties have prompted several approaches to extract the *full symmetry set* from unsegmented gray-scale images. Scott *et al.* [1] propagate waves to recover the full symmetries. They also suggest a convolution approach for implementing the full symmetry set. Pizer *et al.* [2] use a similar approach where by a voting scheme, edges measured at each scale vote for medialness at a point which is a constant proportion of scale away. The ridges of the resulting surface constitute the *core*, a skeleton in x, y and σ (scale). Kelly and Levine [3] use annular symmetry operators in a similar fashion to derive the full symmetry set. In related work, Tari and Shah [4] define symmetries as the curvature maxima of level sets constructed consistently with an edge strength functional. August *et al.* [5] use the notion of a gap skeleton to group certain nearby endpoints identified by a depth separation process.

It has been argued that since the full symmetry set represents all the symmetries of a shape, spurious elements and gaps affect the full symmetry set less than the SAT. We argue that while some of the full symmetry set is revealing, not all of it is useful, and some additional unintuitive branches can infact lead to ambiguities for object recognition, Figures 6 and 8e. Rather, we propose that only in select situations should further symmetries be recovered. First, we observe that the full symmetry set can be viewed as the union of the quench points of a series of waves: the first generation of waves is launched at the edges of the image, while the second is launched at the quench points of the first generation shocks. In general, the nth generation wave is launched at the quench points of the $(n-1)$th generation wave. The union of the multiple generations of shocks constitutes the full symmetry set. Second, we observe that the maze of unwanted symmetries can be avoided by launching the secondary and future generations of shocks *selectively*, *e.g.*, at loops, to bring out relevant symmetries, Section 4.

The computational challenges posed by the ideas of *inter-penetrating waves* and *multiple generation shocks* can be met by a framework based on the contour based distance transform (CEDT). Previously, many approaches were developed to obtain skeletons from the distance transform. However, such schemes

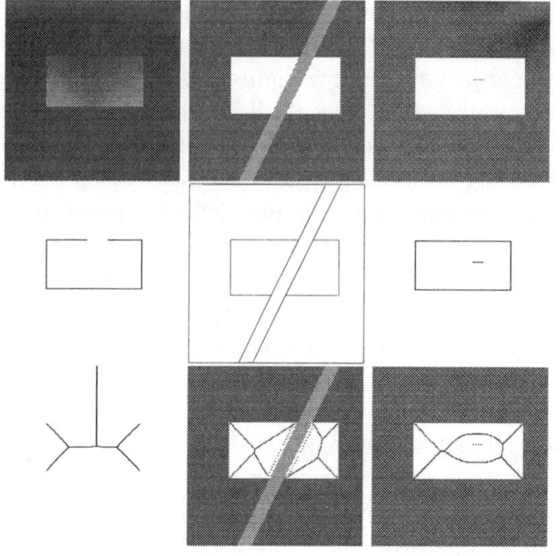

Figure 1: Gaps (a), occluders (b) spurious edges (c) drastically alter object symmetries. Top row: Original image; middle row: edge map; bottom row: skeletons pertaining to the object.

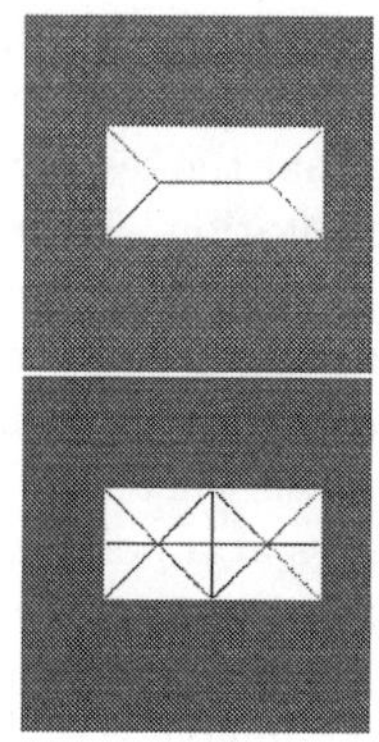

Figure 2: (a) SAT and (b) Full symmetry set from CEDT

do not make propagation of orientation and additional labels explicit. The CEDT not only propagates *distances* but also *orientation* and shock labels such that it is immediately clear at each point on the wavefront not only how far a wave has traveled, but also what the *direction* of propagation is, which point on the original boundary gave rise to it, and whether it is a regular or a rare-faction wavefront. This is the fundamental advantage of the CEDT which we utilize for the recovery of shocks, shock classification, and shock-labeling as an alternative to curve evolution. Two additional key advantages of CEDT over traditional raster-scan based schemes are its lower numerical complexity and its accuracy [6,7].

2 Wave Propagation for Skeleton Computations

The classic paper by Blum [8] has motivated a number of approaches for extracting the symmetries of binary segmented shape in the form of a "skeleton" or "stick figure", including extracting the center of maximally inscribed circles [9], fitting generalized cylinders, computing mid chords of double-tangent circles [10],

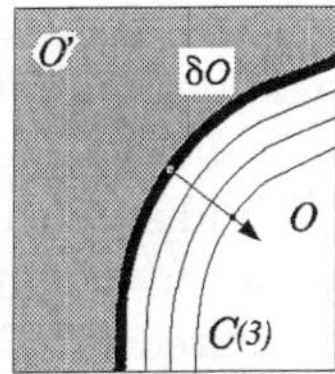

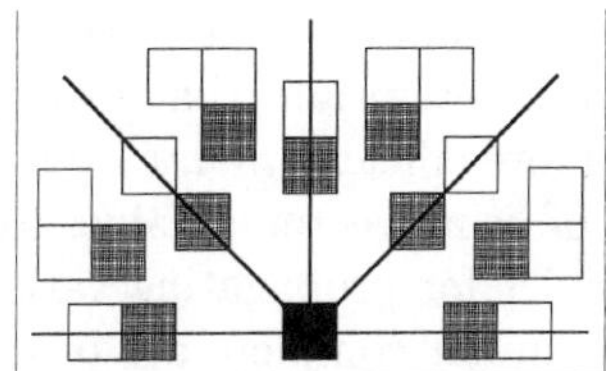

Figure 3: (a) Three iterations of the propagation of a boundary δO at one pixel per iteration. (b) The minimal set of masks (only a mirror image constructs the bottom half of the full picture): The black pixel represents the source while the grey and white pixels represent subsequent propagation of waves. Black lines represent directly supported directions of propagation. for the intermediate directions of propagation, larger masks are required. (Adapted from [6])

extracting ridges of distance transforms [11,12,13], Voronoi diagram methods [14], and thinning algorithms [9]. Blum's original idea was based on a "grass fire" initiated at the contours of the shape which quenches at the skeleton. The reaction-diffusion space and the formation of shocks (singularities) implements and generalizes this idea [15,17,18]. The reaction process can be simulated much more efficiently, however, by the distance transform methods which map a binary image into an image where the value at each point is the Euclidean distance from the object [11]. Each constant distance sets then represents a front where distance represents "time".

Distance transform methods may be classified into those based on raster scans or those that are contour-based. Danielsson showed that Euclidean Distance Transform (EDT) can be computed by comparing neighborhood pixels with vector-valued masks used to evaluate distance steps along the axis of the supporting grid. A raster scan version for EDT (REDT) was described in [19] and later extended to signed EDT [20] and then to contour-based EDT (CEDT) [6,7]. Previously, REDT and CEDT have been considered of similar usefulness when used for wave propagation and symmetry computation mainly because REDT is relatively simpler to implement, due to independence of embedded shapes. In addition, CEDT implementations for symmetry set elicitation have relied upon dilation/erosion of chain-coded representations of contour [21,22], requiring a pre-processing of contour features. Thus, CEDT has received relatively little attention. However, for simulating wave propagation, we propose that CEDT has a key advantage over REDT in that it provides an explicit representation of *orientation* in addition to *distance* of propagation. This is particularly attractive since CEDT can be initiated at points, open and closed contours, and surface patches, without requiring chain-code pre-processing, leading to a more efficient and direct simulation of wave propagation.

The basic design of CEDT follows ideas originated in Montanari [23], brought to the foreground by more recent work, *e.g.*, [24,22] and, Ragnemalm [6,7]. While Montanari had the key insight that wave propagation from boundary feature was potentially more efficient than raster-scan sequential DT, Ragnemalm imported the idea of using vectored values for DT [19] and studied different masks and their properties for propagating various metrics from contours. Figure 3 illustrates the minimal complete set of masks required for Euclidean metric propagation on a 2D rectangular distance grid from a point source. Each masks maintains a distance vector (L_x, L_y) from its origin, thus *explicitly* representing the direction and distance of the propagating wavefront. Note that the distance vector values may in addition propagate other features, *e.g.*, a labeling of original front waves into regular or rarefaction, Section 3. The metric $L^2 = (L_x^2 + L_y^2)$ is also carried to optimize operations. A further optimization uses *buckets* to store wavefront distance values in order of metric L^2, thus leading to constant speed propagation. Other advantages of CEDT include: CEDT is exact, is nearly optimal in terms of numerical complexity when compared to raster-scan based DT, and is easily extended to 3D by defining additional masks.

The extraction of skeleton from distance transform is faced with a number of difficulties. First, most approaches for computing skeletons from DTs rely on non-Euclidean metrics giving rise to highly inaccurate results, and in particular failing to provide rotation invariance [11,25]. Second, approaches relying on a raster-scan implementation to compute DTs, extract skeleton by some post-processing of the ridges of the computed distance map [11,26]. Third, approaches based on the retrieval of a smooth contour representation, such as splines, to compute skeletons from a derived distance map [27] suffer from the two major difficulties: (i) an additional complexity due to the contour modeling (finding good nodes) and (ii) the creation of artifacts due to non-smooth contour features. Finally, extensions to the third dimension usually leads to high numerical complexity. We now consider an alternative approach by tailoring a previous framework based on curve evolution to use CEDT.

3 Shock Detection and Classification by CEDT

Shape can be completely described as the collection of four types of shocks which form in the course of deformations of shape in the reaction-diffusion space [15,17,18] $\frac{\partial C}{\partial t} = (\beta_0 - \beta_1 \kappa)\vec{N}$. The four types of shocks correspond to intuitive elements of shape, namely, parts, protrusions, and bends [16]. The deformations are implemented via the *curve evolution* paradigm by embedding the curves $C(s,t)$ as the level set of a surface $\{\psi(x,y,t) = 0\}$ evolving by $\frac{\partial \psi}{\partial t} = (\beta_0 - \beta_1 \kappa)|\nabla \psi|$. Table 1 shows a classification of shocks from ψ which

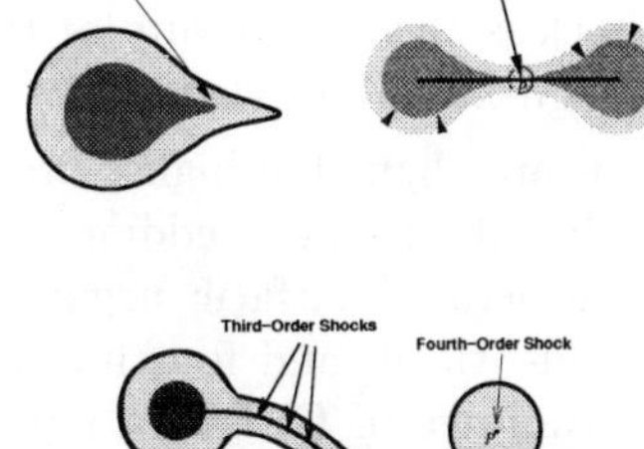

Shock Type	Orientation	Curvature
First–Order	non– vanishing $\nabla\phi$	high level set curvature
Second–Order	isolated vanishing $\nabla\phi$	$\kappa_1\kappa_2 < 0$
Third–Order	non–isolated vanishing $\nabla\phi$	$\kappa_1\kappa_2 = 0$
Fourth–Order	isolated vanishing $\nabla\phi$	$\kappa_1\kappa_2 > 0$

Table 1: This table depicts the classification of shock types based on the the gradient level set curvature and the principal curvatures of the surface.

Figure 4: Each of the four types of shocks each is correlated with a perceptual/semantic category, *i.e.*, *protrusion*, *part*, *bend*, and *seed.*

has been implemented to sub-pixel accuracy [18]. While the derived shock structure when $\beta_1 = 0$ is related to skeletons, several properties of shocks relating to the notions of type, velocity, grouping, salience, and hierarchy are significant. (*i*) certain deformations, *e.g.*, bending, affect shock types selectively, *e.g.*, third-order shocks of a rectangle; (*ii*) the skeletal representation lacks sufficient explicit dimensions for qualitative approximation, *e.g.*, the addition of shock type substantially narrows down the range of shapes it can generate; (*iii*) topological and differential properties of shocks, *e.g.*, velocity, directly reflect boundary properties; (*iv*) the notion of time of formation induces a hierarchy on shocks; and (*v*) a notion of shock grouping and salience based on the diffusion process ($\beta_1 \neq 0$) leading to a stability of representation with small changes.

We now argue that the explicit and simultaneous propagation of orientation and distance in the CEDT leads to an alternate and more efficient framework for the detection and classification of shocks. Observe that each point on the original shape (or even partial contour) can be considered a source for propagation of waves. Since both orientation and distance are available, the source of each point on the front can be determined. Thus, waves arriving at a point from two distinct sources can be identified and distinguished. Since shocks are the quench point of such waves, all image points receiving two or more waves can be easily detected. In addition, since the direction of propagation of each wave is explicit the shock type can be determined. Specifically, the CEDT approach updates the wavefront by propagating each point in the direction where the point had propagated from. In the discrete domain, the propagation continues until the propagating wave meets an incoming wave, as determined by the minimal distance carried by the waves. The collision signals the formation of a shock. Observe that two distinct directions must necessarily have arrived at the shock points. If these two directions are not aligned, a first order shock has formed. The velocity of the shock is the vector sum of the two front velocities; *i.e.*, shock speed is $\frac{1}{sin\frac{\theta}{2}}$ times front speed where θ is the angle between the two fronts. If the two directions are aligned, a higher-order shock has formed. Table 1 shows a classification based on an embedding surface, which in this case we take to be the CEDT generated surface: negative, zero and positive Gaussian curvatures gives second-, third, and fourth-order shocks, respectively. Observe that the crucial advantage of CEDT in representing the angle at which wavefronts meet or cross each other, in contrast to REDT which necessitates a cumbersome and inaccurate post-processing of the distance map [11,26].

The removal of some portions of shape's complete boundary does not simply only lead to the removal of portions of its symmetries, *e.g.*, as represented by shocks, but also to generation of seemingly un-intuitive symmetries, Figure 5. These newly formed "spurious" shocks must be distinguished from shocks common with the previous case. Tek *et al.* [28] suggest that such a distinction should be based on whether propagating waves carry "true" orientation information as supported by the original boundary or carry "bogus" orientation arising from rare-fraction waves, *e.g.*, as arising from a concave corner. This distinction between two types of waves leads to labeling of shocks into three classes [28]:

Definition: Contour points with regular tangent give rise to *regular* wavefronts. Contour points without a uniquely defined tangents give rise to *degenerate* wavefronts. A shock point arising from the interaction of two regular wavefronts is *regular.* A shock point arising from one regular and one degenerate wavefront is *semi-degenerate.* A shock point formed from the interaction of two degenerate wavefronts is *degenerate* [28].

It is suggested that (i) regular shocks represent the only symmetries arising from partial contour segments, (ii) the semi-degenerate shocks are altered form of the underlying symmetries, and (iii) the degenerate shocks arise represent potential candidates for contour continuity and grouping, as in-partitioning shape [29], or arising in completing gaps [30]. The latter statement (iii) has similarities to August *et al.* [5] who use a notion of gap skeleton to group certain nearby endpoints in the edge map segregated by a depth process. However, there are several important distinctions, as (i) they operate on depth-segregated not full edge maps, (ii) our approach is motivated by the notion of orientation propagation and rare-faction waves [28]. Thus, waves simulated by CEDT carry not only orientation and distance but also a rarefaction/regular label which forms the basis of subsequent shock labeling by CEDT, Figures 5. In summary waves can be labeled and propagated, and shocks can be detected, classified, and

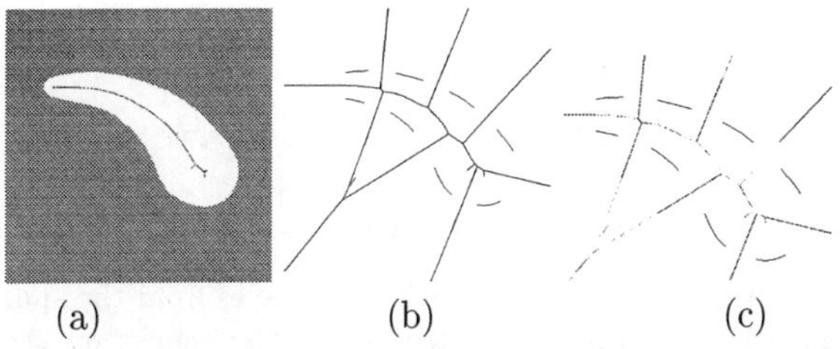

Figure 5: Extracting partial shocks from partial contours. (b) original image with complete boundary and its shocks, (c) partial boundary and the introduction of "spurious" shocks, (d) a labeling of shocks into regular (green, semi-degenerate (yellow) and degenerate (red). Observe that the regular shocks are the partial shocks extracted from partial contour (black).

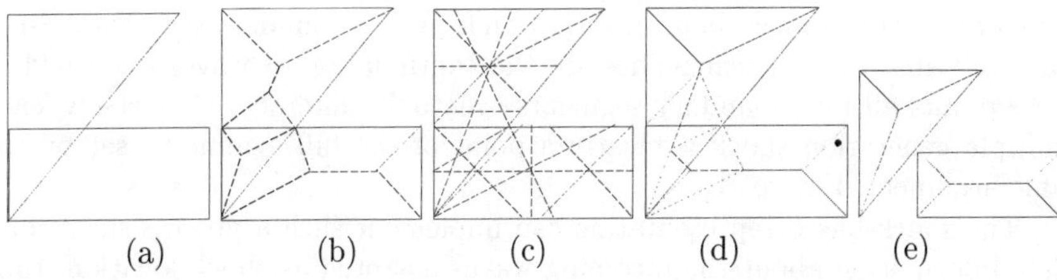

Figure 6: Edge evidence in real images often suggests a multiplicity of groupings, e.g., (a) suggesting a rectangle and a triangle. While the SAT representation does not capture triangular and rectangular symmetries (b) the full symmetry set is capable of bringing out the appropriate symmetries, but also introduces superfluous ones (c). Shocks of secondary waves exclusively initiated at loops (d), however, bring out only the missing pieces leading to two appropriate groupings (e).

labeled via the CEDT framework.

4 Inter-penetrating Waves and Multiple Generation Shocks

The sensitivity of SAT and the ambiguity of the full symmetry set prompts us to propose an alternative which is based on a view of the full symmetry set as the union of quench points of a series of waves:

Definition: The *first generation wave* is the wavefront initiated at the edge map of an image. The *first generation shock set* is the set of quenched points (shocks) arising from the propagation of first generation wave. The nth *generation wave* is the wavefront initialized at the $(n-1)^{\text{th}}$ generation shocks at the time indicated by its formation. The nth *generation shocks* are the shocks corresponding to the nth generation wavefront.

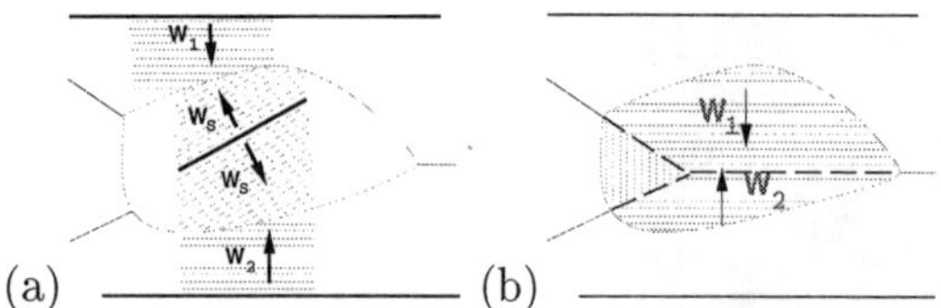

Figure 7: (a) waves W_1 and W_2, are quenched by waves from the spurious boundary, W_s, resulting in a loop in the shock structure. The shocks on the loop can now simulate the passage of the original flow of waves W_1 and W_2 via secondary waves, (b), which are initiated at the shock in a delayed manner, resulting in the formation of shocks due to the top and the bottom boundaries.

Proposition: The union of all generations of shocks is the full symmetry set.
Proof: Each point in the full symmetry set can be viewed as the quench point of two waves traveling without interruption from two boundary segments. Since wave initialized at quench points are the continuation of waves quenched at these points all two boundary segments eventually interact. Conversely, each multiple generation shock is clearly a point of the full symmetry set by the same argument, Figure 7.

The shock-based representation can implement such a process since complete information about the incoming waves is stored as shock location, time of formation, and velocity. The second observation is that multiple generation waves and shocks can recover the distorted or missing symmetries. The idea is to launch second and further generation of waves only at *select groups of shocks* as indicated by special properties of the shock itself. For example, an isolated spurious edge or equivalently a hole in the object interferes with the formation of appropriate symmetries, Figure 6, but also always leads to a *loop* in the shocks arising from it. Thus, selectively launching second generation waves at shock loop effectively removes this element Figure 7 and recovers appropriate symmetries, Figure 8f without generating additional symmetries, Figure 8e. Figure 9 illustrates two interacting spurious shocks requiring a second generation of waves. As a second example consider how symmetries are affected by the appearance of a newly visible part, Figure 10a. The partitioning theory of shape [29] cast in the language of shock labels [28], proposes that salient semi-degenerate and degenerate shocks signal parts. This provides a second criterion for selectively launching a new generation of shock, namely, at these semi-degenerate shocks and at a hypothesized limb part-line, Figure 10b to recover each object's part symmetry axes. A similar argument holds for gaps, which are viewed as "null parts" [30], Figure10e-g. Observe the need for multiple generation shocks to lead to an appropriate grouping essential for segmentation and recognition tasks, *e.g.* in indexing into image databases, Figure 11.

5 References:

1. Guy L. Scott *etal.* *IVC*, 7(1):63–70, 1989.
2. S. M. Pizer and C. A. Burbeck. *Vision Research*, 35,13:1917-1930, 1995.
3. M. F. Kelly and M. D. Levine. ICCV, pages 1016–1021, 1995.
4. S. Tari, J. Shah, and H. Pie. In *IEEE Work. Math. Meth. Bio. I. A.*, 1996.
5. J. August, K. Siddiqi, and S. W. Zucker. In *ICPR*, 1996.
6. I. Ragnemalm. Licenciate Thesis No 206, Linkoping University, Sweden, 1990.
7. I. Ragnemalm. *CVGIP: Image Understanding*, 56(3):399–409, 1992.
8. Harry Blum. *J. Theor. Biol.*, 38:205–287, 1973.
9. C. Arcelli and G. Sanniti di Baja. *IVC*, 11(3):163–173, 1993.
10. M. Brady and H. Asada. *Robotics Research*, 3(3), 1984.
11. F. Leymarie and M. D. Levine. *PAMI*, 14(1):56–75, January 1992.
12. Carlo Arcelli and Gabriela Sanniti di Baja. *PAMI*, 11(4):411–414, 1989.
13. C. Arcelli and G. Sanniti di Baja. *Patt. Rec. Let.*, 13(4):237–243, 1992.
14. R. L. Ogniewicz and O. Kübler. *Pattern Recognition*, 28(3):343–359, 1995.
15. B. Kimia, A. Tannenbaum, and S. W. Zucker. In *ECCV I*, pages 402–407.
16. B B. Kimia, A. Tannenbaum, and S W. Zucker. In IWWF 1993.
17. B. Kimia, A. Tannenbaum, and S. W. Zucker. In *IJCV I*, 15:189–224, 1995.
18. K. Siddiqi and B. Kimia. In *CVPR*, 1996.
19. P.E. Danielsson. *CVGIP*, 14:227–248, 1980.
20. Q.-Z. Ye. In *ICPR*, volume 1, pages 495–499, Bejing, China, 1988.
21. Y. Xia. *PAMI*, 11(10):1076–1086, 1989.
22. Luc Vincent. In *CVPR*, pages 520–525, Maui HI, 1991.
23. U. Montanari. *JACM*, 15(4):600–624, October 1968.
24. B.J.H. Verwer. In *ICPR*, pages 137–142, 1988.
25. F. Leymarie and M. D. Levine. *CVGIP*, 55(1):84–94, January 1992.
26. B. Kruse. Tech. Rep. LiTH-ISY-I-1116, Linkoping U., Sweden, 1990.
27. M. W. Wright, R. Cipolla, and P. J. Giblin. *PAMI*, 13(5):367–375, 1995.
28. H. Tek, P. Stoll, and B. B. Kimia. In CVPR 1997.
29. K. Siddiqi and B. Kimia. *PAMI*, 17(3):239–251, March 1995.
30. K. Siddiqi, K. Tresness, and B. Kimia. In *IWVF*, pages 507–521, Italy, 1994.

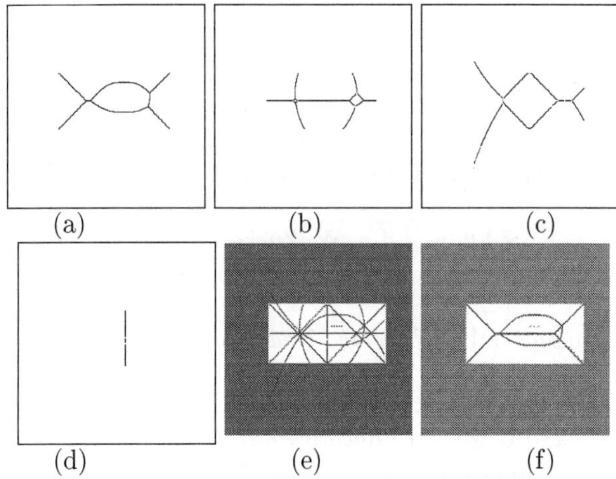

Figure 8: Multiple generation shocks of the image is Figure 1c; (a), (b), (c), and (d) depict first-, second-, third-, and fourth-generation shocks, respectively. (e) the superposition of all generations of shocks constitutes the full symmetry set. Observe that un-intuitive nature of the full symmetry set; (f) second generation of waves exclusively initiated at the loops gives rise to shocks which complete the rectangular symmetry set.

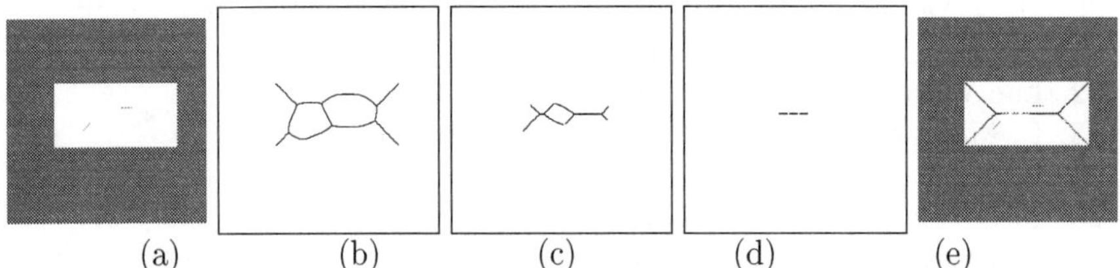

Figure 9: (a) original image; (b) first generation of shocks: (c) and (d) loop transformations to remove the effect of spurious edge elements. (e) the superposition of all generations of shocks.

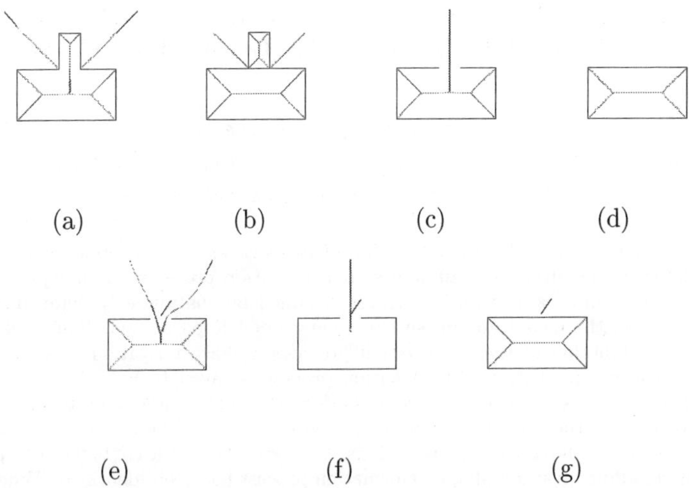

Figure 10: (a) A shape with two parts and its shocks. (b) The recovery of individual part's shocks by shock labeling followed by a second generation shocks of waves initiated at limbs. (c) a shape with a gap (null part) and its shocks. (d) Second generation waves initiated at salient limbs remove the degenerate shocks and correct for the distortion at semi-degenerate shocks. (e) a spurious edge element's interference with contour grouping can be removed by considering multiple generation of shocks as shown in (f) where second generation shocks arising from the shocks loops (completed by the image boundary) generate a new grouping hypothesis thus completing the rectangle symmetries (g).

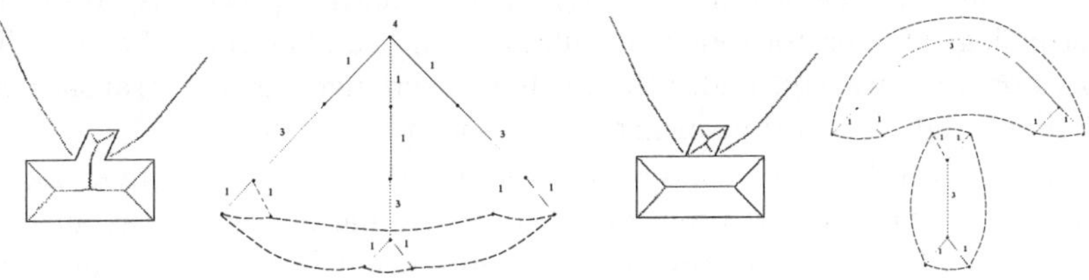

Figure 11: Role of interpenetrating wave in the segmentation of shape and the resulting graphs.

AFFINE INVARIANT DEFORMATION CURVES A TOOL FOR SHAPE CHARACTERIZATION

REIN VAN DEN BOOMGAARD
Faculty of Mathematics, Computer Science Physics and Astronomy
University of Amsterdam, The Netherlands

In this paper we describe a combination of two well-known concepts: morphological deformation curves and affine invariant evolution processes. A morphological deformation curve is a shape descriptor obtained by continuously deforming the shape and in the meantime measuring some geometric parameter. This measurement as a function of the deformation provides a characterization of the shape. In classical morphology the deformation process is taken to be a morphological operator (erosions, dilations and combinations thereof). These operators are only invariant under the Euclidean symmetry group (translation and rotation) and (relative) invariant under isotropic rescalings. Only recently in the context of computer vision, an affine invariant shape deformation process has been identified. When we measure the area of the object while it is deformed in this way we obtain a function that provides a characterization of a shape in an affine invariant way. In this paper an affine invariant deformation curve is introduced and some preliminary experiments are described.

1 Introduction

In this paper we describe a combination of two well-known concepts: morphological deformation curves and affine invariant evolution processes. A morphological deformation curve is a shape descriptor obtained by continuously deforming the shape and in the meantime measuring some geometric parameter. This measurement as a function of the deformation provides a characterization of the shape. In classical morphology the deformation process is taken to be a morphological operator (erosions, dilations and combinations thereof). These operators are invariant under the Euclidean symmetry group (translation and rotation) and (relative) invariant under isotropic rescalings.

Only recently in the context of computer vision, an affine invariant shape deformation process has been identified[10,3]. Affine invariance (as an approximation to the projective invariance) is important in viewpoint independent recognition of shapes. When we measure the area of the object while it is deformed in this way we obtain a function that provides a characterization of a shape in an affine invariant way.

In this paper the "time" parameter is crucial. Our goal is to obtain absolute invariant curves. Therefore we have to look closely at the "time deformation" as well when transforming shapes. Most of the reported applications of the geometry guided diffusion processes just end the diffusion when a pleasing result is obtained.

In this paper an affine invariant deformation curve is introduced and some preliminary experiments are described. To the best of our knowledge this morphological use of a technique from non-linear scale-space theory is not reported before in the literature.

2 Deformation Curves

The common way to deal with shape on a quantitative basis in mathematical morphology is to study the behaviour of a shape while deforming it. The classical morphological tools are granulometries [8], pattern spectra [9] and erosion curves [5].

Let X represent the shape of interest and let Ψ^t denote a one parameter family of shape deformation operators. Applying these operators on the shape under study X, a family of shapes $\Psi^t X$ is obtained. Let m denote some scalar measurement on a shape, i.e. $m(X) \in \mathbb{R}$. The function that is obtained by applying m on all deformed shapes Ψ^t will be called the *deformation curve*:

$$\mu_X(t) = m(\Psi^t X).$$

For shape characterization we would like the deformation curve to be an absolute invariant under the class of space transformations that leave the interpretation of the shape the same. Often encountered classes are the group of Euclidean transforms (rotations and translation) and the isotropic scalings. More complex invariants are also considered in practice (like the projective transforms and the affine transforms as approximations of the projective ones). Let $\mathcal{T}$ denotes the shape transform class considered, then the deformation curve μ_X is said to be absolute invariant iff:

$$\forall T \in \mathcal{T}, \forall t \geq 0 : \mu_X(t) = \mu_{TX}(t).$$

Absolute invariance is seldomly achieved. In practice some normalization of the deformation curve is needed to arrive at a curve that is independent of the—unknown—transform $T \in \mathcal{T}$.

In this paper we only look at the deformation operators Ψ^t and the symmetry classes $\mathcal{T}$ such that the deformation curve μ_X is a relative invariant of the form:

$$\forall T \in \mathcal{T}, \forall t \geq 0 : \mu_{TX}(t) = \alpha\mu_X(\frac{t}{\alpha}). \tag{1}$$

where α only depends on the transform T. Note that the function μ_{TX} is an *umbral scaled* version of the original function μ_X (see figure 1). In a practical

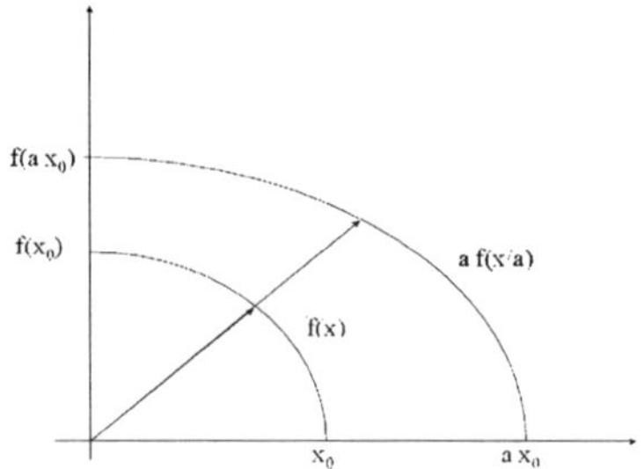

Figure 1: **Umbral Scaling.** Umbral scaling of a function $f(x)$ results in the function $af(x/a)$ that is geometrically scaled with respect to the origin.

application the umbral scaling is unknown and the only possibility to construct an absolute invariant curve is to use the shape measurement to rescale the curve. The easiest way to do so is to (umbral) scale the measured curve in such a way that for the new curve the measurement at $t = 0$ equals a normalized value. We thus arrive at the following absolute invariant deformation curve:

$$\hat{\mu}_X(t) = \frac{\mu_X(\mu_X(0)t)}{\mu_X(0)}.$$

The above deformation curve provides a $\mathcal{T}$-invariant shape characterization. This is easily proved by substituting eq. (1) into the above expression for $\hat{\mu}_X$ and showing that $\hat{\mu}_{TX} = \hat{\mu}_X$. Whether this characterization provides enough information to recognize and classify shapes depends on the shapes to be recognized, on the deformation operator used and on the symmetry group describing the "interpretation-invariant" space transforms. Such an analysis is beyond the scope of this paper.

The deformation curves discussed in this paper all fit within the framework described above. In section 3 the classical morphological deformation curve based on the erosion as the deformation operator will be discussed. In section 4 the deformation is taken to be a non-linear geometry-driven diffusion process. In this case an explicit expression for the deformation operator Ψ^t cannot be formulated. The deformation operator is given as an infinitesimal generator describing how to derive the shape $\Psi^{t+dt}X$ from the shape $\Psi^t X$. Therefore the entire one-parameter family of deformations has to be generated.

In all examples the shape measurement will be the area of the shape. This choice is motivated by the fact that the area (or volume in case of functions) can be measured with great precision and is insensitive to noise. A second motivation is that the area of shapes is a (relative) invariant of the symmetry groups considered in this paper.

3 Erosion Curves

Consider the deformation curve that is obtained by choosing the erosion as the deformation operator (i.e $\Psi^t = \epsilon_{tB}$, the erosion with a disk shaped structuring element of radius t). The shape measurement is the (square of the) area of the shape (i.e. $m(X) = \sqrt{\text{area}(X)}$). The transformations that leave the interpretation of the shape intact are taken from the group of Euclidean transforms (rotations and translations) and the group of isotropic scalings.

This results in what is known in mathematical morphology as the *erosion curve*[a]:

$$\hat{\mu}_{\epsilon,X}(t) = \frac{m(\epsilon_{tB/m(X)}X)}{m(X)}. \tag{2}$$

The fact that this curve is invariant under the Euclidean transforms is evident because all morphological operators involved are translation invariant and because the structuring element in the erosion is a disk (which is itself invariant under rotation). Invariance under isotropic rescalings can be proven using the fact that an isotropic rescaling distributes over the erosion: $\lambda \circ \epsilon_A = \epsilon_{\lambda A} \circ \lambda$ (here λX denotes the set obtained by isotropic scaling of X with factor λ). Also note that the area of a scaled set λX equals λ^2 times the area of the set X.

A generalization of the erosion curves are the morphological granulometries[8] constructed using openings and closings instead of erosions and dilations. The pattern spectrum[9] is another well-known extension to the idea of the erosion curve. The erosion curve (as well as the other morphological deformation curves) prove to be powerful shape descriptors. Schmidt[5] theoretically derived results concerning the equivalence classes (the "shape metameres"). He proved that the erosion curve is not only invariant to the transformations indicated above, but also that the shape may be "bend" as long as the skeleton does not change its topology (and distance measure along the skeleton). Especially for biological shape characterization this is an important property.

In figure 2 the erosion curves for 4 simple shapes are shown. The bumps in the curves are mostly caused by discretizaton effects. This does not imply that the curves in the continuous case are smooth. The second order derivative is not even continuous. This is closely linked to the fact that the underlying

---

[a] The standard definition of the erosion curve does not include the square root.

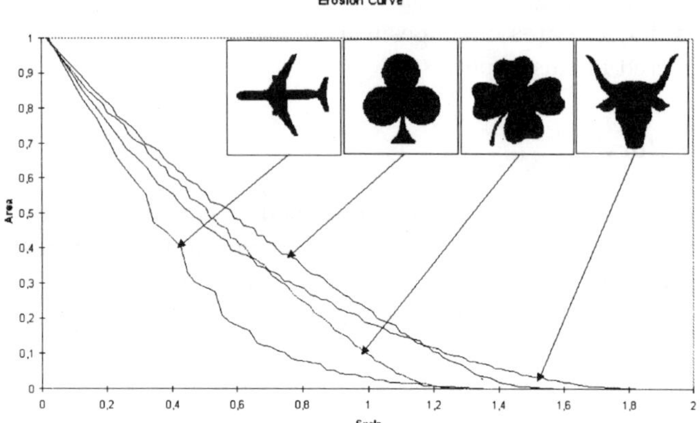

Figure 2: **Erosion Curves.**

deformation operator (the erosion) does not keep the shape connected. The jumps in the second order derivative are linked to the branch points in the skeleton of the shape under study. For details concerning the geometrical interpretation of the erosion curve we refer to Schmidt[5].

4 Diffusion Curves

The one-parameter family of shapes resulting from eroding the original shape X with a disk of increasing size, can also be constructed by an infinitesimal generator which links the contour of the original shape at "time" t with the contour at time $t + dt$. In case the contour of the shape at time t is given by the vector $C(p, t)$ (with p some parameter along the curve) then the change in contour is given by:

$$\frac{\partial C}{\partial t} = -N$$

where N is the outward pointing normal[3,10]. When the curve is embedded in a function $F(x, t)$ (such that the level set at $F = 0$ is equal to the curve) the equivalent evolution of this function is given by

$$\frac{\partial F}{\partial t} = -\|\nabla F\|.$$

It can be easily shown that the solution to the above PDE is given by the erosion of the initial condition $F(x,0) = f(x)$ with a disk of radius t. The above "diffusion" equations[b], interpreted as the infinitesimal generators of a deformation process, are thus equivalent with the erosion curve as discussed in the previous section. We have done some experiments to see whether the PDE formulation is also numerically equivalent to the macroscopic morphological erosion formulation introduced in the previous section. In figure 3 the erosion curves obtained using both techniques are shown. The correspondence between both curves is very close.

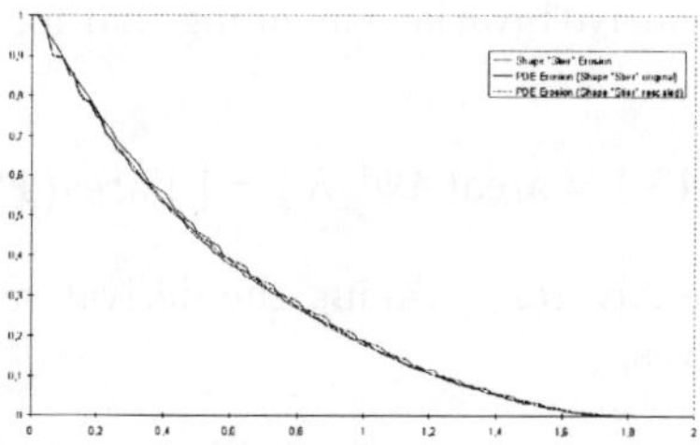

Figure 3: **Erosion Curves.** In the figure the erosion curves for "stier" (bull's head) shape are shown. One of the erosion curves is calculated using the macroscopic erosions, the other two are calculated using the PDE formulation of the constant motion flow.

A disadvantage of pure morphological deformation as the basis of shape description is that it looks impossible to incorporate affine invariance into the deformation. It has been shown by Alvarez[3] and by Sapiro[10] that the affine invariant deformation requires geometry guided diffusion:

$$\frac{\partial F}{\partial t} = -\kappa^{\frac{1}{3}}\|\nabla F\|.$$

Here κ is the curvature of the isophote. In the contour formulation we thus have:

$$\frac{\partial C}{\partial t} = -\kappa^{\frac{1}{3}}N.$$

[b]these are strictly speaking not diffusion equations but reaction equations, nevertheless these types are often discussed along with other types of "non-linear diffusion equations".

Compared to the erosion deformation there is a striking difference: connected objects are guaranteed to stay connected whereas in the erosion one object may split into several parts. It depends on the application whether this is an advantage or not. Kimia[7] introduced the combination of a pure erosion and a pure diffusion to balance these two effects.

We propose to use the above *affine flow* as the underlying deformation in constructing a deformation curve. Just as in the erosion curve we measure the area of the deformed shapes (in the embedding formulation we could equally well use the grey volume: i.e. the sum of all grey values in an image). In order to arrive at an absolute affine invariant deformation curve we should prove that the area of the deformed shapes can be expressed in the form given in equation 1. The area of the shape at time t is given by:

$$\mu_X(t) = \text{area}(\Psi^t X)$$

The affine evolution is relative invariant meaning that for some affine transform A:

$$\mu_{AX}(t) = \text{area}(\Psi^t AX) = \text{area}(A\Psi^{t'} X) = |A|\text{area}(\Psi^{t'} X) = |A|\mu_X(t')$$

where $t' = t'(t, |A|)$ (see Alvarez). Taking the derivative to t on both sides of the above expression gives:

$$\dot{\mu}_{AX} = |A|\dot{\mu}_X \frac{\partial t'}{\partial t} \tag{3}$$

It has been shown by Sapiro[10] that every infinitesimal step in time decreases the area of the shape with the *affine perimeter length* L_X (assuming that $C(p,t)$ is a parametrization of the contour at time t):

$$\dot{\mu}_X = -L_X = -\int [C_p, C_{pp}]^{\frac{1}{3}} dp.$$

where C_p and C_{pp} denote the first order derivative and second order derivative of C to the path parameter p respectively and $[C_p, C_{pp}]$ denotes the determinant of the matrix with column vectors C_p and C_{pp}. Thus:

$$\dot{\mu}_{AX} = |A|^{\frac{1}{3}} \dot{\mu}_X.$$

Substituting this into equation 3 we get:

$$\frac{\partial t'}{\partial t} = |A|^{-\frac{2}{3}},$$

which leads to:

$$t' = |A|^{-\frac{2}{3}}t + k$$

where the constant k equals zero because the shape X at $t = 0$ should correspond with the transformed shape AX at $t' = 0$. To cast the deformation dependent area measurement into the required umbral scaling form we look at:

$$\mu_{AX}^{\frac{2}{3}}(t) = |A|^{\frac{2}{3}}\mu_X^{\frac{2}{3}}(\frac{t}{|A|^{\frac{2}{3}}})$$

Thus whereas in the erosion curve we have to look at the square root of the area to obtain an absolute invariant curve, in the affine deformation curve we have to look at $(\text{area}(X))^{\frac{2}{3}}$. The absolute invariant in this case is:

$$\hat{\mu}_X(t) = \frac{\mu_X^{\frac{2}{3}}(\mu_X^{\frac{2}{3}}(0)t)}{\mu_X^{\frac{2}{3}}(0)}$$

Again note that the value of $|A|$ is eliminated from the final expression by normalization using the area of the original set.

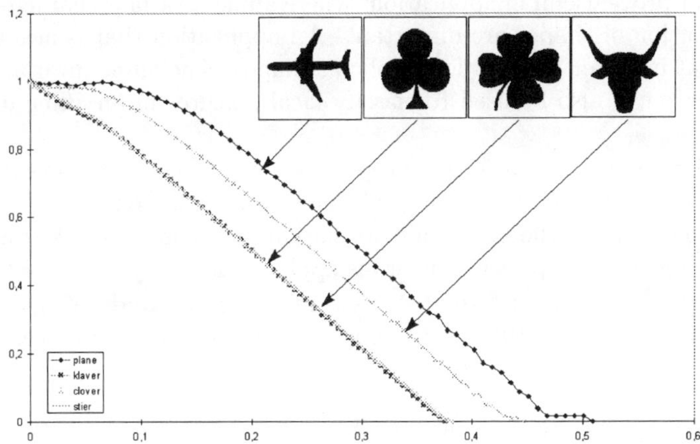

Figure 4: **Affine Invariant Deformation Curves.**

In figure 4 the affine invariant deformation curves for the same 4 shapes as used in figure 2 are shown. Note that the two shapes "Clover" and "Klaver" within this characterization are very much the same.

A special note on the calculation of the affine invariant flow should be made. At first we did the experiments by using the fuzzy derivatives in a simple explicit Euler scheme to solve the affine flow. This resulted in a sequence of images which looked very nice but where the "time axis" was somehow warped beyond prediction. We think this was due to the fact that the fuzzy derivatives themselves are not affine invariant. Only when the scale of differentiation was chosen very small we obtained reproducable results. It even proved just as robust and very much faster to use a simple difference scheme in a 3×3 neighbourhood (as described by Sapiro [10]). Nevertheless the resulting process of calculating the deformations is quite slow (especially when compared to the erosion curve which of course can be calculated using a Euclidean distance transform[1] in well under one second). It might be worthwhile to look at more elaborate (implicit) solution schemes for calculating the affine invariant flow (like the ones described by Weickert[6]).

5 Conclusions

In this paper we have introduced an affine invariant deformation curve. Such a curve might prove useful in applications where affine invariant characterization and recognition of shapes are important. An application that comes to mind is viewpoint invariant recognition of planar shapes. The affine invariant deformation curve can also be used to classify local textures in an affine invariant way.

The deformation curve is a concept originating from mathematical morphology. For the pure morphological deformations like erosions, dilations, openings and closings the power of deformation curves in characterizing shape has been shown in the past in numerous applications.

The affine invariant deformation used in this paper underlying the affine shape characterization still has to prove its usefulness in practice. Future research will look into:

- more theoretical insight into the geometrical interpretation of the affine deformation curve,
- more robust and faster algorithms to calculate the affine invariant deformation and
- efficient ways to use the deformation curves to classify shapes.

Acknowledgements

I would like to thank Erik Engbers who was willing to serve as the "first listener" for the ideas reported in this paper although it was his first week as a PhD student in our group.

References

[1] R. v.d. Boomgaard, The Morphological Equivalent of The Gauss Convolution, Nieuw Archief voor Wiskunde (in English), vol. 10, No. 3, pp. 219—236, November 1992.

[2] R. v.d. Boomgaard, L. Dorst, J. Schavemaker and A.W.M. Smeulders, Quadratic Structuring Functions in Mathematical Morphology, in Mathematical Morphology and its applications to signal processing 3, 1996.

[3] L. Alvarez, J-M. Morel, Morphological Approach to Multiscale Analysis: From principles to Equations, in Geometry Driven Diffusion in Computer Vision, B. ter Haar-Romeny (ed), Kluwer Academic Publisher, 1994.

[4] R. v.d. Boomgaard and A.W.M. Smeulders, The Morphological Structure of Images, The Differential Equations of Morphological Scale-Space, IEEE PAMI, Vol. 16, No. 11, pp. 1101—1113, November 1994.

[5] J. Mattioli, M. Schmitt, Inverse Properties for granulometries by Erosion, Journal of Mathematical Imaging and Vision, vol. 2, pp. 217—232, 1992

[6] J. Weickert, Anisotropic diffusion in image processing, PhD. thesis, University of Kaiserslautern, Germany, 1996

[7] B.B. Kimia, A. Tannenbaum and S.W. Zucker, Towards a Computational Theory of Shape, An Overview, in Proceedings of the First European Conference on Computer Vision, O. Faugeras (ed), 402—407, 1990

[8] J. Serra, Image Analysis and Mathematical Morphology, Academic Press, 1982

[9] P. Maragos, Pattern Spectrum and Multi-Scale Shape Representation, IEEE Transactions on Signal Processing, no. 7, vol. 43, pp. 701—716, 1989

[10] G. Sapiro, A. Tannenbaum, Affine Invariant Scale-Space, Journal of Computer Vision, vol. 11, pp. 25—44, 1993

CONTOUR-BASED SHAPE DISSIMILARITY ANALYSIS USING ARC LENGTH WARPING

G.W.A.M. VAN DER HEIJDEN
DLO Centre for Plant Breeding and Reproduction Research (CPRO-DLO)
P.O.Box 16
6700 AA Wageningen, The Netherlands
E-mail: g.w.a.m.vanderHeijden@cpro.dlo.nl

A.M. VOSSEPOEL
Pattern Recognition Group, Faculty of Applied Physics
Delft University of Technology
Lorentzweg 1, 2628 CJ Delft, The Netherlands
E-mail: albert@ph.tn.tudelft.nl

Contour-based shape dissimilarity can be overestimated due to a strict parameterization convention of contour representations. We present a method, Arc Length Warping (ALW), similar to Dynamic Time Warping (DTW), which allows for a more flexible parameterization. The formulation for ALW is slightly different from DTW, such that a more generic weighting function can be applied. We show that the ALW-based dissimilarity measure is not a metric, but that a measure can be formed, fulfilling our conditions. The method is demonstrated using flowers of *Solanum* species.

1 Introduction

It is not a difficult task to determine whether two (2-D) objects are strictly identical in digital images: there should be a pixel to pixel correspondence. If not, they are not identical. If one allows the objects to be translated, rotated or scaled with respect to each other, the difficulty increases, but it is still fairly simple. The problem becomes more difficult if one wants to determine a quantitative measure of (dis)similarity between objects. Two objects can be regarded as (dis)similar with respect to many different aspects such as size, color, texture, position, orientation and shape. With respect to shape, we can distinguish between internal and external shape features.

In this article we want to study the dissimilarity of 2-D objects with respect to their external shape only, i.e. the shape difference between the outer contours, irrespective of translation, rotation and scaling. In spite of this rather severe restriction, the problem is still complex and many different approaches exist, such as region-based — comprising cross-correlation [3], Hausdorff metrics [2,5] and structural methods such as shape partioning [8] —, based on medial axis and skeletons [6], based on landmarks [1,4] and based on contour representations [10].

A generally applicable shape dissimilarity measure of 2-D objects should meet the following conditions:
C1. The measure should be invariant to scaling, translation and rotation since these equiform operations do not influence the shape of the object.
C2. Dissimilarity between identical objects should be zero (or, in the digital case, within the digitization error bounds).
C3. Dissimilarity between different objects should be larger than zero.
C4. Dissimilarity between object A and B is identical to that between object B and A (symmetric).

With respect to C2, C3, and C4, we see that these closely resemble the requirements of a metric: if the dissimilarity measure is a metric, these conditions are fulfilled. For a true metric, the triangle inequality ($D(A,C) \geq D(A,B) + D(B,C)$) has to apply as well.

Some dissimilarity measures based on cross-correlation or Hausdorff dimensions are provable metrics, but it is difficult to implement them invariant to equiform operations. Therefore, measures based on these approaches are not our first choice. Dissimilarity measures based on shape partitioning or medial axis approaches are often rather application specific. In general, measures based on these approaches do not fulfill all our conditions. Due to the fact that only a few points are used in landmark-based approaches, which do not capture all information present in the contour, C3 will not be fulfilled. Therefore these approaches are all discarded in this study. It can be proven that for contour-representations metric shape dissimilarity measures can be formulated and that hence all conditions can be fulfilled [10]. Therefore we will restrict ourselves in this paper to these measures.

2 Contour representations for shape dissimilarity measures

A parametric contour representation has a starting point, and its position on the contour can vary from object to object. Therefore a fifth condition for a generally applicable dissimilarity measure is added:
C5. The measure should be independent of the starting point of the contour representation.

Not all contour representations are suitable for forming dissimilarity measures. In order to yield a metric dissimilarity measure, a contour representation has to fulfill the following requirements [cf. 10]:

• *single-valuedness*: the representation should have just one value for each different value of the parameter. A similarity measure can not be a metric if there is ambiguity on the value to be used.

• *completeness*: all information should be present. If not, objects differing only in information not present in the representation, will yield a zero dissimilarity and will hence violate C3.

• *continuity*: no large jumps should be present. If sudden jumps occur in the sequence of the function values, the dissimilarity between two almost identical objects will be overestimated.

• *periodicity*: since the starting point on the contour of the representation is not fixed, and we want continuous representations, we also need periodicity of the representation.

• *uniform size*: a representation should have the same extent for all objects. In digital form: the contour representation consists of an equal number of (preferably equally spaced) points for all objects.

Several contour representations which are based on the arc length of the contour can be shown to fulfill the above requirements. Often the arc length parameter is normalized such that a complete tour around the contour has a length of 2π, to fulfill the uniform size requirement. We will symbolize the normalized arc length parameter by t. Van Otterloo [10] has examined the arc-length based representations extensively and he describes several contour representations that fulfill the requirements, such as the position function $z=x+iy$, i.e. the (x,y) coordinates of the contour as function of t, and the curvature κ as function of t.

A contour representation based on t that does not fulfill the requirement of completeness is the radial distance representation r, in which only the magnitude (radius) and not the phase (angle) is used of the contour points with respect to a certain reference point (often the contour average). Since the phase information is missing, two differently shaped objects can have identical representations.

Contour representations differ with respect to their (in)variance to equiform operators. E.g. the contour representation z is variant with respect to all equiform operations, whereas curvature κ is invariant with respect to translation and rotation. All are dependent on the position of the starting point.

A suitable shape dissimilarity measure D for contour representations is based on the minimum of the p-norm between contour representations f_A of object A and f_B for object B over all possible equiform operations and starting point positions τ:

$$D^p(A,B) = \min_{equiform,\tau} \left\| f_A - f_B \right\|_p \qquad (1)$$

For p=1, the measure is global and is the average deviation between the contours. For p=2, it is the square root of the mean square deviation. For $p=\infty$ the measure is local and expresses the maximum difference between the contour representations.

It is practically impossible to calculate this measure optimally, if the contour representation is variant to the equiform operations. So some type of normalization is required. Since z is the original contour representation, it is a logical choice to normalize this representation with respect to translation (average of z = (0,0)) and scaling ($\|z\|_p = 1$). In order to fulfill the uniform size requirement, resampling of the contour points to N equidistant points is also applied. From this normalized contour representation, other contour representations can be derived.

We can express the digital contour representation of contour A and B as a sequence of discrete sampled feature vectors:

$$A = f_A[1], f_A[2], \ldots, f_A[i], \ldots, f_A[N]$$
$$B = f_B[1], f_B[2], \ldots, f_B[i], \ldots, f_B[N]$$

where $f_A[.]$ and $f_B[.]$ can stand for any parametric discrete sampled contour representation.

We can formulate a dissimilarity D^p between objects A and B as the minimum difference between translation and scaling normalized contour representations over all possible starting point positions τ and rotation angles φ as :

$$D^p(A,B) = \min_{\tau,\varphi} \left(\sum_{i=1}^{N} \left| f_A[i] - f_B[i] \right|^p / N \right)^{1/p} \qquad (2)$$

If the contour representation is invariant to rotation (like κ), only optimization over the starting point position is required.

3 Arc length warping

Although the normalized arc length parameter t is a suitable parameter for contour representations, it has some disadvantages: similar objects may have large dissimilarity measures, due to local mismatches in the contour. These local mismatches can be caused by a simple enlargement of a single blob, giving a larger arc length, or by a shift of peaks as is shown by the cat-faces in Fig. 1. Van der Heijden & Vossepoel [9] tried to account for this problem by imposing a common model to all objects under study. This approach was however rather specific and relied heavily on finding all landmarks constituting the common model. A more generic approach would be welcome. Van Otterloo [10] suggested the use of arc length warping (ALW), in analogy with dynamic time warping (DTW), as a possible method to relax the strict parameterization convention.

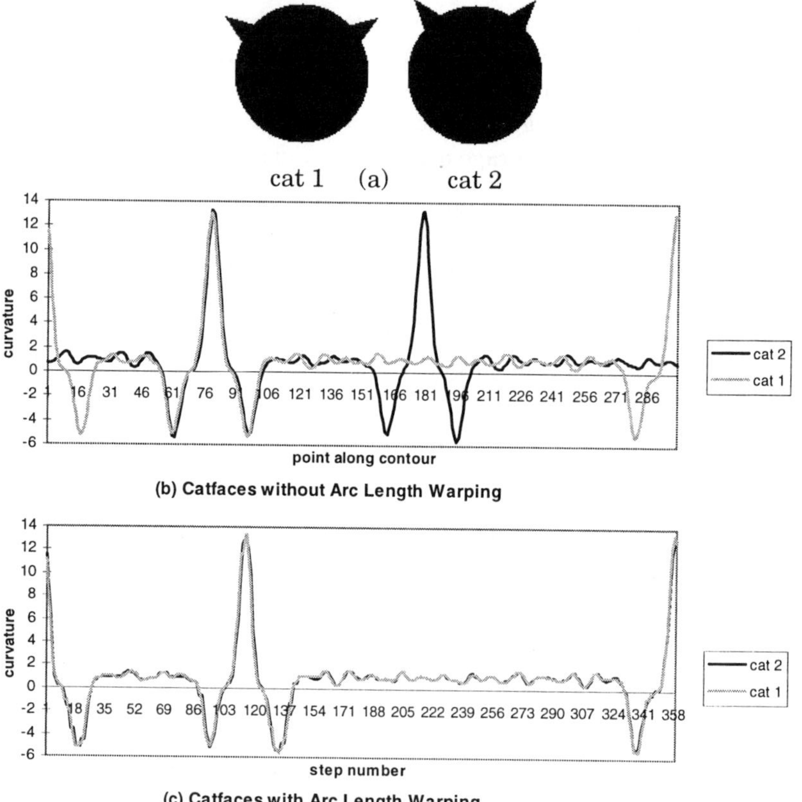

Fig 1. (a) Two 'catfaces' with a different angle between the ears are more dissimilar from each other than they are from a circle, using e.g. contour representation κ; (b) optimal matching without arc length warping. Note that the left ear of cat 1 is at point 0 (300), of cat 2 at point 80. The right ears are at point 80 and 180 respectively; (c) optimal matching with arc length warping. The left ears are at step 0, and the right ears at step 115.

We will demonstrate here the use of ALW almost identical to the DTW that has been proposed by Sakoe and Chiba [7] and we will follow their formulation quite closely. Consider the discrete contour representations $f_A[.]$ and $f_B[.]$. We can relax the strict parameterization convention of t, by allowing differences between the value of t (index i or j) of $f_A[.]$ and $f_B[.]$. These spatial differences can be described by a warping function F consisting of a sequence of points $c=(i_A,j_B)$:

$$F=c(1),c(2),\ldots,c(k),\ldots,c(K) \tag{3}$$

where $c(k)=(i(k),j(k))$ with $c(1)=(1,1)$ and $c(K)=(N,N)$.

This means that we allow a stand-still of the parameter in one of the contour representations, while increasing the other one. The total path will now be longer ($K \geq N$), its length depending on the number of stand-stills in both contour representations. An example is shown in Fig. 2, where a diagonal step indicates no warping and an off-diagonal step indicates warping.

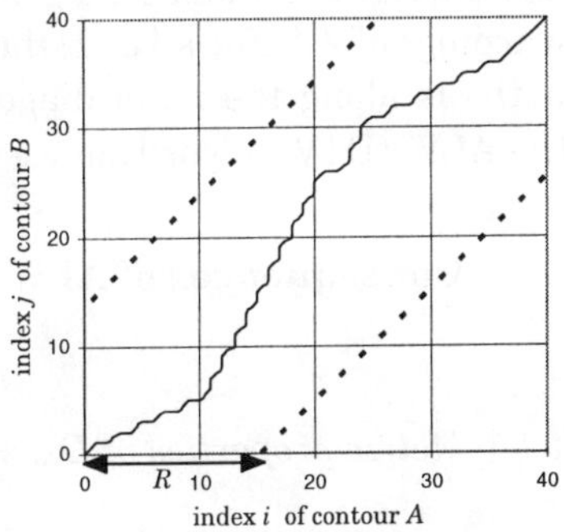

Fig 2. The warping function F allows for stand-stills in either i or j. R is the window size.

Sakoe and Chiba put constraints on the shape of the warping function, using a parameter R, indicating the maximum of $|i\text{-}j|$ that can be taken by the warping function. A smaller value of R reduces the search space and hence the computing time considerably.

We can formulate a weighted dissimilarity measure D_F^p between contour A and B with warping function F as [cf. 7]:

$$D_F^p(A,B)=\sum_{k=1}^{K}\left\{\left|f_A[i(k)]-f_B[j(k)]\right|^p.w(k)\right\} \tag{4}$$

where $w(k)$ is a non-negative weighting coefficient. This dissimilarity measure can be normalized and minimized over all possible warping functions to D_{ALW}^p as:

$$D_{ALW}^p(A,B)=\left(\min_F D_F^p(A,B)/\min_F \sum_{k=1}^{K} w(k)\right)^{1/p} \tag{5}$$

This formulation is different from the one by Sakoe and Chiba [7]. In [7] the minimum over F is taken for the total ratio and not for the numerator and denominator separately. Our formulation allows a more general weighting function to be used in combination with the dynamic programming algorithm. The denominator is employed to compensate for the effect of the number of points, analogous to N in Eq. (2).

If we consider $c(k)$ as a complex number $i(k)$ + i$j(k)$, we can define the following weighting function:

$$w(k) = \|c(k) - c(k-1)\|_q \qquad (6)$$

or written in terms of i and j: $w(k)=(|i(k)-i(k-1)|^q + |j(k)-j(k-1)|^q)^{1/q}$

This means that an off-diagonal step of F (either i or j is increased) has a weight of 1 and a diagonal step (i and j increase simultaneously, no warping) of $2^{1/q}$. For all $q \geq 1$, the minimum sum of weights over all possible paths is along the main diagonal and yields $N \times 2^{1/q}$. For more details on the ALW (DTW) algorithm we refer to [7].

4 Consequences of ALW for shape dissimilarity measures

4.1 Metric properties of D_{ALW}

If, using the warping function F, two contours can be fit on each other perfectly, the dissimilarity measure is zero (regardless of penalties for off-diagonal steps). Thus C3 is not fulfilled. One way out of this, is to calculate, next to D^p_{ALW}, also the original D^p. The difference between the two is a measure for the increase in similarity due to warping. If wanted, one may combine the two as follows:

$$D^{p,\gamma}_{COMB} = \gamma D^p(A,B) + (1-\gamma) D^p_{ALW}(A,B) \qquad 0 \leq \gamma \leq 1 \quad (7)$$

Taking into consideration that $D^p(A,B)$ fulfills C3 (it is a metric), it can easily be seen that $D^{p,\gamma}_{COMB}$ also fulfills C3 for any $0<\gamma\leq 1$. However, it can be shown that the triangle inequality will still not hold, and hence $D^{p,\gamma}_{COMB}$ is not a true metric.

4.2. The position function versus the radial distance function

Although ALW can deal without problems with a complex valued function like the position function z, ALW is not a good solution for z. The warping function only affects the relation between the parameter i and j in both contour representations and not the actual values (x,y) of $z_A(i)$ or $z_B(j)$. The latter is what is needed to account for local mismatches. The radial distance representation r is more suitable in this respect, although it is not information preserving. The loss of the magnitude information can lead to situations where dissimilarity is underestimated.

4.3. Starting point normalization

A major disadvantage of ALW is the computing time. The time required to calculate the dissimilarity is $O(N^2)$ for contour representation κ without warping, but is at least a factor of $2R$ (size of window of F) larger with warping. To avoid excessive use of computing time, we can try to reduce the number of possible starting points (normalization of the starting point). In literature [10] two possibilities are described:

• use the moments to normalize the orientation of the object and use e.g. the crossing point with the positive X-axis as starting point.

• use the Fourier coefficients of contour representation z. Select two coefficients (e.g. the two most significant ones) and solve the starting points using the phase information of the coefficients (c.f. [10] for details).

The first method can only be used if the objects are not too circular. The second one is noise sensitive. Therefore we suggest a third approach:

• use dominant points (points with high curvature) as possible starting points. From the curvature representation κ, local extrema can be selected and used as possible starting points. The idea is that dominant points determine the shape of the contour considerably and that the optimal configuration for two rather similar contours will coincide at a dominant point.

5. Experiments

The experiment is based on a collection of binary images of potato flowers, 6 different species, 5 flowers per species, so a total of 30 objects (Fig. 3). The flowers are characterized by a five-fold rotational symmetry. Each flower consists of five petals merged together. The five sharp points of each flower are the tips of the original petals. The number of contour points of each flower varied between 266 and 514 with an average of 372 points. The number of resampled points N was set to 300.

We have applied the use of ALW to calculate dissimilarity measures based on contour representations r and κ. The curvature κ was calculated using the Freeman resampling method with $\sigma = 3.0$ points [11].

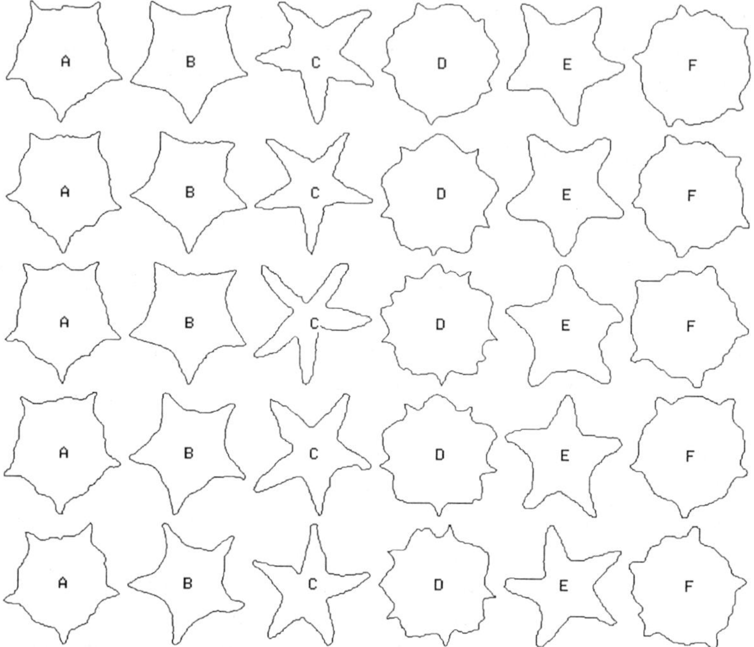

Fig. 3. Six different species of *Solanum*, five flowers each.

To limit the number of possible starting points, dominant points were extracted from the curvature function κ using a local maximum filter (size 30 points). The dissimilarity measure was calculated using only the dominant points (5 per contour) as possible starting points.

The p-norm of the dissimilarity measure was 2. Parameter settings used for ALW were: q=1 (i.e. no penalty for off-diagonal elements, see Eq. (6)) and R=15. The parameter γ in Eq (7) is set to 0.1.

The dissimilarities for all pairs of objects were combined in a lower triangular matrix and this dissimilarity matrix was analyzed using principal coordinates. This technique enables an optimal linear represention of the matrix in a two-dimensional space. A minimum spanning tree is overlaid on the plot, connecting the nearest objects in multi-dimensional space. The tree is an indication for the goodness of representation of the dissimilarity matrix in two-dimensional space. Results are shown for contour representation r (Fig. 4) and κ (Fig. 5).

6. Discussion

Arc length parameterized contour representations are suitable for defining metric shape dissimilarity measures. However, the strict parameterization convention can cause local mismatches, resulting in overrated dissimilarity. We have presented Arc Length Warping as a method to relax this parameterization. The thus obtained dissimilarity measure did not fulfill all conditions C1–C5. By combining, with a parameter γ, this measure with the dissimilarity measure without warping, a measure was obtained that did fulfill the conditions, although it was not a true metric. In our experiment, it was not necessary to introduce γ, but otherwise small values (0.1) will probably suffice.

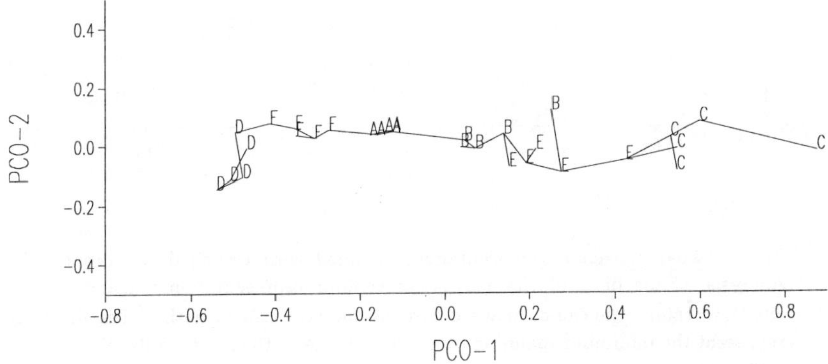

Fig 4. Two-dimensional representation, obtained with Principal Coordinates Analysis, of the dissimilarity matrix for contour representation r using arc length warping. One can clearly see that the species cluster together, The lines represent the minimum spanning tree, which connects the most similar flowers in the multi-dimensional space.

The dissimilarity measures with ALW were capable of measuring overall-shape dissimilarity of objects, as is demonstrated in Fig 4-5. ALW can not be used efficiently for the position function z. A substitute for z is the radial distance function r. As can be seen, r gives less variation within a species than κ. This indicates that r may be the preferred representation to discriminate between the species. It is, however, not completely information preserving and hence violates condition C3.

We have suggested a slightly modified measure of dissimilarity for ALW with respect to DTW to account for a more general weighting function. The parameter q in the weighting function can be used to introduce penalties for warping. This can replace the slope constraint suggested in [7]. Our experiments showed that q should be chosen close to 1, i.e. only small penalties should be introduced.

Since ALW is a computation intensive algorithm, we have reduced the number of starting points by using only dominant points as possible starting points. This kept computation time within reasonable limits.

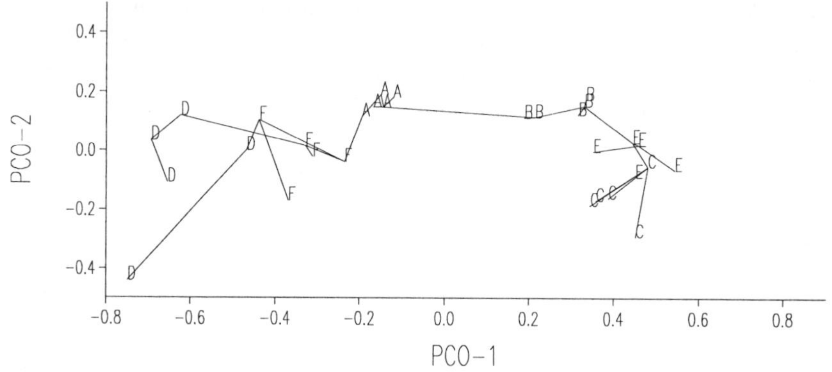

Fig 5. Two-dimensional representation, obtained with Principal Coordinates Analysis, of the dissimilarity matrix for contour representation κ using arc length warping. One can clearly see that the species cluster together, The lines represent the minimum spanning tree, which connects the most similar flowers in the multi-dimensional space.

7. References

[1] F.L.Bookstein, *The Measurement of Biological Shape and Shape Change*, Berlin (Germany): Springer-Verlag (Lecture Notes in Biomathematics, Vol. 24), 1978.

[2] M.-P.Dubuisson and A.K.Jain, "A modified Hausdorff distance for object matching", in: *Proc. 12th Int. Conference on Pattern Recognition* (Jerusalem, Oct.9-13, 1994) Vol. 1, Track A:, Los Alamitos (USA): IEEE Computer Society Press, pp.566-568, 1994.

[3] R.C.Gonzalez and R.E.Woods, *Digital Imaging Processing*, Reading, Massachusetts (USA): Addison-Wesley, 1992.

[4] C.Goodall, "Procrustes methods in the statistical analysis of shape", *Journal of the Royal Statistical Soc. B*, 53 (2) pp. 285-339, 1991.

[5] D.P.Huttenlocher, G.A.Klanderman and W.J.Rucklidge, "Comparing images using the Hausdorff distance", *IEEE Trans. Pattern Anal. Machine Intell.* 15 (9) pp. 850-863, 1993.

[6] B.S.Morse, S.M.Pizer and C.A.Burbeck, "General shape and specific detail: Context-dependent use of scale in determining visual form", in: C. Arcelli, L.P. Cordella, G. Sanniti di Baja (eds.), *Aspects of Visual Form Processing*, Singapore: World Scientific, pp. 374-383, 1994.

[7] H.Sakoe and S.Chiba, "Dynamic programming algorithm optimization for spoken word recognition", *IEEE Transactions on Acoustics, Speech, and Signal Processing*, 26 (1) pp. 43-49, 1978.

[8] K.Siddiqi, K.J.Tresness and B.B.Kimia, "On the anatomy of visual form", in: C. Arcelli, L.P. Cordella, G. Sanniti di Baja (eds.), *Aspects of Visual Form Processing*, Singapore: World Scientific, pp. 507-521, 1994.

[9] G.W.A.M.van der Heijden and A.M.Vossepoel, "A landmark-based approach of shape dissimilarity", in: *Proc. 13th Int. Conference on Pattern Recognition* (Vienna, Austria, Aug.25-29, 1996) Vol. 1, Track A:, Los Alamitos (USA): IEEE Computer Society Press, pp.120-124, 1996.

[10] P.J.van Otterloo, *A Contour-Oriented Approach to Shape Analysis*, Hemel Hampstead (UK): Prentice-Hall, 1991.

[11] M.Worring and A.W.M.Smeulders, "Digital curvature estimation", *CVGIP - Image Understanding*, vol. 58, no. 3, 1993, 366-382.

HYBRID AND ADAPTIVE ARCHITECTURES FOR FACE AND HAND GESTURE RECOGNITION

H. WECHSLER
Department of Computer Science
George Mason University
Fairfax, VA 22030
Email: wechsler@cs.gmu.edu
WWW: http://chagall.gmu.edu

One of the most challenging tasks for visual form ('shape') analysis and object recognition is the understanding of how people recognize each other's face or interpret each other's hand gestures, and the development of corresponding computational models. As the main functionality for both face and hand gesture recognition is that of pattern ('shape') classification AND as hierarchical, modular and adaptive processing has been shown to support such cognitive tasks, we consider herein the potential of hybrid and adaptive architectures for developing robust biometrics and Human-Computer Interaction (HCI) systems. Adaptation is addressed in terms of (short term) learning, (long term) evolution, and their symbiotic interactions. The feasibility of our hybrid and adaptive architecture has been successfully assessed using the standard FERET facial data base, video forensic ('surveillance') sequences, and still photos of hand gestures.

1 Introduction

One of the most challenging tasks for visual form ('shape') analysis and object recognition is the understanding of how people recognize each other's face or interpret each other's hand gestures, and the development of corresponding computational models. Face and gesture recognition, part of the growing field of Human - Computer Interaction (HCI), are becoming important for applications related to biometrics, digital libraries and multimedia, telecommunications and HDTV, medicine, and virtual reality. Automated face and gesture recognition has proved so far to be quite difficult mostly because of the inherent variability of the image formation process in terms of image quality and photometry, geometry, and/or occlusion, change, and disguise. As the main functionality for both face and gesture recognition is that of pattern ('shape') classification AND as hierarchical, modular and adaptive processing has been shown to support such cognitive tasks, we consider herein the potential of hybrid ('Divide et Impera') and adaptive architectures for developing robust biometrics and HCI systems. Adaptation is addressed in terms of (short term) learning, (long term) evolution, and their symbiotic interactions. As an example, such architectures could consist of Decision Trees (DT), Ensembles of Radial Basis Functions (ERBFs), Finite State Automata (FSA) ('HMM'- like) and Genetic Algorithms (GAs) modules, each of them addressing a specific analysis ('categorization') subtask. As more and more (biometrics) information is becoming available on video, we consider also the transition from still imagery ('photo') to video processing of time-varying imagery. An important aspect of biometrics and HCI is eventually that of performance evaluation for existing systems. The feasibility of our hybrid and adaptive architecture is therefore assessed using the standard FERET facial data base,[1] video forensic ('surveillance') sequences, and still photos of hand gestures. The tasks investigated were those of match ('ID verification') and surveillance and CBIR (contents based image retrieval) for face recognition, interpretation for hand gestures and the average performance exceeded 95% accuracy.

2. Shape and Form Analysis

As the topic of interest here is that of visual form analysis it becomes important to define the terms involved and to properly place them in the context of pattern recognition[2] in general, and face and hand gesture recognition in particular. A brief survey of Webster's Dictionary explains the above terms as

shape *n* **1 a**: the visible makeup characteristic of a particular item or kind of item **b** (1): spatial form (2): a standard or universally recognized spatial form.

form *n* **1 a**: the shape and structure of something as distinguished from its material **b**: the component of a thing that determines its kind **d**: a visible and measurable unit defined by a contour 9 **a**: one of the different modes of existence, action or manifestation of a particular thing or substance PATTERN or SCHEMA **c** : the structural element, plan or design *vt* to make up or CONSTITUTE.

analysis *n* [fr. analyein to break up] **1**: separation of a whole into its component parts **2 a**: an examination of complex, its elements, and their relations.

It becomes apparent that the above { SHAPE, and FORM} terms are highly correlated, that face and gesture constitute quite interesting (3D) forms (see face and gesture definitions below), that recognition is a proper type of analysis, and that both face and hand gesture recognition represent challenging shape and form analysis problems in search of robust and efficient solutions.

face *n* **1**: the front part of the human head including the chin, mouth, nose, cheeks, eyes, and usu. the forehead **2**: *archaic*: PRESENCE, SIGHT **3 a**: facial expression **b**: GRIMACE **c**: MAKEUP **4 a**: outward appearance **b**: DISGUISE, PRETENSE **5**: SURFACE **a** (1) : front, upper, or outer surface.

gesture *n* **2**: the use of motions of the limb or body as a means of expression.

Perception in general, and form analysis in particular are important not because they can merely describe things, but as Aristotle realized long ago, because they make us know and 'bring to light' many differences between things so we can categorize and recognize things and respond properly to such affordances. Once forms are represented ('described') their most important functionality is thus to serve for recognition (discrimination and classification). Recognition is thus based on both perceptual form and functionality. Form analysis considers things like the average (shape) prototypes and/or the similarity holding between them, while functionality would carve the perceptual layout according to innate physical and geometrical constraints and corresponding sensory motor affordances. According to this view functional and purposive recognition take precedence over form reconstruction.

As things are always changing and constancy is just an illusion, visual form recognition requires prototyping through generalization so adaptation becomes necessary. As we prototype we should realize that for the purpose of recognition not all forms are equally important and that training to recognize only requires those forms spanning functional boundaries, like the ones used for classification.[3] What visual form analysis does not require is that during the very operation of determining what things are made of we take them to bits, and in ways that destroy the very relations that may be of essence. As Lewontin would say 'one murders to dissect'. To further emphasize the important role functionality plays in perception it's instructive to recall Oliver Sack's best known story, "The Man Who Mistook his Wife for a Hat". The story describes someone who can see, but not interpret what he sees: shown a glove, the man calls it "a receptacle with five protuberances". The moral of the story is that people see not only with the [eyes], but with the [brain]. In other words, SEEING involves a whole and purposive cognitive process.

3. Learning and Hybrid Systems

Form recognition requires modeling and prototyping the forms of interest via generalization. In the framework of predictive learning, estimating a model from finite data requires specification of three concepts: a set of approximating functions (i.e., a class of models : DICTIONARY or KERNELS), an inductive principle, and an optimization (parameter estimation) procedure. The notion of inductive principle is fundamental to all learning methods. Essentially, an inductive principle provides a general prescription for what to do with the training data in order to obtain (learn) the model. In contrast, a learning method is a constructive implementation of an inductive principle (i.e., an optimization or parameter estimation procedure) for a given set of approximating functions in which the model is sought (such as feed forward nets with sigmoid units or radial basis function networks). Once a family of models is chosen one estimates the model using an inductive principle and an optimization procedure. It's only later on that one has to interpret ('describe') the results. There is just a handful of known inductive principles (Regularization, Empirical and Structural Risk Minimization (ERM and SRM), Bayesian Inference, Minimum Description Length), but there are infinitely many learning methods based on these principles. Note that finding the model minimizing future prediction error is an ill-posed problem, since all we have is a finite training sample. In fact accurate estimation of prediction error (risk) is a very difficult problem and involves specifying a model of optimal complexity for a given training sample.[3,4] Finally learning requires both POSITIVE and NEGATIVE examples.

The integration of various learning strategies is an active area of research in artificial intelligence in general, and machine learning in particular (see as an example multistrategy learning). Hybrid learning is a subfield of the more general area known as hybrid (intelligent) systems. The need for hybrid architectures has been discussed earlier by Kanal[2] in the context of pattern recognition, suggesting that "no single model exists for all pattern recognition problems and no single technique is applicable for all problems. Rather what we have in pattern recognition is a bag of tools and a bag of problems". Minsky[5] also supports the hybrid concept when he says that "it is time to stop arguing over which type of pattern classification technique is best because that depends on our context and goal. Instead we should work at a higher level of organization and discover how to build managerial systems ('society of minds') to exploit the different virtues and evade the different limitations of each of these ways of comparing things".

Hybrid learning architectures consider different elements of hierarchical knowledge in terms of concept granularity and specific interfaces. Examples of such elements include connectionist, fuzzy, symbolic and/or evolutionary modules, with each element possibly consisting of a hybrid ('ensemble') architecture by itself. Note that the elements can be structured using different topologies not necessarily hierarchically organized in terms of concept granularity. As the level of abstraction increases, we witness a corresponding degree of data compression leading to more powerful reasoning methods being deployed but on reduced amounts of data. The advantages provided by each element of such a hybrid architecture are:

1) Connectionism can handle the whole range of sensory inputs and their variability ('noise'). Its distributed nature provides for fault tolerance to missing and incomplete data. The output of such modules, known to have a well defined maximum likelihood (ML) probabilistic interpretation, can be combined across ensembles of such networks. Last but not least, the output of such modules yields the sought after fuzzy or symbolic units needed for later stages of processing.

2) Fuzzy elements work on compressed but more abstract data. They provide for flexibility in terms of handling its command variables and adjusting them for enhanced behavioral control. It is this level that first provides for linguistic variables leading later on to full symbolic processing and/or explanation capabilities.

3) Symbolic elements are compact and can fuse data from different sensory modalities and cognitive modes. As a consequence one can make sense of the sensory input and interpret ('explain') it using meaningful coding units as it would be the case with Bayesian nets.

4) Evolutionary elements are appropriate when the range of non-linear combinations and the size of the search space makes adaptation computationally not feasible. Survival of the fittest sifts through and supports effective learning through something akin to symbiotic (Baldwin)[6] adaptation.

Autonomous agents must continuously decide when and when not to learn. According to Wilson,[7] "the decision to learn is fundamentally a choice between acting based on the best information currently possessed vs. acting other than according to what is apparently best - i.e., most remunerative - in order perhaps to gain new information that may permit higher levels of performance later. Learning risks a short-term cost - the "opportunity cost" of not doing the apparent best - in order to achieve higher returns in the longer run. Not learning risks those potentially higher returns in order to get known benefits now. The tension between learning and performance is often described as the "explore/exploit dilemma"[8].

4. Face and Hand Gesture Recognition

The functionality of interest for both face and gesture recognition is that of pattern recognition leading one to consider adaptive methods for achieving robust performance. Major tasks falling under the heading of face recognition include face modeling and knowledge acquisition, computational models, learning robustness and scaling - up performance (our emphasis here), and benchmark (human vs. machine) studies. Face modeling can address issues such as feature based vs. holistic template vs. caricatures modeling, the use and relevance of color, preferential views (3/4), and 2D vs. 3D. Computational models include discriminant analysis, deformation and elastic models, natural and universal bases, and most recently support vector machines (svm)[3].

As hierarchical and modular modes of processing, also referred to as hybrid, have been shown to be fundamental for cognitive behavior, we take a similar approach for developing robust face and gesture recognition schemes. Modular or hybrid design is a common practice where solutions to complex problems are found through a stepwise decomposition of the task into successive modules. The hybrid approach for face and hand gesture recognition involves specific levels of knowledge where the hierarchy is defined in terms of concept granularity and specific interfaces, while modularity is defined in terms of specific stepwise functionality. The hybrid design described below, consists of an **E**nsemble of connectionist networks - **R**adial **B**asis **F**unctions (ERBF) - and inductive decision trees (DT), and it has been shown to be successful for both face and hand gesture recognition[9,10,11]. The reason behind using (E)RBFs is their ability for clustering similar images before classifying them. Decision trees (DT) implement the next symbolic stage using the ERBF outputs.

A hybrid architecture, appropriate for face and hand gesture recognition tasks, is shown in Fig.1. Face recognition usually starts through the detection of a pattern as a face and boxing it, proceeds by normalizing the face image to account for geometrical and illumination changes using information about the box surrounding the face and/or eyes location, and finally it identifies the face using appropriate image representation and classification algorithms.

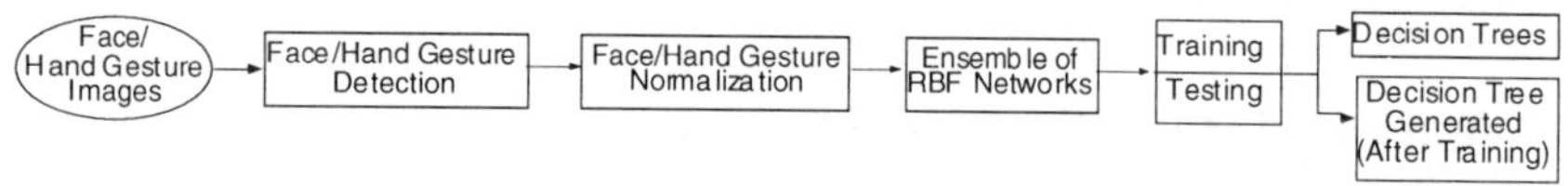

Figure 1. Automated Face / Hand Gesture Recognition (AFHGR) Architecture

In the case of hand gesture recognition, same processes apply as above but normalization now ensures that all the hand gestures are of equal size. We describe here only the tools developed to realize and implement those stages of face (hand gesture) recognition involved in classification and recognition tasks. Examples of normalized faces and hand gestures used by the hybrid classifiers are shown in Fig. 2.

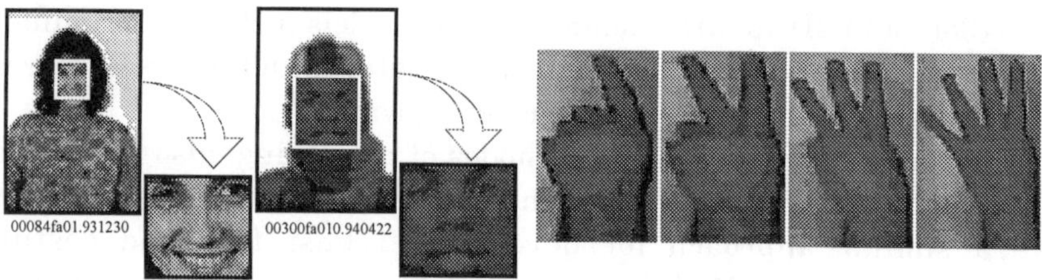

Figure 2. Examples of Normalized Face and Hand Gesture Images

4.1 *Ensemble of Radial Basis Function (ERBF) Networks*

An RBF classifier has an architecture very similar to that of a traditional three-layer back-propagation network. Connections between the input and middle layers have unit weights and, as a result, do not have to be trained. Nodes in the middle layer, called basis functions (BFs) nodes, produce a localized response to the input using Gaussian kernels. The BFs used are Gaussians , where the activation level y_i of the hidden unit i is given by:

$$y_i = \Phi_i(\|X - \mu_i\|) = \exp\left[-\sum_{k=1}^{D}\frac{(x_k - \mu_{ik})^2}{2h\sigma_{ik}^{\ 2}}\right]$$

where h is a proportionality constant for the variance, x_k is the kth component of the input vector X=[x_1, x_2, ..., x_D], and m_{ik} and σ^2_{ik} are the kth components of the mean and variance vectors, respectively, of basis function node i. Each hidden unit can be viewed as a localized receptive field (RF). The hidden layer is trained using **k**-means clustering.

For a connectionist architecture to be successful it has to cope with the variability available in the data acquisition process. One possible solution to the above problem is to implement the equivalent of query by consensus. ERBFs are defined in terms of their specific topology (connections and RBF nodes) and the data they are trained on. Specifically, both original data and distortions caused by geometrical changes and blur can be used to induce robustness to those very distortions via generalization.

4.2 *Decision Tree (DT)*

The basic aim of any concept-learning symbolic system is to construct rules for classifying objects given a *training set* of objects whose class labels are known. The objects are described by a fixed collection of attributes, each with its own set of discrete values and each object belongs to one of two classes. The rules derived in our case will form a decision tree (DT).

The decision tree employed for face recognition is C4.5[12]. C4.5 uses an information-theoretical approach, the entropy, for building the decision tree. It constructs a decision tree using a top-down, divide-and-conquer approach: select an attribute, divide the training set into subsets characterized by the possible values of the attribute, and follow the same procedure recursively with each subset until no subset contains objects from both classes. These single-class subsets correspond then to leaves of the decision tree. The criterion that has been used for the selection of the attribute is called the *gain ratio criterion*.

The decision tree employed for hand gesture recognition is AQDT.[13] AQDT learns a decision structure/tree from decision rules or examples by iteratively selecting an attribute to be a node in the structure, generates as many branches as the number of values of the selected attribute, and associates all rules or examples with the appropriate branch. If all the rules or examples at any branch belong to one decision class, the system creates a leaf node for that decision class; otherwise, it repeats the same process.

4.3 ERBFs and DT (C4.5, AQDT) Hybrids

Inductive learning, as applied to building a decision tree requires a special interface for numeric-to-symbolic data conversion. The ERBF output vectors chosen for training are tagged as 'CORRECT' (positive example) or 'INCORRECT' (negative example) and are quantized. The input to the C4.5 (AQDT) consists of a string of learning (positive and negative) events, each event given as a vector of discrete attribute values. Training involves choosing a random set of positive events and a random set of negative events. The C4.5 (AQDT) builds the classifier as a decision tree whose structure consists of

- *leaves*, indicating class identity, or
- *decision nodes,* that specify some test to be carried out on a single attribute value, with one branch for each possible outcome of the test.

The decision tree is used to classify an example by starting at the root of the tree and moving through it until a leaf is encountered. At each decision node a decision is evaluated, the outcome is determined, and the process moves on.

5. VIDEO BASED PERSON AUTHENTICATION

As more and more biometrics information becomes available on video we consider now the Automatic Video-Based Biometrics Person Authentication (AVBPA) problem. Possible tasks and application scenarios under consideration involve detection and tracking of humans and human (ID) verification. Authentication corresponds to ID verification and involves actual (face) recognition for the subject(s) detected in the video sequence. The architecture for AVBPA takes advantage of the active vision paradigm and it involves difference methods or optical flow analysis to detect the moving subject, projection analysis and decision trees (DT) for face location, and connectionist networks, **R**adial **B**asis **F**unction (**RBF**), for authentication. Subject detection and face location correspond to video break and key frame detection, respectively, while recognition itself corresponds to authentication. The active vision paradigm is most appropriate for video processing where one has to cope with huge amounts of image data and where further sensing and processing of additional frames is feasible. As a result of such an approach video processing becomes feasible in terms of decreased computational resources ('time') spent and increased confidence in the (authentication) decisions reached despite sometime poor quality imagery.

The scenario discussed here involves video sequences consisting of moving subjects approaching the video camera[14]. The overall architecture for such an AVBPA scenario is shown in Fig. 3. Preprocessing, not shown in Fig. 3, first reduces the amount of future processing by skimming the video sequence at reduced sample rates (six rather than thirty frames per second). The contents of frames from the skimmed video sequences are then assessed as of low vs. high signal-to-noise ratio. Our architecture consists basically of three main stages, those of (frame) detection of the moving subject ('video break'), location of subjects' faces ('key frames'), and authentication ('MATCH - recognition') of persons appearing in the video sequence. The first stage, that of frame detection, can be achieved using any of two methods: (i) difference method and (ii) optical flow. Once the moving subject is identified the second stage is activated. The second stage, that of face location, locates the subject's face using inductive decision trees. The face location stage goes on iteratively until a (key) video frame is found where the face is properly located. Following the location of the face projection analysis yields a box surrounding the face where the next stage, that of authentication, is restricted to take place. Should boxing the face fail the whole process is restarted from the next frame. The boxed face is recognized (MATCHed) using an RBF network. If the confidence associated with authentication is 'low', the whole process described above is repeated starting from the last key frame detected.

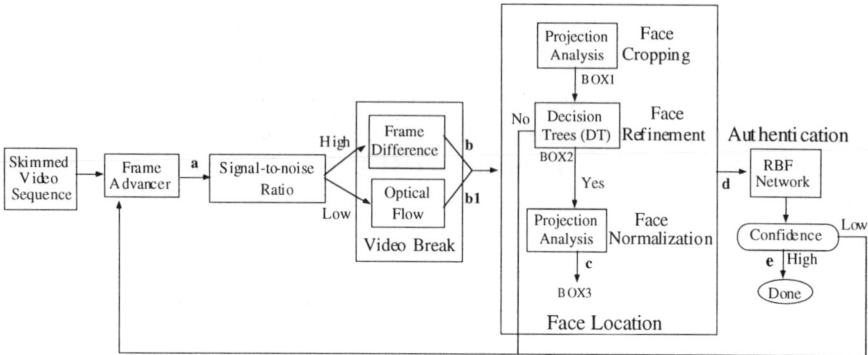

Figure 3. Automatic Video-based Biometrics Person Authentication (AVBPA) Architecture

The feasibility of our AVBPA architecture has been tested on three FERET video sequences acquired in different lighting conditions. The first sequence (one subject) was taken indoors, the second sequence (two subjects) was taken outdoors, and the third (outdoor) sequence was taken during stormy conditions so it displays low signal-to-noise ratio. The three sequences are shown in Fig. 4.

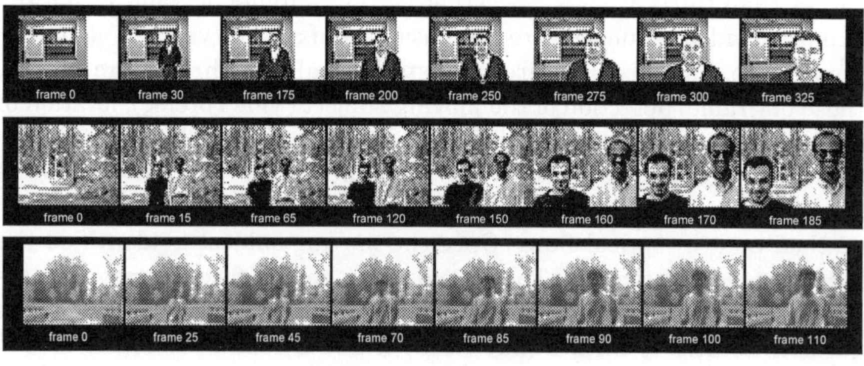

Figure 4. Video Sequences

The goal for each of the three sequences is to detect the moving human subject, locate its face, and verify its identity (ID), i.e., if he/she ('probe') belongs to the given database (DB) of subjects ('gallery'). The generic procedure involves (**a**) video skim (using reduced sampling rate), (**b or b1**) subject detection (using difference or optical flow methods), (**c**) face location, (**d**) face refinement, and (**e**) authentication (using RBF). The (**a**) through (**e**) indicators correspond to the processing points shown in Fig. 3. The three video sequences were acquired at a rate of 30 frames/sec. Video skim was achieved by subsampling the three sequences at a frame rate of 6 frames/sec yielding, 325, 185, and 110 frames, respectively.

The full stepwise (**b - e**) results obtained for the three sequences are displayed next. Positive and negative authentication of the probe is indicated using **+** and **-** signs (Fig. 5), respectively. The probe for the 1st sequence belongs to the gallery, for the 2nd sequence, the left person belongs to the gallery and the right person does not belong to the gallery, while for the 3rd sequence the probe belongs to the gallery. The corresponding (still photos) gallery consists of a total of 20 images. Please note that the stepwise decisions are marked (using an arrow) when a robust decision can be first made regarding detection, location, and authentication, respectively. All authentication decisions made by RBF were correct and were achieved with high confidence.

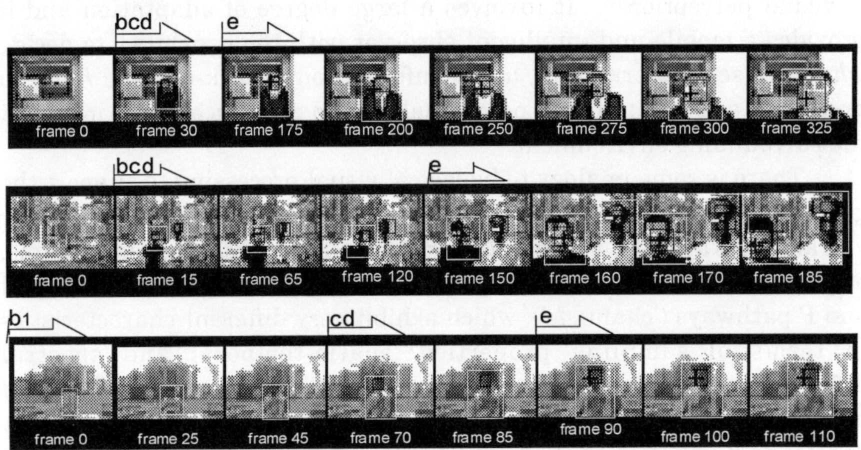

Figure 5. Positive and Negative (ID) Authentication of Subjects

6. Animats, Visual Routines and Eye Detection

As both the position of the eyes and the interocular distance are relatively constant for most people, eye detection provides an excellent framework for image normalization and it also confines the search for other facial landmarks. We briefly describe an adaptive methodology for developing eye detection routines drawing on both learning and evolutionary components[15]. The goals of such an architecture for eye detection are twofold: (**i**) derivation of the saliency attention map ('M - pathway'), as a result of achieving consensus between navigation routines, encoded as finite state automata (FSA) exploring feature landscapes and evolved using genetic algorithms (GAs), and (**ii**) optimal selection of features and derivation of DT (decision trees) for eye classification ('P - pathway') schemes using genetic algorithms (GA) on the most salient locations identified earlier. As saliency is determined first using FSAs and consensus methods, the method is not affected by facial image size.

As the facial landscape to be explored is quite large it becomes necessary to assess the saliency of each facial region in terms of its likelihood that it covers one of the two eyes. Towards that end **A**ctive and **S**elective **V**ision (**ASV**) plays a major role. ASV, known also as directed perception, has advanced the widely-held belief that intelligent data collection rather than image recovery and reconstruction is the goal of visual perception[16]. It involves a large degree of adaptation and it provides a mobile and intelligent observer with the capability to decide *where* to seek information, *what* information to pick up, and *how* to process it, so eventually the perceptual system can successfully interpret the surrounding environment.

There is some analogy to biological visual processing to support the goals of the architecture mentioned above. We know that the two major visual pathways, the *magnocellular* (M) and *parvocellular* (P) streams, originate within the retina and project to low level cortical areas. The M and P pathways ('channels'), which exhibit very different characteristics in terms of sampling properties, spatio-temporal and spectral differentiation as well as processing strategies, form the basis of analyzing *motion* and *form*. The M pathway, which evolutionary developed much earlier than the P pathway, is primarily viewed to be responsible for the analysis of motion while the P pathway performs *recognition tasks* and the detailed analysis of form and color. These two fundamental visual tasks of *object localization* and *object identification* are often referred to as the *where* and *what* problems in the computer vision literature, and would correspond here to eye saliency and recognition, respectively.

As part of behavior-based AI, Maes[17] has proposed autonomous agents (animats) as sets of modules, each of them having its own specific but limited competence. Behavior-based AI has advanced the idea that for successful operation (and survival) an intelligent and autonomous agent should (**i**) consist of multiple competencies ('routines'), (**ii**) be "open" or "situated" in its environment, and (**iii**) monitor the domain of application and figure out, in a competitive fashion, what to do next while dealing with many conflicting goals simultaneously. A similar behavior-based like approach for pattern classification and navigation tasks is suggested by the concept of visual routines[18] recently referred to as a visual routine processor (VRP) by Horswill[19]. The VRP assumes the existence of a set of visual routines that can be applied to base image representations (maps), subject to specific functionalities, and driven by the task at hand. Eye detection can be then viewed as a face recognition (routine) competency, whose inner workings include screening out the facial landscape to detect ('pop-out') salient locations for possible eye locations, and labeling as 'eye' only those salient areas whose feature distribution 'fits' what the eye classifier has been trained to recognize as such. In other words, the first stage of the eye detection routine would implement attention mechanisms whose goal is to create a saliency 'eye' map, while the second stage processes the facial landscape filtered by the just created saliency map for actual eye recognition.

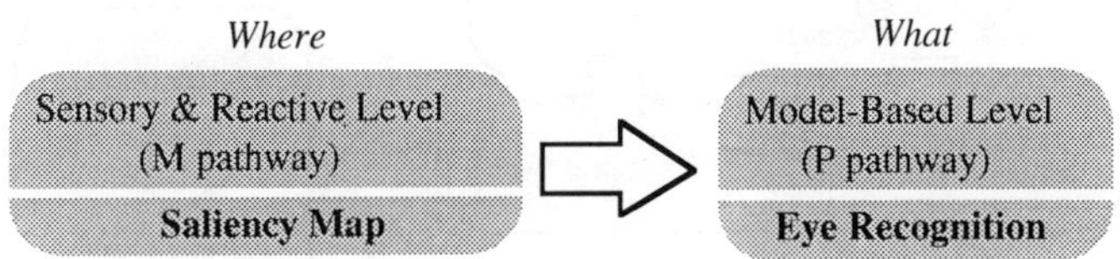

Figure 6. Architecture for Eye Detection

The corresponding architecture, shown in Fig. 6, consists of two components whose tasks are those of eye saliency and eye recognition, respectively. The ('sensory-reactive') saliency component has to discover most likely eye locations, while the ('model-based') eye recognition component probes the suggested locations ('candidates') for actual eye detection.

The derivation of the saliency map (see Fig. 7) is described in terms of tasks involved, computational models, and corresponding functionalities. The tasks involved include feature extraction and data compression, conspicuity derivation, and integration of outputs from several visual routines. The corresponding computational model has access to feature maps, while GAs are used to generate finite state automata (FSA) as appropriate policy (action) functions. Collective intelligence, another expression of hybrid cognitive architectures, considers the scenario when several agents work together towards solving a specific detection problem. The internal (FSA) connections, part of the agent ('animat'), correspond to 'local/autonomous' information, while the external connections would enforce 'global/coordination' constraints. The test bed for the collective behavior of a multi-agents society is the cooperation of eye detection routines towards the derivation of the saliency 'eye' map. Several animats ('agents'), each of them specialized on the same eye detection task, cooperate by exchanging information about their activities and findings. One possible solution to coordinate amongst different agents and the one adopted here is based on consensus methods. The inherent variability of the facial landscape input is handled by starting the eye detection routines from close by points. The motivation behind a consensus strategy is based on the assumption that while it is possible to 'fool' a single agent all of the time one cannot mislead all of them, all of the time.

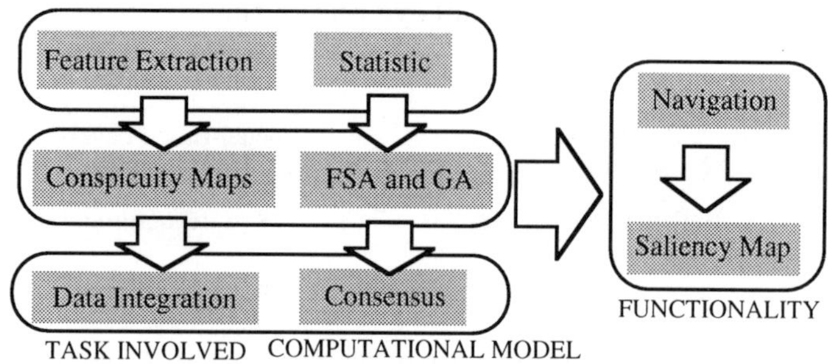

Figure 7. Derivation of the Saliency Map

Eye recognition is performed on the original facial image primed by the saliency map derived earlier. The hybrid eye recognition architecture consists of GA and ID3, where ID3 is an induction decision tree. Final results for eye detection are shown below in Fig. 8.

Figure 8. Final Results for Eye Detection

7. Conclusions

We have shown in this paper the important and constructive role hybrid and adaptive architectures play in face and hand gesture recognition. As the scope of both HCI and video processing expands, such architectures will become even more important. Annotation of video sequences using both captions and speech require appropriate data fusion and integration methods for enhanced performance in terms of both efficiency and accuracy. Furthermore, as most of the hand gestures co-occur with and augment speech in the context of human communication[20] we envision a situation where advanced HCI systems will require the integration of (face) ID verification, analysis of face expression, hand gesture recognition, speech analysis and processing of (text) annotations. As HCI operates over time using time-varying information there is the need for invariance. One possible approach we are now pursuing is that of competitive learning and spatiotemporal consensus[21].

This paper has addressed the topic of hybrid and adaptive architectures in terms of classification and recognition as adaptive abilities only. As it is commonly recognized, however, representations are even more important than learning for biological systems. Distributed and scalespace representations, such as conjoint spatial/spectral representations (Wigner, Gabor, and wavelets), are the counterpart of hybrid classifiers, and together with distributed strategies ('collective intelligence') define the Parallel and Distributed Computation (PDC)[16] One fundamental question remains regarding image and signal representations has been actively pursued recently and relates to the role ('functionality') of sensory coding[22,23]. In particular, the question being addressed compares the merits of PCA like encodings ('factorial coding') vs. sparse coding ('minimum entropy coding') in the context of developing natural bases for image representation using unsupervised ('competitive') learning and redundancy. As PCA does not capture phase information it lacks the ability to account for localization of information. Sparse coding, on the other hand, accounts for phase information and leads to the formation of receptive fields (RFs) similar to those found in the mammalian visual system. As examples of sparse coding one can consider the conjoint spatial/spectral representations ('wavelets') referred to above. We are now pursuing the challenging task of developing hybrid and adaptive architectures in terms of both representations and classification. Towards that end we are working at the intersection between natural bases and universal approximators using hybrid evolutionary and learning methods.

8. References

[1] P. J. Phillips, H. Wechsler, J. Huang, and P. Rauss, "The FERET Database and Evaluation Procedure for Face Recognition Algorithms",, *Image and Vision Computing*, 1997 (under review).

[2] L. N. Kanal, On Patterns, "Categories and Alternate Realities", *University of Maryland Technical Report*, pp. 93 - 05, 1972.

[3] V. Vapnik, 1996, *Statistical Learning Theory*, Springer Verlag.

[4] V. Cherkassky and F. Mulier, *Learning from Data: Statistical, Neural Network and Fuzzy Modeling*, Wiley, 1997 (to appear).

[5] M. Minsky, "Logical versus Analogical or Symbolic versus Connectionist or Neat versus Scruffy", *AI Magazine*, 12 (2), pp. 34 - 51, 1991.

[6] J. Bala, K. DeJong, J. Huang, H. Vafaie, and H. Wechsler, "Using Learning to Facilitate the Evolution of Features for Recognizing Visual Concepts", *Evolutionary Computation* , 4 (3), pp. 297-312, 1996.

[7] S. W. Wilson, "Explore / Exploit Strategies in Autonomy". *Proceedings of the Fourth International Conference on Simulation of Adaptive Behavior*, pp. 325 - 332, MIT Press, 1996.

[8] J. H. Holland, *Adaptation in Natural and Artificial Systems*, MIT Press, 1992.

[9] S. Gutta, J. Huang, I. Imam, and H. Wechsler, "Face and Hand Gesture Recognition Using Hybrid Classifiers", *2nd Int. Workshop on Automatic Face and Gesture Recognition*, Killington, VT, 1996.

[10] S. Gutta and H. Wechsler, "Face Recognition Using Hybrid Classifiers", *Pattern Recognition*, 1997 (to appear).

[11] S. Gutta, I. Imam, and H. Wechsler, Hand Gesture Recognition Using Ensembles of Radial Basis Functions (ERBFs) and Decision Trees (DTs), *Int. Journal of Pattern Recognition and Artificial Intelligence,* 1997 (to appear).

[12] J. R. Quinlan, "The Effect of Noise on Concept Learning", in *Machine Learning: an Artificial Intelligence Approach* 2, R.S. Michalski, J. G. Carbonell, and T. M. Mitchell (Eds.), pp. 149-166, Morgan Kaufmann, 1986..

[13] I. F. Imam and R. S. Michalski, "Learning Decision Trees from Decision Rules: A Method and Initial Results from a Comparative Study", *Journal of Intelligent Information Systems (JIIS)*, 2 (3), pp. 279-304, 1993.

[14] H. Wechsler, V. Kakkad, J. Huang, S. Gutta, and V. Chen, "Automatic Video-Based Person Authentication Using the RBF Network Surveillance and Authentication (VSA)", *1st Int. Conf. on Audio - and Video - Based Biometrics Person Authentication*, Crans-Montana, Switzerland, 1997.

[15] J. Huang and H. Wechsler, "Visual Routines for Eye Detection Using Learning and Evolution", *Image and Vision Computing, 1997* (under review).

[16] H. Wechsler, *Computational Vision,* Academic Press, 1990.

[17] P. Maes, Behavior-Based AI, in J. A. Meyer, H. L. Roitblat, and S. W. Wilson (Eds.), *From Animals to Animats 2,* MIT Press, 1992.

[18] S. Ullman, "Visual Routines", *Cognition,* Vol. 18, pp. 97-159, 1984.

[19] I. Horswill, "Visual Routines and Visual Search", *Int. Joint Conf. on Artificial Intelligence*, Montreal, Canada, 1995.

[20] J. Cassell, "What You Need to Know About Natural Gesture", *2nd Int. Workshop on Automatic Face and Gesture Recognition*, Killington, VT, 1996.

[21] P. Foldiak, "Learning Invariances from Transformation Sequences", *Neural Computation*, Vol. 3, pp. 194-200, 1991.

[22] D. J. Field, "What is the Goal of Sensory Coding?", *Neural Computation*, Vol. 6, pp. 559-601, 1994.

[23] A. J. Bell and T. J. Sejnowski, "Edges are the "Independent Components" of Natural Scenes, *Neural Information Processing Systems (NIPS),* Vol. 9, 1997.

A GRAPH THEORETIC APPROACH TO RECONSTRUCTION OF 3D OBJECTS FROM 2D ENGINEERING DRAWINGS

MIRI WEISS and DOV DORI

Faculty of Industrial Engineering and Management
Technion, Israel Institute of Technology
Haifa 32000, Israel
E-mail: {iemiri, dori} @ie.technion.ac.il

A graph theoretic approach to the reconstruction of 3D objects from engineering drawings is presented. Building on the results supplied by the Machine Drawing Understanding System (MDUS), topological and dimensioning analysis is applied to construct a minimal constraint graph for each 2D view. The minimal graphs are combined into a composite graph representing a 3D object by initial and complete matching. The complete composite graph is then converted into solid 3D object. This approach is demonstrated by a simple non-manifold example.

1 Introduction and Motivation

Engineering drawings have been traditionally used for designing and communicating object information among designers, customers, subcontractors and quality assurance professionals. Significant progress in scanning devices and storage technology has made the reconstruction of 3D objects from paper engineering drawings a viable research issue.

This paper presents a new approach for reconstruction of 3D objects from engineering drawings that extends the work described in Dori and Weiss [7]. A number of approaches and algorithms have been developed over past two decades to automatically interpret user-supplied orthographic views for the purpose of 3D object reconstruction.

The two main reconstruction approaches are the *wireframe-oriented bottom up* approach and the *volume oriented* approach. Existing algorithms within each approach are categorized into those handling only planar surfaces and those which manage more general surfaces, including cylindrical, canonical spherical and toroidal. The use of wireframe-oriented bottom up algorithms is widespread [10,11,13,14,16,17,20]. It employs fundamental topological ideas and features four major steps: transformation of 2D vertices extracted, from orthographic views into 3D vertices, generation of 3D edges from the 3D vertices, construction of faces from the 3D edges and, formation of 3D objects from the 3D faces. *Volume-oriented* Algorithms are based on constructing 3D primitive subparts through translation sweep operations and combining them to generate the complete object. Aldefeld [1,2] suggested to view a complex part as being composed of elementary objects belonging to a set of predefined classes. Recognition of these objects is done by making use of knowledge about the class-dependent pattern of their 2D representation. The term 'primitive' denotes a basic element of 2D representation, such as arc, line, or circle. An object for a 3D representation is termed 'composed part'. Further works can be found in [3,4,9,14,15].

2 Scheme of a proposed approach for 3D reconstruction

The proposed approach for reconstructing 3D objects from 2D engineering drawing is based on the following three stages:

(1) High level 2D orthographic view understanding;

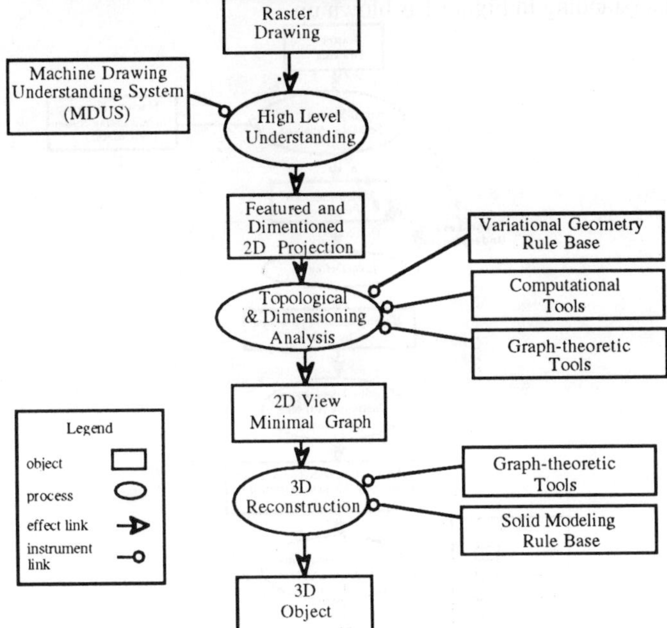

Fig. 1. A Top-Level OPD of the proposed approach for 3D object reconstruction

(2) Analyzing topological relations and dimensioning schemes in each 2D view

using variational geometry elements; and
(3) 3D reconstruction using graph theoretic methods and solid modeling tools..

The top-level view of the approach is described in the object-process diagram (OPD) of Figure 1. An OPD (Dori [5]) is a graphic representation of the objects and processes in the system with their structural and procedural relations. As the legend of Figure 1 shows, objects and processes are represented as rectangles and ellipses, respectively. Effect links (arrows) lead from an affected object to a process in which it takes part, or from a process to a resulting object. An instrument link (a line ending with blank circle) leads from an enabling object - the instrument - to the enabled process.

3 High level 2D orthographic view understanding

For the high-level information of an engineering drawing to be extracted, it ought to be viewed as a dual, two-faceted entity: the image, or geometry layer, which includes projections of the object, and the language, or annotation layer, which includes dimensioning and other functional symbols. In Figure 2 the process of High-Level Understanding in Figure 1 is blown up.

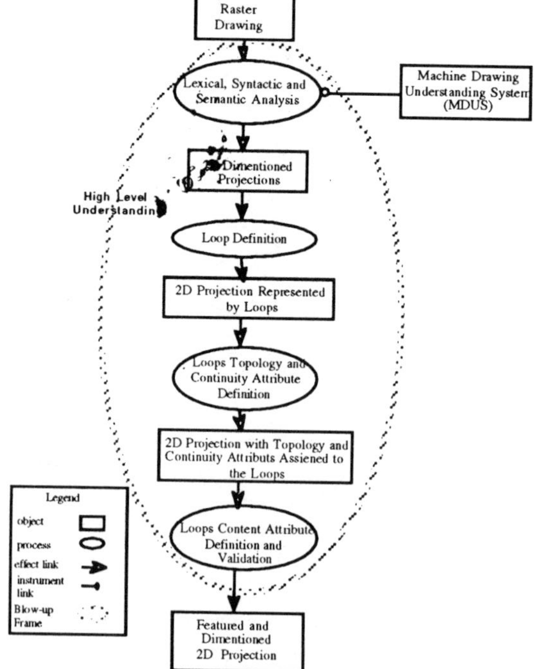

Fig. 2. High Level Understanding process of Figure 1 blown up.

Dori [6] divide the understanding process into three phases: lexical - early vision, syntactic - intermediate vision and semantic -high level vision. The lexical phase is preceded by scanning, noise removal, enhancing, thresholding and other preprocessing operations. Lexical analysis includes recognition of primitives - basic elements found in most engineering drawing: bars (straight line segments), arcs, text and arrowheads. At the syntactic level, the primitives are aggregated into semantically correct groups, such as dimension-sets. The semantic phase involves obtaining complete (image and annotation) 2D views of the object described in the drawing. The process of automated feature recognition from the 2D drawing is performed next and detailed in Weiss and Dori [19]. It includes the following sub-processes: finding all vertices connecting or intersecting bars and arcs in the 2D orthographic view; finding all possible loops based on the definition of a loop as a minimal closed consecutive set of wires; determining the loops' topology and continuity attribute values; determining the loops' content attribute value; and validation and extension of loops' contents.

4 Analyzing topological relations and dimensioning schemes.

Following the 2D understanding of engineering drawings we propose to analyze each one of the projections by means of topological relations. Given an orthographic view, we automatically extract geometric constraints which describe explicit and implicit dimensions.

In Figure 3, the process 'Topological and Dimensional Analysis' of Figure 1 is blown up, exposing three main processes: Constraint Evaluation, Proper Dimensioning Check and Graph Representation & Dependencies Matching.

The basic primitives comprising a 2D orthographic view of an engineering drawing are bars, arcs and circles. Each dimension and topological relation is formulated as a constraint which defines the positioning of each vertex. The variational geometry rule base defined and used in this work is described in detail by Weiss and Dori [18]. Dimensions define geometric constraints, such as distance between two points, distance between a point and a bar, and an angle between two bars. Spatial relations define topological constraints as tangency, parallelism, and perpendicularly. The constraints extracted from each 2D view represent relations among explicit and implicit characteristics. The resulting expressions are mostly non-linear equations. A graph representation of a constraint-set expresses the relations among parameters in more than one constraint. Following the constraint definitions and proper dimensioning check for each 2D orthographic view, we combine the constraints into a minimal graph. The motivation for this operation is to find the minimal set of relations that fully represent the 2D view. The minimal graph representation provides a compact mapping of relations among the parameters. The algorithm is fully described and exemplified in [7].

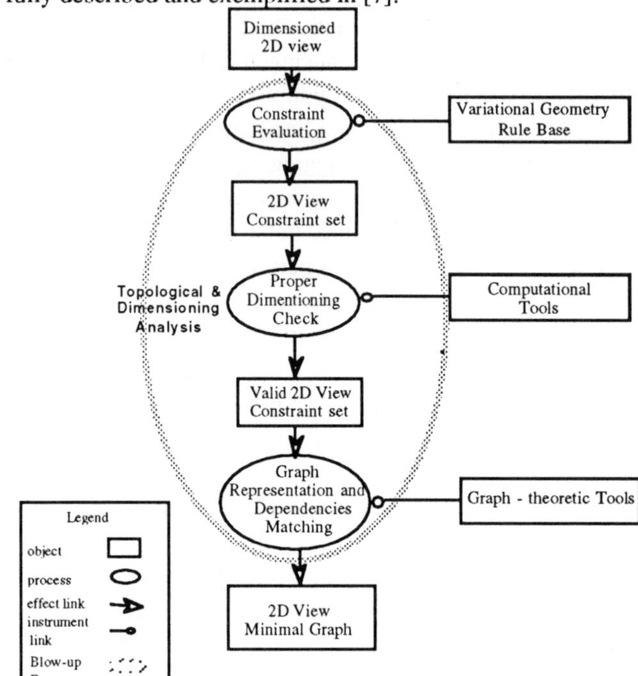

Fig.3. The topological and dimensioning analysis process of Figure 2

5 3D Reconstruction

Having obtained the 2D minimal undirected graph for each 2D orthographic view we reconstruct the 3D object. In Figure 4 is the 3D reconstruction process shown in Figure 1 is blown up, showing that the 3D reconstruction process consists of three major procedures: Initial Matching, Complete Matching and Graph-to-Object Conversion

The processes of Initial Matching and Complete Matching use the set of separate 2D minimal undirected graphs constructed in the previous stage. These graphs are analyzed for matching and merging conditions. A schematic illustration is shown in Figures 5 and 6. Figure 5 illustrates the starting point, in which each 2D view has an independent minimal graph representation. Figure 6 illustrates the complete graph generated by adding new edges (the dashed lines) which connect vertices in the various 2D view graphs.

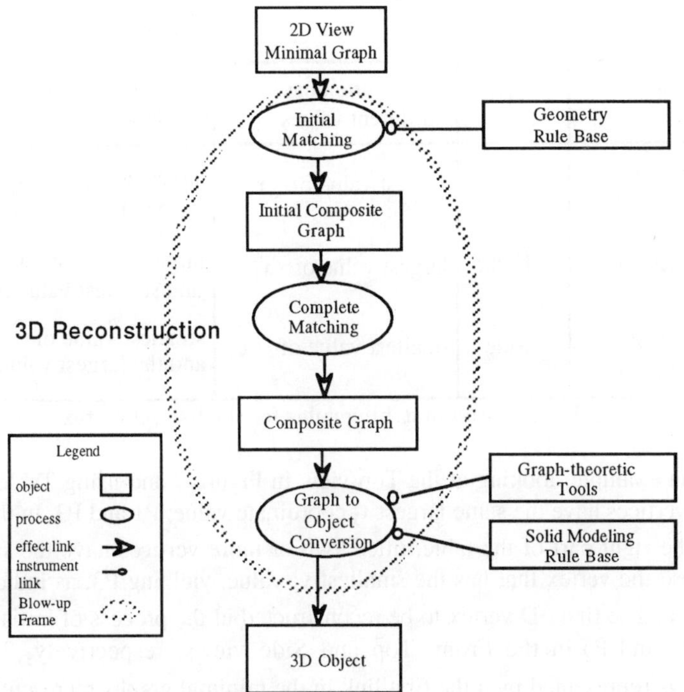

Fig. 4. 3D Reconstruction process blown -up

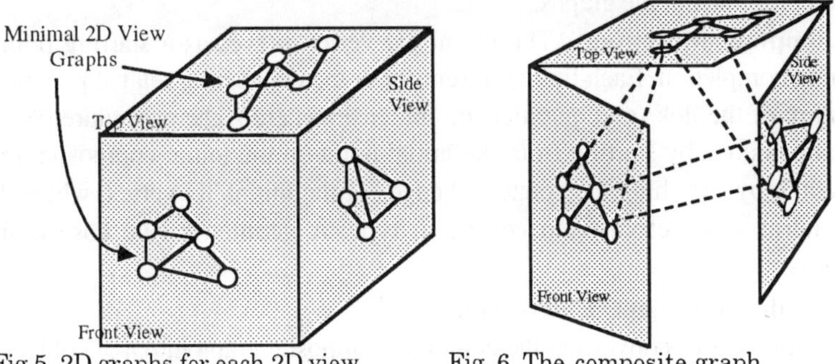

Fig.5. 2D graphs for each 2D view

Fig. 6. The composite graph

Initial matching The system of projections used in our work is based on 'first angle projection'. Matching the first 3D vertex is based on searching each one of the 2D projections for different plane representation of the vertex. These matched vertices from the projections are matched simultaneously in the representing graphs. The matching rules are described in Table 1.

Plane	View	Each vertex has different values	Two or more vertices have the same value
(X,Y)	Top	largest value of x_i	largest value of x_i and smallest value of y_i
(X,Z)	Front	largest value of x_i	largest value of x_i and smallest value of z_i
(Y,Z)	Side	smallest value of z_i	smallest value of z_i and the largest value of y_i

Table 1: Initial matching rules for the fist 3D vertex

As an example, looking at the Top view in Figure 7 and using Table 1, we see that two vertices have the same largest x_i coordinate value: P1 and P3. In this case we refer to the right part of the table, titled 'two or more vertices have the same value' and choose the vertex that has the smallest y_i value, yielding P3, as indicated by a solid circle. The first 3D vertex to be reconstructed in the process of initial matching is P_1 , P_3 and P_2 in the Front, Top and Side views, respectively. This initial matching is represented by a the first link in the minimal graphs representing the 2D views. This procedure yields an initial composite graph containing all three Minimal 2D View graphs, where one node of each such graph coincides with the first 3D vertex represented in the graphs.

Complete Matching - The initial 3D vertex serves as a starting point to the matching completion. Each link represents both the connecting related parameters and the nature of the link (e.g., parallelism, dimensions, etc.) The procedure of complete matching is done by starting from the initial point on the initial composite graph and proceeding by searching the connected edges of the initial 3D vertex, while checking two criteria: connectivity and constraint type. A geometric rule base is used for feasibility.

Graph to Object Conversion

The process of converting the complete composite graph into a 3D object is done by translating the links, connections and constraint types into geometry and topology. This process is based on using graph theoretic tools for retrieving information from the graph and using the results from the feature recognition process which was done in the High level understanding of the 2D views.

All the information represented by the complete Composite Graph composed is used. We use the Chinese Postman Problem (CPP) algorithm [8] for arc routing all the vertices in the graph and traversing all edges by criteria of minimal total distance.

Starting from an arbitrary node, each triplet (two nodes and a connected edge) is translated into geometry or topology of the 3D object, depending on the constraint type and value. For non manifold (genus 0) 3D objects, a partial Boundary representation (B-rep) is reconstructed. Using the results from the feature recognition process and sweeping procedures, a 3D solid is finally reconstructed.

6 An Example

The following simple example illustrates the 3D reconstruction object from two 2D dimensioned views of an engineering drawing.

Constraint Evaluation and Proper Dimensioning Check.

In this example we use the following parameters for the points found in the two 2D views. In each of the views (Front, Side and Top) there are four points: P_1, P_2, P_3 and P_4. Each point is defined in terms of the coordinates of the plane in which it is represented.

Two rules from the variational geometry rule base are used:

Rule # 1 - Euclidean distance between two points

Rule # 2 - Perpendicularity

To prevent solid body translation, we fix a selected point, called *anchor point*, as the origin (0,0). All the points are defined relative to this anchor point. To prevent solid body rotation, we choose a particular bar to be horizontal, i.e., parallel to the horizontal axis.

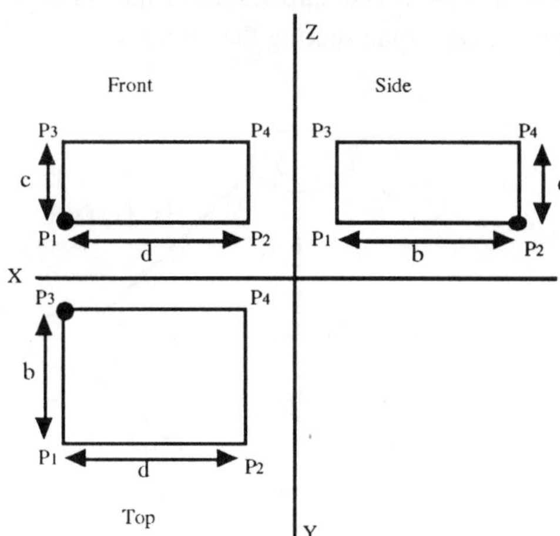

Fig.7. Top, Side and Front views of an engineering drawing

We have chosen this simple example of a non manifold 3D object because the representation of constraints and the resulting minimal graphs are similar for all three views. Equations 1-8 are defined for the Top view. The constraint attribute will differ according to the plane represented, as shown in Table 1, and the Source values will differ according to the dimensioning schemes found in the engineering drawing for each view.

Rule #	Source	Constraint
1	d	$f_1: \quad (x_2-x_1)^2+(y_2-y_1)^2-d^2=0$
1	b	$f_2: \quad (x_3-x_1)^2+(y_3-y_1)^2-b^2=0$
1	d	$f_3: \quad (x_4-x_3)^2+(y_4-y_3)^2-d^2=0$
1	b	$f_4: \quad (x_4-x_2)^2+(y_4-y_2)^2-b^2=0$
2	$P_1P_2 \perp P_1P_3$	$f_5: \quad (x_1-x_2)(x_3-x_1)+(y_1-y_2)(y_3-y_1)=0$
	x anchor	$f_6: \quad x_1=e=0$
	y anchor	$f_7: \quad y_1=a=0$
	orientation	$f_8: \quad y_2-y_1=0$

We calculated a 8x8 Jacobian matrix from Equations 1-8. The rank of this matrix was found to be 8, indicating proper dimensioning and constraint definition of each one of the views.

Graph Representation - For each one of the 2D views a minimal graph is constructed. Figure 8 is an example of the minimal graph representing the Top View. The nodes represent the tuple coordinate values of the vertices and the arcs represent connectivity and type of constraint linking the vertices.

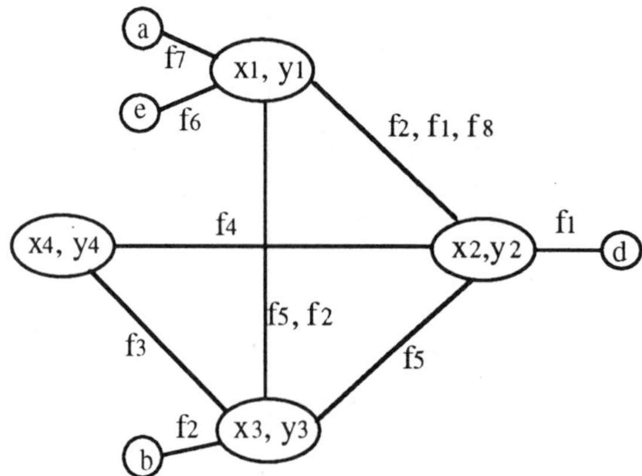

Fig. 8. Minimal graph for the top view

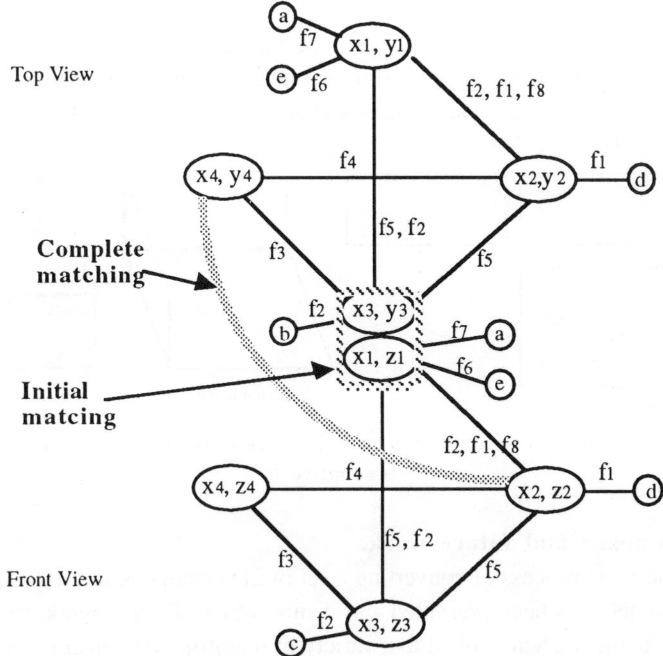

Fig. 9. Composite graph for the Front and Top views

Initial matching - According to the rules in Table 1 which were demonstrated earlier, we matched the first 3D vertex. The matching is indicated by the three solid circles in P3, P1 and P2 in the Top, Front and Side views, respectively. For clarity of presentation, Figure 9 is only a part of the composite graph. As indicated by the gray area the initial matching in the graph represents the coincidence of P1 on the Front view and P3 in the Top view. This is a representation of the same first 3D vertex in two different 2D views.

Complete matching - Starting from the initial matching vertex representation in the composite graph we traverse the edges and nodes connected to it, each time from a different minimal graph representing a different view, simultaneously. Looking at Figure 9, P4 (x_4, y_4) in the Top view was matched with P2 (x_2,z_2) in the Front view. With respect to these two 2D views no other links were found, meaning that no more coincident vertices are represented in the graph which could appear as 3D vertices in the 3D object.

Graph to Object Conversion - Figure 10 shows the results of the graph to 3D object process conversion process. On the left hand side, there are the simple feature recognition results of the High Level Understanding procedure, indicating that each view is composed of one loop, which represents Matter in the 'content attribute value' [19]. The partial B-rep in the middle is based on translating the composite graph to faces by using geometry and topology considerations. Vertices, edges and faces were reconstructed using solid modeling rules detailed in Mantyla [12]. On the right hand side the 3D non-manifold object is finally reconstructed.

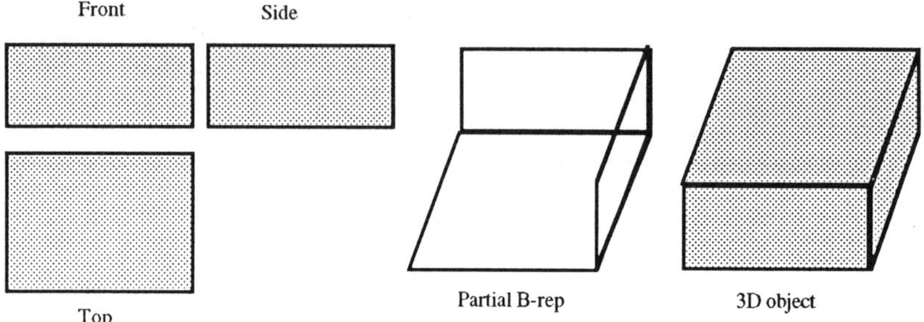

Fig. 10. Feature recognition, partial B-rep and 3D object of the example in Figure 7.

7 Summary and future work.

A complete process of converting a set of 2D orthographic views of a 3D object into that object has been presented and demonstrated. Further work must be done to prove correctness when applied to a variety of manifold 3D object types. Once these are studied and well understood we plan to implement the algorithm in the Machine Drawing Understanding System (MDUS).

8 References

1. Aldefeld, B., On Automatic Recognition of 3D Structures from 2D Representations, *CAD*, Vol. 15, No. 2, 1983.

2. Aldefeld, B. and Richter H., Semiautomatic Three Dimensional Interpretation of Line Drawings, *Computers and Graphics*, Vol. 8, No. 4, pp. 371-380, 1984.

3. Bin, H., Inputting Constructive Solid Geometry Directly from 2D Orthographic Views, *CAD, Vol.* 18, No. 3, pp. 147-155, 1986.

4. Chen, Z. and Perng, D., Automatic reconstruction of 3D solid objects from 2D orthographic views, *Pattern Recognition*, Vol. 21, No. 5, pp. 439-449, 1988.

5. Dori, D., Object Process Analysis: Maintaining the Balance Between System Structure and Behavior, *J. of Logic Computation*, Vol. 20, pp. 227-249, 1995

6. Dori, D., Dimensioning Analysis: a Step Toward Automatic High Level of Understanding of Engineering Drawings, *Comm. of the ACM*, Vol. 35, pp. 92-103, 1992.

7. Dori, D., Weiss, M., A Scheme for 3D Object Reconstruction from Dimensioned

Orthographic Views, *Eng. Applic. Artif. Intell.*, Vol. 9, No. 1, pp. 53-64, 1996.

8. Evans, R. J., Mineika, E., Optimization Algorithms for Network and Graphs, Marcel Dekker, N.Y., 1992

9 Gujar, U. G. and Nagendra, I. V., Construction of 3D Solid Objects from Orthographic Views, *Computers and graphics*, Vol. 13, No. 4, pp. 502-521, 1989.

10. Idesawa, M., A System to Generate a Solid Figure from Three View, *Bulletin of the JSME,* Vol. 16, No. 92, pp. 216-225, 1973.

11. Lequette, R., Automatic Construction of Curvilinear Solids from Wireframe Views, *CAD*, Vol. 20, No. 4, pp. 171-180, 1988.

12. Mantyla, M., An Introduction to Solid Modeling, Computer Science Press, 1988.

13. Markowsky, G. and Wesley, M. A., Fleshing out Wireframes, *IBM J. of Research and Development*, Vol. 24, No. 5, pp. 582-597, 1980.

14. Martson, R. E. and Kuo, M. H., Reconstruction of 3D Object from Three Orthographic Projections using a Decision Chaining Method, *IAPR MVA'94, Workshop on Machine Vision Applications*, Kawasaki, Japan, 13-15 Dec. 1994.

15. Nagasami, V. and Langrana, N. A, Reconstructing of Three-dimensional Object using a Knowledge-based Environment, *Engineering with Computers,* Vol. 7, pp. 23-35, 1991.

16 Preiss, K., Constructing of the Solid Representation from Engineering Projections, *Computers and Graphics,* Vol. 8, No. 4, pp. 381-389, 1984

17. Sakurai, H. and Gossard, D. C., Solid Model Input Through Orthographic Views, *Computer Graphics (SIGGRAPH)*, Vol. 17, No. 3, 1983.

18 Weiss, M. and Dori, D., Variational Geometry as a Tool for Dimensioning Validation of Recognized 2D Views in Engineering Drawing., Dori D. and Bruckstein F. (Eds), *Shape and Structure in Pattern Recognition*, World Scientific, 1995.

19 Weiss, M. and Dori, D., Automatic Resolution of Object Features from Engineering Drawing for 3D Reconstruction, Perner P., Wang P., and Rosenfeld A. (Eds), *Advances in Shape and Structure in Pattern Recognition*, Leccture Notes in Computer Science 1121, 1996.

20. Wesley, M. A. and Markowsky, G., Fleshing out Projections, *IBM J. of Research and Development*, Vol. 25, No. 6, pp. 934-953, 1981.

SURFACE RECONSTRUCTION USING A VARIANCE CONTROLLED ADAPTIVE MESH

RICHARD C. WILSON, EDWIN R. HANCOCK
Department of Computer Science,
University of York,
York, Y01 5DD, UK

This paper describes an active mesh representation for surface reconstruction. The mesh is active in the sense that it is capable of adapting to surfaces of varying curvature and noise. Our surface representation has a dual structure. The control points which sparsely sample the surface are represented by a triangulated mesh. Raw data-points associate to the triangular faces of the mesh. By collecting groups of faces we construct support neighbourhoods whose geometry is dependent on the local mesh configuration. The points encompassed by these neighbourhoods are used to compute the maximum likelihood parameters for local quadric patches. The region over which each quadric patch has influence is therefore closely coupled to the local mesh topology. Our mesh adapts itself to the surface-structure of the raw-data points in a two-step iterative process. Firstly, mesh nodes lying within the local triangulated neighbourhoods migrate to fall on the surface of their best-fit quadric patch. This leaves the mesh topology unchanged. In the second step, the topology of the mesh adapts itself to the surface through a series of edit operations which split and merge the triangular faces.

1 Introduction

Adaptive meshes are a powerful tool for reconstructing surfaces from raw data-points. The basic idea is to describe the surface in terms of a set of nodes representing control points on the surface and a set of edges which inter-connect the nodes. The surface adaptation process therefore requires two ingredients. The first of these is a description of the accuracy of the mesh. The second ingredient is a means of defining the optimal distribution of control points on the surface.

Attempts at realising this process have been numerous. One of the first was the regularised surface mesh of McInnery and Terzopoulos which controls vertex placement using a finite element method [8,9]. Cohen *et al* have realised the update process using Lagranges equations [3]. Neuenschwander *et al* have developed a "Velcro surface" which constrains itself using the surface normals at a number of control points [11]. Each of these methods use a mesh of fixed topology. This can be regarded as optimising the vertex positions without regard for any requirement for a change in the numbers of mesh-points. Stoddart *el al* have addressed this issue by developing a mesh with adaptive topology. The nodes of this mesh represent B-spline surfaces [16]. The spline mesh adapts in a coarse-to-fine manner through the process of surface refinement [13]. Bulpitt and Efford have also realised the surface refinement process using curvature and goodness of fit criteria [1].

Based on this brief review of the literature, we conclude that the bulk of existing adaptive meshes are based on elastic analogies or are of fixed mesh-topology. The exceptions are provided by the coarse-to-fine meshes of Stoddart *et al* [16] and of Bulpitt and Efford [1]. However, here the adaptation of topology is unidirectional. Our aims in this paper are twofold. In the first instance, we aim to realise the surface control as a maximum likelihood fitting process. Our second aim is to control the adaptation of topology in an omnidirectional manner driven by the statistical properties of the raw data-points. In other words, we would like to be able to both coarsen and refine our surface representation. In doing this we aim to avoid the explicit use of information concerning the local differential structure of the surface [3,4] since this is invariably unreliable [17] or difficult to quantify [12]. Instead we drive the process using fit residuals.

Our first step is to describe an adaptive mesh surface which builds on the simplex mesh studied by Delingette [5,7]. The raw data-points associate with surface-triangles of closest perpendicular distance. We demonstrate that the natural local representation of the surface is in terms of piecewise quadric patches, and show how both under- and over-parameterisation of the underlying surface can be prevented using statistical properties of the raw datapoints. This leads to a two stage iterative model. The local extent of a quadric patch is controlled by the mesh density and the mesh density is adjusted in its turn according to the accuracy of the surface representation.

The adaptive surface has a number of important properties which distinguish it from the alternatives reported elsewhere in the literature. Because we employ vertex insertion and deletion processes, the mesh can change its density at high curvature locations without relocating existing vertices. The mesh adopts a level of representation which is consistent with the noise level of the raw surface datapoints. Moreover the process does not employ physical node dynamics or high-order surface derivatives, instead it is driven by the statistics of the datapoints.

The outline of this paper is as follows. Section 2 outlines the details of our surface mesh representation. In Section 3 we describe the representation of the surface in terms of piecewise quadric patches. Section 4 provides details of the mesh reconfiguration proceedure. Section 5 provides some experimental analysis of the method and finally Section 6 offers some conclusions.

2 Surface Mesh Representation

2.1 *Surface mesh*

The first component of our surface representation is a simplex mesh. The positions of the vertices of this mesh will be used to define the reconstructed surface S. The mesh consists of a set of vertices V which are connected by a set of edges $E \subseteq V \times V$ which triangulate the vertices. In constructing our adaptive mesh we will use the vertices of the mesh as control points on the estimated surface. Associated with each vertex $i \in V$ there is a vector of position co-ordinates $\vec{p_i} = (x_i, y_i, z_i)^T$.

2.2 *Surface Triangulation*

In order to establish a surface-covering representation we turn to the faces of the triangulated mesh. Faces are adjacent if they share a defining surface-mesh edge. The set of surface triangles is indexed by the set D and consists of triples of mesh vertices $(a, b, c) \in V \times V \times V$. Each element of the face-set is a triple of vertices such that each vertex pair is itself an edge. In contrast to the mesh representation which provides topological information, the surface triangulation is a surface-filling representation; each triangle defines a physical area on the surface. Raw data-points are assigned to triangles on the basis of minimum perpendicular distance to the plane of a triangle. Each data-point in this set has an associated position vector $q_l = (x_l, y_l, z_l)^T$. The data-points associated with a particular triangle are used to provide local surface characteristics such as normals and statistical information about the surface. The data available to the triangle indexed j is $N_j = \{\vec{d_i} | 0 \leq i < n_j\}$.

3 Piecewise Quadric Patch Representation

We commence by assuming that the underlying surface S which generated the raw datapoints can be represented by a twice differentiable function f, such that surface points with co-ordinates (x, y, z) can be decribed by $z = f(x, y)$. In order to construct a local description of the surface we establish a local co-ordinate system at some point of interest on the surface $\vec{o}$. We then construct a z-axis for the new coordinate system which is normal to the surface S at point $\vec{o}$. The x and y axes are chosen arbitrarily to lie within the tangential plane of the surface at $\vec{o}$ and are orthogonal to one-another. This creates a Cartesian coordinate system around $\vec{o}$. The transformation into the local coordinate system is realised by constructing the matrix $\Theta = (\vec{x}, \vec{y}, \vec{z})$. The position of

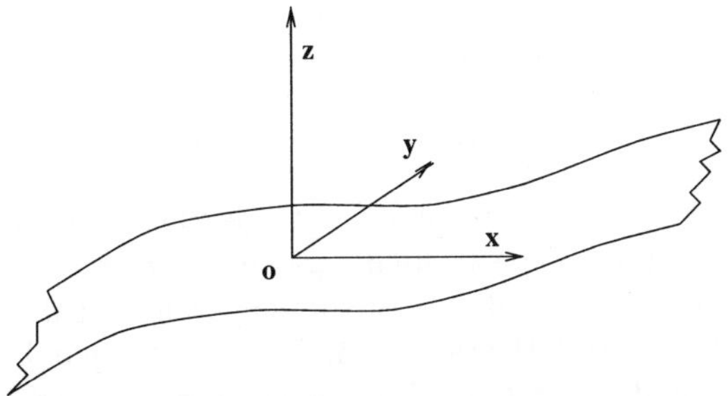

Figure 1: A two-dimensional example of how the local coordinate system relates to the surface.

the point $\vec{q}$ in the new coordinate system is given by

$$\vec{q'} = \Theta_i^{-1}(\vec{q} - \vec{o}) \tag{1}$$

In practical terms the underlying surface is not known and all of these quantities must be estimated. The tangent plane of the surface at point $\vec{o}$ may be determined approximately either by the plane of the mesh triangle containing $\vec{o}$ or by a least-squares plane through a set of N datapoints nearest to $\vec{o}$ if there are sufficient local datapoints.

We now require a local representation of the function f in terms of some simple patch function. A piecewise combination of these patches will be used to represent the surface S relative to a number of local coordinate systems. Consider the Taylor expansion of $z = f(x, y)$ around the point $\vec{o}$.

$$\begin{aligned} z &= f(x_o, y_o) + \left\{\frac{\partial f}{\partial x}\right\}_{\vec{o}} (x - x_o) + \left\{\frac{\partial f}{\partial y}\right\}_{\vec{o}} (y - y_o) \\ &+ \left\{\frac{\partial^2 f}{\partial x^2}\right\}_{\vec{o}} (x - x_o)^2 + \left\{\frac{\partial^2 f}{\partial x \partial y}\right\}_{\vec{o}} (x - x_o)(y - y_o) + \left\{\frac{\partial^2 f}{\partial y^2}\right\}_{\vec{o}} (y - y_o)^2 \\ &+ O(x^3) \end{aligned} \tag{2}$$

In the local coordinate system, the origin of the surface is $(0, 0, 0)$ and the surface is tangent to the x-y plane at the origin; this considerable simplifies the expansion (Equation 3).

$$z = \left\{\frac{\partial^2 f}{\partial x^2}\right\}_{\vec{o}} x^2 + \left\{\frac{\partial^2 f}{\partial x \partial y}\right\}_{\vec{o}} xy + \left\{\frac{\partial^2 f}{\partial y^2}\right\}_{\vec{o}} y^2 + O(x^3) \tag{3}$$

It is now clear that the natural approximate representation of this surface in the local coordinate system is a quadric patch

$$z = ax^2 + bxy + cy^2 \tag{4}$$

where $\vec{\rho} = (a, b, c)^T$ represent estimates of the second order differentials of the surface around $\vec{o}$ in the local coordinate system. The optimal values $\hat{a}, \hat{b}, \hat{c}$ are given by a maximum likelihood estimate of the parameters delivered by the raw datapoints which lie within the range of influence of the patch. The datapoints belonging to the quadric patch provide a noisy representation of the underlying surface. More specifically we assume that the points are independent, identically distributed. and that the measurement errors are characterised by a Gaussian distribution of the perpendicular distance between a data-point $\vec{q_i'}$ and the surface S. The maximum likelihood parameter set for the data-points belonging to the triangles forming the patch Γ_i is the one that satisfies the condition

$$\vec{\rho} = \arg\max_{\vec{\rho}} \prod_i \frac{1}{\sigma\sqrt{2\pi}} \exp\left[-\frac{(z_i' - p(x_i', y_i'))^2}{2\sigma^2}\right] \tag{5}$$

The maximum likelihood parameter estimation process reduces to a simple weighted least squares problem, i.e. the maximum likelihood parameter vector minimises the quantity $\sum_i (z_i' - p(x_i', y_i'))^2$. Each surface patch is represented by the local frame-vector $\vec{\Phi}_j = (\vec{o}_j, \Theta_j, \vec{\rho}_j)^T$.

The global surface is then described by the piecewise combination of surface patches.

4 Adjusting the mesh density

The patch representation describes the surface in a local region up to third order terms. However the accuracy of this representation decreases with increasing distance from the patch origin. It is for this reason that a piecewise representation is adopted; the surface is represented globally by a number of local patches. Controlling the extent of these patches is vital to prevent over- or under-parameterisation of the surface by the patches. Under-parameterisation causes over smoothing of surface features, whereas over-parameterisation leads to noise susceptibility and the creation of false surface features.

In order to control the patch extent we couple the patch to the surface mesh. Each patch represents a grouping of a constant number of triangles on the surface mesh (see Figure 2). The area which the patch covers is therefore inversely proportional to the triangle density in a particular region of the mesh.

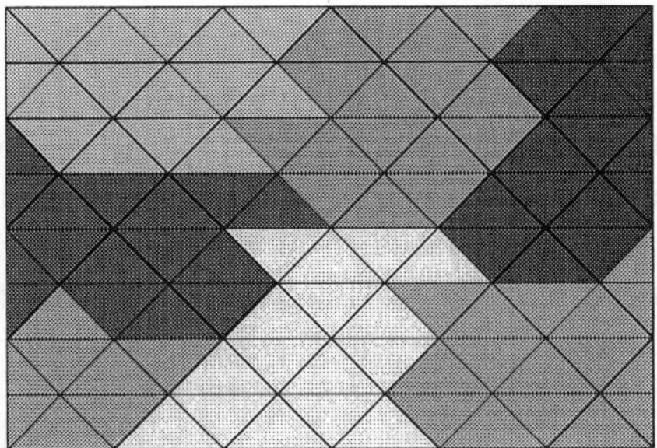

Figure 2: The grouping of triangular faces into patches. Each patch is comprised of 16 triangles which are represented by the same colour.

The size of patches can be controlled by adjusting the density of the mesh triangles.

4.1 A criterion for controlling mesh density

The difference between the true surface $z = f(x,y)$ and the piecewise patch representation, which we will denote $z = p(x,y)$ is characterised by the mean square difference between the the underlying surface and the patch function. By specifying a target quantity for this deviation, the required accuracy of the representation can be controlled. In other words, we need to find a patch which satisfies the condition

$$\frac{1}{A}\int_A [p(x,y) - f(x,y)]^2 = k^2 \tag{6}$$

where A is the area of the patch on the surface and k^2 controls the accuracy of the representation. Of course the underlying surface function $f(x,y)$ is unknown. The surface is infact represented by a set of noisy datapoints, which we denote $d_i = f(x_i,y_i) + n_i$ where n is a noise function which perturbs the datapoints from the true surface. The representation condition therefore becomes

$$\begin{aligned}\frac{1}{N}\sum_{i=1}^{N}[p(x_i,y_i) - d_i]^2 &= \frac{1}{N}\sum_{i=1}^{N}[p(x_i,y_i) - f(x_i,y_i) + n_i]^2 \\ &= \frac{1}{N}\sum_{i=1}^{N}[p(x_i,y_i) - f(x_i,y_i)]^2 + \sigma^2\end{aligned}$$

$$= \quad k^2 + \sigma^2 \tag{7}$$

In other words, if the variance of the datapoints to the patch is greater than $k^2 + \sigma^2$ then the density of triangles in that region must be increased. Similarly if the variance is less than $k^2 + \sigma^2$ then the density must be decreased. By splitting or merging mesh faces in any region according to this criterion we can adjust the mesh density to the required degree of representation and ensure that the closeness of the surface to the patch representation is exactly k^2.

5 Experiments

5.1 Experiments with synthetic images

In this set of experiments we use data-points generated from a damped-cosine surface. These data-points have additive Gaussian noise of varying magnitude σ applied to them and are used as the raw data for our surface reconstruction algorithm. The surface is initialised with a coarse mesh seeded from points sampled from the raw dataset. In these experiments the target closeness k^2 has been set to 0.5 and the resulting surface is compared to both the raw data-points and to the generating surface. Ideally the resultant variances should be 0.5 to the underlying surface and $\sigma^2 + 0.5$ to the raw data-points. The results of these experiments are summaried in table 1.

Noise	Initial		Final	
	Point Var.	Surface Var	Point Var.	Surface Var
0.0	2.87	1.90	0.31	0.70
1.0	4.95	2.86	1.20	0.73
2.0	5.67	3.72	2.17	0.97
3.0	7.51	4.27	2.85	1.02
4.0	7.91	4.82	3.92	1.30
5.0	8.77	3.92	4.80	1.32
6.0	9.59	5.22	5.29	1.51

Table 1: Performance of damp-cos surface with varying degrees of noise

The initial results are recorded after 6 iterations of the patch fitting algorithm, but without split and merge operations on the surface. In other words the mesh is optimised in terms of node position but not density. The final results demonstrate that a large improvement is provided by applying split and merge operations in conjuction with the fitting process. Infact the recovered surface degrades only slowly with increasing noise the raw data points.

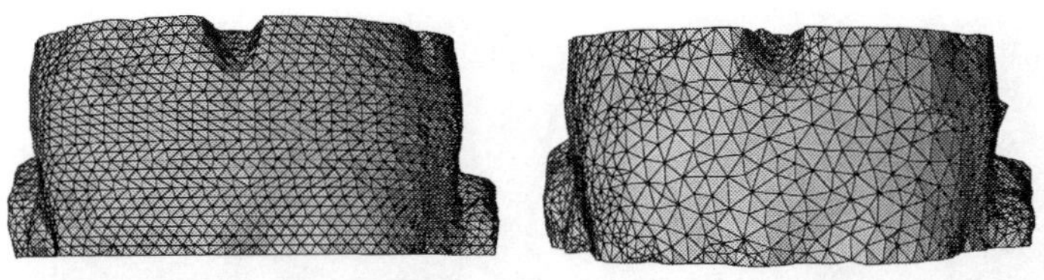

Figure 3: Initial and final configuration of the mesh over a view of the forehead.

5.2 Fitting to iso-surface data

The surface data-points here represent the outer iso-surface in a CT scan. The initial triangulation is dense and contains some 3365 surface triangles. The initial variance of the data-points from the seeded surface is 12.19 and the mean deviation is 0.03. After application of the surface-fitting algorithm with a target variance of 7.0, the triangle density is reduced over the cranium and increased around the ears. The total number of triangles is reduced to 2657, the variance of the data-points around the recovered surface is reduced to 8.3 and the mean deviation is 0.001. The algorithm therefore produces a more efficient triangulation. There are both fewer triangles and a more accurate representation of surface detail.

5.3 Fitting a surface to edge-features

In this example we extract connected contours on individual slices in the CT volume by applying an edge following to the individual slices in the CT stack. The snake attaches itself to the cranial boundary on each slice. The recovered 3D data-points lie on the boundary surface of the head. The data-set studied represents a frontal view (Fig 4).

Initially, the surface-mesh is relatively noisy. The triangulation provides only a rough initial surface representation. The initial number of triangles is 2582, the initial datapoint variance is 5.4 and the mean datapoint deviation is -0.04. After application of the fitting algorithm with target variance 4.5, the number of triangles is reduced to 2102, the datapoint variance is 4.3 and the mean to the surface is 0.02. Examination of the final configuration of the mesh (Figure 4) reveals that the density has been increased in areas of high curvature such as the nose and eyes, and decreased across the cranium.

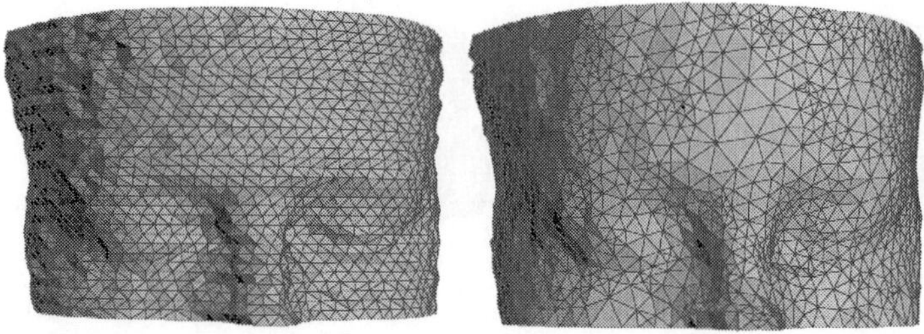

Figure 4: Initial and final configuration of the mesh over a surface extracted from 3D slice data

6 Conclusions

Our main contribution in this paper has been to describe how a mesh of adaptive density can be coupled to a piecewise quadric patch model to achieve a surface representation of any required degree of accuracy (up to the limits of the datapoint noise). The mesh uses both split and merge operations to adapt itself to the structure of volumetric data-points. The adaptive behaviour is controlled by the variance of the data-point positions about maximum-likelihood quadric patches. Our experiments on both synthetic and real-world data have shown that the mesh can improve the quality of a surface representation both in terms of reducing the number of control points required and increasing the accuracy of the surface model. These results show that the method has the effect of increasing the mesh density in areas of high curvature and conversely decreasing the density in relatively flat areas. This property suggests that such a mesh may be useful for labelling the surface in terms of curvature.

1. A.J. Bulpitt and N.D. Efford, "An efficient 3d deformable model with a self-optimising mesh", *Image and Vision Computing*, **14**, pp. 573–580, 1996.
2. Xin Chen and F. Schmill. Surface modeling of range data by constrained triangulation", *Computer-Aided Design*, **26**, pp. 632—645 1994.
3. I. Cohen, L.D. Cohen and N. Ayache, "Using deformable surfaces to segment 3D images and infer differential structure", *CVGIP*, **56**, pp. 243–263, 1993.
4. I. Cohen and L.D. Cohen, "A hybrid hyper-quadric model for 2-d and 3-d data fitting", *Computer Vision and Image Understanding*, **63**, pp. 527–541, 1996.
5. H. Delingette, M. Hebert and K. Ikeuchi, "Shape representation and image segmentation using deformable surfaces", *IEEE Computer Society Conference on Computer Vision and Pattern Recognition*, pp. 467–472, 1991.
6. L. De Floriani, " A pyramidal data structure for triangle-based surface description", *IEEE Computer Graphics and Applications*, **9**, pp. 67–78, 1987.

7. H. Delingette, "Adaptive and deformable models based on simplex meshes", *IEEE Computer Society Workshop on Motion of Non-rigid and Articulated Objects*, pp. 152–157, 1994.
8. D. McInerney and D. Terzopoulos, "A finite element model for 3D shape reconstruction and non-rigid motion tracking", *Fourth International Conference on Computer Vision*, pp. 518–532, 1993.
9. D. McInerney and D. Terzopoulos, "A dynamic finite-element surface model for segmentation and tracking in multidimensional medical images with application to cardiac 4D image-analysis", *Computerised Medical Imaging and Graphics*, **19**, pp. 69–83, 1995.
10. J. O. Lachaud and A. Montanvert, "Volumic segmentation using hierarchical representation and triangulates surface", *Computer Vision, ECCV'96, Edited by B. Buxton and R. Cipolla, Lecture Notes in Computer Science, Volume 1064*, pp. 137–146, 1996.
11. W. Neuenschwander, P. Fua, G. Szekely and O. Kubler, "Deformable Velcro Surfaces", *Fifth International Conference on Computer Vision*, pp. 828–833, 1995.
12. P.T. Sander and S.W. Zucker, "Inferring surface structure and differential structure from 3D images", IEEE PAMI, **12**, pp 833-854, 1990.
13. F. J. M. Schmitt, B. A. Barsky and Wen-Hui Du, "An adaptive subdivision method for surface fitting from sampled data", *SIGGRAPH '86*, **20**, pp. 176–188, 1986
14. L. Scarlatos and T. Pavlidis, "Hierarchical triangulation using cartographic coherence", *CVGIP: Graphical Models and Image Processing*, **54**, pp. 147-161, 1992.
15. W.J.Schroeder, J.A. Zarge and W.E. Lorenson, "Decimation of triangle meshes", *Computer Graphics*, **26** pp. 163–169, 1992.
16. A.J. Stoddart, A. Hilton and J. Illingworth, "SLIME: A new deformable surface", *Proceedings British Machine Vision Conference*, pp. 285–294, 1994.
17. M. Turner and E.R. Hancock, "A Bayesian approach to 3D surface fitting and refinement", *Proceedings of the British Machine Vision Conference*, pp. 67–76, 1995.
18. G. Turk, "Re-tiling polygonal surfaces", *Computer Graphics*, **26**, pp. 55–64, 1992.
19. M. Vasilescu and D. Terzopoulos, "Adaptive meshes and shells", *IEEE Computer Society Conference on Computer Vision and Pattern Recognition* , pp. 829–832, 1992.

OPTIMAL MATCHING BETWEEN SHAPES VIA ELASTIC DEFORMATIONS

LAURENT YOUNES
Groupe DIAM, CMLA (URA 1611)
Ecole Normale Supérieure de Cachan
61, avenue du Président Wilson
94 235 Cachan CEDEX
email: younes@cmla.ens-cachan.fr

We describe an elasting matching procedure between plane curves based on computing a minimal deformation cost between the curves. We also build a complete optimal deformation process, which allows to interpolate between any plane curves.

1 Introduction

Matching deformable shapes is an important matter in image analysis, for example in contexts such as medical or biological imaging. A typical situation can be formalized as follows. A model (or template) of a shape in a given category is given, and some other shape in the same category is observed, the observation being subject to non-rigid deformations. The problem is to match the points of the template to those of the observed shape.

Consider the case when the shape outline is represented as a parametric plane curve, which will be formally expressed as a function

$$\left(m : s \in I \to m(s) \in \mathbb{R}^2\right) ,$$

I being a bounded interval. Given another curve $\tilde{m}$ defined on another interval $\tilde{I}$, the problem is thus to find a one-to-one correspondence $u \leftrightarrow \tilde{u}$ between the abscissa of the points of m and the points of $\tilde{m}$. In other terms, one must determine a one-to-one mapping ϕ from I onto $\tilde{I}$.

In most applications, the approach to estimate ϕ is variational. Assuming enough regularity (for example, that it is a diffeomorphism), one performs the minimization of some functional $E(\phi, m, \tilde{m})$ which generally provides a trade-off between the similarity of the functions m and $\tilde{m} \circ \phi$ and some measure of the regularity of ϕ. For example, denoting by κ and $\tilde{\kappa}$ the curvature functions of m and $\tilde{m}$, the functional used in [2] is

$$E = \frac{1}{2} \int (\tilde{\kappa} \circ \phi(u) - \kappa(u))^2 du + \int \left\| \frac{\partial}{\partial u} (\tilde{m} \circ \phi(u) - m(u)) \right\|^2 du$$

We also propose a variational formula for optimal matching between curves. The associated functional, which has been introduced in [7], will have other interesting properties. It first provides a distance between the curves (this was the motivation of [7]). Moreover, it is based on an interpretation of the matching process as a continuous deformation of one curve into another. This implies that our matching does not only provide a one-to-one correspondance between the points of the curves, but also an optimal way of realizing this correspondance through a continous transformation. This allows, for example, to interpolate between shape outlines, on the basis of an intrinsic mathematical analysis, as described below.

2 Main results

2.1 Optimal matching

We consider plane curves which are parametrized by arc-length, ie. functions ($m : [0, L] \to \mathbb{R}^2$), with a normed gradient ($\|\dot{m}_s\| \equiv 1$), L being therefore the length of m. We furthermore identify curves which may be deduced one from another by a combination of homotheties, translations and rotations, and, following [5], we shall call such an equivalent class a shape.

For such a curve m, we let $\theta(s)$ be the angle between the tangent to m at the point $m(s)$ and the horizontal axis, so that $\dot{m}_s = (\cos\theta, \sin\theta)$; ($\theta : [0, L] \to [0, 2\pi[$) will be called the angle function associated to m. A translation of m has no effect on θ, and an homothetie with factor λ simply transforms the function ($\theta : [0, L] \to [0, 2\pi[$) into the function ($\theta_\lambda : [0, \lambda L] \to [0, 2\pi[$) with $\theta_\lambda(s) = \theta(s/\lambda)$. Thus a curve modulo translation and homothetie may be represented by its normalized angle function $\theta_{1/L}$, which is defined on $[0, 1]$, ie. it may be assumed that the curve length is 1. Finally, a rotation of angle c acting on m transforms the function $\theta(.)$ into the function $\theta(.) + c$ (modulo 2π), or equivalently the function $e^{i\theta(.)}$ into the function $e^{ic}e^{i\theta(.)}$.

Letting $\zeta(.) = e^{i\theta(.)}$, we thus represent shapes by functions

$$\zeta : [0, 1] \to \Gamma = \{z \in \mathbb{C}, |z| = 1\},$$

keeping in mind that two functions ζ and $\tilde{\zeta}$ are identified as soon as $\tilde{\zeta}/\zeta$ is constant. We denote by $[\zeta]$ the equivalence class of ζ.

Our matching will thus act on such equivalence classes, and will be based on a peculiar definition of deformations. If ϕ is an increasing diffeomorphism of $[0, 1]$, and r a complex function defined on $[0, 1]$, with values in Γ, we define the action

$$(\phi, r) \star [\zeta] = [r.\zeta \circ \phi].$$

The diffeomorphism ϕ (or more precisely its differential $\dot{\phi}_s$) may be interpreted as a tangential stretching of the curve, and $r(s)$ as a torsion of the curve at the point of arc-length s. Note that, because of rotation invariance, the action of a constant r has no effect. One may show that this action may be interpreted as a group action if one sets

$$(\phi_1, r_1).(\phi_2, r_2) = (\phi_2 \circ \phi_1, r_1.r_2 \circ \phi_1) .$$

Define now the cost of a deformation (ϕ, r) by

$$E(\phi, r) = \min_{\gamma \in \Gamma} \arccos \int_0^1 \sqrt{\dot{\phi}_s} \left| \Re \left(\gamma \sqrt{r(s)} \right) \right| ds .$$

where $\Re(z)$ is the real part of the complex number z. The ambiguity on the complex square-root is removed by the absolute value, and we have, as it should be $E(\phi, \gamma.r) = E(\phi, r)$ for any complex number γ of modulus one. Finally, let

$$\Delta([\zeta], [\tilde{\zeta}]) = \inf\{E(\phi, r), (\phi, r).\tilde{\zeta} = \zeta\} ,$$

which is interpreted as the minimal cost required to transform $\tilde{\zeta}$ into ζ. This may be rewritten as

$$\Delta([\zeta], [\tilde{\zeta}]) = \inf_{\phi, \gamma} \arccos \int_0^1 \sqrt{\dot{\phi}_s} \left| \Re \left(\gamma \sqrt{\tilde{\zeta} \circ \phi(s) / \zeta(s)} \right) \right| ds . \quad (1)$$

The following result is proved from [7].

Theorem 1 *Δ is a distance on the set of shapes.*

When the infimum in (1) is attained for some ϕ^* and γ^* (sufficient conditions for this will be provided in a forthcoming theoretical paper), we shall say that ϕ^* is an optimal matching for the shapes $[\zeta]$ and $[\tilde{\zeta}]$.

2.2 Deformation path

In fact, more information may be recovered from ϕ^*, because of the cost function is built as a Riemannian distance on some infinite dimensional manifold of shapes, and the associated geodesics can be recovered. We give here an informal description, refering to [7] for a rigorous presentation.

Consider the function

$$\Lambda(\phi, r) = \arccos \int_0^1 \sqrt{\dot{\phi}_s} \left| \Re \left(\sqrt{r(s)} \right) \right| ds ,$$

and assume that the deformation is small, thus $\phi(s) \simeq s$ and $r(s) \simeq 1$. Let $\xi = \phi(s) - s$ and $\rho = r(s) - 1$. We have $\sqrt{\dot{\phi}_s} \simeq 1 + \dot{\xi}_s/2 - \dot{\xi}_s^2/8$, and, writing

$r = e^{i\theta}$ with $\theta \simeq 0$, $\sqrt{r} \simeq 1 + i\theta/2 - \theta^2/8$ so that $\Re(\sqrt{r}) \simeq 1 - \theta^2/8 \simeq 1 - |\rho|^2/8$. We thus get, noting that $\xi(0) = \xi(1) = 0$,

$$\begin{aligned}
\int_0^1 \sqrt{\dot\phi_s}\left|\Re\left(\sqrt{r(s)}\right)\right| ds &\simeq \int_0^1 (1 + \dot\xi_s/2 - \dot\xi_s^2/8)(1 - |\rho|^2/8) ds \\
&\simeq 1 + \int_0^1 \dot\xi_s ds - \int_0^1 (\dot\xi_s^2/8) ds - \int_0^1 (|\rho|^2/8) ds \\
&= 1 - \int_0^1 (\dot\xi_s^2/8) ds - \int_0^1 (|\rho|^2/8) ds
\end{aligned}$$

Thus, since $\arccos(1 - x) \simeq \sqrt{2x}$ for small x,

$$\Lambda(Id + \xi, 1 + \rho)^2 \simeq \frac{1}{4}\int_0^1 (\dot\xi_s^2 + |\rho|^2) ds,$$

and this formula approximates the cost of a small deformation.

Let us consider now a deformation $(\phi(t,.), r(t,.))$ depending on another parameter $t \in [0,1]$. We shall call such a process a deformation path. Such a path may be realized (through a limit argument) by a succession of small deformations, and its cost can naturally be defined by the sum of the costs of these small deformations. After a little differential calculus, and if one orders the small deformations from left to right, one obtains that the cost of the deformation path is given by the formula

$$L(\phi(t,.), r(t,.)) = \int_0^1 \left[\int_0^1 \left(\frac{\ddot\phi_{ts}^2}{\dot\phi_s} + \dot\phi_s |\dot r_t|^2 ds\right) dt\right]^{1/2}.$$

The following theorem is also a consequence of the results in [7]

Theorem 2 *Let ϕ^*, r^* be a deformation with $\dot\phi_s^* > 0$ almost everywhere. The minimum of $L(\phi(t,.), r(t,.))$ among all sufficiently regular paths such that*
i) $\phi(0,s) = s$, $r(0,s) = 1$
ii) $\phi(1,s) = \phi^*(s)$, $r(1,s) = r^*(s)$
is given by $L^* = \Lambda(\phi^*, r^*)$. Moreover, the optimal path is given by the formula

$$\dot\phi_s(t,s).r(t,s) = \left[\cos(L^* t) + \frac{\sqrt{\dot\phi_s^*(s) r^*(s)} - \cos L^*}{\sin L^*}\sin(L^* t)\right]^2$$

where the complex square root is taken with positive real part.

Note that the last formula uniquely defines $\phi(t,s)$ and $r(t,s)$ since $\dot{\phi}_s > 0$ and $|r| \equiv 1$.

Thus, returning to our matching problem, assume that an optimal matching ϕ^* can be obtained with $\dot{\phi}^*_s > 0$ almost everywhere. To built the optimal deformation path between $[\tilde{\zeta}]$ and $[\zeta]$, it suffices to apply theorem 2 with $r^* = \zeta/\tilde{\zeta} \circ \phi^*$. Thus, setting

$$Z(t,.) = (\phi(t,.), r(t,.)) * [\tilde{\zeta}(.)]\,. \tag{2}$$

Thus $Z(t,.)$ provides an interpolation of minimal deformation cost between the shapes $[\tilde{\zeta}]$ and $[\zeta]$.

3 Case of closed curves

In the discussion above, we have assumed that the curves are given with arc-length parametrization defined on $[0,1]$. This implicitely assumes that a starting point and an end point have been selected on the curves. In the case of open curves, these points must coincide with the extremities of the curves and if the curve is oriented, the parametrization is uniquely defined (if the curve is not oriented, there are two possible choices). In the case of (oriented) closed curves, the starting point and the end point coincide and may be any point in the curve. This implies that the arc-length parametrization is defined modulo a translation of the starting point along the curve. This should be taken into account in the matching, in which the cost function should be minimized over all choices for the origins of the curve parametrizations.

Another problem comes with the curve interpolation. Assume that two closed curves are matched, so that correct starting points are selected for the parametrizations. Let ζ and $\tilde{\zeta}$ be the complex representations of directions of the tangents ; the fact that a curve is closed is equivalent to the identity $\int_0^1 \zeta(s)ds = 0$. However, the optimal interpolation $Z(t,.)$ defined in equation (2), one does not have, in general, that $\int_0^1 Z(t,s)ds = 0$ for $t \in]0,1[$ (this is of course true for $t=0$ and $t=1$). This means that the optimal deformation path generally breaks closed curves. This is not a problem as far as matching is concerned, but this is surely an undesirable feature for interpolation, since one would expect that an interpolation of closed curves is closed.

For this reason, we build a suboptimal interpolation path in which all curves remains closed. We however want this deformation path to be similar to the optimal one $Z(t,.)$, so that we look, for all t to the function $\tilde{Z}(t,.)$ which is the closest to $Z(t,.)$ with the constraint that for all t

$$\int_0^1 \tilde{Z}(t,s)ds = 0\,. \tag{3}$$

A consistent way to decide of the similarity of the functions $Z(t,.)$ and $\tilde{Z}(t,.)$ would be to use the distance Δ of equation (1). In such a case, one should compute, for all t, the maximum, over all ϕ and all $\tilde{Z}(t,.)$ satisfying the constraint (3), of

$$\int_0^1 \sqrt{\dot{\phi}_s}\left|\Re\left(\sqrt{\tilde{Z}(t,s)/Z(t,\phi(s))}\right)\right| ds\,.$$

This would however, result in a very large computation cost, so that it is preferable to make some approximations. We shall first impose $\phi = \mathrm{Id}$, so that, letting $Z(t,.) = \exp[i\alpha(t,.)]$ and $\tilde{Z}(t,.) = \exp[i\tilde{\alpha}(t,.)]$, the problem boils down to maximize

$$\int_0^1 \left|\cos\left[\frac{\tilde{\alpha}(t,s)-\alpha(t,s)}{2}\right]\right| ds\,.$$

Using the fact that $1-\cos(x/2) \simeq (1-\cos x)/4$ and $\cos x > 0$ for small x, we get a further simplification and maximize

$$\int_0^1 \cos\left[\tilde{\alpha}(t,s)-\alpha(t,s)\right] ds\,.$$

with the constraints $\int_0^1 \cos\tilde{\alpha}(t,s)ds = \int_0^1 \sin\tilde{\alpha}(t,s)ds = 0$.

This problem becomes much more amenable to computation (recall that the unknown is $\tilde{\alpha}(t,.)$), and its solution provides an efficient and visually satisfying way for "closing an open curve" (cf. figure 1).

4 Experimental results

Numerical procedures for obtaining the optimal matching are described in [7]. They rely on a simplification of the cost function in the case when the curves are polygonal, and use a dynamic programming algorithm.

We now show a few computed matchings of silhouettes of planes, together with the associated interpolation paths (since these curves are closed, we have applied the procedure of section 3 to perform the interpolation). We draw in a single figure the whole deformation process, and in order to make the visualisation possible, we continously scale the deformed curves during this process (note that we work on shapes, so that we see curves independently of

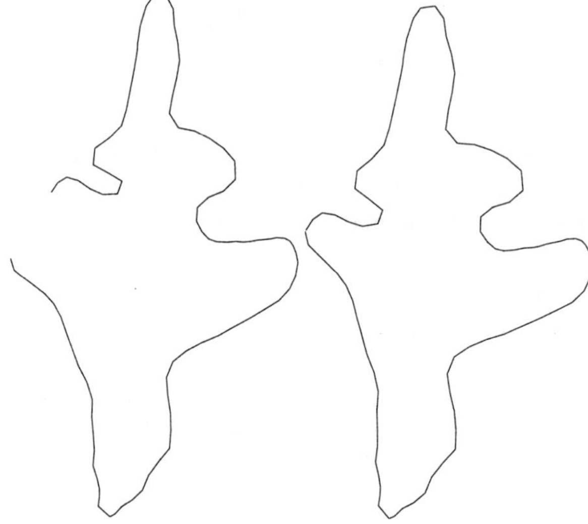

Figure 1: An open curve (left) and the result of the closing operation (right)

scales). The curves are moreover stacked one above the other in 3D-space, so that the output looks is a 3D surface seen from above. Transversal lines on this surface show the trajectory of each point during the process, so that their endpoints provides the optimal matching between the original shapes.

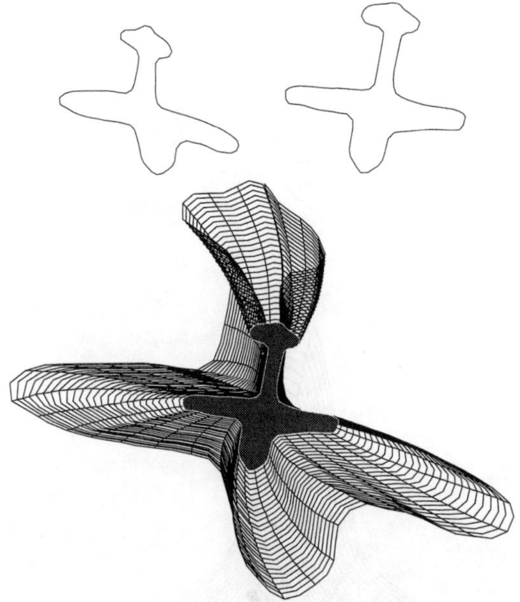

Figure 2: Up: matched shapes ; down : matching and deformation process. Deformation cost: 0.28

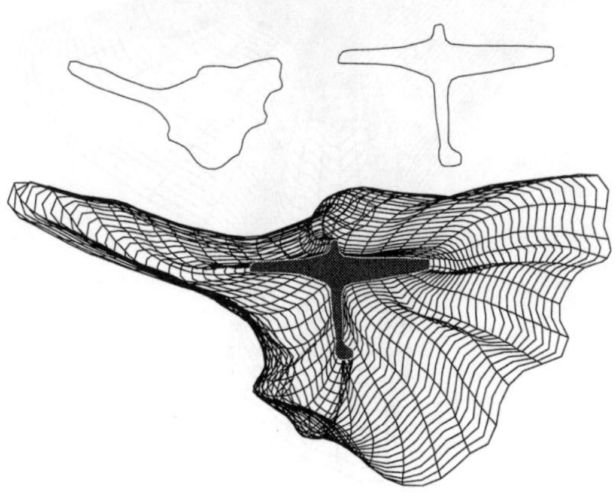

Figure 3: Up : matched shapes ; down : matching and deformation process. Deformation cost:0.70

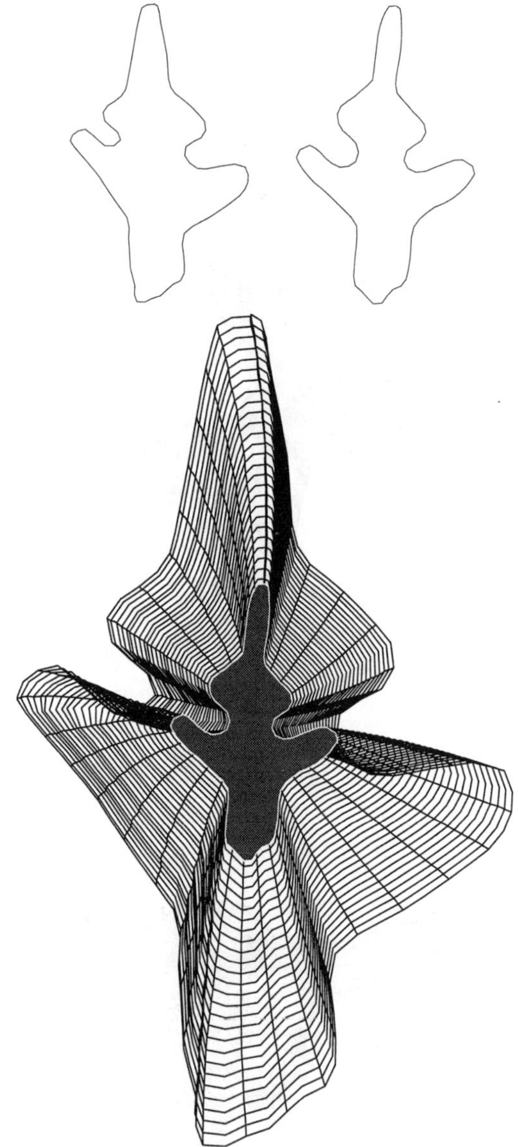

Figure 4: Up : matched shapes ; down : matching and deformation process. Deformation cost: 0.29

5 References

1. R. Azencott : Deterministic and random deformations ; applications to shape recognition. Conference at HSSS workshop in Cortona, Italy (1994).
2. I. Cohen, N. Ayache, P. Sulger : Tracking points on deformable objects using curvature information, *in Computer Vision - ECCV'92* G. Sandini (ed.) pp 458-466 (1992).
3. M. P. Do Carmo : *Riemannian geometry.* Birkaüser.
4. U. Grenander and D. M. Keenan : On the shape of plane images : Siam J. Appl. Math. vol 53, No 4 1072-1094 (1991).
5. D. G. Kendall : Shape manifolds, procrustean metrics and complex projective spaces. *Bull. London Math. Soc., 16, 81-121* (1984).
6. S. Lang : *Introduction to differentiable manifolds*, Interscience, New-York (1962).
7. L. Younes : Computable elastic distances between shapes, To appear in *SIAM J. of Applied Math.*

SPATIAL SAMPLING EFFECTS ON SCANNED 2-D PATTERNS

J.Y. ZHOU, D. LOPRESTI
Matsushita Information Technology Laboratory
Two Research Way, Princeton, NJ 08540

P. SARKAR, G. NAGY
Electrical, Computer and Systems Engineering
Rensselaer Polytechnic Institute, Troy, NY 12180

The bitmap obtained by scanning a printed pattern depends on the exact location of the scanning grid relative to the pattern. We consider ideal sampling with a regular lattice of delta functions. The displacement of the lattice relative to the pattern is random and obeys a uniform probability density function defined over a unit cell of the lattice. The resulting random-phase sampling noise affects the edge-pixels of scanned bitmaps. The number of distinct bitmaps and their relative frequencies can be predicted from a mapping of the original pattern boundary to the unit cell (called a modulo-grid-diagram).

1 Introduction

Digitization is the process of spatial, intensity, and temporal quantization of an analog pattern. In this paper, we study one aspect of digitization – the variability of pixel configurations under uniform random-phase sampling of printed patterns. This variability is the result of the uncontrollable displacement of the sampling grid relative to the page. Unlike other types of noise in scanners, random phase noise is an intrinsic consequence of finite sampling resolution.

We demonstrate that the relationship between the analog pattern and the digital configuration can be captured by what we call the *modulo-grid-diagram*. The modulo-grid-diagram is formed by overlaying the pattern boundaries in each cell of the digitizing grid on the unit cell. We prove that the modulo-grid-diagram decomposes the spatial displacement space into regions of equivalent digital representations of a given pattern. Furthermore, the areas of these equivalence regions correspond to the relative frequencies of the digital patterns.

A qualitative discussion of this phenomenon, emphasizing the correlated nature of the resulting edge-noise in OCR, appears in an early paper by Nagy.[1] Proof for the equivalent one-dimensional result was developed by Sarkar,[2] and some applications to OCR were presented in a paper by Nagy *et al.*[3] The modulo-grid approach to spatial sampling was originated by Havelock.[4] Havelock introduced the concept of a "locale," which is precisely a union of equivalent regions of the modulo-grid-diagram. Pavlidis investigated conditions under which the connectivity and shape of bi-level patterns are preserved under digitization.[5] Related work on the sub-pixel localization of edges and circles was presented in a paper by O'Gorman.[6]

The modulo-grid-diagram is presented in Section 2. Section 3 presents our main results in the form of two theorems. Section 4 contains some examples that illustrate possible applications to OCR, and Section 5 mentions potential generalizations and unsolved problems.

2 The Modulo-Grid Diagram

When a bi-level spatial pattern is sampled with a lattice (or grid) of delta functions, the result depends on the positioning of the grid relative to the pattern itself. An example of this connection is shown in Figure 1, which represents the different pixel configurations (bitmaps) obtained by digitizing a disk.

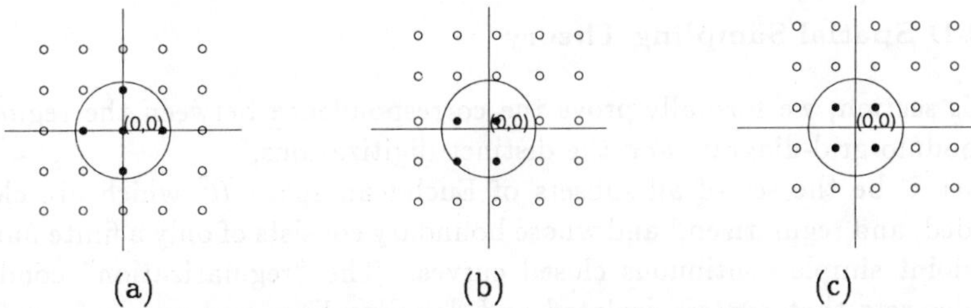

Figure 1: Digitizations of a circular disk resulting from different grid positions.

A pattern digitized by a sampling grid at different locations may give rise to isomorphic digital patterns. For example, the two grid placements in Figure 1(b) and (c) result in equivalent pixel configurations. On the other hand, a pattern may be digitized into distinguishable bitmaps by different translations of the grid. Figures 1(a) and 1(b) show two bitmaps resulting from the same analog pattern.

This relationship between the analog pattern and the digital configuration can be captured by what we call the *modulo-grid-diagram.* The diagram is formed by taking segments of the pattern's boundary contour that lie in each of the "grid cells" and retracing them at their coordinates, modulo one, with respect to both axes.

An example of a modulo-grid-diagram for a circular disk pattern is shown in Figure 2. To understand how the modulo-grid-diagram works, slide the grid around, with its origin confined to the unit cell. Each time the origin crosses over an edge from one region to another, a sampling point at some location moves in or out of the pattern, and vice versa. Different bitmap configurations, therefore, correspond to different regions in the modulo-grid-diagram.

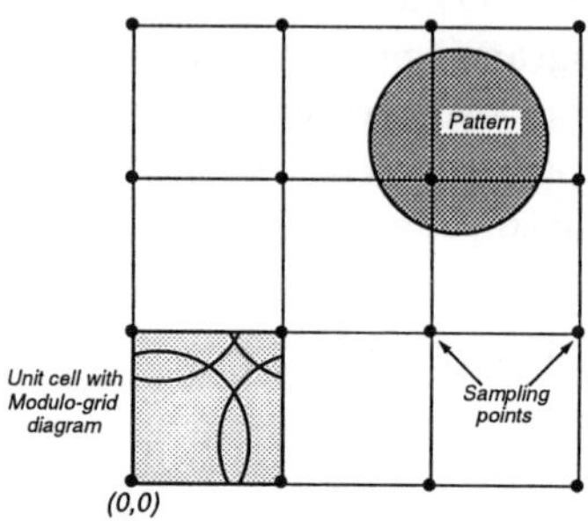

Figure 2: The modulo-grid-diagram for a disk whose diameter equals 1.2 pixel lengths.

3 2-D Spatial Sampling Theory

In this section, we formally prove the correspondence between the regions of the modulo-grid-diagram and the distinct digitizations.

Let $\Im$ be the set of all subsets of Euclidean space R^2 which are closed, bounded, and regularized,[a] and whose boundary consists of only a finite number of disjoint simple continuous closed curves. The "regularization" condition excludes sets that contain isolated and dangling lines and points from $\Im$, so that the formalization is not complicated by patterns that do not occur in reality.

We define an analog pattern in R^2 to be a function $f(\mathrm{x})$, $\mathrm{x} \in R^2$, which is non-zero on a region $X \in \Im$. X is called the *support* of f. Usually $f(\mathrm{x})$ represents the intensity or brightness of the pattern and in applications such as OCR, it is a two-valued function ("1" where the pattern is black and "0" where it is white, or vice versa). X then just represents the pattern and $R^2 - X$ represents the background.

Spatial quantization of an analog pattern is a mapping of $f(\mathrm{x})$ from its continuous support X to a discrete set of ordered pairs:

$$\{(\mathrm{x}, f(\mathrm{x})) : \mathrm{x} \in \textit{ a discrete set of points in } R^2\}$$

In practice, a *sampling grid* or *lattice* is overlaid on R^2 space and $f(\mathrm{x})$ is measured at the grid intersections. In the case of black and white (or binary)

[a]A regularized set is a set that equals the closure of its interior.

patterns, however, specifying the set of grid intersections that lie within the support of the pattern completely defines the spatial quantization; so we use $\{\mathbf{x}\}$ to define a digitization, rather than $\{(\mathbf{x}, f(\mathbf{x}))\}$. In fact it also allows us to separate the spatial quantization effects from amplitude or intensity quantization, which we shall not discuss in this paper (though it is possible to treat non-binary patterns in a similar framework).

Let $\mathbf{u}, \mathbf{v}$ be two base vectors of R^2. A sampling grid, $G(\mathbf{p})$, "positioned" at a point $\mathbf{p}$, is defined as

$$G(\mathbf{p}) = \{\mathbf{g} : \mathbf{g} = k_1\mathbf{u} + k_2\mathbf{v} + \mathbf{p}, \quad k_1, k_2 \in Z\}$$

where Z is the set of all integers. Associated with G is a unit cell, C.

$$C = \{\mathbf{c} : \mathbf{c} = w_1\mathbf{u} + w_2\mathbf{v}, \quad 0 \le w_1 < 1, \quad 0 \le w_2 < 1\}$$

Digitization of X by grid G at position $\mathbf{p}$ is then defined as the set

$$D_{\mathbf{p}} = \{\mathbf{d} : \mathbf{d} \in X \cap G(\mathbf{p})\}$$

Since any grid, as defined above, can be converted to a square lattice and back by linear transformations on R^2, we shall restrict our discussion to square grids.

Let $T(D, \ \mathbf{t}) = \{\mathbf{d} + \mathbf{t} : \mathbf{d} \in D\}$ denote set D translated by $\mathbf{t}$. Two digital patterns D and D' are *isomorphic* or *equivalent* if $\exists \mathbf{t} \in R$ such that $T(D, \ \mathbf{t}) = D'$. The equivalence relation is denoted as $D \equiv D'$.

Note that digitizations, by definition, carry information regarding the location of the grid-origin, unlike *bitmaps* that we obtain from scanners. This makes it necessary to keep in mind the relationship between bitmaps and digitizations: a bitmap is a translation-invariant representation of a digitization, and all equivalent digitizations correspond to the same bitmap.

As we have mentioned earlier, our tool in analyzing these variations is the modulo-grid-diagram. We can now define the modulo-grid operation, "$\mathbf{p}$ mod C", as:

$$\mathbf{p} \bmod C = (p_1 - \lfloor p_1 \rfloor)\,\mathbf{u} + (p_2 - \lfloor p_2 \rfloor)\,\mathbf{v}, \quad \text{where } \mathbf{p} = p_1\mathbf{u} + p_2\mathbf{v}$$

It is easily shown that $D_{\mathbf{p}} \equiv D_{\mathbf{p} \bmod C}$. So we only need to consider grid locations within the unit cell C.

Let X^b denote the boundary of a given analog pattern X ($X^b = X - X^o$, where X^o is the interior of X.) The modulo-grid-diagram, introduced in our earlier discussion, is formally defined as the result of superimposing the boundary X^b over the unit cell C:

$$X_C^b = \{\mathbf{p} : \mathbf{p} = \mathbf{x} \bmod C, \ \mathbf{x} \in X^b\}$$

Such a superimposition creates a mesh of boundary segments in C, which partitions C into non-overlapping, open, connected sets π_i, bounded by points in X_C^b. Each such set is called a region. We have for $i \neq j$, $\pi_i \cap \pi_j = \emptyset$, and $C - \bigcup \pi_i = X_C^b$.

Two points, $\mathbf{p}$, $\mathbf{p}' \in C$ are said to be in the same *locale* if digitizations by $G(\mathbf{p})$ and $G(\mathbf{p}')$ yield the same bitmap. Formally, a locale is a maximal set of points Λ such that

$$\mathbf{p}, \mathbf{p}' \in \Lambda \Leftrightarrow D_{\mathbf{p}} \equiv D_{\mathbf{p}'}$$

For the disk pattern and the grid shown in Figure 2 or 3, each region enclosed by the curve-segments in the modulo-grid-diagram belongs to a single locale, as Theorem 1 will show.

In the following, we formally prove that each region belongs to a single locale. First, we introduce a lemma, the notation for which is illustrated in Figure 3.

Lemma 1 *If* $\mathbf{p}, \mathbf{p}' \in \pi_i$, *then* $\forall \mathbf{x}^* \in G(\mathbf{0})$, *either* $(\mathbf{x}^* + \mathbf{p})$ *and* $(\mathbf{x}^* + \mathbf{p}')$ *are both elements of* X *or are both elements of* $\bar{X} = R^2 - X$.

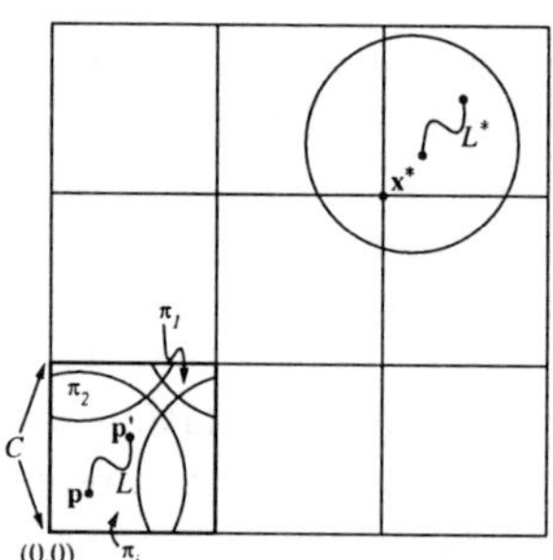

Figure 3: Illustration for Lemma 1.

Proof: Since $\mathbf{p}, \mathbf{p}' \in \pi_i$ and π_i is a connected open set by definition, there exists a continuous path L that starts at $\mathbf{p}$ and ends at $\mathbf{p}'$ such that $L \subset \pi_i$. Consequently,

$$L \cap X_C^b = \emptyset \tag{1}$$

Let us define the curve $L^* = \{\mathbf{x}^* + \mathbf{x} : \mathbf{x} \in L\}$ for any $\mathbf{x}^* \in G(\mathbf{0})$. L^* is a continuous path connecting $(\mathbf{x}^* + \mathbf{p})$ and $(\mathbf{x}^* + \mathbf{p}')$. Figure 3 illustrates the proof for a particular value of $\mathbf{x}^*$. It follows that $\mathbf{y} \in L^* \Rightarrow (\mathbf{y} - \mathbf{x}^*) \in L$. We claim that $L^* \cap X^b = \emptyset$, *i.e.*, L^* does not include any point on the pattern boundary. Indeed if this were not the case, then there must exist some $\mathbf{y} \in L^* \cap X^b$.

But then, $(\mathbf{y} \bmod C) = (\mathbf{y} - \mathbf{x}^*) \in X_C^b$ (since $\mathbf{y} \in X^b$) and $(\mathbf{y} - \mathbf{x}^*) \in L$ (since $\mathbf{y} \in L^*$). Consequently, $(\mathbf{y} - \mathbf{x}^*) \in L \cap X_C^b$. This contradicts Eq. 1.

The presence of a continuous curve L^* between $(\mathbf{x}^* + \mathbf{p})$ and $(\mathbf{x}^* + \mathbf{p}')$, that never cuts the boundary X^b, implies by the Jordan's Curve Theorem that $(\mathbf{x}^* + \mathbf{p})$ and $(\mathbf{x}^* + \mathbf{p}')$ are either both in X or both in $\bar{X}$. □

Theorem 1 formally states that all grid positions in a region are in the same equivalence class or locale, as suggested in Section 2. The proof follows the reasoning that in moving from a shift of $\mathbf{p}$ to a shift of $\mathbf{p}'$, none of the points in the digitizing grid G moves in or out of the pattern.

Theorem 1 $\forall i, \quad \mathbf{p}, \mathbf{p}' \in \pi_i \Longrightarrow D_\mathbf{p} \equiv D_{\mathbf{p}'}$

Proof: Let $\mathbf{x} \in D_\mathbf{p}$. This means that $\mathbf{x} \in G(\mathbf{p})$ and $\mathbf{x} \in X$. From $\mathbf{x} \in G(\mathbf{p})$, we have $\mathbf{x} = \mathbf{x}^* + \mathbf{p}$, where $\mathbf{x}^* \in G(\mathbf{0})$.

Let $\mathbf{x}'$ be defined as $(\mathbf{x} + \mathbf{p}' - \mathbf{p})$. Evidently, $\mathbf{x}' = (\mathbf{x}^* + \mathbf{p}') \in G(\mathbf{p}')$. Furthermore, $\mathbf{x} = (\mathbf{x}^* + \mathbf{p}) \in X \Rightarrow (\mathbf{x}^* + \mathbf{p}') = \mathbf{x}' \in X$ by the premise of this theorem and Lemma 1. Therefore,

$$\mathbf{x}' \in G(\mathbf{p}') \cap X = D_{\mathbf{p}'}$$

Thus we see that $\mathbf{x} \in D_\mathbf{p} \Rightarrow \mathbf{x}' = (\mathbf{x} + \mathbf{p}' - \mathbf{p}) \in D_{\mathbf{p}'}$. Lemma 1 can be similarly used to show that $\mathbf{x} \notin D_\mathbf{p} \Rightarrow \mathbf{x}' = (\mathbf{x} + \mathbf{p}' - \mathbf{p}) \notin D_{\mathbf{p}'}$. Thus $T(D_\mathbf{p}, \mathbf{p}' - \mathbf{p}) = D_{\mathbf{p}'}$ and consequently, $D_\mathbf{p} \equiv D_{\mathbf{p}'}$. □

In Theorem 2, we show that if all grid positions are equally likely, then the number of distinct bitmaps induced by a pattern is statistically bounded above by the number of regions in its modulo-grid-diagram.

Theorem 2 *If the position* $\mathbf{p}$ *of the sampling grid* $G(\mathbf{p})$ *is a random variable that is uniformly distributed in probability over the unit cell* C*, then the number of different bitmaps induced by a pattern* $X \in \Im$ *that can appear with non-zero probability is bounded above by the number of regions* π_i *in the modulo-grid-diagram of* X.

Proof: Since $X \in \Im$, X^b has a Lebesgue measure of zero. Since X^b maps onto X_C^b, the Lebesgue measure of X_C^b also equals zero. Under the assumption of uniform distribution, the Lebesgue measure of a set equals its probability measure. Thus all digitizations $D_\mathbf{q}$ such that $\mathbf{q} \in X_C^b$, put together account for a zero probability of appearance. All *probable* equivalent digitization classes therefore correspond to grid displacements $\mathbf{p}$ that lie within the regions.

By Theorem 1 two different bitmaps, being non-equivalent, cannot belong to the same region π_i and hence the result.

Corollary 1 *The relative frequency of each distinct bitmap, under the assumption of uniformly distributed grid-shifts, is proportional to the area of the corresponding locale.*

The upper-bound in Theorem 2 is valid only statistically because grid positions on the boundary of the pattern can actually correspond to new bitmaps, though such bitmaps occur with zero probability. The pattern on the left in Figure 4 shows an example of a bitmap that can be generated only by the unique grid position shown.

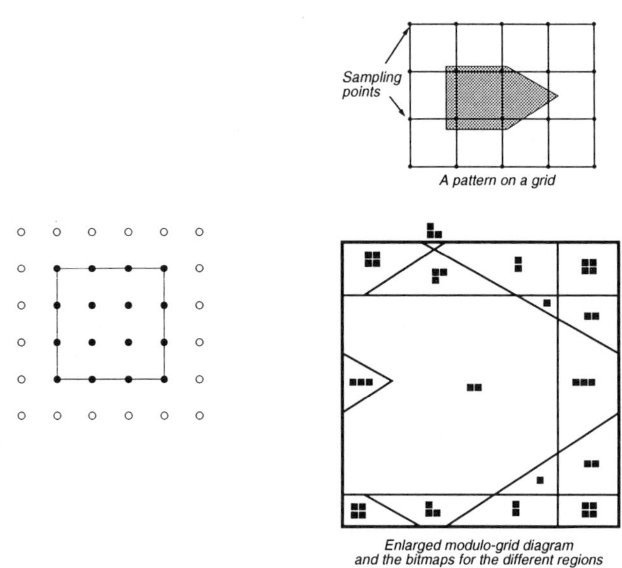

Figure 4: Left: grid location at a boundary point produces a new pattern. Right: an example of two separated regions in a diagram yielding the same bitmap.

Theorem 2 proves that the number of regions is an upper bound for the number of locales and therefore the number of bitmaps for a given analog pattern. Since the modulo process is periodic in nature, the unit cell can be wrapped around. Topologically, the modulo-grid-diagram forms a pattern on a torus: the top and bottom sides, the left and right sides, as well as the four corners respectively are equivalent. This is evident in the example shown on the right in Figure 4, where the bitmap corresponding to each region is indicated on the modulo-grid-diagram. Thus we can get a tighter upper-bound by counting as one the regions that merge together on wrapping around. However, even regions that are not contiguous on the torus can belong to the same locale, as noted by Havelock and illustrated by the example in Figure 4. In this example, the two regions corresponding to the bitmap of a single black pixel are not contiguous on the torus.

4 Experimental Verification

The correlated nature of edge noise in scanned character bitmaps was observed and reported by Nagy as far back as 1968.[1] Zhou and Lopresti observed that simply scanning a document page thrice with the same scanner and taking a vote among OCR results reduced recognition errors by 30%.[7] Since other scanning parameters were the same, this pointed to variable alignment of the page with respect to the scanner grid as a major factor in OCR performance.

Consequently, the random phase sampling effect should be considered in the design of pseudo random defect models for OCR classifiers.[2] Figure 5 demonstrates this effect in scanned characters. Experiments were run on 1,000 bitmaps of 12 point Helvetica e's. Two different sets of bitmaps were synthesized and a third set was obtained by printing and scanning. The first set of synthetic data was obtained by applying an independent threshold noise only, while the second set had the combined effects of random grid shifts and threshold variation. For each set of data, we computed the chain codes of the character contours. We matched each chain code with that of a canonical reference character and plotted the distribution profile of string edits along the chain. Figure 5 presents the results. As expected, independent threshold variation alone results in a uniform distribution profile. But the model using random grid shifts shows peak variation locations that match up well with real scanned characters. This result emphasizes the correlated nature of edge-pixel noise that results from random grid translations.

5 Conclusions

In this paper, we have applied the notion of locales to printed patterns, established an upper bound on the number distinct bitmaps that can be generated by displacements of the scanning grid with respect to an analog pattern under ideal conditions, and provided a tool to compute the frequency of occurrence of each bitmap under uniformly random grid displacements. These extensions of Havelock's ideas open up several interesting areas of investigation.

The dependence of the number of distinct bitmaps on the size of the patterns, with additional allowances made for threshold noise, provides a basis for establishing an acceptable sample size for training OCR classifiers.

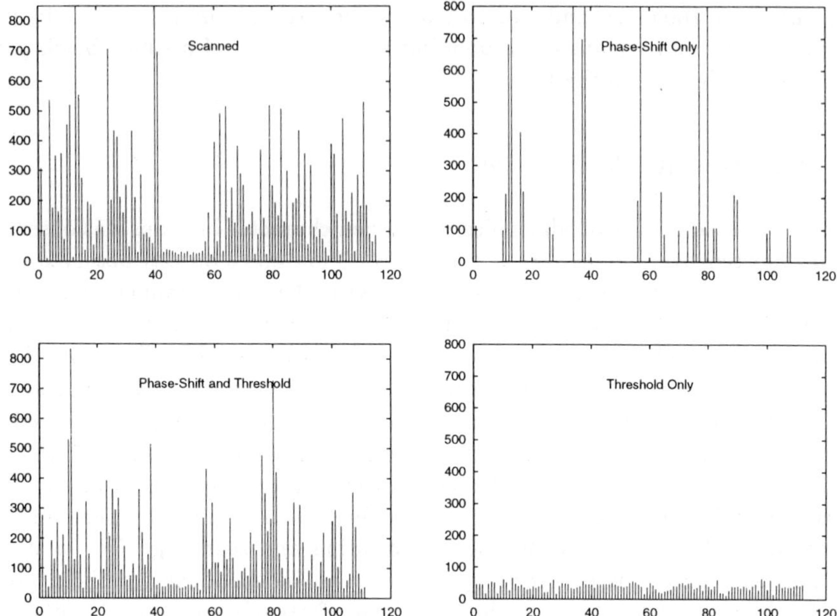

Figure 5: Characteristics of chaincode edits from different noise simulation models.

Predicting, rather than just counting, all possible bitmap representations of a printed character as a function of the spatial sampling rate leads to the minimum sampling resolution that guarantees a given Hamming distance between bitmaps of characters of different classes. A more difficult problem is determination of the effect of random-phase sampling noise on the types of features used in OCR. Although OCR system designers have for decades attempted to construct features that are resistant to edge noise, there is now hope of introducing quantitative considerations into the design process.

Our work also provides a foundation for pseudo-random defect models. Such models are enjoying increasing popularity for generating large sets of identified character bitmaps, but there has been little success so far in estimating their underlying parameters. Random phase sampling appears to reproduce accurately the observed variation among scanned characters. Conversely, it should be possible to reconstruct an analog pattern optimally from a set of digitized samples that differ primarily with regard to the grid displacement.

We conclude that the correspondence between locales and distinct bitmaps offers a rich field of study that extends well beyond the applications proposed in earlier papers.

Acknowledgments

George Nagy and Prateek Sarkar gratefully acknowledge the support of Nortel Technology. A portion of this work was conducted at the New York State Center for Automation, Manufacturing and Robotics at Rensselaer Polytechnic Institute. The CAT is partially funded by a block grant from the New York State Science and Technology Foundation.

References

[1] G. Nagy. On the auto-correlation function of noise in sampled typewritten characters. In *IEEE Region III Convention Record*, New Orleans, LA, 1968.

[2] P. Sarkar. Random phase spatial sampling effects in digitized patterns. Master's thesis, Rensselaer Polytechnic Institute, 1994.

[3] G. Nagy, P. Sarkar, D. Lopresti, and J.Y. Zhou. Spatial sampling effects in optical character recognition. In *Proceedings of the Third International Conference on Document Analysis and Recognition*, 1995.

[4] D.I. Havelock. Geometric precision in noise-free digital images. *IEEE Trans. on Pattern Analysis and Machine Intelligence*, PAMI-11(10):1065–1075, October 1989.

[5] T. Pavlidis. *Algorithms for Graphics and Image Processing.* Computer Science Press, 1982.

[6] L. O'Gorman. Subpixel precision of straight-edged shapes for registration and measurement. *IEEE Transactions on Pattern Analysis and Machine Intelligence*, 18(7), July 1996.

[7] J.Y. Zhou and D. Lopresti. Repeated sampling to improve classifier accuracy. In *Proceedings of the IAPR Workshop on Machine Vision Applications*, Kawasaki, Japan, December 1994. To appear in *Pattern Recognition.*

AUTHOR INDEX